T0321691

Resource Management and Efficiency in Cloud Computing Environments

Ashok Kumar Turuk
National Institute of Technology Rourkela, India

Bibhudatta Sahoo
National Institute of Technology Rourkela, India

Sourav Kanti Addya
National Institute of Technology Rourkela, India

A volume in the Advances in Systems Analysis,
Software Engineering, and High Performance
Computing (ASASEHPC) Book Series

www.igi-global.com

Published in the United States of America by
    IGI Global
    Information Science Reference (an imprint of IGI Global)
    701 E. Chocolate Avenue
    Hershey PA, USA 17033
    Tel: 717-533-8845
    Fax: 717-533-8661
    E-mail: cust@igi-global.com
    Web site: http://www.igi-global.com

Library of Congress Cataloging-in-Publication Data

Library of Congress Cataloging-in-Publication Data

Names: Turuk, Ashok Kumar, 1963- editor. | Sahoo, Bibhudatta, 1967- editor. |
  Addya, Sourav Kanti, 1985- editor.
Title: Resource management and efficiency in cloud computing environments /
  Ashok Kumar Turuk, Bibhudatta Sahoo, and Sourav Kanti Addya, editors.
Description: Hershey, PA : Information Science Reference, 2017. | Includes
  bibliographical references and index.
Identifiers: LCCN 2016043916| ISBN 9781522517214 (hardcover) | ISBN
  9781522517221 (ebook)
Subjects: LCSH: Cloud computing.
Classification: LCC QA76.585 .R3785 2017 | DDC 004.67/82--dc23 LC record available at https://lccn.loc.gov/2016043916

This book is published in the IGI Global book series Advances in Systems Analysis, Software Engineering, and High Performance Computing (ASASEHPC) (ISSN: 2327-3453; eISSN: 2327-3461)

British Cataloguing in Publication Data
A Cataloguing in Publication record for this book is available from the British Library.

For electronic access to this publication, please contact: eresources@igi-global.com.

Advances in Systems Analysis, Software Engineering, and High Performance Computing (ASASEHPC) Book Series

Vijayan Sugumaran
Oakland University, USA

ISSN:2327-3453
EISSN:2327-3461

MISSION

The theory and practice of computing applications and distributed systems has emerged as one of the key areas of research driving innovations in business, engineering, and science. The fields of software engineering, systems analysis, and high performance computing offer a wide range of applications and solutions in solving computational problems for any modern organization.

The **Advances in Systems Analysis, Software Engineering, and High Performance Computing (ASASEHPC) Book Series** brings together research in the areas of distributed computing, systems and software engineering, high performance computing, and service science. This collection of publications is useful for academics, researchers, and practitioners seeking the latest practices and knowledge in this field.

COVERAGE

- Software Engineering
- Performance Modelling
- Network Management
- Computer Networking
- Distributed Cloud Computing
- Computer System Analysis
- Computer graphics
- Engineering Environments
- Enterprise Information Systems
- Virtual Data Systems

IGI Global is currently accepting manuscripts for publication within this series. To submit a proposal for a volume in this series, please contact our Acquisition Editors at Acquisitions@igi-global.com or visit: http://www.igi-global.com/publish/.

Titles in this Series

For a list of additional titles in this series, please visit: www.igi-global.com

Handbook of Research on End-to-End Cloud Computing Architecture Design
Jianwen "Wendy" Chen (IBM, Australia) Yan Zhang (Western Sydney University, Australia) and Ron Gottschalk (IBM, Australia)
Information Science Reference • copyright 2017 • 507pp • H/C (ISBN: 9781522507598) • US $325.00 (our price)

Innovative Research and Applications in Next-Generation High Performance Computing
Qusay F. Hassan (Mansoura University, Egypt)
Information Science Reference • copyright 2016 • 488pp • H/C (ISBN: 9781522502876) • US $205.00 (our price)

Developing Interoperable and Federated Cloud Architecture
Gabor Kecskemeti (University of Miskolc, Hungary) Attila Kertesz (University of Szeged, Hungary) and Zsolt Nemeth (MTA SZTAKI, Hungary)
Information Science Reference • copyright 2016 • 398pp • H/C (ISBN: 9781522501534) • US $210.00 (our price)

Managing Big Data in Cloud Computing Environments
Zongmin Ma (Nanjing University of Aeronautics and Astronautics, China)
Information Science Reference • copyright 2016 • 314pp • H/C (ISBN: 9781466698345) • US $195.00 (our price)

Emerging Innovations in Agile Software Development
Imran Ghani (Universiti Teknologi Malaysia, Malaysia) Dayang Norhayati Abang Jawawi (Universiti Teknologi Malaysia, Malaysia) Siva Dorairaj (Software Education, New Zealand) and Ahmed Sidky (ICAgile, USA)
Information Science Reference • copyright 2016 • 323pp • H/C (ISBN: 9781466698581) • US $205.00 (our price)

Modern Software Engineering Methodologies for Mobile and Cloud Environments
António Miguel Rosado da Cruz (Instituto Politécnico de Viana do Castelo, Portugal) and Sara Paiva (Instituto Politécnico de Viana do Castelo, Portugal)
Information Science Reference • copyright 2016 • 355pp • H/C (ISBN: 9781466699168) • US $210.00 (our price)

Emerging Research Surrounding Power Consumption and Performance Issues in Utility Computing
Ganesh Chandra Deka (Regional Vocational Training Institute (RVTI) for Women, India) G.M. Siddesh (M S Ramaiah Institute of Technology, Bangalore, India) K. G. Srinivasa (M S Ramaiah Institute of Technology, Bangalore, India) and L.M. Patnaik (IISc, Bangalore, India)
Information Science Reference • copyright 2016 • 460pp • H/C (ISBN: 9781466688537) • US $215.00 (our price)

www.igi-global.com

701 E. Chocolate Ave., Hershey, PA 17033
Order online at www.igi-global.com or call 717-533-8845 x100
To place a standing order for titles released in this series, contact: cust@igi-global.com
Mon-Fri 8:00 am - 5:00 pm (est) or fax 24 hours a day 717-533-8661

Editorial Advisory Board

Table of Contents

Preface..xiii

Acknowledgment xviii

Chapter 1
Ubiquitous and Cloud Computing: Ubiquitous Computing 1
    Pinar Kirci, Istanbul University, Turkey

Chapter 2
Using Value-Based Approach for Managing Cloud-Based Services................................... 33
    Salah Eddin Murad, Damascus University, Syria
    Salah Dowaji, Damascus University, Syria

Chapter 3
Cloud Service Footprint (CSF): Utilizing Risk and Governance Directions to Characterize a
Cloud Service.. 61
    Mohammad Shalan, JEA, Jordan

Chapter 4
Cloud Security Issues and Challenges 89
    Srinivas Sethi, IGIT Sarang, India
    Sai Sruti, IGIT Sarang, India

Chapter 5
Cyber-Security Concerns with Cloud Computing: Business Value Creation and Performance
Perspectives.. 105
    Ezer Osei Yeboah-Boateng, Ghana Technology University College, Ghana

Chapter 6
Dynamic Virtual Machine Placement in Cloud Computing 136
    Arnab Kumar Paul, Virginia Tech, USA
    Bibhudatta Sahoo, National Institute of Technology Rourkela, India

Chapter 7
Metaheuristic Approaches to Task Consolidation Problem in the Cloud 168
    Sambit Kumar Mishra, National Institute of Technology Rourkela, India
    Bibhudatta Sahoo, National Institute of Technology Rourkela, India
    Kshira Sagar Sahoo, National Institute of Technology Rourkela, India
    Sanjay Kumar Jena, National Institute of Technology Rourkela, India

Chapter 8
Real Time Task Execution in Cloud Using MapReduce Framework 190
    Sampa Sahoo, National Institute of Technology Rourkela, India
    Bibhudatta Sahoo, National Institute of Technology Rourkela, India
    Ashok Kumar Turuk, National Institute of Technology Rourkela, India
    Sambit Kumar Mishra, National Institute of Technology Rourkela, India

Chapter 9
Resource and Energy Efficient Virtual Machine Migration in Cloud Data Centers 210
    Subrat Kumar Dhal, National Institute of Technology Rourkela, India
    Harshit Verma, National Institute of Technology Rourkela, India
    Sourav Kanti Addya, National Institute of Technology Rourkela, India

Chapter 10
Network Virtualization: Network Resource Management in Cloud 239
    Kshira Sagar Sahoo, National Institute of Technology Rourkela, India
    Bibhudatta Sahoo, National Institute of Technology Rourkela, India
    Ratnakar Dash, National Institute of Technology Rourkela, India
    Mayank Tiwary, C. V. Raman College of Engineering, India
    Sampa Sahoo, National Institute of Technology Rourkela, India

Chapter 11
Software as a Service, Semantic Web, and Big Data: Theories and Applications 264
    Kijpokin Kasemsap, Suan Sunandha Rajabhat University, Thailand

Chapter 12
Software Development Methodology for Cloud Computing and Its Impact 286
    Chhabi Rani Panigrahi, C. V. Raman College of Engineering, India
    Rajib Mall, Indian Institute of Technology Kharagpur, India
    Bibudhendu Pati, C. V. Raman College of Engineering, India

Compilation of References 308

About the Contributors 345

Index 349

Detailed Table of Contents

Preface xiii

Acknowledgment xviii

Chapter 1

Ubiquitous and Cloud Computing: Ubiquitous Computing 1
Pinar Kirci, Istanbul University, Turkey

Recently, great developments in computing and telecommunication technologies caused big amounts of data flow over Internet, especially due to increasing smart device users. Within the last few years, ubiquitous communication has improved with new telecommunication and transmission infrastructures and also enriched with new services. The focus of ubiquitous computing is presenting environments including computing and communication abilities that are integrated with users. Mobile and pervasive computing present many opportunities about exploring various factors all over the world with searching large habitats and species. The services and applications are presented via a heterogeneous environment over many different devices by the ubiquitous system. Accordingly, ubiquitous computing is becoming more popular because of the new research developments and great technological advances in wireless communication networks, cloud computing, Internet technologies, mobile and distributed computing.

Chapter 2

Using Value-Based Approach for Managing Cloud-Based Services 33
Salah Eddin Murad, Damascus University, Syria
Salah Dowaji, Damascus University, Syria

Software-as-a-Service (SaaS) providers are influenced by a variety of characteristics and capabilities of the available cloud infrastructure resources (IaaS). As a result, the decision made by business service owners to lease and use certain resources is an important one in order to achieve the planned outcome. This chapter uses value based approach to manage the SaaS service provided to the customers. Based on our approach, customer satisfaction is modeled not only based on the response time, but also based on the allotted budget. Using our model, the application owner is able to direct and control the decision of renting cloud resources as per the current strategy. This strategy is led by a set of defined key performance indicators. In addition, we present a scheduling algorithm that can bid for different types of virtual machines to achieve the target value. Furthermore, we proposed the required Ontology to semantically discover the needed IaaS resources. We conduct extensive simulations using different types of Amazon EC2 instances with dynamic prices.

Chapter 3

Cloud Service Footprint (CSF): Utilizing Risk and Governance Directions to Characterize a
Cloud Service.. 61
Mohammad Shalan, JEA, Jordan

Cloud Computing (CC) services have made substantive advances in the past few years. It is rapidly changing the landscape of technology, and energizing the long-held promise of utility computing. Successful jump into CC is a considerable task, since the surroundings are not yet mature and the accompanied risk and governance frameworks are still evolving. This effort aims to portray an identity for CC services by employing risk and governance directions among other elements and techniques. Cloud Service Footprint (CSF) is considering practical aspects surrounding the CC paradigm and prescribing the associated directions. CSF will help Cloud Service Providers (CSPs) to characterize their service and benchmark themselves. The Client Enterprises (CEs) can utilize CSF dimensions to find a better way to navigate through CC service arena and to understand its parameters. Along with cost and functional capabilities, the Cloud Service Footprint (CSF) can provide enough information for business executives to evaluate CC services and make informed decisions.

Chapter 4

Cloud Security Issues and Challenges 89
Srinivas Sethi, IGIT Sarang, India
Sai Sruti, IGIT Sarang, India

Cloud computing refers to the basic setup for an emerging model of service delivery, that has the advantage of decreasing the cost by sharing computing, infrastructure including storage resources. This can be combined with on-demand delivery mechanism relying on a pay-per-use model. Cloud computing offers an added level of risk because of essential services provided by it to a third party, which makes it difficult to maintain data privacy and security. Security in cloud computing is a critical aspect, which has various issues and challenges related to it. Cloud service providers/ brokers and the cloud service users should make aware of safety cloud. That is the cloud is safe enough from all kinds of the threats, so that the users do not face any problem like; loss of data or data theft. There is a possibility that, a malicious user can enters the cloud by imitating an authentic user, thus corrupt the entire cloud. It can affect many users who are sharing these types of clouds. This chapter mentions the list of parameters that disturb the security of the cloud. This also explores the cloud security issues and challenges faced by cloud service provider/brokers and cloud service users like; data, privacy, and infected application. Finally, it discusses the countermeasure for handling these issues and its challenges.

Chapter 5

Cyber-Security Concerns with Cloud Computing: Business Value Creation and Performance
Perspectives.. 105
Ezer Osei Yeboah-Boateng, Ghana Technology University College, Ghana

Information is modeled into virtual objects to create value for its owner. The value chain involves stakeholders with varied responsibilities in the cyber-market. Cloud computing emerged out of virtualization, distributed and grid computing, and has altered the value creation landscape, through strategic and sensitive information management. It offers services that use resources in a utility fashion. The flexible, cost-effective service models are opportunities for SMEs. Whilst using these tools for value-creation is imperative, a myriad of security concerns confront both providers and end-users. Vulnerabilities and threats are key concerns, so that value created is strategically aligned with corporate vision, appropriated and sustained. What is the extent of impact? Expert opinions were elicited of 4 C-level officers and 10 security operatives. Shared technology issues, malicious insiders and service hijacking are considered major threats. Also, an intuitive strategic model for Value-Creation Cloud-based Cyber-security is proposed as guidance in fostering IT-enabled initiatives.

Chapter 6
Dynamic Virtual Machine Placement in Cloud Computing 136

Arnab Kumar Paul, Virginia Tech, USA
Bibhudatta Sahoo, National Institute of Technology Rourkela, India

The aim of cloud computing is to enable users to access resources on demand. The number of users is continuously increasing. In order to fulfil their needs, we need more number of physical machines and data centers. The increase in the number of physical machines is directly proportional to the consumption of energy. This gives us one of the major challenges; minimization of energy consumption. One of the most effective ways to minimize the consumption of energy is the optimal virtual machine placement on physical machines. This chapter focuses on finding the solution to the problem of dynamic virtual machine placement for the optimized consumption of energy. An energy consumption model is built which takes into account the states of physical machines and live migration of virtual machines. On top of this, the cloud computing model is built. Unlike centralized approaches towards virtual machine placement which result in many unreachable solutions, a decentralized approach is used in this chapter which provides a list of virtual machine migrations for their optimal placement.

Chapter 7
Metaheuristic Approaches to Task Consolidation Problem in the Cloud 168

Sambit Kumar Mishra, National Institute of Technology Rourkela, India
Bibhudatta Sahoo, National Institute of Technology Rourkela, India
Kshira Sagar Sahoo, National Institute of Technology Rourkela, India
Sanjay Kumar Jena, National Institute of Technology Rourkela, India

The service (task) allocation problem in the distributed computing is one form of multidimensional knapsack problem which is one of the best examples of the combinatorial optimization problem. Nature-inspired techniques represent powerful mechanisms for addressing a large number of combinatorial optimization problems. Computation of getting an optimal solution for various industrial and scientific problems is usually intractable. The service request allocation problem in distributed computing belongs to a particular group of problems, i.e., NP-hard problem. The major portion of this chapter constitutes a survey of various mechanisms for service allocation problem with the availability of different cloud computing architecture. Here, there is a brief discussion towards the implementation issues of various metaheuristic techniques like Particle Swarm Optimization (PSO), Genetic Algorithm (GA), Ant Colony Optimization (ACO), BAT algorithm, etc. with various environments for the service allocation problem in the cloud.

Chapter 8

Real Time Task Execution in Cloud Using MapReduce Framework 190

Sampa Sahoo, National Institute of Technology Rourkela, India
Bibhudatta Sahoo, National Institute of Technology Rourkela, India
Ashok Kumar Turuk, National Institute of Technology Rourkela, India
Sambit Kumar Mishra, National Institute of Technology Rourkela, India

Cloud Computing era comes with the advancement of technologies in the fields of processing, storage, bandwidth network access, security of internet etc. The development of automatic applications, smart devices and applications, sensor based applications need huge data storage and computing resources and need output within a particular time limit. Now users are becoming more sensitive towards, delay in applications they are using. So, a scalable platform like Cloud Computing is required that can provide huge computing resource, and data storage required for processing such applications. MapReduce framework is used to process huge amounts of data. Data processing on a cloud based on MapReduce would provide added benefits such as fault tolerant, heterogeneous, ease of use, free and open, efficient. This chapter discusses about cloud system model, real-time MapReduce framework, Cloud based MapReduce framework examples, quality attributes of MapReduce scheduling and various MapReduce scheduling algorithm based on quality attributes.

Chapter 9

Resource and Energy Efficient Virtual Machine Migration in Cloud Data Centers 210

Subrat Kumar Dhal, National Institute of Technology Rourkela, India
Harshit Verma, National Institute of Technology Rourkela, India
Sourav Kanti Addya, National Institute of Technology Rourkela, India

Cloud computing service has been on the rise over the past few decades, which has led to an increase in the number of data centers, thus consuming more amount of energy for their operation. Moreover, the energy consumption in the cloud is proportional to the resource utilization. Thus consolidation schemes for the cloud model need to be devised to minimize energy by decreasing the operating costs. The consolidation problem is NP-complete, which requires heuristic techniques to get a sub-optimal solution. The authors have proposed a new consolidation scheme for the virtual machines (VMs) by improving the host overload detection phase. The resulting scheme is effective in reducing the energy and the level of Service Level Agreement (SLA) violations both, to a considerable extent. For testing the performance of implementation, a simulation environment is needed that can provide an environment of the actual cloud computing components. The authors have used CloudSim 3.0.3 simulation toolkit that allows testing and analyzing Allocation and Selection algorithms.

Chapter 10

Network Virtualization: Network Resource Management in Cloud 239

Kshira Sagar Sahoo, National Institute of Technology Rourkela, India
Bibhudatta Sahoo, National Institute of Technology Rourkela, India
Ratnakar Dash, National Institute of Technology Rourkela, India
Mayank Tiwary, C. V. Raman College of Engineering, India
Sampa Sahoo, National Institute of Technology Rourkela, India

Cloud computing is a novel paradigm which relies on the vision of resource sharing over the Internet. The concept of resource virtualization, i.e. hiding the detail specification of the resources from the end users is the key idea of cloud computing. But the tenants have limited visibility over the network resources.

The Network-as-a-Service (NaaS) framework integrates the cloud computing services with direct tenant access to the network infrastructure. The Network virtualization (NV) is such a platform that acts as a mediation layer to provide NaaS to tenants. NV supports the coexistence of multiple virtual networks, which is the collection of virtual nodes and virtual links on the same underlying physical infrastructure. Prior to set up a virtual network in an NV Environment, resource discovery and resource allocation are the primary job. In this chapter, we have discussed on basic NV architecture, surveyed the previous work on the resource allocation along with ongoing research projects on network virtualization.

Chapter 11
Software as a Service, Semantic Web, and Big Data: Theories and Applications 264
    Kijpokin Kasemsap, Suan Sunandha Rajabhat University, Thailand

This chapter explains the overview of software as a service (SaaS); SaaS and application service provision (ASP); the security concern of SaaS; the perspectives on SaaS adoption; the challenges of SaaS in the digital age; the overview of the Semantic Web; the current trends in the Semantic Web services; the overview of Big Data; the concept of Big Data analytics; and the prospects of Big Data in the digital age. SaaS offers a wide range of business applications through the cloud computing service providers toward enhancing organizational performance. The Semantic Web extends beyond the capabilities of the current Web 2.0, thus enabling more effective collaborations and smarter decision making in modern operations. Big Data from the cloud computing platforms provides the significant advantage, if the essential data sources are hosted by the same SaaS and enhanced by the Semantic Web technologies.

Chapter 12
Software Development Methodology for Cloud Computing and Its Impact 286
    Chhabi Rani Panigrahi, C. V. Raman College of Engineering, India
    Rajib Mall, Indian Institute of Technology Kharagpur, India
    Bibudhendu Pati, C. V. Raman College of Engineering, India

This chapter emphasizes mainly on the software development methodology basically agile methods of software development in cloud computing platforms and its impact on software development processes. This chapter also covers the benefits of agile development methodology in cloud computing platform. Along with this all traditional software development phases are analyzed to discuss the differences between the traditional software development processes and software development in cloud computing environment. This chapter also includes a brief description of programming models such as MapReduce, BSPCloud, and Dryad etc. available in the literature to handle big data in SaaS cloud. Finally, we highlight the challenges and future scope of software development process in cloud computing environment.

Compilation of References 308

About the Contributors 345

Index 349

Preface

OVERVIEW

Cloud computing is an emerging computing technology that uses Internet and central remote servers to maintain data and applications. It allows consumers and businesses to use applications without installation and access their personal files at any computer with the help of Internet. It can be defined as anything that provides hosted service over the Internet. Further, it facilitates to collaborate on business activities of multiple organizations across geographic locations. This technology is expected to be much more efficient than the presently available technology by centralizing the storage, memory, processing and bandwidth. Technologies, that made cloud computing feasible are virtualization, cyber-infrastructure, and service orient infrastructure. Apart from cloud computing, big data is another cutting edge technology for global data storage and data handling. These two new technologies are evolving across the globe. Now- a-days, IT organizations are moving towards a concept of seamless computing and real-time processing of data with high degree of resource scalability. Collaboration of these two technologies, enable the scope of another emerging technology Internet-of-Things (IoT). With the help of cloud and big data networking, today it is possible to envision pervasive connectivity, storage and computation which in turn, gives rise to different IoT solutions. In the present globalization scenario cloud services can provide speed and cost effective solutions. These benefits will enable enterprises to become competitive in the market.

Cloud Providers offer services that can be grouped into three service model:

1. **Software as a Service (SaaS):** In this model, a complete application is offered to the customer, as a service on demand. A single instance of the service runs on the cloud and multiple end users are serviced. On the customers' side, there is no need for upfront investment in servers or software licenses, while for the provider, the costs are lowered. Since, only a single application needs to be hosted and maintained. Today SaaS is offered by companies such as Google, Salesforce, Microsoft, Zoho, etc.

2. **Platform as a Service (Paas):** In this service model, a layer of software environment is encapsulated and offered as a service. Other higher levels of services can be built upon it. Customers have the freedom to build his own applications, which runs on the provider's infrastructure. To meet scalability requirements of the applications, PaaS providers offer a predefined combination of OS and application servers. Google"s App Engine, Force.com, etc are some of the popular PaaS examples.

3. **Infrastructure as a Service (Iaas):** This service model provides the basic storage and computing capabilities as standardized services over the network. Servers, storage systems, networking equipment, data centre space etc. are pooled and made available to handle workloads. The cus-

tomer would typically deploy his own software on the infrastructure. Some common examples are Amazon, GoGrid etc.

Enterprises can choose to deploy applications on Public, Private or Hybrid clouds. Cloud integrators can play a vital part in determining the right cloud path for each organization.

1. **Public Cloud:** Public clouds are owned and operated by third parties. They deliver superior economies of scale to customers, as the infrastructure costs are spread among a mix of users, giving each individual client an attractive low-cost, "Pay-as-you-go" model. All customers share the same infrastructure pool with limited configuration, security protections, and availability variances. These are managed and supported by the cloud provider. One of the advantages of Public cloud is that they may be larger than an enterprises cloud. Thus providing the ability to scale seamlessly, on demand.
2. **Private Cloud**: Private clouds are built exclusively for a single enterprise. They aim to address concerns on data security and offer greater control, which is typically lacking in a public cloud. There are two variations of private cloud:
   a. **On-Premise Private Cloud:** On-premise private clouds are also known as internal clouds are hosted within one's own data center. This model provides a more standardized process and protection, but is limited in aspects of size and scalability. IT departments would also need to incur the capital and operational costs for the physical resources. This is best suited for applications which require complete control and configurability of the infrastructure and security.
   b. **Externally Hosted Private Cloud:** This type of private cloud is hosted externally with a cloud provider, where the provider facilitates an exclusive cloud environment with full guarantee of privacy. This is best suited for enterprises that do not prefer a public cloud due to sharing of physical resources.
3. **Hybrid Cloud:** Hybrid clouds combine both public and private cloud models. With a Hybrid Cloud, service providers can utilize third party cloud providers in a full or partial manner thus increasing the flexibility of computing. The Hybrid cloud environment is capable of providing on-demand, externally provisioned scale. The ability to augment a private cloud with the resources of a public cloud can be used to manage any unexpected surge in workload.

BENEFITS

Enterprises would need to align their applications, so as to exploit the architectural models that cloud computing offers. Some of the typical benefits are listed below:

1. **Reduced Cost:** There are a number of reasons to attribute cloud technology with lower costs. The billing model is pay as per usage; the infrastructure is not purchased thus lowering maintenance. Initial expense and recurring expenses are much lower than traditional computing.
2. **Increased Storage:** With the massive infrastructure that is offered by Cloud providers today, storage and maintenance of large volumes of data is a reality. Sudden workload spikes are also managed effectively and efficiently, since the cloud can scale dynamically.

3. **Flexibility:** This is an extremely important characteristic. With enterprises having to adapt, even more rapidly to changing business conditions, speed to deliver is critical. Cloud computing stresses on getting applications to market very quickly, by using the most appropriate building blocks necessary for deployment.

TARGET AUDIENCES

The proposed book would be a reference for research scholars, a course supplement to the students pursuing computer science related subjects specially distributed systems and a resource for software professionals.

GIST OF THE CHAPTERS

Pinnar Kirci in the chapter titled "Ubiquitous and Cloud Computing: Ubiquitous Computing" has described the evolution of ubiquitous computing. They have also explained how an ambient intelligence infrastructure exists due to increased information exchange among users, devices and environment where applications of ubiquitous computing can be deployed. In this chapter they have described the techniques for interoperability of ubiquitous systems, applications, and standards of ubiquitous computing.

Murad and Dowaji in their chapter titled "Using Value-Based Approach for Managing Cloud-Based Services" have discussed about different cloud deployment model and pricing mechanism. According to the authors, work reported in the literature can be classified either from business perspective or from technical perspective. A few are driven by the provider objective, while others are driven by the customer. They said the objective of the provider can be defined by a value. This can be done by providing a quantitative measure using a value based approach derived from the value metrics measurement techniques. They have addressed the business objectives of the business service owner. The objectives are driven by a set of key performance indexes that specify the providers' priorities at the current stage. They have presented an algorithm for resource allocation to achieve the target value of service owner.

Shalan in his chapter titled "Cloud Service Footprint (CSF): Utilizing Risk and Governance Directions to Characterize a Cloud Service" discussed the challenges to cloud computing. These challenges arises due to the adoption of cloud computing service that might begin outside the technology organization or against a client enterprise strategy leading to loose association. It investigates the effects of maturity status on the enhancement of key cloud computing service features and its value position. This chapter also introduces a new term called cloud service foot print (CSF) to portray an identity for a cloud computing service. According to the author CSF provide enough information for business executives to evaluate cloud computing service and make informed decision.

Sethi and Sruti in their chapter titled "Cloud Security Issues and Challenges" list the parameters that affects cloud security. According to the author virtualization is critical to host security. Therefore, virtualization layer must be kept secured. They have discussed in details the host security for different cloud computing model such as SaaS, PaaS, IaaS. They have also analyzed the security issues and their countermeasures in cloud computing.

Yeboah-Boating in his chapter titled "Cyber-Security Concerns with Cloud Computing: Business Value Creation and Performance Perspectives" said cloud computing has profoundly altered the business value creation landscape, through IT enabled strategic information management. It is essential to store the sensitive data securely and effectively. This chapter examines cyber-security concerns with cloud computing, both from perspective of cloud service providers and end-users using small-to-medium enterprise in developing economies as a case study. The author noted that it is impossible to eliminate threat. Therefore, protection against them without disruptively business innovation and growth should be the utmost priority.

Paul and Sahoo in their chapter titled "Dynamic Virtual Machine Placement in Cloud Computing" have built an energy consumption model to calculate total energy consumption of physical machines, taking into account different states of virtual machines. They approach the decision making process for dynamic virtual machine placement in a decentralized manner. Two scenarios are considered; one when the physical machines cooperate with one another as in the case of private cloud and the other when they act in a selfish manner in case of hybrid cloud. The authors use cooperative and non-cooperative game theory for the two scenarios respectively for optimal placement of virtual machines onto physical machines to minimize energy consumption.

Mishra et al. in their chapter titled "Metaheuristic Approaches to Task Consolidation Problem in the Cloud" have explained the cloud computing environment along with its various service models. They have also explained the importance of energy consumption in a cloud data center, and different techniques to conserve energy. They have redefined the existing problem, of task scheduling in the cloud environment along with the importance of virtualization technique. Authors have explained the applicability of metaheuristic approaches in scheduling cloud environments. They hae also mentioned the implementation issues of various metaheuristic techniques like Genetic Algorithm (GA), Particle Swarm Optimization (PSO), Ant Colony Optimization (ACO), BAT algorithm with various environments for the service allocation problem in the cloud.

Sahoo et al. in their chapter titled "Real Time Task Execution in Cloud Using MapReduce Framework" have proposed a cloud system model for real-time task processing in the cloud. As many applications like smart devices and sensor-based tasks, generate a significant amount of data that has a time constraint, a scalable platform like cloud computing is required to process it. The authors have also discussed a real-time MapReduce framework in cloud computing used for massive data processing. Various MapReduce scheduling quality attributes are studied, and scheduling algorithms are reviewed based on these characteristics.

Dhal et al. in their chapter titled "Resource- and Energy-Efficient Virtual Machine Migration in Cloud Data Centers" have said that the recent advances in cloud computing services have led to increasing amount of energy consumption in data centers. Thus consolidation schemes for virtual machines (VMs) on physical machines on cloud data centers. Consolidation scheme being NP-complete requires heuristic techniques to get a sub-optimal solution. The authors have proposed an adaptive threshold based consolidation scheme for VMs by improving the host overload detection phase with appropriate measure of statistical dispersion and combined with minimum migration time policy of selecting the VMs for migration. This reduces the performance metric involving energy consumption and the level of SLA violations.

Sahoo et al. in their chapter titled "Network Virtualization: Network Resource Management in Cloud" have stated that virtualization provides a number of benefits to the service providers and everyday users. Virtualization technologies have recently shifted from server virtualization to network virtualization. It can deliver a new platform upon which new network architecture can fabricate and experimented. Since network virtualization in a cloud environment is a new research topic, in this chapter authors have trying to discuss various benefits, different research challenges and under taken projects on network virtualization. Resource discovery and resource allocation are two important task in network virtualization. A mathematical formulation on resource allocations is present in this chapter.

Kasemsap in his chapter titled "Software as Service, Semantic Web, and Big Data: Theories and Applications" consolidated the available literature on SaaS, Semantic web and Big data. The author has described the current issues and trends with SaaS, Semantic web and Big data in order to maximize the technological impact in modern operation. He also explained the perspective of SaaS adoption and challenges of SaaS in the digital age, overview and current trend in Semantic web, Overview, concept and prospect of Big data in the digital age.

Panigrahi et al. in their chapter titled "Software Development Methodology for Cloud Computing and Its Impact" have mentioned that a single software development process model cannot work for all types of project. Software development model is an evolving process which is affected by nature of the project, types of product to be developed etc. They have mentioned how software projects can be developed for cloud computing platform and the impact of cloud computing on software development. They have highlighted the benefit of software development and the agile method of software development in cloud computing platform.

IMPACT OF THIS BOOK

This book outlines advancements in the state-of-the-art, standards, and practices of cloud computing, in an effort to identify emerging trends, research and developments that will ultimately define the future of the cloud and relation with Big Data and IoT. A valuable reference for academics and practitioners alike, this title covers topics such as virtualization technology, Service oriented architecture (SOA), utility computing, cloud application services (SaaS), grid computing, Big Data and IoT.

Ashok Kumar Turuk
National Institute of Technology Rourkela, India

Bibhudatta Sahoo
National Institute of Technology Rourkela, India

Sourav Kanti Addya
National Institute of Technology Rourkela, India

Acknowledgment

At the outset, we would like to thank all the chapter authors for their excellent contributions. We would like to offer my special thanks to IGI Global for the opportunity to edit the publication.

We would like to acknowledge the role of the reviewers and editorial team for their support. Finally, we thank to our family for their continuous encouragement and support in our scholastic pursuits.

Ashok Kumar Turuk
National Institute of Technology Rourkela, India

Bibhudatta Sahoo
National Institute of Technology Rourkela, India

Sourav Kanti Addya
National Institute of Technology Rourkela, India

Chapter 1
Ubiquitous and Cloud Computing:
Ubiquitous Computing

Pinar Kirci
Istanbul University, Turkey

ABSTRACT

Recently, great developments in computing and telecommunication technologies caused big amounts of data flow over Internet, especially due to increasing smart device users. Within the last few years, ubiquitous communication has improved with new telecommunication and transmission infrastructures and also enriched with new services. The focus of ubiquitous computing is presenting environments including computing and communication abilities that are integrated with users. Mobile and pervasive computing present many opportunities about exploring various factors all over the world with searching large habitats and species. The services and applications are presented via a heterogeneous environment over many different devices by the ubiquitous system. Accordingly, ubiquitous computing is becoming more popular because of the new research developments and great technological advances in wireless communication networks, cloud computing, Internet technologies, mobile and distributed computing.

INTRODUCTION

Today, the term of ubiquitous computing, also called as *pervasive computing* was introduced in (Weiser,1991). The basic idea behind the ubiquitous computing is providing a surrounding intelligence at anywhere and anytime with accomplishing every kind of tasks by many network devices to provide more comfortable life for people.

Day by day, the sensor usage increases by mounting them at many devices to be able to utilize at inside or outside of a definite area. Today, most of the world population use these computations and sensing capable devices in their daily life together with the improved and new generation mobile devices that have data processing and storage capabilities. Because, the amount of information transmission between users, devices and environments increase and human activity contexts are produced. Thus, an

DOI: 10.4018/978-1-5225-1721-4.ch001

ambient intelligence (AmI) infrastructure is presented for the pervasively existing intelligence at the covering area around which is delicate to the human presence and also ubiquitous computing (UbiComp) applications are deployed. Human centric ubiquitous computing systems own the facilities of mobility and pervasiveness. A ubiquitous computing system should be fault tolerant, robust and it should be able to adapt the changing factors around itself. Also, in a ubiquitous computing system, the heterogeneity of hardware, networks and operating systems should be masked and also novice users should be able to utilize the system easily. Ubiquitous computing systems combine multi-disciplinary research areas, thus security and privacy is the most important topics for each one of the multidisciplines.

To provide security, there should be interdisciplinary collaboration between the networking, security, software, sensing and architecture disciplines. Ubiquitous computing systems own an interaction through multimodal interfaces that have non visual sensitivity. In addition to this, the system includes implicit interaction with mere presence of the user, human computer interaction, human physical interaction and intelligent agents interaction. Because of having an interdisciplinary structure, the system benefits from the developments at the considered disciplines like energy consumption and green transportation, lately (Zaharakis & Komninos, 2012).

Basically, ubiquitous and pervasive computing focuses on developing an intelligent area by seamless service access for users with determining the applications and needs. And another aim of ubiquitous computing is developing service provisioning to improve the life quality of people by the help of the basic computing and networking infrastructures. Besides, providing resources for the high level requirements of applications that include context and needs of the users together with providing efficiency is also one of the main aims of the system. Some of the considered applications are health care, social networking, assisted living, smart spaces and logistics. These applications have reliability, adaptability, context-awareness and flexibility properties.

The system is composed of wireless communications and Bluetooth, Zigbee, LTE and Wi-Fi are the most known of them. Furthermore, these smart device technologies are also used with Radio Frequency ID (RFID) tags, sensors, wearable computers and smart phones by the help of the last improvements about small sensors to provide ubiquitous services and enlarge their usage areas. Here, with the system, multiple device programming and providing interaction between them is performed. Also, service management, context and data facilities are performed together with solving the battery insufficiency problem at resource constraints.

Ubiquitous computing systems can not directly utilize from middleware design methods which are generally used at distributed computing systems. The reasons can be summarized as three layers. The first one is about the power consumption and energy limits of the devices. Because of the collaboration of the system with embedded devices and sensors, it needs a lightly implementing middleware since these devices occupy finite energy. Next, the heterogeneity and complexity of the network structures, operating systems and devices should be hidden in and between them because the heterogeneity at ubiquitous computing systems is higher than mobile and distributed structures. Third, in ubiquitous computing systems, the applications need context awareness and service orientation facilities to serve situation aware services. Here, to be able to provide the derivation of higher level context, the collection and processing of raw context with some mechanisms are used. Eventually, these systems own vital facilities about commerce, health care, traffic and transport management applications. To support these applications, there should not be an interruption or the users should not be disturbed. Especially, health care applications should work permanently, the interruptions in milliseconds may affect the life qualities of old and disabled people who need permanent medical care during their lifes' definite period. Also, the traffic management of airplanes and vehicles need crucial consideration, because the system could not handle system collapse easily (Raychoudhury, Cao, Kumar & Zhang, 2013).

In this chapter, ubiquitous and mobile computing techniques are briefly presented. Also, most remarkable applications and standards are described. The chapter is organized as follows. In Section 1, basic ttechniques for interoperability of ubiquitous systems are surveyed. In Section 2, most important ubiquitous computing applications are given. In Section 3, ubiquitous network structure is presented. In Section 4, an overview is provided about the standards of ubiquitous computing applications. The conclusion part, provides a summary and concludes the chapter.

TECHNIQUES FOR INTEROPERABILITY OF UBIQUITOUS SYSTEMS

Internet is a communication and data transmission platform and also an ubiquitous communication field. It continues its development with more distributed, secure and high complexity owning structure to provide more private and better social interactions. Especially, with online cooperation, the data transmission over mobile devices become more popular.

In Figure 1, the presented network structure is utilized for providing the connection and transmission of new services as ubiquitously. In the ubiquitous and pervasive manner, the communication is performed as anytime, anywhere and over any device via a determined communication technology in a heterogeneous environment with the cooperation of nearly all type of networks including wireless, satellite, broadcasting and wired networks (Torres, Nogueira & Pujolle, 2013).

Figure 1. Future network infrastructure
Source: Torres, Nogueira, Pujolle, 2013

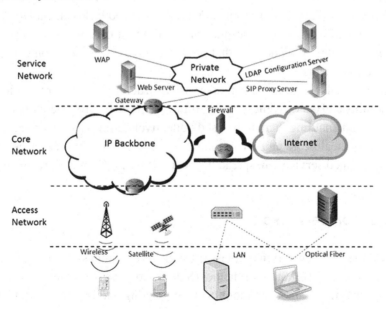

Mobile Technology

In recent years, internet usage rates ascended together with the increasing number of internet users and the current state caused new technological developments in wireless networks for instance in cellular networks, wireless LAN (WLAN) and WiMAX (worldwide interoperability for microwave access). They are the most important of these presented technologies. WLAN technologies become very popular in a short time period because of being cheap and having easy installation procedure. Besides, the technology reaches high data transmission values with IEEE 802.11. Today, a big city may be encompassed with some access points (AP) by WLANs that are conducted with different IP subnets. Such as, wireless Philadelphia or wireless London are one of the most quickly spreading wireless networks all over the world. With the insuppressible developments in WSNs, the expansion of the technology accelerated recently as ubiquitous WLAN structure mostly.

The communication of a mobile node with Internet is provided by an access point according to the coverage in WLAN. Here, the mobile nodes need to have many handovers over various IP subnets. Mobility management schemes like mobile IP (MIP) and mobile stream control transmission protocol (mSCTP) are used to provide the wireless and mobile connection during the IP address changes. A mobile node of a ubiquitous wireless LAN may go from one access point to another during application utilizations (Kashıhara, Tsukamoto & Oie, 2007).

In WSNs, mobility is utilized in military, environmental, commercial and civil areas together with localization. Furthermore, in commercial areas, the service robots are constructed for nursing to patients at home, providing security at definite areas and servicing people in houses, hotels and restaurants. The software design of these robots include permanent localization. In housekeeping robot applications, map of the rooms are produced to walk in the rooms by using sensors. Also, in civil usage area, there are many WSN usage examples, in the first one, pothole detectors are employed for streets that are carried by the cars. The next one is about emergency situations, in the advanced 911 emergency service which is wireless E91, the position of the caller is found when the service is called, by localization methods (Ararez, Chaouchi & Gurkas, 2011; Amundson & Koutsoukos, 2009; Roxin, Gaber, Wack & Nait-Sidi-Moh, 2007; Yu & Wang, 2008).Today, smartphones and PDAs are very common and they are known as the most used personal computing devices that present many services and contents depending on the users' interests and requirements.

In the future, Internet will be composed of a pervasive structure with heterogeneity owning devices and resources. In mobility and pervasiveness having future Internet, heterogeneous resources over mobile devices are managed with enabling them to be used collectively, thus user generated content sharing at content-centric services, healthcare and area monitoring at environmental services and mobile social networking at social oriented services are spread between the users (Conti, Giordano, May & Passarella, 2010).

Wireless and Sensor Networks

Main research aim of the next generation wireless networks is encompassing the coverage of ubiquitous high data rates with high spectral efficiency schemes (Salem, Adinoyi, Yanikomeroglu & Falconer, 2010). Lately, WSNs are getting more famous in monitoring, collecting and processing data at many different areas. Sensors present remarkable benefits for space researches, wild area investigations, remote health monitoring and war area monitoring systems. Sometimes, the sensors are left to the corresponding areas at random. They are mostly left at steep areas. And for monitoring their environment, these sensors (nodes) have to find out at first their own location in some situations. Besides, in some applications of remote medical systems, the sensors are mounted to the elder people or patients to detect only their locations because the location detection of these people may be vital in some emergency situations (Ma, Yang & Zhao, 2013).

In wild areas, small sized and autonomous sensors are left with an ad hoc style to gain information reports with sampling from the environment, storing the collected information and sending the gained information to the base station. In air change monitoring, war area monitoring and animal monitoring, event detection and storage applications are provided. In event detection, the collected data is evaluated if it is useful or not for sending to the base station. Then, the sensors store the collected data as in database like storages, in event based systems (Kulkarni, Förster & Venayagamoorthy, 2011).

The improvement of wireless sensor networks (WSN) still proceed under many subtitles. Each one of all these subtitles include great resources for users, thus they are examined, evaluated and utilized with many protocols and algorithms by researchers. Especially, the developments in sensor technology cause wireless sensor networks (WSNs) to attract an ever growing attention. WSNs are used in different areas: disaster, battlefield supervision and tracking as a reliable, cheap and functional solution. The vital part of the introduced WSN solutions is the collected location information by the sensors. Detection of a sensor's position with less expenditure and exact place indication is known as sensor localization problem in WSNs.

A sensor node includes many parts: sensing part, processor, transmitter, mobilizer, position finding system and power units. Data sensing and gaining about an area with considering the surrounding circumstances is provided by the sensors. Then, the collected data is converted into signals to transmit and process. The sensor nodes on the sensor field send the gained data to the sink over a multihop structure. WSN is mostly used in medical care monitoring, distributed computing, stock monitoring and rescue managements with collecting, processing and transmitting data by many sensors.

Routing tables and latest routing informations are used in routing of static nodes. In routing mobile nodes, the data at the routing table or routing history informations become old and useless in a very short time period. So, these informations need to be renewed frequently with extra cost and time, thus localization researches consider minimizing these extra needs. Furthermore, more channel capacity, more transmission pathways and accuracy at the gathered data are presented by the network mobility also less number of hops in transmission distance is provided for the messages which traverse base stations. The localization of network nodes is one of the most important titles in WSNs. In some scenarios, the nodes know their own places during information sensing process, thus they can transmit the information with their position data. In many indoor and outdoor applications, the positions of the nodes should be known, thus the localization problem attracts great attention of researchers' lately. Most of the localization studies are about static network structure, but in some applications, mobile network structure may be more useful, because the monitored area can be examined more easily with the help of the mobile sensors. Recently, treatment, rescue and chasing in health system, environmental area, locomotion and dead-reckoning applications are supported by WSNs. GPS is commonly used but rather expensive method in outdoor position estimation of nodes. In GPS, satellites transmit epheremis data and transmission time containing messages to mobile receivers, so the receivers can estimate their location with the help of lateration method (Kirci, Chaouchi & Laouiti, 2014).

Recently, many different needs and requirements of mobile users are provided by wireless access technologies that are in a tremendous evolution period. The basic aim of next generation all-IP network architecture is integrating many diverse but complementary technologies under an internet like common infrastructure. So, an ubiquitous, anytime, anywhere connectivity and transmission will be constructed. To be able to cooperate with each other, the basic structure of wireless networks is compatible with ubiquitous network structures (Xu, He, Zhang, Chen & Xu, 2013).

Localization of mobile users and management of their mobility over the whole network are the basic issues at the improvement of context aware applications in ubiquitous environments and also for the intelligent utilization of its full potential. But the considered idea has some difficulties about the inter-operability of heterogeneous networks and the seamless switching between them. Searching about potential synergies of them may give some opportunities about tackling many problems and providing different functionalities at the envisioned multi access networks for improving user's experience. And also in the telecommunication and navigation fields, localization with radio signals has attracted considerable attention, lately.

Global Positioning System (GPS) is one of the mostly used and satellite based positioning technology. Also, the technology is very successful about tracking users at outdoor environments. In wireless networking, localization of a sensor is very significant and vital because knowing the exact positions of sensors are needed for some of the applications, routing protocols and algorithms. Manually determining the exact places of sensors may be very hard and may cause high costs in steep and upstate environments and for localization, using GPS for each one of the sensors in the network is also expensive and hard. Besides, GPS is known as the best and exact position determining technology for localization between other technologies. GPS technology is composed of 24 satellites to indicate the positions of mobile nodes. These satellites are controlled by delicate clocks and monitor stations. Furthermore, there should be some equipment at the mobile nodes to receive the GPS signals, in the system the receivers at the users are used for measuring the travel time of the GPS satellite signals. And for the receivers, timing is an essential factor in GPS transmission. By the way, during the localization, the generated long lasting delays are the most significant disadvantages of the GPS.

In GPS, WSN structure includes numerous wireless sensors, some of them are manually arranged but most of them are randomly scattered. But, manually arranged GPS based wireless sensors consume more time and cause high costs. For this reason, wireless sensors are scattered as randomly over the area and then, their positions are determined by localization algorithms. Data about the locations of the sensors is significant for improving the efficiency of the network protocols. Obtaining the target sensor position is vital for managing the catastrophic facts in emergency situations and the data collected from the sensor nodes that know their positions may be used for monitoring, redirecting and conducting people at the emergency services during the disasters.

Otherwise, for indoor environments, GPS based wireless sensors are not appropriate, because the inability of satellite signals to penetrate buildings causes GPS to fail in indoor environments. The indoor radio propagation channel is characterized as site specific and low probability of line-of-sight (LOS) signal propagation among transmitter and receiver to make accurate indoor positioning very challenging. Infrared, WiFi and RFID wireless technologies are presented for indoor location sensing. Additionally, in literature, many techniques are given to find the locations of sensors with distance estimation, position calculation and localization algorithms (Kirci, Chaouchi & Laouiti, 2014).

RFID Technology

In medical area, radio frequency identification (RFID) is another developing technology, with reducing medical errors, providing more secure access and improving the healthcare quality in hospitals by monitoring and identifying patients, hospital personnel and hospital equipment. To be able to monitor patients, personnel and staff in hospital, RFID is needed because of many vital reasons. RFID provides security and time saving while serving patients, at especially emergency situations. At the beginning, RFID tags were implanted to animals, afterwards low frequency (LF) and high frequency (HF) RFID systems were mounted on the bodies but these systems were limited because of their short ranges and very low data rates. The main reason of the disadvantages is about the attenuation of the signal. The ultra-high frequency (UHF) and microwave RFID systems have larger operation ranges and higher data rates because of their strong attenuated signals inside the body tissues. Today, they are also implanted in the human body instead of wearing over the body, thus there will be no risk about losting of the tags and it will not be perceptible from outside with its invisible manner. Also, other than tagging applications, RFID can be used at integrated sensing and signal processing areas. In monitoring with sensor applications, the usage of RFID tags with RFID based personal area networks may be useful in gathering data about the patients (Sani, Rajab, Foster & Hao, 2010).

Many electronic tags are needed to be able to ensure the pervasive interconnection with things at the industrial process monitoring, security surveillance and at the habitat controlling to be able to connect over objects as presented in Figure 2. RFID technology, lets its physical state to be noticed and provides a digital code to correlate with an object in a wireless manner. According to the merging styles and functionalities, RFID tags can be equipped with many sensors. Wider operating areas and higher data rates are provided by active RFID tags with a true microcontroller and independent batteries, but ensuring these facilities cause high costs. Furthermore, the presented technology have a limited lifetime. By the way, passive RFID tags have a battery free structure and for monitoring applications, they can be mounted as tagged objects.

Figure 2. Sensing with RFID readers
Source: Marrocco, 2010

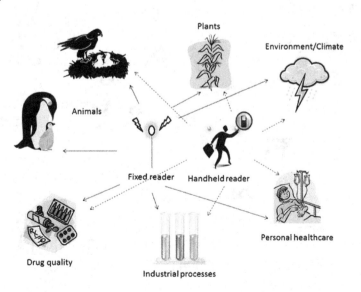

RFID tag is a kind of small computer which works with the combination of microchip data type digital structure and analog antenna that is known as low power radio. Here, the data at the reader is encoded as digital. The management of the backscattered power is performed as analog with the orientation between the reader and tags, also by the interaction with objects around. So, the data gathering can be done by using RFID without using sensors (Marrocco, 2010).

UBIQUTIOUS COMPUTING APPLICATIONS

Ubiquitous Computing in Monitoring Animals and Plants

With wireless sensor networks (WSNs), it is easy to cover large fields over the world depending on the technology and basic requirements with consuming less power and lower cost compared with the proposed communication technologies. By the help of the great functionality of their structure, WSNs are used in many fields: in environment monitoring by gathering data about the wildlife of animals, climate, pollution rates in air, water and soil as given in Figure 3. Also, the disaster and battlefield monitoring can be used to take precautions such as at volcanic eruptions, earthquakes, flood disasters and tornados.

And, the technology can be utilized to increase the productivity in agriculture and farming in big farms. At an animal farm, a basic WSN production monitoring system includes a network structure composed of farm indoor/outdoor sensors, the management part together with the veterinary part and access devices: gateway and public communication networks. Wireless networks enable people to reach network resources in their homes, schools or primary networking environments. Today, many applications: e-agriculture, e-livestock and e-education are based on computers and mobile phones, because of the ever increasing computer and mobile phone usage.

Figure 3. Farm monitoring system
Source: Schoofs, Daymand, Sugar & Mueller, et al., 2009

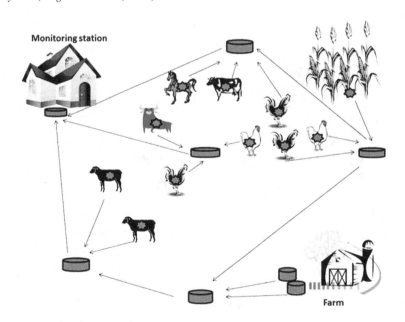

During the last twenty years, hens and other animals are laid at cages or small areas but this system is out of date. Especially, egg producers and farmers have decided to raise the hens and farm animals at non-cage and larger fields, recently. Because small fields and in cage areas cause stagnancy and stress on animals. Thus, weak, unhealthy and ill animals are produced in the farms. Due to these factors, the gained egg, milk and meat production quality and rates become worse and less in time. To follow the animals at non cage areas and larger fields is a challenging situation. Most of the researches focused on the egg, milk, meat and other gained products' production rates. Also, water, nutrition, medicine consumption rates of the animals and the indoor environment temperature, moisture and oxygen rates are considered and examined. While monitoring daily routine of an animal, many different factors and parameters are considered. In (Banerjee, Biswas, Daigle & Siegford, 2012) wearable sensors are mounted on the hens to monitor the daily activities of them. Many vital illnesses influence the health of the farm animals and their productivity rates. For this reason, it will be very useful to follow these illnesses with sensors. Infected chickens and animals by viruses are examined and inspected deeply but initial diagnosis is more important. Because if there is an infected animal at the farm area, the virus spreads very quickly from animal to animal, thus it is very important to be able to define the first infected animal before infecting other animals in the farm area. Here, a temperature sensor and an accelerometer owning wireless sensor is mounted to the hens, to follow the movements, body temperatures and to detect the unusual states of hens caused by the virus. When the sensors sense fever at the hens or weakness at the movements of hens, then, the manager is informed by sending a health information report as in (Okada, Itoh, Suzuki, Tatsuya & Tsukamoto, 2010). To be able to detect this kind of changes immediately at farm animals, most of the researchers are concentrated on wearable sensors.

For cattle, generally static sensors are used in the farms. The animals are easily followed when they are in the monitoring area of the static sensors which are attached at definite places in the farms. Furthermore, for big animals, leg or neck collars are used. These collars are mostly utilized at cattles to gather information: body temperature, breath rates, heart rates, movement speeds, periods and time (Kwong, Sasloglou, Goh & Wu, 2009). Accordingly, collecting vital and real time data about the farm animals will be easier by the help of the pervasive structure based technologies.

Ubiquitous Computing in Public Transport Accessibility

Nowadays, the subject of smart cities getting more popular in pervasive computing. In smart cities, to develop the services that are needed at the cities, sensors are used. The people who live in the city and the considered objects are used as sensors. Also, various sensors and data are conceived as digital traces. And to be able to gather traces, pervasive devices and systems are employed. Monitoring the mobility of people with pervasive data, supplies real time and actual information about old and disabled people, because this kind of people get lost easily, forget to interchange, get on or get off at the wrong stations and lose time and money. Therefore, to monitor these people while using city services during their wandering in the city, will help to determine the usage rates of the stations. To benefit from pervasive mobility data, gives comprehension about the characteristics of urban transportation network. In consequence of such explorations, the problems, the drawbacks of the already presented solutions reveal. Thus, proper, adequate and qualified solutions can be presented for ensuring efficient investments (Ferrari, Berlingerio, Calabrese & Curtis-Davidson, 2013).

Sensor Network Applications and Healthcare Systems in Ubiquitous Computing

In remote health care applications, wireless sensor networks (WSNs) are mostly used to detect body temperature, body pressure, heart pulses and activity rates of people. With the sensors, a wide range of medical and general information of people can be collected easily. Furthermore, with these valuable information, vital results can be produced for medical systems. By the way, mobile application usage rates affected by the great increase in the number of smartphone users. Especially in medical applications, utilizing from cheap and light sensors with smartphones is crucial for patients and old people who need medical care. To mount the wireless and wearable sensors on patients, simplifies collecting data about physical and physiologic states of patients at everywhere.

To monitor and gather the medical situation data of patients with wireless sensor methods and send them to a remote center is a significant topic in both communication and medical areas as represented in Figure 4. With the new advances in communication and informatique, composing a portable and wireless remote health monitoring system gets simpler and cheaper. With these systems, monitoring of patients out of the hospital and informing related people and institutions immediately is possible in emergency situations. Also, long term recording of diagnosis of definite illnesses is possible, thus these systems improve the life standards of patients and medical care needing people.

Medical monitoring systems are introduced as analog electrocardiogram (ECG) systems at the beginning of 20th century. Medical monitoring systems and wireless technologies have progressed over time. Initially, portable monitoring devices are proposed and consequently wireless medical monitoring devices are put on the markets.

To provide multiparametric and remote monitoring, outside the hospital by patient's mobile phone will decrease the hospitalization of patients who suffer from chronic diseases. In addition to collecting and sending vital signals from personal body area of a patient to the remote medical center system may

Figure 4. Basic healthcare system architecture
Source: Kirci, Kurt & Omercikoglu, 2014

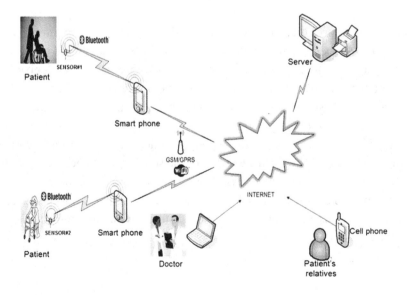

interact and cooperate with other people around the patient. Other mobile users around the patient: other patients, care givers and the sensors around, can be utilized to determine the environment. The state of the patient, the communication and contact history of the patient and the received stimuli can be monitored, so the functionality of the system can be enriched (Kirci, Kurt & Omercikoglu, 2014).

In our century, the people communicate with each other easily by using internet and mobile devices: mobile phones and computers. Mobile and sensor technology in remote monitoring is used in many states: controlling of patients' behaviors after operations, following the medicine effects on patients, following daily fever rates, following heart rate and weight values. All of the considered data can be gathered by medical systems, then they are examined and reported to the medical centers. Thus, the system will help patients to improve their health state in a short time. Wireless technology simplifies networking by enabling multiple computers to simultaneously reach resources: broadband internet connection, data files, streaming audio and video at home, school or café. And also it allows to utilize many applications without using additional wiring or technology. At the beginning, computer users were single and stand-alone but today, they are using multiple devices over networks by owning different operating systems and varying peripheral hardwares, thus resource sharing become more popular for computer users (Chen, Shen, Huo & Xu, 2010).

People have stressful lives and many health problems because of living in crowded cities and working for long hours. Thus, the number of medical treatment needing people increases day by day. Unfortunately, there is not sufficient number of medical centers or medical staff for providing the needs of all patients. In addition to this, many old and incapable people require medical treatments in their own homes but this kind of medical care for patients is rather expensive. Thus, remote and mobile medical management is gaining attention recently, to present medical care for patients especially in their homes. Monitoring, gathering and processing the psychological data of a person gives very valuable results for doctors and the psychology science. Because even in hospitals it is impossible to follow people's behaviors and movements in a psychological manner during the day. By following patients or elder people after serious treatments and surgeries, we can learn more about the effects of medicines on people, recovery periods of surgeries, traumas and diseases. And also, body reactions to many factors: stress, fear and cold between different ages, genders and races can be detected. Eventually, all of these factors can be examined easily and cheaply without disturbing patients and doctors by remote medical systems (Liu, Wu & Hou, 2012).

Ubiquitous Systems for Physiological Personal Health

The things, actions and facts that effect our physiology can be detected and measured. Wearable bio physiological sensors sense many parameters around us and from our experiences. By wearable sensors, it is possible to monitor, gather and record the data of our physiological signals during the twenty-four hours in a day and seven days in a week, thus we may determine which actions or choices influence our physiology. Do our sleeping hours, eating and working habits and other daily actions influence our activity levels, general performance and quality of our life? To answer these questions, physiological signals should be collected and labeled with contextual informations which are gained by self-reports of patients' diaries and logs or by observation of patients' activities with monitoring. Contextual information contains many states: position, activity, nutrition, social activities and sleeping. Contemporarily, various contextual data about patients are collected by mobile phones and sensors in many researches (Ayzenberg & Picard, 2014).

A Ubiquitous System for Learning of Children with Autism

For children with autism, to focus on a task and process an information is not easy. Also, to recognize, understand and express their emotions are difficult for them. According to some psychologists, emotional changes of the children may affect their attention changes. Generally, discrete trial teaching method is used with dividing tasks into smaller ones which are named as trials, in the education of children with autism. As a second education method, stimulus response reward is used with utilizing from physical objects and devices to teach attention management like basic skills. But, these methods are not as useful as expected, because according to most of the children, it is very boring to repeat tasks many times and also the used objects do not seem interesting and attract their attention. Thus, most of the children are not interested in their education tasks and consume their time to no avail. Teachers use many different methods to attract the attention of children. Teachers utilize from giving reward method when the children give right answers to the asked questions together with utilizing from physical, verbal prompts and putting explanations on the physical objects.

At some therapies, to be able to attract the attention of children with autism to the physical objects, digital words are used in Mobile Object Identification System (Mobis). In the system, digital explanations can be put on the physical objects with the mobile reality application at the therapies. Furthermore, the effectiveness of the system is examined if it is useful for improving the selective attentions and revealing the positive emotions of children with autism, during the therapies. One of the most important advantages of the mobis system is the easy integration of the system with other pervasive technologies in the therapy classes. To provide such an opportunity will improve the effectiveness of the teachers in the classrooms about easy following and catching the contextual information considered with the attention of the children and also that factor will be helpful to increase the children's improvement (Escobedo, Tentori, Quintana & Favela, et al, 2014).

Mobile Social Networks (MSN) and Ubiquitous Computing

At the pervasive communication platform based mobile social networking, users can make searches with using their smartphones on the Internet. To obtain the needed information, they can make neighboring peer queries with mobile social networking. Latest and most popular social networking sites: Facebook and Twitter have nearly 1.3 billion users all over the world. The popularity of social networking depends on both the ubiquitous connections of Internet networks and the recent technological developments of smartphones. Because of these factors, social networking becomes more accessible among mobile users. With mobile social networking, reaching real time worldwide news and staying up to date are the basic facilities provided by the system. And also sending and receiving messages at anytime, anywhere and from anybody related is achieved by the pervasive communication platform which is composed of smartphones, network infrastructures and social networking as illustrated in Figure 5. The popularity of MSN is increased with the mobile applications. Mobile applications allow their users to control their social updates, watch online videos and share photos, files over a mobile field with the transmissions among smartphone users and Internet service providers. Also, in location based applications, data is basically downloaded from Internet. Initially, the positions of the smartphones are determined by the GPS and then the gathered information is sent to Internet service providers. Consequently, the gathered information is mostly preferred and used by Facebook and Foursquare. Also, the communication of smartphone users with neighbor smartphone users and local service providers over Bluetooth and WiFi Direct is known as autonomous mobile applications.

Figure 5. Mobile social network structure
Source: Liang, Zhang, Shen & Lin, 2014

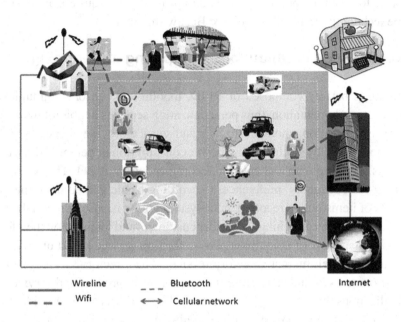

Smartphone users use many different technologies to communicate with other smartphone users, Internet service providers and local service providers by mobile applications (Liang, Zhang, Shen & Lin, 2014).

Agriculture with Pervasive Wireless Sensor Networks

People need agriculture, water and animals to be able to provide best life standards, thus people should use water resources and lands over the world as efficiently and carefully as possible. Lately, to provide these needs, pervasive and wireless sensor network based smart farms are used for animal management in farms. Besides, agricultural monitoring is a growing research area. Because by following many factors: farm products, crop, soil and animals, their productivity and yield will be increased. Here, the main aim is improving the farm productivity with less labor and cost. In monitoring with sensor nodes, they sense and measure many factors: temperature and humidity of plants to determine the crop quality, the state of pastures with following the moisture by sensors, the pasture assessment of grass coverage, grass height and greenness level by the cameras (Wark, Corke, Sikka & Klingbeil, 2007).

Pervasive computing technology belonging sensor systems collect information over the environment. Temperature values, lighting rates, moisture, the movement and presence of people and many more aspects of the environment and the species can be collected with sensors. According to the needs of the determined products, the requirements are provided by the designed monitoring system results and produced solutions. In the vineyard systems, frost is considered as a problem in winter period because it affects vines in a bad way, as a solution, night temperatures are followed in winter period against sudden frost affects with an alert system. And also, with following the temperature, ripeness of the grapes' can be understood so the harvest time can be decided, also powdery mildew risk may be realised with the temperature data promptly and the gained data can be used to decide which part of the vineyard should spray itself immediately to prevent the spreading risk. Agriculture needs delicate care during twenty-four hours and seven days, to give the optimum yield and to provide this requirement, pervasive computing is the most suitable technology (Burrell, Brooke & Beckwith, 2004).

Personalization Services in Ubiquitous Computing at Shopping

Ubiquitous computing is basicly composed of RFID, mobile and sensor communication devices as network technologies at implementation, thus personalization services in ubiquitous computing spreads with utilizing seamless interaction among customers and service providers' speciality. Ubiquitous personalization should cover privacy, security, low power consumption at personal devices for a customer network in ubiquitous shopping with a client side recommendation model. The proposed system has a learning ability about the customers' preferences. According to the gained data, the system produces recommendation lists of items with a recommender system which is based on collaborative filtering in minimum computational time by searching for similar customers and focusing on their local relationship.

To have the help and support of ubiquitous personalization service based ubiquitous shopping applications is better and more helpful than directory services. The directory services which are presented in the shopping environments include and present common store, product and service lists but in ubiquitous shopping applications the data is customized according to the users as individually and separately by providing current recommendations. Actually, reaching big amounts of data sources by many users with ubiquitous networks is provided by recommendation techniques in the ubiquitous personalization services. Here, the personal mobile device users having similar choices are connected over presented system and offered them a convenient shopping experience (Kim, Kim & Ryu, 2009).

UBIQUITOUS NETWORKS

The undeterred expanding of Internet due to the major improvements in telecommunication and technological area, takes place in our century. Internet provides many services: e-applications, advertising and entertainment according to the users' demands in social and business areas having wireless structures that is suitable for the construction of anywhere, anytime computing which is named as ubiquitous computing by ensuring multiple of computers to be in a convenient situation at a physical environment as invisible in Figure 6. Ensuring the computing at anywhere and at any time as staying at the background for end users is the focus of ubiquitous computing. Networking and ubiquitous computing can cooperate with each other because of the virtual nature of Internet with wireless and mobile networks. In ubiquitous computing, many different devices: cell phones, laptops and PDAs operate on many wireless technologies: Wi-Fi, Bluetooth and Wi-MAX.

Ubiquitous networks are examined under two categories with consisting of LAN and across networks. Ubiquitous LAN network is composed of windows, Linux and Mac PCs like dissimilar devices but an across network based ubiquitous network structure is composed of different technologies like wireless/ Ethernet and LAN connecting to a cellular network. Consequently, the connection of these networks constructs a ubiquitous WAN but there may be some incompatibilities in between the networks such as packet losses may occur during mobility or while switching in the network, delays may emerge.

Figure 6. Ubiquitous network architecture
Source: Obaidat, Denko & Woungang, 2011

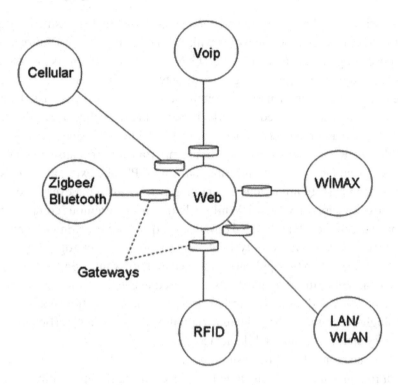

Ubiquitous network architecture is composed of three hierarchies as LANs, WAPs (Wireless Access Point) or RBS (Relay Base Stations) and the Internet/IP backbone. There is an internal connection between LANs and the connection to the Internet is provided by theWAPs or RBS which is serving as a gateway. LANs cover smaller environments like home and office with WMNs (Wireless Mesh Networks), PANs (Personal Area Networks), MANETs (Mobile Ad hoc Networks). And the interconnected LANs own their LAN managers, for performing QoS, performance and privacy issues. Base stations emerge in computer and radio communication networks as mostly in fixed state. According to the placements of base stations, they are categorized as remote base station, relay base station and home base station. They are used as central hubs in wireless networks and gateways among wired and wireless networks. And, TCP/IP backhaul is the backbone infrastructure at the connection phase of these networks because TCP/IP is the networking standard protocol.

Diverse technologies are used together with multiple of component networks in the complicated ubiquitous network architecture. Because of its complicated structure, to be able to manage an ubiquitous network structure, autonomic networking is based on at the setup, configuration, maintenance and administration processes as a solution. Ubiquitous computing may cooperate with autonomic networking, thus ubiquitous network structure will be administrated easily because the network will have a more practical structure (Obaidat, Denko & Woungang, 2011).

STANDARDS OF UBIQUITOUS COMPUTING APPLICATIONS

Information transmission including personal and context data constructs transmission and communication systems mostly over heterogeneous networks which is the main part of ubiquitous systems. Basicly, the system is composed of gateways and end nodes. Gateways are mostly in fixed structure and they are used for providing the communication among the sub networks with their high computing power and also end nodes send and receive information through the network over gateways. Ubiquitous systems are composed of both wireless and wired networks for ensuring the robustness. The data transmission of wireless devices may be assured over wireless networks and by backbone networks.

Besides, in wireless networks context awareness is an important topic because in some of the ubiquitous system applications, the collected context information from GPS like external devices or the wireless network itself is the main part. In ubiquitous computing, with ensuring at everywhere, anytime access over every device provide users a new world. While utilizing from ubiquitous computing, they might not realize that they make use of the computational devices. Ubiquitous computing is comprised of essential technologies and standards, basicly: mobility, context-awareness and heterogeneity.

To enable users to utilize from the applications whenever they want and whichever place they prefer and also as mobile, makes ubiquitous applications to be used in everyday life and conglutinated to many activities. To assure mobility and succeed seamless access, some necessities should be ensured on communication technologies and standards: indulgencing failures and roaming efficiently with the limited bandwidth and battery source owning mobile devices.

In mobility, the connections should be ensured permanently for the moving users from one place to another during their roaming and wandering together with ensuring the applications and data to be alive. But there are some issues arise about data coherence and synchronization, because of keeping a copy of data and pervasive dependability problem on every day systems. Due to these reasons, proposed solutions should have limited resource including cheap and simple devices. In service selection procedure, users want to make free selections but it is hard to provide this kind of dynamic environments at daily activities. Also, broken link failures due to mobility should be considered and system adaptation should be provided. Additionally, security and privacy are the crucial factors in ubiquitous systems that provide mobility. To ensure simple, easy, extemporary access and transmission for users over heterogenous environments of many standards and devices, new solutions are needed.

Using of data to determine the state of an entity as location, object and people is known as context awareness. Most important one of these entities is location which includes location based service type definite localization with tracking by sensor network, GPS or over wireless network by some methods.

Besides, dynamic adaptation to user requirements and choices with personal awareness is also a considerable factor. Most appropriate and best services can alter due to the choices and criterias of users' contexts. The context in ubiquitous systems include spontaneous, occasional user interaction and transparent, natural user interaction in the related issue. By the way, temporal awareness that includes time scheduling of events and device awareness with processing power and battery are also important factors. In personal awareness, the private and individual data of people is utilized and transmitted as digital like the position data of people in context aware applications. Here, the vital problem is ensuring the privacy for every one of the users in public and private places by anonymous storing or information deletion after a while.

Today, in our tremendous technological environment there are various kinds of systems, appliances and networks that make the environment considerable in especially ubiquitous systems and they are named as heterogeneous environments. Heterogeneity is a crucial topic for ubiquitous systems because ubiquitous systems need heterogeneous and dynamic environments more than others and to be able to utilize heterogeneity, a unifying middleware layer is defined at the appliances and services. In distributed systems to deal with the heterogeneity, a software layer is used as middleware by locating among the operating system and applications, because it provides a general interface for every kind of devices without considering their network technology and hardware types, thus middleware is a vital structure for ubiquitous systems. Through the considered layer, software complexity is reduced and a homogeneous interface is presented for the system's upper layers but there are still incompatible standards appear that require an integration framework (Obaidat, Denko & Woungang, 2011).

CLOUD COMPUTING

Cloud computing includes the aim of transparency and virtualization of resources more than grid computing. Also, it provides the use of processing and storage capacities of servers, they are distributed over the world and linked with a network, like the Internet.

The main principle of grid computing and cloud computing is similar. They differ in implementation. In cloud computing, users do not have the computer servers providing the infrastructure. External resources are accessed as online without having to manage the underlying hardware. Because it is complicated for installing, configuring and keeping up-to-date, and also it is subject to failures. The economic model is based on the reciprocity of supply and maintenance of resources in the grid. But the user pays per use, such as, to rent a remote processor for a few hours in cloud computing. The data are not deployed on the user's local computer, but in a cloud composed of many interconnected remote servers. The results are retransmitted to the client or transmitted over sites. Access to the service is provided over a standard application, a web browser. The user invokes a job execution service by using a specific description language, in the grid. To be able to use the computing power, an access service to virtual resources is utilized in the cloud. The cloud provides an abstract infrastructure supplying resources and their associated services over the Internet. Management, communication and business application is capable of using the resource services presented by cloud computing technology. It is available at any computer that connects to the Internet. There are many different clouds are available: A storage cloud provides storage, a data cloud presents data-management services and a computing cloud gives data-processing services (Viat-Blanc, Soudan, Guillier & Goglin, 2011).

Ubiquitous Computing in Cloud Environment: Ubiquitous Cloud

In the ubiquitous computing, the adaptive ubiquitous services are a serious problem because of their dynamic adaptation of behaviors to contexts. To overcome this problem and utilize ubiquitous service resources, a ubiquitous cloud platform which is based on cloud computing is proposed. With the presented platform, it is encouraged to use ubiquitous objects in application levels, infrastructure and platform. The architecture of the presented platform is composed of the adaptive resource finder, the service resource registry, the service concierge and the context manager. And with and without the proposed ubiquitous cloud, a practical adaptive service is improved in a home network system.

To administer service resources for adaptive ubiquitous applications with services, an architecture is presented with Service Resource Registry, Adaptive Resource Finder, Context Manager and Service Concierge. Service Resource Registry presents an infrastructure providing ubiquitous resources utilizable as atomic Web services and it is positioned in the IaaS layer. Adaptive Resource Finder determines best service operations for users according to user contexts and it is positioned in the PaaS layer. Context Manager collects contextual data that belongs to real world by the underlying sensor services and it is positioned in the PaaS layer. Service Concierge performs published adaptive applications and it is positioned in the SaaS layer. Thus, with the presented ubiquitous cloud platform, the considered problem is solved and ubiquitous service resources are efficiently utilized (Egami, Matsumoto & Nakamura, 2011).

Ubiquitous Computing in Cloud Environment: Hybrid Pervasive Mobile Cloud Computing

The Hybrid Pervasive Mobile Cloud Computing (HPMCC) is composed of mobile, pervasive and cloud computing technologies with many benefits, for instance localized elastic scalability and multidimensional perception. Thus, it provides efficient human-machine interaction with preventing insufficient connectivity, security and sensing.

Pervasive systems own inadequate structures, thus they cannot detect differences, conceive context data, sustain seamless connectivity and provide security for the system. A restricted geographical area is utilized and executed by using all of the considered resources together with energy constraint entities. Distant clouds, nearby desktops, crowd of proximate SMDs, near/far mobile and fixed heterogeneous computing entities including new hybrid multi-tier architecture is proposed with HPMCC. Unlimited resources and context are provided but localized scalability is restricted. There is a low propagation delay between service consumer and provider over short distances, thus utilization time is advanced. Pervasiveness of SMDs together with sensing abilities raise smartness in ubiquitous systems with decreasing localized scalability. Ubiquitous systems use multidimensional perception over ubiquitous SMDs. But ubiquitous system's energy resources are limited. The hybrid multi-tier infrastructure provides smartness, perception and localized scalability. Thus, most of the ubiquitous problems such as smartness, context-awareness and localized scalability can be eased by HPMCC (Sanaei, Abolfazli, Khodadadi & Xia, 2014).

Ubiquitous and Cloud Applications: Healthcare

A pervasive healthcare monitoring (PHM) system is proposed in (Chen, Lin & Huang, 2011). The system includes medical wearable wireless sensors and planar super wideband (SWB) antenna. These cloud devices provide the needs of ubiquitous healthcare. The presented system is convenient for healthcare monitoring applications and mobile patient station (MPS) because of its cloud devices. It will have more cloud resources with higher channel capacity. Utilized cloud device provide radio cloud resources and their impedance bandwidths cover 1.69~20GHz. The broadband cloud device has compact characteristic. It ensures short/long distance transmitting cloud resources, together with Bluetooth, WiMAX2600, ZigBee, LTE2500, DCS, UWB, and PCS system. Also, it provides healthcare monitoring for mobile and nomadic patients and old people with cloud computing (Chen, Lin & Huang, 2011).

In a hospital, E-Healthcare data management is a vital topic because of the produced big amounts of data with latest diagnostic techniques. Too much time is consumed to keep and process medical data records. By the way, for Clinical Decision Support Systems (CDSS), fast data retrieval, and presentation services are needed. Large computing resources from Cloud Service Providers (CSP) is very important for outsourcing information services. Electronic Patient Record (EPR) management needs excellent security. Integrity, security availability and cross CSP mobility are problems that need to be solved. For ubiquitous services about data acquisition archiving and supplying in Cloud, E-Healthcare models are proposed in (Ahmed & Abdullah, 2011). In the cloud domain, a ubiquitous model of E-healthcare is given with data acquisition, presentation, archiving, and decision support services. A service architecture is utilized for management and security in cloud domains. The Cloud Services Architecture (CSA) based model is composed of communication and storage systems with Wireless Sensor Networks. In medical treatment and follow up procedures, E-Healthcare is vital. Internet is widely utilized in healthcare services, thus the scope of healthcare services is enlarged. Because of the ubiquitous connectivity and availability, cloud computing is getting remarkable (Ahmed & Abdullah, 2011).

Today, people pay attention for their health and health care because of their improving life styles. Thus, the cost of healthcare systems rise. There are many researches about improving the quality of health care services with lower costs. Ubiquitous life care (u-life care) is presented as a qualified, flexible, and cost-effective health care infrastructure. Also, for health care services, cloud computing ensures high cost savings and high throughput. Consequently, Secured Wireless Sensor Network (WSN) named platform architecture is presented (Khattak, Pervez, Ho, Lee,et al, 2010). The platform architecture is composed of an integrated cloud computing for u-Life Care with many wireless sensors. These wireless sensors gather and send data to cloud server over cloud gateway. Thus, the system ensures real-time home care, safety, information sharing and patient monitoring (Khattak, Pervez, Ho, Lee,et al, 2010).

Intelligent manipulation of activities with Context-aware Activity Manipulation Engine (CAME) which is base of Human Activity Recognition Engine (HARE) is studied. Context analysis of the activities are processed with utilizing wearable sensor based, video based and location based activity recognition engines. CAME receives real time, low level activity information from Activity Recognition Engines. Then, it makes situation analysis and with processing of activities by their corresponding data, it produces appropriate decisions. For processing of data, two phase filtering technique is used. The experimental results of activity information process, produced comparatively adequate accuracy (Khattak, Pervez, Ho & Lee, et al, 2010).

Lately, global patient information containing Personal Health Records (PHRs) have increased. PHRs are very important for many different systems in healthcare and the tax Payers. Emergency medical systems (EMS) are one of these systems. EMS starts when the time of a call is received to an ambulance service and ends at the time of patient's discharge from a hospital, thus collaboration is crucial for emergency healthcare services. For this reason, a PHR-based EMS is studied in a cloud computing environment in (Koufi, Malamateniou & Vassilacopoulos, 2010). The system is based on supplying pervasive access to medical data which is stored and exchanged in emergency cases. Cloud-based services access easily and immediately to a patient's information at anywhere and over nearly any device. Thus, in emergency health care supply, cloud based services are very useful. Recently, to improve the flexibility and dexterity of healthcare systems and increase the quality of patient care, healthcare providers choose cloud computing (Koufi, Malamateniou & Vassilacopoulos, 2010).

Ubiquitous and Cloud Applications: Education

The importance of utilizing cloud computing in education is noticed in some universities. Because of its simple and easy to use structure and configuration, educators will spend their time on teaching and researching instead of spending their time on complex computer configurations. Most important advantages of Cloud computing for E-Learning and education are: minimizing complexity, providing virtualization and centralized data storage. Thus, universities start to utilize cloud computing before government and commerce (Ghazizadeh, 2012).

In E-Learning and education, using Cloud Computing owns advantages and disadvantages. Cloud Computing provide accessing to applications at anywhere. By the way, some of the applications do not run in cloud. It may be open to business environments but it may have security problems for sensitive data. It may improve the functional capabilities but insufficient standards are a problem. The advantages of cloud computing in mobile learning are: lower cost, increased data reliability, improved performance, device independence and universal document access. Thus, Cloud computing services, architecture and advantages for electronic and mobile learning is considered in (Ghazizadeh, 2012). Here, a cloud computing service provide ubiquitous communication over mobile devices and applications ensured with cloud service providers. In education, it provides educational applications, resource storage tools and databases for students and teachers. It will develop the quality of today's education system at an affordable cost (Ghazizadeh, 2012).

Latest progress and improvements in mobile technology strengthen learners in education. With utilizing the mobile technology, education can be more pervasive. Mobile technology provides a pedagogical shift between teacher based to student based learning. Also, it ensures a pervasive learning environment. Improving the power of mobile learning technologies is studied in (Bai, 2010) for augmenting storage, evolving teaching efficiency, and providing green technology without applying extra cost on school and faculty. A mobile learning framework was improved with native functions of mobile devices and Web 2.0 applications. Some Web 2.0 platforms are reachable over the cloud at little or no costs. Hybrid application presents non-technical instructors to improve mobile learning content. Web 2.0, is a social media form, which is used to change passive learning students into active learning students with providing making conversation between students. It is well accepted in both cognitive constructivism and social constructivism that effect creative, constructive and attentive part of learning. Consequently, Cloud Computing will improve the quality of today's education system with ensuring a pervasive learning environment.

Ubiquitous and Cloud Applications: Robotics

Recently, applications of cloud computing in robotics have attracted great attention. Complex computations and storing large scale knowledge bases can be done on dedicated server hardware with less computing power and less memory on the robot. Cloud robotics is basically application of these concepts to robotics. There are many studies about integrating the robot control programs with cloud that are composed of remotely managing partly autonomous robots, sharing knowledge and coordinating robot teams.

Simplification of management and deployment of distributed robotic applications is considered over networked robot architectures. Application modularize is focused with presenting in a formal knowledge base which is shared between the robots and service applications. Robot control decisions will be formulated with inference tasks. These tasks are evaluated with the considered knowledge while task execution. The explicit and modular knowledge representation provides human operators to integrate the respective parts of the knowledge independently. This idea is applied with associating the knowledge representation methods of the ROBOEARTH project with the distributed task execution capabilities of the Ubiquitous Network Robot Platform (Tenorth, Kamei, Satake & Miyashita, et al, 2013). The Ubiquitous Networked Robot Platform (UNR-PF) is presented as a framework for distributed task coordination and control (Kamei, Nishio, Hagita, Sato, 2012). The UNR-PF provides a generic interface which will be utilized by application developers to develop hardware independent robotic services. UNR-PF will provide suitable devices which will be controlled remotely for needed components. A hierarchy of local and global platforms are ensured with the UNR-PF. Remotely starting, supervising and task coordination on diverse physical robots is provided.

Ubiquitous and Cloud Applications: Various Applications

The smart home system is composed of communication technology and wiring technology basically. The main aim of the smart home is ensuring amenity, security and convenience of family members. An ordinary house consists of many household appliances that works with electronic techniques and all of these household appliances will take place in the smart home system. Thus, the smart home systems become more complex, various and hard to overcome. Nevertheless, the Cloud Computing provides amenity and convenience for the users with the capability of computer infrastructure. It is a large scale distributed computing paradigm with storage, managed computing power and platforms. Also, it has services which are delivered on demand to external customers over the Internet (Gu, Diao, Liu, Zhang, 2011).

Lately, the smart home attracts great attention and it is obvious that it will play a significant role in future researches for intelligent life of people. The smart homes will be smart space environments in the future with the help of the pervasive computing. The smart home is a concept of the ubiquitous computing, and it becomes important for the people utilizing the high technology. A Cloud Computing based smart home system is proposed to minimize local workload with gaining the real time information over Web browser directly. The collected experimental results reveal that the presented smart home platform has amenity, high efficiency and low cost. Also, because of Cloud Computing the platform presents many network resource, and ensures the users data security (Gu, Diao, Liu & Zhang, 2011).

A new cloud service whose name is Sensing Instrument as a Service (SIaaS) is presented. The proposed cloud service provides users to utilize data acquisition instruments shared over cloud infrastructure in a ubiquitous service. It has an interface to administer physical sensing instrument. Furthermore, it utilizes cloud computing for gained data storage and process. SIaaS ensures the access of geographically distributed users over an internet connected device without installing a program (Lauro, Lucarelli & Montella, 2012).

Lately, the number of pervasive devices rise. The Smart Home and Ambient Assisted Living like systems which are Internet of Things based application domains also increase. And, these factors make it difficult for device integration solutions to involve an extensive set of devices. Device integration need to be considered with device abstraction mechanisms. Thus, the complexity of the physical device layer will be hidden from the application layer. The OSGi (OSGi Alliance, 2015) based device integration middleware is proposed to combine a modular integration approach. Thus, loading and deploying needed integration knowledge from Cloud repositories on demand will be provided, with a category based abstraction mechanism (Kliem & Koner, 2015).

Internet of Things (IoT) and Cloud computing effect distributed systems. Recently, a new distributed system which is known as IoT Cloud is utilized. The system is composed of many smart IoT devices/sensors that are interconnected over a remote Cloud platform, or infrastructure. A flexible IoT Cloud system with energy management strategy is proposed to provide and optimize the distribution of geographically localized smart sensors. The presented IoT Cloud system is given as a mesh of IoT Cloud providers. Defined IoT Cloud providers are interconnected to ensure a decentralized sensing and actuating environment where everything is driven by agreements in a pervasive infrastructure (Giacobbe, Celesti, Fazio & Villari, et al, 2015).

In big data applications, context-awareness is different from that of traditional applications. Because, it is becoming difficult to gain the contexts from big data since the complexity, velocity, and variety, particularly for big video data. In big data, the awareness of contexts is hard, thus an in-depth context-awareness framework is presented for a pervasive video cloud based on deep learning techniques and it is supported by both online and offline cloud computing technologies. So, underlying contexts in big video data will be obtained easily. The results imply that the presented framework is efficient for real-time context-awareness in a pervasive video cloud. A deep awareness architecture is given in the study which can be utilized to achieve deep context-awareness for pervasive video cloud (Zhang, Duan, Li & Lu, et al, 2015).

Today's cloud computing is based on Internet to access resources and services from cloud service providers. But, in disaster, underdeveloped and rustic areas, there may not always be available Internet connectivity. In Ubiquitous Computing Cloud (UCC), cloud resources and services may be located on every reachable node. The UCC offers the maintenance of local and ad hoc clouds, enabling pervasive cloud computing whenever and wherever required. Ubiquitous resource-infinite computing paradigm owns many advantages: enhanced efficiency, reduced cost for organizations and improved on-demand resource availability for extreme environments. To realize UCC, a distributed ubiquitous computing cloud platform, named as PlanetCloud is presented. A Global Resource Positioning System (GRPS) helps the creation of mobile computing clouds with ensuring a dynamic real-time resource scheduling and tracking system which can be accessed over the iCloud interface. Also, an analytical model is presented to calculate the resource request-response time. As a result, the number of pervasive devices and applications increase. And, cloud computing states the usage of many applications, services, data and infrastructure (Khalifa & Eltoweissy, 2012).

FUTURE RESEARCH WORK AND DIRECTIONS

More users utilize from cloud computing technologies because of the provided accessibility and flexibility of resources, ease of use and ubiquitous availability. Because of the ubiquitous character of cloud computing, data can be reached at anywhere and at any time. Furthermore, u-commerce was presented as a new commercial paradigm including network ubiquity and universality together with accessibility at anywhere and at any time (Filippi, 2013).

Today, big amounts of computing units and servers are hosted by infrastructures. In the future, the considered amounts will rise. Also, the interaction of infrastructures with variable resources will increase. Infrastructures' scale increase together with complexity and heterogeneity. For this reason, the management of the area becomes more challenging. Thus, to develop the manageability of infrastructures, novel methods are required. Cloud computing has emerged to provide the requirements of big hosting infrastructures, internet provided services and applications (Schubert & Jeffrey 2012).

CONCLUSION

Interactive, adaptive and reliable digital environments based ubiquitous computing makes people's lives easier and improve their life quality. The interaction of the user in physical worlds, virtual worlds and the awareness of the objects are provided by mobile computing in ubiquitous computing (Gorai & Agarwal, 2012).

The basic aim of ubiquitous computing is to design and construct a surrounding intelligence with network devices for ensuring on going and confidential connectivity and services. Contemporarily, designing and producing smart environments, applications and global accessibility with ubiquitous computing systems is easy to construct, because of the considerable and ever growing evolution in computing, networking and telecommunication platforms. Most notable of them are embedded devices, wireless networking, power management and cloud computing, with the cooperation of them, pervasive computing systems are constructed. Autonomously acting and providing users' requirements in a context and situation aware way is the basic facility of the system with managing resource discovery, routing, localization, tracking, monitoring, activity recognition, device communication and the learning of user preferences at the background of the system. Through diverse devices, millions of applications are easily attainable: remote health monitoring, remote agriculture, animal tracking, disaster, battlefield monitoring and responding are the most remarkable ones of the utilized applications.

Consequently, with millions of users together with their mobile phones over the world, the considered system is composed of huge amounts of data which is transmitted via heterogeneous networks and computing platforms to make peoples' lives easier, thus ubiquitous computing gives an idea about the technological and computing improvements that will emerge in the future (Cook & Das, 2012).

Cloud computing defines the improvement of many existing technologies in computing. Application and information resources are separated from the underlying infrastructure by Cloud. Furthermore, agility, availability and collaboration are augmented by Cloud. Also, cloud defines the utilization of many applications, services, data and infrastructure consist of network, data, and storage resources. These components can be easily implemented and decommissioned (Security Guidance for Critical Areas of Focus in Cloud Computing V2.1, 2009)

Cloud computing and ubiquitous computing improve permanently and in the future it will evolve the quality of the education system, E-Learning, healthcare, robotics, smart homes, communication and data transmission with providing many benefits to enterprises, universities, hospitals and governments.

REFERENCES

Ahmed, S., & Abdullah, A. (2011). E-Healthcare and Data Management Services in a Cloud. *8th International Conference on High-capacity Optical Networks and Emerging Technologies*. Retrieved on June 10, http://ieeexplore.ieee.org/xpl/articleDetails.jsp?arnumber=6149827&newsearch=true&query Text=E-Healthcare%20and%20Data%20Management%20Services%20in%20a%20Cloud

Amundson, I., & Koutsoukos, X. D. (2009). A Survey on Localization for Mobile Wireless Sensor Networks. Mobile entity localization and tracking in GPS-less environments. *Lecture Notes in Computer Science, 5801*, 235-254. Retrieved on June 8, http://link.springer.com/chapter/10.1007%2F978-3-642-04385-7_16

Ararez, L., Chaouchi, H., & Gurkas, Z. (2011). Performance Evaluation and Experiments for Host Identity Protocol. *International Journal of Computer Science*, 8(2), 74-83. Retrieved on June 8, http://ijcsi.org/papers/IJCSI-8-2-74-83.pdf

Ayzenberg, Y., & Picard, R. W. (2014). FEEL: A System for Frequent Event and Electrodermal Activity Labeling. *IEEE Journal of Biomedical And Health Informatics*, 18(1), 266-277. Retrieved on June 1, http://ieeexplore.ieee.org/xpl/articleDetails.jsp?arnumber=6579690&newsearch=true&queryText=FEEL:%20A%20System%20for%20Frequent%20Event%20and%20Electrodermal%20Activity%20Labeling

Bai, X. (2010). Affordance of Ubiquitous Learning through Cloud Computing. *Fifth International Conference on Frontier of Computer Science and Technology*. Retrieved on June 8, http://ieeexplore.ieee.org/xpl/articleDetails.jsp?arnumber=5575671&newsearch=true&queryText=Affordance%20of%20Ubiquitous%20Learning%20through%20Cloud%20Computing

Banerjee, D., Biswas, S., Daigle, C., & Siegford, J. M. (2012). Remote activity classification of hens using wireless body mounted sensors. *The 9th International Conference on Wearable and Implantable Body Sensor Networks*. Retrieved on June 6, http://ieeexplore.ieee.org/xpl/articleDetails.jsp?arnumber=6200546&newsearch=true&queryText=Remote%20activity%20classification%20of%20hens%20using%20wireless%20body%20mounted%20sensors

Burrell, J., Brooke, T., & Beckwith, R. (2004). Vineyard Computing: Sensor Networks in Agricultural Production. *Pervasive Computing, 3*(1), 38-45. Retrieved on June 9, http://ieeexplore.ieee.org/xpl/articleDetails.jsp?arnumber=1269130&newsearch=true&queryText=Vineyard%20Computing:%20Sensor%20Networks%20in%20Agricultural%20Production

Chen, K. R., Lin, Y. L., & Huang, M. S. (2011). A Mobile Biomedical Device by Novel Antenna Technology for Cloud Computing Resource toward Pervasive Healthcare. *11th IEEE International Conference on Bioinformatics and Bioengineering*. Retrieved on June 9, http://ieeexplore.ieee.org/xpl/articleDetails.jsp?arnumber=6089820&newsearch=true&queryText=A%20Mobile%20Biomedical%20Device%20by%20Novel%20Antenna%20Technology%20for%20Cloud%20Computing%20Resource%20toward%20Pervasive%20Healthcare

Chen, Y., Shen, W., Huo, H., & Xu, Y. (2010). A Smart Gateway for Health Care System Using Wireless Sensor Network. *Fourth International Conference on Sensor Technologies and Applications 2010*. Retrieved on June 5, http://ieeexplore.ieee.org/xpl/articleDetails.jsp?arnumber=5558128&queryText=A%20Smart%20Gateway%20for%20Health%20Care%20System%20Using%20Wireless%20Sensor%20Network&newsearch=true

Conti, M., Giordano, S., May, M., & Passarella, A. (2010). From Opportunistic Networks to Opportunistic Computing. *IEEE Communications Magazine*, 48(9), 126-139. Retrieved on June 3, http://ieeexplore.ieee.org/xpl/articleDetails.jsp?arnumber=5560597&newsearch=true&queryText=From%20Opportunistic%20Networks%20to%20Opportunistic%20Computing

Cook, D. J., & Das, S. K. (2012). Pervasive Computing at Scale: Transforming the State of the Art. *Journal Pervasive and Mobile Computing*, 8(1), 22-35. Retrieved on June 1, http://www.sciencedirect.com/science/article/pii/S1574119211001416

Egami, K., Matsumoto, S., & Nakamura, M. (2011). Ubiquitous Cloud: Managing Service Resources for Adaptive Ubiquitous Computing. *IEEE International Conference on Pervasive Computing and Communications Workshops*. Retrieved on June 10, http://ieeexplore.ieee.org/xpl/login.jsp?tp=&arnumber=5766853&url=http%3A%2F%2Fieeexplore.ieee.org%2Fxpls%2Fabs_all.jsp%3Farnumber%3D5766853

Escobedo, L., Tentori, M., Quintana, E., Favela, F., & Garcia-Rosas, D. (2014). Using Augmented Reality to Help Children withAutism Stay Focused. *IEEE Pervasive Computing / IEEE Computer Society [and] IEEE Communications Society*, *13*(1), 38–46. doi:10.1109/MPRV.2014.19

Ferrari, L., Berlingerio, M., Calabrese, F., & Curtis-Davidson, B. (2013). Measuring Public-Transport Accessibility Using Pervasive Mobility Data. *IEEE Pervasive Computing*, *12*(1), 26-33. Retrieved on June 1, http://ieeexplore.ieee.org/xpl/login.jsp?tp=&arnumber=6353419&url=http%3A%2F%2Fieeexplore.ieee.org%2Fiel5%2F7756%2F5210084%2F06353419.pdf%3Farnumber%3D6353419

Filippi, P. D. (2013). Ubiquitous Computing in the Cloud: User Empowerment vs. User Obsequity. In *User Behavior in Ubiquitous Online Environments*. IGI Global. Retrieved on June 1, https://halshs.archives-ouvertes.fr/hal-00855712/document

Ghazizadeh, A. (2012). Cloud Computing Benefits And Architecture In E-Learning. *Seventh IEEE International Conference on Wireless, Mobile and Ubiquitous Technology in Education*. Retrieved on June 8, http://ieeexplore.ieee.org/xpl/articleDetails.jsp?arnumber=6185026&newsearch=true&queryText=Cloud%20Computing%20Benefits%20And%20Architecture%20In%20E-Learning

Giacobbe, M., Celesti, A., Fazio, M., Villari, M., & Puliafito, A. (2015). A Sustainable Energy-Aware Resource Management Strategy for IoT Cloud Federation. *IEEE International Symposium on Systems Engineering* (ISSE). Retrieved on June 8, http://ieeexplore.ieee.org/xpl/articleDetails.jsp?arnumber=7302751&newsearch=true&queryText=A%20Sustainable%20EnergyAware%20Resource%20Management%20Strategy%20for%20IoT%20Cloud%20Federation

Gorai, M., & Agarwal, K. (2012). A Survey on Pervasive Computing. *International Journal of Scientific & Engineering Research*, *3*(6), 1-7. Retrieved on June 2, http://www.ijser.org/researchpaper%5CA-Survey-on-Pervasive-Computing.pdf

Gu, H., Diao, Y., Liu, W., & Zhang, X. (2011). The Design of Smart Home Platform Based on Cloud Computing. *International Conference on Electronic & Mechanical Engineering and Information Technology*. Retrieved on June 8, http://ieeexplore.ieee.org/xpl/articleDetails.jsp?arnumber=6023915&newsearch=true&queryText=The%20Design%20of%20Smart%20Home%20Platform%20Based%20on%20Cloud%20Computing

Kamei, K., Nishio, S., Hagita, N., & Sato, M. (2012). Cloud networked robotics. *IEEE Network Magazine*, *26*(3), 28–34. Retrieved on June 8, http://ieeexplore.ieee.org/xpl/articleDetails.jsp?arnumber=6201213&newsearch=true&queryText=Cloud%20networked%20robotics

Kashihara, S., Tsukamoto, K., & Oie, Y. (2007). Service-Oriented Mobility Management Architecture For Seamless Handover in Ubiquitous Networks. *IEEE Wireless Communications*, *14*(2), 28 - 34. Retrieved on June 8, http://ieeexplore.ieee.org/xpl/articleDetails.jsp?arnumber=4198163&newsearch=true&queryText=Service-Oriented%20Mobility%20Management%20Architecture%20For%20Seamless%20Handover%20in%20Ubiquitous%20Networks

Khalifa, A., & Eltoweissy, M. (2012). A Global Resource Positioning System for Ubiquitous Clouds. *International Conference on Innovations in Information Technology* (IIT). Retrieved on June 2, http://ieeexplore.ieee.org/xpl/articleDetails.jsp?arnumber=6207720&queryText=A%20Global%20Resource%20Positioning%20System%20for%20Ubiquitous%20Clouds&newsearch=true

Khattak, A. M., Pervez, Z., Ho, K. K., Lee, S., & Young-Koo Lee, Y. K. (2010). Intelligent Manipulation of Human Activities using Cloud Computing for u-Life Care. *10th IEEE/IPSJ Annual International Symposium on Applications and the Internet.* Retrieved on June 10, http://ieeexplore.ieee.org/xpl/articleDetails.jsp?arnumber=5598159&newsearch=true&queryText=Intelligent%20Manipulation%20of%20Human%20Activities%20using%20Cloud%20Computing%20for%20u-Life%20Care

Kim, H. K., Kim, J. K., & Ryu, Y. U. (2009). Personalized Recommendation over a Customer Network for Ubiquitous Shopping. *IEEE Transactions on Services Computing*, 2(2), 140-151. Retrieved on June 8, http://ieeexplore.ieee.org/xpl/articleDetails.jsp?arnumber=4815203&newsearch=true&queryText=Personalized%20Recommendation%20over%20a%20Customer%20Network%20for%20Ubiquitous%20Shopping

Kirci, P., Chaouchi, H., & Laouiti, A. (2014). Cluster-Based Protocol Structures in WSNs. *21st International Conference on Systems, Signals and Image Processing* (IWSSIP 2014). Retrieved on June1, http://ieeexplore.ieee.org/xpl/articleDetails.jsp?arnumber=6837661&newsearch=true&queryText=Cluster-Based%20Protocol%20Structures%20in%20WSNs

Kirci, P., Chaouchi, H., & Laouiti, A. (2014). Wireless Sensor Networks and Efficient Localisation. *2014 International Conference on Future Internet of Things and Cloud.* Retrieved on June 4, http://ieeexplore.ieee.org/xpl/articleDetails.jsp?arnumber=6984181&newsearch=true&queryText=Wireless%20Sensor%20Networks%20and%20Efficient%20Localisation

Kirci, P., Kurt, G., & Omercikoglu, M. A. Y. (2014). Remote Monitoring of Heart Pulses with Smart Phone. *CIE44&IMSS14 Proceedings.* Retrieved on June 5, https://www.researchgate.net/publication/289263211_Remote_monitoring_of_heart_pulses_with_smart_phone

Kliem, K., Koner, M., Weißenborn, S., & Byfield, M. (2015). The Device Driver Engine - Cloud enabled Ubiquitous Device Integration. *IEEE Tenth International Conference on Intelligent Sensors, Sensor Networks and Information Processing* (ISSNIP). Retrieved on June 8, http://ieeexplore.ieee.org/xpl/login.jsp?tp=&arnumber=7106921&url=http%3A%2F%2Fieeexplore.ieee.org%2Fxpls%2Fabs_all.jsp%3Farnumber%3D7106921

Koufi, V., Malamateniou, F., & Vassilacopoulos, G. (2010). Ubiquitous Access to Cloud Emergency Medical Services. *Proceedings of the 10th IEEE International Conference on Information Technology and Applications in Biomedicine.* Retrieved on June 10, http://ieeexplore.ieee.org/xpl/articleDetails.jsp?arnumber=5687702&newsearch=true&queryText=Ubiquitous%20Access%20to%20Cloud%20Emergency%20Medical%20Services

Kulkarni, R. V., Förster, A., & Venayagamoorthy, G. K. (2011). Computational Intelligence in Wireless Sensor Networks: A Survey. *IEEE Communications Surveys & Tutorials*, 13(1), 68 - 96. Retrieved on June1, http://ieeexplore.ieee.org/xpl/articleDetails.jsp?arnumber=5473889&newsearch=true&queryText=Computational%20Intelligence%20in%20Wireless%20Sensor%20Networks:%20A%20Survey

Kwong, K. H., Sasloglou, K., Goh, H. G., Wu, T. T., Stephen, B., Gilroy, M., . . . Andonovic, I. (2009). Adaptation of wireless sensor network for farming industries. *Sixth International Conference on Networked Sensing Systems* (INSS). Retrieved on June 3, http://ieeexplore.ieee.org/xpl/login.jsp?tp=&arnumber=5 409951&url=http%3A%2F%2Fieeexplore.ieee.org%2Fxpls%2Fabs_all.jsp%3Farnumber%3D5409951

Lauro, R. D., Lucarelli, F., & Montella, R. (2012). SIaaS - Sensing Instrument as a Service Using cloud computing to turn physical instrument into ubiquitous service. *10th IEEE International Symposium on Parallel and Distributed Processing with Applications*. Retrieved on June 8, http://ieeexplore.ieee.org/xpl/articleDetails.jsp?arnumber=6280396&newsearch=true&queryText=SIaaS%20-%20Sensing%20 Instrument%20as%20a%20Service%20Using%20cloud%20computing%20to%20turn%20physical%20 instrument%20into%20ubiquitous%20service

Liang, X., Zhang, K., Shen, X., & Lin, X. (2014). Security And Privacy in Mobile Social Networks: Challenges And Solutions. *IEEE Wireless Communications, 12*(1), 33–41. doi:10.1109/MWC.2014.6757895

Liu, Y., Wu, M., & Hou, H. (2012). The Design and Implement of Mobile Heath Management Software Base on the Android Platform. *International Symposium on Information Science and Engineering 2012*. Retrieved on June 6, http://ieeexplore.ieee.org/xpl/articleDetails.jsp?arnumber=6495353&newsearch=tr ue&queryText=The%20Design%20and%20Implement%20of%20Mobile%20Heath%20Management%20 Software%20Base%20on%20the%20Android%20Platform

Ma, M., Yang, Y., & Zhao, M. (2013). Tour Planning for Mobile Data-Gathering Mechanisms in Wireless Sensor Networks. *IEEE Transactions on Vehicular Technology, 62*(4), 1472 - 1483. Retrieved on June 2, http://ieeexplore.ieee.org/xpl/articleDetails.jsp?arnumber=6359890&queryText=Tour%20 Planning%20for%20Mobile%20DataGathering%20Mechanisms%20in%20Wireless%20Sensor%20 Networks&newsearch=true

Marinescu, D. C. (2012). Cloud Computing and Computer Clouds Department of Electrical Engineering & Computer Science. Orlando, FL: University of Central Florida. Retrieved from https://www.cs.ucf. edu/~dcm/Teaching/CDA5532-CloudComputing/LectureNotes.pdf

Marrocco, G. (2010). Pervasive Electromagnetics: Sensing Paradigms By Passive Rfid Technology. *IEEE Wireless Communications, 17*(6), 10-17. Retrieved on June 6, http://ieeexplore.ieee.org/xpl/articleDetails. jsp?arnumber=5675773&newsearch=true&queryText=Pervas%C4%B1ve%20Electromagnetics:%20 Sensing%20Paradigms%20By%20Passive%20Rf%C4%B1d%20Technology

Obaidat, M. S., Denko, M., & Woungang, I. (2011). *Pervasive Computing and Networking*. John Wiley & Sons. Retrieved on June 8, http://eu.wiley.com/WileyCDA/WileyTitle/productCd-0470747722.html

Okada, H., Itoh, T., Suzuki, K., Tatsuya, T., & Tsukamoto, K. (2010). Simulation study on the wireless sensor-based monitoring system for rapid identification of avian influenza outbreaks at chicken farms. *IEEE Sensors Conference*. Retrieved on June 4, http://ieeexplore.ieee.org/xpl/articleDetails.jsp?arnumb er=5690089&newsearch=true&queryText=Simulation%20study%20on%20the%20wireless%20sensor-based%20monitoring%20system%20for%20rapid%20identification%20of%20avian%20influenza%20 outbreaks%20at%20chicken%20farms

OSGi Alliance. (2015). *OSGi Core Release Specification 5.0*. Retrieved on June 8, http://www.osgi.org/

Raychoudhury, V., Cao, J., Kumar, M., & Zhang, D. (2013). Middleware for pervasive computing: A survey. *Pervasive and Mobile Computing, 9*(2), 177-200. Retrieved on May 27, http://www.sciencedirect.com/science/article/pii/S1574119212001113

Roxin, A., Gaber, J., Wack, M. & Nait-Sidi-Moh, (2007). A Survey of Wireless Geolocation Techniques. *IEEE Globecom Workshops 2007.* Retrieved on June 9, http://ieeexplore.ieee.org/xpl/articleDetails.jsp?arnumber=4437809&newsearch=true&queryText=A%20Survey%20of%20Wireless%20Geolocation%20Techniques

Salem, M., Adinoyi, A., Yanikomeroglu, H., & Falconer, D. (2010). Opportunities and Challenges in OFDMA-Based Cellular Relay Networks: A Radio Resource Management Perspective. *IEEE Transactions on Vehicular Technology, 59*(5), 2496–2510. Retrieved on June 3, http://ieeexplore.ieee.org/search/searchresult.jsp?newsearch=true&queryText=Opportunities%20and%20Challenges%20in%20OFDMA-Based%20Cellular%20Relay%20Networks:A%20Radio%20Resource%20Management%20Perspective

Sanaei, Z., Abolfazli, S., Khodadadi, T., & Xia, F. (2014). Hybrid Pervasive Mobile Cloud Computing: Toward Enhancing Invisibility. *Information, 16*(11), 8145-8181. Retrieved on June 10, https://umexpert.um.edu.my/file/publication/00001293_110375.pdf

Sani, A., Rajab, M., Foster, R., & Hao, Y. (2010). Antennas and Propagation of Implanted RFIDs for Pervasive Healthcare Applications. *Proceedings of the IEEE, 98*(9), 1648-1655. Retrieved on June 6, http://ieeexplore.ieee.org/xpl/articleDetails.jsp?arnumber=5523906&newsearch=true&queryText=Antennas%20and%20Propagation%20of%20Implanted%20RFIDs%20for%20Pervasive%20Healthcare%20Applications

Schoofs, A., Daymand, C., Sugar, R., Mueller, U., Lachenman, A., Kamran, S. M., . . . Schuster, M. (2009). IP-based testbed for herd monitoring. *International Conference on Information Processing in Sensor Networks, 2009* (IPSN 2009). Retrieved on June 4, http://ieeexplore.ieee.org/xpl/articleDetails.jsp?arnumber=5211913&newsearch=true&queryText=IP-based%20testbed%20for%20herd%20monitoring

Schubert, L., & Jeffrey, K. (2012). *Advances in clouds, research in future cloud computing.* European Union. Retrieved on June 10, http://cordis.europa.eu/fp7/ict/ssai/docs/future-cc-2may-finalreport-experts.pdf

Security Guidance for Critical Areas of Focus in Cloud Computing V2 . 1. (2009). Cloud Security Alliance. Retrieved on June 1, https://cloudsecurityalliance.org/csaguide.pdf

Tenorth, M., Kamei, K., Satake, S., Miyashita, T., & Hagita, N. (2013). Building Knowledge-enabled Cloud Robotics Applications using the Ubiquitous Network Robot Platform. *IEEE/RSJ International Conference on Intelligent Robots and Systems* (IROS). Retrieved on June 8, http://ieeexplore.ieee.org/xpl/articleDetails.jsp?arnumber=6697184&newsearch=true&queryText=Building%20Knowledgeenabled%20Cloud%20Robotics%20Applications%20using%20the%20Ubiquitous%20Network%20Robot%20Platform

Torres, J., Nogueira, M., & Pujolle, G. (2013). A Survey on Identity Management for the Future Network. *IEEE Communications Surveys & Tutorials, 15*(2), 787-802. Retrieved on June 7, http://ieeexplore.ieee.org/xpl/articleDetails.jsp?arnumber=6275425&queryText=A%20Survey%20on%20Identity%20Management%20for%20the%20Future%20Network&newsearch=true

Viat-Blanc, P., Goglin, B., Guillier, R., & Soudan, S. (2011). *Computing Networks from cluster to cloud computing*. Wiley. Retrieved on June 10, http://eu.wiley.com/WileyCDA/WileyTitle/productCd-1848212860.html#

Wark, T., Corke, P., Sikka, P., Klingbeil, L., Guo, Y., & Crossman, C. … Bishop-Hurley, G. (2007). Transforming Agriculture through Pervasive Wireless Sensor Networks. *IEEE Pervasive Computing, 6*(2), 50-57. Retrieved on June 9, http://ieeexplore.ieee.org/xpl/articleDetails.jsp?arnumber=4160605&newsearch=true&queryText=Transforming%20Agriculture%20through%20Pervasive%20Wireless%20Sensor%20Networks

Weiser, M. (1991). The Computer for the 21st Century. *Scientific Am., 265*(3), 66-75. Retrieved on May 17, https://www.ics.uci.edu/~corps/phaseii/Weiser-Computer21stCentury-SciAm.pdf

Cloud Computing. (n.d.). In *Wikipedia*. Retrieved on June 5, 2016 https://en.wikipedia.org/wiki/Cloud_computing

Xu, X., He, G., Zhang, S., Chen, Y., & Xu, S. (2013). On Functionality Separation for Green Mobile Networks: Concept Study over LTE. *IEEE Communications Magazine, 51*(5), 82-90. Retrieved on June 4, http://ieeexplore.ieee.org/xpl/articleDetails.jsp?arnumber=6515050&newsearch=true&queryText=On%20Functionality%20Separation%20for%20Green%20Mobile%20Networks:%20Concept%20Study%20over%20LTE

Yu, G. J., & Wang, S. C. (2007). A Hierarchical MDS-based Localization Algorithm for Wireless Sensor Networks. *16th IST Mobile and Wireless Communications Summit*. Retrieved on June 1, http://ieeexplore.ieee.org/xpl/articleDetails.jsp?arnumber=4299079&queryText=A%20Hierarchical%20MDSbased%20Localization%20Algorithm%20for%20Wireless%20%20%20Sensor%20Networks&newsearch=true

Zaharakis, I. D., & Komninos, A. (2012). Ubiquitous Computing – a Multidisciplinary Endeavour. *IEEE Latin America Transactions, 10*(3), 1850 – 1852. Retrieved on May 27, http://ieeexplore.ieee.org/xpls/abs_all.jsp?arnumber=6222593&tag=1

Zhang, W., Duan, P., Li, Z., Lu, Q., Gong, W., & Yang, S. (2015). A Deep Awareness Framework for Pervasive Video Cloud. *IEEE Access, 3*, 2227 - 2237. Retrieved on June 2, http://ieeexplore.ieee.org/xpl/articleDetails.jsp?arnumber=7315021&newsearch=true&queryText=Zhang,%20W.,%20Duan,%20P.,%20Li,%20Z.,%20Lu,%20Q.,%20Gong,%20W.%20.AND.%20Yang,%20S.%20A%20

ADDITIONAL READING

Al-Dubi, A., Ali, S., Liu, L., & Zhu, D. (2014). Special Issue on Ubiquitous Computing and Future Communication Systems. *Future Generation Computer Systems, 39*, 1–2. doi:10.1016/j.future.2014.05.003

Bayramusta, M., & Nasir, V. A. (2016). A fad or future of IT?: A comprehensive literature review on the cloud computing research. *International Journal of Information Management, 36*(4), 635–644. doi:10.1016/j.ijinfomgt.2016.04.006

Bosse, S. (2015). Unified Distributed Computing and Co-ordination in Pervasive/Ubiquitous Networks with Mobile Multi-Agent Systems using a Modular and Portable Agent Code Processing Platform. *Procedia Computer Science*, 63, 56-64. Retrieved on May 12, 2016 from http://www.sciencedirect.com/science/article/pii/S1877050915024400

Chou, D. C. (2015). Cloud computing risk and audit issues. *Computer Standards & Interfaces*, 42, 137–142. doi:10.1016/j.csi.2015.06.005

Corredor, I., Martínez, J. F., & Familiar, M. S. (2011). Bringing pervasive embedded networks to the service cloud: A lightweight middleware approach. *Journal of Systems Architecture*, 57(10), 916–933. doi:10.1016/j.sysarc.2011.04.005

Cook, D. J., & Das, S. K. (2012). Pervasive computing at scale: Transforming the state of the art. *Pervasive and Mobile Computing*, 8(1), 22–35. doi:10.1016/j.pmcj.2011.10.004

Huang, T. C., & Zeadally, S. (2015). Flexible architecture for cluster evolution in cloud computing. *Computers & Electrical Engineering*, 42, 90–106. doi:10.1016/j.compeleceng.2014.08.006

Iivari, A., & Ronkainen, J. (2015). Building a Simulation-in-the-loop Sensor Data Testbed for Cloud-enabled Pervasive Applications. *Procedia Computer Science, 56, 357-362.* Retrieved on June 02, 2016 from http://www.sciencedirect.com/science/article/pii/S1877050915017007

Jones, S. (2015). Cloud computing procurement and implementation: Lessons learnt from a United Kingdom case study. *International Journal of Information Management*, 35(6), 712–716. doi:10.1016/j.ijinfomgt.2015.07.007

Khan, M. A. (2016). A survey of security issues for cloud computing. *Journal of Network and Computer Applications*, 71, 11–29. doi:10.1016/j.jnca.2016.05.010

Li, X., Qian, Z., You, I., & Lu, S. (2014). Towards cost efficient mobile service and information management in ubiquitous environment with cloud resource scheduling. *International Journal of Information Management*, 34(3), 319–328. doi:10.1016/j.ijinfomgt.2013.11.007

Loke, S. W. (2012). Supporting ubiquitous sensor-cloudlets and context-cloudlets: Programming compositions of context-aware systems for mobile users. *Future Generation Computer Systems*, 28(4), 619–632. doi:10.1016/j.future.2011.09.004

Luo, S., & Ren, B. (2016). The monitoring and managing application of cloud computing based on Internet of Things. *Computer Methods and Programs in Biomedicine*, 130, 154–161. doi:10.1016/j.cmpb.2016.03.024 PMID:27208530

Ochoa, S. F., & López-de-Ipiña, D. (2014). Distributed solutions for ubiquitous computing and ambient intelligence. *Future Generation Computer Systems*, 34, 94–96. doi:10.1016/j.future.2014.01.004

Ogiela, L. (2015). Intelligent techniques for secure financial management in cloud computing. *Electronic Commerce Research and Applications*, 14(6), 456–464. doi:10.1016/j.elerap.2015.07.001

Prasad, A., Green, P., & Heales, J. (2014). On governance structures for the cloud computing services and assessing their effectiveness. *International Journal of Accounting Information Systems*, 15(4), 335–356. doi:10.1016/j.accinf.2014.05.005

Riahi, G. (2015). E-learning Systems Based on Cloud Computing: A Review. *Procedia Computer Science, 62, 352-359*. Retrieved on May 20, 2016 from http://www.sciencedirect.com/science/article/pii/S1877050915025508

Salim, F., & Haque, U. (2015). Urban computing in the wild: A survey on large scale participation and citizen engagement with ubiquitous computing, cyber physical systems, and Internet of Things. *International Journal of Human-Computer Studies, 81*, 31–48. doi:10.1016/j.ijhcs.2015.03.003

Schniederjans, D. G., & Hales, D. N. (2016). Cloud computing and its impact on economic and environmental performance: A transaction cost economics perspective. *Decision Support Systems, 86*, 73–82. doi:10.1016/j.dss.2016.03.009

Shiau, W. L., & Chau, P. Y. K. (2016). Understanding behavioral intention to use a cloud computing classroom: A multiple model comparison approach. *Information & Management, 53*(3), 355–365. doi:10.1016/j.im.2015.10.004

Siewe, F. (2016). Towards the modelling of secure pervasive computing systems: A paradigm of Context-Aware Secure Action System. *Journal of Parallel and Distributed Computing, 87*, 121–144. doi:10.1016/j.jpdc.2015.09.008

Vroom, R. W., & Horváth, I. (2015). Ubiquitous computing-based design tools and systems. *Computer Aided Design, 59*, 158–160. doi:10.1016/j.cad.2014.11.007

Wang, L., & Qu, W. (2014). Advances in ubiquitous computing and communications. *Future Generation Computer Systems, 38*, 11–12. doi:10.1016/j.future.2014.04.005

Yu, P., Ma, X., Cao, J., & Lu, J. (2013). Application mobility in pervasive computing: A survey. *Pervasive and Mobile Computing, 9*(1), 2–17. doi:10.1016/j.pmcj.2012.07.009

Zdravković, M., Noran, O., & Trajanović, M. (2014). Interoperability as a Property of Ubiquitous Healthcare Systems. *IFAC Proceedings Volumes, 47*(3), 7849-7854. Retrieved on June 01, 2016 from http://www.sciencedirect.com/science/article/pii/S1474667016428491

KEY TERMS AND DEFINITIONS

ARPANET: Advanced Research Projects Agency Network was the preliminary network to apply the protocol suite TCP/IP.

Bandwidth: It is a measure of the width of a range of frequencies.

Carrier: The intermediary which ensures connection of cloud services among providers and consumers.

Cloud Distribution: Transmission of cloud data among Providers and Cloud.

Distributed Computing: It is a computer science area which works distributed systems.

Distributed System: In the system, components are placed on networked computers communicate and manage their actions with passing messages.

General Packet Radio Service (GPRS): It is a packet oriented mobile data service over the 2G and 3G cellular communication system's global system for mobile communications (GSM).

Global System for Mobile Communications (GSM): It is a standard developed by the European Telecommunications Standards Institute (ETSI) to define the protocols for second generation (2G) digital cellular networks utilized by mobile phones.

Grid Computing: It is a kind of distributed and parallel computing that process very large tasks.

Mainframe Computer: It is a robust computer utilized by big organizations for important applications (Wikipedia, 2016).

Mobile Endpoints-Fixed Endpoints: A device which ensures a machine interface to cloud services (Wikipedia, 2016; Marinescu, 2012).

Peer-to-Peer: It is a distributed architecture where central coordination is not needed.

Service Deployment: Whole of the actions required to make a cloud service available.

Service-Oriented Architecture (SOA): It is an architectural pattern in computer software design in which application components provide services to other components over a communications protocol.

Chapter 2
Using Value–Based Approach for Managing Cloud–Based Services

Salah Eddin Murad
Damascus University, Syria

Salah Dowaji
Damascus University, Syria

ABSTRACT

Software-as-a-Service (SaaS) providers are influenced by a variety of characteristics and capabilities of the available cloud infrastructure resources (IaaS). As a result, the decision made by business service owners to lease and use certain resources is an important one in order to achieve the planned outcome. This chapter uses value based approach to manage the SaaS service provided to the customers. Based on our approach, customer satisfaction is modeled not only based on the response time, but also based on the allotted budget. Using our model, the application owner is able to direct and control the decision of renting cloud resources as per the current strategy. This strategy is led by a set of defined key performance indicators. In addition, we present a scheduling algorithm that can bid for different types of virtual machines to achieve the target value. Furthermore, we proposed the required Ontology to semantically discover the needed IaaS resources. We conduct extensive simulations using different types of Amazon EC2 instances with dynamic prices.

INTRODUCTION

The high cost and effort required to operate traditional business applications makes it very important to improve organizational efficiency and to reduce operational cost. With cloud computing, the shared infrastructure and services made it possible to mitigate those issues by presenting it as a utility, where you only pay for what you need and transfer the headache of operation, maintenance and upgrade to the other party.

DOI: 10.4018/978-1-5225-1721-4.ch002

Figure 1. Cloud computing deployment models

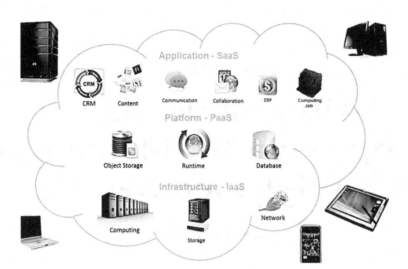

The use of Cloud systems leads to promising business models and benefits for both of the providers and end-users (Armbrust et al., 2009). These benefits may include greater efficiency, increased agility, improved compliance, reduced costs, and limitless ability to scale and to provide on-demand resources.

As illustrated in Figure 1, a cloud can offer three service models: Software as a Service, Platform as a Service, and Infrastructure as a Service (Litoiu, Ng, & Iszlai, 2010).

Software as a Service (SaaS)

Software as a Service is the delivery of software functionality through the internet, this functionality is similar to the one installed on a local machine. Buyya et al. (2010) provide examples of the SaaS services including the services that are provided by Google for office automation, this includes Google Mail, Google Documents, and Google Calendar. SalesForce.com is a provider of commercial solution which provides online CRM (Customer Relationship Management). Another commercial solution provider is Clarizen.com which provides a project management services. Appirio is an integrated solution that provides complete support for any management aspect of modern enterprises from project management to resource planning.

Platform as a Service (PaaS)

It is a service model where all resources required to build applications are provided through the internet without the need to install software. Examples of such platforms are the application servers and database servers. Google AppEngine, Microsoft Azure, and Manjrasoft Aneka are examples of PaaS services and their providers.

Infrastructure as a Service (IaaS)

It is a service model where the hardware is provided to the consumer as a service, this includes the processing capability, network connectivity, memory, and storage space in the form of a set of virtual machines. Amazon EC2, Amazon S3, Nirvanix, GoGrid are examples of IaaS services and providers.

The remainder of the chapter is organized as follows: background section comes next, followed by a detailed literature review. Research methodology is summarized in a separate section, while the developed model is presented in the problem description section. The value based management framework section describes the proposed framework including the needed components to implement the model. Experimental setup section describes the simulation set up of the proposed model. The evaluation and experiments of our approach are presented in the evaluation section Last, the summary and future works is presented.

BACKGROUND

The different available service models of Cloud Computing paradigm have made it more feasible for service providers to deliver their services as a utility to the customers in different methods. According to Litoiu et al. (2010), this is mainly and specifically due to: Virtualization and Software as a Service Model. Virtualization is a process in which the organization provides its physical resources through a set of virtual resources. Those virtual resources may have different characteristics and may work using different configurations on the top of the physical resources. Using this virtualized environment allows for physical resource utilization.

Four main deployment models can be recognized for clouds (Smyth, 2009):

- Private clouds (internal clouds) are a proprietary computing architecture, owned or leased by the organization. It is usually refers to providing services to the organization customers or users behind the firewall within the organization. The services and applications in the private cloud are only accessible by the permitted users. Private clouds are a secure environment that are protected by the organization's firewall and usually used by the organizations that own them (Zafar & Omar, 2013).
- Community Cloud is a multi-tenant environment which ensures a common computing environment shared by all the organizations of the cloud. Community cloud supports a certain community (Hefner, 2012). Example of the community clouds may include the cloud of community of universities or community of governmental offices.
- Public clouds environments where organizations can use the services provided by third party provider and can run their applications online through that provider. The provider could be responsible for providing the infrastructure, servers, storage and networking necessary to ensure the availability and scalability of the applications. The provider can also provide public services and platforms to be leased and used by external customers and users. This provides a lower up-front investment for many parties especially the small to medium enterprises and the individual initiatives where users can develop and deploy their applications in the cloud with very little cost.
- Hybrid clouds environments where some applications, or parts of applications, could run in the public cloud while others run in the private cloud. This hybrid approach results in a system with new demands especially in resource management.

The relation between the cloud service provider and the customer is usually governed by a set of defined characteristics of the cloud service that are agreed between the both parties. Pricing model, usage model, and security are examples of the parameters used usually to define the service level agreement (SLA). For instance, the provider warrants to provide a minimum level of the response time or storage. In this context, the provider will be liable for any violation of the agreement through a specific agreed penalty model. In this chapter, both of the response time and the budget allotted by the customer for request processing are considered.

From financial perspective, many pricing models are used by the service providers in cloud environments. Although the current cloud computing literature considers the pricing of cloud services, the discussion is almost mention the pay per use mechanism of cloud services (Jaakko, 2010). There are often various pricing schemes (Voorsluys, Garg, & Buyya, 2011): the on-demand market, which offers standard virtual machines (VMs) at a fixed cost, and the spot market, which offers unused capacity in the form of variable price VMs. Osterwalder (2004) categorized the pricing mechanisms into three categories as presented in Table 1.

According to (Buyya, Pandey, & Vecchiola, 2013), "the market oriented computing in industry is getting real as evidenced by developments from companies such as Amazon. For example, EC2 started with flat pricing then moved to pricing based on service difference and lately introduced auction based models, using spot instances." In such model, the prices of instances differ according to offers and demands. Amazon EC2 offers spot instances of VMs for lease in a price lower than the standard fixed price of the similar instances. Based on that, the utilization of the spot instances to run the services in lower cost in comparison with the fixed price model is a feasible advantage.

This technology, Cloud Computing, holds many challenges, and requires influential decisions to be taken. Resources selection and management are one of the major issues in determining the degree to which the objectives of the business service providers are met. The value based approach presented in this chapter is driven by prioritized business metrics provided by the provider to ensure the desired decision is reached.

Table 1. Pricing mechanisms

Category	Pricing Mechanism	Description
Fixed Pricing	Pay per use	Customer pays in function of the time or quantity he consumes of a specific service.
	Subscription	Customer pays a flat fee in order to access the use of a product or to profit from a service.
	List price / menu price	A fixed price that is often found in a list or catalog.
Differential Pricing	Service feature dependent	Price is set according to service configuration. Includes also bundling of different services.
	Customer characteristic dependent	Price is tailored to the characteristics of every single customer.
	Volume dependent	Differentiates prices on the basis of purchased volumes.
Market pricing	Bargaining	The price outcome depends on the existing power relationships between the parties involved.
	Yield management	The best pricing policy for optimizing profits is calculated based on real-time modeling and forecasting of demand behavior.
	Auction	Price is set as buyers bid in increasing increments of price.
	Reverse auction	Price is set as sellers bid in decreasing decrements of price.
	Dynamic market	Price is the outcome of a large number of buyers and sellers that have indicated their price preference, but are not able to influence this price as individual sellers.

(Osterwalder, 2004)

LITERATURE REVIEW

Several works have been proposed in the field of cloud computing to deal with different issues. There have been a number of attempts that focused on the technical perspective of the computing model including performance enhancement (Alsolami, 2013; Roy & Dutta, 2013), availability (Birman, Chockler, & van Renesse, 2009), data storage (Gheorghe, Neuhaus, & Crispo, 2010; Pretschner, Hilty, Schutz, Schaefer, & Walter, 2008) and privacy (Unruh & Muller, 2010; Kunzler, Muller, & Raub, 2009; Dowsley, Muller, & Nascimento, 2009). Other researches ranged from computer networking, distributed file systems, distributed database to computational job scheduling problems (Chun & Culler, 2002; Coleman, Norris, Candea, & Fox, 2004).

Many other works proposed different approaches to identify and define the issue of business driven resource allocation. Authors in (Li & Chinneck, 2009), presented a method for achieving optimization in clouds by using performance models in the development, deployment and operations of the applications running in the cloud. In comparison with our model, their presented optimization model only considers the target of reducing the cost and uses the response time to determine the quality of the service (QoS) provided to the customer.

Minimization of the costs of running the servers is presented by authors in (Ardagna, Turbian, & Zhang, 2004). The system they consider is based on a centralized network dispatcher which controls the allocation of applications to servers. The dispatcher can also decide to turn on or off servers depending on the system load. Their model always tries to assign the application components to the machines with the lower costs. In our model, we take into consideration other factors besides the cost in the placement decision and resources selection.

In (Burge, Ranganathan, & Wiener, 2007), the authors proposed algorithms for a cost-aware provider to maximize its profit. Their approach addressed which data centres to use considering the energy cost of having the data centre on or off. Sauv´e et al. proposed a model that realizes the best service value for the provider, but their model only considered the business losses due to IT service failure or performance degradation. In addition, their work uses a static method for resource allocation and depends only on the response time threshold and the minimum service availability to determine the level of the service provided to the customer.

Profit maximization of using cloud resources has been presented by authors in (Tsakalozos et al., 2011). Their approach answers the question of how many resources a consumer should request from the seemingly endless pool provided by the cloud. However, they modelled the budget constraint as a function of response time. In comparison to our approach, our model doesn't depends on the response time only but on the degree to which the customer target is fulfilled. Authors in (Dash, Kantere & Aliamaki, 2009) presented financial model which uses budget constraint to manage the cloud environment. The approach responds to user QoS requirements by building new data structures and modelled the budget as a function of response time, at the same time it can't adapt with the number of VMs deployed.

A budget constraint scheduling of a workflow applications presented by authors in (Yu & Buyya, 2006), they proposed a scheduling approach to minimize the execution time while meeting the specified budget for delivering the result. Eventually, this can conflict with the strategy of the provider in some stages in which a longer execution time can be allowed for the sake of cost reduction.

A general architecture has been introduced by Aiber et al. (2004), they presented a set of methodologies and technologies to enable autonomic optimization according to different business level objectives. However, this architecture considered only the objective of income maximization of a single e-commerce site. Another framework for managing a utility computing environment has been presented by authors in (Aib, Salle, Bartolini, & Boulmakoul, 2005). This framework only takes into account the provider's view point and requires human intervention to apply the management actions. Our approach allows the provider to take into consideration the customer targets while setting the provider objectives.

Authors in (Oriol & Guitrt, 2011) presented an architecture for business driven IT management. They outlined a number of challenges that apply to the cloud computing environment. This architecture uses three layers: cloud layer, business layer and the execution layer. Adopting this architecture by the cloud providers will allow for a business level governance.

In (Lioiu et al., 2010), authors discuss several facets of optimization in cloud computing and propose an architecture for corresponding challenges. They consider a layered cloud where various cloud layers virtualize parts of the cloud infrastructure. Their architecture takes into account different stakeholders in the cloud (infrastructure providers, platform providers, application providers and end users).

Customer satisfaction models appeared in work presented in (Zhang, Wang, Zhao, & Cattani, 2012), where an improved trapezoidal fuzzy number is used to express the satisfaction. Compared with our model, customer satisfaction in their work is only modelled as a function to the response time only.

In order to augment the private cloud resources using resources from public providers, Luiz et al. (2011) presented a scheduling algorithm that optimizes the cost of the resources to be leased. The aim is to provide the needed computing resources to run a workflow within a required time. Their work doesn't consider the case of migrating depending tasks to different public clouds and the cost associated with that scenario.

The issue of minimizing the cost of workflow execution while meeting the time constraint appeared in the work presented by (Yu, Buyya, & Tham, 2005). Their scheduling algorithm utilizes the grid resources by rescheduling the failed jobs by migrating them into the available working resources. The decision to use certain resources only take into account the cost factor.

The work presented in (Chen & Sion, 2011) studies the feasibility of cloud computing. This is done by comparing the saving in the cost generated by using public resources with any associated deployment. The comparison made in that work depends on a solely cost-centric perspective using two scenarios, "unified client" and "multi-client" scenarios. A Pareto Optimal approach is used by authors in (Hoseiny et al., 2013) to schedule Bag-of-Tasks (BoT) applications using hybrid cloud resources. The scheduling decision considers the user's required deadline or budget or a trade-off between them.

Authors in (Marshall, Keahey, & Freeman, 2010) proposed a model to extend a site by using external cloud resources on demand, they developed a model of an elastic site that adapts services provided within a site to take advantage of elastically provisioned resource. The presented architecture adds an additional layer capable of monitoring the demand of applications and responding by acquiring or releasing cloud nodes, but only for the simpler cloud-bursting case and uses IaaS cloud resources only.

The comparison designed by authors in (Assun, Costanzo, & Buyya, 2009) investigated the benefits of using Cloud Computing providers to augment the computing capacity of the local infrastructure. Different scheduling strategies are studied to address how these strategies achieve a balance between performance and usage cost when there is a need to allocate additional resources from a Cloud infrastructure.

In (Bossche, Vanmechelen, & Broechove, 2010), authors deal with the scheduling of independent tasks on hybrid clouds. They propose a binary integer program to decide which cloud provider to choose when outsourcing a task that cannot be currently executed in the private cloud. The aim is to minimize the cost of running the tasks in the cloud, while the quality of service constraints are met. Their approach proved to become less feasible in a hybrid cloud setting due to very high solve time.

Authors in (Siva & Poobalan, 2012) presented a framework in which Cloud Computing systems can utilize the power of Semantic web technologies to provide the user with capability to efficiently store and retrieve data for data intensive applications. They proposed an algorithm that is guaranteed to provide a query plan whose cost is bounded by the log of the total number of variables in the given SPARQL query.

Chauhan (2011) has provided a general framework for vendor-independent cloud management, which chooses and executes cloud management actions that are optimal businesswise. He extends the WS-Policy4MASC to support the management actions and metrics.

Elmroth et al. (2009) propose an accounting and billing architecture between the consumers and the infrastructure provider in a federated cloud infrastructure. The objective is to cope with the migration of virtual machines by managing pre-paid and post-paid payment schemes according to the users' needs.

Li et al. (2013) introduce an approach for improving the availability guarantee of software applications by optimizing the availability considering the performance and cost. Their approach considers how sharing the VM resource with many users can affect the availability.

From a provider perspective, the minimization of the cost while meeting the SLA has been deliberated by Karve et al. (2006). A management algorithm is proposed to maximize the utilization of active virtual machines and minimize the SLA violation. Khajemohammadi et al. (2014) used levelled multi-objectives Genetic Algorithm in order to reduce the scheduling time when running workflows on grid environment. The aim is to allocate each task in the workflow on the most appropriate resource in the grid based on the user requirements, cost, and deadline.

A new approach to schedule Bag of Tasks (BoTs) with increase in parallel process presented by Pingale and Mogal (2015). They proposed an algorithm for multi-objectives scheduling. The optimized objectives are the execution time, the network bandwidth, and the storage requirements.

Alkhanak et al. (2015) discussed the challenges of workflow scheduling that affect the workflow cost. They classified the cost-aware relevant challenges of workflow scheduling in cloud computing depending on the Quality of Service (QoS) performance, system functionality and system architecture. Ultimately they provided a taxonomy set in order to facilitate the selection of the appropriate approach from the available alternatives.

The aforementioned works uses different objectives, either from technical perspective or from business perspective. Some approaches are driven by the provider objectives, while others are driven by the customer. Our work differs from the other works in coupling the provider objectives with the customer targets without losing the control of the provider, who still able to define the proper strategy as per needed. Therefore, the objective of the provider can be defined finally by a value, this is done by providing a quantitative measure using a value based approach, derived from the value metrics measurement technique. This method will allow the business service provider to express the result of serving the customer request and his planned outcome as values, i.e. business values or service values. In this sense, the service owner is able to manage and control the computing resources to be used in more practical manner and in alignment with his current strategy.

We will address the business objectives of the business service owner. These objectives are driven by a set of key performance indexes (KPIs) that specify the provider's priorities at the current stage. Churn, monthly recurring revenue and average revenue per customer are examples of those potential KPIs (Metrics blog, 2014). At the same time, those objectives are integrated with the customer preferences as well, the budget and the desired response time.

An algorithm to make the resource allocation decisions is presented to achieve the targeted value of the service owner. It considers using multiple types of infrastructure resources with different capabilities and dynamic prices similar to Amazon EC2 spot instances model (Amazon, 2014). To achieve this, we modelled the target value of service owner, the customer request value (or customer satisfaction), revenue, cost, budget and response time.

Furthermore, we will present the issue of cloud resources discovery through the usage of Semantic Web and propose the required Ontology to describe the IaaS resources.

RESEARCH METHODOLOGY

A procedure has been created to manage the research progress starting from an extensive search of the high-related keywords over the most important search engines and repositories like IEEE Xplore, Science Direct, Google Books and Google Scholar. A set of more than 40 academic papers have been collected and reviewed. It mainly included sources from books, journals, conference proceedings and available working papers related to Cloud Computing, Management of Cloud Computing, Business Driven Management and other related topics.

A new model has been built and a study of the most adaptable simulation frameworks and tools has been carried out including:

iCanCloud: A simulation platform aimed to model and simulates cloud computing systems, which is targeted to those users who deal closely with those kinds of systems. The main objective of iCanCloud is to predict the trade-offs between cost and performance of a given set of applications executed in a specific hardware, and then provide to users beneficial information about such costs (Castane, & Nunez, & Carretero, 2012).

CloudSim: A Framework for Modelling and Simulation of Cloud Computing Infrastructures and Services (Calheiros et al., 2011).

In this chapter, CloudSim simulation framework is used to test and assess the proposed model.

Following are the detailed steps followed in the research:

- Searching for Cloud Computing management related papers.
- Classify papers by similarity using affinity diagram.
- Papers shortlisting.
- Link the result of each paper with its factors using Ishikawa diagrams.
- Set traceability matrixes to define the research tracks and how they are related to each other.
- Define the business objectives to be used.
- Development of the conceptual model
- Two simulation frameworks have been investigated (CloudSim and iCanCloud).
- CloudSim is used and model extension is developed and integrated for the simulation.
- Simulation Scenarios are defined
- Data generation, simulation scenarios are conducted for assessment (variance analysis assessment, regression analysis, precision and accuracy tests).
- Conclusion and future work planning.

PROBLEM DESCRIPTION

The efficiency of IT activities requires the ability to measure performance and cost across all cloud services, from infrastructure to applications as a service. The proposed value based management model "VBM" makes those aspects of cloud services transparent to organizations and provides a measurement method of the provided service. Therefore, it enables fact based decisions to be aligned with business goals.

As SaaS Owner providing my services to clients, I need to make suitable deployment choices of my application using resources provided in form of IaaS service (such as Amazon EC2) to process customer requests. This choice is driven by a set of business objectives and at the same time has to take into account the customer's requirements and priorities. These priorities are specified per processing request. As a result, the value of the provided service is determined according to those choices. In this sense, the question is, what are the best infrastructure resources to select in order to realize the best value of the service?

The placement decision will consider the following:

1. **Profit:** The application owner charges the customer for the provided service, the price is not constant and depends on the value presented to the customer as per agreed in the SLA between the two parties. The cost is also variable and depends on the type and prices of the set of the VM instances used to deliver the service to the client at the moment of renting.
2. **Customer Satisfaction:** Client satisfaction will be quantified based on the budget allocated by the customer for his request and based on the response time. The customer is also allowed to specify the compromising between the budget and the response time according to his needs.
3. **Current Priority and Trend:** The priorities of the service provider changes over time based on strategy, focus on the customer satisfaction could be preferred in some stages while the profit could be the most important in others. In this sense, the provider needs to control the operation accordingly. This control can be derived from a set of KPIs that are updated on time upon serving each customer, as a result, these KPIs can provide real time directions of the current priorities. Discussion of the best KPIs to use for that purpose is out of scope of this chapter.

The service value presented to the customer is denoted by BV, which is the sum of weighted values of all business objectives under concern which in turn are calculated based on the defined value metrics for each. Therefore, this value is generally formulated as follows:

$$BV = \sum_{j=1}^{k} x_j \, BO_j \tag{1}$$

The objective function is defined as

$$\max \ BV = \sum_{j=1}^{k} x_j \, BO_j$$

$$\text{s.t. } \sum_{j=1}^{k} x_j = 100$$

Where

$\mathcal{BO}_j$ The value of business objective j;

x_j Weight of $\mathcal{BO}_j$, $0 \leq x_j \leq 100$.

The business objectives that we are concerned about in our model are the profit and customer satisfaction. To model the service value, let's suppose we have N customers' request (R), each of them is modelled by the tuple $(R_{Size}, B_{Dsrd}, \text{þ}, PT_{Dsrd}, w1, w2)$, where R_{Size} presents the request size that reflects the computing needs to execute the request, B_{Dsrd} and PT_{Dsrd} represent the allocated desired budget to execute the job R within the desired processing time respectively, by achieving these two parameters the provider achieves the baseline value to the customer. þ is the ceiling price, i.e. the maximum value, that the customer is willing to pay according to the value he receives of his request, it, therefore, presents an incentive for the provider to get higher pay in relation to the quality of service he provides to the customer, the compromising between the budget and response time is done using the rates $w1$ and $w2$ which are provided by the customer, where $w2 = 100 - w1$.

On the other hand, the service provider has his own priorities, these priorities can be presented in the same way using the tuple (P_r, ρ_1, ρ_2), where ρ_1 and ρ_2 represent the importance degree of the provider's profit and the customer request value to his business value, i.e. service value, where $\rho_2 = 100 - \rho_1$.

The profit of the application owner changes according to the revenue gained from the customer and the cost of the used cloud resources as presented in formula 2.

$$P_r = \mathcal{V}_r(Q_r(B, PT)) - \sum_{i=1}^{M} C_i \qquad (2)$$

Where

M VM instances used to process the customer request;

C_i The price of using VM instance i;

$Q_r(B, PT)$ The customer request value which measures the customer satisfaction;

$\mathcal{V}_r(Q_r)$ Revenue function of serving request r which indicates the price the customer is willing to pay according to the value he receives;

In fact, there could be no limitation for the formulation of $\mathcal{V}_r(Q_r(B, PT))$, while the expected form of the function in our model is to depend on the value presented to the customer in ascending manner and limited by a ceiling price þ upon delivering the maximum value to the customer; i.e. $\mathcal{V}_r(Q_1) > \mathcal{V}_r(Q_2), \forall Q_1, Q_2 \in (0, Q_{max}] s.t. Q_1 > Q_2$. This can be described in the function types presented in Figure 2.

Figure 2. Typical revenue functions: (a) step function; (b) concave function; (c) convex function

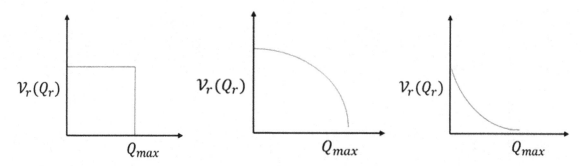

For simplicity but, without losing generality, we'll model the revenue as a step function with set of ranges to determine the result as follows:

$$
V_r\left(Q_r\left(\text{B}, \text{PT}\right)\right) = \begin{cases} \text{Þ} & Q_r \geq 2.5 \\ \text{B}_{Dsrd} & 1.5 \leq Q_r < 2.5 \\ \text{B}_{Dsrd} - \gamma & 1 \leq Q_r < 1.5 \\ \text{B}_{Dsrd} - 2\gamma & Q_r < 1 \end{cases} \tag{3}
$$

Where γ is a penalty rate determined by the SLA, Þ is the maximum price the customer tolerates to pay. The values of Q_r can be different per agreement with each customer as a part of the SLA.

The final customer satisfaction, i.e. customer request value, $Q_r\left(\text{B}, \text{PT}\right)$, is determined by the degree to which the acceptable value of the request is satisfied as shown in formula 4.

$$
Q_r(\text{B}, \text{PT}) = W1\text{B} + W2(\sum_{i=1}^{M}\text{PT}_i + \mu) \tag{4}
$$

Where

M VM instances used to process the customer request;
 PT_i The elapsed time to process the customer request on the instance i;
μ The total waiting time of request when its status is pending.

To quantify the customer request value $Q_r(\text{B}, \text{PT})$, we'll use the value metrics technique to evaluate the actual delivered value to the customer in comparison with the baseline value. Figure 3 presents an example of this metric for budget and processing time objectives between the provider and consumer.

As shown in this example, the Q_r is "two" when the desired objective value is reached, "one" or "three" values are when the output is worst or better than the desired range by 10% to 20% respectively, Q_r is "zero" or "four" when the output is worst or better than the desired result by more than 20% re-

Figure 3. Value metrics chart

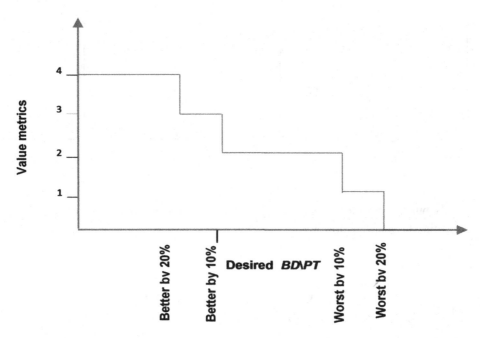

spectively. Table 2 reveals an example of how to quantify the customer request by calculating the Q_r as a model of customer satisfaction.

As a result the objective functio C^t n is formulated as in 5.

$$BV = MAX(\rho_1(V_r(Q_r) - \sum_{i=1}^{M} C_i) + \rho_2 Q_r) \tag{5}$$

During the selection of the best instances at each time slot of the processing time frame, the total cost and the processing time are calculated cumulatively as follows:

$$C^t = C^{ac} + R^{rs} C^c \tag{6}$$

$$R^{rs} = S^c / CC \tag{7}$$

Table 2. Q_r Calculation example

Component	Weight	Desired Range	Actual	Value
Budget	20%	0.08-0.12	0.07	2.5 * 0.2 = 0.5
Response Time	80%	400-500	450	2 * 0.8 = 1.6
				$Q_r = 2.1$

$$PT = PT^{ac} + R^{rs} + \mu + \alpha \tag{8}$$

The total cost,, of request processing at each time slot, presented in formula 6, equals to the accumulated cost (C^{ac}) of previous assignments of this request to VMs in the previous computing rounds plus the multiplication of the cost of renting a certain VM at the current round (C^c) and the remaining request size (R^{rs}), where R^{rs} is given by formula 7. S^c represents the remaining unprocessed part of the request, and CC is the computing capacity of the nominated VM to be selected. This capacity is compared to a standard VM capacity.

The other component of the customer request is the needed processing time which is calculated at each round using formula 8 based on the accumulated processing time (PT^{ac}). The waiting time, μ, is the idle period in which the request status is either not started or waiting for bidding on the new rent in the next round, α is added as an error factor.

In this model, the next proposed algorithm (Provider Business Value- PBV) is used to assign the N customers' requests to combination of M resource (VM) type. An illustration of the high level interaction of the model's parts are presented in Figure 4. Figure 5 illustrates the mapping between the requests and the used resource class.

During each scheduling window the algorithm tries to specify the best type of VM resource (that achieve the best business value for the service provider) to lease from the spot instance IaaS provider for each customer request. A resource of the selected type will be rent to host and execute that request within the next time slot.

Figure 4. High level illustration of model interaction

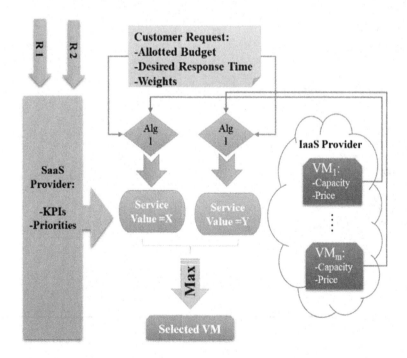

Figure 5. Request/resource class mapping

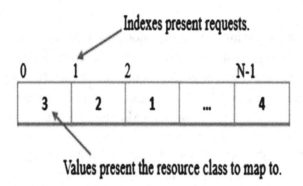

Table 3. PBV algorithm

Algorithm 1 Calculate Business Value of request processing (PBV Algorithm)

//R listofType Request, RC listofType //ResourceClass, P1 and P2 typeof Integer
CalculateBusinessValue(R,RC,SLA,P1,P2)
if R <> ⊙
foreach ri in R
PT= μ
foreach rcj in RC
 	
R^{rs} (ri)= S^{c} (ri) / CC(rcj)
 	
C^{t} (ri) = C^{ac} (ri) + R^{rs} (ri) * C^{c} (rcj)
 	
PT+= PT^{ac} (ri)+ R^{rs} (ri)+ α
CV=CalculateCostValue()
PTV=CalculatePTValue()
 	
Q_{ri} =CalculateCRV(PTV,CV,w1,w2)
 	
V_{ri} =CalculateRevenu(Q_{ri} ,SLA)
 	
P_{ri} = V_{ri} - Cost
 	
BV=CalculateBusinessValue(P_{ri} , Q_{ri} , P1,P2)
If BV > LastBusVal
LastBusVal= BV
SelectedRC=rcj
end if
end for
ResultArray← ResultArray ∪ {[rj,rcj]}
end for
for each item in ResultArray
SelectedRC=Rent (item["rc"])
Assign rj to SelectedRC for execution
end for
else
return Null
end procedure

Depending on the request size and the computing capacity of each type of potential resources, PBV algorithm calculates the processing time and the cost of the request if assigned to each type. The cost includes the current price of the prospective VM type and the accumulated cost of the same request during the previous processing slots if any. Based on the calculated cost and processing time, the customer satisfaction (customer request value) is calculated considering the other required input from the customer, i.e. desired budget, desired time, w1, and w2. At the same time, the B is calculated and the VM type that is associated with the maximum BV value is then selected.

As per described above, the proposed model uses both of SaaS and IaaS models to provide the service. Looking for the IaaS resources to be used to host the SaaS services can be performed statically by pre-defining a potential list of IaaS providers or IaaS resources, or it can be performed in more flexible manner by discovering the IaaS resources that meet a specific configuration and technical requirements.

Cloud computing, with its multiple models, enabled a lot of vendors to introduce various services. As a result of this diverse and heterogeneous space of services, interoperability and portability issues came to surface. This made it harder to get the full potential of this technology, especially when the need is for dynamic discovery of resource (as in our case) or for integration of services. In this regards, the semantic web becomes an important development in the information technology world to help solving such kinds of problems. Generally, semantic web can be used to support the discovery of the infrastructure resources using specific ontologies, and also can be used to discover and use services or to compose new services using ontologies like OWL-S (DARPA, 2008) and S_3OS (Murad, 2013).

The semantic web is considered as a new generation of the web, where the information is machine interpretable and understandable (Lee, Hendler, & Lassila, 2001).

The discovery operation for the suitable, matched, resources requires a representation of functional, non-functional, or even data descriptions of that resources in machine interpretable form. Therefore, looking for public IaaS resources, to host some tasks by the SaaS provider based on the customer requests, requires to model the configuration of the virtual machine (VM) instances at the first side and the task infrastructure minimum requirements on the other side. For that purpose, we propose the Ontology illustrated in Figure 6 for describing the IaaS resources.

A simple language, i.e. domain-specific-language (DSL) (Shetch & Ranabahu, 2010), is used to describe the characteristics of those resources in relation to the abovementioned ontology. Following is an example of IaaS resource configuration.

It is clear that this scenario requires the IaaS resources to be semantically described. Whenever we have described resources and described the requests' requirements, the discovery of those resources can be performed dynamically by matching the two description semantically and proposing the resources with the high matching degree to be used by the VBM model. In similar way, semantic can also add a value to enable the service consumer of IaaS resource to look for infrastructure resources providers based on the characteristics of the resource instances they provide.

VALUE BASED MANAGEMENT FRAMEWORK

The value based management framework, illustrated in Figure 7, presents multi-tiers architecture. Service Layer, Business Management Layer, and Operation Management Layer.

The Service Layer is the layer in which the services are presented by the provider to the customers, this layer receives the processing requests from the clients and binds them to the processing queue until

Figure 6. IaaS resource ontology

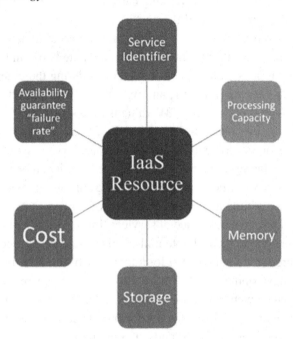

it is assigned to a computing resource for execution. The second layer is the Business Management Layer which contains the components that are related to the business perspective, these components are the Dashboard which provides the direction for determining the business objectives and the Cloud Solver, the Solver is responsible for the placement decision making for each processing request based on set of factors. The third layer is the Operation Management Layer which is responsible for the operational part of the process through the Cloud Broker and the Executor and Monitor components, the first works with the computing resources providers to bid for certain resources and the second works to dispatching the requests to their selected resources and gets the feedback of what has been executed. The last layer is the Infrastructure Layer where the available computing resources of the infrastructure providers come from.

Process wise, the time frame is divided into number of time slots as illustrated in Figure 8, the processing of customer requests is performed during those slots. The windows between those slots are the

Table 4. IaaS resource configuration description

```
Config: cost do
Param: max {
: value => 1,
: unit => dollar,
: duration => hour,
: Identifier => rdf:resource="#resource_cost"
}
Config: guarantee do
Param: uptime {
: value => 95%,
: Identifier => rdf:resource="#availability_ guarantee"
}
....
```

Figure 7. representation of the VBM framework

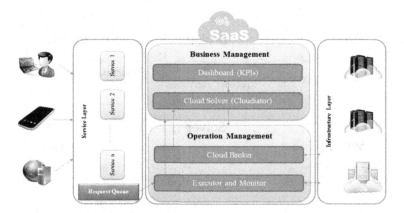

period in which the rent decision is taken by the system owner and the bidding for the selected VM types are done with the infrastructure provider. The processing request of the customer can be received at any time and it has to wait until the next time slot to be considered by the SaaS owner; this waiting time will be considered as a part of the request response time. If the execution of the request is not completed during the current slot, the remaining unexecuted part will be moved to the next time slot. The remaining part of all incomplete requests and the new coming requests are subject to bidding for new resources during the next bidding window. The type of resources, which can be rent for the remaining part of the request in the next slot, could be different from the ones which were used in the previous slots, this is determined by how the business value gets better.

Back to the Business and Operation Management Layers and in more details, the role of the Cloud Solver is to find the best assignment decision of the service request to the computing resources proposed by the Cloud Broker. It depends on their cost and computing capacity in order to achieve the required value for executing the service request. The role of the Cloud Broker is to propose, at each bidding window, the available resources "VM instances" to the Solver in a vendor independent manner, and makes the needed resources' reservation as per requested by that Solver. Thus, upon the customer processing

Figure 8. Scheduling process time-frame

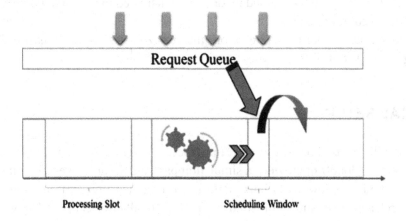

Figure 9. UML representation of VBM

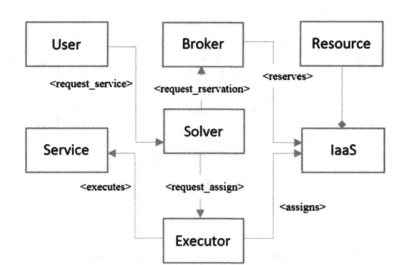

Table 5. The configurations of types of spot instances on Amazon

Instance type	CPU (core)	Memory (GB)	Storage (GB)
t2.micro	1	1	EBS only
t2.small	1	1	EBS only
m3.meduim	1	3.75	1 X 4
m3.2xlarge	8	30	2 X 80
c3.xlarge	4	7.5	2 X 40
c3.2xlarge	8	15	2 X 80
r3.large	2	15.25	1 X 32
r3.8xlarge	32	244	2 X 320

request, the Cloud Solver and Cloud Broker will work closely in order to take a decision and rent the needed VM instance respectively in each time window.

Therefore, both of an IaaS and SaaS cloud models are considered in our model. UML representation of this model is presented in Figure 9.

The IaaS cloud service model is inspired from the Amazon EC2 Spot (Amazon, 2014). Table 5 presents a configuration list of different types of spot instances on Amazon.

EXPERIMENTAL SETUP

As our assessment will be based on Amazon EC2 instances (Amazon, 2014) and will use CloudSim as a simulation platform, "CloudSim provides a simulation package library developed on the top of Sim-Java that can run on both Windows and Linux platforms. It inherits from GridSim programming model and supports research and development of cloud computing" (Calheiros et al., 2011), we developed the needed extension to CloudSim in order to implement our model for cloud resources selection process. We configured four types of VMs in the simulation environments using the characteristics described in Table 6. We defined five main testing scenarios (as per detailed in the next section), each scenario has its parameter set up which are randomly generated using defined ranges, as per provided in Table 7. Generally, number of repeated runs have been performed using different and randomly generated set of parameters that simulates each scenario and case. The average value of the outcomes has been used to evaluate and analyze the results of the simulation.

Evaluation

This section presents the evaluation of the simulation we conducted to our model and algorithm based on Amazon EC2 instances and CloudSim, The experiments aim to check the behaviour of VBM model when using different parameters, priorities and weights, computing capacities and prices of instances of different VM types. We will evaluate how much it is significant to specify the provider priorities and how it may affects his profitability, the effectiveness of different customer and provider preferences, and the value of using different types of computing resources to handle the same processing request in comparison with using homogeneous instances only.

The Importance of Provider Priorities

To present how missing or under estimating the provider's business objectives may affect the result of renting, we run a simulation of two cases as an example, each case has different provider objectives using the parameters shown in Table 8.

Table 6. The configurations of used types of VMs

VM Type	VM memory (GB)	CPUs	VM size (MB)
Small VM	1	1	1000
Medium VM	4	2	1000
Extra VM	8	4	10000
Super VM	15	8	10000

Table 7. Simulation parameters template

Parameter	Value
# of runs	How many times the simulation is repeated
# of requests	Number of customer requests per run
# of requests per round	Number of received requests during each time slot
Request size	Range of requests' sizes
instances	small, medium, extra, super
P1/P2 – W1/W2	Provider priorities and customer preferences

Table 8. Parameters of different provider objectives simulation

Parameter	Value	
# of runs	10	
Request size	400 -1400 MIPS	
# of requests	1000	
# of requests per round	20	
instances	small, medium, extra, super	
instance prices	Amazon spot instances price history	
Simulation Case	**Case 1**	**Case2**
W1	25%	25%
W2	75%	75%
P1	20%	80%
P2	80%	20%

In this experiment, we generated 1000 requests with different sizes and repeated the simulation for 20 times, we used 4 different types of VM instances with their prices as per provided by Amazon Spot Price history console.

To show the impact of the provider's objectives we set w1 and w2 to 25% and 75% respectively; this means that the processing time is the most important objective from the customer point of view.

Results presented in Figure 10 show how highly considering the customer objective (*P1* is 80%), who in his turn prefers the processing time over the budget objective, may cause provider profit loss (0.0674-0.002=0.0654$) in comparison to case 2 when the profit is the most important objective (*P1* is 80%). This shows how it is important to specify the priorities of the provider to avoid undesired outcomes.

Figure 10. The importance of provider priorities

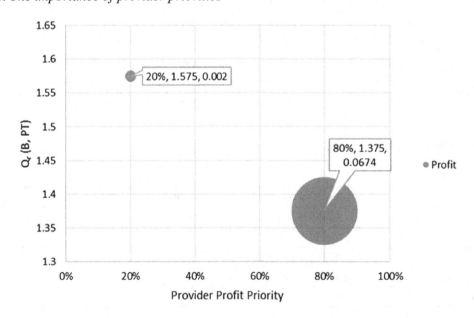

The Relationship Between the Cost, Processing Time and Profit

Using randomly generated parameters presented in table 9, Figure 11 shows the result of our simulation. As expected, it shows that the processing time goes down as the cost increases. This is back to using instances of higher price with greater performance capabilities. At the same time, the experiments show that the profit will decline in instances where rent is more expensive, this is back to having a smaller profit margin.

Therefore, when the processing time is the most important factor to the customer and the customer satisfaction value is the most important for the provider, the provider has to utilize the more expensive resources with the greater computing capacity and so with higher price and as a result will have less profit.

Table 9. Randomly generated parameters

Parameter	Value
# of runs	15
Random Request size	400 -1400 MIPS
# of requests	15,000
# of requests per round	25
instances	small, medium, extra, super
instance prices	Amazon spot instances price history
W1, W2, P1, P2	Random [0-100]

Figure 11. The relation between the cost, processing time and profit

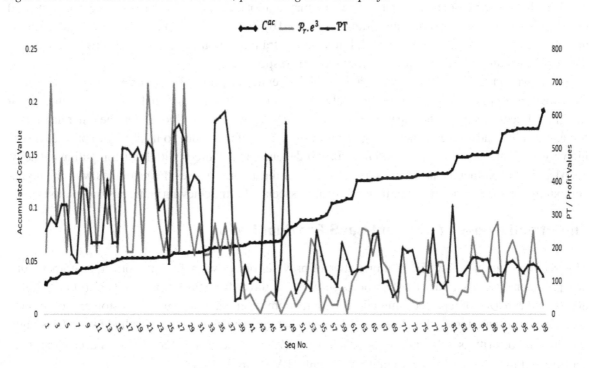

Figure 12. Using different instances types

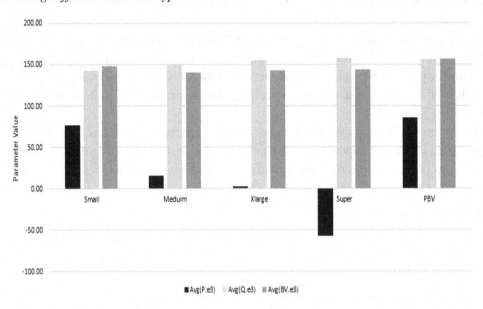

As a conclusion, the provider can realize better gain with customers that care of cost rather than the response time, this is back to using the cheaper computing resources even if the request response time went up.

Different Instances Types

To check how using more than one instance type may improve the provider performance, we compared our algorithm with three baseline algorithms introduced by Zomaya (2011), named as BL-small, BLlarge and BL-xlarge, which always rent Small, Large and Extra Large homogeneous instances from the candidate VM instance type set to process user requests respectively.

As shown in Figure 12, our model achieves the higher average of profit and provider business value. BL-Small comes next in profit because it always uses cheap resources which means a higher profit margin, while the usage of the super resources leads to a negative profit (loose). On the other hand, BL-Super has a little advantage in achieving better customer satisfaction due to its ability to provide a very high rate of response time to the customer, since it depends on resources with high computing capacity.

Also, it is clear that the profit goes down whenever the algorithm uses the resources with the higher computing capacity, at the same time this is generally associated with achieving better customer satisfaction.

The Effectiveness of Different SaaS Provider Ratios

This section examines how different priorities of provider objectives affects the profit, customer value and provider business value. For this purpose we used three different ratios of *P1/P2* (50/50, 20/80, 80/20) and run a set of repeated simulations with randomly generated weights of customer metrics (*W1* and *W2*) as presented in Table 10. Figure 13 shows that the average profit (multiplied by 1000) is highest when its priority is 80% and lowest when it is 20%. Q_r also had different values according to its priority and its value got larger when it's 80% while BV changes slightly.

Table 10. Parameters of randomly generated weights of customer preferences

Parameter	Value
# of runs	10
# of requests	10,000
# of requests per round	20
Request size	400 -1400 MIPS
instances	small, medium, extra, super
P1/P2	50/50, 20/80, 80/20

Figure 14. The effectiveness of different customer ratios

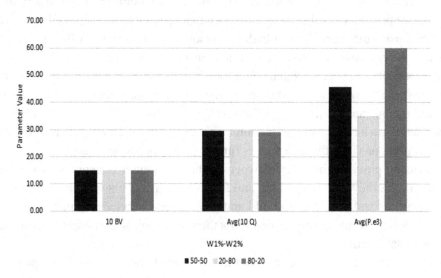

Figure 13. Provider business objectives

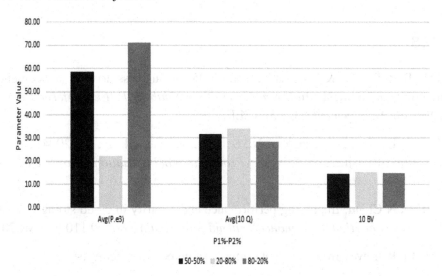

The Effectiveness of Different Customer Ratios

To measure the impact of customer preferences on the provider business value, we used various *W1/W2* ratios, 50/50, 20/80 and 80/20. As presented in Figure 14, when customer prefers the processing time over the cost, the provider will have a smaller margin to achieve profit because the broker will try to rent the instances with the high price and high performance capacity.

SUMMARY AND FUTURE WORK

Clouding systems management is complex operation because of the diversity, complexity, and scale of cloud systems. It can be done using technical metrics, which may not optimise business metrics.

In this chapter, we presented a value based approach that accounts for business driven preferences of SaaS provider when using different kinds of IaaS VM resources. This model, VBM, mainly coupled two factors that reflect the business objectives, profit and customer satisfaction, and can be generalized to include other components and attributes that count for the final value, either from the customer perspective or the service owner perspective. In this sense, the system management is driven by a set of KPIs that are aligned to the business objectives of the service owner at the current stage. Defining the IaaS resources to be used is performed using a semantic web approach for autonomic resources discovery.

From practical point of view, this research is further endeavor towards the motivation of the adoption of cloud service. It provides the service owners in the cloud environments with a model to control and manage the services they own in dynamic and flexible manner. This will encourage even the small and mid-size enterprises and providers to build and provide new services for public and to reach new customers with the least upfront investment and adapt their decisions in alignment to their strategy focus, i.e. profit, customer satisfaction.

Future work will focus on the utilization of our model in the hybrid environment, private and public clouds, in order to make the most suitable hosting decision based on the enterprise objectives and environment characteristics.

REFERENCES

Aib, I., Salle, M., Bartolini, C., & Boulmakoul, A. (2005). A business driven management framework for utility computing environments. In *Proceedings of the Ninth IFIP/IEEE International Symposium on Integrated Network Management (IM'05)*. IEEE.

Aiber, S., Gilat, D., Landau, A., Razinkov, N., Sela, A., & Wasserkrug, S. (2004). Autonomic self-optimization according to business objectives. In *Proceedings of International Conference on Autonomic Computing* (ICAC'04).

Alsolami, F. (2013). N-Cloud: Improving performance and security in cloud storage. *2013 IEEE 14th International Conference on High Performance Switching and Routing*. doi:10.1109/HPSR.2013.6602319

Amazon EC2. (n.d.). Retrieved from http://aws.amazon.com/ec2/instance-types

Ardagna, D., Trubian, M., & Zhang, L. (2004). SLA based profit optimization in multi-tier web application systems. In *Int'l Conference On Service Oriented Computing*.

Armbrust, M. (2009). *Above the clouds: A berkeley view of cloud computing*. EECS Department, University of California, Berkeley, Tech. Rep. UCB/EECS-2009-28.

Assun, M., Costanzo, A., & Buyya, R. (2009). Evaluating the Cost-benefit of Using Cloud Computing to Extend the Capacity of Clusters. In *Proceedings of the 18th ACM International Symposium on High Performance Distributed Computing (HPDC 2008)*.

Berners-Lee, T., Hendler, J., & Lassila, O. (2001). The Semantic Web. *Scientific American Magazine*.

Birman, K., Chockler, G., & van Renesse, R. (2009). *Toward a cloud computing research agenda*. SIGACT News.

Burge, J., Ranganathan, P., & Wiener, J. (2007). Cost-aware scheduling for heterogeneous enterprise machines (CASH'EM). In *Cluster Computing, 2007 IEEE International Conference on*.

Buyya, R., Pandey, S., & Vecchiola, C. (2013). *Market-Oriented Cloud Computing and the Cloudbus Toolkit*. The University of Melbourne. doi:10.1002/9781118640708.ch14

Calheiros, R., Ranjan, R., Beloglazov, A., De Rose, C. A. F., & Buyya, R. (2011). CloudSim: A Toolkit for Modeling and Simulation of Cloud Computing Environments and Evaluation of Resource Provisioning Algorithms. *Software: Practice and Experience, 41*(1), 23-50.

Castane, G. G., Nunez, A., & Carretero, J. (2012). iCanCloud: A Brief Architecture Overview. *Parallel and Distributed Processing with Applications (ISPA), 2012 IEEE 10th International Symposium on*. doi:10.1109/ISPA.2012.131

Chen, Y., & Sion, R. (2011). To cloud or not to cloud? Musings on costs and viability. In *Proc. of Symp. on Cloud Computing, SOCC '11*. doi:10.1145/2038916.2038945

Chun, B. N., & Culler, D. E. (2002). User-centric performance analysis of market-based cluster batch schedulers. In *Proceedings of the 2nd IEEE/ACM International Symposium on Cluster Computing and the Grid (CCGRID)*. doi:10.1109/CCGRID.2002.1017109

Coleman, K., Norris, J., Candea, G., & Fox, A. (2004). Oncall: defeating spikes with a free-market application cluster. In *Proceedings of the 1st International Conference on Autonomic Computing*.

DARPA. (2016). *The DARPA agent mark-up language*. Retrieved from http://www.daml.org/

Dash, D., Kantere, V., & Ailamaki, A. (2009). An Economic Model for Self-Tuned Cloud Caching. In *Proc of the 25th IEEE International Conference on Data Engineering*. doi:10.1109/ICDE.2009.143

Dowsley, R., Muller-Quade, J., & Nascimento, A. C. A. (2009). *A cca2 secure public key encryption scheme based on the mceliece assumptions in the standard model*. In CT-RSA. doi:10.1007/978-3-642-00862-7_16

Gheorghe, G., Neuhaus, S., & Crispo, B. (2010). ESB: An Enterprise Service Bus for Access and Usage Control Policy Enforcement. In *Proc. Annual IFIP WG 11.11 International Conference on Trust Management*.

Hefner, K. (2012). *Search cloud storage, community cloud*. Retrieved from http://searchcloudstorage. techtarget.com/definition/community-cloud

Hoseiny Farahabady, M., Dehghani Samani, H. R., Leslie, L., Lee, Y. C., & Zomaya, A. (2013). Handling Uncertainty: Pareto-Efficient BoT Scheduling on Hybrid Clouds. *Parallel Processing (ICPP), 2013 42nd International Conference on.*

Karve, A., Kimbrel, T., Pacifici, G., Spreitzer, M., Steinder, M., Sviridenko, M., & Tantawi, A. (2006). Dynamic Placement for Clustered Web Applications. In *15th International Conference on World Wide Web*. ACM. doi:10.1145/1135777.1135865

Khajemohammadi, H., Fanian, A., & Gulliver, T. A. (2014). Efficient Workflow Scheduling for Grid Computing Using a Levelled Multi-objective Genetic Algorithm. *Journal of Grid Computing, 12*(4), 637–663. doi:10.1007/s10723-014-9306-7

Kunzler, R., Muller-Quade, J., & Raub, D. (2009). *Secure computability of functions in the IT setting with dishonest majority and applications to long-term security*. In TCC. doi:10.1007/978-3-642-00457-5_15

Li, J., & Chinneck, J. (2009). Performance Model Driven QoS Guarantees and Optimization in Cloud. *Software Engineering Challenges of Cloud Computing*. doi:10.1109/CLOUD.2009.5071528

Li, J., Lu, Q., Zhu, L., Bass, L., Xu, X., Sakr, S., ... Liu, A. (2013). Improving Availability of Cloud-Based Applications through Deployment Choices. *IEEE 6th International Conference on Cloud Computing*.

Litoiu, M., Ng, J., & Iszlai, G. (2010). A Business Driven Cloud Optimization Arcitecture. In *Proceedings of 2010* (pp. 380–385). ACM SAC.

Litoiu, M., Woodside, M., Wong, J., Ng, J., & Iszlai, G. (2010). A business driven cloud optimization architecture. *Proceedings of 2010 ACM SAC*.

Luiz, F. B. (2011). HCOC: A Cost Optimization Algorithm for Workflow Scheduling in Hybrid Clouds. *Journal of Internet Services and Applications, 2*(3).

Marshall, P., Keahey, K., & Freeman, T. (2010). Elastic Site Using Clouds to Elastically Extend Site Resources. In *Proceedings of the 10th IEEE/ACM International Symposium on Cluster, Cloud and Grid Computing (CCGrid 2010)*. doi:10.1109/CCGRID.2010.80

Murad, S. E. (2013). Using Semantic Services in Service-Oriented Information Systems. *IEEE Potentials Magazine., 32*(1), 36–46. doi:10.1109/MPOT.2012.2187806

Must Have Metrics for Your SaaS Business. (2012). Retrieved from https://blog.kissmetrics.com/5-metrics-for-saas

Oriol, F., & Guitart, J. (2011). Initial Thoughts on Business-driven IT Management Challenges in cloud Computing Providers. *6th IFIP/IEEE International Workshop on Business Driven IT Management*.

Osterwalder, A. (2004). *The Business Model Ontology - A Proposition In A Design Science Approach* (Doctoral thesis). University of Lausanne.

Pingale, S.H., & Mogal, V. (2015). New Approach to Schedule Bag of Tasks (BoTs) with Increase in Parallel Process. *International Journal of Innovative Research in Computer and Communication Engineering, 3*(7).

Pretschner, A., Hilty, M., Schutz, F., Schaefer, C., & Walter, T. (2008). Usage control enforcement: Present and future. In *Security & Privacy* (pp. 44–53). IEEE.

Roy, A., & Dutta, D. (2013). Dynamic Load Balancing: Improve Efficiency in Cloud Computing. *International Journal of Emerging Research in Management &Technology, 2*(4).

Sauv'e, J., Marques, F., Moura, A., Sampaio, M., Jornada, J., & Radziuk, E. (2005). SLA Design from a Business Perspective. In *Proceedings of the 16th IFIP/IEEE International Workshop on Distributed Systems: Operations and Management* (DSOM'05). Citeseer.

Shetch, A., & Ranabahu, A. (2010, August). Semantic Modeling for Cloud Computing. *IEEE Internet Computing.*

Siva, M., & Poobalan, A. (2012). Semantic Web Standard in Cloud Computing. *International Journal of Soft Computing and Engineering, 1.*

Smyth, P. (2009). *Cloud Computing A Strategy Guide for Board Level Executives.* Kynetix Technology Group.

Tsakalozos, K., Kllapi, H., Sitaridi, E., Roussopoulos, M., Paparas, D., & Delis, A. (2011). *ICDE '11 Proceedings of the 2011 IEEE 27th International Conference on Data Engineering.*

Unruh, D., & Muller-Quade, J. (2010). Universally composable incoercibility. In IACR Cryptology. doi:10.1007/978-3-642-14623-7_22

Van den Bossche, R., Vanmechelen, K., & Broeckhove, J. (2010). Cost-Optimal Scheduling in Hybrid IaaS Clouds for Deadline Constrained Workloads. In *3rd International Conference on Cloud Computing,* (pp. 228–235). doi:10.1109/CLOUD.2010.58

Voorsluys, W., Garg, S. K., & Buyya, R. (2011). Provisioning Spot Market Cloud Resources to Create Cost-effective Virtual Clusters. In *Proceedings of the 11th IEEE International Conference on Algorithms and Architectures for Parallel Processing* (ICA3PP-11). Springer.

Yu, J., & Buyya, R. (2006). A Budget Constrained Scheduling of Workflow Applications on Utility Grids using Genetic Algorithms. In *Workshop on Workflows in Support of Large-Scale Science (WORKS).* doi:10.1109/WORKS.2006.5282330

Yu, J., Buyya, R., & Tham, C. (2005). Cost-based Scheduling of Scientific Workflow Applications on Utility Grids. In *Proceedings of the 1st International Conference on e-Science and Grid Computing* (e-Science 2005).

Zafar, F., & Omer, A. (2013). *Social, Dynamic and Custom-Based Clouds: Architecture, Services and Frameworks.* Springer London.

Zhang, J., Wang, W., Zhao, Y., & Cattani, C. (2012). Multiobjective quantum evolutionary algorithm for the vehicle routing problem with customer satisfaction. Mathematical Problems in Engineering.

Zomaya, A. Y. (2011), Maximizing Profit and Pricing in Cloud Environments. *12th International Conference on Web Information System Engineering (WISE 2011)*.

KEY TERMS AND DEFINITIONS

Business Driven IT Management: The ability to take a technology management related decisions based on business drivers like: profit, customer satisfaction, etc.

Cloud Computing: A technology term refers to providing services and resources over internet as a utility, therefore, it can be seen as a utility computing paradigm.

Dynamic Resource Discovery: The ability to look for the needed computing resources based on their description in run time.

Resource Management: A set of actions to define, allocate, initiate, operate, maintain, and release the computing resources as needed.

Semantic Web: A machine interpretable web in which the information can be described and discovered based on an Ontology.

Value-Based Metric: A quantified measure that can be defined and tracked numerically.

Virtual Resource: A logical resource with specific characteristics which can be initiated and used by the users in isolation from the physical resource that hosts it.

Chapter 3
Cloud Service Footprint (CSF):
Utilizing Risk and Governance Directions to Characterize a Cloud Service

Mohammad Shalan
JEA, Jordan

ABSTRACT

Cloud Computing (CC) services have made substantive advances in the past few years. It is rapidly changing the landscape of technology, and energizing the long-held promise of utility computing. Successful jump into CC is a considerable task, since the surroundings are not yet mature and the accompanied risk and governance frameworks are still evolving. This effort aims to portray an identity for CC services by employing risk and governance directions among other elements and techniques. Cloud Service Footprint (CSF) is considering practical aspects surrounding the CC paradigm and prescribing the associated directions. CSF will help Cloud Service Providers (CSPs) to characterize their service and benchmark themselves. The Client Enterprises (CEs) can utilize CSF dimensions to find a better way to navigate through CC service arena and to understand its parameters. Along with cost and functional capabilities, the Cloud Service Footprint (CSF) can provide enough information for business executives to evaluate CC services and make informed decisions.

INTRODUCTION

Cloud computing (CC) is increasingly asserted as the technology with the potential to change the way internet and information systems are being utilized into client enterprises (CEs). CC has emerged as a growing trend of scalable, flexible and powerful computing, capable of introducing a paradigm shift in how technology is delivering value to the business. With significant global investments, CC is showing the power to completely revolutionize the business mindset and to promote new business characteristics such as on-demand self-service, broad network access, shared resources, rapid provisioning and minimal intervention. However, CC benefits are not coming hassle free; several risks, technical concerns, contracting and compliance issues are surrounding the CC services.

DOI: 10.4018/978-1-5225-1721-4.ch003

Some challenges arise because the adoption of CC services might begin outside the technology organization (TO) or against the CE strategy leading to loose associations. Other challenges are due to immaturity of particular CC service measures, even worse is the reduced maturity of CC associated risk and governance models. Business and technology teams have to increase correlation and communication to collectively agree upon the right balance.

This chapter consider few surroundings to portray a picture for CC deliberate challenges. It investigates the effects of maturity status on the enhancement of key CC service features and its value propositions. It then researches the governance abilities to orchestrate heterogeneous environments, setting rules and responsibilities, leading the way to maintain the CC phenomena. Risk management (RM) is called-out to handle the associated risks in a reliable and trustworthy way. This chapter devote to define a new term called Cloud Service Footprint (CSF) to portray an identity for a CC service.

The trust and trace natures of CC services provide a major motivation to characterize the CSF. When correlated to cost and functional capabilities, CSF deemed to be the third element to provide enough information for business executives to evaluate CC services and make informed decisions. This aligns to an early lesson, whereas realizing value from new services requires a mature organization that can recognize associated benefits and own the tools for effective performance management.

CSF dimensions and parameters are categorized in a systematic manner as related to the CC concepts to separate the potentially significant business benefits and threats from the hype and hyperbole that are surrounding. The conferred CSF components provide first pass among a jungle of elements that shape the CC structure. These components include architecture dimensions, data considerations, licensing and agreements, collaborations and adaptations in addition to the ethical and legal aspirations.

This chapter is factorizing the CSF dimensions as evidence-based insights while looking at CC benefits, associated risk elements and governance contributions. It appeals to both academics and practitioners. Its length and design precludes extensive treatment of each area, but highlighting some key concepts and practices that can help smoothing the CSF consideration and evaluation.

BACKGROUND

Cloud Computing (CC) represents the network of business platforms (Baya, Mathaisel & Parker, 2010). It is a new way to conceptualize and manage the integration between business and technology. Yet, there is no universal way to measure business and technology alignment in literature (HBR, 2011; De Haes & Grembergen, 2009). Risk and governance are gaining more space to reshape the cloud era. The parameters of CC services are extensively discussed in literature, similarly are risk management and governance. But, they are evolving with plenty of research dedicated to each topic individually or bi-combined (Aven, 2008; Ackermann, 2012; Goranson, 1999). We are jointly correlating these topics. The joint understanding is unique since everyone know these topics individually, but limited client enterprises (CEs) are doing all of it.

CC and technology transformations have reshaped significantly the business domains (Menken & Blokdijk, 2008). Usually we used to say that technology must support business strategy, nowadays, there are times when technology will lead into the next realm of the previously unthinkable (Vice, 2015). This is obvious today with many CEs are establishing technology in the core of their operations (Turban, Leidner, McLean & Wetherbe, 2008). This shift will require more collaboration between business people and technology organization (TOs) with both parties are invited to understand the terminologies and concepts of each other.

Researchers agree that CEs are facing a continuously changing business environment and a highly complex set of rules and regulations. Collaboration is required to establish a governance model for CEs based on utility driven computing which is started to stay and grow (Shawish & Salama, 2014). The movement towards CC adoption is in line with the global trend of moving from product procurement to service procurement. That is why board members are being directly accountable for technology and requiring strong governance in analogy to their responsibility for enterprise objectives and key assets (Hardy, 2006). With such speedy progressing and emerging, it becomes crucial to understand and characterize all aspects about the CC services and associated technologies. Here comes the introduction of the CSF.

CC chaos is passing a hurdle with everyone is asking; What is a cloud services? Why do I need to move to the cloud? What is a service lifecycle? Who are service owners? CSF is introduced to help executives answer such question and take informed decisions. CC practitioners are trying to take a more structured approach to the art of governing, and turn it, as much as possible, into a science (Brown & Laird & Gee & Mitra, 2008). Risk Management is the process enables the enterprise to set the risk tolerance, identify potential risks and prioritize them based on the enterprise's business objectives in association with internal controls (AAIRM, 2002). Plenty of books and articles have defined and discussed risks, the enterprise risk management and the risks associated with CC (Hillson, 2008; Brotby, 2006; Davis, Schiller, & Wheeler, 2006; Schlarman, 2009).

Plenty of articles are trying to answer the practitioners concerns when asking why do we need the new esoteric terms when evaluating the CC services? (Stantchev & Stantcheva, 2013). The advent of CC has enabled every CE to acquire software, often without the need for technology team support or capital (Marks, 2015). Thus it is more important to set new rules and define parameters that everyone may understand.

In summary, it can be argued that recent progress in CC and technology environments have promoted more research on enterprise risk management and governance (Abram, 2009; Segal, 2011). The main differentiator of this chapter is the orchestration of a wide spectrum of elements to help executives, practitioners and researches understand correlations and plan necessary CC service elements and supporting functionality. Joint understanding produces the CSF as a scalable, measurable, sustainable, and defensible term that is continually improving.

CLOUD SERVICE FOOTPRINT (CSF)

In its original and primary form, the footprint is a tracing that contains lots of information about the identity and nature of the beast that made it. This chapter is introducing the Cloud Service Footprint (CSF) as an invented term to identify aspirations and interdependencies of a given cloud service. CSF is intended as a control element that provides client enterprises (CEs), cloud service providers (CSPs) and regulatory bodies with necessary visibility to measure each CC service independently or collectively. CSF is intended to work in discrete and continuous basis. This section is providing few insights to define, generate and correlate CSF, additionally it will look into its feasibility and motivations. CSF is crafted for CEs considering to implement CC services. It provides a multi-category approach to evaluate the CC impacts on the CE from various angles. Yet, it also adds value for CSPs who are trying to bench mark their CC services. CSF helps to clarify the service transformation mechanisms and fit it within the CE governance, service management and operations. Overall, the CSF dimensions help to move away from reactive and unreliable CC services evaluations.

Definition

In analogy to the original definition of a footprint, the Cloud Service Footprint (CSF) is intended to provide a tracing that contains lots of information about the identity and nature of a given CC service. At one place, CSF is used to describe the trails and traces left online. On the other hand, it can contain weighted indices that consider the service risks, controls, maturity and momentum considerations. CC associated risks are understood, mapped, segmented, weighted and monetized by the CSF.

CSF will enhance the CE technology decision-making processes and assist CSPs in communicating the value proposition of their products and services. Additionally, this helps to demonstrate, justify and realize the tangible value of CC initiatives by senior management and key business stakeholders. It also assists CSPs in winning, serving and retaining customers.

Motivations

When applied to CC, controls that exist today need to be stretched and distressed to cope with the demands placed on it. Modifications may be insufficient, this assures the need for new mechanisms and parameters to control various CC aspects and associated risks. CC services should have adequate internal controls, applied security levels or enhanced values for each business area. CSF is intended to touch on the scope of technical controls required to mitigate threats. It draws from the quality management procedures and the governance models to introduce a simple to use and easily-to-understand parameters or techniques that can be easily dictated and managed.

CC increasingly require the management of Middle Circle Contractors (MCCs) or the "men-in-the-middle". CSF shed special light and controls for selecting and contracting a suitable MCC or CSP. The critical elements of CC service deployment boil down to "trust and trace". An appropriate CSP will maintain sustainability and quality to prevent loss of data and vendor or technology lock in. A malicious user can move from one CE to another through the CSP environment because CSPs are providing support and services for multiple CEs on a shared basis. Furthermore, if an MCC is using common devices it is important to separate the interfaces between CEs with distinct accounts separate privileges and folders. CSF can summaries such roles and help the CSP or MCC to "commensurate with the level of risk to which the CE is exposed to" (CSA, 2015).

CEs utilizing CC services need to develop robust service schema in collaboration with CSPs. This schema is required to achieve agreed-upon goals to support the business mission and technology goals regardless of the service or deployment model. CSF may act to adjust the defined roles and responsibilities in the combined schema based on the respective scope of control. The deployment model may define accountability and expectations based on risk assessment. CSF is trying to combine many parameters to help CEs, MCCs and CSPs and enhance the common understanding.

Derivation

CSF was derived through a reverse engineering process for several CC implementations. Lessons learnt were collected and the development elements were analyzed. To find the best fit, attained data were categorized with respect to the main CSF dimensions and subs. Every CC service were examined based on composite expectations of CEs or considering the characteristics of a specific CE. Controls modeling and risk adjustment were deliberated based on highlighted issues and concerns. Such tunings played a key part in the CSF crafting to outfit categories that include a broad range of details or in situation that have a large number of outside forces.

Feasibility

CC increasingly emphasized the trend of separate independent services that run in the background. Multiple services are invoked together to make an action. CSF can demonstrate an increased value as a facilitator for these "off-the-shelf" services. In this context, CSF can provide the power needed to seamlessly automate processes and manage CC services effectively. CSF is introduced to give business and technology organizations the necessary visibility and control for continuous improvement of CC services. Factoring in, CSF is intended as an essential element to better identify the merits of a selected CC service. Promoting clarity and transparency, CSF may derive an efficient delivery process with optimum performance to control costs, maintain compliance and reduce vulnerability.

Solid measurements provided by CSF allow CEs to enumerate action delivery and optimize the operation. Better service understanding produced by CSF enhances the mechanism to improve the value calculations of CC services and technology investments, such as total cost of ownership (TCO) and the return on investment (ROI). It helps to standardize the CEs and CSPs interaction processes with each other also with various stakeholders. With enhanced asset and business orchestration, CSF is expected to affect the CC strategy, analysis and decision hierarchy and to reduce the traditional sophistication of technology. CSF may synthesize various results to provide a clear picture of the total impacts of a CC service.

Correlations

Three elements are claimed to provide enough information for business executives to evaluate CC services and make informed decisions. In addition to the CSF, cost and functional capability can provide the basis for prioritizing CC and technology initiatives in a manner that saves huge struggle among CEs. The correlation between these three elements can produce an effective business value and ensures that CC service benefits can be realized.

Cost signify the investment necessary to achieve certain value and acquire the associated benefits of the proposed service. Cost combine all investments and expenses necessary to deliver the proposed value. Additionally, it captures incremental or ongoing payments over the existing environment if it is associated with the service. Costs must be tied to the benefits that are generated. Direct benefits and functionalities represent one part of the investment, although it is typically used as the primary way to justify the service attainment. Another significant part is related to measuring the strategy alignment of the CC service or the expected drawbacks on the CE future. Flexibility represents the value that can be generated if new features are built on top of the acquired service.

Functional capability represents the operational value derived from the proposed CC service as measured by the entire CE combining the technology organization (TO) and/or business units (BUs). Benefit estimates involve a clear dialogue with the CE stakeholders to comprehend the specific value being created. Prior to cloud era, functional justification focus on one business silo, leaving little room to analyze the effect on the entire CE strategy. CC services are enabled across the CE and effects its entire environment, consequently it promotes full examination and places variable weights to measure benefits and capabilities.

CSF can be hired to ensure CC service sustainability and ability to perform as promised, in a secure, trusted and reliable way. It enables better design, evaluation and management of CC services. This defines a clear line of accountability that can be considered whether the focus is external from the public cloud, or within a private cloud inside the CE. CSF may also consider the side effects or enhancements of a CC service. For instance, acquiring an industry accredited service can potentially increase standardization and efficiency. However, an embedded collaboration feature may translate to greater worker productivity if activated. The bottom line is that correlating CSF with cost and functional capability provides the ability to measure multiple dimensions related to CC services and to capture their future and strategic values.

CSF BUILDING DERIVES

CC is positioned in a convergence mode as a technology adoption that inherits business risks. Problems are typically associated with the newly emerging business models. Substantive advances occurred for the CC service delivery models in the past few years. But, associated risk and governance practices have not matured at a similar rate. The dynamic scalability of CC enhances the possibility of quick upsizing and downsizing, but there exist some roadblocks. Business and technology teams have to increase correlation and communication to collectively agree upon the right balance.

Some internal and external factors add up to increase the efficiency of CC services, including the compliance strategies and risk based auditing. CC aspirations encourage governance in its participatory form as the job of every stakeholder, particularly the most vulnerable. The board of directors are playing a main role in CC governance under the corporate governance umbrella while aligning the CE strategy. Understanding CC service aspirations and alignment help in setting related policies and ensuring the CE credibility.

This section is putting risk and governance in the heart, looking at service maturity and momentum to introduce Cloud Service Footprint (CSF) as a guideline to evaluate the CC services. It supports moving business infrastructure, processes and applications into the cloud while increasing the navigation clarity through the fear, uncertainty and doubt. It also provides answers to improve the understanding of CC adoption in a structured and systematic approach.

Risks Management

The ISO Guide 73:2009 define risk as the "effect of uncertainty on objectives" (ISO:2009). This includes uncertainties caused by ambiguity or lack of information. According to COSO "Risk is the possibility that an event will occur and adversely affect the achievement of objectives" (COSO, 2012). Positive and negative uncertainties are contained within the CC services and their surroundings. Tracking and measuring risks, enhances the opportunity to meet original projections. Risk Management (RM) is the act of aligning exposure and capability to handle risks as per the stakeholders' guidelines. In this regard, it acts as a primary means to support technology decisions triggered to protect the confidentiality, integrity, and availability of CC services and assets. Different categorization of risks may be introduced to allow stakeholders understanding the qualitative distinctions between the types of risks that CEs can face.

Although some categorizations defined before the cloud era, they are now becoming more recognized and deep (Kaplan, & Mikes, 2012).

Business risk mapping is the process used to identify and segment contemplations that can hinder the normal business flow. CC services enable cross functionality with all business processes introducing a joint risk arena. Hence, CC related risks need to be delineated in the functional space and categorized along functional lines to identify their inter-dependencies. No two industries will have a common generic set of functional risks. "After the risk management plans are implemented, there is a need to follow-on actions as part of a comprehensive assessment and continuous monitoring program for effectiveness" (Alnuem, Alrumaih & Al-Alshaikh, 2015). Risk assessment is crucial to help management evaluating the risk events associated with its cloud strategy. This will help to determine the potential impact of the risks associated with each CC option (Broder, 2006). The ability to make risk assessment more accurate depends on whether the CE has a comprehensive, accurate, and current inventory of risks. The outcomes of risk treatment plans should be incorporated into service agreements where applicable to analyze risks' likelihood, acceptance levels and criteria.

RM functions are critical to every CE. It includes the valuation of CC assets and the analysis of associated threats and vulnerabilities. Risk likelihoods are usually based on a related probability density functions The underlying impacts of risk scenarios necessitate the development of risk action plans defining the proper risk technique either being mitigation, avoidance, transfer and acceptance. "The occurrence of an event, which is associated with the adoption and use of cloud computing can have undesirable consequences or impacts on user companies" (Dutta, Peng & Choudhary, 2013). CC can affect critical focal points of RM including the CE risk profile which encompasses the entire risk population. This profile should be extended by the inclusion of a subset of the risk universe associated with business units, CSPs and MCCs. The inherent and residual risk levels of CC options can be either greater or less than those as the non-cloud computing solutions. Similar changes occur to the likelihood and impact in many cases when CC solutions are adopted.

There are many variables, values and risks in any CC opportunity or program that affect the business decisions. Risk types may not be affected if CC services are procured, but some of them may have different characteristics. However, the CE level of risk thresholds will, in most cases, change based on CC purpose and how far the CC solutions will be adopted. As CC services are going through, some changes are associated with the CSP who has been engaged. "With cloud computing poised to move from its nascent phase to a more robust growth phase, a systemic understanding of the risk space enveloping cloud is becoming important" (Warrier & Shandrashekhar, 2006).

Each CE has to weigh few variables to decide for cloud appropriate solutions with the executive board to be engaged when required. Some risks can be managed through a rules-based model; others may require alternative approaches. CEs acquiring services from CSPs should ask whether their own management has defined risk tolerances with respect to CC services and accepted any residual risks. Normally, a CSP should demonstrate comprehensive and effective RM processes in association with its services. The CE should carefully evaluate the risk behaviors of a CSP in conjunction with their own abilities to compensate for the potential RM gaps. Risk assessment approaches between CSPs and CEs should be consistent or mapped. They should jointly develop risk scenarios for the cloud service. Such scenarios should be intrinsic to the CSPs' design of service and to the CE assessment of CC service risks.

Governance

To be effective, CEs must establish clear chains of responsibility to empower people and to widen the communication channels to keep all stakeholders informed. This should be accompanied by measurements to gauge effectiveness and policies to guide the entire CE toward its goals. On top of this control mechanisms are necessary to ensure compliance and strategy alignment. Governance is a strategic lesson learned the hard way over the past decade but it need to be revisited in the cloud era to handle all challenges and controls. Governance represents a set of processes, customs, policies, laws, and institutions affecting the way an enterprise is directed, administered or controlled. It also controls the relationship among involved stakeholders.

There exist plenty of good governance principles, including four major pillars:

- Accountability obligation to report, explain and be answerable for the consequences of decisions that was made on behalf of the stakeholders.
- Transparency to enable stakeholders understanding the decision-making process and follow the consistent rule of law to achieve justice.
- Responsive to serve the entire stakeholders in a responsible manner while balancing competing interests appropriately. It also produces a positive timely response to change.
- Effectiveness to implement decisions and follow processes with efficiency. The best out of the available people, resources and time will be utilized to produce superior results in equity and fairness.

Good governance is based on the acceptance of the shareholders' rights as the true owners of the CE and the role of senior management as trustees. Governance lead to "establishing chains of responsibility, authority, and communication to empower people carry out their roles and responsibilities while establishing measurement, policy, and control mechanisms" (Brown, Moore, & Tegan, 2006). There are many governance practices that follows similar basic principles in terms of audit behaviors, board and management structures, corporate responsibility and the exercise of control rights.

As cloud correlates business with technology, governance will enhance both executive and non-executive oversight. Business directors will gain significant benefits as they have limited amount of time to devote to the CE, but almost unlimited responsibilities. Governance need to start with the decision makers who are building cloud architectures. It is aimed as a constitution that is required to articulate a common agreement about cloud definitions and follow the best possible process for decision making. Good CC Governance is expected to deliver well-defined solutions that will satisfy stakeholders and resolve any conflicts. Cloud governance roadmap is a sub-journey of the governance roadmap with long-term view to deliver short term solutions with a coherent vision.

CSF acts to maximize business value by incorporating effective business-driven management and governance tools into the CC applications from the ground up. It also aims toward minimal disruption of business, technology operations and stakeholders inconvenience. CSF is a critical success factor for both achieving standardization, reducing costs and improving business process flexibility. CSF is ultimately turning business agility from a platitude to reality. Typical governance paradigm includes requirements of technology infrastructure, employee behavior, and business processes. These components are often recorded, implemented and measured in silos, CSF acts to cross link these capabilities. Effective governance will be produced as executives break down the walls between business silos and devise common approaches. CC technologies helped in resolving the trade-offs between diverse, sometimes conflicting, needs and interests.

Governance will be utilized as a mechanism to orchestrate heterogeneous elements in the cloud environment, setting rules and responsibilities, leading the way to review the cloud phenomena and the associated risks in a reliable and trustworthy way. It should be noted that migrating to the cloud is not an abdication of responsibility. Even, the outsourced service still need to be governed. The opposite understanding may place the whole enterprise at risk of falling over technical and compliance barriers. CSF helps to embed and link the governance practices inside CC lifecycle end-to-end. The cycle includes requirements gathering, planning, architecture design, deployment, bursting, CSP switching and off-boarding from cloud.

Maturity

The National Institute of Standards and Technology (NIST) defines CC as: "A model for enabling ubiquitous, convenient, on-demand network access to a shared pool of configurable computing resources (e.g. networks, servers, storage, applications, and services) that can be rapidly provisioned and released with minimal management effort or service provider interaction" (Mell & Grace, 2011). The NIST definition aimed towards a mature setup, which is not the situation today where CC means various things to different stakeholders. Developers often equate CC and web services as one and the same. Designers view CC as a set of implementation patterns that should be applied during development. Business executives and technology leaders consider CC as a core underpinning to their information and technology strategy. CSF supports creating a shared vision and definition to achieve the promised benefits as expected by every stakeholder in a mature, responsible and diverse environment.

Cloud metrics are stacking without clear capabilities and boundaries, even "the terminology of cloud service measurements is not well defined" (NIST, 2015). Different interpretations exist between CSPs, CEs and regulatory bodies who should monitor, control, and report on CC services. This require more transparency to precisely align CC services, expenses and demands. Effective measurement of CC services is still evolving to optimize resource utilization and enhance controls. Mature and unified metering will impose unique benefits on the top of every CC service. Various stakeholders are expected to benefit from enhanced controls. CSF supports leveraging the CC metering capability according to a suitable level of abstraction in order to enable fair judgement on the reliability and effectiveness of CC measures.

In its mature setup, CC offers a value proposition that is different from traditional technology environments. It enables the CEs to provision computing capabilities based on self-service model and on-demand requirements. It offers economies of scale that would otherwise be unavailable. For example, CC enabled computing resources such as servers and network storage to be acquired and upgraded automatically without requiring physical intervention or human collaboration. Effective resource pooling is a value that is enhanced along with CC maturity. The CSP resources may serve multiple CEs using a multi-tenant model. Different physical and virtual resources can be assigned or reassigned as per CE demand. "Resources can be rapidly and elastically provisioned" (Shinder, 2013). With rapid elasticity, resources often appear as unlimited and can be purchased in any quantity at any time. CSF acts to standardize and formalize the CC value proposition including its various elements.

To cover the requirements of CEs across the whole business spectrum, CC are utilizing four main topology deployment models. These models are progressively elaborating to cover a wide matrix of cost and features. Private clouds are dedicated to a single enterprise for private use. Public clouds are owned and provided by external CSPs, their services are priced based on actual consumption basis. Hybrid clouds blend the benefits of public and private clouds by enabling CEs to retain confidential information in a private cloud, while providing access to the wider choice of applications available in a public cloud. Community clouds share collaborative resources between number of CEs with common interests. CSF is considering the topology deployment model while accounting for the maturity of a CC service.

To support multi-layers on-demand services, CC encompasses a variety of service delivery models (SDMs). These models are evolving to provide different service forms while spanning all computing layers. Infrastructure-as-a-Service, IaaS, is generally the CE first step into CC. Platform-as-a-Service, PaaS, acts at the platform level to provide an environment that supports rapid evolution for key business application development. Software-as-a-Service, SaaS, are available at the application level, via standard browsers to support device independence and anywhere access. Database-as-a-Service, DBaaS, is a cloud-based approach to store and manage structured data, with similar functionality to relational database management systems (RDBMS). The maturity levels of these models vary significantly in accordance to their spread. CSF measures the disruptive behaviors of these models as they deliver new functionalities.

Positive correlation exists between CC maturity levels and the refined organizational practices. Maturity helps to realize CC benefits and measurement instruments, especially when there is no common agreement to define the service elements. Effective maturity assessment is a key to measure readiness and to establish CC roadmaps and improvement plans. Immaturity may affect CC decisions explicitly causing a disturbed enterprise architecture and service agility. Even the project and portfolio management approaches should be unique and mature to deploy CC services as a holistic single overall process. CSF consider correlations, measurements and deployment techniques to help producing a transparent blueprint for CC services.

Getting optimal value from CC requires maturity at the strategic and operational levels. Strategy can enhance alignment and governance while operation can provide continuous measurements and performance enhancements. The combination of activities at both levels augments the conditions for adequate value delivery. A robust governance framework operates at the highest levels to enable the transition and operation of CC. Such framework may compensate for some immaturity or weaknesses. A high level steering committee is recommended to operate at the executive level to align with business strategy and enterprise architecture. Overall, the CSF is introduced to enhance CC maturity, provide visibility to the business, communicate uniform maturity measurements and define clear tradeoffs if necessary.

Service Momentum

Plenty of CC services are spread across the arena. CEs select and adopt new services based on their future economic benefit or utility. The concept of service potential was described in ITIL as "the total possible value of the overall capabilities and resources of the IT service provider" (Axelos, 2016). In its definition, service potential relates to the service providers' ability to better utilize their resources and capabilities in a way that will allow their CEs to deliver business outcomes. It drives up the demand for services from CEs and reduces the idle capacity of the service providers.

The proposed service momentum approach complements the service potential landscape. It covers broader service areas and use additional variables to evaluate the CC service capabilities and predict its future. Service momentum is meant to measure the ability of a CC service to deliver value at any point in its life and support the CE business that is committed for. It identifies collaboration junctions with various business elements to achieve efficiency and absorb the CC service as a strategic business asset that can last onwards. It also includes the service capacity to deliver an economic output from the moment when the service is first acquired in addition to benefits from subsequent upgrades.

During CC service implementations, service momentum helps to validate the ecosystem components. It can be viewed as a broad-scale assessment and spatial mapping of every component. This may determine the overall service relevance to CE policies, business scope and the expected success likelihood. Service momentum can achieve an integrated assessment to represent the expected business value without masking the individual contribution of each component. It includes the identification of the key service-specific processes and the relationships with the targeted ecosystem services.

To measure the future sustainability of CC service, service momentum may include selected predictor variables to establish a scoring scheme that is allied with the service attributes. Various techniques can be used to identify the scores associated with each attribute. Thresholds can be accompanied based on accepted standards and relative observations. Reliable spatially explicit data may enhance the key business processes and support the management decisions. Sometimes there exist no clear thresholds or attributes to support the identification and development of quantitative future estimations. Modifications can be triggered based on the service performance and business relevance.

Service momentum is sought out to utilize the best available approaches to assess the current and future capabilities of each individual CC service based on abstract and expert opinion. This allows service momentum to act as a quality indicator to ensure CC service availability and feasibility. Service momentum approach is not yet complete; it needs further analysis to develop. Hands-on practical experience, market research, deep knowledge and industry relationships are utilized here to tentatively measure the service momentum for every CSF dimension or component.

CSF DIMENSIONS

CSF penetrates various fields to create an identity for every CC service and help both CEs and CSPs to better utilize resources, conduct the contracting and handle CC projects implementation operation and service management. CSF is encompassing various aspects including the architectural dimensions, data considerations, licensing and agreements, service collaboration, and legal aspirations. All dimensions, parameters and sub-parameters are shown in figure 1 below.

Figure 1. A list of all dimensions and sub-parameters of the Cloud Service Footprint (CSF)

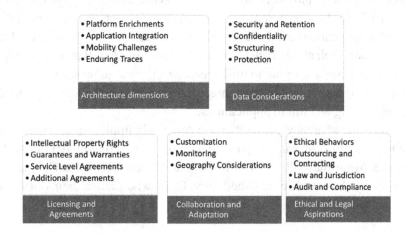

Architectural Dimensions

When planning CC projects, suitable architecture is considered among the most natural and necessary prerequisites. It determines few dimensions related to the CC service such as the number of users, transactions and its price list. One challenge is to determine the unique scope and parameters to provide an optimal relationship between service cost and effectiveness. This section is considering CSF capabilities to boost and optimize CC architectural elements including the platform enrichment, application integration and mobility challenges.

Platform Enrichments

While acquiring new CC service, CEs are expected to assess how this service can be utilized to enhance their technology adoption and promote business integration. Stakeholders may require to satisfy specific technical constrains, especially for unique requirements or sensitive information. Understanding technology concepts is important to determine what efforts are reasonable to address the CC risks. The CEs ability to assess the CC platform is important to give informed consent to forgo certain measures. CEs must be competent to assess the architecture related to the CC services or consult with someone who is. Number of platform measures and concepts are important to achieve the planned integration or correlation with on-premises technologies. Platform enrichment may consider the effect of various technologies on the CE future and adaptation.

CC services requires well-structured platform that foster adaptive implementations and accept sets of standards. Enriched platform need to leverage all solutions, share and re-use the existing infrastructure in a repeatable and cumulative means. A successful CC implementation may require blending of traditional on-premises infrastructure with public shared systems. Poor integration can prohibit the realization of multiple benefits. Infrastructure ownership can be a differentiator where some CSPs don't own their CC servers and instead use Amazon or Microsoft infrastructure for storing data and backing it up. Such a case creates an issue if the CSP defaults on a payment to servers' owner who might immediately cut off access.

Application Integration

CEs are looking to modernize and enhance their entire business applications environment. CC services attracted CEs to focus on rapid-deployment implementations that is delivering simple and scalable solutions. They encourage CEs to abandon the engagement in expensive implementations and customizations of protracted enterprise applications that is based on specific vertical solutions. Instead the applications based on CC services proofs their ability to deliver cost-friendly solutions that address a specific business processes in a short time. CSPs are trying to utilize best practices to jump start CEs with new efficient applications in smaller time frame. Application integration is meant to facilitate smooth connectivity of CC services with the existing and future applications.

The CC applications are what they are, as they are "generally implemented on the provider's terms, thus the degree of negotiability pales in comparison with the contracting model in traditional services" (Opelt, Gloger, Pfarl & Mittermayr, 2013). There is a general recognition that CEs have to start at CSP configurations, especially those well-established large CSPs who dictate their rules. Consequently, if a CE expects customization with genuine configurations of service parameters, then there should be special considerations related to the acquired solutions or components.

Mobility Challenges

The 3 As (Anytime, Anywhere and on Any device) phenomenon resulted from the prioritized mobile access (Mastorakis, Mavromoustakis, & Pallis, 2015). Mobility required by CEs to engage with their customers, business partners and employees. Mobile engagement is increased to enrich customer experience and transform data into actionable insights. However, it exposes applications and data on a small, light and always-on portable device. Every CC service should be evaluated against its mobility practices and its engagement with mobile service providers (MCPs). CSPs are expected to manage mobile application distribution and governance by considering several MCPs and public application stores.

Mobility is located at the front end of the new interaction system, which is people-centric as opposed to traditional systems, which was record or process-centric. CC services should support effective mobility platform that has a scalable hierarchy and architecture and can progressively deliver the optimum service based on existing resources. It should respond timely to the iterative, faster lifecycles, fragmented mobile devices with various operating behaviors. CSPs are expected to accommodate advanced mobile services such as push notifications and geo location services. CSPs are expected to have a robust mobile strategy to reduce risks across the CE infrastructure including mobile devices (endpoint) and other mobile stacked layers.

Enduring Traces

While information is transmitted online via website registration, emails, attachments or any other forms of uploads, they leave identifying traces and information. Such traces can be seen by others online or it may leave a permanent effect in the supporting platform architecture. CEs can be susceptible to security flaws originating from the leak of personal information via this digital footprint.

A CC service should be evaluated against the trace it leaves online. Network technologies tend to leave large traces due to its spread and expansion. Functional technologies tend to leave fairly small footprints as they may not be used outside a specific silo. One functional example is Computer Aided Drafting (CAD) system which is used only by engineering department. Some technologies or services can have small footprints or very large ones based on their complexity and usage. One example is the Enterprise Resources Planning (ERP) and Customer Relationship Management (CRM). Technology borders should be set up carefully when moving any functionality to the cloud. The enduring traces can play a major role in the complexity and cost of CC service.

Data Considerations

When contracting a CSP or an MCC to process data on its behalf, the CE will continue to be accountable and responsible for what the third party does with the data. This means that the CE could be liable if the data handled by the CSP is lost or destroyed. The CE has an obligation to ensure that the contracted third party has adequate measures in place to protect data securely against unauthorized or unlawful processing, accidental loss, destruction and damage. The CE also should consider data confidentiality, structuring, protection and backward collection when the contract is ceased. CSF is considering such dimensions as described in this section.

Security and Retention

CEs are required to ensure that all data processing under their responsibility is handled in adherence to their data protection principles. Whether data handling is outsourced or being processed internally within CE data controllers. CEs can manage those requirements by including a security schedule within the CSP contract to outline data handling mechanisms. This includes:

- How the CE data is separated from others' data?
- Applicable restrictions on data and the associated security measures.
- Responses to security breaches of all kinds
- Reactions to legal requirements under various scenarios

CEs need to validate the CC service dimensions in relation to data disposal and retention schedules. Legal obligations and committed practices should be cascaded when the data is hosted and processed in the cloud. Data procedures need to comply with the stakeholder agreed schema and clarified during the contracting with the CSP or an MCC.

Confidentiality

There are many occasions when data access is restricted to authorized CE staff. Prior to signing a CC service agreement, CE seniors need to test CC solutions for data confidentiality and compromising immunity. It is required to assess whether the cloud is an appropriate place to store and work with classified data where confidentiality is critical. Outlining provisions in the contract may be required to detail the processes required to protect confidentiality (JISC, 2014).

CSP standard terms and conditions vary in the degree they undertake to maintain the data confidentiality. Some CSPs state that they have no duty of confidentiality regarding CE data and place the responsibility on the CE. Therefore, it is desirable to state clearly in the contract the confidentiality terms and obligations between CEs, CSPs & MCCs.

Structuring

The ownership of CC services and applications may not be available for licensing on CE systems outside of CSP provision. This pressures the importance to keep a copy of data locally under CE control to have the ability to download and use data in a native standardized format. Alternatively, the CSP should be able to move data to a different host if the CE becomes dissatisfied or otherwise wants to change providers. The CE need to confirm the CSP capability to purge and wipe any copies of the data according to different scenarios. This goes in line with data usage rights where the ownership of data supplied by the CE to the CSP need to be clearly disclosed. Even the ownership of metadata and other statistical information should be considered with the purposes it may be used for.

Data format may consider the portability and interoperability features to ensure that all CE data can be exported to multiple standardized format at any stage of the service delivery. Data encryption responsibilities should be completely understood by the CE if the provider encrypts confidential data, including who can determine the encryption sufficiency and how it should be used in all data transport-ability scenarios.

Protection

CSP should back up data adequately to include data, configuration items, settings, files, documents, operating systems, applications and permissions. Backup frequency can be either immediate, hourly, daily, weekly or monthly and the storage location can be offshore or offsite with pre-determined relative location and distance from the location of the data being backed up. Access to backup data or archived data should be clearly articulated including the method it is available through and the management of restoration requests. The timeframe that it will be commenced within and the backup data retention period. The permission of client audits of backup data. Regular maintenance program is also required to ensure the reliability and stability of CSP resources and service offerings. If any service is paid the expected costs should be mentioned

CSP is expected also to take every reasonable action to protect data and guard against unauthorized attempts of access. Breaches include unauthorized access to confidential CE information by the CSP employees, MCCs or by outside parties like hackers. There should be procedures to be triggered if the CE discover that his data has been lost or compromised and policies to notify CEs of security breaches and next actions. CSF in intended to mask the complexity of data structures and protection allowing the CE to make informed decisions. It simplifies the CC data interaction with the systems and can be utilized easily to optimize operational decisions.

Licensing and Agreements

The nature of CC services allows information to be continuously generated, constantly added, removed and modified. It is important to agree upon the ownership of this data and to ensure that the CSP contract terms are clear. In certain conditions, it is essential to state in the contract that all data will continue to be owned by the CE including the residual database rights.

Intellectual property rights, warranties and guarantees should be considered while crafting the agreement accord. The CE, as data controller, will remain responsible for the adequate protection of their stakeholders' data. Combined with CC contracts there should be some agreements or provisions in order to clearly define the acceptable behavior of personnel from both parties including the service level agreement (SLA). Contract and agreements accord are important for both CEs and CSPs and is considered as a crucial part of the CSF dimensions

Intellectual Property Rights

CEs and CSPs need sloid arrangements to manage the intellectual property rights (IPRs). It is important to consider those rights from the outset of the service agreement as CC services are usually operated from the CSP cloud. CSPs can claim the ownership of the service itself, but CEs need to have the own-ership of unique processes, contents and data uploaded by their users. A reviews for the CSP standard terms and conditions should be conducted at the early start-head to validate the IPR. Negotiations may be required to modify certain terms and conditions especially for emerging conditions. One scenario is to set out how intellectual property rights are assigned for new materials created as part of the jointly launched CC service.

Software Escrow Agreements (SEAs) is a smart, simple way of protecting intellectual property rights for software owners while ensuring the long-term availability of business-critical systems for end-users. SEAs are used to ensure continued use of critical business systems by depositing the software systems source code with a neutral third party escrow agent (Olson & Peters, 2011). SEAs can be used effectively in CC.

Guarantees and Warranties

Certain services or applications may require a guarantee that only named authorized persons can use certain resource and on local servers only. Using CC services create a possibility of third party access including the CSP or MCC staff, additionally data location may not be specified. This necessitate that contractual agreements between CE stakeholders or clients to be reflected in the CC service contracts if correlated. CE should guarantee preventing unlicensed users and any unauthorized usage of the licensed resources.

CE should also consider to have necessary warranties related to the performance of the CC services. It is important to examine the terms and conditions of any warranties provided by the CSP according to its requirements. If a special warranty is required, it should be negotiated at the service start-head.

Service Level Agreements (SLAs)

When CEs utilize CC environments, they are inherently giving up control over certain aspects of the provided services. Service Level Agreements (SLAs) define the acceptable service levels to be provided by the CSP in measurable terms. SLA acts to define the necessary roles and responsibilities appendices to provide careful delineation between the accountabilities and relationships among all parties. As a best practice, SLAs should clearly define how CSPs monitor their service levels, provide timely notifications of failures or upgrades and submit evidences that problems have been resolved or mitigated. Issue reporting, communication mechanisms and response times for support requests should be defined and classified into reasonable agreed scenarios. If an SLA is not met, the consequences can be catastrophic to CEs.

Service Level Agreements (SLAs) represent an important component under the umbrella of the overall CC contracting between CSPs and CEs. SLA performance clauses should be consistent with other performance clauses within the contract. SLA should be fully contemplated by both of them prior to procuring CC services. SLA usually includes provisions that detail how end-users may use the services, responsibilities of the CSP, and how the CSP will deal with customer requirements. It is noteworthy that the definitions, measurements/metrics and enforcement of this performance vary widely among CSPs. Therefore, a CE "need to fully understand any ambiguities in the definitions of the terms in order to know what levels of service to expect" (Metheny, 2013). The bottom line is that value is provided where terms are clearly defined and performance metrics are measured and guaranteed.

Additional Agreements

CC contracts may require to set out additional agreements or workflow processes to be activated in case of non-performance, breach of contract or even the special scenarios. Consortium agreements handle the special case when several CEs are working together on a private cloud to outline the terms and conditions of collaborative working. Software Escrow Agreements (SEAs) are necessary for business continuity and more crucial in CC to mitigate the inherent risks resulted because CEs rely on the CSP tools and applications. It ensures that the systems utilized by CEs can be made available in severe cases with an access the source code and documentation. The source code is released to the licensee (CE) if the licensor (CSP or MCC) vanishes out or fails to maintain and update the software as specified in the software license agreement.

Some CEs may require that CSP and MCC personnel to sign Non-Disclosure Agreements (NDAs) when dealing with their data to ensure that they protect sensitive non-public information or details. The acceptable behavior prescribed by NDAs requires reasonable oversight, including examining its clauses and monitoring some end-users' activities. CSF is shedding the light on the additional agreements to ensure reliable CC service is provided. On top of this, there may be a need for specific service agreements, rights and responsibilities clauses, license arrangements, security schedules and what is required.

Service Collaboration

Unlike traditional applications, temporary interruption in CC services may be the norm, not the exception. Each CSP can define its own service approach and limitations which is outside the CE controls. Cloud and related technologies have promoted new service status including the "always on" concept, Omni-channel experience and the versioning control tracking. Multiple dimensional synchronization poses a new set of requirements, as customers demand seamless uniform look and feel.

CSF is considering necessary parameters to ensure that CC services are effectively designed, well-documented and closely monitored and collaborated by the CSPs and CEs. It provides the ability to have a continuous experience across multiple brands, formats and devices that is completely bespoke. CSF is considering the promise of new thinking and marketing ways that has been fabricated by the CC and associated services.

Customization

There are areas where CEs need to show their naivety by asking for changes that directly contradict the commoditized nature of the service offering. Usually little changes are accepted by the CSP who may comply with CE's complex requests only at a very high cost. Special requirements take backseats with CSPs who prefer to incorporate any processes changes to all CEs. The management of specific application changes for every CE will drive down CC efficiencies and raise costs. Silo implementations may delay the CSP strategy, root-in the ability of swift change reactions and necessitate setting new policies.

CC enables the most sophisticated analytic tools and applications along with increasingly diverse data sets. CC resources are being put in use to solve problems in ways people can scarcely imagine. CSPs utilize an infrastructure that enables CEs to deliver value more quickly. This is leading the way for context-driven variability by understanding CEs and engaging them in more authentic or personalized ways. CC services changed the collaboration obligation and technologies in a manner that is very useful for CEs as they reduce the costs associated with expensive travel and communication. Cloud also converted the ways data transactions are facilitated along plenty of industries and activities.

CSF needs to measure the easiness and effectiveness of CC service to deliver new applications to a broader set of users. Collaboration benefits and parameters need to be measured by the CSF to improve operational efficiency and facilitate effective mechanism and an integral element.

Monitoring

CEs may require their usage of the CC services not to be monitored by CSPs either due to concerns regarding the outcome of such monitoring or their fear to disclose confidential data. CSPs consider different monitoring policies to control the nature/pattern of use or to ensure good quality service provision. Monitoring may be used for statistical analysis or to enforce the acceptable use policy (AUP). CSF is opening the CE eyes to examine the contract details related to the level of monitoring and to confirm that associated terms are consistent with their own requirements.

Geography Considerations

CSPs are likely to store and move data around multiple servers situated in a number of jurisdictions which are most likely located in different countries. Some jurisdictions do not allow the transfer of data abroad unless the hosting country has an adequate level of protection or transparency (JISC, 2014). CEs will need to find out where the CSP is processing data an ensure satisfactory geographical location are chosen to store and archive data. Some major CSPs offer a number of "regional zones" in which a customer may be assured the data will remain. Yet, it is good practice that CE ask for warranty or legal assurance of data location during the contracting phase. The CE should also verify that reporting and auditing mechanism are compliant with local requirements.

CSF consider such geographical information to evaluate service reliability and spread. Additionally, this gives a description of how much territory the CC service is intended to cover, utilize and reach functionally.

Legal Aspirations

CEs, CSPs and MCCs usually follow the contractual agreements but also they need to consider ethical rules and other applicable laws. Behavioral and legal circumstances should be closely considered by the CEs when acquiring a CC service. The experience and reputation of a CSP is important as well its geographical spread, divisional and functional reach and its service coverage. CEs are expected to do their due diligence or consult for recommendations to choose a CSP with a proven record of ethics and functionality.

This section is pinpointing few CSF dimensions related to legal, ethical, law and jurisdiction controls. It also looks at to determine the outsourcing and contracting recommended behaviors and some considerations related to audit and compliance surroundings for CC.

Ethical Behaviors

Inadvertent disclosure or unauthorized interception may pose a great effect on the CEs and their clients and partners. CEs should ask themselves how bad it would be if unauthorized parties gained access to information in bulk or case-by-case basis. The CE should take the proper precautions and measures to prevent access or disclosure. Some measures are easy to set up and then run without additional input while advanced or custom measures may require expert knowledge.

One reason why ethics are important, is the difficulty of evaluating every functionality and implementation of safeguards in particular. Some measures are less likely to be deemed necessary as they may prevent service access or disrupt the flow of practices. Therefore, it is preferred to compensate by a CSP ethics to provide a holistic assurance of safeguards and functionality measures. Service can be re-visited occasionally and selectively to verify or advise situations where additional considerations are necessary.

When evaluating CSPs, CSF imposes a considerable scoring weight to the possibility of expected breach and handling ethics. The extent to which ethical behaviors affect the CEs' ability to collaborate with stakeholders is considered. CSF is required to validate some ethics and conditions to reduce the likelihood of the disclosure and to determine when it is necessary to implement additional safeguards.

Outsourcing and Contracting

Trust and confidence are key factors when the CE decide to participate-in or engage-with a project or a program. In the CC era, these factors are further complicated due to multiple interdependencies. CSPs and middle circle contractors (MCCs) are major players in the CC supply chain loop. The lack of physical control over infrastructure in many CC deployments necessitate mechanisms and parameters to reduce deployment and operation concerns. Stakeholders are more likely to engage with CC projects when they have sufficient confidence that the CSP and other MCCs can control and deliver the desired business outcomes in a consistent manner as they are contracted to.

Prior to the CC era, the failure due to purely external challenges was limited, however this is increasingly being a possible reason of failure. Clashes between various parties may occur due to the inadequacy in understanding the functional and technical specifications or their rigidity to be accommodated into new business realities. The terms of the agreement for CC services should always be read with particular attention to the CSP mechanisms. CEs should ask questions to fully understand how service is implemented, information is protected and how it is aligned to their business goals. It is important to identify the legal and ethical surroundings of the jurisdictions, especially, when the CSP is located overseas. To avoid clatters and disappointments, the CE need to ensure that the CSP or MCC understanding and protocols are on par with the CE expectations. Confusion may affect many stakeholders and increases the likelihood of external action to curtail the actions of the CE. The CC deployment teams need to place huge efforts to avoid loss of confidence and participation which is pervasive in change management.

CEs need to ensure that CC service contracts are adequate to handle their requirements and concerns and to respond to the future expectations. Policies and procedures in the contract need to comply with the CE obligations, strategies and policies. CC contracts can vary in format and wording depending on the CSP and the type of procured solution. For all CC contracts, it is a good practice to ensure that legal obligations are managed according to the CE satisfaction. An important factor at the contract stage is to ensure that the CSP will take reasonable steps to meet the CE's existing legal duties while they are providing the service (JISC, 2014).

CC service contracts are expected to handle the obligation to comply with data protection legislations and obligations. Appropriate management of intellectual property rights, licensing of resources and law enforcement obligations may be detailed to the appropriate level. CEs need to consider also the CSP's take-down policy for its internal and external published content if some materials are declared to break the law. The procedure, authorization and CE involvement in removing such material should be assessed and documented.

CSF visualize the CC projects to have deep engagement with business strategy, thus large-scale failure in them could be part of the board agenda. There are times when, in spite of all care and consideration, projects get so far off-the track, thus there is no alternative to pulling the plug. CSF aims to examine and assess the CSPs and MCCs relationships and dependencies to the extent possible. The CSF is intended to provide the stakeholders with enough visibility to navigate the trust and confidence factors. CSF aims to make all stakeholders, including the board, more aware of the consequences and prepared to make decisions from the early days of the project.

Law and Jurisdiction

Due to its nature, multiple legal jurisdictions are involved in off-shore CC services. Relevant jurisdictions are likely to include the country in which the CE is based and the country where the CSP headquarters are located, in addition to the locations where CSP servers and its MCCs reside. Defining which country's laws apply to a particular issue and which country's courts will hear a particular dispute can be complex. The resolution may vary according to the area of law and the jurisdiction in which the question arises. However, some general observations are possible.

A CSP normally specifies within the contract terms the governing laws of a specific country and that disputes will be heard in which country's courts. Usually jurisdiction is performed in the country where the cloud provider has its principal place of business, but occasionally it may be the legal system where the CE is based. The law typically places few restrictions on this type of contractual clause, except the situations of specifying a totally irrelevant jurisdiction or stringent controls.

In the event of a dispute CEs need to avoid enforcing contractual terms or defending an action in an overseas jurisdiction and under foreign law. They may therefore have to consider the possible additional costs, efforts and impacts if the CSP choose to apply a foreign law and jurisdiction against the benefits of that particular service.

Audit and Compliance

Due to the on-demand provisioning and multi-tenant aspects of CC, traditional forms of audit and compliance may not be available, or may need to be modified. CC enforced major changes in the auditing arena causing external and internal audits to stretch, also continuous auditing concept is introduced. Similarly, the compliance is expanded to propagate into the CC service insides and not to stop at the boundary of the CSP. The embedded audit and compliance procedures need to provide the required value to all stakeholders including CEs, CSPs and regulatory bodies. New parameters and techniques need to be invented to accommodate the audit and compliance techniques that are appropriate and necessary for the CC service and the CE circumstances.

CSF may consider adding reasonable care for any CSP or MCC related restrictions or missing contractual exceptions. Its parameters will simplify CC audits and will enhance some behaviors, components and related aspects. CSF behavioral involvements will reduce the misunderstanding between various stakeholders and provide more visibility and awareness. CSF is intended to achieve higher degrees of communication, comprehension, and buy-in of all the stakeholders. Thorough audit and compliance processes can avoid regulatory fines and reputational damage and reduce disruption. Ultimately, this will give CC platforms the ability to implement system changes and refinements faster and in a more cost-effective manner.

FUTURE RESEARCH DIRECTIONS

The relation between technology organizations (TOs) and business users is being rephrased leading to a wide change in mentality and collaboration of both teams. Risk accompanies change, it is an inherited component of life. The willingness to take and accept risk is crucial for development and progress. Governance is setting the roles to enable stakeholders benefiting from change while minimizing the negative consequences. Technology is now everywhere, and cloud computing (CC) is extending its reach and stretching services so it can be used without significant capital expenditure or even the involvement of technology organization (TO). It is the time to promote unique measures to help business and technology stakeholders including executives to compare CC services and understand associated risks and implications. This is triggering a joint research in CC risk and governance, along with the business and technology alignment in the CC era.

Cloud computing (CC) and associated technologies opens a wide research terrain in theories, characterization and measurements of CC services. Cloud Service Footprint (CSF) is a measure that is introduced in this chapter to provide self-characterization of CC services. It enables the CC service to be utilized everywhere with a standardized business implications and approaches. It also endorses advanced measurement techniques for CC services and mini-services structures, paving the way for independent CC services and extensible enterprise transformation. It aims also to enhance scalability, reduce costs, simplify service management and the decision making process. However, all these phenomena are improving gradually while the CC services are maturing. Extensive research is required to accompany these phenomena, enhance the CSF dimensions and produce effective measures.

In summary, this chapter suggests two main research topics, the first is related to the development of an effective measures for CC services based on risk and governance concepts. This effort, in order to be successful, requires the participation of a very wide range of stakeholders and to benefit from existing frameworks, theoretical bases and practices. The second is to widen the CSF dimensions to include all possible aspects of the CC services whenever they can be realized and measured. Qualitative description and analysis to be conducted continuously, comprehensively and while quantitative description of the CSF dimensions need to be added, if applicable, at a later stage. Quantitative analysis is suggested to follow the weighted average mechanism considering the risk, governance, service maturity and momentum levels.

CONCLUSION

Cloud computing (CC) is reshaping the future, plenty of benefits are justifying its acceptance both from technical and management perspectives. However, it is important to re-invest the savings obtained from CC utilization to attain additional controls, ongoing assessments and more optimization. This chapter studied some CC aspirations including risk, governance, service maturity and momentum levels. It then defined a combined factor that can measure continuously the CC service performance and validate business benefits. Cloud Service Footprint (CSF) is introduced to evaluate a CC service, certify if accepted challenges are rewarded and to identify if the acquired CC service is adequate. CSF as a footprint consider all dimensions and subs surrounding the CC service and the traces that can be residual out of any dimension.

CC services are undoubtedly forming the dynamic heart of the next transformation and utility based computing. Practice has shown that associated CC technologies and risks are often not well understood by the key stakeholders in the client enterprises (CEs) including board members and executive management. However, without a clear understanding, major stakeholders have no point of reference for prioritizing and managing CC services and align them with the CE objectives. CSF is designed to provide executives with more clarity to navigate into the CC journey with long-term view to deliver short term solutions in a coherent vision.

CC service benefits are introduced through evaluation and deployment phases but become measurable during the utilization and operation. This chapter define some CSF dimensions to help business and technology stakeholders working for the CEs, CSPs, MCCs or even regulatory bodies to evaluate and compare CC services. It is intended to support the selection and rollout of CC services with sure steps to satisfy the integration and isolation rules on the way towards well governed "off-the-shelf" CC services. In this regard, the CSF measure the CC service dimensions related to the supporting architecture, data considerations, licensing, service collaboration and legal aspirations. In every dimension and subsequent branches lookup items are identified and commented to achieve the best performance.

CSF is expected to apply equally to existing services and future components and to help in deriving the policies, mechanisms and metrics associated with a CC service. It also needs to judge new components of CC services as well the pre-defined ones. Well-governed CC services can help to regenerate the CE processes and fit business areas. Clear, fact-based efforts and communications are required to lay the foundation of CC service measurements and to include standardized methodologies.

By introducing the CSF, this chapter attempts to present an effort and aspirations to ignite fruitful discussion that will eventually lead to an increased number of research studies in the field of CC service characterization based on governance, risk, service maturity and momentum. This field is really important as it is paving the way to enhance the standardization of CC service and associated technologies. The ultimate goal is to help CEs evaluate existing CC services while the CSPs can brand and benchmark their services in standardized formats

REFERENCES

AAIRM. (2002). *A risk management standard.* London UK: The Institute of Risk Management, the National Forum for Risk Management in the Public Sector and the Association of Insurance and Risk Managers.

Abram, T. (2009). The hidden values of it risk management. *Information Systems Audit and Control Association Journal, 2009*(2), 40-45.

Ackermann, T. (2012). *IT Security Risk Management: Perceived IT Security Risks in the Context of Cloud Computing.* Berlin, Germany: Springer-Gabler.

Alnuem, M., Alrumaih, H., & Al-Alshaikh, H. (2015). *Enterprise risk management from boardroom to shop floor.* Paper presented in The Sixth International Conference on Cloud Computing, GRIDs, and Virtualization, Nice, France.

Aven, T. (2008). *Risk analysis: Assessing uncertainties beyond expected values and probabilities*. West Sussex, UK: John Wiely and Sons, Ltd. doi:10.1002/9780470694435

AXELOS. (2011). *ITIL® glossary and abbreviations*. Retrieved April 07, 2016 from https://www.exin. com/assets/exin/frameworks/108/glossaries/english_glossary_v1.0_201404.pdf

Baya, V., Mathaisel, B., & Parker, B. (2010). The cloud you don't know: An engine for new business growth. PWC Journal of Technology Forecast, 1(4), 4-16.

Broder, J. (2006). *Risk analysis and the security survey*. Burlington, MA: Butterworth-Heinemann Elsevier.

Brotby, W. (2006). *Information security governance: Guidance for boards of directors and executive management*. Rolling Meadows, IL: IT Governance Institute.

Brown, W. A., Moore, G., & Tegan, W. (2006). *SOA governance—IBM's approach*. Somers, NY: IBM Corporation.

Brown, W., Laird, R., Gee, C., & Mitra, T. (2008). *SOA Governance: Achieving and Sustaining Business and IT Agility*. Indianapolis, IN: IBM Press.

COSO. (2012). Enterprise Risk Management for Cloud Computing. Durham, NC: The Committee of Sponsoring Organizations of the Treadway Commission (COSO).

CSA (The Cloud Security Alliance). (2011). *Security guidance for critical areas of focus in cloud computing v3.0*. Retrieved September 09, 2015, from https://downloads.cloudsecurityalliance.org/initiatives/guidance/csaguide.v3.0.pdf

Davis, C., Schiller, M., & Wheeler, K. (2006). *IT auditing: Using controls to protect information assets*. Emeryville, CA: McGraw-Hill Osborne Media.

De Haes, S., & Grembergen, W. (2009). *Enterprise governance of information technology: Achieving strategic alignment and value*. New York: Springer. doi:10.1007/978-0-387-84882-2

Dutta, A., Peng, G. C., & Choudhary, A. (2013). Risks in enterprise cloud computing: The perspective of IT experts. *Journal of Computer Information Systems*, *53*(4), 39–48. doi:10.1080/08874417.2013.11645649

Goranson, H. (1999). *The agile virtual enterprise: Cases, metrics, tools*. New York: Quorum Books.

Hardy, G. (2006). New roles for board members on IT. *Governance Journal*, *13*(151), 11–14.

HBR (Harvard Business Review). (2011). *Harvard Business Review on Aligning Technology with Strategy*. Boston: Harvard Business School Publishing.

Hillson, D. (2008). Why risk includes opportunity. *The Risk Register Journal of PMI's Risk Management Special Interest Group*, *10*(4), 1–3.

ISO-International Organization for Standardization. (2009). *ISO GUIDE 73:2009*. Geneva, Switzerland: International Organization for Standardization.

JISC Legal Information. (2014). *User Guide: Cloud Computing Contracts, SLAs and Terms & Conditions of Use*. Retrieved February 5, 2016, from http://www.webarchive.org.uk/wayback/archive/20150703224546/http://www.jisclegal.ac.uk/ManageContent/ViewDetail/ID/2141/User-Guide-Cloud-Computing-Contracts-SLAs-and-Terms-Conditions-of-Use-31082011.aspx

Kaplan, R., & Mikes, A. (2012). Managing Risks: A new framework. *Harvard Business Review, 90*(6), 48–63.

Marks, N. (2015). *The myth of IT risk*. Retrieved September 09, 2015, from https://normanmarks.wordpress.com/2015/08/28/the-myth-of-it-risk/

Mastorakis, G., Mavromoustakis, C., & Pallis, E. (2015). *Resource Management of Mobile Cloud Computing Networks and Environments*. Hershey, PA: IGI Global. doi:10.4018/978-1-4666-8225-2

Mell, P., & Grace, T. (2011). The NIST Definition of Cloud Computing. NIST Special Publication, 800-145. Gaithersburg, MD: National Institute of Standards and Technology (NIST).

Menken, I., & Blokdijk, G. (2008). *Virtualization: The complete cornerstone guide to virtualization best practices*. Brisbane, Australia: Emereo Pty Ltd.

Metheny, M. (2013). *Federal Cloud Computing: The Definitive Guide for Cloud Service Providers*. Waltham, MA: Elsevier.

NIST (National Institute of Standards and Technology). (2015). *Cloud computing service metrics description*. Retrieved September 09, 2015, from http://www.nist.gov/itl/cloud/upload/RATAX-CloudServiceMetricsDescription-DRAFT-20141111.pdf

Olson, D. & Peters, S. (2011). Managing Software Intellectual Assets in Cloud Computing, Part 1. *Journal of Licensing Executives Society International, H*(3), 160-165.

Opelt, A., Gloger, B., Pfarl, W., & Mittermayr, R. (2013). *Agile Contracts: Creating and Managing Successful Projects with Scrum*. Hoboken, NJ: John Wiley & Sons. doi:10.1002/9781118640067

Schlarman, S. (2009). IT risk exploration: The IT risk management taxonomy and evolution. *Information Systems Audit and Control Association Journal, 2009*(3), 27-30.

Segal, S. (2011). *Corporate Value of Enterprise Risk Management: The Next Step in Business Management*. Hoboken, NJ: John Wiley & Sons.

Shawish, A., & Salama, M. (2014). Cloud Computing: Paradigms and Technologies. In F. Xhafa & N. Bessis (Eds.), *Inter-cooperative Collective Intelligence: Techniques and Applications* (pp. 39–67). Berlin, Germany: Springer-Verlag. doi:10.1007/978-3-642-35016-0_2

Shinder, D. (2013). *Selecting a Cloud Provider*. Retrieved September 09, 2015, from http://www.cloudcomputingadmin.com/articles-tutorials/architecture-design/selecting-cloud-provider-part1.html

Stantchev, V., & Stantcheva, L. (2013). Applying IT-Governance Frameworks for SOA and Cloud Governance. In M. D. Lytras, D. Ruan, R. D. Tennyson, P. Ordonez De Pablos, F. J. García Peñalvo, & L. Rusu (Eds.), *Information Systems, E-learning, and Knowledge Management Research* (pp. 398–407). Berlin, Germany: Springer-Verlag. doi:10.1007/978-3-642-35879-1_48

Turban, E., Leidner, D., McLean, E., & Wetherbe, J. (2008). *Information technology for management: Transforming organizations in the digital economy.* John Wiley and Sons Inc.

Vice, P. (2015). *Taking risk management from the silo across the enterprise.* Retrieved September 9, 2015, from http://www.aciworldwide.com/-/media/files/collateral/aci_taking_risk_mgmt_from_silo_across_enterprise_tl_us_0211_4572.pdf

Vice, P. (2015). *Should IT Risks Be Part of Corporate Governance?* Retrieved September 09, 2015, from http://insurance-canada.ca/blog/2015/08/30/should-it-risks-be-part-of-corporate-governance/

Warrier, S., & Shandrashekhar, P. (2006). A Comparison Study of Information Security Risk Management Frameworks in. Paper presented in the Asia Pacific Risk and Insurance Conference, Tokyo, Japan.

ADDITIONAL READING

Aljawarneh, S. (Ed.). (2012). Cloud Computing Advancements in Design, Implementation, and Technologies. Hershey, PA, USA: IGI Global Australian Government. (2013). Negotiating the cloud – legal issues in cloud computing agreements. Sydney, Australia.

Ben Halpert, B. (2011). *Auditing Cloud Computing: A Security and Privacy Guide.* Hoboken, NJ, USA: John Wiley & Sons. doi:10.1002/9781118269091

Bento, A., & Aggarwal, A. (Eds.). (2013). *Cloud Computing Service and Deployment Models: Layers and Management.* Hershey, PA, USA: IGI Global. doi:10.4018/978-1-4666-2187-9

Bostrom, A. (Ed.). French, S. (Ed.), & Gottlieb, S. (Ed.). (2008). Risk assessment, modeling and decision support: Strategic directions. Heidelberg, Germany: Springer-Verlag

Buyya, R., Broberg, J., & Goscinski, A. (Eds.). (2010). *Cloud Computing: Principles and Paradigms.* Hoboken, NJ, USA: John Wiley & Sons.

Chao, L. (Ed.). (2012). *Cloud Computing for Teaching and Learning: Strategies for Design and Implementation.* Hershey, PA, USA: IGI Global. doi:10.4018/978-1-4666-0957-0

Cornelius, D. (2013, October). *SMAC and transforming innovation.* Paper presented at the meeting of the 2013 PMI Global Congress. New Orleans, Louisiana.

Daecher, A., & Galizia, T. (2015). *Ambient computing. Deloitte Journal of Tech Trends 2015, 6 (1)* (pp. 34–49). United Kingdom: Deloitte University Press.

Easwar, K. L. (2014). Segmentation of Risk Factors associated with Cloud Computing. Paper presented at 2nd International Conference on Cloud Security Management [ICCSM], Reading, UK.

Fit'o, J., & Guitart, J. (2014). Introducing Risk Management into Cloud.[Elsevier Science Publishers B. V. Amsterdam, The Netherlands.]. *Journal of Future Generation Computer Systems, 32*(1), 41–53.

Grembergen, W. (Ed.). (2003). *Strategies for information technology governance.* Hershy, Pennsylvania, USA: Idea Group Publishing.

Hogan, M., & Sokol, A. (Eds.). (2013). NIST Cloud Computing Standards Roadmap, NIST Special Publication, 500-291. Gaithersburg, MD, USA. National Institute of Standards and Technology (NIST).

Hoogervorst, J. (2009). *Enterprise governance and enterprise engineering*. Diemen, Netherlands: Springer. doi:10.1007/978-3-540-92671-9

Information Resources Management Association (Ed.). (2015). Cloud Technology: Concepts, Methodologies, Tools, and Applications (Vols. 1–4). Hershey, PA, USA: IGI Global.

ISACA. (2013). COBIT5 for Risk. Rolling Meadows, IL, USA. Information Systems Audit and Control Association (ISACA).

Jayaswal, K., Kallakurchi, K., Houde, D., & Shah, D. (2014). *Cloud Computing Black Book*. New Delhi, India: Dreamtech Press.

Khidzir, N, Z., Mohamed A. & Arshad, N. H. (2013). ICT Outsourcing Information Security Risk Factors: An Exploratory Analysis of Threat Risks Factor for Critical Project Characteristics. *Journal of Industrial and Intelligent Information Vol. 1, No. 4, December, 1*(4), 218-222.

McDonald, K. (2010). *Above the Clouds: Managing Risk in the World of Cloud Computing, Cambridge shire*. United Kingdom: IT Governance Ltd.

Moran, A. (2014). *Agile Risk Management*. New York, USA: Springer. doi:10.1007/978-3-319-05008-9

Niemann, K. (2008). *From Enterprise architecture to IT governance: Elements of effective IT management*. Wiesbaden, Germany: Springer-Verlag.

Poppendieck, M., & Poppendieck, T. (2013). *The Lean Mindset: Ask the Right Questions*. Westford, Massachusetts: Addison-Wesley.

Ramirez, D. (2008). IT risk management standards: The bigger picture. *Information Systems Audit and Control Association (ISACA) Journal, 2008*(4), 35-39.

Renn, O. (2008). *Risk governance: Coping with uncertainty in a complex world*. London, United Kingdom: Earthscan Publications Ltd.

Rodrigues, J., Lin, K., & Lioret, J. (2013). *Mobile Networks and Cloud Computing Convergence for Progressive Services and Applications (Advances in Wireless Technologies and Telecommunication)*. Hershey, PA, USA: IGI Global.

Rothstein, H., Borraz, O., & Huber, M. (2013). Risk and the Limits of Governance. Exploring varied patterns of risk-based governance across Europe. *Regulation and Governance Journal. Wiley Publishing Asia Pty Ltd, 7*(2), 215–235.

Sargut, G., & McGrath, R. (2011). Learning to Live with Complexity. *Harvard Business Review, 89*(9), 68–76. PMID:21939129

Shalan, M. A. (2010). Managing IT Risks in Virtual Enterprise Networks: A Proposed Governance Framework. In S. Panios (Ed.), *Managing Risk in Virtual Enterprise Networks: Implementing Supply Chain Principles* (pp. 115–136). Hershey, PA, USA: IGI Global. doi:10.4018/978-1-61520-607-0.ch006

Shelton, T. (2013). *Business Models for the Social Mobile Cloud: Transform Your Business Using Social Media, Mobile Internet, and Cloud Computing*. Indianapolis, Indiana, USA: John Wiley & Sons. doi:10.1002/9781118555910

Soili, N., Thomas, B., & Jaakko, K. (Eds.). (2015). *Flexibility in Contracting*. Rovaniemi, Finland: University of Lapland.

Thuraisingham, B. (2013). Developing and Securing the Cloud, Poca Raton, FL, USA: CRC Press: Taylor & Francis Group. doi:10.1201/b15433

Türke, R. (2008). *Governance: Systemic foundation and framework*. Heidelberg, Germany: Springer-Verlag. doi:10.1007/978-3-7908-2080-5

Udoh, E. (Ed.). (2011). *Cloud, Grid and High Performance Computing: Emerging Applications*. Hershey, PA, USA: IGI Global. doi:10.4018/978-1-60960-603-9

Wells, J. (2013). *Complexity and Sustainability*. New York, NY: Routledge.

KEY TERMS AND DEFINITIONS

Client Enterprise (CE): An organization that uses the professional, networking or computing services provided by Cloud Service Providers (CSPs) according to a signed contract against some agreed financial charges. This is compared to ITIL:2011 definition of "business customer" as a comprehensive term for a recipient of a product or a service from the business.

Cloud Service Footprint (CSF): An invented term intended as a control element that provides client enterprises (CEs), cloud service providers (CSPs) and regulatory bodies with necessary visibility to measure each cloud service independently or collectively in order for stakeholders to make informed decisions.

Cloud Service Provider (CSP): An entity that provides computing services based on their existing platforms and apply certain rules for these services.

Governance: A set of processes, customs, policies, laws, and institutions affecting the way an enterprise is directed, administered or controlled. If added to a specific area such as technology it has similar meaning in addition to alignment between that area and the enterprise strategy.

Middle Circle Contractor (MCC): An external or internal person, group or organization that is appointed to perform work or to provide goods/services at a certain price or within a certain time. The MCC appears as a middle person who usually disappears after the specified task is complete.

Risk Management: The act of handling the risk exposure through mitigation, acceptance, sharing and avoidance. It includes the ability to handle information and technology risks based on stakeholders' risk parameters.

Service Momentum: Is meant to measure the ability of a CC service to deliver value at any point in its life and support the business that is committed for. It complements the service potential landscape to evaluate the CC service capabilities and predict its future.

Take-Down Policy: A process operated by online hosts including Cloud Service Providers (CSPs) that is developed to balance the risk between continued availability of data content that may infringes certain law and the damage that may result from wrongful take-down. It may be activated as a response to court orders or personal allegations.

Technology Organization (TO): A team either inside the client enterprise (CE) or outside it, that is in charge of establishing, monitoring and maintaining technology systems and services. In addition, the "TO" supports strategic planning to ensure that all technology initiatives support business goals. It was referred to as the information technology (IT) department which does not reflect the entire spectrum of technology usage nowadays.

Chapter 4
Cloud Security Issues and Challenges

Srinivas Sethi
IGIT Sarang, India

Sai Sruti
IGIT Sarang, India

ABSTRACT

Cloud computing refers to the basic setup for an emerging model of service delivery, that has the advantage of decreasing the cost by sharing computing, infrastructure including storage resources. This can be combined with on-demand delivery mechanism relying on a pay-per-use model. Cloud computing offers an added level of risk because of essential services provided by it to a third party, which makes it difficult to maintain data privacy and security. Security in cloud computing is a critical aspect, which has various issues and challenges related to it. Cloud service providers/ brokers and the cloud service users should make aware of safety cloud. That is the cloud is safe enough from all kinds of the threats, so that the users do not face any problem like; loss of data or data theft. There is a possibility that, a malicious user can enters the cloud by imitating an authentic user, thus corrupt the entire cloud. It can affect many users who are sharing these types of clouds. This chapter mentions the list of parameters that disturb the security of the cloud. This also explores the cloud security issues and challenges faced by cloud service provider/brokers and cloud service users like; data, privacy, and infected application. Finally, it discusses the countermeasure for handling these issues and its challenges.

INTRODUCTION

Albeit there is no established definition for cloud computing, a definition that is adopted in a conventional manner which is provided by the National Institute of Standards and Technologies (NIST) of United States as:

Cloud computing is a model for enabling ubiquitous, convenient, on-demand network access to a shared pool of configurable computing resources (e.g., networks, servers, storage, applications, and services) that can be rapidly provisioned and released with minimal management effort or service provider interaction. (Mell & Grance, 2009)

DOI: 10.4018/978-1-5225-1721-4.ch004

Cloud computing is a prototype for conducive and on-demand networking platform to a shared group of configurable computing resources that can be expeditiously coupled and unconstrained with minimal management efforts. Cloud computing performs as a computational paradigm with distribution architecture. The main objectives of cloud computing concept are to provide quick, convenient, secure data storage and clear computing service, with all available computing resources treated as services and delivered over the Internet (Zhao et al., 2009; Zhang et al., 2010). The cloud augments fraternization, dexterity; extensibility, opportunity, competency to acclimate to fluctuations based on demand, accelerates the development works as per the users requirements, and provides the potential for cost reduction by optimized, effective and efficient computing in the cloud. The cloud computing concept is to make administer scalable with low-cost on-demand computing resources and it provides good quality of service levels. This type of computing is basically used to shares the distributed large scale resources which is cost effective and location independent. Resources available in the cloud can be used by the different client and designed and developed by the vendors such as Google, Amazon, IBM, Microsoft, Salesforce, Zoho, Rackspace, etc. It shares necessary software and various on-demand tools for different IT Industries to achieve enormous benefits of cloud computing. The most vital point for the customers/ client is that, the customers/ clients don't need to buy any resource from a third-party vendor. They can use the resource available in the cloud and pay for it as a service. Therefore, it helps a lot to the customers for saving the time and money. Clouds are not only for Multinational large companies but also being used by small and medium organisations (Lord CrusAd3r, n.d.). Although there are various advantages to adopting cloud computing concept, there are also some consequential obstacles to adopt this concept in the organisation.

Security is one of the most primary barriers to adopt this concept. Cloud computing is a relatively new computing prototype in the recent era. So, there is a major difficulties to include the security concept in various areas like; network, host, application, and data levels of cloud computing. These difficulties have consistently led information for executives to security concern and this is their number one concern with cloud computing implementation (KPMG, 2010). The architecture of the cloud computing consist of numerous cloud components, which are interacting with each other about the various data in different locations they are holding. This assists the users to get the desired data on a faster rate with reliability. The front end and the back end are two different parts focused on data when it comes to cloud. The front end is at user end at which required data is highly essential and users are mostly confined to secure data. Whereas, at the back end, the numerous data storage device, servers available in the Cloud (Lord CrusAd3r, n.d.). There are three kinds of cloud according to their characteristics and usage. They are named as private cloud, public cloud and hybrid cloud. The private cloud is owned by a single enterprise or organization and it provides greater control and better flexibility on the cloud. Whereas, public cloud is shared on a larger scale by the organization or companies for their use. Hybrid cloud is a mixing of private and public cloud which is exploited by most of the industries. The advantages of cloud computing technology may be very appealing but it also involvements several malfunctions. Cloud has different issues when it comes to security point of view, particularly on data theft, data loss and its privacy (Lord CrusAd3r, n.d.). However, in the cloud computing concept, it has a better impact as there are more numbers of people interact with the cloud. It influences many present technologies such as web browsers, web services, and virtualization.

In the cloud, data storage and virtualization are the most critical components and an attack to one of them can do the most harmful in the cloud. In the other part, attacks to one layer have more impact to the other layers. It can put more importance on threats, which is associated with data being stored and processed remotely with sharing the resources and the usage of virtualization in the cloud. All types of attacks are applicable to a computer network system and the data in transportation equally relates to cloud based services. Some of the threats in this category are available for networking system such as phishing, man-in-the-middle attack, sniffing, eavesdropping, etc. Distributed Denial of Service (DDoS) attack is a major attack in the cloud. So, security and its issues are most important concern in the cloud computing environment.

The rest of the chapter are discussed as follow. Section 2 discusses the cloud deployment and service models followed by security in cloud in section 3. Security issues in cloud computing has been discussed in section 4. Section 5 analysed the security issues in cloud computing followed by counter measures in section 6. Section 7 concludes the chapter.

CLOUD DEPLOYMENT AND SERVICE MODELS

Cloud computing technology refers to the fundamental setup which may be very complex one. This may delivers services to users via defined interfaces. There are different layers of services available in the cloud computing technology, which refer to different kinds of *service model in the cloud*. Each offering distinct capabilities in cloud computing. The major layers are discussed as follow.

- **Infrastructure as a Service (IaaS):**Tthe supply of the computing infrastructure resources as a service, which includes virtual machines and other abstracted hardware used in the cloud. The computing resources may be managed through application program interface (API). The user rents these computing resources rather than purchasing them and installing them in data centre. The resources are often dynamically scalable and effective paid for on a usage basis. One of the pioneers of *IaaS* was a storage provider called Storage Networks, which was set up in the late 1990s in Waltham, Massachusetts. They marketed storage-as-a-utility with a pay-per-use billing. They offered a menu of services such as data archiving, backups, and replication. Today, with the robust virtualization technologies (such as Xen from Citrix, Hyper-V from Microsoft and open software), high speed broadband, businesses are looking to buy or rent only what they need for the day. *Iaas* is the solution for them. Examples include Amazon EC2 and S3. The *IaaS* service must include the following:
  - Utility-style computing service with pay-per-use billing
  - Superior, world class IT infrastructure and support
  - Virtualized servers, storage, and network to form a shared pool of resources
  - Dynamic scalability of memory, bandwidth, storage, and servers to meet user needs in real-time
  - Flexibility for users to add more or reduce the allocated resources
  - Automation of administrative tasks
  - Ability to view and manage resource utilization
- **Platform as a Service (PaaS):** This allows user to develop new applications using API organized and constituted remotely. The user can organize developed applications or it can be created by programming languages and tools maintained by the provider. Developers can create applications on cloud platform which is treated as PaaS using APIs or website portals or gateway software

Figure 1. Cloud service models

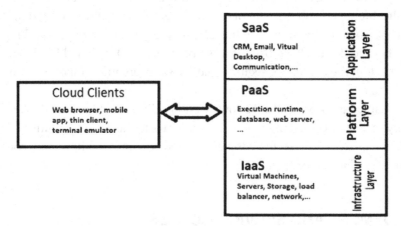

installed on the cloud servers in the cloud computing. Examples of PaaS include Google App Engine, Microsoft Azure and Force.com.

- **Software as a Service (SaaS):** In simple multi-occupancy or multi-tenancy, each user has its own resources in the cloud that are separated from other users. A more efficient form of SaaS is multi-occupancy, where all the available resources are shared, except that user data and access abilities are separated within the application. The delivery of applications as a service, available on-demand basis and paid for on per-use basis. Examples of SaaS include online word processing, online spread sheet tools, web content delivery services and customer relationship management (CRM) services.

These three services models in cloud computing are placed in Figure 1

Security is the best highlighted aspect for any kind of computing and making it a noticeable expectation that security issues in cloud environment are crucial. Confirmation of eligible users' identifications and protecting such authorizations are part of the security issues in the cloud computing.

SECURITY

Conservation of reliability, accessibility and privacy of data/information with other assets such as consistency, liability and faithfulness is known as Security (ISO: 27001, 2005). To certify the safety measures of handling out the information, suitable technological and managerial techniques must be implemented by the data controllers to defend it from:

- **Illegal Access:** Where the data are transmitted over a network
- **Demolition:** Unintended destruction or failure
- **Adaptation:** Improper modification
- **Unlawful Use:** Other illegal forms of analyzing the data

The security of the virtualization software is the responsibility of the cloud provider. It is the software which facilitates the user to build and erase virtual machines. In infrastructure as a service (IaaS) environment, each one of the virtual machine is possessed by a customer. The virtual machines appear by means of an operating system like Linux, Microsoft and Windows. Whereas in platform as a service (PaaS) and Software as a Service (SaaS), the virtual machines were collectively used or shared by several customers. As all the cloud providers are using virtualization and is significant to host security, a detail mechanism should be provided to the user which can be mostly implemented to secure the layers of the virtualization.

Host Security for SaaS

If a SaaS customer asks for the host information then the user will receive no data or least amount of data. This is because the provider itself manages the servers, applications and networks. The provider generally refuses to give any of the details regarding OS, security measure implementation etc, to maintain the data/information away from the hackers which may exploit the information. There are various means used by the users/customer to obtain assertion of security:

- Users may enquire about the security status as soon as they sign a Non-Disclosure Agreement (NDA) with the provider.
- They may enquire if the provider has security evaluation report such SysTrust report.
- They may also enquire about security certifications like ISO 27002.

Moreover, SaaS providers are not compelled to give user details but a high-level SLA will be given for data backups and recovery.

Host Security for PaaS

In a PaaS environment, the total control and access of information/data users can be able to get for servers, as similar to that of SaaS. However, PaaS gives an environment to build up products, kernel-level parameters and access to libraries.

Alike SaaS, the operating system is also hidden from the user in the PaaS. But in PaaS, the customer can access the abstraction layer over the OS. A number of Application Programming Interfaces (APIs) is provided by the cloud provider which is indirectly accessed by the PaaS users to the abstraction layer that hides the OS. The Figure 2 represents how PaaS customers can utilize APIs.

The administration host is the accountability of the cloud provider in PaaS. But in other hand, it grounds a huge loss of control on the host operating situations. Again, it is the responsibility of the users, to maintain the data in cloud, value the security which cloud provider has introduced, and to check if it is adequate for the customer and community developer.

Host Security for IaaS

In IaaS, users have full right to process the server, its assets like memory, bandwidth, CPU, ports as well as administrator password. Customers themselves decide which OS modules need to be installed and activated.

Figure 2. PaaS users utilize APIs to host the abstraction layer

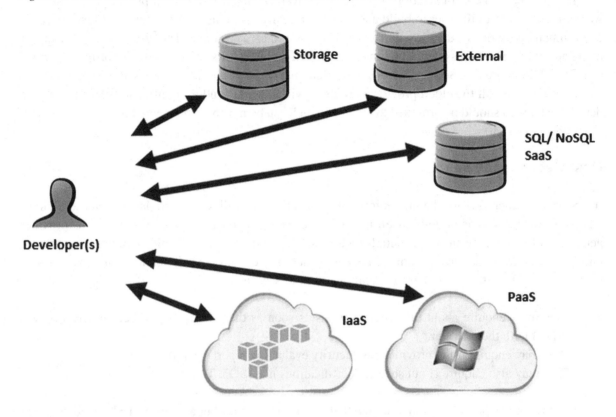

It is essential to identify the implicit hosts in the cloud which are available to one and all to protect it from attacks. Therefore, strategies must be implemented by the users to restrict the access. At a time, only one port should be opened as and when it is required.

SECURITY ISSUES

Software-as-a-Service (SaaS) Security Issues

SaaS offers application services like business applications, email and conferencing software. SaaS customers have least control on security along with the three delivery models in the cloud.

- **Application Security:** These are mainly carried by means of the Internet through Web browsers. On the other hand, mistakes in web applications may generate vulnerabilities. Attackers using the web to negotiate user's system execute malicious actions such as stealing some perceptive data. In SaaS the security challenges are similar to the web application technology, but the traditional approaches do not successfully protect it from attacks, so new techniques are compulsorily required. Ten most critical security threats of web applications are being identified by the Open Web Application Security Project (OWASP) (Cloud Security Alliance, 2012). Since there are many more security issues, but for securing web applications it is a good start.

- **Multi-Tenancy:** SaaS applications grouped into maturity models which are mainly identified by scalability, multi-tenancy and configurability. In the first maturity model each user has their own modified illustration of software (Keene, 2009). It has several limitations, but security problems are good in comparison to other models. In second model, the retailer offers several occurrences of applications for each and every user, but all the occurrences access the same code. Customers can alter some structure preferences to meet up their requirements. In third maturity model since multi-tenancy is supplemented, so a single instance serves all the users (Chandramouli & Mell, 2010; Jaeger & Schiffman, 2010). This strategy facilitates more effective exploitation of resources but scalability is restricted. Since data/information from multiple tenants is supposed to be accumulated in the same database, the threat of data leakage is very high. The policies regarding securities are required to make sure that customer's data are reserved apart from other users. The final model can scale up the applications by moving the application to the most powerful server if required.
- **Data Security:** A widespread distress for any type technology, but now it has become a major factor when SaaS customers have to depend upon their suppliers for appropriate security. In SaaS, organizational data are generally accessed in plain text and accumulated in the cloud (Xu, Zhang, Song, & Song, 2009). The SaaS provider is in charge of security of the data while processing and storing. On the other hand, keeping a backup of data is an important phase to smoothen the recovery in case of disaster, but it also initiates security concerns as well. In addition to that, large compliance principles do not imagine conformity with the policy in the world of Cloud Computing. In SaaS, the course of compliance is very complicated because the information/data is situated in the supplier's data centres and may bring up complicated issues like privacy, security and isolation that may be imposed by the provider.
- **Accessibility:** Using applications on the internet through the web browser makes the utilization easier, including mobile devices and open computers. It also interprets the provision to more security issues (Dawoud, Takouna, & Meinel, 2010). The Cloud Security Alliance has unconstrained a certificate that shows the existing status of mobile computing and the mostly occurred threats such as information leaking malware, apprehensive networks (Wi-Fi), problems in the OS and hacking.

Platform-as-a-Service (PaaS) Security Issues

PaaS assists the consumption of cloud-based applications with no cost of importing and preserving hardware and software levels. In comparison to SaaS with IaaS, PaaS depends on a secure with consistent network and web-browser. PaaS application security consists of two software layers. They are Security of the PaaS platform and Security of customer applications on a PaaS stage. PaaS sources are in charge of securing the software load that involves the runtime mechanism that executes the user applications. Similar to SaaS, PaaS also carries data security matters and other challenges as mentioned below:

- **Third-Party Relationships:** PaaS gives traditional programming languages and offers third-party web services (like mashups). Mashups merges more than one element into a distinct integrated unit (Jaeger & Schiffman, 2010). So, PaaS models inherit security problems associated to mashups like data and security. In addition to this, a PaaS user depends on both security development tools and third-party services.

- **Development Life Cycle:** Developers face the difficulty for building secure applications from the perspective view of the application development that may be hosted in the cloud (Jasti, Shah, Nagaraj, & Pendse, 2010). The speed with which the applications are changing in the cloud, affects both the Security and System Development Life Cycle. PaaS applications should be updated regularly, so that their application development procedure becomes flexible to keep up with the changes (Hashizume, Yoshioka, Fernandez, 2013; Owens, n.d.). Besides these security development techniques, developers need to instruct about the authorized issues, so that the data/information will store in an appropriate location.

- **Underlying Infrastructure Security:** In PaaS, providers are in charge of securing the infrastructure as well as the applications services because developers do not have the right to access the essential levels. They are not sure that the environmental tools provided by a PaaS provider are secure even when the developers have the power of security of their applications. As a result, there are least materials in the document about security problems in PaaS (Wu, Ding, Winer, & Yao, 2010). SaaS provides software which is then delivered over the web while PaaS provides development implementations to generate SaaS applications. Though, both of them use multi-tenant structural design so numerous synchronized users can exploit the identical software. The security of data processing, transferring, and storing depends on the provider.

Infrastructure-as-a-Service (IaaS) Security Issues

IaaS provides a group of assets in the form of virtualized scheme, which are exploited through the Internet. Users are unrestricted to access any software with complete control and maintenance on the assets appointed to them. Cloud users have superior control above the security as compared to the other models as long as no security outlet is there in the effective machine monitor (Reuben, 2007). They are accountable to organize the security strategy accurately. IaaS suppliers must assume a considerable attempt to protect their organization in order to reduce the threats which are created from formation, communication, observation, adaptation, and mobility. Some of the security issues related to IaaS are follows:

- **Virtualization:** It permits the customer to generate, duplicate, split, transfer, and turn round effective machines, which may permit them to run a diversity of applications. However, it also initiates new prospects for invaders because additional layer must be provided security (Xiaopeng, Sumei, & Xianqin, 2010). Virtual machine security is important as physical machine security, and any error in whichever might influence the other (Hashizume, Yoshioka, & Fernandez, 2013). Virtualized environments are susceptible to all kinds of attacks; but security is a bigger dispute as virtualization gives more interconnection difficulty.

- **Virtual Machine Monitor (VMM):** VMM is liable for virtual machines segregation; therefore, if the VMM is negotiated, its virtual machines may possibly be negotiated as well (Winkler, 2011). It is low-level software that controls and checks its virtual machines (VMs). The VMM are kept as uncomplicated and minute as possible in order to reduce the threat of security occurrences. Furthermore, virtualization establishes the skill to transfer virtual machines among physical servers for error easiness, maintenance or load balancing. An attacker can settle the transfer module in the VMM and may migrate a victim VM to a malicious server. Also, VM migration interprets the content to the network, which assists its data veracity and privacy (Venkatesha, Sadhu, & Kintali, 2009; Popovic & Hocenski, 2010). A malicious VM can be moved to another host with another VMM.

- **Shared Resource:** VMs are situated on the same server, shares the CPU, memory, etc. Sharing resources among VMs may diminish the security of each VM (Ranjith, Chandran, & Kaleeswaran, 2012), such as a malicious VM can deduce some information/data regarding other VMs through shared memory without negotiating the hypervisor. Two VMs can commune ignoring all the rules of the security module of the VMM using convert channels (Bisong & Rahman, 2011). Thus, a malicious Virtual Machine can observe shared resources with any notice, so the attacker can deduce some data/information about other virtual machines.

- **Public VM Image Repository:** A VM image is a pre-packaged software template consisting of configuration files that are accessed to build VMs. Thus, these images are basic for the whole security of the cloud. One can create their own VM image from scratch, or can utilize any image stored in the supplier's repository (Owens, n.d.). Like Amazon provides a public image storehouse where legal users can upload or download a VM image. Malicious customers can accumulate images containing malicious code into public storerooms settling other customers or the cloud system, such as an attacker with applicable account can build an image having malicious code as Trojan horse. If other user makes use of this image, the virtual machine will get infected with the hidden malware. In addition, involuntarily data seepage can be established by VM reproduction (Townsend, 2009). Some private information/data such as login passwords or keys can be traced when a picture is being formed. If the picture is not clear and error free, the information/data can be showed to other users. VM images are hidden artifacts that are difficult to patch while they are offline.

- **Virtual Machine Rollback:** Virtual machines are proficient to go back to their earlier states if any error occurs. But doing this can expose them to security vulnerabilities that were re-enabling previously disabled passwords or accounts (Popovic & Hocenski, 2010). In order to give rollbacks, copy or snapshot of the virtual machine should be made which can consequence in the proliferation of composition faults and other problems.

- **Virtual Machine Life Cycle:** It is essential to appreciate the lifecycle of the VMs and their alteration in status as they shift throughout the environment. VMs may be on, off or suspended which makes it difficult in detecting malware. They can be susceptible even when the virtual machines are offline. This malicious imagery can be the preliminary stage of the propagation of malware by introducing malicious code within other virtual machines in the formation process (Ristenpart, Tromer, Shacham, & Savage, 2009).

- **Virtual Networks:** Network components are collectively shared by various occupants because of resource pooling. As sharing resources agrees to attackers to initiate cross-tenant attacks, Virtual Networks amplifies the VMs interconnectivity which is an essential security dispute in Cloud Computing. The most protected way is to clasp each VM with its host by using enthusiastic substantial channels. Although, most hypervisors makes use of virtual networks to link VMs to converse directly and economically (Wang & Jiang, 2010). Most virtualization stages such as Xen provide two methods to construct virtual networks i.e., bridged and routed, but these approaches enlarges the possibility to carry out a few attacks such as sniff and spoof virtual network.

ANALYSIS OF SECURITY ISSUES IN CLOUD COMPUTING

Here it has been systematically analysed the existing security vulnerabilities with threats of Cloud Computing environment. For each threat and vulnerability, it has been identified which cloud service model(s) can be exaggerated by these security complications. The analysis delivers a brief explanation of the vulnerabilities, and specifies the cloud service models(s) can be exaggerated by them. For this, it has been focused on technology-based vulnerabilities in cloud computing. But there are other kind of the vulnerabilities that are common to any organization and are to be taken into consideration since they have negative impact on the security of the cloud computing and its primary platform. Some of the vulnerabilities are discussed as follow:

- Lack of employee screening with poor hiring practices: some of the cloud providers may not make background screening of their employees or cloud providers. Cloud administrators typically have unrestricted access to the cloud data.
- Lack of customer background checks: most of the cloud providers generally not check their customer's background, and so, anyone can open their cloud account with a valid credit card and email identity. Accounts having questionable authenticity, (i.e., the apocryphal accounts can perform any malicious activity in the cloud without being identified.
- Lack of security education: people can be continued with a weak point in information security in the cloud.

The above vulnerabilities usually occur in any type of organization. But in the cloud environment, it has a greater impact as there are more numbers of people interact with the cloud such as cloud providers, suppliers, organizational customers, third-party providers, and end-users. Cloud computing influences many existing technologies; like web-browsers, web-services, and virtualization, which have main role to the evolution of cloud computing. Therefore, any vulnerability related to these concepts also affects the cloud, and it can have a significant impact in the cloud.

Table 1 represents an analysis of different kind of vulnerabilities in Cloud Computing environments. From Table 1, it has been observed that data storage and virtualization in the cloud are the most critical point. An attack to the cloud can be ensured the most harm in the cloud. Table 1 also mentioned the threats that are associated with the concept used in cloud computing environments, and it indicates the particular cloud service models are visible to these threats. It can put more importance on threats that are connected with cloud data being stored in the cloud and handled remotely, sharing the resources and the usage of virtualization in the cloud computing.

COUNTERMEASURES

It is highly required to protect from malicious activities in the cloud. Here, it has been provided a brief description of some countermeasure, which are listed earlier.

Table 1. Threats that are related to the technology in different layers

Threats	Description	Layer
1. Account or service hijacking	An account theft can be performed by different ways such as social engineering and weak credentials. If an attacker gains access to a user's credential, he can perform malicious activities such as access sensitive data, manipulate data, and redirect any transaction.	SPI
2. Data scavenging	Since data cannot be completely removed from unless the device is destroyed, attackers may be able to recover this data.	SPI
3. Data leakage	Data leakage happens when the data gets into the wrong hands while it is being transferred, stored, audited or processed.	SPI
4. Denial of Service	It is possible that a malicious user will take all the possible resources. Thus, the system cannot satisfy any request from other legitimate users due to resources being unavailable.	SPI
5. Customer-data manipulation	Users attack web applications by manipulating data sent from their application component to the server's application. For example, SQL injection, command injection, insecure direct object references, and cross-site scripting.	S
6. VM escape	It is designed to exploit the hypervisor in order to take control of the underlying infrastructure.	I
7. VM hopping	It happens when a VM is able to gain access to another VM (i.e. by exploiting some hypervisor vulnerability)	I
8. Malicious VM creation	An attacker who creates a valid account can create a VM image containing malicious code such as a Trojan horse and store it in the provider repository.	I
9. Insecure VM migration	Live migration of virtual machines exposes the contents of the VM state files to the network. An attacker can do the following actions: a) Access data illegally during migration b) Transfer a VM to an untrustworthy host c) Create and migrate several VM causing disruptions or DoS	I
10. Sniffing/Spoofing virtual networks	A malicious VM can listen to the virtual network or even use ARP spoofing to redirect packets from/to other VMs.	I

Wang, Wang, Ren, & Lou (2009)

Countermeasures for Account or Service Hijacking

- Cloud Security Alliance is a non-profitable organization that encourages the use of best practices in order to provide security concept in cloud computing environments. It has issued an Identity and access management guidance, which offers a list of suggested best experienced to assure characteristics and secure access management (Wang & Jiang, 2010). This includes centralized directory, identity management, access management, user access certifications, role-based access control, privileged user, access management, separation of duties, and identity with access reporting.

Countermeasures for Data Leakage

- Fragmentation-redundancy-scattering technique: The aims of this technique to provide intrusion tolerance with secure storage. This technique consists of first breaking down delicate data into irrelevant fragments. So, fragments have not any significant information by itself. Then, fragments are distributed in a redundant manner across different sites of the distributed system.

- Digital signatures: Digital signature with RSA encryption algorithm (Somani, Lakhani, & Mundra, 2010) try to secures data, while data is being transferred over the Internet. RSA encryption algorithm is claimed to protect data in cloud environments (Wang, Wang, Ren, & Lou, 2009).
- Homomorphic encryption: Transfer, store, and process are three basic operations of cloud data. Encryption techniques of data can be used to secure data in cloud while it is being transferred in and out of the cloud or it may be stored in the provider's premises. Cloud providers have to decrypt the data to get the actual data in order to process it, which raises the privacy concerns in the cloud. Many encryption methods are based on the application of fully homomorphic encryption to provide in the security of clouds. Fully homomorphic encryption methods allow performing random computation on texts without being decrypted. Current homomorphic encryption methods support limited number of homomorphic operations like: addition and multiplication (Fernandez, Yoshioka, & Washizaki, 2009). It has been provided some real-world cloud applications where some basic homomorphic operations are needed to implement in the cloud. However, it needs a vast processing power which may impact on power consumption and user response time.
- Encryption: it has been used for long time to secure sensitive data in the network system. Sending encrypted data and its storing in the cloud will ensure that the data is in secure. However, it is assuming that the encryption techniques are strong as compared to others. There are some well-known encryption techniques such as Advanced Encryption Standard (AES) have been used in cloud computing environment. Moreover, it can be used to stop side channel attacks on cloud storage de-duplication. However, it may leads to offline dictionary attacks releasing personal keys (Somani, Lakhani, & Mundra, 2010).

Countermeasures for Customer Data Manipulation

- Web applications can be easy to target, as they are exposed to the public. A web application scanner is an application which scans web applications using the front-end of the web-application in order to identify vulnerabilities. Web application firewall in the cloud routes all web traffic by the firewall which inspects specific threats in the cloud.

Countermeasures for Sniffing/Spoofing Virtual Networks

- It presents a virtual network framework, which secures the communication process among different VMs. This structure offers two configuration modes for virtual networks such as "bridged" and "routed". This model is composed of three layers viz., firewall, routing layers, and shared networks, which can be prevented VM from sniffing and spoofing. Web-services are the prime technology in cloud computing environments. However, this also leads to several issues and challenges that need to be talked. Security in web-services standards describes how to secure communication occurs between applications through confidentiality, integrity, authorization and authentication. There are several security standard specifications such as WSSecurity, Security Assertion Markup Language (SAML), XML Digital Signature, XML Encryption, Extensible Access Control Markup Language (XACML), Key Management Specification (XKMS), WS-Secure Conversation, WS-Federation, WS-Trust and WS-Security Policy. The NIST Cloud Computing Standards Roadmap Working Group has collected high level standards that are related for Cloud Computing (Harnik, Pinkas, & Shulman-Peleg, 2010).

CONCLUSION

Cloud Computing is a current trend burning topic that presents benefits for its users. But, it has some security problems that may slow down its use. Understanding the vulnerabilities exist in the Cloud will helps to organizations for making the shift towards the Cloud. It provides advantages of many technologies by using cloud computing with inherit their security issues in it. Traditional web-applications, virtualization and data hosting have been looked over. Whereas, some of the solutions presented are immature. It has been presented security issues in cloud models: SaaS, PaaS, and IaaS, which are depending on the cloud models. Particularly, virtualization, storage, and networks are the biggest security concerns in Cloud. So, it can be identify the vulnerabilities contribute to the implementation of the threats and make the model more healthy. It also listed some current solutions in this context in order to mitigate these threats. However, new security concepts are needed, which can work with cloud architectures. Conventional security concepts may not work well in cloud computing environments as it is a complex architecture, which is a combination of different technologies.

There are many other security challenges have been observed. It will be difficult to realize end-to-end security due to the complexity of the cloud. However, the challenges in the cloud are to ensure more secure operations even if some parts of the cloud fail. For many applications, we need information assurance with mission assurance. Therefore, the objective is to frustrate the challengers, so that the enterprise has time to carry out the mission even if challengers have entered the system. As such, secure applications from whole components will be a key aspect with respect to security in the cloud. Cloud computing is used to share the resources on a larger scale, which is cost effective and location independent. Cloud computing resources on the cloud can be used by the client and deployed by the vendor such as Salesforce, Zoho, Amazon, Rackspace, Google, IBM, and Microsoft. It also shares software and on-demand tools for various information technology Industries. Cloud is sharing by not only for Multinational companies but also being used by Small and medium enterprises (Lord CrusAd3r, n.d.). Because if the cloud computing concept represents a relatively new computing model, there is a great deal of ambiguity about how security in various areas such as; network, host, application, and data levels can be performed. That ambiguity has steadily managed information executives to state that security is their important concern with Cloud Computing (KPMG, 2010).

Cloud has many issues when it originates to security point of views, especially on Data theft, Data loss and Privacy (Lord CrusAd3r, n.d.). This is possible in any type of organization. Cloud Computing influences many existing technologies like: web browsers, web services, and virtualization, which contribute to the evolution of cloud computing environments. So, any vulnerability associated with these technologies also impacts the cloud. Use of the different cloud services may lead to security for the users, if they are not well conscious with the particulars of the services.

REFERENCES

Bisong, A., & Rahman, S. (2011). An overview of the Security concerns in Enterprise Cloud Computing. *International Journal of Network Security & Its Applications*, *3*(1), 30–45. doi:10.5121/ijnsa.2011.3103

Chandramouli, R., & Mell, P. (2010). State of Security readiness. *Crossroads*, *16*(3), 23–25. doi:10.1145/1734160.1734168

Cloud Security Alliance. (2012). *Security guidance for critical areas of Mobile Computing*. Available: https://downloads.cloudsecurityalliance.org/initiatives/mobile/Mobile_Guidance_v1.pdf

Dawoud, W., Takouna, I., & Meinel, C. (2010). Infrastructure as a service security: Challenges and solutions. In *The 7th International Conference on Informatics and Systems* (INFOS). Potsdam, Germany: IEEE Computer Society.

Fernandez, E. B., Yoshioka, N., & Washizaki, H. (2009). Modeling Misuse Patterns. In *Proceedings of the 4th Int. Workshop on Dependability Aspects of Data Warehousing and Mining Applications (DAWAM 2009), in conjunction with the 4th Int.Conf. on Availability, Reliability, and Security (ARES 2009)*. Fukuoka, Japan: IEEE Computer Society. doi:10.1109/ARES.2009.139

Garfinkel, T., & Rosenblum, M. (2005). When virtual is harder than real: Security challenges in virtual machine based computing environments. In *Proceedings of the 10th conference on Hot Topics in Operating Systems*. USENIX Association.

Harnik, D., Pinkas, B., & Shulman-Peleg, A. (2010). Side channels in Cloud services: Deduplication in Cloud Storage. *IEEE Security and Privacy*, *8*(6), 40–47. doi:10.1109/MSP.2010.187

Hashizume, K., Yoshioka, N., & Fernandez, E. B. (2013). Three misuse patterns for Cloud Computing. In D. G. Rosado, D. Mellado, E. Fernandez-Medina, & M. Piattini (Eds.), *Security engineering for Cloud Computing: approaches and Tools* (pp. 36–53). IGI Global. doi:10.4018/978-1-4666-2125-1.ch003

ISO. (2005). *27001: Information Security Management – Specification with Guidance for Use*. London: ISO.

Jaeger, T., & Schiffman, J. (2010). Outlook: Cloudy with a chance of Security challenges and improvements. *IEEE Security and Privacy*, *8*(1), 77–80. doi:10.1109/MSP.2010.45

Jasti, A., Shah, P., Nagaraj, R., & Pendse, R. (2010). Security in multi-tenancy cloud. In *IEEE International Carnahan Conference on Security Technology (ICCST)*. IEEE Computer Society.

Ju, J., Wang, Y., Fu, J., Wu, J., & Lin, Z. (2010). Research on Key Technology in SaaS. In *International Conference on Intelligent Computing and Cognitive Informatics (ICICCI)*. Hangzhou, China: IEEE Computer Society.

Keene, C. (2009). *The Keene View on Cloud Computing*. Available: http://www.keeneview.com/2009/03/what-is-platform-as-service-paas.html

KPMG. (2010). *From hype to future: KPMG's 2010 Cloud computing survey*. Available: http://www.techrepublic.com/whitepapers/from-hype-to-futurekpmgs-2010-cloud-computing survey/2384291

Mell, P., & Grance, T. (2009). *A NIST definition of cloud computing*. National Institute of Standards and Technology. NIST SP 800–145. Retrieved from: http://www.nist.gov/itl/cloud/upload/cloud-def-v15.pdf

Owens, K. (n.d.). *Securing virtual compute infrastructure in the Cloud*. SAVVIS. Available: http://www.savvis.com/en-us/info_center/documents/hoswhitepapersecuringvirutalcomputeinfrastructureinthecloud.pdf

Popovic, K., & Hocenski, Z. (2010). Cloud Computing Security issues and challenges. In *Proceedings of the 33rd International convention MIPRO*. IEEE Computer Society.

Lord CrusAd3r. (n.d.). *Problems Faced by Cloud Computing*. Retrieved from dl.packetstormsecurity. net/.../ProblemsFacedbyCloudComputing.pdf

Ranjith, P., Chandran, P., & Kaleeswaran, S. (2012). On covert channels between virtual machines. *Journal in Computer Virology Springer, 8*(3), 85–97. doi:10.1007/s11416-012-0168-x

Reuben, J. S. (2007). *A survey on virtual machine Security*. Seminar on Network Security. Retrieved from http://www.tml.tkk.fi/Publications/C/25/papers/Reuben_final.pdf.

Ristenpart, T., Tromer, E., Shacham, H., & Savage, S. (2009). Hey, you, get off of my cloud: exploring information leakage in third-party compute clouds. In *Proceedings of the 16th ACM conference on Computer and communications security*. ACM. doi:10.1145/1653662.1653687

Somani, U., Lakhani, K., & Mundra, M. (2010). Implementing digital signature with RSA encryption algorithm to enhance the data Security of Cloud in Cloud Computing. In *1st International conference on parallel distributed and grid Computing* (PDGC). IEEE Computer Society. doi:10.1109/PDGC.2010.5679895

Townsend, M. (2009). Managing a security program in a cloud computing environment. In *Information Security Curriculum Development Conference* (pp. 128–133). ACM. doi:10.1145/1940976.1941001

Venkatesha, S., Sadhu, S., & Kintali, S. (2009). *Survey of virtual machine migration techniques*. Technical report, Dept. of Computer Science, University of California, Santa Barbara. Retrieved from http://www.academia.edu/760613/Survey_of_Virtual_Machine_Migration_Techniques

Wang, C., Wang, Q., Ren, K., & Lou, W. (2009). Ensuring data Storage Security in Cloud Computing. In *The 17th International workshop on quality of service*. IEEE Computer Society. doi:10.1109/IWQoS.2009.5201385

Wang, Z., & Jiang, X. (2010). HyperSafe: a lightweight approach to provide lifetime hypervisor control-flow integrity. In *Proceedings of the IEEE symposium on Security and privacy*. IEEE Computer Society. doi:10.1109/SP.2010.30

Winkler, V. (2011). *Securing the Cloud: Cloud computer Security techniques and tactics*. Waltham, MA: Elsevier Inc.

Wu, H., Ding, Y., Winer, C., & Yao, L. (2010). Network Security for virtual machine in Cloud Computing. In *5th International conference on computer sciences and convergence information technology* (ICCIT). IEEE Computer Society.

Xiaopeng, G., Sumei, W., & Xianqin, C. (2010). VNSS: a Network Security sandbox for virtual Computing environment. In *IEEE youth conference on information Computing and telecommunications (YC-ICT)* (pp. 395–398). Washington, DC: IEEE Computer Society. doi:10.1109/YCICT.2010.5713128

Xu, K., Zhang, X., Song, M., & Song, J. (2009). Mobile Mashup: Architecture, Challenges and Suggestions. In *International Conference on Management and Service Science*. IEEE Computer Society.

Zhang, S., Zhang, S., Chen, X., & Huo, X. (2010). Cloud Computing Research and Development Trend. In *Second International Conference on Future Networks* (ICFN'10). IEEE Computer Society. doi:10.1109/ICFN.2010.58

Zhao, G., Liu, J., Tang, Y., Sun, W., Zhang, F., Ye, X., & Tang, N. (2009). Cloud Computing: A Statistics Aspect of Users. In *First International Conference on Cloud Computing (CloudCom)*. Springer Berlin. doi:10.1007/978-3-642-10665-1_32

Chapter 5
Cyber–Security Concerns with Cloud Computing:
Business Value Creation and Performance Perspectives

Ezer Osei Yeboah-Boateng
Ghana Technology University College, Ghana

ABSTRACT

Information is modeled into virtual objects to create value for its owner. The value chain involves stakeholders with varied responsibilities in the cyber-market. Cloud computing emerged out of virtualization, distributed and grid computing, and has altered the value creation landscape, through strategic and sensitive information management. It offers services that use resources in a utility fashion. The flexible, cost-effective service models are opportunities for SMEs. Whilst using these tools for value-creation is imperative, a myriad of security concerns confront both providers and end-users. Vulnerabilities and threats are key concerns, so that value created is strategically aligned with corporate vision, appropriated and sustained. What is the extent of impact? Expert opinions were elicited of 4 C-level officers and 10 security operatives. Shared technology issues, malicious insiders and service hijacking are considered major threats. Also, an intuitive strategic model for Value-Creation Cloud-based Cyber-security is proposed as guidance in fostering IT-enabled initiatives.

INTRODUCTION

Emerging technologies in ICT have transformed the way we live, we work or we play. One such technologies is digitization of information, be it represented in voice, data or image. They are said to be modeled into virtual objects (ITU-T, 2007) and create value. Emerging technologies in ICT are facilitated by digitization, computerization and packet-based switching. These are utilized in the data design, production, processing and transmission and distribution, which in turn creates invaluable business value chains.

DOI: 10.4018/978-1-5225-1721-4.ch005

The value chain creation involves various stakeholders with varied roles and responsibilities in the cyber-market. Indeed, "controlling the digital information value chain, i.e. the infrastructure and the content" (ITU-T, 2007, p. 54), is bedeviled with challenges such as cyber-security concerns in this context.

Cloud computing which emerged out of virtualization, distributed computing and grid computing, has profoundly altered the business value creation landscape, through IT-enabled strategic information management. It is imperative to ensure that corporate sensitive data is produced, processed and stored securely and effectively.

The flexible, CAPEX free and cost-effective service models are opportunities for businesses, especially small-to-medium enterprises (SMEs) in developing economies. In essence, cloud computing simplifies the complexities of installation, configuration and maintenance of computing resources for end-users.

In addressing the security context of the communication infrastructure, (ITU-T, 2007) posits that cyber-security must be viewed as the cornerstone activity and service used in the creation of other value-added services as well as to generate business value.

Cloud computing is a service delivery paradigm offering computing resources as a service, rather than a product, with capabilities to share or use resources in utility fashion supplied over an Internet enabled infrastructure. Many businesses, especially SMEs in developing economies, are taking advantage of the opportunities offered by cloud computing facilities to create value for their customers (Yeboah-Boateng E. O., 2013a). Whilst utilization of these tools is indispensable for successful value creation and performance, there are some cyber-security concerns that both providers and end-users are confronted with, which need urgent attention (Yeboah-Boateng E. O., 2013a) (Microsoft, 2005).

Cloud computing as a business model offers on-demand resources from a pool of shared configurable computing tools and applications, with the capability of rapid provisioning, scalability and minimal management efforts required of end-users.

Cloud computing is used to create business value by, say, automating certain business processes, or for the provisioning of IT-enabled resources such as network infrastructure, software and business applications; thus, contributing to efficient utilization of scarce corporate resources.

As organizations apply cloud computing services, they find opportunities to add value to their value chain, in effective and efficient manner.

Generally, technology and its implications on appropriate business strategy is of key concern to most chief-level (C-level) officers, especially in developing economies. By adopting cloud computing services, firms could focus on core competencies and harness the capabilities offered by ubiquitous business tools and techniques to create value for their customers. In adding value, cloud service providers (CSPs) could create value for end-users through unique cyber-risk mitigation measures that would not exceed the customer willingness-to-pay (CWP) (Piccoli, 2013). Furthermore, CSPs could also work with their security providers and create incentives for them to furnish the needed resources for less supplier opportunity cost (SOC) (Piccoli, 2013). It must be noted that cyber-security has become a core component of the customer value proposition (McKinsey & Co., 2012). Cyber-security could represent a business opportunity as they create end-to-end customer experiences that are both convenient and secure.

This study examines cyber-security concerns with cloud computing, both from the perspectives of CSPs and end-users, using SMEs in developing economies as a case sample. Key issues confronting the service delivery are inherent vulnerabilities, facilities and utilization, such as susceptibilities with confidentiality, integrity and availability (CIA). Similar studies allude to these concerns as well (Sahandi, Alkhalil, & Opara-Martins, 2013; Vaquero & Moran, 2011; Sood & Enbody, 2013). Some cloud customers have also expressed concerns about security vulnerabilities associated with cloud configuration (Singh, 2013).

It must be noted that in addressing the cyber-security challenges, eliminating threats is impossible, so protection against them without disrupting business innovation and growth is of utmost priority of C-level officers.

The US government identified cyber-security as "one of the most serious economic and national security challenges" the nation faces (US Gov't, 2009). Businesses are constantly battling against cyber-attacks. The threats of cyber-criminals, disgruntled employees or insiders disclosing sensitive corporate information, "selling" intellectual property to competitors, or engaging in online fraud are some concerns for all corporate executives. In view of the incessant, complex and dynamic nature of threats (coupled with sophisticated threat agents), businesses must adopt cyber-risk mitigation measures to protect critical business information without stifling innovation and growth. Another concern in doing business is the interconnectedness of the supply chain. For example, businesses persuade and invite vendors and customers to join their networks, thus creating some vulnerabilities or security concerns.

Problem Formulation

The emergence of cloud computing has altered the dynamics of conducting business amongst all stakeholders. With more adoptions, concerns have been raised on data confidentiality, data integrity and data and resource availability. Especially, as perennial commercial power outages is a common business operative in developing economies.

It is not uncommon for organizations, be it large corporation, government or military or an SME, to loose control of its information. In some instances, the organization, when probed further, would admit that it lacks a clear appreciation of what information assets it owns, or where that information assets are stored, or what is the asset value. Indeed, many more organizations are attacked almost on a daily basis, corporate, sensitive or confidential information are breached in an unprecedented manner. Often, these compromises go on for months undetected, thus exposing the victim organization and eroding or depleting their strategic value. In other instances, the organization will fail to recover from the catastrophic attacks (Yeboah-Boateng E. O., 2013a).

Data confidentiality and integrity are issues that are of utmost concerns, in view of the mission critical nature of the business applications and processes involved in delivering value to their customers.

Though benefits accrue to SMEs by adopting cloud computing, the level of awareness amongst those in developing economies could be a barrier to its acceptance (Yeboah-Boateng & Essandoh, 2013). Coupled with education and massive sensitization on cloud computing to ensure its uptake in emerging markets (Yeboah-Boateng & Essandoh, 2013), a number of key questions ought to be addressed.

Smallwood (2012) asserts that vulnerabilities inherent in organizations that subsequently leads to "data spills and breaches" can be placed, strategically at the doorstep of corporate executives. He calls it "poor management, [which] presents an avoidable business risk" (Smallwood, 2012, p. 5). The business value of any organization reside with its corporate information assets or cyber-assets, such as trade secrets, intellectual property, confidential files, financial records, corporate strategic plans, customer records, confidential emails, exclusive product releases, etc.

This study critically examines those cyber-related vulnerabilities, threats and risks associated with cloud computing and its implications on business performance. Sixty-five (65) SMEs in developing economies were surveyed on security and business metrics. Strategic interviews were conducted with 4 C-level officers purposively chosen from CSPs and 10 out of 65 respondents randomly selected cyber-security functionaries to ascertain some observed constructs accrued from the survey.

Key Research Questions and Objectives

Key research questions and objectives for this study are presented hereunder:

- What are the threats that impact on business value creation?
- How do C-level officers ensure that their cloud computing services are secured?
- How should the C-level officers evaluate the cyber-risks associated with cloud computing adoption, implementation and operations?
- How can cloud computing add business value, whilst mitigating any cyber-risks?
- What are the cyber-risk concerns of cloud computing?

The objectives of the study are as follows:

- To identify opprotunities to create value with cloud resources, and to design and develop value adding cloud security related strategic initiatives;
- To assess the cyber-security concerns with using cloud services and to prefer an appropriate mitigation measures;
- To design a value creation model to examine the cyber-security concerns in cloud computing;

Highlights of Findings

Key findings are the taxonomy of cloud-related threats as major concerns that could impact adversely on CSPs and end-users, with the possibility of eroding any value added. The major threats are deemed to shared technology issues, malicious insiders and service hijacking. An intuitive strategic model aimed at assisting stakeholders as a guide in formulating appropriate cloud-based strategy that could be sustained is proposed.

Significance of the Chapter

The study's appeal with perspectives from value creation and sustainability is an enhancement to the discussion that cyber-security practitioners, C-level executives, IT managers and researchers would find useful.

Assumptions and Limitations

The key assumptions are the study's definition of SMEs and developing economy (as adopted from (Yeboah-Boateng E. O., 2013a)). Here, SMEs are defined as business entities with less than 10 employees as micro enterprises, small enterprises have employees between 10 and 50, whilst medium enterprises have between 50 and 250 employees. The sample size used in the analysis could hamper a bit on generalization of findings, albeit empirically sound and reliable results. The actual identities of CSPs and SMEs are ethically kept confidential.

Outline of the Chapter

The introductory section dealt with overview of cyber-security concerns with cloud compucting. Followed by related works on cyber-security challenges, cloud computing paradigm, business value creation and appropriation. Fuzzy multi-attribute decision-making, with fuzzy similarity measures are discussed. Computations to rank the taxonomy of threats follows, and then conclusion and recommendations.

BACKGROUND: RELATED LITERATURE

This section gives the definitions, theoretical underpins and synthesis with literature, as it advances arguments for the chosen research approach.

Cloud Computing

Cloud computing is a novel paradigm that leverages on innovative Information and Communications Technologies (ICTs) to create IT efficiency and business agility. It is characterized by efficient resource utilization, virtualized physical resources, service-oriented architecture, with the abstraction of infrastructure, applications and data into layers, dynamic scalability of resources, elastic and automated self-provisioning of resources, ubiquity (i.e. device and location independence) and operational expense model.

The companies that provide cloud services are known variously in literature, such as Cloud Services Provider (CSP), Cloud Application Provider, Cloud Storage Provider, network provider; in this study, CSP is used to represent these providers.

Cloud computing holds "real potential for new types of on-demand dynamic IT services" (Oltsik, 2010, p. 3). It is akin to information system, which transcends IT into other disciplines such as business and strategy. It is characteristic of data center consolidation and server virtualization, with transition from physical to virtual IT assets, and coupled with dynamic service delivery. It is used to provision a combination of the following resources: networks, servers, storage, applications and services, processing, memory, bandwidth and virtual machines, etc. It offers economics of scale by spreading the costs across clients. It matches clients' computing needs to consumption, in a flexible manner, near real-time provisioning (Smallwood, 2012), with utility-based, scalable and modulated business models. Cloud computing is also characterized by on-demand computing, offering off-site backups, and some form of security. It is innovative and has cost savings, as it eliminates capital outlays. Its agility is manifested by offering on-demand provisioning of computing resources, and has the potential to align IT with business strategies. Resources are shared with dynamic access, coupled with ubiquity or remote access:

- **IaaS**: End-users are provisioned with virtual machines (VMs), storage capacity, network bandwidth, and they are billed for the amount of time or resources utilized, rather than on contractual basis of procuring switches, storage arrays, servers or routers. IaaS offerings are implemented as APIs and associated services, such as management access for end-users, using web applications and service technologies.
- **PaaS**: Provides the development capability and tools needed to build upon or deploy applications on an abstracted IaaS. Typically, CSPs offer multiple application components that align with specific development models and programming tools of end-users. For example, Microsoft based

stack (i.e. Windows, .NET, IIS, SQL server, etc.) or an open source based stack (i.e. the "LAMP" stack containing Linux, Appache, MySQL and PHP).

- **SaaS**: Here an entire business or a set of IT applications are provisioned via the Internet and implemented as web applications. It is delivered over the telecommunications networks, such as the internet, or a virtual private network (VPN), with some committed security level. Typically, users access these applications over the cloud using a thin client interface such as a Web browser; e.g. Gmail from Google, Microsoft "Live" offerings, and saleforce.com.

There are 3 key technologies which are the pillars of cloud computing, namely web applications and services, virtualization and cryptography.

- Web applications and services technologies facilitate the service models. These technologies are utilized in the provisioning of cloud services, which relies on the cloud servers or VM components installed on the backend infrastructure; e.g. IaaS. The ubiquity attribute of cloud computing is thus made a reality as users can access services virtually from anywhere using a web browser.
- Virtualization enables the capacity to share or pool computing resources, such as servers and storage devices. For example, it provides for the capability to divide a physical server into many virtual servers, with different operating systems (OSs) in a logical manner (Shelly & Vermaat, 2011). The obvious advantage is that an end-user can be provisioned with just a fraction of the computing capacity, whilst sharing the remaining resources with other users. Also, the virtual server can be provisioned, configured, and managed in a dynamic fashion and with ease (Zhu, 2010).

Grid computing is the technology whereby numerous servers and/or PCs are networked to perform as one large computer, leveraging on the cumulative computing power (Shelly & Vermaat, 2011). Coupled with virtualization is automation of system resources using "template" technology. This facilitates the provisioning of certain resource configurations, whilst giving end-users the ability to customize some functions or capabilities as well (Zhu, 2010). Through self-management and self-organization, end-users are to provision their computing resources automatically, without service provider's interventions.

- Cryptography is the practice of providing security for the information assets, whether at rest (in storage) or in transit (in transmission). To ensure secure communications over the Internet, cryptographic algorithms or techniques are used to provide security in the midst of unauthorized third party entities. Many cloud computing security requirements are solved or implemented by using cryptographic techniques.

Cloud computing has been defined variously in literature. This study adopts that of Kramer and the National Institute of Standards and Technology (NIST) which are as follows:

Kramer (2012) asserts that cloud computing is a "new paradigm that provisioned on-demand technology resources, purchased and scaled over the Internet, with service contracts that specify availability, data–loss prevention, liability, flexibility and pricing" (Kramer, 2012, p. 60).

Kramer's (2012) definition takes into account the business perspectives as it emphasizes the economic and strategic aspects of cloud computing thereby giving it a better appreciation.

On the other hand, the NIST definition (Mell & Grance, 2011) is more technical in focus.

Cloud computing is a model for enabling ubiquitous, convenient, on-demand network access to a shared pool of configurable computing resources (e.g., networks, servers, storage, applications, and services) that can be rapidly provisioned and released with minimal management effort or service provider interaction (Mell & Grance, 2011, p. 2).

Using the NIST definition of cloud computing, the following key characteristics are deduced:

- **On-Demand Self-Service**: Users can order and manage services (provisioning and de-provisioning) without human interaction with the service provider, using web portal and management interface.
- **Ubiquitous Network Access**: Cloud services are accessed via the Internet, using standard mechanisms and protocols.
- **Resource Pooling**: Computing resources using homogeneous infrastructure to provide shared cloud services.
- **Rapid Elasticity**: Resources are scaled up and down rapidly and elastically.
- **Measured Service (Utility)**: Resources usage is constantly metered, supporting optimization of resource usage, customer usage reporting, and pay-as-you-go business models.

Enumerated below are key cloud computing performance objectives:

- Maximizing throughput;
- Resource utilization;
- Financial benefits – with user needs such as low cost and response time and maximum availability.

It must be noted that the price to pay for any system optimization is increased system complexity.

Cyber-Security Concerns

In spite of the benefits that inure to the customers, cyber-security concerns are always seen as inhibitors to the full uptake of the cloud paradigm. Vulnerabilities, limitations to bandwidth for certain data intensive applications, and the problem of short-lived virtual computers in carrying out digital forensics are just a few concerns.

Cloud security controls must be tested, audited, whereas the actual enforcement must be carried out by the management. Cloud computing can be affected by both malicious attacks and infrastructure failures, such as power outages. Such attacks can affect the Internet, DNS servers, prevent access to clouds or directly affect cloud operations. The following exemplify the point (Marinescu, 2014):

- **June 15, 2014:** Akama Technologies had DNS outage; Google Inc., Yahoo! Inc., had major blackouts;
- **May 2009:** Google news & Gmail were down for several days due to denial of service (DoS) attack;

- **June 29-30, 2012:** Lightning strike – utility power fluctuations caused outage of Amazon Web Services (AWS) cloud;
- Failure to switch to backup Genset before exhausting UPS;
- Bugs in Elastic Load Balancing (ELB) used for switching/routing traffic to servers with availability capacity.

Typically, CSPs implement different security policies to address issues with different service and deployment models. Another inherent vulnerability is associated with the unpredictable interactions between load balancing and other reactive mechanisms could lead to dynamic instabilities. The unintended coupling of independent controllers that manage the load, power consumption, and elements of the infrastructure could lead to undesirable feedback and instability similar to the ones experienced by the policy-based routing in the Internet Border Gateway Protocol (BGP).

Clustering resources in data centers distributed in different geo-locations as a means to lower the probability of catastrophic failures (Marinescu, 2014). Cloud computing inherited some challenges from some technological antecedents, such as parallel and distributed computing. Cloud computing is beset with inherent challenges emanating from the delivery models in use. Additionally, there are inherent challenges from the utility computing mechanisms, which is based on resource sharing and virtualization, with attendant requirements of completely different trust model from the regular user-dependent ubiquitous model. The most significant of all cloud computing challenges is, by far, security. It is paramount, therefore, to address the security concerns if CSPs are to leverage the value added measures for the uptake of mass market cloud services. For various cloud computing services, the users interact with the cloud eco-system using well defined interfaces. These interfaces have inherent vulnerabilities that could adversely impact on the cloud security value chain.

Data in storage is vulnerable to DoS and other malicious attacks, especially, data replication necessary to ensure continuity of service; this could be a business value creation metric. Data encryption may protect data in storage, but may be decrypted for processing and possible attacks.

IaaS model can expose the CSPs network to new or different attacks, which may be initiated with cloud resources. Virtualization is also susceptible to attacks that could target the hardware and the Hypervisor, as well as the management OS. The virtual machine (VM) can be saved to facilitate migration and recovery, which is another source of vulnerability. Typically, threats and associated threat agents do not fizzle off, they rather mutate over time; i.e. they change their states from either dormant or dead, inactive or active, and sometimes even acquire new capabilities (Vidalis & Jones, 2005). An infected VM can be inactive upon system clean up, but may wake up later to infect other systems.

Resource management could also serve as a source of vulnerabilities. The management system uses the controllers which are tasked to implement several policies, such as admission control, capacity allocation, load balancing, energy optimization, and QoS guarantees and provisioning (Marinescu, 2014). The controllers need accurate information about the global state of the system. In view of the dynamic nature of individual resources and requirements, the controllers must be able to function with incomplete or approximate knowledge of the system state.

Self-management and self-organization attributes of cloud computing could also pose some risks; they raise the bar for implementation of logging and auditing procedures, which is critical to the security and trust in the provisioning of services. Under self-management, it becomes next to impossible to identify the reasons that a certain action that resulted in a security breach was taken (Marinescu, 2014).

Vendor lock-in – a major concern here is that a user is tied to a particular CSP for service. Standardization would support interoperability and thus alleviate some of the fears that a critical service may be unavailable for an extended period or the vendor may fold up business. Caution must be taken not to stifle innovation with imposition of standards at a time when the paradigm is still evolving (Marinescu, 2014).

Basic Elements of Cyber-Security

The ITU-T Recommendation X.805 stipulates eight (8) cyber-security properties: authentication, authorization, availability, confidentiality, communications security, integrity, non-repudiation and privacy (ITU-T, 2005). Though other properties exist, invariably, for any good and viable security solutions, the cyber-security triad of Confidentiality, Integrity and Availability (CIA) are deemed as the fundamental elements or bedrock of cyber-security initiatives. In view of the above, this study focuses the discussions on the CIA triad and adapted the definitions of (Yeboah-Boateng E. O., 2013a).

- **Confidentiality:** Implies, for example, that *end-users* expect that the privacy of their transactions, their user credentials, sensitive data, and any other information shared during cloud service provisioning will be secured. Thus, "*Confidentiality* is the property that information is not made available or disclosed to unauthorized individuals, entities, or processes, either in storage or in transmission" (p. 3).
- **Integrity:** Implies, for example, that end-users expect that the contents of documents stored in the cloud are not altered and inventory processed on the cloud are accurate, authentic and complete. Thus, "*Integrity* is the property that data has not been altered in an unauthorized manner during transmission or storage" (p. 3).
- **Availability:** Implies, for example, that end-users expect to be able to access or process cloud services whenever convenient for them, and the Internet bandwidth is provisioned and functional without disruption. Thus, "*Availability* is the property that the system has always honored any legitimate requests by authorized principals or entities" (p. 4). *Availability* ensures that cloud resources are accessible whenever needed. It is an important property since any disruption of service may adversely affect business operations of CSPs and end-users.

In perspective, cyber-security is defined as the ability to safeguard the digital assets of information systems and to ensure that the confidentiality, integrity and availability of the data they contain are not compromised, whether in processing, in storage or in transmission.

This study seeks to critically assess the cyber-security concerns with the adoption and operation of cloud computing amongst SMEs in developing economies, and the need to mitigate the associated risks in order to create value and leverage the full performance using IT-enabled strategies.

This study seeks to design a value creation model to examine the cloud-based cyber-security constructs. The media for exchanging communications and/or processing data are basically unsecure and untrusted. There wouldn't have been any concerns if end-users were to communicate via secure and trusted channels. In reality, end-users subscribe to cloud services from providers that they have never met. Just like, email messages are sent and e-Commerce activities are transacted over the Internet, which are susceptible and prone to all manner of attacks. In order to initiate any such interactions, the entities involved instantiate communication session by exchanging entity credentials to ascertain their identities (i.e. authentication), as well as to establish non-repudiation and confidentiality (Walker, 2009). To realize the full potentials of cloud computing, there is the need to address the numerous concerns holistically, especially those bothering on cyber-security with militating adverse effects on business value and performance.

The discussion on the basic elements of cyber-security would be incomplete without the treatment of the cyber-risk parameters – which are the asset value, threats and vulnerabilities.

Risk Parameters

This study is inspired by the cyber-risks treatise of (Yeboah-Boateng E. O., 2013a), which advocated for the holistic risk assessment using fuzzy risk relational function, with vulnerabilities, threats and asset value as functional arguments. The basic assumptions are that human knowledge and business decision-making are fraught with lots of uncertainties, and are generally fuzzy in nature. Business decisions are made in fuzzy linguistic terms, such as the cloud services are "secured" or "vulnerable"; sometimes, as "highly secure" or "slightly vulnerable". Also, cyber-security concerns are very uncertain and that any analytical metric used in its assessment to capture the very essence of information and its attributes, must be based on fuzzy-related possibility measures (Zadeh, 1978).

Assets Value

Generally, assets are any items which have economic value, either convertible to equivalent cash, or owned by an entity or an organization (Yeboah-Boateng E. O., 2013a). A cyber-asset is the very embodiment of an organization, upon which business is conducted (Ozier, 2002). It could be tangible or intangible asset. The tangible assets are the typical information supportive-and/or-enabled items, such as PCs, laptops, hardware, storage media, web servers, networking equipment and devices, etc. Whereas, intangible assets include the information asset itself (called content), goodwill, corporate image and reputation, intellectual property, etc.

In view of the critical nature of information assets, organizations ought to appoint custodians who are responsible for ensuring that asset value is sustained. Admittedly, estimating the asset value could be a daunting task for all organizations. The organization needs to classify the assets based on its value, which is estimated through fuzzy constructs such as criticality, urgency, sensitivity, as well as the regulations, compliance and business objectives. The asset value determines the level of protection that would be offered, and the extent and severity of any adverse impact is directly correlated with it. Since the asset value and associated attractiveness to threat agents wane or appreciate with time, it is only appropriate to re-classify the assets periodically.

Cyber-asset is herewith defined as the very embodiment of provisioning cloud services, such as the servers, networks, and the data that is processed or stored, and its value as the value at risk that could compromise the confidentiality, integrity and availability attributes of the asset (Yeboah-Boateng E. O., 2013a). Those assets are attractive targets to numerous threat agents and threats (Whitman & Mattord, 2005).

Vulnerabilities

Vulnerabilities are weaknesses inherent or associated with an asset, which renders the asset susceptible to various threats or attacks. Vulnerabilities, typically are systemic weaknesses that could be exploited to violate the CIA properties of the cloud resources. Generally, the systems, networks, infrastructures and applications are fraught with weaknesses that result in compromises of the CIA properties whenever they are exploited by threat agents. Vulnerabilities can be classified as being due to technical, human, physical, operational and sometimes, business commissions and omissions (Hermann, 2003).

This study examines the cloud vulnerabilities holistically from business value and performance perspectives, such that any compromises debase its value and erodes the potentials to leverage competitive advantage. Thus, the vulnerabilities hamper on harnessing the potentials of cloud computing, especially security attributes, towards appropriating sustainable value-added offerings.

Also, in view of the subjective nature of business decision-making, the vulnerability attributes were assessed using fuzzy linguistic tuples, such as "highly vulnerable", "slightly vulnerable", rather than the often probabilistic "overly binary outlook" (Yeboah-Boateng E. O., 2013a).

Enumerated below are some cloud characteristic vulnerabilities, adopted from (Grobauer, Walloschek, & Stocker, 2011):

- **Unauthorized Access to Management Interface:** Through on-demand self-service; e.g. insufficient security audit possibilities; certification schemes and security metrics aren't adapted to cloud computing.
- **Internet Protocol Vulnerabilities:** Associated with network access, which is usually the Internet; e.g. IP vulnerabilities such as man-in-the-middle attacks.
- **Data Recovery Vulnerabilities:** Associated with pooling and elasticity of resources – implies that memory and storage resources allocated to one user is re-allocated to another user – which has the possibility of data recovery written by the previous user; cross-tenant storage access and network access; almost impossible with media sanitization in cloud.
- **Metering and Billing Evasion:** Associated with metering data used for optimization of service delivery and billing – possibilities of metering and billing data manipulation and billing evasion.
- **Injection Vulnerabilities:** e.g. SQL injection, in which the input contains SQL code that's erroneously executed in the database backend.
- **Command Injection:** In which the input contains commands that are erroneously executed via the OS.
- **Cross-Site Scripting:** In which the input contains javascript code that's erroneously executed by a victim's browser.
- **Weak Authentication Mechanisms:** Weak dictionary based passwords; e.g. insecure user behavior, weak or re-use password; inherent limitations of one–factor authentication mechanisms.
- The possibility that an attacker might successfully escape from a virtualized environment lies in virtualization's very nature, which is an intrinsic vulnerability; insufficient network-based controls; limited IP-based network zoning; difficulty of distinguishing friendly network vulnerability scanning from attacks.
- **Web Application Technologies:** Have the inherent vulnerability of implementing session handling. In view of the HTTP protocol's requisite stateless protocol nature, whereas web applications require some session state-hold. This creates susceptibility to session riding and hijacking. Virtualization implies that network traffic occurs on both real and virtual.
- **Cryptanalysis Advances:** Can render any cryptographic mechanism or algorithm insecure as novel methods of breaking into them are discovered. For instance, flaws within cryptographic algorithm implementations render them weak, though needed for the protection of data confidentiality and integrity in the cloud. Difficulties with poor key management procedures, e.g., hardware security module (HSM) storage. Lack of standard security metrics for cloud infrastructures.

Threats

Generally, an attack or threat is said have been realized, whenever a vulnerability is exploited. The attacker is also known as the threat agent. Various threat agents militate against the cloud ecosystem; they could be human, such as end-users, with intentional or unintentional motives, but grave consequences. Threats could emanate from internal sources, such as corporate espionage agents, or insiders or disgruntled employees or contractors, as well as from external sources, often referred to as intruders, hackers or crackers. Threats could also be attributed to non-human, such as hardware failure, power outages, software failures, malicious codes or malwares, etc.

This study evaluates threats by assessing the possibility of attacks and appraise their attributes based on the threat agent's capability and motivation, and the opportunity presented for an attractive cloud asset (Pedrycz & Gomide, 2007). In practice, it may not be possible to measure all vulnerability attributes and their severity, so expert opinions are elicited with some educated guesstimates (Yeboah-Boateng E. O., 2013a).

This study defines cyber-threat as any event, situation, or occurrence that possibly could cause harm, loss, damage or compromise an information asset or pose risk to the cyber-asset. These threats are deemed to exploit the weakness in systems in order to compromise the confidentiality, integrity and availability properties of the cloud assets or resources.

Some of the threats militating against cloud services and resources are malicious, unintentional, compromised sensitive data, deleted data, altered data, storage on unreliable media, unauthorized entities having access or gaining access to sensitive data, etc. There are increased threat activities due to more interactions, with corresponding inherent vulnerabilities and they are persistent.

Cloud specific threats include the following (Grobauer, Walloschek, & Stocker, 2011; Marston, Li, Bandyopadhyay, Zhang, & Ghalsasi, 2011): insecure points of cloud connection – APIs are used for cloud services, such as provisioning, management, billing and reporting, etc., anonymous logins, reusable passwords, man-in-the-middle (MITM) attacks, insufficient authentication, authorization and audit (AAA) controls to regulate login access, ineffective encryption, hardware failures - such as server crashes, lack of effective asset disposal policies, data center reliability, backup, disaster recovery and business continuity related issues.

Also, issues with multi-tenancy and resource pooling could pose serious threats. For example, the Hypervisor inadvertently enables guest OS to gain inappropriate levels of controls or influence on the underlying platform (c.f. Joanna Rutkowska's Blue Pill rootkit) (Smallwood, 2012; Kortchinsky, 2009). The study adopted some of the top threats cited by the Cloud Security Alliance (CSA) as metrics for benchmarking threat taxonomy (Ko & Lee, 2013).

Risk

There are various definitions for what constitutes risk. It could be said to be possibility of losses due to CIA compromises with adverse impact on the cloud ecosystem (McEachem, 2001).

Generally, risk could be evaluated by assessing the cost-benefits, return-on-investment or the likelihood of a threat being realized or the likelihood of a successful compromise of a cloud asset. The issue is these notions are based on probabilistic computations, which erroneously assume the randomness of attacks. This approach, according to the US department of Homeland Security (DHS) (2006), could lead to a grievous error thus misleading the decision process.

Indeed, they recognize that a viable risk assessment must take into account the lots of uncertainties in risk evaluations and that, it is best to estimate risk qualitatively. DHS (2006) actually recommends the utility of building a consensus with expert opinions or judgment.

Katsikas (2009) asserts that evaluating cyber-risk using only probabilistic computations is very simplistic and that it avoids the complexities and uncertainties associated with cyber-security.

So, this study takes a holistic stance on cyber-risk and adapts the definition used by (Yeboah-Boateng E. O., 2013a), which is:

The possibility of the occurrence or realization of a threat, due to compromises of the confidentiality, integrity and availability (CIA) of the system and the associated adverse impact on business. (p. 89)

This approach takes into account the uncertainties and renders an assessment of the cloud ecosystem taking into consideration the imprecision, vagueness and "incomplete knowledge" metrics of the entire cloud set-up (Yeboah-Boateng E. O., 2013; Ngai & Wat, 2005).

Following the footsteps of (Shaurette, 2002), this study evaluated the risks using intuitive fuzzy inferences to capture and aggregate the consensus of experts' advice on cloud–related cyber-security concerns. In simple terms, for a higher asset value of cloud resources, with a higher vulnerability, which is exploited by a high threat, would lead to a higher risk (Ye, 2008). It must be noted that, an asset may have numerous vulnerabilities, and may be exploited by multiple threats as well.

The following are some ways that an organization could be adversely impacted due to information breaches (Abatan, 2011, p. 143):

- Erosion of the perceived business value;
- Waning of investor confidence;
- Lack of control on information assets storage (so no clue where corporate information resides – no knowledge when it spills);
- Lack of control of confidential information, once sent to third party;
- Transmission of confidential information to third party, inadvertently;
- Lack of knowledge of when IP is taken out without permission and when used in a way that may be detrimental to your business.

Cyber-attacks can affect the ability of information processing, storage and transmission of information resources or assets (ITU-T, 2007). They can also cause harm or damage to intangible assets, productivity and adversely impair the decision making processes within the organization (ITU-T, 2007) and could have direct or indirect socio-economic impacts. It's herewith reckoned that the mitigation measures for cloud vulnerabilities and risks, require a multi-faceted approach that takes into consideration social, economic, legal, human and technical dimensions of the solutions.

The CSVA Model

This section discusses the cyber-security vulnerabilities assessment (CSVA) model (Yeboah-Boateng E. O., 2013a) and relate it to this study. First of all, the CSVA is discussed herein in view of its multi-disciplinary perspectives based on fuzzy relational cyber-risk formulation. There are four (4) layers, namely the vulnerabilities, threats, assets value and risk (impact) layers, in the order of lowest to the highest.

Figure 1. CSVA model
Source: Adapted from Yeboah-Boateng, 2013

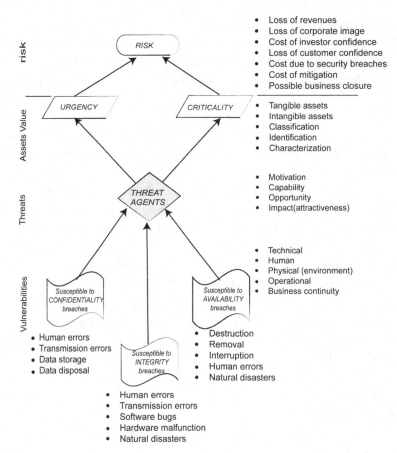

The CSVA model is used to assess or characterize the uncertainties, such as the vulnerabilities or threats. The unique distinction here is that perceived or abstract notions rather physical quantities of cyber-security are assessed.

The cyber-security concerns with cloud computing are discussed from business value creation and performance perspectives, or the lack thereof, using the CSVA multi-faceted model.

The CSVA model conveys an understanding of how to characterize vulnerabilities and to recommend the eminent risks associated with information systems. It assists in the explanation of complexities and uncertainties of vulnerabilities and threats. It presents the key cyber-security challenges confronting CSPs and highlights on the contributory roles of asset value, vulnerabilities, threats, risks and associated impact, as well as policies needed to build a secure cloud ecosystem.

The CSVA model is used to explain the security posture of the CSPs and it assists in the understanding of the effects or implications of threats on vulnerabilities, as well as utilizing the model for the prediction of risk impact on the organization.

The essence of the CSVA model is to safeguard business assets against vulnerabilities and threats to cyber-security, so as to ensure business continuity and optimum performance, which are sustainable value-added and appropriation metrics.

Layer 1

Layer 1 of the CSVA model is the vulnerabilities layer and the lowest in the model. At this layer, weaknesses in the systems, networks, infrastructures, and applications are identified and assessed. The objective is to estimate the extent to which the systems are rendered susceptible to cyber-attacks. The assessment takes into consideration the possibilities of multiple threats and estimate the combined effects of multiple and sequential incidents.

The CSVA model offers CSPs a very good understanding of the assets that ought to be safeguarded, the threats against which those assets ought to be safeguarded, the vulnerabilities of these particular assets as well as the existing risk as a result of those threats and exposure (ITU-T, 2006).

In assessing the vulnerabilities, due recognition is taken for the fact that typical weaknesses or flaws in cyber-assets could be exploited to compromise any of the CIA security properties in a number of ways. In accordance with ITU-T X.800 (ITU-T, 2006), the following vulnerabilities could be exploited:

- Those associated with weak, unenforceable policies;
- Those inherent in design and specifications, which could be omissions or commissions;
- Those that emanate from poor configurations or inappropriate utilization of resources choices;
- Those that are due to implementation errors.

The CSVA model is also used to classify the vulnerabilities into technical, human, physical, operational and business susceptibilities. Similarly, and in accordance with (Hermann, 2003), the CSVA model can classify the vulnerabilities into such categories as type, source and severity. Vulnerability identification and classification are used in recommending appropriate and effective mitigation solutions to CSPs.

Layer 2

Layer 2 of the CSVA model is the threats layer and it deals with the evaluation of any events or situations or actions that can possibly exploit weaknesses in the ecosystems to cause harm and/or pose risk to a given cloud-asset or resource.

Typically, vulnerabilities in the systems are exploited by threat agents to facilitate the realization of a threat, whose impact is the risk. The CSVA model is used to assess the possible threat agents, which could be either human (end-users), insiders, hackers or technical (such as systemic or operational) or environmental in nature.

Though there's a tall list of threat agents that can militate against the cloud ecosystem, this study deals with just a limited list. So the CSVA model in its assessment identifies and evaluates the type, sources and possibilities of realization of threats. Threat agents capitalize on the opportunities afforded to them by the susceptibilities in the systems. The CSVA evaluates threat agents' motivations and capabilities, as well as the attractiveness of the resource at stake. Through the identification and assessment of threat agents, the CSVA model serves as a decision analysis technique which facilitates and prioritizes resources allocated to mitigate possible risks.

The model can also be used to evaluate historical dataset, if available, to give an indication or predict the possibilities of certain threats being realized.

Finally, the threats layer is utilized to assess threat agents and account for their transitional states as the agents actually "mutate over time" (Vidalis & Jones, 2005). For example, a script kiddie may have acquired new skills or gathered additional capabilities to hack into a corporate system with fresh motivation, though at some point in time, his activities might have been deemed inactive or dormant.

Layer 3

Layer 3 of the CSVA model is the asset layer. Cyber-assets in this study has been attributed to those cloud resources that are utilized in the value creation and appropriation chains.

In view of that, this layer evaluates cyber-assets and endeavors to estimate the cumulative asset value involved. The process involves appropriate assets identification and classification. The classification facilitates the exact estimation or assessment of the criticality or importance label assigned to each cyber-asset, based on parameters such as business risk (upon compromise), actual asset value (purchased price with depreciation rules applied), sensitivity, governance and compliance requirements.

This layer also estimates the urgency parameters of the given resources. In accordance with (Fisch & White, 2000), the asset value is also computed by taken into account the time required for its maintenance and repairs, its sensitivity to the CSPs, as a measure of the urgency with which restoration will be required upon compromise.

The CSVA model allows for intuitive assessment of the cyber-assets based on the assessor's expertise to assign values using qualitative fuzzy criteria, such as purpose, pleasure and ideals. To make the evaluation objective, one can use the organization's asset classification policy, if available, as a guide. Also, through the use of the CSVA model, other policies which depend upon the assets classification policy can be re-formulated.

Two (2) important metrics of criticality and urgency are used to ascertain the extent or severity of impact upon cyber-attack or compromise.

Finally, it must be noted that the asset value is proportional to the impact or risk level to the CSPs; that is, the asset value is positively correlated to the risk to the CSPs. In fact, the asset value is a "disutility" and it reflects the extent of possible losses (e.g. revenue loss, loss of reputation, possible lawsuits, etc.) to be incurred upon compromise.

Layer 4

The highest layer of the CSVA model is the cyber-risk layer. It is the culmination of the essence of the CSVA model; depicting the ultimate expression of the consequences resulting from a threat agent exploiting an opportune vulnerability in a given asset.

The cyber-risk layer is used to express the fuzzy relationships existing amongst the other lower layers. It estimates qualitatively the resultant risk value upon assessing the nature and extent of vulnerabilities and the possibility of exploitation and associated severity, should a threat matures for a given cyber-asset (Katsikas, 2009). This evaluation is carried out by taking into account all possible (including potential) threats, with the notion that a vulnerability might be exploited by multiple threat agents.

The CSVA model takes an approach in assessing and evaluating the risks by deducing the cumulative relational impact of a compromise on an asset.

The implication is that, a higher asset value (which is treated as disutility or negative utility), and a higher vulnerability value (i.e. highly susceptible asset) and/or a higher threat value (i.e. highly motivated threat agent, equipped with necessary capabilities in an opportune moment) will create a high impact or risk to the SME (Ye, 2008).

Business Value Creation

A business process is a set of business activities that together contribute to achieving the business objectives in an organization. Strategy is an intention to establish a plan to reach an objective. Strategy actually involves decision making using the best possible options for projects, alternatives and programs.

When there is a set of complex choices to be made, be they comparable or not, subject to restrictions and limitations, and when it is necessary to perform a selection and ranking, it is convenient to use strategic management to solve this system. It involves the use of sequential procedures, usually with a lot of feedback to find the most convenient alternative.

According to (Piccoli, 2013), the key characteristics of any business value creation are as follows:

- Value can be tangible or intangible;
- Creation of value is not necessarily appropriation;
- Competitive advantage and added value are closely related;
- Value is in the eyes of the customer;
- Customer willingness-to-pay (CWP) is not equated with price.

The essence of leveraging the use or adoption of cloud computing is to deploy these information systems for business value creation and appropriation of economic value within the organization. What does it mean to create value? Why would an organization want to engage in value creation (and indeed who cares?)? How does the organization ensures that the benefits from its value creation strategies and initiatives are sustained?

Piccoli (2013) asserts that economic value is created whenever "something worthwhile" and novel is initiated (p. 252). In other words, those new technologies and/or products must mean "something " to someone, and in essence must solve a problem to merit value-added. The technologies or products and services must be transformed in their "next best utilization" (Piccoli, 2013, p. 252) if it has to create value to the end-users. Indeed, no value is created if the input resources were not transformed and rather remained in its original state or form.

"The input resources are represented by any factor of production" according to (Piccoli, 2013, p. 253), in this context the so-called cloud computing resources. Considering cloud computing ecosystem, the transformation process for the business value creation involves set-up, installation and configuration of virtual machines and servers in order to provision cloud services for which the end-users are willing to pay for. Here, the willingness-to-pay for a secured and reliable network bandwidth and storage, are typical security related cloud computing value-added services.

Value Appropriation

Value appropriation is the process of splitting the total value created into the contributory quotas. It assigns the value contributed by each of the business units or partners in realizing the value addition transformation. In this study, value appropriation is seen as a performance metric in respect of ensuring that the value created is not eroded. Bartlett et al. (2006) posit that research has shown that organizations which succeed are those with fixed and strong core values or corporate cultures, but have dynamic business strategies with endless change adaptation. That is their core purposes do not change, although strategies and practices adapt endlessly to change.

It is reckoned that IT in general, and cloud computing per se, do not have the characteristics for "rarity and inimitability" (Piccoli, 2013, p. 360), so a holistic approach or framework is needed to ensure that the value created is sustained or appropriated over time. The fact that cloud security by itself may not be valuable, rare and inimitable doesn't mean the value created solutions are non-sustainable. Concerted efforts must be adopted to harness the potentials as the CSPs mitigate against any vulnerabilities and threats. These concepts of value creation and appropriation have their antecedents from the industry analysis grounded Five Forces model (Porter, 1980).

Piccoli (2013) posits that "no matter how much value a firm contributes to creating, unless the firm can be unique in their value creation, they will quickly compete away this value to customers" (p. 259).

This study seeks to identify some opportunities to create value with cloud computing resources and to mitigate the cyber-security concerns. The object is that once these variables have been identified informed choices are made to select those measures that hold greatest potential for value creation and appropriation.

Fuzzy Multi-Attribute Decision Making (MADM)

It is observed that the approach used to propose any multi-faceted mitigation mechanisms in dealing with cloud security concerns, is one of multi-attribute decision-making (MADM).

This approach is employed to rank the decision alternatives in multiple attribute decision-making problem of enlisting threats as perceived by the sample experts. The objective is that given a set of threats deduced from the main study as alternatives, then fuzzy MADM techniques are used to rate them in the order of most-to-least.

Fuzzy triangular numbers are used herewith for simplicity and ease of computation. For instance, it can be showed that similar treatment with fuzzy trapezoidal numbers would yield similar results.

Fuzzy Similarity Measures is one of the basic concepts in human cognitive endeavors (Beg & Ashraf, 2009). It finds applications in multi-attribute decision-making (MADM) such as taxonomy, recognition, case-based reasoning (Beg & Ashraf, 2009). There are various aspects of fuzzy similarity measures, which are applied for variety and specific purposes (Anisseh & Yussuf, 2011; Deng, Kang, Zhang, Deng, & Zhang, 2011) etc.

Fuzzy similarity measures find applications in fuzzy ordering or ranking as well as fuzzy analysis of various risk constructs. In this study, fuzzy similarity measures are utilized in ranking various threat agents that confront cloud services providers and end-uers in developing economies.

Beg & Ashraf (2009) classified similarity measures into three (3) groups, namely:

1. Metric-based measures;
2. Set-theoretic based measures; and
3. Implicators based measures.

This study dwells on an aspect of the set-theoretic based similarity measures. Indeed, set theoretic similarity measures come in two (2) types: crisp logic based and fuzzy logic based. Here again, this study narrows down to the fuzzy logic similarity measures or fuzzy similarity measures, for brevity.

Similarity measures are sometimes referred to in literature as degrees or measures of similarity.

Now, let the fuzzy linguistic variables be defined by the tuples $S = \{s_i : i = 1, 2, ..., n\}$ such that $s_i < s_j$ iff i < j.

In this study, $S = \{s_1 = $ very minor, $s_2 = $ minor, $s_3 = $ important, $s_4 = $ vital, $s_5 = $ critical$\}$ and the experts are $E_i = \{E_1, E_2, ..., E_n\}$, where n is the total number of experts.

From the study (c.f. Figure 2), expert E_1 is deemed the most important and assigned relative importance of $r_1 = 1$. Then, relative importance of the other experts, based on professional experience attribute, are computed using the equation below.

Degrees of importance can be computed from the equation

$$w_i = \frac{r_i}{\sum\limits_{i=1}^{n} r_i};$$

(1)

Figure 2. Depicting the results computed from the empirical data
Source: Yeboah-Boateng, 2016

	$\hat{Z}_i$ FTN	$\hat{I}_i$ FTN	$S_{(\hat{z}_*, \hat{z}_i)}$	Min-max method	Xu's method	Rank
Natural Disasters	(4.19 5.56 6.94)	(6.94 8.09 9.24)	$S_{(\hat{z}_*, \hat{z}_1)}$	0.75	0.77	8th
Power Failure	(4.74 6.10 7.46)	(5.43 6.72 8.00)	$S_{(\hat{z}_*, \hat{z}_2)}$	0.82	0.84	6th
APIs	(3.53 5.06 6.59)	(4.93 6.40 7.86)	$S_{(\hat{z}_*, \hat{z}_3)}$	0.68	0.71	9th
Malicious Insiders	(5.07 7.03 8.30)	(6.64 7.85 9.06)	$S_{(\hat{z}_*, \hat{z}_4)}$	0.95	0.95	2nd
Data Leakage	(4.87 6.22 7.50)	(5.78 7.10 8.42)	$S_{(\hat{z}_*, \hat{z}_5)}$	0.84	0.85	5th
Service Hijacking	(5.51 6.80 8.10)	(6.80 7.90 9.00)	$S_{(\hat{z}_*, \hat{z}_6)}$	0.92	0.92	3rd
Share Technology Issues	(5.69 7.07 8.45)	(6.40 7.65 8.90)	$S_{(\hat{z}_*, \hat{z}_7)}$	0.95	0.96	1st
Hardware Failure	(4.25 5.76 7.27)	(5.40 6.95 8.50)	$S_{(\hat{z}_*, \hat{z}_8)}$	0.78	0.79	7th
Abuse & Nefarious Usage	(3.34 4.93 6.52)	(4.90 6.40 7.90)	$S_{(\hat{z}_*, \hat{z}_9)}$	0.69	0.69	10th
Hypervisor Errors	(6.91 8.07 9.23)	(8.00 9.00 10.00)	$S_{(\hat{z}_*, \hat{z}_{10})}$	0.92	0.92	4th

For any given fuzzy sets $A = \{a_i\}$ and $B = \{b_i\}$, $\forall$ i = 1,2, ..., n , the grade of similarity (or agreement degree) of the fuzzy relations is given by

$$S_{(R_i,R_j)} = \frac{\sum_i (a_i \wedge b_i)}{\sum_i (a_i \vee b_i)} \tag{2}$$

Equation [eqn-2] is known as the min-max similarity method (Hsu, Hsi-Mei & Chen-Tung Chen, 1996), and the fuzzy sets A and B are said to be approximately equal if and only if (iff), there exists a proximity measure, ε, (Pappis & Karacapilidis, 1993) such that $S_{(R_i,R_j)} \equiv S_{A,B} \leq \varepsilon$.

Another useful method is that of Xu (Xu, 2005) for similarity measure given by

$$S_{(R_i,R_j)} = 1 - \frac{|a_2 - a_1| + |b_2 - b_1| + |c_2 - c_1|}{8q} \tag{3}$$

Where q = 3 for fuzzy triangular numbers and q = 4 for fuzzy trapezoidal numbers.

It is noted that $S_{(R_i,R_j)} \in [0,1]$ and $S_{(R_i,R_j)} \to 1$ implies that R_1 and R_2 are closer to each other. So $S_{(R_i,R_j)} = 1$ iff $R_1 = R_2$ and also that $S_{(R_i,R_j)} = S_{(R_j,R_i)}$

Assume that the fuzzy set $X = \{x_1, x_2, ..., x_n\}$ be the set of alternatives and $U = \{u_1, u_2, ..., u_m\}$ be the set of attributes. Then for a given degree of importance or weights vector $w = \{w_1, w_2, ..., w_m\}$; $\forall$ $w_i \geq 0$; i = 1,2, ..., m. the linguistic decision matrix or agreement fuzzy matrix (AM) is computed as

$$AM_{mxn} = \begin{bmatrix} S_{11} & S_{12} & \cdots & S_{1n} \\ \vdots & \vdots & \ddots & \cdots \\ S_{m1} & S_{m2} & \cdots & S_{mn} \end{bmatrix} \tag{4}$$

Or $AM_{mxn} \equiv (a_{ij})_{mxn}$ where $a_{ij} = [a_{ij}^a \ a_{ij}^b \ a_{ij}^c] \in S$ is the attribute value, which takes the form of a fuzzy triangular linguistic variable, given by the decision maker, for the alternative $x_j \in X$ with respect to the attribute $u_i \in U$. It follows that for a vector of attribute values $a_j = (a_{1j}, a_{2j}, ..., a_{mj})$ it corresponds with the alternative $x_j : j = 1, 2, ..., n$.

There exists an ideal point of attribute values, where $I_i = [I_i^a, I_i^b, I_i^c]$ such that $I_i^a = \max\{a_{ij}^a\}$, $I_i^b = \max\{a_{ij}^b\}$, $I_i^c = \max\{a_{ij}^c\}$.

Using the data on the 14 experts, 10 key cloud-related threats were identified and enlisted in the order of most-to-least severe impacts on the CSPs were deduced.

The essence of the strategic interviews was to elicit expert opinions to formulate expert knowledge for the fuzzy rule-base inference model and also to aggregate consensus for the evaluation of taxonomy of threats and vulnerabilities. Here, the 14 respondent experts' opinions are aggregated into a group consensus opinion. First, the index of consensus of each expert relative to other experts are defined using fuzzy similarity measures. Opinions were aggregated based on both the index of consensus and the relative importance of the experts.

The issue at stake is such that each expert has ranked the assets, vulnerabilities and the threat agents by their own subjectivity and perceived knowledge. This explains the essence of using fuzzy based multi-attribute decision making approach in estimating the consensus aggregation function. Within the multi-attribute decision-making techniques, a couple of fuzzy similarity methods are utilized in the final evaluation or ranking of the taxonomies.

METHODOLOGY

Based on extensive literature review, a set of vulnerabilities, threats and cloud assets were identified (CSA, 2011) (NIST, 2008), and a set of questions were carved out. The study targeted CSPs and cloud consumers in the SMEs sector.

The samples were characterized as experts, i.e. those with requisite educational background in ICT, professional cyber-security practitioners, system administrators and corporate chief-level executives.

Initially, about 200 end-users who are currently using one form of cloud resources were purposively identified and recruited for the study. The necessary study objectives and ethics were explained to them. Only 65 responses were received, which were collated and categorized, and used as the basis for designing the semi-structured questions used to conduct the strategic interviews, and also to validate the results.

As a follow-up, the contacts of the 65 were randomized and the first 10 were selected to participate in the interviews. Four (4) C-level officers of CSPs were purposively recruited to participate in the interview, which sought their expert opinions on various cyber-security concerns with cloud computing and business value creation metrics.

The research approach commenced with the interviews of the target samples. Dhillon & Torkzadeh (2006) studied the business values that stakeholders attached to information systems security. They solicited the perceptions of samples on access to information, identified problems and shortcomings in cloud computing, Internet convergences, understand goals and policies, constraints and evaluation of perspectives.

A 3-prong approach used by Keeney (1992) was adopted to identify and organize the cyber-security concerns with cloud computing, from their business value creation and performance perspectives.

1. First, interviews were conducted to elicit the constructs;
2. Second, the constructs were "normalized" into common contexts and meanings, e.g. similar constructs were grouped together to create one variable;
3. Third, the constructs were categorized into key security vulnerabilities or threats.

Using the CSVA model and supported by the 3D cloud security method (Pande & Jog, 2014), the sample responses were evaluated and categorized into vulnerabilities and threats. For example, a sample assigns the perceived level of susceptibility due to confidentiality, integrity and availability. The perceived assignment indicates the level of data confidentiality with cloud storage, or the reliability of provisioned resource being assured to be of service (i.e. level of availability).

RESULTS AND ANALYSIS

Key Findings

The key motivation for this study has been to critically examine the cyber-security concerns with cloud computing, in respect of harnessing (or the lack thereof, hampering) business value creation and performance perspectives. Here, cloud security challenges and proactive mitigation measures are being implemented to create unique value. In view of the performance metric, the created value added must be appropriated over time so that it is not eroded away.

The key findings of this study are as follows:

- First, a taxonomy of ten (10) threats are benchmarked – that could impact adversely on the cloud ecosystem (andcompared with a similar analysis by the Cloud Security Alliance (CSA) (2010); and
- The Value Creation Cloud-based Cyber-security (VC3) model is proposed – to assist CSPs and end-users to assess or evaluate their security posture in the ecosystem.

Taxonomy of Threats

Using fuzzy similarity measures, the 10 top threats deduced from the study employing the experts' opinions were ranked. The min-max and Xu's methods were used in the computations. The results are depicted on Figure 2 below.

Deducing from the above, the ranking of alternative threats are:

$$Z_7 > Z_4 > Z_6 \approx Z_{10} > Z_5 > Z_2 > Z_8 > Z_1 > Z_3 > Z_9$$

The taxonomy of threats as perceived by CSPs and end-users in developing economies are from the most likely attacks to the least, as follows:

1. Shared Technology Issues
2. Malicious Insiders
3. Service Hijacking
4. Hypervisor Errors
5. Data Leakage
6. Power Failure
7. Hardware Failure
8. Natural Disasters
9. APIs
10. Abuse & Nefarious Usage.

Interestingly, some of the rankings corresponding with that of CSA, whilst some key threats are not in conformity with a similar study by (Yeboah-Boateng, 2013a, 2013b):

Shared Technology Issues

Here, the concept of multiple end-users sharing the same servers or resources could pose some security concerns. There could be capacity issues for servers designed for single users, rather than multiple simultaneous users – introducing availability concerns. This is considered the most threaten concerns amongst the CSPs and end-users that were studied (c.f. CSA #4). Basically, shared technology issues include cloud–related concerns with respect resource pooling and multi-tenant architecture, disk partitioning, CPU caches, memory and registry pooling, guest OSs, etc.

Though, the concept of multi-tenant facility adds value by economies of scale, at the same time, there are risks of over-provisioning which could result in denial-of-service – an availability concern. Also, multi-tenancy could introduce resource contention with adverse effects on latency sensitive applications – which could be degraded in performance.

Also, overt malicious attacks also threaten the value-added multi-tenancy (Steiner, 2012).

Malicious Insiders

Insiders are legitimate end-users with authorized access credentials, but who assume an ulterior motives to carry out nefarious acts within the system. Here, the list includes corporate espionage agents or spies, disgruntled employees, etc. Even trusted employees can pose enormous risks to the CSPs and consumers. The severity of these threats emanate from the fact that, insiders are privy to knowledge on inherent vulnerabilities of the systems and they could exploit them. Also, insiders have legitimate access rights for which they can elevate their privileges. Studies show that the impact of malicious insiders is usually loss of sensitive data, loss of corporate resources, and even market share (Yeboah-Boateng E. O., 2013c)

Service and Account Hijacking

The CSA ranked is threat as 6th. Account and service hijacking is a process whereby an end-user's email account, login-credentials, or any other account-based resource or service is stolen or hijacked by an unauthorized entity. Once the account credentials is stolen, the entity-thief can use it to carry out some nefarious activities.

Indeed, the threat of abuse and nefarious usage was ranked 10th in this study, whereas CSA ranked it 1st. This is not as surprising as probably our expert samples reckon this as a byproduct of other threats. Invariably, any threats that intercept communication session or account information is likely to abuse it. These include malicious insiders, regular hacking activities and man-in-the-middle attacks, etc.

Another impact could be due to unwarranted usage charges or bills, since the cloud ecosystem is metered upon usage. The "thief" could be running your services on your behalf.

Hypervisor Errors

CSA didn't rank this threat separately, but accounted for it in the shared technology issues. The hypervisor is an abstraction that implements and controls the virtualization of the physical hardware. Errors in the hypervisor could be exploited to isolate runtime environment using a guest domain. This attack is said to be catastrophic to the virtualized system (Oracle, n.d.). Threats emanating from hypervisor errors are quite a lot. These could be due to failed state, no physical machines that are associated with the hypervisor; connection problems as well as login issues. Issues of changed passwords not properly effected could raise concerns. Corrupted hypervisor and intercepting hosting provider's password system (c.f. Turkish hacker group that hijacked service providers' password system on Dec. 29, 2013).

Virtualized environment do not necessarily improve security (Vogl, n.d.), efforts must be made to ensure the hypervisor is adequately protected. Unintended misconfiguration could create unwarranted communications channels that could be exploited to compromise the systems.

Data Leakage or Losses

CSA also ranked this threat as 5th. Data loss or leakage is unauthorized disclosure of data to an unauthorized entity. It may be due to human error, malware infection, hardware malfunctioning, natural disasters, etc. These threats include accidental deletion of data without proper backup, malicious access – with unauthorized disclosure of sensitive information. These could result from insufficient authentication methods, operational failures, asset disposal without due process to data leakages.

Power Failure

There is perennial power outages in the case example country where the study was undertaken. So comes as a bit of surprise that power supply is ranked 6th, instead of within the third. Possibly, cognizant of the problem the providers and the end-users have equipped their systems with standby power supply. That said, power failure hampers on operations eroding the valuable gains made by the organization. It also raises a number of security concerns – availability and causing malfunctioning due instability and fluctuations.

Hardware Failure

This is manifested as malfunction of electronic and/or electromechanical components. The influencing causes could be power failure. Hardware failure impacts heavily on business continuity. It causes loss of critical corporate data. It also results in data loss and a possible solution often preferred is by duplicating copies or backups. This in turn creates another threats as data is vulnerable to theft or leakage, etc.

Natural Disaster

It quite interesting that this threat ranked 8th. A similar study amongst similar samples rated natural disaster very high. It's probably because this cloud computing where most of the resources are not located within the study setting.

Value Creation Cloud-Based Cyber-Security (VC3) Model

The VC3 model is 4 phased model that seeks to assist CSPs and end-users in examining their corporate strategy in respect of cloud computing. This study utilized the intuitive reasoning of the expert samples in designing the model solution. Intuitive reasoning is said to be based on human intelligence and understanding of the issues at stake (Yeboah-Boateng E. O., 2013a). Literature support the use of intuitive reasoning and perceived uncertainty measures in eliciting expert opinions or judgments (Ayyub B. M., 2001; Ayyub & Lai, 1992; Lai, 1992).

It starts with the adoption phase where the end-user accepts to use cloud services. This is strategic decision as it could impact on operations, both positively and negatively.

Figure 3. Value creation cloud-based cyber-security (VC3) model

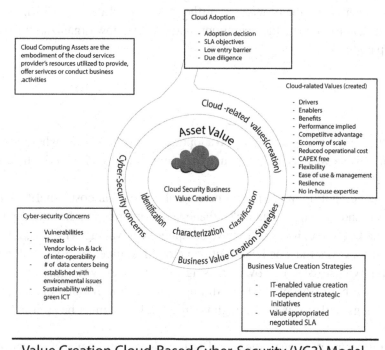

Value Creation Cloud-Based Cyber-Security (VC3) Model

The organization must articulate its corporate strategy by spelling out it as a service level objective. This can assist in negotiating a good availability metrics with the CSP.

The next phase is the cyber-security concerns. Here, various security challenges must be identified and addressed. For instance, vulnerabilities and threats with the choice of cloud resource must be thoroughly understood and assessed.

The business value creation phase follows with the strategy for harnessing IT-enabled and IT-dependent opportunities. The key question is, how the organization can leverage on the cloud services to add value to its products and services, especially ensuring that security concerns are mitigated to appropriate the gains. The essence is to commit the value added into a sustainable competitive advantage over time; i.e. appropriated over time.

The last phase is that of cloud-related value creation. Here, emphasis is on the drivers, enablers and benefits and constantly create value through innovation.

Throughout these phases, the cloud assets or resources would need to be strategically identified, re-classified so that appropriate and commensurate protection measures can be offered.

FUTURE RESEARCH

Though the findings were empirically based, they had some limitations due to the study setting and sample size used. Within the study setting, it's difficult to find the exact quantum of the cloud services population; partly due to lack of a regulator. For example, one doesn't need any permissions to subscribe to Google apps. So in future, the study would extend coverage to a larger sample and then also to segregate the consumers from the providers. Further research will assess which resources are more susceptible to attacks, and to monitor the operations, and observe how organizations are actually leveraging on the cloud paradigm.

CONCLUSION

SMEs usually take the "crawl-walk-run" model in adopting cloud computing, whereby they deploy basic server virtualization, which evolves into a responsive dynamic internal IT, and finally, advances to cloud computing (Oltsik, 2010, p. 5).

Migration to cloud computing might inure operational and capital cost benefits, but how about the numerous applications and their performance? Whenever an organization has the capacity to do something that is unique and valuable, it is said to have competitive advantage (Piccoli, 2013).

For strategic reasons, CSPs must be able to utilize cloud resources to create value by either reducing supplier opportunity cost (SOC) or by increasing the customer willingness-to-pay (CWP) for its products and services or both (Piccoli, 2013). An important lesson that any organization would learn in business value strategy is that it is not enough to create value, it must be appropriated over time so that it is not eroded.

From the security perspective once the cloud is introduced, the perimeter security is said to be "non-existent", i.e. it is gone. At the same time, there are voluminous data which is valuable, and being transmitted at the "speed-of-light" velocity and in variety of forms. Incidentally, the threats are more persistent than they used to be a decade ago, and with sophisticated attacker profiles.

The VC3 model is intended to assist stakeholders in mitigating cloud security concerns, whilst strategizing to take the benefits of cloud computing to add value and to sustain it. The fact that appropriate mitigation measures can be identified, in itself would have positive impact on the organization.

As regards the taxonomy of threats, the list would aid stakeholders to benchmark the risk levels and know which issues and systems ought to be protected adequately. It also offers a common platform to assess the threats and proactively deploy protective, detective and deterrence mechanisms.

It is noted that cloud computing saves money by reducing the capital expenditure on hardware and software, as well as creating value and efficiency. It is clear that using cloud computing resources is more economical than building a network internally. It also simplifies the management of the infrastructure with less people to maintain it.

REFERENCES

Abatan, P. (2011). *What could Happen if you don't Employ Enterprise Rights Management*. Retrieved July 01, 2014, from www.enterprisedrm.info/

Anisseh, M., & Yussuf, R. b. (2011). A Fuzzy Group Decision Making Model for Multiple Criteria based on Borda Count. *International Journal of the Physical Sciences*, 6(3), 425–433.

Ayyub, B., & Lai, K.-L. (1992). Structural Reliability Assessement with Ambiguity & Vagueme=ness in Failure. *Naval Engineers Journal*, 104(3), 21–35. doi:10.1111/j.1559-3584.1992.tb02221.x

Ayyub, B. M. (2001). *Elicitation of Expert Opinions for Uncertainty & Risks*. CRC Press LLC. doi:10.1201/9781420040906

Beg, I., & Ashraf, S. (2009). Similarity Measures of Fuzzy Sets. *Applications & Computational Mathematics*, 8(2), 192–202.

CSA. (2010). *Top Threats to Cloud Computing V1.0*. CSA.

CSA. (2011). *Security Guidance for Critical Areas of Focus in Cloud Computing V3.0*. CSA.

Deng, Y., Kang, B. Y., Zhang, Y. J., Deng, X. Y., & Zhang, H. X. (2011). *A Modified Similarity Measure of Generalized Fuzzy Numbers. In Chinese Control & Decision Conference* (pp. 2173–2175). CCDC.

Dept. of Homeland Security. (2006). *Security Guidelines for the Petroleum Industry*. American Petroleum Institute (API) Publications.

Dhillon, G., & Torkzadeh, G. (2006). Value-focued Assessment of Information System Security in Organizations. *Information Systems Journal*, 16(3), 293–314. doi:10.1111/j.1365-2575.2006.00219.x

Fisch, E., & White, G. (2000). *Secure Computer & Networks: Analysis, Design & Implementation*. Boca Raton, FL: CRC Press.

Grobauer, B., Walloschek, T., & Stocker, E. (2011, March/April). Understanding Cloud Computing Vulnerabilities. *IEEE Security and Privacy*, 9(2), 50–57. doi:10.1109/MSP.2010.115

Hermann, D. S. (2003). *A Practical Guide to Security Engineering & Information Assurance*. Auerbach Publications, CRC Press.

Hsu, H.-M., & Chen, C.-T. (1996). Aggregation of Fuzzy Opinions Under Group Decision Making. *Fuzzy Sets and Systems*, 79(3), 279–285. doi:10.1016/0165-0114(95)00185-9

ITU-T. (2005). *International Telecommunications Union (ITU) - Telecoms Standards Recommendation X.805*. Geneva: ITU.

ITU-T. (2006). Security in Telecommunications and Information Technology: An Overview of Issues and the Deployment of Existing ITU-T Recommendations for Secure Telecommunications. Geneva: International Telecommunications Union (ITU).

ITU-T. (2007). Cyber-security Guide for Developing Countries. Geneva: International Telecommunications Union (ITU).

Katsikas, S. K. (2009). Risk Management. In J. R. Vacca (Ed.), Computer & Information Security Handbook (pp. 605-625). Morgan-Kaufmann, Inc.

Ko, R., & Lee, S. S. (2013). Cloud Computing Vulnerability Incidents: A Statistical Overview. *IEEE Spectrum*, 49(12).

Kortchinsky, K. (2009). *CloudBurst: A VMware Guest to Host Escape Story*. Las Vegas, NV: Immunity, Inc.

Kramer, F. (2012). *Musings on the Cloud - A Customer Oriented Comcept Formation to Cloud computing with respect to SME.* EMCIS2012 European Mediterranean & Middle Eastern Conference on Information Systems, Munich, Germany.

Lai, K.-L. (1992). *Generalized Uncertainty in Structural Reliability Assessment.* College Park, MD: University of Maryland.

Marinescu, D. (2014). *Cloud Computing: Cloud Vulnerabilities.* Retrieved July 6, 2014, from TechNet Magazine: www.technet.microsoft.com/en-us/magazine/dn271884.aspx

Marston, S., Li, Z., Bandyopadhyay, S., Zhang, J., & Ghalsasi, A. (2011). Cloud Computing: The Business Perspective. *Decision Support Systems, 51*(1), 176–189. doi:10.1016/j.dss.2010.12.006

McEachem, C. (2001). Technology Risks: Don't Panic - Financial Services Firms Seem to Have Cyber-Risk Under Control. *Wall Street Technology, 38.*

McKinsey & Co. (2012). *Perspectives of Digital Business.* McKinsey Center for Business Technology.

Mell, P., & Grance, T. (2011). *The NIST Definition of Cloud Computing.* National Institute of Standards and Technology (NIST). Retrieved June 2014, from www.csrc.nist.gov/publications/nistpubs/800-145/SP800-145.pdf

Microsoft. (2005). *Security Guide for Small Businesses.* Microsoft Corporation. Retrieved from www.asbdc-us.org

Ngai, E., & Wat, F. (2005). Fuzzy Decision Support System for Risk Analysis in e-Commerce Development. *Decision Support Systems, 40*(2), 235–255. doi:10.1016/j.dss.2003.12.002

NIST. (2008). *Taxonomies of Security Metrics. National Institute of Standards & Technology (NIST). doi:Elizabeth Chew.* Marianne Swanson, Kevin Stine, Nadya Bartol, Anthony Brown & Will Robinson.

Oltsik, J. (2010). *What's Needed for Cloud Computing? - Focus on Networking and WAN Optimization. Enterprise Security Group.* ESG.

Oracle. (n.d.). *Oracle VM Server for SPARC 3.1 Security Guide.* Retrieved from Oracle Technology Network: www.docs.oracle.com/cd/E38405_01/

Ozier, W. (2002). Risk Assessment. In *Information Security Management Handbook.* CRC Press.

Pande, D., & Jog, V. (2014). Study of Security Problem in Cloud. *International Journal of Engineering Trends & Technology*, 34-36.

Pappis, C., & Karacapilidis, N. (1993). A Comparative Assessment of Measures of Similarity of Fuzzy Values. *Fuzzy Sets and Systems, 56*(2), 171–174. doi:10.1016/0165-0114(93)90141-4

Pedrycz, W., & Gomide, F. (2007). *Fuzzy Systems Engineering: Towards Human Centric Computng.* John Wiley & Sons. doi:10.1002/9780470168967

Piccoli, G. (2013). *Information Systems for Managers: Text & Cases* (2nd ed.). John Wiley & Sons, Inc.

Porter, M. E. (1980). *Competitive Strategy: Techniques for Analyzing Industries & Competitors.* New York: Free Press.

Sahandi, R., Alkhalil, A., & Opara-Martins, J. (2013). Cloud Computing from SMEs Perspectives: A Survey-based Investigation. *Journal of Information Technology Management, 24*(1), 1–12.

Shaurette, K. M. (2002). The Building Blocks of Information Security. In Information Security Management Handbook.Academic Press.

Shelly, G. B., & Vermaat, M. E. (2011). *Discovering Computers: Living in a Digital World*. Course Technology, Cengage Learning.

Singh, S. (2013). *Data Security Issues and Strategy on Cloud Computing. Moradabad: International Journal of Science, Engineering and Technology Research*.

Smallwood, R. F. (2012). *Safeguarding Critical e-Documents: Implementing a Program for Securing Confidential Information Assets*. John Wiley & Sons, Inc. doi:10.1002/9781119204909

Sood, A., & Enbody, R. (2013). Targeted Cyber-attacks: A Superset of Advanced Persistent Threats. *IEEE Security and Privacy, 11*(1).

Steiner, T. (2012). *An Introduction to Securing a Cloud Environment*. SANS Institute.

US Gov't. (2009, May). *The White House*. Retrieved July 01, 2014, from The Comprehensive National Cybersecurity Initiative: www.whitehouse.gov/issues/foreign-policy/cybersecurity/national-initiative

Vaquero, L. R.-M., & Moran, D. (2011, January). Locking the Sky: A Survey on IaaS Cloud Security. *Computing, 91*(1), 93–118. doi:10.1007/s00607-010-0140-x

Vidalis, S., & Jones, A. (2005). Analyzing Threat Agents & Their Attributes. Pontypridd, UK: School of Computing, University of Glamorgan.

Vogl, S. (n.d.). Secure Hypervisor. *Technische Universitat Muncheon*.

Walker, J. (2009). Internet Security. In J. R. Vacca (Ed.), Computer & Information Security Handbook (pp. 93-117). Morgan-Kaufmann, Inc. doi:10.1016/B978-0-12-374354-1.00007-8

Whitman, M. E., & Mattord, H. (2005). Principles of Information Security (2nd ed.). Thomson Course Technology.

Xu, Z. (2005). An Approach Based on Similarity Measure to Multiple Attribute Decision Making with Trapezoid Fuzzy Linguistic Variables. In J. C. Siekmann (Ed.), Fuzzy Systems & Knowledge Discovery (LNAI), (Vol. 3613, pp. 110-117). Springer. doi:10.1007/11539506_13

Ye, N. (2008). *Secure Computer & Network Systems: Modeling, Analysis & Design*. John Wiley & Sons. doi:10.1002/9780470023273

Yeboah-Boateng, E. O. (2013a). *Cyber-Security Challenges with SMEs in Developing Economies: Issues of Confidentiality, Integrity & Availablity (CIA)*. Aalborg University.

Yeboah-Boateng, E. O. (2013b, February). Fuzzy Similarity Measures Approach in Benchmarking Taxonomies of Threats against SMEs in Developing Economies. *Canadian Journal on Computing in Mathematics, Natural Sciences. Engineering in Medicine*, 34–44.

Yeboah-Boateng, E. O. (2013c, December). Of Social Engineers and Corporate Espionage Agents: How Prepared Are SMEs in Developing Economies? *Journal of Electronics and Communication Engineering Research*, 14-22.

Yeboah-Boateng, E. O., & Essandoh, K. A. (2013, November). Cloud Computing: The Level of Awareness amongst Small and Meduim Enterprises (SMEs) in Developing Economies. *Journal of Emerging Trends in Computing & Information Sciences*, 832-839.

Zadeh, L. (1978). Fuzzy Sets as a Basis for a Theory of Possibility. *Fuzzy Sets and Systems*, *1*(1), 3–28. doi:10.1016/0165-0114(78)90029-5

Zhu, J. (2010). Cloud Computing Technologies and Applications. In B. F. Escalante (Ed.), Handbook of Cloud Computing (pp. 21-45). Springer Science & Business Media. doi:10.1007/978-1-4419-6524-0_2

ADDITIONAL READING

Andress, J. (2011). *The Basics of Information Security: Understanding the Fundamentals of InfoSec in Theory and Practice*. Elsevier Inc.

Graaf, S. V. D., & Washida, Y. (2007). *Information Communications Technologies and Emerging Business Strategies*. Idea Group Publishing. doi:10.4018/978-1-59904-234-3

Hayden, L. (2010). *IT Security Metrics: A Practical Framework for Measureing Security & Protecting Data*. The McGraw Hill Companies.

Keeney, R. L., & von Winterfeldt, D. (2011). A Value Model for Evaluating Homeland Security Decisions. *Risk Analysis*, *31*(9), 1470–1487. doi:10.1111/j.1539-6924.2011.01597.x PMID:21388426

Meyer, M. A., & Booker, J. M. (2001). *Eliciting and Analyzing Experts Judgment: A Practical Guide. American Statistical Association & the Soceity for Industrial & Applied Mathematics. Cox, Earl (1994). The Fuzzy Systems Handbook: A Practitioner's Guide to Building, Using and Maintaining Fuzzy Systems.* Academic Press, Inc.

Munier, N. (2011). *A Strategy for Using Multicriteria Analysis in Decision Making: A Guide for Simple and Complex Environmental Projects*. Springer Science Business Media. doi:10.1007/978-94-007-1512-7

Taticchi, P. (2010). *Business Performance Measurement and Management: New Contexts, Themes and Challenges*. Springer-Verlag Berlin Heidelberg. doi:10.1007/978-3-642-04800-5

Turban, E., Volonino, L., & Wood, G. R. (2013). *Information Technology for Management: Advancing Sustainable Profitable Business Growth*. John Wiley & Sons, Inc.

KEY TERMS AND DEFINITIONS

Appropriating: This is a concept of strategy aimed at ensuring that the value created is not eroded away, especially with substituted products or services. Appropriating one's value implies ensuring that the product or service is costly and difficult to imitate, and measures are in place to sustain it over time.

Benchmarking: The process of comparing an organization's business or security metrics with those of its sectoral best practices. It assumes that a measured or an observed construct is compared with an acceptable best practice in order to make informed strategic decisions. So, the taxonomies are geared towards creating acceptable benchmarks within the sector.

Concerns: Interests expressed in business activities or issues, especially when they could affect the operations if ignored. They are usually challenges that influence the way business transacts are conducted. Concerns are issues that crave for the attention of business executives to effect changes so that the business objectives can be met and sustained.

Cyber-Security: A business concern, rather than a technical problem. It seeks to ensure that functions of the business are protected, and to ensure the smooth and secure operations and applications of the business systems and processes. It also protects the data produced, processed and stored by the business entity. In essence, cyber-security is to safeguard the information and technology assets of the organization.

Strategy: An intent to establish a set of activities to achieve the set objectives. It involves making the best possible decision choices amongst options available, given certain constraints. So, business strategy is simply the executive decision choices on how to create value and ensure that the created value is sustained over long time.

Value-Added: Value is anything unique and worthy to someone. It is usually convertible to cash and expressed in moentary terms. Value-added connotes the enhancements that a business makes on its products and services. It gives the organization an edge or competitive advantage over its competition.

Chapter 6
Dynamic Virtual Machine Placement in Cloud Computing

Arnab Kumar Paul
Virginia Tech, USA

Bibhudatta Sahoo
National Institute of Technology Rourkela, India

ABSTRACT

The aim of cloud computing is to enable users to access resources on demand. The number of users is continuously increasing. In order to fulfil their needs, we need more number of physical machines and data centers. The increase in the number of physical machines is directly proportional to the consumption of energy. This gives us one of the major challenges; minimization of energy consumption. One of the most effective ways to minimize the consumption of energy is the optimal virtual machine placement on physical machines. This chapter focuses on finding the solution to the problem of dynamic virtual machine placement for the optimized consumption of energy. An energy consumption model is built which takes into account the states of physical machines and live migration of virtual machines. On top of this, the cloud computing model is built. Unlike centralized approaches towards virtual machine placement which result in many unreachable solutions, a decentralized approach is used in this chapter which provides a list of virtual machine migrations for their optimal placement.

INTRODUCTION

Cloud computing is a technique for helping users to have access to computing resources on demand with very minimal effort in management. It has emerged as a popular computing model in order to support processing of large scale data. There are several cloud service providers, for example, Amazon, Microsoft, Google, IBM and Yahoo which have built platforms for other enterprises and cloud users in order to access the services provided in the cloud.

The areas in which cloud computing is used vary from nuclear physics to geothermal experiments. Thus we need data centers to help provide powerful computation resources for these vital areas. A Data Center (DC) consists of a large number of Physical Machines (PM) arranged on racks and packed densely

DOI: 10.4018/978-1-5225-1721-4.ch006

in order to increase space utilization. In cloud computing, one of the key concepts for data center management is virtualization. The most important advantage of virtualization is the capacity to run many instances of operating system in a single PM thus making maximum use of the hardware capacities of the PM which helps immensely in saving money for energy and hardware costs. These individual instances of operating system are called Virtual Machines (VM). Thus, in cloud computing, users access the computing resources of a DC with the help of VMs.

The scheduling of VMs in DCs and VM scheduling on PMs form an important part in cloud computing now more than ever because of the growing number of users. VM scheduling has a massive effect on the system's performance and throughput. Thus, the two types of placement of VMs include Virtual Machine Placement (VMP) over DCs and VMP over PMs. The effect that VMP provides is directly related to the Quality of Service (QoS) provided by the services in the cloud. The major objective of VMP is to make maximum utilization of a data center, thus making use of a lesser number of DCs. This helps in achieving more availability and flexibility of DCs, while reducing the costs incurred during operating and maintaining hardware.

Anatomy of Cloud Computing

In cloud computing, virtualization is the most important factor in giving dynamic and scalable architectures. Apart from providing the important aspects of resource sharing and scalability, virtualization also contributes to the capability of virtual machine migration between PMs in order to balance the load (Jones, 2010).

Figure 1 depicts the key elements in a single node in the environment of cloud computing. The component of virtualization in a cloud node is given by the Hypervisor, which is also called as the Virtual Machine Monitor (VMM). This layer is responsible for providing the interface of executing many instances of operating systems in one PM. Thus, hypervisors create virtual machine objects which provide encapsulation for operating system, applications and configuration. Another important aspect in a cloud node known as device emulation is given either in the hypervisor or as a VM. VM management takes place both in local PMs as well as in global DCs.

Thus in order to form a DC, the cloud node shown in Figure 1 is multiplied over a network provided with the management orchestration over the complete infrastructure:

- **Hypervisors:** This is the initial level of a PM (a single cloud node). It provides the virtual operating platform, thus managing the execution of guest operating systems, known as VMs. The VMs share the virtualized hardware resources of the cloud node. One of the best examples of hypervisors for production environments is the Linux Kernel Virtual Machine (KVM).
- **Device Emulation:** Hypervisors are responsible for providing the platform for sharing virtualized physical resources. But in order to achieve complete virtualization, the whole cloud node must be virtualized. This is the job of a device emulator. QEMU is the example of a complete package combining emulator and hypervisor.
- **Virtual Networking:** As the number of cloud users grow, the number of VMs increases. In order to achieve intensified networking system, virtual machines are required to communicate on a virtualized network rather than on a physical level. This reduces the load on the physical infrastructure of the system. Virtual switches are also introduced for effective communication among the VMs.

Figure 1. Core elements of cloud node

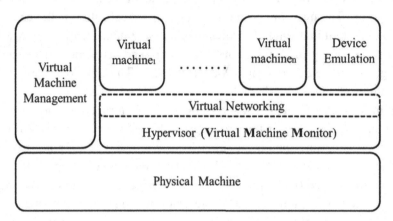

Figure 2. Cloud computing architecture

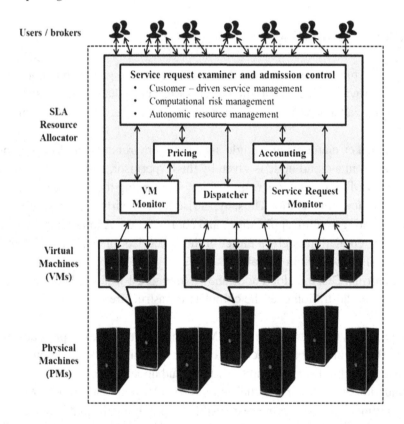

Cloud Computing Architecture

In the environment of cloud computing, cloud users are dependent on Cloud Service Providers (CSP) for fulfilling their needs. Therefore, certain QoS parameters need to be maintained by CSPs which are mentioned in the Service Level Agreement (SLA). To achieve this, traditional resource management architecture cannot be used. Thus, we have market oriented architecture of cloud computing which is shown in Figure 2.

The market oriented architecture of cloud computing has the following components.

Users or brokers acting on behalf of the cloud users, submit their job requests to the cloud data center for processing.

The interface between CSP and user is provided by the SLA Resource Allocator. When a user submits a user request, a decision is made by the Service Request Examiner whether to accept or reject the request. It checks the requirements of the QoS parameters. It takes the decision by looking at the information of the resource availability provided by the VM Monitor and workload availability provided by the Service Request Monitor, to ensure no overloading of resources occur. After consideration of these parameters, user requests are assigned to the VMs and a decision is taken regarding the resource requirements of the allotted VMs.

Pricing operation takes decisions regarding the prices to be charged from the cloud users. These prices can be charged on the basis of the user request, or the time of submission, or availability of cloud resources, or simply a fixed rate. This aids in prioritizing the resource allocation process in a cloud DC.

Another important operation is known as Accounting which keeps an account of the actual consumption of resources. This helps in the calculation of the final price to be charged from the cloud user. It also helps in making an informed decision by the service examiner by keeping a tab of the historical resource usage consumption.

VM Monitor keeps a periodic check on the requirements of various resources and the availability of VMs. Dispatcher is accountable for initiating the execution of the user requests on the VMs allotted. Service Request Monitor has the important task of maintaining an account of job requests' execution.

Virtual Machine Placement in Cloud Computing

A two-tiered approach is followed when distributing the VM requests. There are a large number of PMs in a DC. A CSP can have many DCs. The first step is to optimally distribute the VM requests over DCs. Next, the requests are distributed over PMs.

The virtual machine placement can be of the following two types.

- Static virtual machine placement
- Dynamic virtual machine placement

Static Virtual Machine Placement

Static VMP is performed when system is in offline mode or during startup of the system. This forms the initial VMP in the environment of cloud computing. There isn't any previous VM mapping. This VMP does not take into consideration the VM states, PM states and the rate of VM requests.

Below is the diagrammatic explanation of the centralized model for static virtual machine placement following the two tier approach. First, VM placement over data centers and then the placement of requests over PMs in a particular data center are shown.

Figure 3 represents the flow of VM Requests from the users till they are distributed over data centers.

Cloud users use the services provided by the cloud service provider and issue requests. These requests are in the form of virtual machine requests since every request will be completed on a virtual machine

Figure 3. Static virtual machine placement over data centers

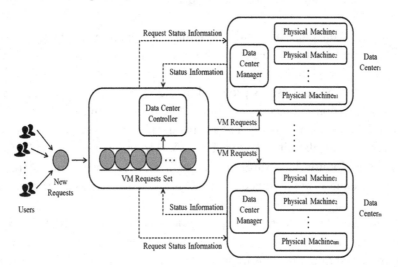

on top of a physical machine. The VM requests comprise the VM Requests Set. Every data center has multiple physical machines and a Data Center Manager to control all the PMs. In order to control all the data centers, a Data Center Controller is used.

The data center controller receives the VM requests set. It then requests status information from all the data center managers which have the information of their respective data centers. The VM requests contain information of the resources (CPU, RAM, Network etc.) needed in order to complete the request. The data center managers send information of the available resources to the controller. The data center controller optimally distributes VM requests to the data center managers following a heuristic algorithm. This approach to distribute VM requests is a Centralized Approach, where the decision to schedule requests depends on the central controller.

Figure 4 depicts the static placement of virtual machine requests in physical machines in a single data center.

In a data center, there are multiple physical machines on top of which lies the Virtual Machine Monitor [VMM] (Hypervisor). The VMM has the responsibility for virtualization in PMs. The data center manager sends requests to the VMMs to provide the status information of all the physical machines. The data center manager already has the VM requests' information. Upon arrival of the status information from the VMMs, the DC manager places the VM requests to the individual physical machines in order to process them and sends back the response to the cloud users. The placement of VM requests over physical machines is also a centralized approach as the decision is taken by a central authority, in this case the data center manager.

Dynamic Virtual Machine Placement

If an existing mapping of VMs onto PMs is present, we go for dynamic placement of virtual machines. The main goal of dynamic VM placement is to achieve optimum solutions from the already available mapping of VMs at minimal cost. The optimality parameters may vary from minimization of the response

Figure 4. Static virtual machine placement over physical machines

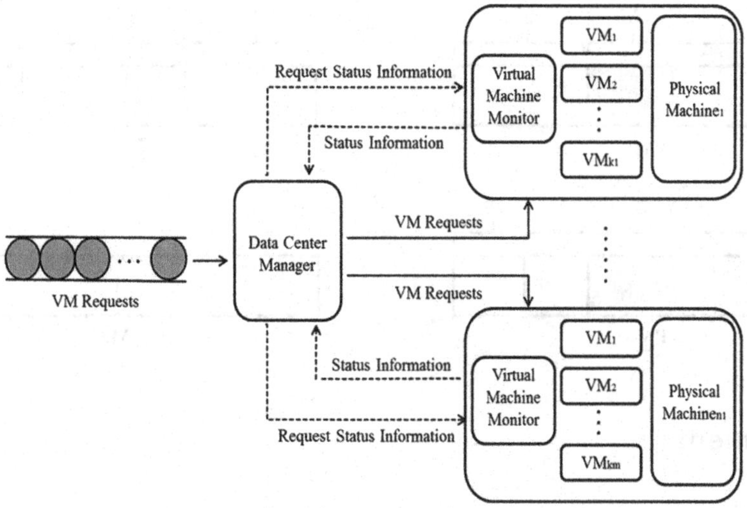

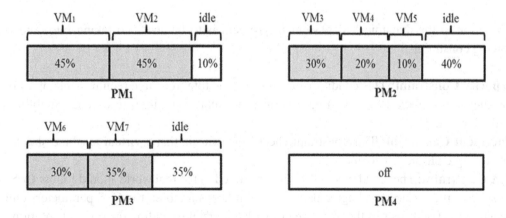

time to the minimization of energy consumption or a combination of multiple parameters. The rate of arrival of user requests as well as the states of both VMs and PMs needs to be considered while taking a decision. Below is an example of dynamic virtual machine placement.

Figure 5 shows the initial solution (i) for the dynamic VM placement problem. Seven VMs are placed over four PMs. PM_4 is in off state since no VM is running on it. Assuming that all the PMs have same amount of resources, the VMs should be dynamically distributed over different PMs in order to reduce energy consumption.

One such solution is shown in Figure 6. In order to reach solution s_1 from (i), live migrations need to be performed. The list of migrations is: VM_5 from PM_2 to PM_3, migration of VM_1 from PM_1 to PM_2 and finally migrate VM_4 from PM_2 to PM_1.

Dynamic VMP is explained in detail later in the chapter.

Figure 5. Initial solution i

Figure 6. Target solution s₁

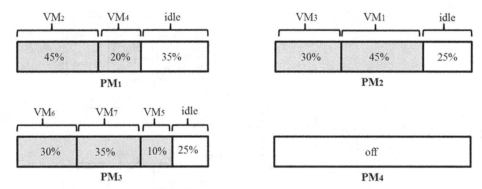

Problem Statement

The dynamic virtual machine placement problem has been solved by many researchers. But they haven't considered the live migrations and thus may provide unreachable solutions to the problem. The primary objective of the research in this chapter is to model a cloud computing framework such that the dynamic virtual placement problem can be solved while providing the live VM migrations to be executed, in order to reach the solution.

This can be elaborated as follows:

- The motive is to model the dynamic placement problem in such a way that the states of virtual machines and physical machines are taken into account. Also the list of executable live VM migrations must be provided so that the optimal solution can be obtained.
- The problem if solved using centralized evolutionary techniques has a risk of providing unreachable solutions. Thus, decentralized approach using congestion game model must be used in order to provide the solutions to the dynamic virtual machine placement problem.
- In real world scenario, physical machines may act selfishly and not cooperate to achieve an optimal solution to the problem. Thus both cooperative and non-cooperative approaches should be discussed in order to reach to an optimal solution.

The solution to the dynamic VM placement problem is to be achieved taking into consideration the following constraints:

- **Capacity Constraint**: This condition ensures that the total resource requirements of all the VMs running on a specific PM should be less than or equal to the total resource availability of that particular PM.
- **Placement Constraint**: This constraint checks the criteria that a virtual machine should run on only a single physical machine.
- **SLA Constraint**: The cloud model to be incorporated in the real world should follow QoS parameters. Thus the service level agreement constraint keeps a tab on the QoS parameters enlisted in the agreement and ensures that they are not violated when providing the optimal solution.

BACKGROUND

Dynamic VM Placement in Cloud Computing

Dynamic placement of VMs places VMs based on an existing mapping which is in contrast to the static placement of VMs which starts with no mapping. Dynamic VM placement aims to reach optimal solutions from the existing mapping at minimum cost. This would not shut down or stop the already running VMs, thus the placement solution should provide the list of live migrations to be executed in order to reach the optimal state from the existing state. The whole process is in contrast to the static placement of VMs where VMs can be stopped and restarted which increases the energy consumption and thus degrades the complete system performance. In order to execute dynamic placement of VMs, states of physical machines should also be considered.

Dynamic VM Placement problem can be illustrated in Figures 5, 6, and 7. Figure 5 shows the initial solution (i) for the dynamic VM placement problem. Distribution of seven VMs over four PMs is shown. PM_4 is in off state since no VM is running on it. Assuming that all the PMs have same amount of resources, the VMs should be dynamically distributed over different PMs in order to reduce energy consumption. One such solution is shown in Figure 6. The list of migrations has already been given in a previous section. We can reach another solution s_2 from (i) as shown in Figure 7. Since there isn't much space in PM_1 and PM_2 for the direct interchange of VM_1 and VM_3, there needs to be an involvement of PM_3. Thus the migrations needed for solution s_2 to be reached are: the extra migration of VM_3 from PM_2 to PM_3, VM_1's migration from PM_1 to PM_2 and migrating VM_3 from PM_3 to PM_1. But in order to reach s_2 from (i) will result in more cost than to reach solution s_1 from (i) because of the migrations involving larger VMs. VM_1 and VM_3 could have been stopped and restarted in order to facilitate direct interchange but that would involve more cost. Also the involvement of PM_4 for the interchange of VM_1 and VM_3 would result in higher costs since it would then consider the cost of state change for PM_4.

Dynamic virtual machine placement problem is NP-hard. There have been existing researches where attempts have been made to map the dynamic VM placement problem to bin-packing problem which led to the development of evolutionary algorithms like, genetic algorithms or particle swarm optimization algorithm. As explained before, many problems arise when VMs have to be placed dynamically. While the evolutionary algorithms like genetic algorithms tries to provide optimal solutions to the problem, there may be solutions which are unreachable.

Figure 7. Target solution s_2

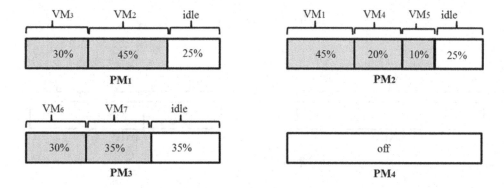

Figure 8 shows an example of unreachable solution to the dynamic VM placement problem. Figure 8(a) shows the placement of 4 VMs onto 2 PMs which form the initial solution sol_0. The optimal solution 'sol' is shown in Figure 8(b) which brings down the energy consumption by a considerable amount. But the solution is unreachable since there is no executable migration route from (a) to (b). In order to achieve the solution, a third PM has to be switched on to handle the migrations which will again consume more energy. Thus, in case of evolutionary algorithms, judgment has to be made whether the optimal solution is reachable or not.

In this chapter, decentralized decision making is used with the help of congestion game theory in order to find solutions to the dynamic VM placement problem. In Congestion Games, a group of players is modeled to share a resource set. Every player selects a subset of resources from the resource set in order to maximize the payoff (Milchtaich, 1996). Here, PMs will be modeled as players which will select a subset of VMs from the VM set in order to minimize the consumption of energy. Nash Equilibrium is attained after a finite number of iterations. This intelligent algorithm uses the initial mapping to obtain the optimum solution and also generates the list of executable VM live migrations to reach the optimal state. Thus no solution is unreachable.

Game Theory

Turocy et al. (2001) defines game theory as the formal study of cooperation and conflict. Hotz (2006) describes a game as a set of players and their possibilities to play the game by following some rules (strategies). The players can be individuals, agents or organizations. The main subject of game theory is the situation where the result is mattered not only by the decision of a single player but others as well.

The earliest instance of formal game theoretic analysis is Antoine Cournot's study of duopoly in 1838. In 1921, a formal theory of games was suggested by Emile Borel. This was further studied upon by John von Neumann's theory of parlor games in 1928. The basic terminology and setup of game theory was established in Theory of Games and Economic Behavior by von Neumann and Oskar Morgenstern in 1944. John Nash in 1950 showed that the games with finite number of players always have a point of

Figure 8. Unreachable solution

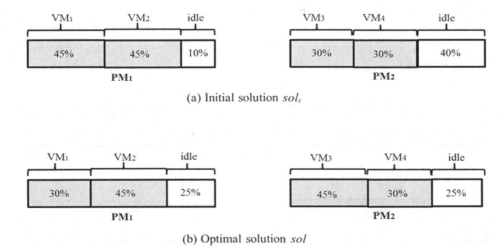

(a) Initial solution sol_0

(b) Optimal solution sol

equilibrium where the players choose their best strategy taking into consideration the strategies of other players. This equilibrium is known as Nash Equilibrium, named after John Nash. This pivotal point in non-cooperative game theory has been used in various fields from sociology, biology to computer science.

There are mainly two types of game scenarios:

- Cooperative Game
- Non-Cooperative Game

Cooperative Game

Xhafa et al. (2010) defines cooperative game as the game scenario where players form coalitions in advance to discuss their actions. Cooperative game theory investigates such coalition games by studying how successfully a coalition divides its proceeds.

The applications of cooperative game theory are mainly seen in cases related to political science or international relations. In cloud computing, cooperative game theory is used when data centers are managed by a single service provider or the providers form a coalition such that the strategies of virtual machine placement are known by all the physical machines and respective actions are taken to maximize the payoffs of all the SPs.

Non-Cooperative Game

The term non-cooperative implies that this type of game models the process of players who are making choices thinking about their own interest.

The non-cooperative game theory relates to realistic cloud computing where the service providers do not form coalitions and a decision is made considering the selfish actions of individual providers who want to maximize their profit.

Games in Normal Form

The representation of a game in normal form or strategic form is given by Jackson (2011):

- The set of players $N = \{1 \ldots n\}$.
- Player i has a set of actions a_i which are normally referred to as pure strategies.
- The set of all pure strategies is denoted by $a = (a_1 \ldots a_n)$.
- Player i has a payoff represented as the function of the action vectors is denoted by $u_i: A \rightarrow I R$, where u_i (a) is i's payoff if a is the strategy taken.

Normal form games are often represented in the form of a table. The most common example is prisoner's dilemma represented in Figure 9.

In prisoner's dilemma, the number of players is two with each having two pure strategies, where $a_i = \{C, D\}$; C is for cooperate and D is for defect. C indicates the payoff to the row player (player 1) as a function of the pair of actions, while D is the payoff to the column player (player 2). The game is

Figure 9. A prisoner's dilemma game

Player 2

		C	D
Player 1	C	-1, -1	-3, 0
	D	0, -3	-2, -2

explained as follows. Both the players are caught committing a crime and are investigated in different cells in a police station. The prosecutor comes to each of them and tells each of them:

If you provide a confession and accept to testify against the other; and if the partner doesn't confess; you will be set free. If both of you accept committing the crime, you will be both sent to jail for two years. If you do not accept committing the crime but your partner does, you will be given a sentence of three years imprisonment. If none of you confess; only one year punishment will be given due to the lack of evidence.

So the payoff matrix shows the imprisonment time in years. The term cooperate means that the partners cooperate with each other. The term defect means that you are accepting the crime and agreeing to testify, and so you are breaking the agreement which you two have.

Nash Equilibrium

If a set of strategies for the players constitute a Nash Equilibrium, it means that none of the players can benefit by altering his/her strategy unilaterally.

A strategy a_i is a best reply, also known as a best response, of player i to a set of strategies $a_{-i} \in a_{-i}$ for the other players if

$$u_i(a_i, a_{-i}) \geq u_i(a'_i, a_{-i}) ; \forall a'_i \tag{1}$$

A profile of strategies $a \in A$ is a pure strategy Nash equilibrium if a_i is a best reply to a_i for each i. That is, a is a Nash equilibrium if

$$u_i(a_i, a_{-i}) \geq u_i(a'_i, a_{-i}) ; \forall i, a'_i \tag{2}$$

A pure strategy Nash equilibrium only states that the action taken by each agent be the best against the actual equilibrium actions taken by the other players, and not necessarily against all possible actions of the other players.

In prisoner's dilemma, Nash Equilibrium occurs if both player 1 and 2 cooperate (C). If any of the players change his/her strategy, no player can benefit.

RELATED WORK

Dynamic VM Placement Problem

Hyser et al. (2008) studied the virtual machine placement scenario by developing an autonomic controller which dynamically maps the virtual machines onto the physical machines by following the users' policies. This work also differentiated the static VM placement and dynamic VM placement. The algorithms dealing with static VM placement start with no initial mapping. There isn't any need for these algorithms to consider the intermediate steps or the number of moves taken to reach the final state. This is in sharp contrast to the algorithms dealing with dynamic VM placement problem which must find optimal solutions from an initial mapping.

In 2007, Wood et al. (2007) presented a system called Sandpiper, which was used for automatic monitoring and detection of system hotspots. It also provided a new mapping of VMs onto physical hosts and initiated the migrations too. Algorithms for hotspot detection focus on signaling a need for migration of VMs whenever SLA violations are detected either implicitly or explicitly. In the same year, Bobroff et al. (2007) implemented an algorithm based on first-fit approximation to find solution to the problem of dynamic VM placement having the goal of price minimization. The problem was mapped as a bin packing one where the minimum number of PMs to be needed for the VMs was calculated and then a remapping was done for VMs onto PMs. The main disadvantage of the algorithm was that, it didn't look for unreachable solutions from the initial mapping.

A two phase process was developed by Hermenier et al. (2009) in order to find solutions to the dynamic VM placement problem. The consolidation manager named Entropy found solutions in two phases. The first phase finds out a placement keeping in mind the constraints, VM set and the CPU requirements. It also provides the likable configuration plan to achieve the desired mapping. The second phase tries to improve the result computed in the first phase. It takes into account a refined set of constraints and tries to minimize the number of migrations required. However very simple parameters are considered in this work and server consolidation is not taken as a factor.

Liao et al (2012) affirmed that dynamic VM placement problem faced three major challenges; multi-dimensional constraints, the initial state and the intermediary steps. They proposed a system called GreenMap which was a VM-based management framework to be able to execute live VM migrations considering the resource consumption of servers and energy consumption. Simulated annealing based heuristic is used for the optimization problem under the constraint of multi-dimensional resource consumption. The two objectives namely, reduction in energy consumption and performance degradation are balanced to give the desired output. But the GreenMap system doesn't address heterogeneous physical hosts which invariably form the real life server clusters.

Cooperative Game Theory

Wei et al. (2010) uses cooperative game theory in order to find solution of the QOS constrained problem of allocation of resources. Here problem solution is done in 2 steps. First optimal problem solution is done by every participant independently without resource multiplexing. Next a mechanism is designed by considering strategies which are multiplexed, of all the players. Existence of Nash Equilibrium is shown if resource allocation problem has feasible solutions. This paper creates a useful analytical tool for the solution of optimal scheduling problem.

No consideration for multi-tier architecture of web services and lack of emphasis on stable placement of applications are the drawbacks in Wei et al. (2010). These disadvantages are removed by Lee et al. (2010) where an evolutionary approach of game theory is designed for stable and adaptive placement of applications. This paper implements Nuage which uses an evolutionary game theoretic approach in order for stable adaptive deployment of applications. The main goal of this work is to deploy N applications on M hosts with the goal that applications adapt their locations and allocation of resources is done on the basis of resource and workload availability. In this work only CPU time share is considered for assignment of resources to each VM.

General colocation game and process colocation game were introduced by Londono et al. (2009) in order to distribute resources to infrastructure providers. This work considers a cooperative game theoretic framework where the objectives for resource management were to maximize resource utilization and minimize total cost of the allocated resources. The work also proves that achieving nash equilibrium is NP-complete. The main drawback of this work is that although it provides best response computation, it is an expensive framework.

Cooperative VM management for multi-organization environment in cloud computing was done by Niyato et al. (2011). Three types of resources are considered for VM management; private cloud, on-demand plans and reservation of public CSP. The algorithm works in two steps. First, an optimization model is formulated for cooperative organizations and then, an optimal VM allocation problem is solved in order to minimize the total cost. This work doesn't consider the stochastic nature of demand.

Resource allocation in Horizontal Dynamic Cloud Federation Platform (HDCF) environment is studied by Hassan et al. (2011).The work presents a cost effective and scalable solution to the resource allocation problem using game theory. It studies both cooperative and non-cooperative resource allocation games as well as both decentralized and centralized algorithms are presented in order to find optimal solutions. The major drawback in this framework is that it doesn't take into consideration the dynamic nature of clouds where hundreds of clouds leave and join the federation in a dynamic manner.

Mao et al. (2013) worked upon the problem of cloud service deployment by modeling it as a congestion game. Only cost and quality of resources were considered. Every service acts as a player which chooses a subset of resources for the maximization of his payoff. It is shown that Nash equilibrium is reached in polynomial time. This work can be further implemented in seeking solution to the placement of multiple cooperative heterogeneous components over many cloud services.

New resource allocation game models (CT-RAG, CS-RAG) were introduced for problem solving in cloud computing by Sun et al. (2014). Existence of Nash equilibrium is shown but the work considers static game with no representation of fairness of tasks. The problem of allocation of resources for PMs in cloud computing based on the uncertainty principle of game theory and coalition formulation was studied by Pillai et al. (2014). It is shown that the solution gives higher request satisfaction and better resource utilization.

Non-Cooperative Game Theory

Teng et al. (2010) introduced a novel Bayesian Nash Equilibrium allocation algorithm in order to find solution to the resource management problem in cloud computing. It analyzes the bid proportion model where users are assigned resources in proportion to their bids. The allocation solutions reach Nash equilibrium by gambling in stages which is further simplified by considering that competition among users is for the same job type consisting of a sequential order of same type of jobs. In this model, the shortcoming is that bidders fix the resource price and problems of response delay are not addressed. In the same year, Sun et al. in (2010) used continuous double auction and Nash equilibrium for the allocation of resources in cloud based on the M/M/1 queueing system. Sun et al. (2010) took performance QOS and economic QOS as optimization objectives. The work in Sun et al. (2010) greatly improves the Quality of Service in terms of performance and economy. It is fair to both resources and users by considering execution cost of 'pay per use' services and the average time of execution of user jobs.

The problem of service provisioning was studied by Ardagna et al. (2011). IaaS providers host applications of SaaS providers such that every SaaS complies with the SLA (revenue and penalty) requirements. SaaS providers maximize revenues while cost of resources by IaaS is minimized. IaaS providers maximize revenue by providing virtualized resources. The following assumptions for SaaS providers are taken in this work.

- A single web service application is hosted on a single VM.
- Same web service application implemented by many VMs can run in parallel.
- All the virtual machines are uniform in terms of CPU and RAM capacity.

IaaS providers offer flat VMs, on-demand VMs and on-spot VMs for which SaaS providers pay. The service provisioning problem is formulated and solved using game theory.

The main drawbacks in this work are listed as follows.

- Validation of the solution is missing by experiments in real world environment.
- The heuristic solutions adopted by IaaS and SaaS providers are not compared.

These drawbacks in 2011 were worked upon by Ardagna et al. (2013).

Kong et al. (2011) worked upon resource allocation among selfish virtual machines by applying stochastic approximation methods. It thwarted non-cooperative behavior of the VMs. The proposed approach is not implemented in a real world virtualized cloud system. A cooperative game theoretic resource splitting solution in cloud computing was formulated by Lu et al. (2012). Here multiple cloud providers cooperate with one another in order to form a cloud federation which ensures greater profit since provider's capability to serve for public cloud users is enhanced. A game theoretic policy is formed to aid SPs in the decision making process. The work's performance is not gauged for many cloud environments.

The co-scheduling problem addressed by Dhillon et al. (2013) involves a central authority which provides solution to constrained optimization problem with an objective function. This works provides an alternate game theoretic perspective using stable matching theory which reduces the Stable Roommates Problem (SRP) to Stable Marriages Problem (SMP). Chen et al. (2014) studied the use of game theory for live migration prediction over cloud computing. It is shown that game theory improves Gilbert-Elliot model for the prediction of the probability on dirty page.

PROBLEM FORMULATION

Energy Consumption Model

The major part of energy consumption in a data center is produced by PMs which are running. There are other causes of energy consumption such as cooling apparatus but they form a much lesser percentage. Here we focus on the energy consumption or PMs which is divided into three sections.

Energy Consumption in Different States

Existing research indicates that energy consumption can be minimized by the adjustment of the states of PMs. Here 4 states of a PM are considered:

- *off* - This state consumes no energy.
- *ready* - PM is on but there are no active VMs on it. This state wastes energy consumption if PM is kept in this state for a long time. But if PM is switched off, much energy and time will be wasted to turn the PM back on to ready state.
- *idle* - This state exists as a result of a trade-off between off and ready states. PMs in this state consume lesser energy than PMs in ready state. Also lesser time and energy will be required to turn a PM on from idle state to ready state.
- *running* - This state consumes the maximum energy.

The states and the transitions allowed are shown in Figure 10.

It is observed that energy consumption varies according to load changes in a PM Xu et al. (2010). Thus energy consumption of a PM depends on the PM's utilization.

Thus the energy consumption for a PM can be modeled as:

$$EC\,(t) = F\,E \times t + x \times L(t)^y \tag{3}$$

In equation 3, EC(t) represents the energy consumed in time period *t*, FE is the energy consumption that is fixed per unit time, L(t) is the load of PM in time *t*, and *x* and *y* are the energy adjusting coefficients.

The above equation can be modified for modeling energy consumption of the ith PM in a particular state, since the fixed energy consumption of a PM in every state is different.

$$EC_i\,(t) = F\,E_i\,(P\,M\,S_i) \times t + x_i \times L_i\,(t)^{y}i \tag{4}$$

Figure 10. States and their transitions

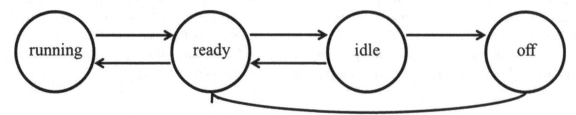

Equation 4 calculates the energy consumption of PM_i in time period t. $FE_i (PMS_i)$ is the fixed energy consumption per unit time of PM_i in state PMS_i. $L_i(t)$ is the load of PM_i for time period t, while x_i is the energy coefficient of the ith PM and y_i is the relationship between load and energy of PM_i.

Energy Consumption During State Switch

Following rules are maintained while calculating energy consumption during switching of states of a PM.

- Energy consumption during switching between running and ready states can be ignored.
- State switching between off and ready states is slower than switches between idle and ready states.
- Switching off a PM costs lesser than keeping the PM in idle state.

Thus we use an array ECS(P X 4) to store the energy consumption of state switches since it is fixed for a particular state transition for a specific PM. The energy consumption during state switching of PM_i according to the array ECS can be seen in Figure 11.

Energy Consumption During Live VM Migrations

The consumption of energy during live virtual machine migrations are of three parts;

- Energy consumption by the source PM for preparation for migration.
- Energy consumption by the target PM for reception and rebuilding of the migrated VM.
- Energy consumption by other physical equipment during VM migration.

We maintain three arrays in order for energy consumption during live VM migration.

EVS (P X V) denotes the energy consumption by source PM during migration. EVS_{ij} is the energy consumed by PM_i for moving VM_j out.

EVT (P X V) denotes the energy consumption by target PMs for receiving the migrated VMs. Thus, EVTij is the energy consumed by PM_i for receiving the migrated VM_j.

EV X (P X P X V) is a three dimensional array which denotes the energy consumption during migration. Thus EVX_{ijk} is the energy consumed during migration of VM_k from PM_i to PM_j.

Figure 11. Energy consumption of state switching

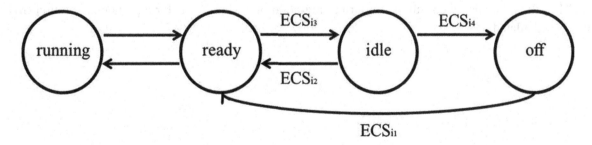

Thus the energy consumption during live VM migrations can be modeled as follows:

$$EVSij = \alpha i \times SZj + \beta i \tag{5}$$

$$EVTkj = \alpha k \times SZj + \beta k \tag{6}$$

$$^{EVX}kj = {}^{\gamma}ik \times {}^{SZ}j \tag{7}$$

where, α_i, β_i, α_k, β_k and $^{\gamma}_{ik}$ are energy adjusting coefficients and SZ_j is the size of VM_j

The Overall Energy Consumption Model

The energy consumption due to the switching of states during the entire migration process can be simplified. On comparison of the array *PMS* before and after the whole migration process, an array *PMST(4 X P)* can be derived, which represents the state switching of all PMs. Thus,

- $PMST_{1i} = 1$ means PM_i need state transition from off to ready.
- $PMST_{2i} = 1$ means PM_i need state transition from idle to ready.
- $PMST_{3i} = 1$ means PM_i need state transition from ready to idle.
- $PMST_{4i} = 1$ means PM_i need state transition from idle to off.

Thus the total energy consumption by state switching of PMs (EPS) for a particular solution (M) of the VM placement problem can be calculated as:

$$EPS(M) = \sum_{i=1}^{P} \sum_{k=1}^{4} (ECS_{ik} \times PMST_{ki}) \tag{8}$$

In order to calculate the total energy consumption during live migration, we create 3 arrays by comparing the array M before and after migration.

Array *VMLM* (P X P X V) is created to show the live migrations for all the VMs. Thus, $VMLM_{ikj} = 1$ means that VM_j's migration from PM_i to PM_k is needed.

Similarly 2 other arrays VMS(P X V) and VMT(P X V) are created to show the sources of migrations and their targets respectively. Thus $VMS_{ij} = 1$ means that VM_j is migrated from PM_i and $VMT_{kj} = 1$ means that VM_j is migrated to PM_k.

Thus the total energy consumption during migration of VMs (EVM) for a particular solution (M) can be calculated as:

$$EVM(M) = \sum_{i=1}^{P} \sum_{j=1}^{V} (EVS_{ij} \times VMS_{ij}) + \sum_{k=1}^{P} \sum_{j=1}^{V} (EVT_{kj} \times VMT_{kj})$$
$$+ \sum_{i=1}^{P} \sum_{k=1}^{P} \sum_{j=1}^{V} (EVX_{ikj} \times VMLM_{ikj}) \tag{9}$$

The total energy consumption by all the PMs in different states (EPM) for a particular solution (M) can be given as:

$$EPM(M) = \sum_{i=1}^{P} EC_i(t) \tag{10}$$

Thus the total energy consumption by the VM placement problem (TEC) from initial solution M' to solution M can be denoted as:

$$TEC(M) = EPS(M) + EVM(M) + EPM(M) - EPM(M') \tag{11}$$

where, EPM(M') is the energy consumption of all PMs under initial solution M'.

System Model

With increasing dependence on Cloud Service Providers (CSP) by consumers for computing needs, there has been an enhanced requirement of a specific level of QoS which has to be followed by the CSPs. CSPs aim to meet the QoS parameters which are specified in the negotiated Service Level Agreement (SLA). Thus, an improved cloud architecture has to be developed which will cater to the needs of the consumers as well as the CSPs. The problem model that has been used in this chapter is depicted in Figure 12.

The cloud architecture being referred here has many entities.

- Users or brokers
- SLA Resource Allocator
- Service Request Examiner
- VM Monitor
- Service Request Monitor

VM requirements are given in the form of a vector $x.(\overrightarrow{cpu}) + y.(\overrightarrow{mem}) + z.(\overrightarrow{cores})$, where $\overrightarrow{cpu}$ is the CPU requirement in GHz, $\overrightarrow{mem}$ is the memory requirement in GB and $\overrightarrow{cores}$ is the requirement for the number of cores. x, y and z are the multiplying factors constraint to x + y + z = 1.

All Physical Machines (PMs) have a PM Controller which accepts the VM Request queue sent from the dispatcher. The PM Controllers are as players for the cooperative game theory which take the decision on the dynamic VM placement problem in order to minimize energy consumption.

Figure 12. Proposed system model

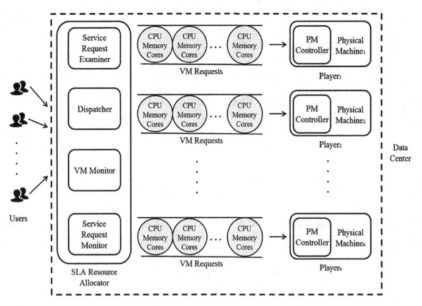

Problem Statement

Figure 12 refers to the system model which is used in order to find the solution to dynamic VM placement problem.

There are *n* Physical Machines (PMs). Every PM has a state associated with it. The states included are: 1 = off, 2 = idle, 3 = ready and 4 = running. Thus we use an array PMS (1 X P) to specify the current state of a PM. For every PM, there are 3 resources, namely CPU (GHz), Memory (GB) and number of cores. Thus we use an array PMR (3 X n) to specify the amount of resources that every PM has. Thus PMR_{ij} specifies the amount of resource$_i$ that PM_j has. The dynamic VM placement problem in this chapter is solved by Cooperative Game Theory where the players are the physical machines. Thus the resource status information is shared by all the PMs which aids in the problem solving process.

There are V_i number of VMs in PM_i. Let the maximum number of VMs present in one particular PM be maxV.

$$\max V = \max(V_i) \quad ; 1 \le i \le n \tag{12}$$

VM requirements are given in the form of a vector $x.(\overrightarrow{cpu}) + y.(\overrightarrow{mem}) + z.(\overrightarrow{cores})$.

Thus a 3-dimensional array VMR (3 X maxV X n) is created in order to forecast requirement of resources for VMs for a certain period of time. Thus VMR_{ijk} indicates the requirement of ith resource by the jth VM residing in kth PM. For all the V VMs where $V = \sum_{i=1}^{n} V_i$, we require I number of performance indicators. In order to represent the performance requirements, we create an array VMP (I X V), where VMP_{ij} is the requirement of the ith performance indicator for the jth VM. This performance indicator acts as the SLA indicator.

The result of the virtual machine placement problem is stored in a mapping array M (P X V). M_{ij} can hold values 0 or 1. The value 1 indicates that j^{th} VM is placed at the ith PM, while the value 0 shows that j^{th} VM is not running on the ith PM. We also require an array MP (I X V) which indicates the level of performance of all the VMs. MP_{ij} means the jth VM is performing at the ith level for a particular solution to the VM placement problem.

The VM dynamic placement problem based on energy consumption (EC) (VDPPEC) can be formulated as follows:

$$VDPPEC = \min TEC(M) \tag{13}$$

where,

$$TEC(M) = EPS(M) + EVM(M) + EPM(M) - EPM(M') \tag{14}$$

such that,

$$\begin{aligned} C_{ri} &\leq PMR_{ri} \\ (C_{ri} &= VMR \times M'; r = 1, 2, \ldots, R; i = 1, 2, \ldots, P) \end{aligned} \tag{15}$$

$$\sum_{i=1}^{P} M_{ij} = 1 \qquad (j = 1, 2, \ldots, V) \tag{16}$$

$$MP_{iv} \geq VMP_{iv} \quad (i = 1, 2, \ldots, I; \ v = 1, 2, \ldots, V) \tag{17}$$

Equation 13 shows the optimization objective of the VM dynamic placement problem, i.e. minimization of energy consumption (EC) for a particular placement solution (M).

The solution is arrived upon satisfying all the three constraints as shown in equations 15, 16 and 17. Equation 15 is the capacity constraint. M' is the transposition of the mapping matrix (M). Placement constraint is represented in equation 16 and equation 17 shows that the SLA should be met in VM placement solution.

SOLUTION

Cooperative Game Theory

In this section, the algorithm based on congestion game theory for cooperative physical machines has been discussed which is used for solving the dynamic VM placement problem. In order for better convenience for description of the algorithm, the symbols along with their meanings have been listed in Table 1.

Table 1. List of symbols and their meanings

Symbols	Meanings
n	Number of physical machines
V	Number of virtual machines
$\rho\, n$	Initial mapping of V VMs onto n PMs
$\delta\, n$	Optimal mapping of V *VMs* onto n PMs after dynamic VM placement
δ_{p-1}^{α}	A strategy α for PM$_{p\text{-}1}$
ϑ	3 dimensional matrix (n * n * V) showing the live migrations to be executed. Thus, $\vartheta_{ikj} = 1$ means that *VMj's* migration from PM_i to PM_k is needed.
S	Strategy matrix to store the collection of strategies for all the PMs. Thus S_{ij} means the jth strategy for i^{th} PM.
$payoff_i(\ \delta_i^{\alpha}\ )$	Total Energy Consumption if strategy α of PM_i is taken.

The algorithm is executed dynamically whenever any SLA constraint is violated. The status of all the physical machines is shared by all the players. Thus, it is cooperative game theory.

Algorithm 1 (Figure 13) is the calling module. It takes the initial mapping of V virtual machines onto n physical machines as input and produces the best strategy or the optimal mapping with minimum energy consumption as the output. Also the migrations needed to reach to the optimal solution are given as output.

The algorithm uses the congestion game model which models a resource set being shared by a group of players. Here every player selects a subset of resources from the resource set in order to maximize his own payoff; here maximizing the payoff means minimizing the energy consumption. Here, the physical machines are treated as players which select a subset of VMs in order to minimize the total consumption of energy. Thus algorithm 1 calls algorithm 2 for each player in order to reach Equilibrium at every step.

Every player, which is each Physical machine, acts as a player and attempts to achieve its own equilibrium by going through algorithm 2.

Algorithm 2 (Figure 14) finds the best strategy for the ith PM. It takes as input the best strategy for (i-1) PMs and gives as output the best strategy of i PMs. First the ith PM looks for the best strategy which will consume the least energy. Then all the (i-1) PMs change their strategies accordingly so that equilibrium

Figure 13. Algorithm 1: Equilibrium of 'n' players

Algorithm 1: Equilibrium for n players

Input: n Physical Machines, V Virtual Machines
      Initial mapping for n players; $\rho^n = (\rho_0^n, \rho_1^n, \ldots\ldots, \rho_{n-1}^n)$
Result: Best strategy for n players; $\delta^n = (\delta_0^n, \delta_1^n, \ldots\ldots, \delta_{n-1}^n)$
      Executable live migrations matrix; ϑ
for $(i = 0; i < n; i++)$ **do**
      | Nash_Equilibrium(i);

Figure 14. Algorithm 2: Nash_Equilibrium(p)

Algorithm 2: Nash_Equilibrium(p)

Input: Best strategy for (p-1) Physical Machines
; $\delta^{p-1} = (\delta_0^{p-1}, \delta_1^{p-1}, \ldots\ldots, \delta_{p-2}^{p-1})$

Output: Best strategy for p players; $\delta^p = (\delta_0^p, \delta_1^p, \ldots\ldots, \delta_{p-1}^p)$

$\exists \delta_{p-1}^\alpha \in S_{(p-1)j}$,

$payoff_{p-1}(\delta_{p-1}^\alpha) \leq payoff_{p-1}(\delta_{p-1})$; $\forall \delta_{p-1} \in S_{(p-1)j}$

$\delta_{p-1}^p \leftarrow \delta_{p-1}^\alpha$

$\delta_i^p \leftarrow \delta_i^{p-1}$, $i \in [0, p-2]$

$\delta^p = (\delta_0^p, \delta_1^p, \ldots\ldots, \delta_{p-2}^p, \delta_{p-1}^p)$

$j = 0$;

for $(i = 0; i < (p-1); i = j)$ **do**

   if $(payoff_i(\delta_i^p) \leq payoff_i(\delta_i)$; $\forall \delta_i \in S_{ij})$ **then**

      j++;

   else

      $\exists \delta_i^\alpha \in S_{ij}$,

      $payoff_i(\delta_i^\alpha) \leq payoff_i(\delta_i)$; $\forall \delta_i \in S_{ij}$

      $\delta_i^p \leftarrow \delta_i^\alpha$

      $j = 0$;

---

is maintained, that is optimal energy consumption takes place. This algorithm thus produces the best strategy for every step for all the *n* physical machines.

There are *n* players (Physical Machines) and *V* virtual machines. So in each step in order to achieve Nash Equilibrium for a player the time complexity will be O(nV). The algorithm for finding out the equilibrium for a particular step has to be repeated for n players. Thus the time complexity to achieve Nash Equilibrium for *n* players will be O(n²V).

Thus this algorithm obtains the Nash Equilibrium in cooperative congestion game for dynamic VM placement at a particular time frame in polynomial time.

Six sets of experiments are performed and the results are compared with results of Best Fit algorithm. Best Fit Algorithm is a centralized algorithm which aims to place VMs into the PM with the least available space and with no SLA violations, such that the PMs are fully utilized. The steps involved in best fit procedure are defined in Algorithm 3 (Figure 15). The results are shown later.

Non-Cooperative Game Theory

In this section, the algorithm based on non-cooperative theory which has been used to solve the problem of dynamic virtual machine placement has been discussed. The symbols used in the algorithm have been listed in Table 2.

Algorithm 4 (Figure 16) shows the procedure for a PM to select its best placement every time such that in every iteration, the energy consumption by that physical machine is lesser than the energy consumption in the previous iteration for that particular PM. Thus, all the PMs act selfishly in order to optimally dynamically place VMs onto PMs such that energy consumption is minimized.

Practically speaking, in order to compute Nash Equilibrium, some coordination must be present among the players; in this case the physical machines. Thus, the non-cooperative procedure shown in algorithm 5 is devised where players (PMs) are synchronized in such a manner that their individual placement strategies are updated in a round-robin fashion.

Figure 15. Algorithm 3: Best Fit Algorithm

Algorithm 3: Best Fit

Input: p Physical Machines, n Virtual Machines
Result: Best Fit placement strategy for n Virtual Machines
for $(i = 0; i < n; i = i + 1)$ **do**
  Sort p PMs in increasing order of free space (remaining capacity)
  for $(j = 0; j < p; j = j + 1)$ **do**
    if $(Requirement(VM_i) \leq Capacity(PM_j))$ **then**
      Place VM_i into PM_j
      break;

Table 2. List of symbols and their meanings

Symbols	Meanings
i	Physical machine number
itr	Iteration number
$energy_i^{(itr)}$	Total energy of ith PM computed at iteration number itr
τ	The accepted tolerance
$\delta p_{-1\alpha}$	A strategy α for PM_{p-1}
en	Tolerance at iteration number itr. $$\sum_{i=1}^{n}\left|energy_i^{(itr-1)} - energy_i^{(itr)}\right|$$
$command$	The instruction given to the neighbor PM. It has two values, *CEASE* and *CARRY_ON*.
$SEND((a, itr, command), i)$	Send message (a, itr, command) to PM_i
$RECEIVE((a, itr, command), i)$	Receive message (a, itr, command) from PM_i
$VMLM\_TEMP$	Temporary live VM migration matrix.
M_TEMP	Temporary VM placement matrix.

Figure 16. Algorithm 4: Best_Placement(i)

Algorithm 4: Best_Placement(i)

Input: VMLM_TEMP, M_TEMP, itr
Output: $energy_i^{itr}$
while (1) **do**
  Find new placement strategy for PM_i;
  Calculate $energy_i^{itr}$
  if $(energy_i^{itr} \leq energy_i^{itr-1})$ **then**
    Update M_TEMP, VMLM_TEMP;
    return($energy_i^{itr}$);

Algorithm 5 (Figure 17) is executed for all the physical machines periodically or whenever SLA violations are made. When the execution of the algorithm is over, the players will have reached Nash Equilibrium, thus the strategies remain the same in equilibrium.

In this algorithm, the tolerance is maintained at a very small value, such that in every iteration, the energy consumption is reduced till a point that very small savings in energy is seen in consecutive iterations. This is the point where the algorithm exits. In order to facilitate the coordination among all the physical machines, messages are sent to the next physical machine. The message consists of three arguments; the energy savings made in that particular iteration, the iteration number and the command. If the command is CARRY_ON, it means that equilibrium has not been reached and best placement strategy needs to be computed again. On the other hand, the command CEASE instructs the next physical machine that it can exit the algorithm as equilibrium is reached. In every iteration, the first PM checks the tolerance for the last iteration and accordingly initiates the command sequence for all the PMs.

SIMULATION AND RESULTS

The simulation has been done using an in house simulation using Java.

Figure 17. Algorithm 5: Non-Cooperative Algorithm

```
Algorithm 5: Non-Cooperative Algorithm
PM i; (i=1, 2, . . . ., n) executes:
1. Initial :
      itr ← 0;
      energy_i^itr ← 0;
      en ← 1;
      sum_energy ← 0;
      command ← CARRY_ON;
      prev = [(i-2) mod n] + 1;
      next = [i mod n] + 1;
2. while (1) do
      if (i = 1) // First PM then
            prev = n;
            if (itr ≠ 0) then
                  RECEIVE((en, itr, command), prev);
                  if (en ≤ τ) then
                        SEND((en, itr, CEASE), next);
                        exit;
            sum_energy ← 0;
            itr ← itr + 1;
      else
            // Other PMs
            RECEIVE((sum_energy, itr, command), prev);
            if (command = CEASE) then
                  if (i ≠ n) then
                        SEND((sum_energy, itr, CEASE), next);
                  exit;
            energy_i^itr = Best_Placement(VMLM_TEMP, M_TEMP, itr);
            sum_energy = sum_energy + |energy_i^(itr-1) - energy_i^(itr)|;
            SEND ((sum_energy, itr, CARRY_ON), next);
```

Simulation Parameters

The series of experiments have been performed considering the capacities of physical machines as each having 12.8 GHz of processor speed, 8 GB memory and is octa-cored. The capacities of VMs are chosen randomly from a fixed set of values.

The values of x_i and y_i are determined via function fitting graph related to CPU utilization and are fixed at 61.06 and 2 respectively. Thus Equation 4 which calculates the consumption of energy by PMs in different states can be written as:

$$EC_i(t) = F E_i(P M S_i) \times t + 61.06 \times L_i(t)^2 \tag{18}$$

It is considered in the experiments that all the PMs are homogeneous in nature. Thus the parameters' values are same for all the PMs.

In order to calculate the consumption of energy by every PM, we use the energy consumption model described in chapter 2. The values for the parameters are shown in Table 3. To determine the energy consumption during live VM migration, the parameters have their values fixed; $\alpha_i = 0.256$, $\beta_i = 10.0825$, $\alpha_k = 0.256$, $\beta_k = 10.0825$ and $\gamma_{ik} = 0.5$.

Experimental Results

The Convergence of Nash Equilibrium

In order to prove that the non-cooperative algorithm converges to the nash equilibrium, we have performed experiments; the results of which is shown in Figure 18 and Table 4. A system of 20 PMs and 50 VMs is considered.

It is observed that the value of en converges to zero as the number of iterations increases. This proves that we are achieving Nash Equilibrium in polynomial time. From this experiment, for further simulations, we fix the value of τ as 0.003.

Figure 19 shows the variation of the number of iterations needed to achieve a value for sum_energy less than τ (0.003) as the number of PMs increase. For this simulation, the number of VMs has been fixed at 50.

Next, we perform a set of experiments keeping the number of PMs available fixed at 40 and increasing the number of VMs from 10 to 150. All the results obtained from the non-cooperative game theoretic algorithm are compared with the results obtained from cooperative game theoretic algorithm and best fit algorithm. The impact of selfishness is seen in the results.

Table 3. Values for the energy consumption parameters

States	Running	Ready	Idle	Off
Running	$FE_i(running) = 32.2708$	-	-	-
Ready	-	$FE_i(running) = 32.2708$	$ECS_{i3} = 3.5$	-
Idle	-	$ECS_{i2} = 7.5$	$FE_i(idle) = 0$	$ECS_{i4} = 5.5$
Off	-	$ECS_{i1} = 0$	-	$FE_i(off) = 0$

Figure 18. en vs No. of Iterations

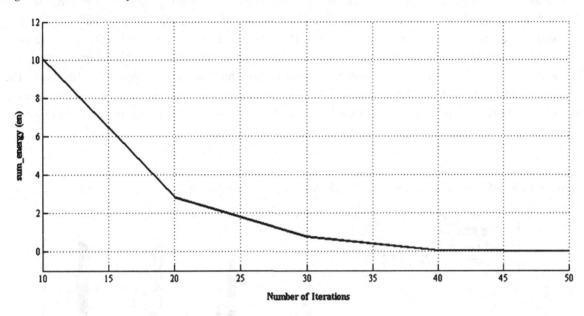

Table 4. sum energy (en) vs No. of Iterations (for 20 PMs, 50 VMs)

Sum Energy (en)	No. of Iterations
10.09	10
2.84	20
0.76	30
0.043	40
0.0027	50

Figure 19. Convergence of non-cooperative algorithm (until en $\leq$ 0.003)

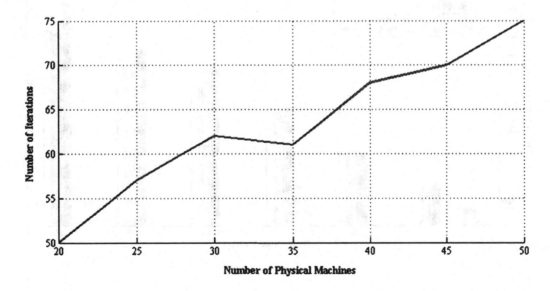

The number of PMs used in order to dynamically place the VMs are projected in Figure 20. The results showing the energy consumption and execution time are shown in Figures 21 and 22 respectively.

From the results, it is observed that number of PMs used and the energy consumption for the non-cooperative game theoretic algorithm are similar to the results obtained from the cooperative game theoretic approach. Both these algorithms give better results than the best fit approach. But due to the non-cooperative nature of the players, that is PMs, the execution time increases for the non-cooperative approach. But the increase in execution time is not drastic so as to discard the algorithm. For minimization of the energy consumption, a slight increase in the execution time can be afforded.

Figure 20. No. of PMs Used vs No. of VMs (Available PMs Fixed at 40)

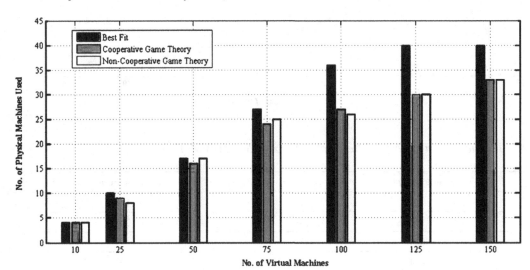

Figure 21. Energy Consumption vs No. of VMs (Available PMs Fixed at 40)

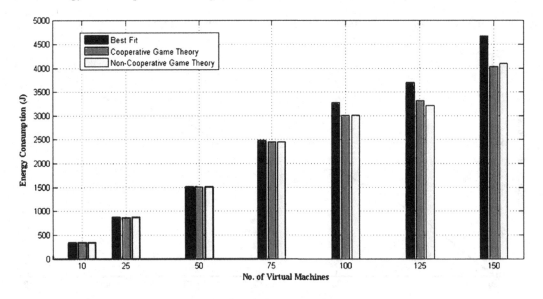

Figure 22. Execution Time vs No. of VMs (Available PMs Fixed at 40)

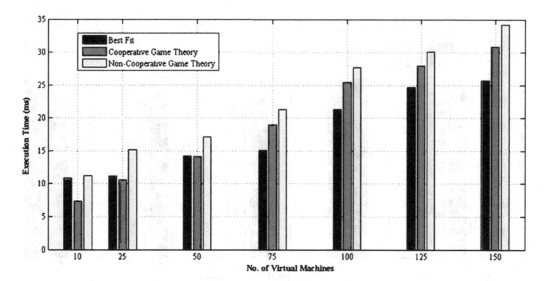

The next set of experiments are performed for a number of VMs fixed at 100 while the number of available PMs are increased from 35 to 95 in equal intervals of 15. The results of the non-cooperative approach along with the comparison with the cooperative procedure and the best fit algorithm are shown in Figures 23, 24 and 25.

Here too, the results obtained from the non-cooperative algorithm are similar to the results of cooperative approach which are better than the best fit procedure's results. But the minimization of energy consumption via non-cooperative approach comes at a cost of increased execution time.

Figure 23. No. of PMs used vs No. of Available PMs (VMs Fixed at 100)

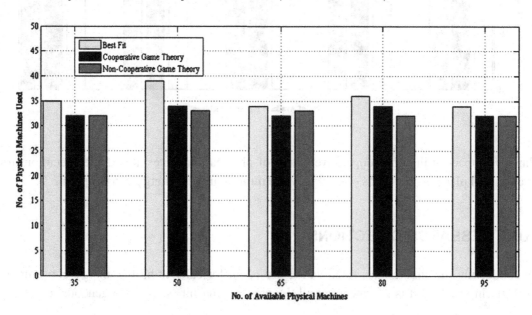

Figure 24. Energy consumption vs No. of available PMs (VMs Fixed at 100)

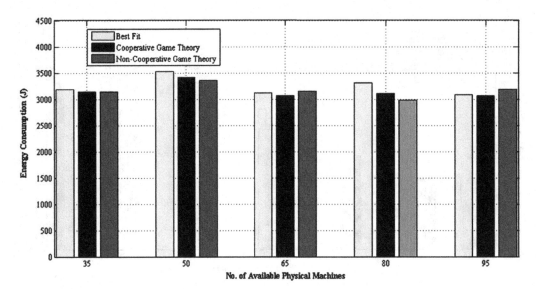

Figure 25. Execution time vs No. of available PMs (VMs Fixed at 100)

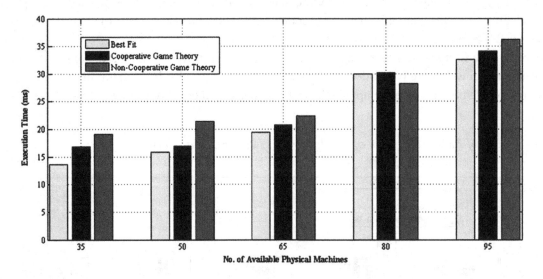

Thus the impact of the non-cooperative nature of physical machines affects the execution time to achieve optimal placement of VMs onto PMs while minimizing the energy consumption.

FUTURE RESEARCH DIRECTIONS

While conducting the simulations, fixed values are taken for calculating the energy consumption of physical machines. Also it is assumed that all the physical machines are homogeneous in nature. For further research, the values of the parameters for calculation of energy consumption should be computed dynamically. Also heterogeneous environment should be considered. In addition to these, energy consumption due to other factors like cooling equipment which have not been considered in this work should be taken into account in future.

CONCLUSION

In this chapter, the problem of dynamic virtual machine placement has been addressed. After a deep analysis of the already existing research work in this area, a decentralized approach using game theory has been proposed here in order to optimize the consumption of energy. First, an energy consumption model is built in view of the complicated process of dynamic placement of virtual machines. Here, three factors have been considered while building the model, namely energy consumption of physical machines in different states, consumption of energy during the state transition of physical machines and during live virtual machine migrations. In this work, both cooperative and selfish nature of physical machines has been considered. Cooperative game theory using the concept of congestion game and non-cooperative game theoretic approaches have been used to propose new algorithms to optimally place virtual machines onto physical machines dynamically. For both the approaches, it is seen that Nash equilibrium is achieved in polynomial time. Both the algorithms guarantee a list of live virtual machine migrations to achieve the target solution from the initial mapping. Simulations are done and the experimental results are compared with the best fit approach. Both cooperative and non-cooperative algorithms help in minimizing the energy consumption, though the non-cooperative game theoretic approach takes a longer execution time to give the optimal result.

REFERENCES

Ardagna, D., Panicucci, B., & Passacantando, M. (2011). A game theoretic formulation of the service provisioning problem in cloud systems. In *Proceedings of the 20th ACM international conference on world wide web*. doi:10.1145/1963405.1963433

Ardagna, D., Panicucci, B., & Passacantando, M. (2013). Generalized nash equilibria for the service provisioning problem in cloud systems. IEEE Transactions on Services Computing, 6(4), 429–442.

Bobroff, N., Kochut, A., & Beaty, K. (2007). Dynamic placement of virtual machines for managing sla violations. In *10th IFIP/IEEE International Symposium on Integrated Network Management, IM'07*. doi:10.1109/INM.2007.374776

Chen, Y.-L., Yang, Y.-C., & Lee, W.-T. (2014). The study of using game theory for live migration prediction over cloud computing. Springer Intelligent Data analysis and its Applications, 2, 417–425. doi:10.1007/978-3-319-07773-4_41

Dhillon, J. S., Purini, S., & Kashyap, S. (2013). Virtual machine coscheduling: A game theoretic approach. In *2013 IEEE/ACM 6th International Conference on Utility and Cloud Computing (UCC)*, (pp. 227–234).

Hassan, M. M., Song, B., & Huh, E.-N. (2011). Game-based distributed resource allocation in horizontal dynamic cloud federation platform. In *Algorithms and Architectures for Parallel Processing* (pp. 194–205). Springer. doi:10.1007/978-3-642-24650-0_17

Hermenier, F., Lorca, X., Menaud, J.-M., Muller, G., & Lawall, J. (2009). Entropy: a consolidation manager for clusters. In *Proceedings of the 2009 ACM SIGPLAN/SIGOPS international conference on Virtual execution environments*. doi:10.1145/1508293.1508300

Hotz, H., (2006). *A short introduction to game theory*. Academic Press.

Hyser, C., Mckee, B., Gardner, R., and Watson, B. J., (2008). *Autonomic virtual machine placement in the data center*. Academic Press.

Jackson, M. O., (2011). *A brief introduction to the basics of game theory*. Academic Press.

Jones, M. T. (2010). *Anatomy of an open source cloud*. Retrieved from http://www.ibm.com/developerworks/opensource/library/oscloud-anatomy

Kong, Z., Xu, C.-Z., & Guo, M. (2011). Mechanism design for stochastic virtual resource allocation in non-cooperative cloud systems. In *2011 IEEE International Conference on Cloud Computing (CLOUD)*. doi:10.1109/CLOUD.2011.82

Lee, C., Suzuki, J., Vasilakos, A., Yamamoto, Y., & Oba, K. (2010). An evolutionary game theoretic approach to adaptive and stable application deployment in clouds. In *Proceedings of the 2nd workshop on Bio-inspired algorithms for distributed systems*. doi:10.1145/1809018.1809025

Liao, X., Jin, H., & Liu, H. (2012). Towards a green cluster through dynamic remapping of virtual machines. *Future Generation Computer Systems*, *28*(2), 469–477. doi:10.1016/j.future.2011.04.013

Londono, J., Bestavros, A., & Teng, S. H. (2009). *Collocation games and their application to distributed resource management. Tech. Rep.* Boston University Computer Science Department.

Lu, Z., Wen, X., & Sun, Y. (2012). A game theory based resource sharing scheme in cloud computing environment. In *2012 IEEE World Congress on Information and Communication Technologies (WICT)*. doi:10.1109/WICT.2012.6409239

Mao, Z., Yang, J., Shang, Y., Liu, C., & Chen, J. (2013). A game theory of cloud service deployment. In *2013 IEEE Ninth World Congress on Services*. doi:10.1109/SERVICES.2013.35

Milchtaich, I. (1996). Congestion games with player-specific payoff functions. *Games and Economic Behavior*, *13*(1), 111–124. doi:10.1006/game.1996.0027

Niyato, D., Zhu, K., & Wang, P. (2011). Cooperative virtual machine management for multi-organization cloud computing environment. In *Proceedings of the 5th International ICST Conference on Performance Evaluation Methodologies and Tools, ICST (Institute for Computer Sciences, Social-Informatics and Telecommunications Engineering)*.

Sun, D., Chang, G., Wang, C., Xiong, Y., & Wang, X. (2010). Efficient nash equilibrium based cloud resource allocation by using a continuous double auction. In *2010 International Conference on Computer Design and Applications (ICCDA)*.

Sun, W., Zhang, D., Zhang, N., Zhang, Q., & Qiu, T. (2014). Group participation game strategy for resource allocation in cloud computing. In *Network and Parallel Computing* (pp. 294–305). Springer. doi:10.1007/978-3-662-44917-2_25

Teng, F., & Magoules, F. (2010). A new game theoretical resource allocation algorithm for cloud computing. In *Advances in Grid and Pervasive Computing* (pp. 321–330). Springer. doi:10.1007/978-3-642-13067-0_35

Turocy, T. L., & Von Stengel, B. (2001). *Game theory: Draft prepared for the encyclopedia of information systems.* Tech. Rep. CDAM Research Report LSE-CDAM-2001-09.

Wei, G., Vasilakos, A. V., Zheng, Y., & Xiong, N. (2010). A game-theoretic method of fair resource allocation for cloud computing services. *The Journal of Supercomputing, 54*(2), 252–269. doi:10.1007/s11227-009-0318-1

Wood, T., Shenoy, P. J., Venkataramani, A., & Yousif, M. S. (2007). *Black-box and gray-box strategies for virtual machine migration* (Vol. 7, pp. 17–17). NSDI.

Xhafa, F., & Kolodziej, J. (2010). Game-theoretic, market and meta-heuristics approaches for modelling scheduling and resource allocation in grid systems. In *2010 IEEE International Conference on P2P, Parallel, Grid, Cloud and Internet Computing (3PGCIC).* doi:10.1109/3PGCIC.2010.39

Xu, J., & Fortes, J. A. (2010). Multi-objective virtual machine placement in virtualized data center environments. In *2010 IEEE/ACM Int'l Conference on Green Computing and Communications (GreenCom) & Int'l Conference on Cyber, Physical and Social Computing (CPSCom).* doi:10.1109/GreenCom-CPSCom.2010.137

KEY TERMS AND DEFINITIONS

Cloud Computing: Cloud computing is a technique for helping users to have access to computing resources on demand with very minimal effort in management.

Cooperative Game Theory: Cooperative game as the game scenario where players form coalitions in advance to discuss their actions.

Game Theory: Game theory is the formal study of cooperation and conflict. A game is described as a set of players and their possibilities to play the game by following some rules (strategies).

Non-Cooperative Game Theory: This type of game models the process of players who are making choices thinking about their own interest.

Virtualization: Virtualization is the capacity to run many instances of operating system in a single PM thus making maximum use of the hardware capacities of the physical machine which helps immensely in saving money for energy and hardware costs.

Virtual Machines: These individual instances of operating system are called Virtual Machines (VM).

Virtual Machine Placement: The scheduling of virtual machines in data centers and virtual machine scheduling on physical machines.

Chapter 7
Metaheuristic Approaches to Task Consolidation Problem in the Cloud

Sambit Kumar Mishra
National Institute of Technology Rourkela, India

Kshira Sagar Sahoo
National Institute of Technology Rourkela, India

Bibhudatta Sahoo
National Institute of Technology Rourkela, India

Sanjay Kumar Jena
National Institute of Technology Rourkela, India

ABSTRACT

The service (task) allocation problem in the distributed computing is one form of multidimensional knapsack problem which is one of the best examples of the combinatorial optimization problem. Nature-inspired techniques represent powerful mechanisms for addressing a large number of combinatorial optimization problems. Computation of getting an optimal solution for various industrial and scientific problems is usually intractable. The service request allocation problem in distributed computing belongs to a particular group of problems, i.e., NP-hard problem. The major portion of this chapter constitutes a survey of various mechanisms for service allocation problem with the availability of different cloud computing architecture. Here, there is a brief discussion towards the implementation issues of various metaheuristic techniques like Particle Swarm Optimization (PSO), Genetic Algorithm (GA), Ant Colony Optimization (ACO), BAT algorithm, etc. with various environments for the service allocation problem in the cloud.

INTRODUCTION

In recent times, a large number of improvements have been done in distributed computing like flexibility, reliability, efficiency, etc. The cloud computing is one of the models which provides verities elastic services by using internet technologies. The term "elastic computing" refers to the ability of dynamically acquiring computing resources and supporting a variable workload. The cloud applications are normally based on the client-server model, and the applications are running on the local machines while the executions are conducted on the cloud. There are three actors (CSU, CSP, and CSN) in the cloud environment.

DOI: 10.4018/978-1-5225-1721-4.ch007

The cloud service user (CSU) is a person or an organization that consumes delivered cloud services. The cloud service provide (CSP) is an organization that provides and maintains delivered cloud services. The cloud service partner (CSN) is a person or an organization that provides support to the building of the service offer by a CSP. The cloud user has to request the cloud service provider for the execution of their tasks, and an agreement has to make between them called service level agreement (SLA). According to the SLA, the CSP provides services to the user. Otherwise, the CSP may give a penalty for the violence of SLA. A cloud service provider maintains a massive infrastructure to support elastic services. Cloud computing is cost-effective due to resource multiplexing and one of the essential terminologies of the cloud computing is virtualization. Virtualization is the creation of a virtual component of different resources of physical computing devices or a single physical machine can run multiple operating systems concurrently, each in its own virtual machine.

The National Institute of Standards and Technology (NIST) has defined the cloud computing system as a model that provides on-demand services from a shared pool of computing resources like storage, servers, network, services, etc. and these services are provided to the user in a faster mode as well as stop the services rapidly (Mell & Grance, 2011). According to NIST definition, the cloud system model has five essential characteristics, four deployment models, and three service models as shown in Figure 1. The difference between the four deployment models is the comparison of scalability, reliability, security, and cost.

Essential Characteristics of Cloud Computing

1. **On-Demand Self-Service:** The cloud resources can be registered by the consumer for their usage without the necessity of human interaction with each CSP. Here, the computing resources include processing power, storage, virtual machines, etc.
2. **Broad Network Access:** Capabilities are accessible to the network system which can access in different ways that advance the system utilization in heterogeneous gadgets, as, for example, electronic devices like laptops, mobiles, and telephones.
3. **Resource Pooling:** The computing resources provided by the CSP serve numerous clients using a multi-tenant model, with various resources assigned and reassigned dynamically as per customer interest. Because of independent location feeling, the client has no knowledge of the exact location of different virtual machines.
4. **Rapid Elasticity:** Availabilities of services can be dynamically provisioned and released automatically by the scale out and scale in by discharging required resources on demand.
5. **Measured Service:** Utilization of cloud resources measured by monitoring CPU time, storage usage, bandwidth usage, etc. Different cloud service provider provides services to the users at a different level of abstraction.

Deployment Models of Cloud Computing

1. **Private Cloud:** This type of cloud infrastructure exclusively used by one organization or company or a group of clients. The name of this kind of infrastructure tells about the higher level of security, and it results in the increase in cost. This type of cloud may be owned, self-managed, and self-operated by any organization. The StACC (Collaborative Research in Cloud Computing) set

up the first private cloud infrastructure in the UK (Lemos, 2009) where they have used Eucalyptus open-source software and 64 virtual machines used in this cloud.

2. **Community Cloud:** This type of cloud infrastructure typically used by multiple organizations for their specific utilization purpose. For example: suppose two universities combine and used this cloud infrastructure, then for specific applications or for specific time span one can accessing those specific services while the other can't.

3. **Public Cloud:** This type of cloud infrastructure used by the general public. Its openness makes the infrastructure insecure because of which it is less expensive. Some large organization provides and controls this kind of cloud infrastructure. Some large organization they provide public cloud infrastructure are Microsoft, Google, Amazon, etc.

4. **Hybrid Cloud:** This cloud infrastructure is a combination of multiple distinct cloud infrastructures. Since this infrastructure is a combination of private, public, and community cloud, it can provide a certain level of security according to the user need.

Service Models of Cloud Computing:

1. **Software as a Service (SaaS):** SaaS model provides services to the client through the internet to use software services which are running on a cloud infrastructure. Here, the client doesn't know about the location of the infrastructure where the specific software is running. The client only uses the required application and pay for that service. Services are accessible from different client devices through some interface like a web browser. SaaS provides application like video conferencing, accounting, web analytics, etc. The client does not have any control over the cloud infrastructure, including different resources like network, servers, storage, and application for any configuration settings. SaaS model is failing when the organization wants a very specific computational need. Salesforce, Concur and Google Docs are examples of the SaaS model. Figure 1 shows the architecture of the service model.

2. **Platform as a Service (PaaS):** PaaS model provides the capability or all the resources to deploy various applications onto the infrastructure of cloud systems. The consumers are allowed to create applications using different programming languages, and some tools those are supported in their

Figure 1. Service model architecture

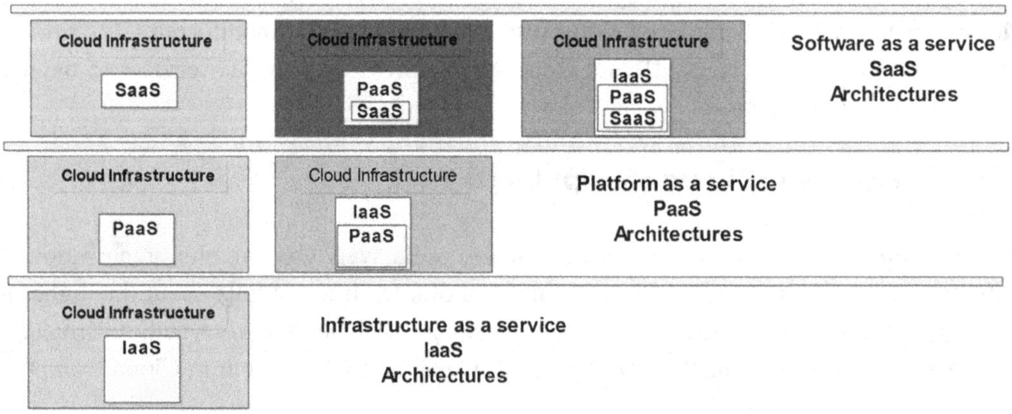

applications. Here also the consumer does not have control the cloud infrastructure, including network, servers, operating systems, or storage, however, they can control all the deployed applications as well as the possible configuration settings for the cloud environment. PaaS provides services like testing, deployment, development, hosting, etc. Google App Engine and Microsoft Azure are two good examples that use PaaS as the cloud computing model.

3. **Infrastructure as a Service (IaaS):** IaaS model provides some provision for accessing the processing, networks, storage, and other infrastructure level computing resources of the cloud system. The consumer can be able to access as well as control the underlying cloud infrastructure where the deployment of resources (servers, storage, operating systems, applications, etc.) and the running of arbitrary software include operating systems, applications and also some control over the network elements. EC2 (Elastic Compute Cloud) and S3 (Simple Storage Service) web services of Amazon are two well-known examples of IaaS.

One can bring only infrastructure from a cloud service provider and deploy their own platform and software. In the same way, one can brought infrastructure and platform, and deploy their own applications, and may bring all the three service models as shown in Figure 1. It is obvious that optimization is applied to everywhere for engineering work and business purpose, even if in day-to-day life also. Typically, all looks for optimizing something to achieve certain quality, profit and also time. As resources in real-world are limited, all have to utilize these valuable limited resources optimally. Different ways of resource management affect the cloud system to provide efficient services to the cloud user since it affects the system performance and cost directly. In the cloud, the resources that may be physical resources or virtual machines are shared among different tasks, and it is often difficult to schedule them optimally. Various types of tasks like CPU intensive, I/O intensive, network intensive, etc. are allocated to the virtual machines of the cloud system (Puthal, Sahoo, Mishra, & Swain, 2015). In such environment, the tasks, as well as the resources are may be homogeneous or heterogeneous. Task scheduling or task allocation is one of such problem to solve that one should go for heuristic algorithms. Several task consolidations heuristic algorithms are proposed by researchers (Kumar & Sahoo, 2014; Alahmadi, Alnowiser, Zhu, Che, & Ghodous, 2014; Mishra, Deswal, Sahoo, & Sahoo, 2015; Sahoo, Nawaz, Mishra, & Sahoo, 2015). These heuristic tasks scheduling strategies help to search for optimal task scheduling in the cloud computing.

Virtualization technology is a way of saving money, by running multiple operating systems (OSs), each OS with their specific tasks to execute on the equivalent server hardware. Virtualization isolates the software from hardware and provide rapid software development and requires no or minimum physical hardware provisioning and thereby significantly reducing the time required for an application to run. For any incoming requests in the cloud, resources are allocated in 2 steps, namely VM Provisioning and Resource Provisioning (Rao, Liu, Xie, & Liu, 2010). The first step is to create multiple instances of VM's on a physical server to host the incoming application requests. Creating VM instances by matching to the specific requirements of the request called as VM provisioning. The next step also called as Resource provisioning maps these incoming requests onto the distributed physical servers. A considerable amount of research work has been done using various resource allocation and software approaches. Virtualization includes modifying the OS kernel to substitute non-virtualizable instructions with hypercalls to communicate immediately with the virtualization layer hypervisor. The hypervisor likewise gives hypercall interfaces for separate critical kernel operations, for example, memory management, interrupt handling, and timekeeping. A hypervisor is a host application that permits a computer to support multiple, identical execution environments through VMs.

A system model with virtualized resources and without virtualization is shown in Figure 2. This unique property of cloud plays a significant role in task scheduling. It is the ability to create multiple instances of virtual machines dynamically on demand and has proved to be an attractive solution to manage the resources of a physical server. Virtualization technology improves the utilization of resources, and also the running independence of a user's applications is ensured. It facilitates the execution of several tasks concurrently on a single physical resource. The various benefits of virtualization include:

1. Isolation of applications from each other
2. Standardization
3. Consolidation
4. Ease of testing

This chapter deliberates about the problem of service allocation in homogeneous as well as in heterogeneous cloud environment. The complete chapter is designed as follows. At first a discussion on the task Consolidation Problem in the cloud system including the system model. Then, an explanation of the consumption of energy in data centers or the cloud system; It follows a presentation on the application of multiple metaheuristic approaches to the task scheduling problem in the cloud, as well as GA, ACO, PSO, BAT, and hybrid metaheuristic algorithms, are demonstrated. Finally, conclude the chapter with future research of the service allocation problem using metaheuristic techniques and definition of some important terminology.

TASK CONSOLIDATION PROBLEM IN THE CLOUD

The task consolidation problem is the process of allocating a set of user requests or tasks to a set of cloud resources, without violating SLAs and without degrading the quality of service (QoS). The cloud system consumes much more energy for processing all the tasks. Therefore, task consolidation plays a

Figure 2. A system model without virtualization and with virtualization

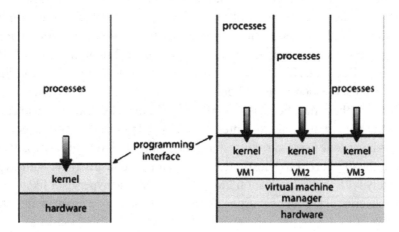

significant role in optimizing the energy consumption. The primary purpose of task consolidation is to maximize the resource utilization and finally to minimize the energy consumption. More precisely, in the task consolidation problem, the resources allocated to a particular task must sufficiently provide the resource (CPU, main memory, storage, bandwidth, etc.) usage of that given task. The resource allocation problem is also a significant challenge in cloud computing because the consumers have unlimited access to the resources over the internet anywhere and at any point in time. The cloud user cannot access the cloud resources directly, but with the help of SOAP (Simple Object Access Protocol) or Restful web APIs that help in mapping the storage and computational request onto the virtualized resources. In a cloud, resources are managed using a centralized or distributed resource manager depending upon the size of cloud (i.e., the number of physical servers). Since the cloud computing model offers almost infinitely available resources, it is capable of supporting on-demand and elastic allocation of resources. But, sometimes this may also lead to non-optimal allocation of resources. In the cloud environment, anything such as memory, CPU, storage, application and bandwidth can be termed as an ICT resource. For an energy efficient data center, it is crucial to utilize the resources properly. The problem of resource allocation in the cloud is an NP-complete problem (Tziritas, Khan, Xu, Loukopoulos, & Lalis, 2013; Kumar & Sahoo, 2014). Hence, no optimal solution can be found. The solution space is exponential and different heuristic algorithms have been developed to search the solution space and get a sub-optimal solution in an acceptable amount of time. The problem of resource allocation is very complex, and its complexity further increases as the cloud infrastructure size increases. Thus, it also requires certain assumption including a set of tasks, a set of operational servers, set of virtual machines, and reduction in energy consumption.

To efficiently utilize the resources various efficient methods have been developed. Methods of memory compression, request discrimination, task consolidation among virtual machines are designed to enhance resource utilization (Hsu, Slagter, Chen, & Chung, 2014). In response to the poor use of resources, Task Consolidation plays the role of an effective technique for maximizing use of resources. Maximizing resource utilization improves various benefits like IT service customization, rationalization of maintenance, and reliable and QoS services.

The cloud infrastructure composed of several data centers. Suppose, D be the set of x number of data centers, $D = \{d_1, d_2, \ldots, d_x\}$. In each data center, there are y number of hosts. Let, H_i be the set of hosts on i^{th} datacenter, $H_i = \{h_{i1}, h_{i2}, \ldots, h_{iy}\}$. All the physical hosts have some resources like processing power, bandwidth, main memory, secondary storage. In the homogeneous environment, each host has same resource capacity. But, in most of the cases, the cloud system environment is heterogeneous. A set of n virtual machines, V_{ij} running on the jth host of ith datacenter and the set $V_{ij} = \{v_{ij}^1, v_{ij}^2, \ldots, v_{ij}^n\}$. All the VMs running on a single host share the resources of that host. The load of the cloud system is the set of user requests or tasks. In real-time, the user requests are submitted to the system in a batch mode, means a small set of tasks submitted to the system at a time. Suppose, there are n number of tasks and the set is $T = \{t_1, t_2, \ldots, t_m\}$. Each task has some attributes: task_id, task length, required number of CPU cores, CPU time requirement, memory requirement, and bandwidth requirement. The tasks submitted to the system and the tasks executed in different virtual machines. The problem of allocation of tasks to the set virtual machine efficiently is known as a task consolidation problem. This multi-objective consolidation problem has the following objectives.

1. Minimize energy consumption
2. Maximize resource utilization

3. Make-span minimization
4. Load Balancing
5. Guarantee quality of service (QoS)
6. Enhance throughput and
7. SLA completion

Recent studies demonstrate that vitality utilization of physical server's shifts directly with the resource usage. Task consolidation can also help in freeing up the resources sitting idle yet consuming huge power. An efficient task consolidation method can improve the performance of the system by the use of the technology called virtualization. It allows running of multiple VMs on a single host at the same time and is a strong approach to be achieved efficient energy utilization of resources in any data center. The task consolidation problem in the Cloud is a multi-objective problem, mostly all give emphasis on the single objective optimization problem. By making some modifications in multiple single optimization problems one can solve a multi-objective problem. Researchers move towards the heuristics and metaheuristic techniques for the task consolidation optimization problem in the cloud due to its NP-complete nature.

ENERGY CONSUMPTION IN DATA CENTER

Nowadays power consumed by servers in a cloud has almost reached an unacceptable level, resulting onto a financial burden on the operating organizations, an environmental burden on society and the infrastructure burden on power utilities (Katsaros, et al., 2013). According to (Dabbagh, Hamdaoui, Guizani, & Rayes, 2015; Zhang, Li, Lo, & Zhang, 2013), around 2% of the global carbon is emitted by ICT itself. The increased use of Cloud computing, resulting the necessary to reduce carbon dioxide emissions and increasing energy costs calls for the energy-efficient technologies that can sustain Cloud data centers. Internet companies like Microsoft and Google have worked to improve the energy savings of their multi-megawatt data centers significantly. According to (Zhang, Li, Lo, & Zhang, 2013; Alnowiser, Aldhahri, Alahmadi, & Zhu, 2014), around 2% of the total electricity consumption in the US is due to data centers. Idle power wastage is one of the primary reasons for inefficient power consumption. At the time of very low utilization (10%) of the resources also the energy consumption is around 50-60% of the peak energy (Lee & Zomaya, 2012; Srikantaiah, Kansal, & Zhao, 2008; Mkoba & Saif, 2014; Valentini, Khan, & Bouvry, 2013; Alahmadi, Alnowiser, Zhu, Che, & Ghodous, 2014; Hu, Jin, Liao, Xiong, & Liu, 2008). This results in reducing system reliability, enormous electricity bills and environmental issues generating due to the emission of carbon in large quantity. The key areas where energy consumption is maximum inside a data center involves various critical computational servers that provide storage and CPU functionalities, power conversion units and cooling systems (Luo, et al., 2012).

The use of low power consumption hardware equipment's like power supplies and CPU for reducing the energy consumption and peak power consumption by looking at the current application workloads and resource utilization (Tang, Gupta, & Varsamopoulos, 2008). Since the power density is in close relation with the temperature, the power factor is associated with the process of calculation of dynamic criticalities in power-aware allocation and scheduling. The most direct and efficient method is to make use of more power efficient components during the hardware designing phase. Other alternatives have also developed that include algorithms to scale down power or even shut down a system when not in use. In this context, the authors in (Hameed, et al., 2014; Beloglazov, Buyya, Lee, Zomaya, & others,

2011) have proposed a high-level taxonomy for the power management which as shown in Figure 3. CSP has to pay the execution cost for the use of data center; this cost is the result of the energy consumption of the computation. According to the energy consumption latter, the CSP fixes a price for the clients.

According to recent research in (Mkoba & Saif, 2014; Beloglazov, Buyya, Lee, Zomaya, & others, 2011; Singh, Pandey, Mandoria, & Srivastava, 2013; Luo, Wu, Tsai, Di, & Zhang, 2013), the major component of power consumption due to the server is shared by the CPU then followed by the storage and then by losses occurring from power supply inefficiency. Also in (Minas & Ellison, 2009), data given by Intel Labs, most of the power in a server is consumed by the CPU and then by the memory. The data in Figure 3 show the power consumed by various components in a server (Singh, Pandey, Mandoria, & Srivastava, 2013). But as a result of continuous improvement in the application of various power saving techniques like DVFS that are capable of enabling active low-power modes and rapidly increasing CPU power efficiency, CPU is no longer dominating in the consumption of power by a server. To minimize the energy consumption in the cloud environment, dynamically optimize the task consolidation problem. To optimize the energy parameter with multiple servers in the cloud environment, the task consolidation should be optimized.

Dynamic power range for all other server's elements are much narrow, i.e., fewer than 25% for disk drives, 50% for DRAM and 15% for the networking switches, and for all additional components are negligible (Beloglazov, Buyya, Lee, Zomaya, el al, 2011). The reason behind is that various active low-power modes are supported only by the CPU, whereas all the other components can either be partially or completely switched off. Most of the techniques for the management of power mainly focused only on the processor; however, the constant increase in capacity and frequency of memory chips, raises the cooling requirements along with the issue of huge energy consumption. These are the reasons that make memory one of the essential components of a server that should be managed efficiently. Latest techniques and approaches for the decline of the memory power consumption have developed. The problem of low

Figure 3. Taxonomy of power management techniques

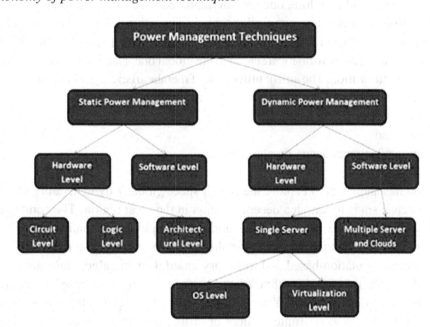

average resource utilization is equally applicable to the disk storage devices in any data center, especially when the disks attached to servers. However, this problem can be somewhat resolved by transferring the disks to an external centralized storage array. To meet this problem effectively, policies should use that will efficiently maintain a storage system containing numerous disks.

METAHEURISTIC TECHNIQUES

The optimization algorithms are classified in two ways:

1. Deterministic algorithm and
2. Stochastic algorithm.

Use of deterministic algorithms for gradient information and the Newton-Raphson algorithm is one of the best examples of a deterministic algorithm. The stochastic algorithm can be classified into two:

1. Heuristic algorithm and
2. Metaheuristic algorithm.

Heuristic means search the solution of the problem in a trial and error basis. The chance of finding a quality solution with the help of a heuristic algorithm is very less. After that, some metaheuristic algorithms are developed. Here, the meaning of metaheuristic means higher level or better level of heuristic algorithms. Heuristic techniques are problem-dependent and because of too greediness nature, they normally get trapped in a local optimum and mostly they failed to reach the global optimum solution. Meta-heuristics techniques are problem-independent, and those techniques are not greedy. However, they may still accept a temporary deterioration of the solution, which allows them to examine more completely the entire solution space, and therefore, one gets an improved solution (occasionally coincide with the global optimum). Recent researchers name all stochastic algorithms as metaheuristic algorithms. All metaheuristic techniques utilize a tradeoff of randomization and local search. Randomization gives a decent approach to running away from local search to the global one. Nearly all metaheuristic techniques are fit for the global optimization. The aim of utilization of metaheuristic algorithms is to obtain a feasible solution in an acceptable amount of time. There are two components:

1. Intensification and
2. Diversification of any metaheuristic algorithms.

Diversification mechanism is to explore the search space globally by generating diverse solutions. Intensification mechanism is to search a decent solution in the local region. The combination of these two components will mostly guarantee the achievability of the global optimality.

Researchers did several classifications for metaheuristic algorithms. The metaheuristic algorithms can be categorized as population-based and trajectory-based. Genetic algorithms are the examples of population-based, whereas the PSO algorithms are the examples of trajectory-based. Probably Alan Turing was the first to use heuristic algorithms (Yang & Press, 2010). The input to the following metaheuristic approaches are the finite task pool, finite number of virtual machines, a matrix for expected time to execute all tasks in different virtual machines. A window size will be chosen according to the requirement for the execution of tasks at a time. A set of task containing window size number of tasks from the pool of tasks. The termination condition for the following iterative-based algorithm is the number that found by dividing the total number of tasks with the window size. Firstly, find different allocation result between the tasks and VMs with the help of the following approaches, and then calculate the energy consumption for those corresponding allocation. Then, optimize the energy consumption of the system.

Metaheuristic Approach-1: GA

Genetic algorithm was first introduced in 1975 and represented as a population based optimization method. In GA, all the solutions are represented as population and the individual population is a chromosome which is a string of genes. Various encoding schemes are used to encode the chromosomes. To start the basic GA, the initial population is chosen randomly. But, to increase the efficiency of the algorithm, researchers used some heuristic techniques for the initial population (Kaur, Chhabra, & Singh, 2010). To verify the chromosome, a function is used called fitness function. Broadly, there are three major operations in this algorithm for each iteration: selection, crossover, and mutation. There are several types of selection operation like roulette wheel selection, Boltzmann selection, tournament selection, rank selection, steady state selection, elitism selection, stochastic remainder selection. Similarly, several types of crossover method like single-point crossover, two-point crossover, multi-point crossover, uniform crossover, matrix crossover, arithmetic crossover, heuristic crossover, position-based crossover. There are also several models of mutation operation such as flip-bit or bitwise mutation, boundary mutation, uniform mutation, non-uniform mutation, Gaussian mutation, shift mutation, exchange mutation.

In present time, to encode the solutions of scheduling for GA, researchers used direct representation (Ge & Wei, 2010; Zheng, Wang, Zhong, & Zhang, 2011), permutation-based representation (Kaur, Chhabra, & Singh, 2010; Yu & Buyya, 2006), and tree-based representation (Gu, Hu, Zhao, & Sun, 2012). Chromosomes are in the form of vectors and the size of the vector is same as the total number of tasks to be allocated to different machines. The Permutation-based representation uses a matrix to represent a chromosome and if the matrix is E, then E_{ij} is 1 if the ith task is allocated to j^{th} VM, otherwise 0. The tree-based representation is used for mapping the relationship between the physical hosts and VMs, and also between the VMs and tasks (Sawant, 2011). In Ai and Tang andFidge, (2010), they have used random key for assigning priority to different tasks. The pseudocode for a GA based task consolidation algorithm in the cloud environment is shown in Figure 4.

A two-stage technique (computing and testing) was used to make a decent introductory solution set or population of the genetic algorithm (Delavar & Aryan, 2011). Firstly, a set of initial candidate solutions can be created using some heuristic algorithms like round-robin, min-min, etc. By using some testing criterion on the set of candidate solutions, some suitable initial solutions to be selected and they applied crossover and mutation on that solution. A hybrid GA for the scheduling of computing resources to the vast amount of tasks optimally (Lin & Chong, 2015). To represent a solution, they have used the Wall coding scheme which was developed in 1996 for project scheduling problems. They have used random initialization. Each genome was encoded as a vector of relative start time. For the generation of new offspring's, they have used Blend crossover (Schaer & Eshelman, 1993). They also proved that the Blend crossover worked better than the arithmetic crossover. They have applied Gaussian distribution to perform the mutation operation. They have mentioned two conditions for the termination of the algorithm. One is the number of generations and second is the number of generations that cannot deliver a better

Figure 4. Pseudocode of GA for task consolidation problem

Procedure GA
1. *Initialization: Generate initial population P consisting of chromosomes.*
2. *Fitness: Calculate the fitness value of each chromosome using fitness function.*
3. *Selection: Select the chromosomes for producing next generation using selection operator.*
4. *Crossover: Perform the crossover operation on the pair of chromosomes obtained in step 3.*
5. *Mutation: Perform the mutation operation on the chromosomes.*
6. *Fitness: Calculate the fitness value of these newly generated chromosomes known as offsprings.*
7. *Replacement: Update the population P by replacing bad solutions with better chromosomes from offsprings.*
8. *Repeat steps 3 to 7 until stopping condition is met. Stopping condition may be the maximum number of iterations or no change in fitness value of chromosomes for consecutive iterations.*
9. *Output best chromosome as the final solution.*

End Procedure

solution. Among these two conditions, whichever is earlier that will be applied. They have added some new ideas like enhancement, local search to the GA.

Normally, the selection procedure of the GA is the evaluation operator and determination operator of metaheuristic techniques. To implement the task scheduling algorithm using GA in the cloud environment, one should take all mappings between tasks and VMs as population and some selected allocation as the chromosome. Mutation procedure is used in finding the most efficient allocation result of mapping between tasks and VMs and not to stop in a local optimum. For designing the fitness functions of the algorithm, several assumptions to be made that affects a lot changes in complexity point of view. In the cloud environment, the design of the fitness functions is effected from different assumptions. During the design of the fitness functions, multiple effective parameters (like communication cost, computation cost, etc.) have to be considered. To calculate the degree of SLA violation for the execution of heterogeneous services, we may follow the following steps:

1. The fitness value can be calculated using the scheduling result, and then
2. Takes a smaller value for the fitness function if certain level of SLA is violated (Ai, Tang, & Fidge, QoS-oriented resource allocation and scheduling of multiple composite web services in a hybrid cloud using a random-key genetic algorithm, 2010).

A task scheduling technique was proposed in (Wang, Liu, Chen, Xu, & Dai, 2014) based on GA and the objectives are makespan minimization and load balancing among VMs. Here, they have used a heuristic for initialization of population and also used probabilistic crossover and mutation in place of using fixed values. (Joseph, Chandrasekaran, & Cyriac, 2015) have used FGA (family genetic algorithm) to mapped VMs and physical machines efficiently to maximize the resource utilization. FGA separates the population into various families and then each family can be processed in parallel to increase the processing capacity of the algorithm. Applying the basic GA operations results in some chromosomes and similar chromosomes are placed in the same family. Here, they have also optimized the energy consumption and the rate of VM migrations. They have taken dynamic mutation probability and that to be self-adjusting. MAGA (multi-agent GA) was introduced by Zhu et al. for load balancing among the VMs (Zhu, Song, Liu, Gao, & Cheng, 2011). This MAGA was compared with the basic GA in the cloud environment resulting the reduction of convergence time. The MEGA technique adjusts both processor utilization and memory usage of VMs.

Crossover and mutation operators in GAs are used for transition purpose (exchange the information between multiple chromosomes or solutions). Two kinds of crossover used in GA: one-point and two-point (Mocanu, Florea, Andreica, & Tapus 2012). After applying crossover, we will have new chromosome set or solution set. The mutation operator is used for exchanging the genes of a chromosome in the algorithm. The two operator's crossover and mutation of GA are redesigned for the representation of the tree (Sawant, 2011). Generally, crossover rate is higher, and it may be static or dynamic. Many researchers have developed and used parallel GA for the optimization of computational time of the algorithm. To do the resource allocation problem, researchers used a coarse-grained parallel genetic algorithm in the cloud. A multi-agent GA was used for representing the population in a grid structure (Zhu, Song, Liu, Gao, & Cheng, 2011). A mechanism called cooperative co-evolutionary GA was used to solve the scheduling problem where deadline acts as a constraint (Ai, Tang, & Fidge, 2011). Almost in maximum cases, two patents or chromosomes are used to make offspring in genetic algorithms. However, 'x' number of chromosomes were used to create offspring and here, 'x' is the population size. Some researchers present heuristics for the scheduling problem as a multi-objective problem (Kessaci, Melab, & Talbi, 2011) and also applied multi-objective genetic algorithms where they can consider multiple optimization parameters (CPU, memory, and bandwidth). In that paper, they considered energy consumption, CO_2 emissions, and cost as parameters to optimize in their multi-objective procedure.

Metaheuristic Approach-2: ACO

ACO is a population-based metaheuristic technique for doing various computational problems or optimization problems. The ACO metaheuristic technique is inspired by the action of ants to locate the shortest path to a source of food. Almost all the real world problems are search problem and the basic idea of finding the solution to those problems by the ACO technique by analyzing the movement of ants in every step. Here, an enormous number of ants are distributed over a network where the network has various cities (or physical nodes) and the path between them. To solve discrete optimization problems where the goal is to find the optimal path, ACO metaheuristic techniques are beneficial. This technique has been applied successfully for solving TSP (travelling salesman problem), multidimensional knapsack problem, job scheduling, quadratic assignment problem, tasks scheduling in the grid and cloud (Kalra & Singh, 2015). The mapping between the ant system and the problem is the first step to using ACO.

The Pseudocode for an ACO based task consolidation algorithm proposed in (Tawfeek, El-Sisi, Keshk, & Torkey, 2013) for the grid and cloud environment is in Figure 5. Their aim is to minimize makespan and the heuristic function is based on the execution time and the transfer time of ith task executed on j^{th} VM. They have used CloudSim as a simulator to simulate their algorithm by varying the number of tasks from 100 to 1000. They have compared their ACO based algorithm with FCFS and round robin algorithms and found 29% to 32% reduction in makespan approximately in ACO based algorithm. A workflow scheduling technique based on the ACS (ant colony system) was proposed in (Chen, Zhang, & Yu, 2007). Their objective is the cost minimization with the deadline as a constraint. They have defined two types of pheromone, one for the makespan minimization and another for the cost minimization. They have defined three different types of heuristic information to guide the direction of the solution. Based on the probabilities controlled, each ant used one heuristic type and one pheromone type in each iteration and those are adjusted in the algorithm.

Researchers provide varieties of solutions for the scheduling or allocation problems on the grid or cloud computing environments by using ACO (Maruthanayagam & Umarani, 2010; Kousalya & Bala-

Figure 5. Pseudocode of ACO for task consolidation problem
Soource: Tawfeek, El-Sisi, Keshk, & Torkey, 2013

Procedure ACO
1. **Initialization:**
   i. *Initialize the pheromone value to a positive constant for each path between tasks and resources*
   ii. *Optimal solution=null*
   iii. *Place the m ants on random resources*
2. **Solution Construction of each ant:**
   Repeat for each ant
   i. *Put the starting resource in tabu list of this ant (for the first task).*
   ii. *For all the remaining tasks*
      a.   *Choose the next resource r_j for the next task t_i by applying following transition rule*

   $$P_{ij} = \frac{(\tau_{ij})^{\alpha}(\eta_{ij})^{\beta}}{\sum_{k\,\varepsilon\,allowed}(\tau_{ik})^{\alpha}(\eta_{ik})^{\beta}} \quad \text{if } j \,\varepsilon \text{ allowed, allowed means not in tabu list}$$
   else 0

      b.   *Put the selected resource in previous step into tabu list of this ant*
   End For
   Until each ant builds its solution
3. *Fitness: Compute the fitness value of the solution of each ant*
4. *Replacement: Replace the Optimal solution with the ant's solution having best fitness value if its fitness value is better than Optimal solution.*
5. *Pheromone Updation:*
   i. *Update local pheromone for each edge*
   ii. *Update global pheromone*
6. *Empty tabu lists of all ants*
7. *Repeat steps 2 to 6 until stopping condition is met. Stopping condition may be the maximum number of iterations or no change in fitness value of ants' solutions in consecutive iterations*
8. *Output: Print Optimal solution*
End Procedure

subramanie, 2009; Kant, Sharma, Agarwal, & Chandra, 2010). Most of them used expected time to compute a task on different virtual machine matrix for their modelling. They calculated the completion time (CT_{ij}) of ith task on j^{th} VM as the addition of the start time of ith task and expected time to compute the ith task of jth VM, and from the CT_{ij}, the makespan of the system is computed. The makespan attribute used to measure the system throughput and QoS is measured from the flow time (Maruthanayagam & Umarani, 2010). The solution of allocation problems using ACO algorithms can be done by assigning resources (such as CPU time, RAM, bandwidth, etc.) to all the tasks. There are four types of heuristic information used:

1. Response time to access different cloud services,
2. Consistency of cloud services,
3. Expense of cloud services, and security to use cloud services (Liu, Xu, & Miao, 2011).

The local search plays a significant role to improve the scheduling performance of ACO algorithm. An advanced local search method is used to interchange the sub-solutions (means the allocation of resources to different tasks) among the various virtual machines (Kousalya & Balasubramanie, 2009). In this technique, the ants may be of various types to improve the efficiency of ACO. In (Kant, Sharma, Agarwal, & Chandra, 2010), they considered red and black ants. Here, to estimate the system resources, the red ants are used and to determine the resource allocation, black ants are used. Kun Li et al. have introduced a method based on LBACO (load balancing ant colony optimization) for the scheduling of tasks (Li, Xu, Zhao, Dong, & Wang, 2011). Their main goal is to minimize makespan of the system and also the load of the system. They have simulated the algorithm in CloudSim and the result shows that the LBACO is much better when compared with FCFS and the basic ACO.

Metaheuristic Approach-3: PSO

An evolutionary computational technique called PSO was added in (Kenndy & Eberhart, 1995) from the behavior of the particles. Each particle of PSO technique has one position vector and one velocity vector. Since both the vectors are used to solve the multi-dimensional problem, it takes several iterations of the algorithm and in each iteration, the vectors are updated based on its best position. This technique merges the local search and the global search to balance the exploration and exploitation. PSO can easily realize and quickly converge the problem so that the scheduling strategy is capable of getting an optimal or suboptimal solution with minimum computational time. The Pseudocode for a PSO based task consolidation problem in the cloud environment is shown in Figure 6. To implement the task scheduling algorithm using PSO in the cloud environment, one should consider the resulted allocation of tasks and VMs is the particle.

To succeed the limitation of the standard PSO technique (i.e. it is easily trapped into the local optima), a self-adaptive learning PSO (SLPSO)-based technique was proposed (Zuo, Zhang, & Tan, 2014). Their key issue is to increase the profit of the service provider while ensuring the QoS. They have formulated the problem as a model called integer programming (IP) and apply an SLPSO technique. Four updating approaches are applied to change the velocity of each particle. After doing experiments, they showed their algorithm raise a cloud provider's profit by 0.25% to 11.56% when compared with the standard PSO. Authors in (Ramezani, Lu, & Hussain, 2014) have proposed method called TBSLBPSO (Task-based System Load Balancing method using PSO) to balance the system load by shifting additional tasks from an overloaded VM to another VM so that there is no need for VM migration. Their aim is to diminish the downtime of migration of VM in the heterogeneous cloud. Their algorithm has a task migration optimization model that reduces the execution time and also transfer time. They validate their method by using Cloudsim and Jswarm packages.

One of the important issues of using PSO is the encoding of the solution. If the particles are task and virtual machines, then the encoding may be the pair or assignment of a task to VM. To have complete knowledge regarding the status of the network, a fuzzy mechanism was introduced for PSO algorithm, where the fuzzy matrix size is same as the expected time to compute matrix (Liu, Abraham, & Hassanien,

Figure 6. Pseudocode of PSO for task consolidation problem

Procedure PSO

1. *Initialization: Initialize position vector and velocity vector of each particle.*
2. *Conversion to discrete vector: Convert the continuous position vector to discrete vector.*
3. *Fitness: Calculate the fitness value of each particle using fitness function.*
4. *Calculating pbest: Each particle's pbest is assigned its best position value till now. If particle's current fitness value is better than particle's pbest, then replace pbest with current position value.*
5. *Calculating gbest: Select the particle with best fitness value from all particles as gbest.*
6. *Updation: Update each particle's position vector and velocity vector using following equations:*
   $V_{i+1} = \omega V_i + c_1 rand_1 * (pbest - x_i) + c_2 rand_2 * (gbest - x_i)$
   $X_{i+1} = X_i + V_{i+1}$
   where
         $\omega = interia$
         $c_1, c_2 = acceleration\ coefficients$
         $rand_1, rand_2 = uniformly\ distributed\ random\ numbers\ and\ \varepsilon\ [0, 1]$
         $pbest = best\ position\ of\ each\ particle$
         $gbest = best\ position\ of\ entire\ particles\ in\ a\ population$
         $i = iteration$
7. *Repeat steps 2 to 6 until stopping condition is met. Stopping condition may be the maximum number of iterations or no change in fitness value of particles for consecutive iterations.*
8. *Output: Print best particle as the final solution.*

End Procedure

2010). Modified fitness functions are employed to designate the network status in the cloud. Sometimes the mutation operator is also applied to PSO to expand the search space of each particle at the time of convergence and like mutation, the crossover operator is also applied to PSO.

Metaheuristic Approach-4: BAT

Yang got inspiration from the echolocation behavior of bats to introduce the BAT algorithm (Yang, 2010). However, bats are flying with a random velocity, they automatically adjust their frequency, pulse rate, and loudness when they are searching for their prey. Bats release a loud and short sound pulse and catch the sound that returns from the surrounding objects by their auricle. Bats may fail to reach their prey, but they slowly progress towards the target, approximately close to the prey. The reduction of loudness and the increase in pulse rate tells that bats approach their target. Bat algorithm was developed to unite the properties of some other metaheuristic algorithms to perform better as compared to algorithms by analyzing the benefits and limitations of those algorithms. These algorithms may comprise the simulated annealing, PSO, and Harmony search. The particle selection process for BAT is similar to PSO for the task scheduling algorithm in the cloud environment.

Bat algorithm fundamentally based on the three parameters of bats: velocity, frequency, and position. The pseudocode of the BAT algorithm for the task consolidation problem is presented in Figure 7. The change of the velocity vector and the position vector of BAT algorithm has a correspondence to PSO algorithm. A model called CBA (cloud model bat algorithm) to advance the convergence rate as well as the precision of bat algorithm was proposed in (Zhou, Xie, Li, & Ma, 2014). They mentioned that the CBA algorithm analyzes the balance between the global optimum and local optimum and also the equilibrium between intensification and diversification. They have considered each position of the bat

Figure 7. Pseudocode of BAT for task consolidation problem

Procedure BAT

1. **Initialization:**
   i. *Initialize bat population -position(x) and velocity(v) of each bat randomly*
   ii. *Initialize echolocation parameters –frequency (f), pulse rate(r) and loudness (A) of each bat*
2. **Generation of new solution:** *Generate new solutions at time step t by updating velocity, position and adjusting frequency (f) using following equations:*

$$f = f_{min} + (f_{max} - f_{min})\beta$$
$$v^t = v^{t-1} + (x^t - xbest)f$$
$$x^t = x^{t-1} + v^t$$

where $\beta \varepsilon$ [0,1] is a random vector drawn from a uniform distribution, xbest is current global best solution which is best among all bats.

3. **Generate a local solution:**
   If (rand(0,1) >r)
   Select a solution among the best solutions
   Create a local solution near the selected best solution.
   Endif
4. **Generate a new random solution:** *Generate a new solution by flying randomly.*
5. *If (rand<A) and (f<f_{best})*
   Accept the new solutions
   Increase r and reduce A
   End if
6. *Repeat steps 2 to 5 for each bat*
7. *Rank the bats and find the current best xbest.*
8. *Repeat steps 2 to 8 until maximum no. of iterations.*
9. **Output:** *Print xbest as the final solution.*

End Procedure

as a candidate solution of the optimization problem. They have simulated how bats search for prey using echolocation approach in a search space under ideal circumstances, where the prey position indicates an optimal solution. To solve the workflow scheduling problem with the aim to minimize processing cost in the cloud, a binary BAT algorithm was applied in (Raghavan, Marimuthu, Sarwesh, & Chandrasekaran, 2015). The algorithm functions better regarding the processing cost as compared to the Best Resource selection (BRS) algorithm. Even they mentioned that the BAT algorithm performs the best among all the other metaheuristic techniques.

Metaheuristic Approach-5: Hybrid Metaheuristic Scheduling Algorithms

The fundamental concept of the hybrid metaheuristic algorithm is to apply multiple basic metaheuristic techniques to a single problem to optimize the objective of the search problem. There are three different types of hybrid metaheuristic scheduling algorithms used in various problems, and those are:

1. Combining population-based algorithm with a single-solution-based algorithm;
2. Combining two population-based algorithms, and
3. Combining metaheuristic algorithm with some other heuristic algorithm (Tsai & Rodrigues, 2014).

If the hybrid metaheuristic algorithm is of the first type, then the solution move towards the global search by using the population-based algorithm and by using the single-solution-based algorithm, the solution is further enhanced. In (Guo-ning, Ting-lei, & Shuai, 2010), authors have used the hybrid metaheuristic scheduling algorithm (combination of SA and GA) in their work.

An aggregate of PSO and GELS (Gravitational Emulation Local Search) algorithm was presented (Pooranian, Shojafar, Abawajy, & Abraham, 2015) for the scheduling of independent task in the grid. Initially, PSO is applied for the allocation of tasks and then GELS is used to enhance the results achieved after PSO, by avoiding local optima. So the efficient solution or allocation depends on the use of GELS algorithm. They have simulated and their result shows that their hybrid algorithm achieves a reduction of 29.2% makespan over the Simulated Annealing algorithm. Shojafar et al. have introduced FUGE (a hybrid approach of GA and fuzzy theory) with the aim of makespan minimization, degrades expense, and load balancing by allocating the tasks in the cloud (Shojafar, Javanmardi, Abolfazli, & Cordeschi, 2015). They have compared their issues with basic GA and ACO techniques. The comparison shows an enhancement of about 45% regarding execution cost and about 50% regarding makespan over GA.

The hybrid metaheuristic algorithm described in (Wang, Shuang, Yang, & Yang, 2012) used PSO as well as TS for the scheduling of jobs. Since in general the population-based metaheuristic algorithms are used to search the global optimum, therefore, people used the second type of hybrid metaheuristic algorithm. The merging of two population-based metaheuristic techniques having different convergence points may delay the convergence time. The hybrid metaheuristic algorithm used in (Sadasivam & Selvaraj, 2010) integrates the GA and PSO algorithms, where the information among the chromosomes are shared by using GA and the best solutions are shared by using PSO. An adaptive hybrid heuristic that combined the genetic algorithm with the dynamic critical path (DCP) was developed to consolidate tasks dynamically in the cloud environment (Rahman, Li, & Palit, 2011). Here, the first phase is to use to find the best allocation having minimum execution time with the help of GA, and the DCP is further used to allocate the tasks on the cloud system dynamically.

CONCLUSION

This chapter extensively reviews the applicability of metaheuristic approaches in the scheduling field in the cloud environments. Since the Metaheuristic techniques are functionally slower, a researcher interested to enhance the convergence speed as well as the quality of the solution. From the literature, it is shown that most of the authors have concentrated on the minimization of makespan, energy consumption, and execution cost, although others have given importance to throughput, response time, flow time and the resource utilization. Data center utilizes an enormous amount of energy, and the reduction of this energy consumption without any performance degradation and SLA violation is a big challenge. Any improvement in this area will potentially provide new insight into the knowledge of how and why metaheuristic techniques work. This study will also assist us to design more dynamic, efficient, often hybrid algorithms for dealing with a wider class of hard optimization problems. In this chapter, several open issues are also addressed that can be taken up for future research.

REFERENCES

Ai, L., Tang, M., & Fidge, C. (2011). *Resource allocation and scheduling of multiple composite web services in cloud computing using cooperative coevolution genetic algorithm*. Neural Information Processing. doi:10.1007/978-3-642-24958-7_30

Ai, L., Tang, M., & Fidge, C. J. (2010). *QoS-oriented resource allocation and scheduling of multiple composite web services in a hybrid cloud using a random-key genetic algorithm*. Academic Press.

Alahmadi, A., Alnowiser, A., Zhu, M. M., Che, D., & Ghodous, P. (2014). Enhanced first-fit decreasing algorithm for energy-aware job scheduling in cloud. *Computational Science and Computational Intelligence (CSCI), 2014 International Conference on*.

Alnowiser, A., Aldhahri, E., Alahmadi, A., & Zhu, M. M. (2014). Enhanced weighted round robin (ewrr) with dvfs technology in cloud energy-aware. *Computational Science and Computational Intelligence (CSCI), 2014 International Conference on*.

Beloglazov, A., Buyya, R., Lee, Y. C., Zomaya, A., & others. (2011). A taxonomy and survey of energy-efficient data centers and cloud computing systems. *Advances in Computers, 82*(2), 47-111.

Chen, W.-N., Zhang, J., & Yu, Y. (2007). Workflow scheduling in grids: an ant colony optimization approach. *Evolutionary Computation, 2007. CEC 2007. IEEE Congress on*, (pp. 3308-3315).

Dabbagh, M., Hamdaoui, B., Guizani, M., & Rayes, A. (2015). Toward energy-efficient cloud computing: Prediction, consolidation, and overcommitment. *IEEE Network, 29*(2), 56–61. doi:10.1109/MNET.2015.7064904

Delavar, A. G., & Aryan, Y. (2011). *A Synthetic Heuristic Algorithm for Independent Task Scheduling in Cloud System*. IJCSI.

Ge, Y., & Wei, G. (2010). GA-based task scheduler for the cloud computing systems. *Web Information Systems and Mining (WISM), 2010 International Conference on*.

Gu, J., Hu, J., Zhao, T., & Sun, G. (2012). A new resource scheduling strategy based on genetic algorithm in cloud computing environment. *Journal of Computers, 7*(1), 42–52. doi:10.4304/jcp.7.1.42-52

Guo-ning, G., Ting-lei, H., & Shuai, G. (2010). Genetic simulated annealing algorithm for task scheduling based on cloud computing environment.*2010 International Conference on Intelligent Computing and Integrated Systems.*

Hameed, A., Khoshkbarforoushha, A., Ranjan, R., Jayaraman, P. P., Kolodziej, J., & Balaji, P. (2014). A survey and taxonomy on energy efficient resource allocation techniques for cloud computing systems. *Computing*, 1–24.

Hsu, C.-H., Slagter, K. D., Chen, S.-C., & Chung, Y.-C. (2014). Optimizing energy consumption with task consolidation in clouds. *Information Sciences, 258*, 452–462. doi:10.1016/j.ins.2012.10.041

Hu, L., Jin, H., Liao, X., Xiong, X., & Liu, H. (2008). Magnet: A novel scheduling policy for power reduction in cluster with virtual machines. *Cluster Computing, 2008 IEEE International Conference on*, (pp. 13-22).

Joseph, C. T., Chandrasekaran, K., & Cyriac, R. (2015). A novel family genetic approach for virtual machine allocation. *Procedia Computer Science, 46*, 558–565. doi:10.1016/j.procs.2015.02.090

Kalra, M., & Singh, S. (2015). A review of metaheuristic scheduling techniques in cloud computing. *Egyptian Informatics Journal, 16*(3), 275–295. doi:10.1016/j.eij.2015.07.001

Kant, A., Sharma, A., Agarwal, S., & Chandra, S. (2010). An ACO approach to job scheduling in grid environment. In Swarm, Evolutionary, and Memetic Computing (pp. 286-295). Springer. doi:10.1007/978-3-642-17563-3_35

Katsaros, G., Subirats, J., Fitó, J. O., Guitart, J., Gilet, P., & Espling, D. (2013). A service framework for energy-aware monitoring and VM management in Clouds. *Future Generation Computer Systems, 29*(8), 2077–2091. doi:10.1016/j.future.2012.12.006

Kaur, K., Chhabra, A., & Singh, G. (2010). Heuristics based genetic algorithm for scheduling static tasks in homogeneous parallel system. *International Journal of Computer Science and Security, 4*(2), 183.

Kenndy, J., & Eberhart, R. (1995). Particle swarm optimization.*Proceedings of IEEE International Conference on Neural Networks*. doi:10.1109/ICNN.1995.488968

Kessaci, Y., Melab, N., & Talbi, E.-G. (2011). A pareto-based GA for scheduling HPC applications on distributed cloud infrastructures. *High Performance Computing and Simulation (HPCS), 2011 International Conference on*, (pp. 456-462).

Kousalya, K., & Balasubramanie, P. (2009). To Improve Ant Algorithm's Grid Scheduling Using Local Search. *International Journal of Intelligent Information Technology Application, 2*(2).

Kumar, D., & Sahoo, B. (2014). *Energy efficient heuristic resource allocation for cloud computing*. Academic Press.

Lee, Y. C., & Zomaya, A. Y. (2012). Energy efficient utilization of resources in cloud computing systems. *The Journal of Supercomputing, 60*(2), 268–280. doi:10.1007/s11227-010-0421-3

Li, K., Xu, G., Zhao, G., Dong, Y., & Wang, D. (2011). Cloud task scheduling based on load balancing ant colony optimization.*Chinagrid Conference (ChinaGrid), 2011 Sixth Annual*, (pp. 3-9). doi:10.1109/ChinaGrid.2011.17

Lin, Y.-K., & Chong, C. S. (2015). Fast GA-based project scheduling for computing resources allocation in a cloud manufacturing system. *Journal of Intelligent Manufacturing*, 1–13.

Liu, H., Abraham, A., & Hassanien, A. E. (2010). Scheduling jobs on computational grids using a fuzzy particle swarm optimization algorithm. *Future Generation Computer Systems*, *26*(8), 1336–1343. doi:10.1016/j.future.2009.05.022

Liu, H., Xu, D., & Miao, H. (2011). Ant colony optimization based service flow scheduling with various QoS requirements in cloud computing. *Software and Network Engineering (SSNE), 2011 First ACIS International Symposium on*, (pp. 53-58).

Luo, L., Wu, W., Di, D., Zhang, F., Yan, Y., & Mao, Y. (2012). A resource scheduling algorithm of cloud computing based on energy efficient optimization methods.*Green Computing Conference (IGCC), 2012 International*, (pp. 1-6).

Luo, L., Wu, W., Tsai, W., Di, D., & Zhang, F. (2013). Simulation of power consumption of cloud data centers. *Simulation Modelling Practice and Theory*, *39*, 152–171. doi:10.1016/j.simpat.2013.08.004

Maruthanayagam, D., & Umarani, R. (2010). Enhanced ant colony algorithm for grid scheduling. *International Journal of Computer Technology and Applications*, *1*(1), 43–53.

Mell, P., & Grance, T. (2011). *The NIST definition of cloud computing*. Academic Press.

Minas, L., & Ellison, B. (2009). Energy Efficiency for Inf ormation Technology: How to Reduce Power Consumption in Servers and Data Centres (Computer System Design). Energy Efficiency for Information Technology: How to Reduce Power Consumption in Servers and Data Centres (Computer System Design). Intel Press.

Mishra, S. K., Deswal, R., Sahoo, S., & Sahoo, B. (2015). *Improving Energy Consumption in Cloud*. Academic Press.

Mkoba, E. S., & Saif, M. A. (2014). A survey on energy efficient with task consolidation in the virtualized cloud computing environment. *International Journal of Research in Engineering and Technology, 3*.

Mocanu, E. M., Florea, M., & Andreica, M. I. (2012). Cloud computing task scheduling based on genetic algorithms.*Systems Conference (SysCon), 2012 IEEE International*, (pp. 1-6).

Pooranian, Z., Shojafar, M., Abawajy, J. H., & Abraham, A. (2015). An efficient meta-heuristic algorithm for grid computing. *Journal of Combinatorial Optimization*, *30*(3), 413–434. doi:10.1007/s10878-013-9644-6

Puthal, D., Sahoo, B., Mishra, S., & Swain, S. (2015). Cloud computing features, issues, and challenges: a big picture. *Computational Intelligence and Networks (CINE), 2015 International Conference on*, (pp. 116-123).

Raghavan, S., Marimuthu, C., Sarwesh, P., & Chandrasekaran, K. (2015). Bat algorithm for scheduling workflow applications in cloud. *Electronic Design, Computer Networks \& Automated Verification (EDCAV), 2015 International Conference on*, (pp. 139-144).

Rahman, M., Li, X., & Palit, H. (2011). Hybrid heuristic for scheduling data analytics workflow applications in hybrid cloud environment. *Parallel and Distributed Processing Workshops and Phd Forum (IPDPSW), 2011 IEEE International Symposium on*, (pp. 966-974).

Ramezani, F., Lu, J., & Hussain, F. K. (2014). Task-based system load balancing in cloud computing using particle swarm optimization. *International Journal of Parallel Programming, 42*(5), 739–754. doi:10.1007/s10766-013-0275-4

Rao, L., Liu, X., Xie, L., & Liu, W. (2010). Minimizing electricity cost: Optimization of distributed internet data centers in a multi-electricity-market environment. *Proceedings of the IEEE*, 1–9.

Sadasivam, S. G., & Selvaraj, D. (2010). A novel parallel hybrid PSO-GA using MapReduce to schedule jobs in Hadoop data grids. *Nature and Biologically Inspired Computing (NaBIC), 2010 Second World Congress on*, (pp. 377-382).

Sahoo, S., Nawaz, S., Mishra, S. K., & Sahoo, B. (2015). *Execution of real time task on cloud environment*. Academic Press.

Sawant, S. (2011). *A genetic algorithm scheduling approach for virtual machine resources in a cloud computing environment*. Academic Press.

Schaer, J., & Eshelman, L. (1993). Real-Coded Genetic Algorithms and Interval Schemata.Foundations of Genetic Algorithms-2-, D. Morgan-Kaufmann.

Shojafar, M., Javanmardi, S., Abolfazli, S., & Cordeschi, N. (2015). FUGE: A joint meta-heuristic approach to cloud job scheduling algorithm using fuzzy theory and a genetic method. *Cluster Computing, 18*(2), 829–844. doi:10.1007/s10586-014-0420-x

Singh, P., Pandey, B. K., Mandoria, H. L., & Srivastava, R. (2013). Review of Energy Aware policies for Cloud Computing Environment. *i-Manager's Journal of Information Technology, 3*(1), 14.

Srikantaiah, S., Kansal, A., & Zhao, F. (2008). Energy aware consolidation for cloud computing.*Proceedings of the 2008 conference on Power aware computing and systems*.

Tang, Q., Gupta, S. K., & Varsamopoulos, G. (2008). Energy-efficient thermal-aware task scheduling for homogeneous high-performance computing data centers: A cyber-physical approach. *Parallel and Distributed Systems. IEEE Transactions on, 19*(11), 1458–1472.

Tawfeek, M. A., El-Sisi, A., Keshk, A. E., & Torkey, F. A. (2013). Cloud task scheduling based on ant colony optimization. *Computer Engineering & Systems (ICCES), 2013 8th International Conference on*, (pp. 64-69).

Tsai, C.-W., & Rodrigues, J. J. (2014). Metaheuristic scheduling for cloud: A survey. *Systems Journal, IEEE, 8*(1), 279–291. doi:10.1109/JSYST.2013.2256731

Tziritas, N., Khan, S. U., Xu, C.-Z., Loukopoulos, T., & Lalis, S. (2013). On minimizing the resource consumption of cloud applications using process migrations. *Journal of Parallel and Distributed Computing*, *73*(12), 1690–1704. doi:10.1016/j.jpdc.2013.07.020

Valentini, G. L., Khan, S. U., & Bouvry, P. (2013). Energy-efficient resource utilization in cloud computing. In Large Scale Network-centric Computing Systems. John Wiley & Sons.

Wang, T., Liu, Z., Chen, Y., Xu, Y., & Dai, X. (2014). Load balancing task scheduling based on genetic algorithm in cloud computing. *Dependable, Autonomic and Secure Computing (DASC), 2014 IEEE 12th International Conference on*, (pp. 146-152).

Wang, Z., Shuang, K., Yang, L., & Yang, F. (2012). Energy-aware and revenue-enhancing Combinatorial Scheduling in Virtualized of Cloud Datacenter. *Journal of Cases on Information Technology*, *7*(1), 62–70.

Yang, X.-S. (2010). A new metaheuristic bat-inspired algorithm. In Nature inspired cooperative strategies for optimization (NICSO 2010) (pp. 65-74). Springer. doi:10.1007/978-3-642-12538-6_6

Yang, X.-S., & Press, L. (2010). Nature-Inspired Metaheuristic Algorithms (2nd ed.). Academic Press.

Yu, J., & Buyya, R. (2006). Scheduling scientific workflow applications with deadline and budget constraints using genetic algorithms. *Science Progress*, *14*(3-4), 217–230.

Zhang, L. M., Li, K., Lo, D. C.-T., & Zhang, Y. (2013). Energy-efficient task scheduling algorithms on heterogeneous computers with continuous and discrete speeds. *Sustainable Computing: Informatics and Systems*, *3*(2), 109–118.

Zheng, Z., Wang, R., Zhong, H., & Zhang, X. (2011). An approach for cloud resource scheduling based on Parallel Genetic Algorithm. *Computer Research and Development (ICCRD), 2011 3rd International Conference on*.

Zhou, Y., Xie, J., Li, L., & Ma, M. (2014). Cloud model bat algorithm. *The Scientific World Journal*. PMID:24967425

Zhu, K., Song, H., Liu, L., Gao, J., & Cheng, G. (2011). Hybrid genetic algorithm for cloud computing applications.*Services Computing Conference (APSCC), 2011 IEEE Asia-Pacific*, (pp. 182-187). doi:10.1109/APSCC.2011.66

Zuo, X., Zhang, G., & Tan, W. (2014). Self-adaptive learning PSO-based deadline constrained task scheduling for hybrid IaaS cloud. *Automation Science and Engineering. IEEE Transactions on*, *11*(2), 564–573.

KEY TERMS AND DEFINITIONS

Host: The host is a network-connected-device (that may be a computer, mobile, etc.). Each host has certain resources (processing speed, main memory, secondary storage, etc.) and provides services to the user.

Service Level Agreement (SLA): SLA is a document explaining expected quality of service and legal guarantees.

Task: It is a unit of execution or a unit of a job. In cloud computing, a task is a user request. Each task has some attributes: task identification, task length, required number of CPU cores, CPU time requirement, memory requirement, and bandwidth requirement.

Task Consolidation Problem: The mapping or the allocation problem of a finite set of tasks to a finite set of virtual machines is termed as a task consolidation problem.

Virtual Machine (VM): A virtual machine is an application installed on host operating system through a hypervisor or VMM, which emulates the hardware resources. In other words, it's an isolated environment that appears to be a whole computer but only has access to a portion of the computer's resources. Virtual machines execute the tasks.

Virtual Machine Monitor (VMM) / Hypervisor: It is a software that securely partitions a computer's resources into one or more VMs. Each VM seems to be running on own hardware, providing the appearance of multiple instances of the same machine. However, all VMs are supported on a single computer.

Virtualization: Virtualization is an abstraction or simulation of hardware resources (e.g., virtual memory).

Chapter 8
Real Time Task Execution in Cloud Using MapReduce Framework

Sampa Sahoo
National Institute of Technology Rourkela, India

Ashok Kumar Turuk
National Institute of Technology Rourkela, India

Bibhudatta Sahoo
National Institute of Technology Rourkela, India

Sambit Kumar Mishra
National Institute of Technology Rourkela, India

ABSTRACT

Cloud Computing era comes with the advancement of technologies in the fields of processing, storage, bandwidth network access, security of internet etc. The development of automatic applications, smart devices and applications, sensor based applications need huge data storage and computing resources and need output within a particular time limit. Now users are becoming more sensitive towards, delay in applications they are using. So, a scalable platform like Cloud Computing is required that can provide huge computing resource, and data storage required for processing such applications. MapReduce framework is used to process huge amounts of data. Data processing on a cloud based on MapReduce would provide added benefits such as fault tolerant, heterogeneous, ease of use, free and open, efficient. This chapter discusses about cloud system model, real-time MapReduce framework, Cloud based MapReduce framework examples, quality attributes of MapReduce scheduling and various MapReduce scheduling algorithm based on quality attributes.

INTRODUCTION

Cloud Computing is an internet-based computing, where resources can be accessed as pay-as-you-go basis over the internet. It enables computing as a utility like electricity, gas, etc. Cloud Computing offers its users a new dimension of viewing the resources i.e. resources as services via internet. Virtualization is the base of Cloud Computing, which creates logical (virtual) machine consisting of all the resources

DOI: 10.4018/978-1-5225-1721-4.ch008

(Operating System, server, storage, and network) similar to a physical machine. We can consider cloud as a network of large groups of servers where resources can be shared and accessed as virtual resources in a scalable and secure manner. The virtualization technique also eliminates the need for maintenance of computing hardware, dedicated space and software. The paradigm shifts from on premise computing to Cloud Computing allows resource sharing and isolation from the underlying hardware. Various advantages of Cloud Computing include on-demand scalability, low cost storage services, parallelization, high computing power, security, etc. On-demand scalability feature allows to scale-in/out resources depending on workload which reduces unnecessary resource usage. On-premise computing users spend a major part of their budget on hardware, software, recovery management, networking, power supply. But, Cloud Computing reduces it as accessing a Virtual Machine (VM) is cheaper than buying and installing a physical resource. Cloud Computing allows parallelization i.e. several VMs can work simultaneously without affecting each other and thus increasing the resource utilization and efficiency of the cloud system. Cloud Computing is an off-premise form of computing, which is changing the expectation of what, how and when computing, allocation and management of storage and networking resources. It is also referred to as ubiquitous (anywhere, anytime) computing which requires only a subscription to use the virtual resources through the internet. In cloud, VM instances are deployed in cloud service provider data centres from where users can use the computational resources. An agreement is signed between client and service provider known as Service Level Agreement (SLA) in terms of price, Quality of Service (QoS) level, penalties associated with SLA violation, etc.

The cloud service model can be categorized as Infrastructure-as-a-Service (IaaS), Platform-as-a-Service (PaaS), and Software-as-a-Service (SaaS). SaaS model provides an interface that can be used to access applications managed by a third party through the internet. Users can use applications directly from a web browser without any downloads or installations, in some cases through plugins. Here everything (data, OS, servers, applications, storage and networking) is managed by third party. Popular SaaS examples are Google Apps, Salesforce, Citrix GoToMeeting, Concur, Gmail, Microsoft Office 365, DropBox, etc. A development environment is provided in PaaS model to build, host, and deploy an application. To run an application hardware and software maintenance is not required at company's workspace. PaaS examples include Google App Engine and SalesForce.com, etc. IaaS model gives infrastructure (computing, storing, networking resources, etc.) like an actual physical infrastructure as a service. It is a self-service model where users can purchase IaaS based on requirement like other utility (electricity, gas, etc.). This model gives users the ability to manage applications, data, OS, middleware, etc. IaaS examples are Microsoft Azure, Amazon Web Services (AWS), Joyent, Google Compute Engine (GCE). The Cloud Computing implementation models are public cloud, private cloud, hybrid cloud and community cloud. In private cloud the services and computing infrastructure are maintained by a particular organization. Here the required software and infrastructure are purchased and maintained in the organization, which offers high security and control. In public cloud services and infrastructure can be accessed over the internet. Here the user has no visibility and control over the computing infrastructure. It can be shared between any organizations, which makes it less secure than private cloud. Hybrid cloud uses the functionality of both private and public cloud features. An organization with the hybrid cloud model can use a private cloud for normal usage and public cloud for high load requirements to handle the sudden increase in computing requirements (Puthal, Sahoo, Mishra & Swain, 2015).

One of the research domains in the cloud is applications that must complete within the deadline (e.g. weather prediction, video streaming). Real-time applications need fast processing of tasks to maintain logical and timing correctness. The development in Internet of Things (IoT) applications, availability of the internet and low manufacturing cost gives rise in development of smart devices or systems. These applications continually generate huge amounts of data and processing all this to get a meaningful information is a tedious job. The numerous data imposes a massive burden on the computational infrastructure, which may fail if load increases beyond a certain limit. The various requirements of real-time applications include real-time responsiveness, huge amounts of task processing, heterogeneity of task (message, image, video, reading from sensors, etc.), fast application development and deployment for changing conditions. Cloud features supporting real-time task processing are:

1. Unlimited parallel computing and vast storage space that can handle a variety of workloads,
2. Virtualization of resources enable cost-effectiveness,
3. On-demand facility allows provisioning of hardware, software dynamically and
4. Elimination for configuration of development environment.

Users are now more sensitive to the latency of services they consume and want the service providers to ensure dynamic allocation and management of resources according to changing demand in real-time. The massive dynamic, fluctuating, heterogeneous real-time data require a Cloud Computing platform to support efficient storage of massive data. Real-time stream data processing problems can be solved in Cloud based on-demand subscribe-use-pay model. Real-time application main requirement is to be completed within the timing constraint failing of which generate penalty for the system depending on whether the task is soft or hard real-time. If a task is soft real-time and it misses its deadline, then system performance degrades. The system is failed if the task is hard real-time and it misses the deadline. Cloud Computing provides a platform where large amounts of data can be hosted and can be consumed by users in a pay-as-you-go manner and it uses NoSQL databases for storing and retrieving information.

The researchers (Kamburugamuve, Christiansen & Fox, 2015) described Internet of Things (IoT) Cloud, which is a platform for real-time processing and control of data from smart devices in the cloud. A robotic application built on this framework is used to measure the performance of the system. The authors (Liu, et al., 2014) have proposed a comprehensive framework for cloud-enabled robotic information fusion system for video tracking application. Here (Gunasekera, Hunter, Canto & Weeks, 2015) deployment of web-based satellite image processing pipelines onto Azure Cloud Computing platform is discussed. The researchers (Khodadadi, Calheiros & Buyya, 2015) have introduced a data-centric framework for development and deployment of IoT applications in the cloud. A mobile Cloud Computing (Mora Mora, Gil, Colom Lopez & Signes Pont, 2015) is presented to overcome the local computational power insufficiency for real-time processing. This paper (Zheng, Wang, Liu & Sun, 2015) discusses about real-time big data processing framework based on Cloud Computing technology, its challenges and solutions. The authors (Rao & Ali, 2015) have discussed various big data applications which depends on quick and timely (real-time) analytic for correct results. Here (Zhang, Cao, Khan, Li & Hwang, 2015) a task-level adaptive MapReduce framework is used for processing real-time streaming data from healthcare applications. The author (Wahner, 2014) has described real-time stream processing and streaming analytic frameworks. Table 1 presents several related studies that deal with real-time applications through Cloud Computing.

Real time applications guarantees following Quality of Service (QoS)/SLA parameters: bandwidth, maximum delay in transmission, delay jitter, loss rate, blocking probability, availability, downtime, time to response, etc. from the underlying network for maintaining the service quality (QoS, n.d.). One of the current processing models for rapid processing of large amount of data in parallel in a more efficient

Table 1. Real-time applications using Cloud

Sl. No.	Application	Challenges	Solution
1.[33]	Robot	Huge Data Processing	Cloud
2.[34]	Robot	Computationally Intensive Tasks	Cloud
3.[35]	Satellite Image Processing	Huge Data Processing	Cloud
4.[36]	Sentiment Analysis of Twitter Data	Huge Data Processing	Cloud
5.[37]	Smart Drive Application	Huge Data Processing, Data storage	Cloud
6.[38]	Smart Grid	Large Data Processing, Heterogeneity	Cloud
7.[39]	Health Care Application	Huge Data Processing	Cloud

manner is called MapReduce. It is a framework that allows large-scale data computation on clusters of machines in a Cloud Computing platform (Daneshyar & Razmjoo, 2012). Hadoop is an open source MapReduce implementation based on Hadoop Distributed File System (HDFS). HDFS is used to partition data sets and minimizes the impact of failures through replication of data sets (Assuncao, Calheiros, Bianchi, Netto & Buyya, 2015). MapReduce is a distributed programming framework used to process large amount of data. Cloud Computing environment is also used to address the processing challenges of massive data sets. The cloud application environment uses MapReduce to process a large amount of data application. The increase in web application and sensor network development led to the processing of large-scale data that are latency sensitive. This gives rise the need for MapReduce real-time scheduling. Hadoop is used by several Cloud providers like Amazon Elastic Compute Cloud (EC2). Cloud providers offer solutions to process real-time stream of data. AWS Kinesis is used for real-time processing of streaming data that can handle multiple sources like building dashboards, event generation, etc. Apache Kafka is a real-time publish-subscribe infrastructure (used by LinkedIn) to process activity data. Apache S4, Storm, Samza, IBM InfoSphere streams are another examples of the framework used for real-time data processing in the cloud (Lai, Chang, Hu, Huang & Chao, 2011). MapReduce is a powerful programming model which can be applied to various data-intensive applications such as search indexing, mining social network, recommendation services, etc. Many applications such as real-time advertising control data centers needs real-time data. Real-time applications using cloud need real-time analysis, which can be handled through the real-time MapReduce framework. Real-time applications are time bounded missing of which may reject the system.

Various challenges of data intensive Cloud Computing include scalability, availability, fault tolerance, elasticity, flexibility and efficient user access, data placement and data locality, efficient storage mechanism, privacy, energy efficiency, etc. (Shamsi, Khojaye, & Qasmi, 2013). Scalability means a large number of users can use the system without any noticeable performance degradation. Availability is related to the system's ability to tolerate faults i.e. the amount of time a system functions properly. Fault tolerance feature deals with the system's ability to sustain different types of failure like network congestion, CPU availability, bandwidth limitation, power faults and disk failures. Elasticity deals with cloud capability to utilize system resources as per the requests and usages. A data-intensive cloud should encourage an adaptable advancement environment in which desired tasks and demands should be easily put into use. Different issues for the big data system include data locality, fast data loading and query processing, efficient storage utilization, reduce network overhead, lower power consumption, etc. Since the data is distributed the storage mechanism must allow fast and efficient document access.

As in cloud data is outsourced and stored on cloud servers, issues of data protection and data privacy arises. Since data intensive cluster consumes high electric power an infrastructure is required with low power consumption. MapReduce has been the most popular programming platform for data-intensive computing. Hadoop is a popular MapReduce framework where tasks use shared resources to execute over a cluster of machines. For real time application resources may compete to meet their timing requirements. In such a scenario resource allocation (or resource scheduling) plays an important part to meet an application's expectation. Hadoop uses a fair scheduler to ensure each user get a minimum number of resources for task execution.

This chapter discusses about cloud system model, real-time MapReduce framework, Cloud based MapReduce framework examples, quality attributes of MapReduce scheduling and various MapReduce scheduling algorithm based on quality attributes.

CLOUD SYSTEM MODEL

A cloud data center consists of n heterogeneous physical hosts. Each host is identified by host id, processing element list, processing speed in terms of MIPS, memory size, total bandwidth, etc. There are C_j number of Virtual Machines running on k^{th} host, $V_{ki} = V_{k1}, V_{k2}, V_{k3}... V_{kCj}$ where, k= {1, 2... n}. A Virtual Machine (VM) can be identified by VM id, processing speed of VM in terms of MIPS, memory size of VM, bandwidth of VM, etc. When a request comes it is assigned to one of the VMs by the scheduler if sufficient resources are there to complete within deadline otherwise, task will be rejected. After the completion, resources used by VM are released and can be used by other request.

Ready queue is used to store task before it is assigned to appropriate VMs. The cloud task processing platform consists of admission controller, SLA negotiator, VM Monitor and Scheduling module. Admission controller decides whether to admit or reject the task. SLA Negotiator negotiates with the cloud

Figure 1. Cloud system model

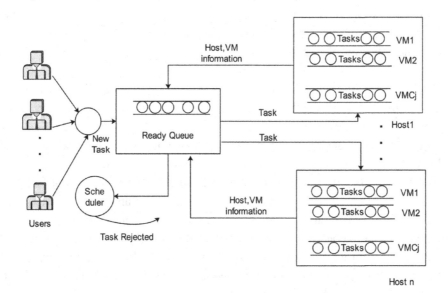

consumer in terms of pricing policy and QoS levels with a cloud provider to make the SLA (Service Level Agreement) between them. VM Monitor keeps track of status of VM i.e. activities and performance of the VM. Scheduler schedules the task to one of the VMs.

MapReduce FrameWork

MapReduce programming framework introduced by Google is used to provide scalable computing to process enormous amounts of data over clusters of computers (Lai, Chang, Hu, Huang, & Chao, 2011). The internet-based applications generate and consume enormous amounts of data. Facebook creates and processes nearly 15 Terabytes of data daily, Akamai captures and processes nearly 75 million events daily. Such huge volumes of data can be processed through a large number of parallel data tasks operating in different parts of the data sets. MapReduce framework generates a sequence of map and reduce tasks for a given input and runs these tasks on multiple nodes (machines) concurrently on different data elements (Tiwari, Sarkar, Bellur & Indrawan, 2015). MapReduce is a data-driven parallel computing model made up of large clusters of commodity machines with local storage. It provides system-level abstraction that hides the details of how computations are carried out and finding the input data for computation. The main aim of this model is to support parallel computation with distributed memory on large datasets. The MapReduce model consists of two phases: Map phase and Reduce phase. The whole process of MapReduce framework can be summarized as follows: in map phase the master node divides the input

Figure 2.

MapReduce Word Count Example

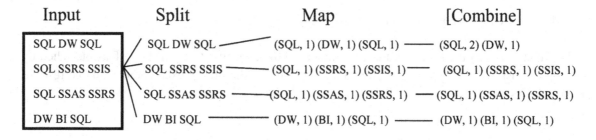

Figure 3.

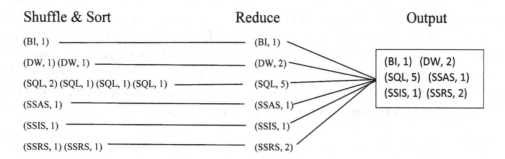

into independent blocks and then assign them to worker nodes. The worker nodes solve the sub problem and sends the results to its master node. The input in the form of <key, value> pair is distributed among the available map tasks. The output of mapper task is a key-value pair and it is transformed to reduce function for further processing. The mapper tasks are independent of each other and reducer task cannot start until all mapper tasks are finished. The intermediate key-value pair is used by reducer to generate output in the form of key-value pairs. Shuffle and Sort phases are the intermediate steps after map and before reduce phase. The advantages of MapReduce framework are fault-tolerance, fair task distribution, move processing to the data, and system-level abstraction from the users (Fernandez, et al., 2014).

REAL-TIME MAPREDUCE TASK

Let TS= $\{t_1, t_2 ... t_n\}$ represents set of task on a MapReduce cluster (Teng, Magoules, Yu, & Li, 2014). A real-time task is expressed as (A_i, C_i, D_i), where A_i is the arrival time of task i, C_i is the computation time, and D_i is the relative deadline of task i. $C_i < D_i$ because any task shouldn't exceed its deadline D_i (Sahoo, Nawaz, Mishra, & Sahoo, 2015) The tasks are partitioned into n_m map and n_r reduce operations each. Let the finishing time of map phase is M_i i.e. time required for completion of n_m map operations. R_i is finishing time of reduce phase i.e. the time to finish n_r reduce operations. Reduce operation can begin only after the completion of all map operations. The overall computation time for task t_i is

$$CT_i = M_i + R_i$$

This computation time must be less than the deadline of task ($CT_i < D_i$). The utilization u_i is defined as the ratio between computation time and its period i.e. $u_i = CT_i / D_i$. The overall utilization U of the system is the sum of utilization for all the tasks in TS.

$$U= (M_1 + R_1)/ D_1 + (M_2 + R_2)/ D_2 +... + (M_n + R_n)/ D_n$$

This metric shows the fraction of cluster time used by a specific task set. For a feasible scheduling solution for task set TS the required computation resources should not exceed the available resources i.e. $U \leq 1$ must be true.

MAPREDUCE FRAMEWORK EXAMPLES

A MapReduce infrastructure ensures availability, fault-tolerance and performance. The TaskTracker on nodes sends a periodic (within a specified time) heartbeat signal to the JobTracker, failing of which marked as node failure. If a node failure is detected by the JobTracker it reschedules all the previously executed map tasks by that node, but reduce task is not rescheduled because of presence in HDFS. Hadoop MapReduce scheduler uses data locality and backup task run to improve fault-tolerance and performance. Hadoop MapReduce considers multiple levels of data locality assuming that nodes are spread over several racks across the data center. Different data locality are:

1. **Node Locality:** A map task is executed on a node (local node) that contains a copy of the required data.
2. **Rack Locality:** Another node (rack local) in the same rack having idle worker node is used to run map a task.
3. **Nonlocality:** An idle (nonlocal) node in the same network switch area is used to execute map tasks.

The order used by a scheduler for data locality to schedule tasks is node locality, rack locality, nonlocality. Hadoop runs backup (speculative) tasks for straggler (slow) tasks to improve job's response time. Straggler tasks are tasks that get delayed due to resource completion on the corresponding node. Relative progress of task compared to the other tasks of a job is used to check whether a task is straggler task or not (Tiwari, Sarkar, Bellur & Indrawan, 2015).

Hadoop is an open source MapReduce framework. MapReduce follows master-slave architecture where one master node manages several slave nodes (Tiwari, Sarkar, Bellur & Indrawan, 2015; Fernandez, et al., 2014). Hadoop working model is explained below:

1. The input data are split into a set of equal-sized chunks (blocks) and distributed on the nodes of the cluster by NameNode (master node) of HDFS. DataNode (worker/slave node) are used to perform operations on data blocks as instructed by the NameNode.
2. JobTracker is a scheduler present in master node that schedules a set of map tasks and reduce tasks to a cluster of nodes (worker node) that run TaskTracker.
3. A map task works on assigned chunk of data and give key-value pairs as the output. The key-value pairs generated by all map tasks are partitioned into R sets (one for each reduce task). The details of the partition are informed to the JobTracker by the TaskTracker.
4. The JobTracker then communicates the partition details to each reduce task via TaskTracker.
5. The reduce task uses shuffling phase to read, sort and group the intermediate data by its corresponding intermediate keys.
6. The reduce task then do reduce operations on intermediate keys and generate output in the form of key-value pairs.

Corona is Facebook's in house scheduling framework for managing its data. Earlier Apache Hadoop was used by Facebook, but its limitations like scalability, inefficiency, less cluster utilization led to the development of a new framework. Hadoop uses slot-based resource management model, where map and reduce slots may be wasted if cluster workload doesn't meet the configuration. For software upgrades all the running jobs must be killed or ceased which results significant downtime. Corona separates cluster resource management from job coordination. The major difference between Hadoop and Corona are:

1. Addition of the cluster manger in Corona to track all the nodes and the amount of free resources available. It is integrated with fair-share scheduler.
2. Corona uses push-based scheduling, whereas Hadoop uses pull-based scheduling (MapReduce, n.d.).

Summingbird is an open sourced MapReduce streaming framework released by Twitter. Execution of code can be done either as Hadoop/MapReduce based batch mode or Storm based storm-mode or hybrid mode. The reason behind development of new framework is that there are issues with fully real-time system execution on Storm as:

1. Historical logs need to be coordinated with Hadoop or streamed through Storm whenever recomputation is performed on it
2. Message passing and random-write databases mechanism of Storm is difficult to maintain.

Summingbird uses Lambda architecture similar to Yahoo's Storm-YARN. Lambda architecture supports both batch and stream processing and can handle data from social media (Twitter, LinkedIn, etc.), financial sector (fraud detection, recommendations, etc.), IoT applications (smart city, wearable, manufacturing, etc.) (Summingbird, n.d.).

Twitter Storm is a distributed, fault-tolerant, real-time computation system. It is used for "stream processing", processing databases and messages in real-time. Storm uses Directed Acyclic Graph (DAG) topology, which can execute until there is some disturbance or system shut down completely. Some of the important features of Storm are:

1. Simple programming model reduces the complexity of real-time data processing
2. Runs any programming language (Java, Ruby, Python are default language)
3. Fault-tolerant
4. Horizontal scalability
5. Guaranteed message processing faster.

Storm cluster is similar to Hadoop cluster, but Storm runs "topologies" and Hadoop runs "MapReduce jobs". The Storm cluster is made up of master node and worker nodes. Master node runs "Nimbus" responsible for code distribution, task assignment and checking for failures. Each worker node runs "supervisor" which is responsible for the start and end of worker processes. Coordination between Nimbus and supervisor is done by Apache Zookeeper. Various terminologies used by Storm are Streams (data being processed), Spouts (data source), Bolts (process the data), Tasks (threads run within a Spout or Bolt), workers (processes that run threads), Stream Groupings (specify type of input to Bolt) and Topology (network of Spouts and Bolts nodes connected by Stream Groupings). Apache Storm can read and write files to HDFS (Storm, n.d.).

Phoenix MapReduce model is based on the shared memory concept. Thread is used to generate parallel map and reduce tasks and shared memory buffer is used to facilitate communication without data copying. Dynamic task scheduling to the available processors helps to achieve load balance and maximum task throughput. Field Programmable MapReduce (FPMR) on the field programmable gate arrays (FPGA) is a multi-level parallel MapReduce framework. It uses bit-level to task-level parallelism for machine learning and data mining. Misco MapReduce framework intended for mobile devices comprises of a master server and several worker client nodes. The master server keeps track of the user applications and application data, schedule tasks to workers. The client node request works from the master server, perform data processing and send results to the server. CLOUDLET is implemented using a Hadoop MapReduce framework for virtualized infrastructures. Mars is a MapReduce framework on graphic processors (GPUs). Here GPU threads are used for map or reduce tasks. Each thread is assigned a small number of key/value pairs to work on. A lock-free scheme is used for the massive tread parallelism of the GPU. Cloud MapReduce (CMR) framework buffers input/output data and intermediate data to queue from where data are supplied to the map and reduce workers. CMR is designed for computing clouds on the Amazon EC2 and optimized based on the Amazon's Simple Queue Service (SQS) for moving messages (Zhao, Tao & Streit, 2016).

Apache Samza is a real-time stream processor at LinkedIn, which uses Apache Kafka for messaging and Apache Hadoop YARN (Yet Another Resource Manager) for fault tolerance, processor isolation, security and resource management. Samza overcomes the high latency messaging issue of Hadoop through low-latency messaging system. Apache Kafka. The building blocks of Samza application are streams and jobs. A stream is a collection of immutable messages of similar type or category and provided by Apache Kafka. A job is the code that consumes and processes set of input streams and append messages to a set of output streams. The basic 3 components of Samza's architecture are:

1. Streaming layer (provide partitioned streams which are replicated and durable)
2. Execution layer (used for scheduling and coordinating tasks across the machines)
3. Processing layer (process the input stream and apply transformations).

Samza supports stateful stream processing and data are brought closer to the stream processor. It provides YARN Application Master and a YARN job (Linkedin-samza, n.d.; Samza, n.d.).

Amazon kinesis processes a large stream of data in real-time. It emit data to other data services such as Amazon Elastic MapReduce (Amazon EMR), Amazon Simple Storage Service (Amazon S3), or Amazon Redshift. Amazon Kinesis Firehose automatically delivers real-time streaming data to destinations (Amazon S3, EMR, redshift). An Elastic MapReduce connector is added to kinesis to analyze streaming data using Hadoop tools such as Hive, Pig and Hadoop streaming. Amazon Elastic MapReduce (Amazon EMR) web service is used for quick and cost-effective big data processing. It provides a managed Hadoop framework to distribute and process vast amounts of data on dynamically scalable Amazon Elastic Compute Cloud (Amazon EC2). DataTorrent is a real-time stream analytics framework used to process, analyze and act on data in motion. It supports today's high-throughput, Big Data analytics applications. DataTorrent can scale automatically (Datatorrent, n.d.).

Apache Spark is an open source big data processing framework that runs on top of Hadoop, Mesos or in the cloud. It provides in-memory cluster computing for high speed and access various data sources like HDFS, S3, HBase. Spark gives a comprehensive, unified framework to manage a variety of data sets such as batch data, real-time streaming data for big data processing. Spark uses less expensive shuffles, in-memory data storage and near real-time processing (Spark, n.d.).

QUALITY REQUIREMENTS OF MAPREDUCE SCHEDULING

Various quality requirements of MapReduce scheduling (Tiwari, Sarkar, Bellur & Indrawan, 2015) are as follows:

- **Fairness:** Fairness means each job gets equal or entitled opportunity execution. To ensure fairness to users and jobs, the resources need to be distributed in a cluster either equally or based on their priorities, size, or speed of execution required for the execution of their tasks. The scheduling algorithm must be such that it ensures fairness among jobs while scheduling.

- **Throughput:** The number of jobs/tasks completed over a given interval of time is known as throughput. Higher throughput can be achieved by improving data localization, energy efficiency and effective utilization of resources.
- **Response Time:** Response time of a job must be honoured agreed-upon SLA response time. Response time SLA adherence is becoming a key requirement for MapReduce jobs.
- **Availability:** Availability is the percentage of time a system is up and running and servicing requests. It is also defined as mean time between failures respond to user requests. For MapReduce job running on different machines or on cloud infrastructure availability is an important point of concern.
- **Energy Efficiency:** The energy efficiency requirement of a MapReduce system demands that node clusters consume as little energy as possible while executing the given workload, without impacting performance. The low utilization levels of servers, due to low load and data duplication, also result in poor energy efficiency in MapReduce clusters. So, the algorithms used for high data volume and use of commodity servers in MapReduce clusters must improve MapReduce energy efficiency.
- **Data Locality:** Data locality means moving task execution near the data storage for local data execution. The increase in data local task executions helps to minimize network contention (i.e., effective resource utilization) which in turn results higher throughput. So, the scheduling algorithm must strive to increase the instances of node or rack local data process executions.
- **Resource Utilization:** Effective resource utilization implies minimization of the time the CPU, I/O, and network resource waste in wait or idle or contention states. In a large shared environment, effective utilization of resources like CPU, memory, and I/O becomes critical in ensuring the best possible use of available resources by as many users/jobs as possible.
- **Security:** The security of a MapReduce cluster can be defined as having highly controlled access to the data, nodes, and processes running on all the nodes to avoid potential misuse and corruption. MapReduce scheduler uses a Kerberos distributed file system for data access security.

SCHEDULING ALGORITHMS BASED ON QUALITY ATTRIBUTES

FCFS is the earliest MapReduce scheduling algorithm implemented in Hadoop. Subsequently, various algorithms proposed are variations of the basic FCFS algorithm. The analysis based on specific quality attributes, namely *Fairness, Throughput, Response time, Availability/Reliability, Energy Efficiency, Data locality*, and *Resource utilization*. Following subsections describe how various algorithms aim to achieve the specific quality attribute based on various entities they schedule and the environmental characteristics to which they adapt for scheduling the given entity.

Data Locality

The increase in the number of interactive cloud applications led to MapReduce real-time scheduling for large scale data processing. MapReduce real-time jobs are affected by data locality and as they are non-pre-emptive shorter deadline jobs may be blocked by a longer deadline job. A MapReduce real-time scheduling framework is provided to guarantee deadline for interactive web applications. The data-locality-aware dispatcher balances the trade-off between runtime blocking and data locality for maximizing performance. Dynamic power management policy is also proposed to save system energy. For energy saving each node is considered to be in active or idle or sleep states. Let the switching time between active to sleep state is T_a and the switching time for active to idle state is negligible. Each node uses (Earliest Deadline First) EDF algorithm for scheduling the tasks (Kao & Chen, 2016).

Network bandwidth is a scarce resource for Cloud Computing systems like MapReduce, Hadoop. So, data locality is important to reduce job completion time. There are many approaches like delay scheduling, flow based algorithm to improve data locality. Since the methods are greedy they overlook global optimization and may suffer from high computation complexity. These problems are addressed by proposed data locality driven Balance-Reduce (BAR) algorithm. At first an initial task allocation is produced then job completion time is reduced by tuning it. BAR uses global view to adjust data locality dynamically based on network state and cluster workload. For overloaded cluster is handled by decreasing data locality so that tasks start early (Jin, Luo, Song, Dong & Xiong, 2011).

MapReduce features like simplicity, fault-tolerance, scalability makes it the most efficient and reliable technique to be used for data intensive Cloud Computing. An algorithm based on Locality-aware and fairness-aware key partitioning (LEEN) is developed to save network bandwidth dissipation during shuffle phase and balance reducer's input. Data locality is improvised in LEEN through asynchronous map and reduce scheme in the cloud. Current Hadoop's hash partitioning is suitable for equally appeared and uniformly stored intermediate keys in the data nodes. The blind hash partitioning lead to network congestion due to the huge amount of shuffled data, unfairness of reducer's inputs, performance degradation as the job's response time is dominated by the slower reduce instance. The network congestion during shuffle phase and unfairness of reducer's inputs is handled by locality-aware concept where intermediate keys buffer to the destination. This is achieved through the consideration of locations with high frequencies along with fair distribution of reducer's inputs (Ibrahim, et al., 2010).

A virtual MapReduce cluster allows enterprises cost-effective analysis of large amounts of data without investing in large infrastructure of their own. Each MapReduce job generates computation load, storage load, and network load. The network load increases during transfer of map tasks to reduce task which in turn deteriorates cloud performance. So, to reduce network traffic data locality is considered for both map and reduce phases of MapReduce workloads. The main goal of data locality is to reduce the network distance between storage and compute nodes i.e. the Virtual Machine (VM) executing the map task must be close to the VM that stores the input data. Similarly for reduce task intermediate data generated by map task VMs to be used as reduce input must be near to the VMs executing reduce task. The advantages of data locality are reduction in job execution time and network traffic. There is improvement in data locality with the use of Purlieus during map and reduce phases. It considers data and VM placement in the cloud. Data access in map and reduce phases and network flows between machines containing input/intermediate data and machines that process the data are used to classify MapReduce jobs. Conventional MapReduce clouds (e.g. Amazon Elastic MapReduce) use a separate cloud for both MapReduce computation and data storage. This framework delays the job execution and do data duplication in the cloud. Purlieus uses dedicated MapReduce cloud for storing the data and execute the jobs locally to nodes containing data (Palanisamy, Singh & Liu, 2015).

MapReduce handles big data by distributing the storage and data processing among a large number of computers (nodes). MapReduce framework provides scalable and fault tolerant environment where users can execute their task without worrying about implementation details as in the case of distributed programming. An important research area is how MapReduce will perform in heterogeneous environments where machines are dissimilar. This paper discusses about MapReduce deployment in heterogeneous cloud. Data is dynamically partitioned before the map phase and use of Virtual Machine mapping in the reduce phase maximize the resource utilization. Data locality is the reflection of the performance of MapReduce as access is faster for local data. MapReduce works in the principle of "moving computation towards data is cheaper than moving data towards computation". The proposed method is used to improve data locality and total completion time of MapReduce in cloud environment (Hsu, Slagter & Chung, 2015).

Data locality is a key factor that affects the performance of MapReduce framework. High Performance Scheduling Optimizer (HPSO) is used to improve data locality for MapReduce jobs. The required input data are preloaded before the launch of tasks to TaskTracker. The completion time for MapReduce jobs is reduced as waiting period of map tasks with rack and rack-off locality is shortened. The prefetching service based task scheduler HPSO combines the task scheduler, prediction and prefetching methods together to exploit data locality. First execution time of map tasks is predicted and then a sequence of nodes free busy slots are evaluated. This node sequence is used by HPSO to predict and assign the most suitable map tasks to nodes ahead of time. After the scheduling decision is made the required input data of the node are preloaded from remote nodes or local disk to memory (prefetching buffer) before the actual task launching. Main issues with prefetching mechanism are size and management. The authors have considered 64 MB prefetch buffer which is the default data block size of HDFS. The prefetching buffer is managed by two buffer units: one for running map task processing and other for preloading of next map task or null (Sun, Zhuang, Li, Lu & Zhou, 2016).

Energy Efficiency

Energy is an important parameter (Mishra, Deswal, Sahoo & Sahoo, 2015). The energy efficiency of data centers is becoming a major concern, and a few scheduling algorithms have been proposed to address it. In this section, we discuss those MapReduce scheduling algorithms designed to improve the energy efficiency of MapReduce systems.

Cloud Computing increases utilization and power savings through consolidation. The flexibility and on-demand feature of cloud environment makes it suitable for big data analysis. The writers have used two Hadoop deployment models one with collocated data and compute services and another with separated data and compute services to understand their performance and power implications. In Hadoop compute layer is provided through the MapReduce framework and HDFS is used to provide data layer. Data Locality helps to minimize data movements for the map tasks. Hadoop assumes co-existence of data nodes and compute nodes and it doesn't support on-demand feature. Scalability is an important feature of cloud environment. Scale-up/down of partitioning VMs is expensive due to the involved time and space overhead. Large amounts of data processing require huge compute and storage infrastructures which in turn consume substantial amounts of energy. The performance evaluation of both the deployment model shows that (i) data locality plays a key role for energy efficiency, (ii) separated data and compute model is feasible at the cost of increased energy consumption (Feller, Ramakrishnan & Morin, 2015).

The energy efficiency of servers is an important component for the overall energy consumption of the data center. The researchers have proposed an energy efficient task scheduling model based on Google's MapReduce framework for Cloud Computing. The scheduling method uses genetic algorithm with their own encoding, decoding methods and genetic operators. The difference between server's optimal points with its CPU utilization after scheduling is used in the energy efficient optimization model. Different ways of reducing energy consumptions are by decreasing energy consumed by supporting systems like servers, cooling system, power distribution equipment, etc., turning off unused devices when possible, and designing energy proportional servers or networks. Energy-proportional servers consume energy in proportional to the amount of work performed and energy proportional network consume energy in proportional to the amount of traffic it is moving (Wang, Wang & Zhu, 2012; Wang, Wang & Cui, 2016).

Energy efficiency is one of the key reasons for migrating to cloud environment. Cost of energy has a large percentage of operational expenditure for computating infrastructure. Radian 6 and Palantir are commercial examples of big-data analysis with cloud-based infrastructures using Hadoop. Different metrics used to demonstrate the energy efficiency of cloud provider are "BREEAM certification", "LEED certification", "energy star rating". These metrics can be combined with other metrics like carbon footprint and energy consumption per VM to give a finer energy usage analysis. The researchers have investigated the energy consumption of Virtual Machines running Hadoop system, over an OpenNebula cloud. The workload used is based on sentiment analysis undertaken over Twitter messages. They have considered different power consumption levels starting from switching on the physical machine to the point it is being shut down. The six power consumption levels are standby mode (machine is connected to the electricity grid), machine is switched on, idle state (machine ready to host VMs), deployment and idle state of the VMs, Hadoop job execution, and switched off (shut down) (Conejero, et al., 2016).

Others

To enhance MapReduce performance identical tasks are allocated to each cloud node. But for heterogeneous cloud this allocation is not applicable due to variation in computing power and system resources between the nodes. Adaptive Task Allocation Scheduler (ATAS) is used to improve the original speculative execution method by accurately determining response time and backup tasks that affect the system. Nodes are divided into two groups: quick node and slow node out of which quick node is given higher priority for allocation of backup tasks (Yang & Chen, 2015).

A backup task is launched on other nodes to handle slow tasks. It helps slow (straggler) tasks finished as soon as possible. Wrong detection of straggler tasks causes many problems like no improvement in execution time due to the presence of real straggler tasks and wastage of system resources as backup tasks are launched for the wrong straggler task. History based Auto Tuning (HAT) MapReduce scheduler is proposed for detection of straggler tasks and to introduce backup tasks efficiently for heterogeneous environments. Straggler task detection and parameter tuning is done based on historical information on each node. The weight of each phase of a map task and a reduce task is tuned by value stored in history task. This weight of the phases is used to calculate the progress of current tasks, which is then used to accurately estimate the remaining time of tasks. Thereafter backup tasks are launched for the tasks with longest remaining time (Chen, et al., 2013).

Paused Rate Monotonic (PRM) algorithm is used to schedule hard real-time tasks on a MapReduce base3d cloud. PRM is a priority driven algorithm that schedules tasks to maximize the number of tasks meeting their deadlines. A short break (Pause) is done between the map and reduce stage. This break is used to partition, sort, combine and shuffle to speedup intermediate data transfers across the network (Teng, Magoules, Yu & Li, 2014).

The researchers have presented Cura a cost-effective MapReduce cloud service model. Here MapReduce profiling is used to form best cluster configuration for the job. Execution delay of certain jobs provides deadline awareness which in turn optimizes cloud providers global resource allocation and reduce cost. Cura provides cost-aware resource provisioning and ensures fast response for short interactive jobs (Palanisamy, Singh & Liu, 2015).

A server is used to record user's behaviour for the recommendation of the most popular TV programs. The server becomes the bottleneck of the system as the number of user increases. This system also requires grouping of users based on similar viewing patterns in a cluster which is time consuming. A cloud based program recommendation system based on MapReduce framework is proposed to lower the server's load. MapReduce version of k-means and k-Nearest Neighbour (kNN) methods are used to group users into clusters and to add a new user into grouped cluster. The weight used for grouping users into clusters is the sum of time periods that users have watched it. The main idea of using the MapReduce framework is to provide scalable and powerful computing for mass information processing for a recommendation system (Lai, Chang, Hu, Huang & Chao, 2011).

Resource stealing is used to improve resource utilization in heterogeneous network environments. In this method residual resources are stolen by idle slots on a node through sub task creation that collaboratively process input data. Speculative execution in Hadoop runs useless speculative tasks, which is reduced by proposed benefit aware speculative execution (Guo & Fox, 2012).

The authors have evaluated the cost of moving MapReduce applications to the cloud. Cloud-based data-intensive applications take advantage of the huge processing and storage capabilities of cloud and MapReduce computation. Amazon elastic MapReduce, Azure MapReduce are examples of MapReduce implementation on cloud. The cost model consists of computational cost (CPU cost), data storage costs and data transfer cost. They have evaluated the performance of 3 MapReduce applications (grep, sort, pipeline MapReduce) in two environments one in Grid'5000 experimental grid testbed and another in a Nimbus cloud with Grid'5000 physical nodes (Moise & Carpen-Amarie, 2012).

MapReduce is designed for data-intensive applications while cloud data center host a huge amount of data. So, MapReduce is a good choice for parallel computing in the cloud. The authors develop a framework for the MapReduce execution on individual Virtual Machines. The framework is able to dynamically include or remove Virtual Machines, MapReduce execution across different cloud platforms. The proposed MapReduce framework was assessed on a private cloud with the OpenNebula cloud middleware. Deployment of MapReduce on the cloud needs cluster management for efficient run of MapReduce application. Due to this inter Cloud Computing is prohibited. The software framework developed enables individual Virtual Machines to execute MapReduce applications in a parallel/collaborative way without introducing a middleware. The research work focus on Single-Sign-On (SSO) security mechanism that enables the remote access to the individual machines (Zhao, Tao, & Streit, 2016).

In (Sahoo, Sahoo, & Tiwary, 2014) a MapReduce approach is used to detect malware present inside unstructured data stored in a distributed file system. Different pattern matching algorithms like Boyer-Moore's algorithm, KnuthMorrisPratt's algorithm, RabinKarp's algorithm are used to search signatures in the content of files.

There are various challenges and requirements of cloud infrastructures to support cloud based data intensive applications that are latency sensitive. Applications like mission critical task, real-time control decision has strict timing requirement and missing of which is undesirable. The researchers have submitted a stream of Hadoop jobs with a deadline to cloud cluster. The main objective is to schedule the job to meet the real-time constraint. The different metrics used are miss rate, i.e. fraction of applications missing their deadline and maximum tardiness i.e. the maximum elapsed time from the deadline for completion time of the applications that miss their deadlines (Phan, Zhang, Zheng, Loo & Lee, 2011).

CONCLUSION

Most of the real time applications need to deal with a variety of data like text, image, video, etc. and huge amount of data. On-premise infrastructure has various issues like scalability, high computing resource, and large data storage for processing such applications. On the other hand Cloud Computing has following essential characteristics: on-demand access, resource pooling, and scalability. So, Cloud Computing is used to process such applications which need huge computing resource, data storage, etc. For processing huge amount of data termed as big data MapReduce framework is used. MapReduce framework has many advantages such as parallel computing, scalable, cost-effective, fast, flexibility, simplicity and security, etc. This chapter discusses about MapReduce framework for real time task, its examples and various MapReduce scheduling algorithms satisfy quality attribute like energy-efficiency, data locality, cost, fairness, etc.

FUTURE SCOPE AND CHALLENGES

Cloud Computing era is due to the advancement of technologies in various fields ranging from processing, storage, providing computational resources on demand, high bandwidth network access and increased security of the internet. Now users are becoming more sensitive towards, delay in applications they are using. The development of automatic applications, smart devices and applications, sensor based applications need huge data storage and computing resources which will increase the capital cost after certain limit. So, a scalable platform like Cloud Computing is required that can provide huge computing resource, and data storage for processing such applicatons. MapReduce framework is used to process huge amounts of data. Data processing on a cloud based on MapReduce would provide added benefits such as fault tolerant, heterogeneous, ease of use, free and open, efficient which most DBMS do not provide. There lies a bright future for processing real time applications in the cloud. Despite several advantages various challenges associated with MapReduce framework include data storage, online processing, analytics, privacy and security. The execution of real time applications in the cloud using the MapReduce framework adds additional challenges as they required timing constraint.

REFERENCES

Assuncao, M. D., Calheiros, R. N., Bianchi, S., Netto, M. A., & Buyya, R. (2015). Big Data computing and clouds: Trends and future directions. *Journal of Parallel and Distributed Computing*, *79*, 3–15. doi:10.1016/j.jpdc.2014.08.003

Chen, Q., Guo, M., Deng, Q., Zheng, L., Guo, S., & Shen, Y. (2013). HAT: History-based auto-tuning MapReduce in heterogeneous environments. *The Journal of Supercomputing*, *64*(3), 1038–1054. doi:10.1007/s11227-011-0682-5

Conejero, J., Rana, O., Burnap, P., Morgan, J., Caminero, B., & Carrion, C. (2016). Analyzing hadoop power consumption and impact on application qos. *Future Generation Computer Systems*, *55*, 213–223. doi:10.1016/j.future.2015.03.009

Daneshyar, S., & Razmjoo, M. (2012). Large-scale data processing using Mapreduce in cloud computing Environment. *International Journal on Web Service Computing, 3*(4), 1–13. doi:10.5121/ijwsc.2012.3401

Datatorrent. (n.d.). Retrieved from https://www.datatorrent.com/product/architecture/

Feller, E., Ramakrishnan, L., & Morin, C. (2015). Performance and energy efficiency of big data applications in cloud environments: A hadoop case study. *Journal of Parallel and Distributed Computing, 79*, 80–89. doi:10.1016/j.jpdc.2015.01.001

Fernandez, A., del Rio, S., Lopez, V., Bawakid, A., del Jesus, M. J., Benitez, J. M., & Herrera, F. (2014). Big Data with Cloud Computing: An insight on the computing environment, MapReduce, and programming frameworks. *Wiley Interdisciplinary Reviews: Data Mining and Knowledge Discovery, 4*(5), 380–409.

Gunasekera, K., Hunter, J., Canto, M., & Weeks, S. (2015). *Accelerating Satellite Image Processing through Cloud Computing.* Academic Press.

Guo, Z., & Fox, G. (2012). Improving mapreduce performance in heterogeneous network environments and resource utilization. *Proceedings of the 12th IEEE/ACM International Symposium on Cluster, Cloud and Grid Computing (Ccgrid 2012).* doi:10.1109/CCGrid.2012.12

Hsu, C.-H., Slagter, K. D., & Chung, Y.-C. (2015). Locality and loading aware virtual machine mapping techniques for optimizing communications in MapReduce applications. *Future Generation Computer Systems, 53*, 43–54. doi:10.1016/j.future.2015.04.006

Ibrahim, S., Jin, H., Lu, L., Wu, S., He, B., & Qi, L. (2010). Leen: Locality/fairness-aware key partitioning for mapreduce in the cloud. *Second IEEE International Conference on Cloud Computing Technology and Science (CloudCom).*

Jin, J., Luo, J., Song, A., Dong, F., & Xiong, R. (2011). BAR: an efficient data locality driven task scheduling algorithm for cloud computing. *Proceedings of the 11th IEEE/ACM International Symposium on Cluster, Cloud and Grid Computing.* doi:10.1109/CCGrid.2011.55

Kamburugamuve, S., Christiansen, L., & Fox, G. (2015). A framework for real time processing of sensor data in the cloud. *Journal of Sensors, 2015*, 1–11. doi:10.1155/2015/468047

Kao, Y.-C., & Chen, Y.-S. (2016). Data-locality-aware mapreduce real-time scheduling framework. *Journal of Systems and Software, 112*, 65–77. doi:10.1016/j.jss.2015.11.001

Khodadadi, F., Calheiros, R. N., & Buyya, R. (2015). A data-centric framework for development and deployment of Internet of Things applications in clouds. *Tenth IEEE International Conference on, Intelligent Sensors, Sensor Networks and Information Processing (ISSNIP).* doi:10.1109/ISSNIP.2015.7106952

Lai, C.-F., Chang, J.-H., Hu, C.-C., Huang, Y.-M., & Chao, H.-C. (2011). CPRS: A cloud-based program recommendation system for digital TV platforms. *Future Generation Computer Systems, 27*(6), 823–835. doi:10.1016/j.future.2010.10.002

Linkedin-samza. (n.d.). Retrieved from http://www.infoq.com/articles/linkedin-samza

Liu, B., Chen, Y., Blasch, E., Pham, K., Shen, D., & Chen, G. (2014). A holistic cloud-enabled robotics system for real-time video tracking application. In Future Information Technology. doi:10.1007/978-3-642-40861-8_64

MapReduce. (n.d.). Retrieved from https://www.quora.com/How-does-Facebook-Twitter-and-Google-use-Map-Reduce-paradigm

Mishra, S. K., Deswal, R., Sahoo, S., & Sahoo, B. (2015). *Improving Energy Consumption in Cloud.* Academic Press.

Moise, D., & Carpen-Amarie, A. (2012). *Mapreduce applications in the cloud: A cost evaluation of computation and storage.* Springer.

Mora Mora, H., Gil, D., Colom Lopez, J. F., & Signes Pont, M. T. (2015). *Flexible Framework for Real-Time Embedded Systems Based on Mobile Cloud Computing Paradigm.* Mobile Information Systems.

Palanisamy, B., Singh, A., & Liu, L. (2015). Cost-effective resource provisioning for mapreduce in a cloud. *IEEE Transactions on Parallel and Distributed Systems*, 26(5), 1265–1279. doi:10.1109/TPDS.2014.2320498

Phan, L. T., Zhang, Z., Zheng, Q., Loo, B. T., & Lee, I. (2011). An empirical analysis of scheduling techniques for real-time cloud-based data processing. *IEEE International Conference on, Service-Oriented Computing and Applications (SOCA)*. doi:10.1109/SOCA.2011.6166240

Puthal, D., Sahoo, B., Mishra, S., & Swain, S. (2015). Cloud computing features, issues, and challenges: a big picture. *International Conference on, Computational Intelligence and Networks (CINE)*. doi:10.1109/CINE.2015.31

QoS. (n.d.). Retrieved from http://www.nptel.ac.in/courses/106105086/pdf/module6.pdf

Rao, K. V., & Ali, M. A. (2015). *Survey on Big Data and applications of real time Big Data analytics.* Academic Press.

Sahoo, A. K., Sahoo, K. S., & Tiwary, M. (2014). Signature based malware detection for unstructured data in Hadoop. *International Conference on, Advances in Electronics, Computers and Communications (ICAECC)*. doi:10.1109/ICAECC.2014.7002394

Sahoo, S., Nawaz, S., Mishra, S. K., & Sahoo, B. (2015). *Execution of real time task on cloud environment.* Academic Press.

Samza. (n.d.). Retrieved from http://thenewstack.io/apache-samza-linkedins-framework-for-stream-processing

Shamsi, J., Khojaye, M. A., & Qasmi, M. A. (2013). Data-intensive cloud computing: Requirements, expectations, challenges, and solutions. *Journal of Grid Computing*, 11(2), 281–310. doi:10.1007/s10723-013-9255-6

Spark. (n.d.). Retrieved from http://www.infoq.com/articles/apache-spark-introduction

Storm. (n.d.). Retrieved from http://www.infoq.com/news/2011/09/twitter-storm-real-time-hadoop

Summingbird. (n.d.). Retrieved from http://www.infoq.com/news/2014/01/twitter-summingbird

Sun, M., Zhuang, H., Li, C., Lu, K., & Zhou, X. (2016). Scheduling algorithm based on prefetching in MapReduce clusters. *Applied Soft Computing*, *38*, 1109–1118. doi:10.1016/j.asoc.2015.04.039

Teng, F., Magoules, F., Yu, L., & Li, T. (2014). A novel real-time scheduling algorithm and performance analysis of a MapReduce-based cloud. *The Journal of Supercomputing*, *69*(2), 739–765. doi:10.1007/s11227-014-1115-z

Tiwari, N., Sarkar, S., Bellur, U., & Indrawan, M. (2015). Classification framework of MapReduce scheduling algorithms. *ACM Computing Surveys*, *47*(3), 49. doi:10.1145/2693315

Wahner, K. (2014). *Real-Time Stream Processing as Game Changer in a Big Data World with Hadoop and Data Warehouse*. InfoQ.

Wang, X., Wang, Y., & Cui, Y. (2016). An energy-aware bi-level optimization model for multi-job scheduling problems under cloud computing. *Soft Computing*, *20*(1), 303–317. doi:10.1007/s00500-014-1506-3

Wang, X., Wang, Y., & Zhu, H. (2012). Energy-efficient task scheduling model based on MapReduce for cloud computing using genetic algorithm. *Journal of Computers*, *7*(12), 2962–2970. doi:10.4304/jcp.7.12.2962-2970

Yang, S.-J., & Chen, Y.-R. (2015). Design adaptive task allocation scheduler to improve MapReduce performance in heterogeneous clouds. *Journal of Network and Computer Applications*, *57*, 61–70. doi:10.1016/j.jnca.2015.07.012

Zhang, F., Cao, J., Khan, S. U., Li, K., & Hwang, K. (2015). A task-level adaptive MapReduce framework for real-time streaming data in healthcare applications. *Future Generation Computer Systems*, *43*, 149–160. doi:10.1016/j.future.2014.06.009

Zhao, J., Tao, J., & Streit, A. (2016). Enabling collaborative MapReduce on the Cloud with a single-sign-on mechanism. *Computing*, *98*(1-2), 55–72. doi:10.1007/s00607-014-0390-0

Zheng, Z., Wang, P., Liu, J., & Sun, S. (2015). Real-time big data processing framework: Challenges and solutions. *Applied Mathematics & Information Sciences*, *9*(6), 3169.

KEY TERMS AND DEFINITIONS

Availability: Availability means the degree to which a system, subsystem or equipment is in a specified operable and committable state.

Data Locality: Data Locality means the vicinity of the data in regard to the Mapper tasks working on the data.

Hadoop Distributed File System: Hadoop Distributed File System (HDFS) is a Java-based file system that supports large cluster of commodity servers. It also makes the data storage, scalable and reliable.

Quality of Services: Quality of Service (QoS) is the degree to which certain level of performance is guaranteed.

Response Time: The response time of a task is the time delay between arrival time of task and task produces its required results.

Scalability: Scalability is the capability of a system, network, or process to handle the increasing amount of work/ user without disruption.

Service Level Agreement: A service level agreement (SLA) is a treaty among the end user and a service provider. SLA defines level of service expected by the end user from a service provider, metrics that measure the service, and the remedies or consequences if required service level is not achieved.

Virtual Machine: A Virtual Machine is a logical machine which has all the features of physical machines and runs an operating system and applications.

Virtualization: Virtualization refers as technique to create a virtual version of something like computer hardware, storage devices, operating systems, computer network resources, etc.

Yet Another Resource Negotiator: Yet Another Resource Negotiator (YARN) is a cluster management technology used in Apache Hadoop. It separates HDFS from MapReduce to make Hadoop environment apt for operational applications.

Chapter 9
Resource and Energy Efficient Virtual Machine Migration in Cloud Data Centers

Subrat Kumar Dhal
National Institute of Technology Rourkela, India

Harshit Verma
National Institute of Technology Rourkela, India

Sourav Kanti Addya
National Institute of Technology Rourkela, India

ABSTRACT

Cloud computing service has been on the rise over the past few decades, which has led to an increase in the number of data centers, thus consuming more amount of energy for their operation. Moreover, the energy consumption in the cloud is proportional to the resource utilization. Thus consolidation schemes for the cloud model need to be devised to minimize energy by decreasing the operating costs. The consolidation problem is NP-complete, which requires heuristic techniques to get a sub-optimal solution. The authors have proposed a new consolidation scheme for the virtual machines (VMs) by improving the host overload detection phase. The resulting scheme is effective in reducing the energy and the level of Service Level Agreement (SLA) violations both, to a considerable extent. For testing the performance of implementation, a simulation environment is needed that can provide an environment of the actual cloud computing components. The authors have used CloudSim 3.0.3 simulation toolkit that allows testing and analyzing Allocation and Selection algorithms.

INTRODUCTION

According to Mell et al. (2011), Cloud computing is "a model for enabling ubiquitous, convenient and on demand network access to a shared pool of configurable computing resources (e.g., networks, servers, storage, applications, and services) that can be rapidly provisioned and released with minimal management effort or service provider interaction."

DOI: 10.4018/978-1-5225-1721-4.ch009

The services offered by the cloud computing model can be classified as:

- **Software as a Service (SaaS):** "The potentiality provided to the user is to use the provider's applications and programs carrying out on a cloud infrastructure. The applications are accessible from several client devices through either a client interface, such as a web browser or a program interface. The user neither manages nor controls the fundamental cloud infrastructure, including storage, networks, servers or operating systems, with the exception of limited application configuration settings."
- **Platform as a Service (PaaS):** "The potentiality provided to the user is to deploy user-developed applications created using programming languages, and tools supported by the provider onto the cloud infrastructure. The user neither manages nor controls the fundamental cloud infrastructure, including storage, networks, servers or operating systems, but has control over the deployed applications and configuration settings for the hosting environment."
- **Infrastructure as a Service (IaaS):** "The potentiality provided to the user is to provision processing, storage, networks, and other underlying computing resources where the user is able to deploy and run discretionary software, which can include operating systems and applications. The user neither manages nor controls the fundamental cloud infrastructure, but has control over storage, operating systems, and deployed applications; and limited control of select networking components (e.g., host firewalls)."

These services are made available to the cloud service users by creating instances of Virtual Machines (VMs) and then consolidating the resource allocation periodically. After virtualization, users' applications can run on the same hardware managed by their own operating system.

Traditionally, organizations have had to own and deploy the hardware, network resources and also run them efficiently. Cloud computing has changed this approach drastically. According to Buyya et al. (2009), the organizations can outsource their computational requirements to the cloud service providers and use the services over the internet, to reduce infrastructure and maintenance costs, instead of dealing with the cost and process of purchasing expensive IT infrastructure and then with periodic upgrades of the same. They can now pay only for the cloud resources they actually use.

A cloud data center consists of a large number of servers and switches for transmitting data between servers or between servers and clients. The infrastructure energy consumed in a data center includes the energy used for computational tasks, the energy used for transmission of data and the energy required for cooling the data center. According to Belady et al. (2007), the cost incurred due to this infrastructure energy has been estimated to be much more than the IT costs. The rise in the use of cloud computing has resulted in the setting up of more and more number of data centers, which has led to a huge increase in the consumption of energy. According to Huang et al. (2014), data centers consume around 110 Billion kilowatt hours of energy per year. This humongous increase in the infrastructure energy consumption in recent times has resulted in a sharp increase in the CO_2 emissions, which contributes towards global warming, according to Hanne (2011). Thus it is imperative that energy consumption in the cloud data centers be reduced, by improving the way in which the cloud resources are provisioned. Some of the ways in which the resource provisioning in the cloud has been improved is by the use of the virtualization technology and live migration techniques, as suggested by Hwang et al. (2013) and Bobroff et al. (2007) respectively.

The most important difference between cloud computing and a traditional method like grid computing, is the use of large scale virtualized environments and devices. Virtualization is advantageous as it partitions the resources of a single server into multiple execution environments, which are isolated from each other. According to Sahoo et al. (2010), this enables a number of Operating systems to run on the same hardware, thus reducing the hardware cost and increasing the return on investment (ROI) for the service providers. Each of these partitioned units is known as a Virtual Machine. Without virtualization, the processing power of a physical server may not be fully utilized if it runs only a single OS. An important concept in Virtualization is that of the Hypervisor or the Virtual Machine Monitor (VMM). Hypervisor is a layer of abstraction between the hardware and the operating system and the applications running on top of it. The virtualization layer is an interface between the users and the infrastructure resources.

The Virtualization layer contains the resource managers and other components that are responsible for energy efficient consolidation and resource allocation. The Virtual Machines behave like Physical Machines (PM), and they can run simultaneously, yet remain isolated from each other, all the while sharing the same physical resources. The hypervisor is responsible for the abstraction of these Virtual Machines from the physical resources and for determining what share of resources each Virtual Machine gets to use. Figure 1 shows the basic architecture of a physical machine along with the hypervisor layer and the VMs running on it.

Live migration is a technique using which VMs can be transferred between PMs with nearly a zero downtime. It enables the VMs to utilize minimal number of PMs based on their present resource requirements. Huang et al. (2011) in their experiment to compare the power consumed in VM consolidation schemes deploying live virtual migration, with the power consumed in regular VM placement strategies without making use of live migration, found out that live VM migration does increase some overhead involved in the consolidation process, but overall, it leads to a significant decrease in the power consumption in the data centers.

Another important concept which is made use of in reducing the energy consumption is switching the idle servers on/off or putting them to sleep (power saving state). This is because an idle server may still use up-to 70% of the peak energy consumption, according to Fan et al. (2007). It is therefore, highly

Figure 1. Virtualization concept

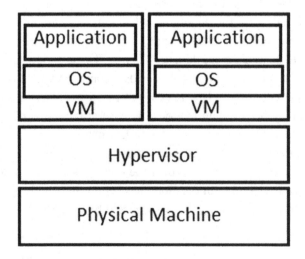

inefficient to keep the underutilized servers running in such a state. So, based on VM selection policies, certain chosen VMs, if possible, may be migrated away from these under-utilized servers and the server can be put to sleep or switched off.

On the other hand, overloading of servers leads to performance degradation of the application workload and hence the occurrence of SLA violations. In the state of over-utilization, the servers are not able to allot the adequate amount of CPU processing power requested by the applications. As a result, the cloud service providers have to pay a previously agreed upon fine, as defined in the Service level agreement (SLA), to the cloud service users based on the level of SLA violations experienced by the applications. Thus overload of servers incurs extra cost to the cloud service providers. Live migration is made use of, to migrate some of the VMs from the overloaded servers.

It is therefore, extremely important for the cloud service providers to find a good balance between keeping the energy consumption down and reducing the SLA violations as both contribute significantly towards the cost incurred by the cloud service providers.

Literature Review

One of the earliest attempts at energy saving in cloud data centers was by Horvath et al. (2009). They made use of the Dynamic voltage and frequency scaling (DVFS) method. In DVFS, the CPU frequency and voltage of the hosts is reduced proportionally to the power required due to the application workloads running on them.

The DVFS method was further improved upon by Heo et al. (2009) by combining it with switching the hosts on/off to further reduce energy consumption. Calheiros et al. (2010) combined the DVFS approach and switching on/off of hosts with live migration of the VMs. They aggressively consolidated the VMs, migrating them after every 5 seconds, based on the CPU utilization of the hosts. Gupta et al. (2003) in their work have suggested considering network infrastructure for reducing energy consumption. They suggest that Network interfaces, switches, routers and links be sent to power saving mode to reduce energy usage. Kusic et al. (2009) have defined the virtual machine provisioning problem as an uncertain sequential optimization problem and they use a technique called Limited Lookahead Control (LLC) for the optimization of the same. Their objective is to reduce power usage and the level of SLA violations. In their work, they predict the future state of the system using Kalman filter and then provision the Virtual Machines, based on these predictions. Srikantaiah et al. (2008) have suggested consolidation using multi-dimensional bin packing to obtain optimal energy consumption. Nathuji et al. (2007) divided the data center resource management into local and global levels. The global level decides whether VM optimization needs to be done, based on the information received from all the local managers and the local manager in each of the hosts is responsible for provisioning the resources locally in the host. For optimizing the VM placements, Verma et al. (2008) migrate the VMs, using live migration, periodically to minimize the power consumption and enhance resource utilization of the hosts. They have used a power-aware First Fit Decreasing heuristic for VM placements. But they do not consider SLA violations in their work. Jung et al. (2008), (2009) in their work of dynamic consolidation of virtual machines employed the technique of live migration and strictly adhering to the SLA. Kumar et al. (2009) in their work proposed consolidating the Virtual Machines based on the stability of the current placement scenario. They estimate the current allocations stability and then decide if further consolidation is needed or not.

Beloglazov and Buyya (2012) proposed self-adapting heuristics which make use of a statistical analysis of the historical data of the resource usage by the virtual machines in the hosts. They have proposed the use of various measures of statistical dispersion for dynamically changing the overload threshold limit. For detecting underload of hosts, they first choose the host with the least CPU utilization and check if all VMs running on it can be migrated or not to other hosts. If it can be done, that host is switched to a power saving state and the VMs are migrated to other hosts. This process is carried on iteratively for all other hosts. For choosing which VMs to migrate they have used three algorithms namely: Minimum number of migrations (MNM), highest potential growth (HPG) and random choice (RC). For placing the VMs a modified power aware version of the Best Fit Decreasing heuristic is used. Their proposed algorithms succeed in reducing energy to a great extent while also maintaining a high level of adherence to the SLA.

Research Statement and Research Questions

The problem consists of devising an efficient VM consolidation scheme that can not only reduce the energy consumption in the data centers but also adhere to the SLA to a great extent. The problem deals with rigorous online monitoring of utilization levels of servers to check for over-utilization and under-utilization, VM selection and VM placement. The consolidation scheme can be divided into 5 phases: *Initial VM placement, Host Underload detection, Host Overload detection, VM Selection* and *VM placement*. While there exist many algorithms for each of the five phases which give good results, the performance of the algorithms can always be enhanced even further to reduce the energy consumption and also lower the level of SLA violations.

The main research questions are:

1. How to formulate the energy and QoS model for an IaaS environment with unknown workloads.
2. When to consider a Host as Overloaded and Underloaded, so that VMs can be migrated away from the host.
3. How to efficiently solve the VM placement problem.
4. How to design the scheme to reduce both energy and the level of SLA violations.
5. How to efficiently choose the VMs for migration.

Goal of the Research

The goal of this research is to propose an improved VM consolidation scheme which reduces the combined performance metric involving the energy consumption in the data center and the level of SLA violations.

Research Objectives

To address the goal of the research, following objectives have been identified:

1. To propose efficient algorithms for each/some of the three phases defined above.
2. To improve the performance of the VM consolidation scheme by maintaining a good balance between energy consumption and the level of SLA violations.
3. To evaluate the performance of the proposed scheme extensively, against the prevalent, most popular consolidation scheme.

Research Methodology

1. The Dynamic VM consolidation process as a whole can be improved by enhancing each/some of the five phases, according to Beloglazov and Buyya (2012), involved in it. In these earlier stages of the research work, the authors have tried to improve the Overload detection scheme of the VM consolidation process, by theoretically analyzing and experimenting with the performance of various measures of statistical dispersion, both robust and non-robust, and applying it to the VM consolidation scheme.

2. They have evaluated and compared the proposed scheme with the most effective scheme, put forward by Beloglazov et al. (2012), which used extensive simulation through the CloudSim 2.0 toolkit by Calheiros et al. (2011).

The simulation and performance evaluation of the consolidation schemes has been done using CloudSim 3.0.3. A simulation tool is chosen instead of real cloud infrastructure because it is very difficult, time consuming, resource and cost intensive to use real cloud infrastructure just for evaluation of the consolidation schemes; real cloud infrastructures are too rigid to be of any use in this regard, while in the cloud simulators, the cloud parameters and the entire setup can be controlled very easily and the provisioning schemes can be developed and tested with different types of workloads and resources. CloudSim provides the facility to actually model and test the performance of the services in large heterogeneous cloud environments with little programming and deployment effort. It provides support for modelling various features of the cloud including the broker policies, overload and underload detection schemes, allocation schemes; it supports virtualized environments; and provides option for choosing between space-shared and time-shared task allocation policies.

For the workload, the authors have used the PlanetLab workload traces as provided in CloudSim 3.0.3. These workload traces represent an IaaS cloud environment and correspond to the system model in question (section 2.1). The data was collected over a period of 10 days as part of the CoMon project.

Contribution

The research contributions for "Energy Efficient Virtual Machine Migration in Cloud Data Centers" of the authors are as follows:

1. They have extended the work done by Beloglazov and Buyya (2012) and proposed the use of a non-robust measure of statistical dispersion for adaptive threshold based overload detection: the MEANMAD 2.5.

2. They have proposed a VM selection scheme Migrate Maximum MIPS (MMM).

The authors have used both these proposed schemes together (MEANMAD MMM 2.5). Performance evaluation has indicated that the proposed consolidation scheme has improved upon the results obtained by Beloglazov et al. in their paper, in terms of reducing both energy and the level of SLA violations as a whole.

SYSTEM MODEL AND VM PLACEMENT STRATEGY

System Model

The authors consider the virtualized data center model with multiple cloud users as by Beloglzov et al. (2012). The cloud environment consists of N Physical hosts. P is the list of Physical Machines, where P = $\left\{ P_1, P_2, \ldots, P_n \right\}$. The Physical hosts are homogeneous i.e. each of the hosts has identical memory, CPU performance capacity (measured in MIPS) and also has same network bandwidth. Each of the Physical hosts has a capacity of A_h. It is assumed that the servers are connected among themselves with LAN of adequate speed and also to the internet. All the hosts have access to a Network Attached Storage (NAS), which is used for enabling the virtualization technology and serves as a storage drive for the VMs.

The authors consider work in an IaaS environment. The data center consists of an admission control manager, a cloud manager and several local managers which are local to each physical host. The admission control manager is responsible for deciding whether a new VM request (for an application) can be allocated or not and whether the Quality of service constraints can be adhered to. If it is possible, then the Service level agreements are signed and the VM request is accepted and sent to the global manager for allocation on a host. The cloud manager is present in the controller node and with data collected from the local managers; it synchronizes, handles and manages the allocation and migration of the Virtual Machines among the Physical hosts. Each of the physical hosts consists of a local manager which is responsible for continual monitoring of all the Virtual Machines on the host and handling resource allocation to the VM and deciding whether VMs need to be migrated from the host or not. This information is then sent to the Global Manager for further action.

Figure 2 shows the view of the data center:

Figure 2. System model

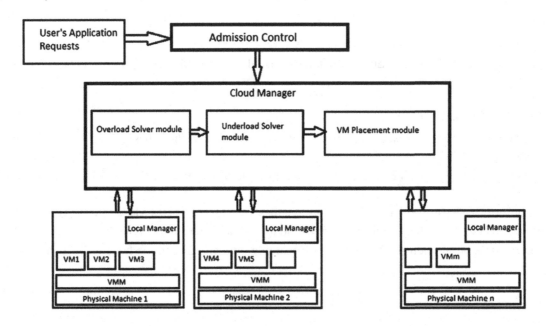

Each node can be described by the following performance parameters: the CPU performance measured in Million instructions per second (MIPS), amount of RAM available and the network bandwidth. The resource management system is not aware of the type of the applications it is managing. Various cloud service users independently submit their requests of handling M heterogeneous Virtual Machines denoted by the set $V = \{V_1, V_2, \ldots, V_m\}$ each of which also can be defined by the characteristics: MIPS, amount of RAM required and network bandwidth requirement. The Virtual Machines have constantly changing demands of resources i.e. the amount of CPU power it requires, but each Virtual Machine can be allotted a maximum of A_v CPU capacity. As the capacity of each physical host is A_h, a maximum of A_h / A_v number of virtual machines can be assigned to a physical host. These Virtual Machines run a wide variety of applications, which may differ greatly from one another and they are to be run simultaneously. The users and cloud service providers agree on a Service Level Agreement, which if not adhered to, will lead to a penalty on the side of the service providers.

Heuristics for VM Placement

Introduction

To provide fast cloud services, it all depends on how the resources are utilized in the data center especially in virtual machine placement. Virtual machine placement is the process of mapping VMs to the most suitable Physical Machine (PM) based on the requirement of VM characteristics to achieve the Quality of Service (QoS) without any violation of the SLA. VM placement is an important approach for improving power efficiency and resource utilization in cloud infrastructures. Virtual machines are of different configuration and cloud computing is a heterogeneous environment, so allocating multiple VMs to PMs has to be done wisely so that a good load balancing is achieved.

A Virtual Machine placement problem is typically a combinatorial optimization problem. Given a set of M virtual machines, each with a resource requirement specification along multiple dimensions $\{k_1, k_2, \ldots, k_m\}$ and a set of N physical machines, each with a capacity along m dimensions, the VM placement algorithm gives a mapping of VMs to PMs. According to Bobroff et al. (2007), mapping the Virtual Machines to the available Physical Machines can be reduced to a Bin Packing Problem, where the Physical Machines can be considered as bins and the Virtual Machines as the objects being filled into the Physical Machines. A set of Physical Machines, not all of the same size and a set of Virtual Machines are given, sizes chosen randomly from a predefined range, the VMs must be placed into (a subset of) these Physical Machines. Naturally, the number of Physical Machines used for placing the VMs has to be minimized.

The placement of the VMs is modelled as a bin packing problem in this work. According to Coffman Jr. et al. (1996) the bin packing problem is combinatorial NP-hard, hence no known polynomial-time algorithm exists for this problem. While there exist other approaches to the VM placement problem like Genetic algorithm or the Stochastic Integer Programming, the Bin Packing approach is useful when dynamic VM consolidation is required where the demand is changing all the time. The bin packing approach being heuristic based may not give us the optimal solution always but it will produce a competitive solution in relatively lesser amount of time. It is also of use when the hosts have the same physical characteristics. Energy costs of the cloud data centers can be minimized by efficiently packing the VMs into the least number of PMs possible. Several works have been done in this area as bin packing problem is one of the most fundamental and most studied problems in computer science history with wide range of applications in various fields. Berkey et al. (1994) compared heuristics like first fit decreasing, systolic packing and harmonic packing based on their performance. They found that these heuristics performed better for smaller bins than for larger bins. Scholl et al. (1997) proposed a new heuristic that incorporates *tabu* search and a branch-and-bound procedure based on known and new bound arguments and a new branching scheme. They have studied various heuristics including the First Fit Decreasing, Best Fit Decreasing, Worst Fit Decreasing and the B2F heuristic. Anily et al. (1994) studied the worst case performance of the heuristics for the bin packing problem. Fleszar et al. (2002) developed a new algorithm which is based on the idea of minimal bin slack. Yang et al. (2003) studied a variant of the bin packing problem known as the open-end bin packing problem, in which, if there is any space remaining in the bin, new items can be further added until the total size of all items in the bin is greater than the size of the bins.

Formalising VM Placement Problem

The one-dimensional problem takes into account only a single dimension which can be any parameter among Processor usage, network bandwidth, storage capacity, memory usage and the Power usage. Broadly, there exist two approaches to the VM placement problem: On-line algorithms and Off-line algorithms. The on-line algorithms place the VMs into the Physical Machines as and when they appear without having any knowledge of the subsequent VMs being arrived. It is implemented on shorter durations, shorter than periods of significant variableness of the resource demand. According to Bobroff et al. (2007), this placement algorithm runs in the background of the application process collecting data. On the other hand, the off-line algorithms have knowledge of the VMs beforehand and they examine the entire list before applying their strategy to place the VMs. Two of the most popular techniques used in the bin packing problem, the First fit decreasing(FFD) and the Best fit decreasing(BFD) are compared and it is analyzed how these two differ from each other. In both the FFD and the BFD algorithms the set of Physical Machines is sorted in ascending order and the following methods are followed:

- **First Fit Decreasing:** The VMs are sorted in decreasing order with respect to their size. The first VM is placed in the lowest numbered bin into which it fits i.e. if there is any partially filled ith PM with capacity of j_{th} VM + remaining capacity of i_{th} PM $\leq$ capacity of j_{th} PM then the current VM is placed in that lowest indexed j_{th} PM. If it does not fit into any open PM, a new one is used and the VM is placed there. This procedure is then repeated for all of the remaining VMs, and the partially filled PMs are kept open so that they can be considered for placing the subsequent VMs into them.

- **Best Fit Decreasing:** Similar to the FFD, the VMs are sorted in decreasing order. The current VM is placed into the PM which leaves the least space left over after the VM is placed in the PM. If the VM does not fit into any PM, a new one is started. Consider a case where the set of the given VMs is: $\{V_1, V_2, \ldots, V_{10}\}$ with capacities as $\{4,8,3,1,6,5,1,4,2,3\}$ respectively. Here, in both the FFD and the BFD algorithms, the VMs would first be sorted in decreasing order i.e. $\{8,6,5,4,4,3,3,2,1,1\}$. In the FFD algorithm the final packing would be as shown in the Figure 3. Since size of PMs is fixed, BFD also achieves the exact same packing in this case.

Figure 3. Packing using BFD and FFD algorithms

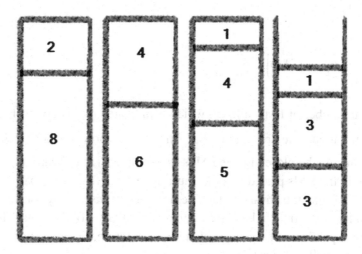

Proposed Model

Given a set of n Physical Machines $\{P_1, P_2, \ldots, P_n\}$ of processing capacity in the range $[u_1, u_2]$ and a set of m Virtual Machines $\{V_1, V_2, \ldots, V_m\}$ with processing capacity in the range $[v_1, v_2]$, it is needed to find the number of bins B such that

$$\sum_{i \in P_k} capacity(V_i) \leq capacity(P_k); \qquad \forall k \in [1, n] \qquad (1)$$

(1) implies that the sum of the processing capacity of all the VMs should not exceed that of the Physical machine.

$$B = \sum_{j=1}^{n} y_j \qquad (2)$$

Subject to

$$\sum_{i=1}^{m} capacity(V_i).t_{ij} \leq capacity(P_j).y_j; \qquad \forall j \in [1, n] \qquad (3)$$

$$\sum_{j=1}^{n} t_{ij} = 1; \qquad \forall i \in [1, m] \qquad (4)$$

$$y_j \in \{0,1\}; \qquad \forall j \in [1,n] \tag{5}$$

$$t_{ji} \in \{0,1\}; \qquad \forall j \in [1,n] \ \forall i \in [1,m] \tag{6}$$

(2) shows the total number of PMs utilized, which is indicated by (5) giving 1 if a particular PM_j is used and 0 if it is not used. The presence of VM_i in PM_j is shown in (6) which is 1 if present else 0. A particular VM can only be placed in one PM is shown in (4). (3) indicates that the sum of the processing capacities of all the VMs placed in a PM must not exceed that of the particular PM.

The placement of VMs into the Physical Machines is done set-wise i.e. by considering a particular set of the VMs are considered at a time to be placed into a particular set of the PMs. This helps in enhancing the fault tolerance capabilities of the entire cloud infrastructure. Figure 4 shows the list of PMs into which the VMs have to be allocated set-wise.

The experiment is conducted by varying the number of Virtual Machines from 50 to 750 at uniform intervals of 50 units i.e. 50, 100, ..., 750. The Virtual Machines have capacities in the range of [15, 30] and the Physical Machines have capacities in the range of [80, 120] units. The VMs are then tried to be placed in the given 100 number of Physical Machines using the modified FFD, the modified BFD and the randomized algorithm. The randomized algorithm is purely for comparative purposes, to gauge the effectiveness of FFD and BFD against random placement of the Virtual Machines.

Algorithm 1 is the main function which calls the modified FFD, modified BFD and Randomized algorithms. It takes the list of VMs and PMs as input and gives us the mapping of VMs onto PMs. *vmUnplaced* denotes the virtual machines yet to be placed and *pmOpen* denotes the physical machines

Figure 4. Placement of VMs set-wise in PMs

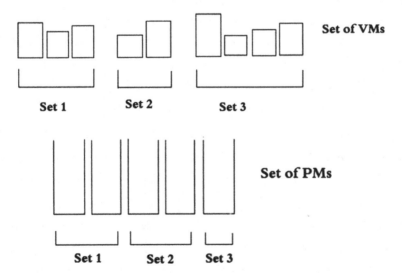

Algorithm 1. The Global Function

```
Input: vmList, pmList
Output: Mapping of VMs to PMs
vmUnplaced   ← numberofVM;
pmOpen    ← numberofPM;
Call First fit algorithm;
Call Best fit algorithm;
Max heapify the VMs;
Call Randomized algorithm;
while All VMs and PMs are not considered do
vmSet   ← Generate a set of VMs;
pmSet   ← Generate a set of PMs;
Call modified FFD algorithm;
Call modified BFD algorithm;
if All VMs placed or All PMs full then
    break;
return mapping;
```

that have enough resources. *vmSet* and *pmSet* are the set of VMs and PMs that have been generated and are to be used for mapping.

Algorithm 2 is the modified FFD algorithm which takes set of VMs and PMs as input and provides the mapping of VMs onto PMs. For each VM in the *vmSet*, it tries to place in the PM which has enough resources for VM and whichever comes first in the *pmSet*.

Algorithm 2. Modified FFD Algorithm

```
Input: vmSet, pmSet
Output: Mapping of VMs to PMs
for each VM in vmSet do
if VM is not placed already then
    for each PM in pmSetdo
        if PM has enough resources then
            if VM can be placed into PM then
                mapping. add(VM, PM);
            if PM is full then
                Close PM;
                pmOpen ← pmOpen - 1;
            if VM is placed then
                Goto next VM;
return mapping;
```

Algorithm 3. Modified BFD Algorithm

```
Input: vmSet, pmSet
Output: Mapping of VMs to PMs
for each VM in vmSet do
    if VM is not placed already then
        for each PM in pmSet do
            MinHeapify the PMs;
            if PM has enough resources then
                if VM can be placed into PM then
                    mapping. add(VM, PM);
                if PM is full then
                    Close PM;
                    pmOpen  ← pmOpen - 1;
                if VM is placed then
                    Goto next VM;
return mapping ;
```

Algorithm 3 is the modified BFD algorithm which takes *vmSet* and *pmSet* as input and provides the mapping of VMs onto PMs. For each VM in the *vmSet*, it tries to place in the PM which has enough resources for the VM and leaves least amount of free resources after placement.

Algorithm 4 is the randomized algorithm that takes *vmSet* and *pmSet* as input and gives VM-PM mapping an output. For each VM in *vmSet*, it tries to place in a randomly chosen PM.

Algorithm 4. Randomized Algorithm

```
Input: vmSet, pmSet
Output: Mapping of VMs to PMs
while All VMs and PMs are not considered do
    vmSet  ← Generate a set of VMs;
    pmSet   ← Generate a set of PMs;
    MinHeapify the PMs;
    for each VM in vmSetdo
        while some PMs are open do
            pmChosen ← Generate a random PM;
            if VM can fit into pmChosen then
                mapping. add(VM, PM);
                break;
    pmOpen ← pmOpen - pmSet;
    vmUnplaced ← vmUnplaced - vmSet;
    if All VMs are placed or No PM has any resource then
        break;
return mapping;
```

Simulation Results

The algorithms were implemented and the following results were obtained. Also it has to be said that the timing is not accurate for smaller test cases which take small running times. This is because of the *CLOCKS_PER_SEC* macro which has been used for measuring the running times of the programs. Hence in some cases, same running times will appear, but actually the running times differ by a very small amount. Also, for smaller test cases the running time for the program may be 0 seconds but actually they have very small values not big enough to be measured by the macro.

Figure 5. Number of PMs used vs Number of VMs used (for 100 PMs)

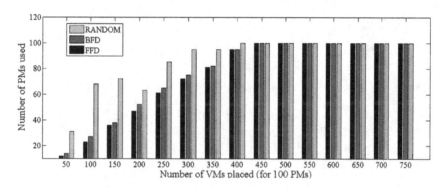

Figure 6. Number of PMs used vs Number of VMs used (for 150 PMs)

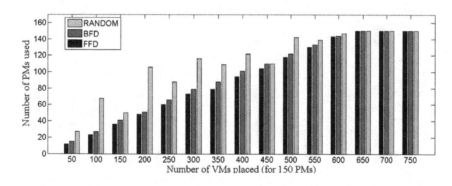

Figure 7. Number of PMs used vs Number of VMs used (for 200 PMs)

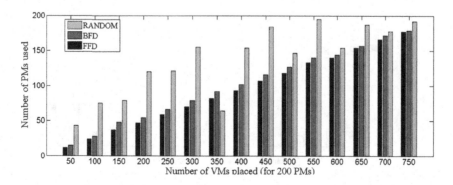

From Figure 5, Figure 6 and Figure 7, it can be observed that the modified FFD algorithm uses lesser number of Physical Machines for placing the VMs closely followed by the modified BFD algorithm. The modified BFD algorithm takes the slightly more number of PMs than the modified FFD algorithm in each case because in BFD the Physical Machine list is to be sorted in each iteration for placement.

From Figure 8, Figure 9 and Figure 10, it can be observed that the modified FFD algorithm takes the least amount of time for placing the VMs into the Physical Machines closely followed by the modified BFD algorithm. This is because in modified BFD, the Physical Machines are sorted in ascending order according to the space remaining in them.

Figure 8. Time taken vs VMs placed (100 PMs)

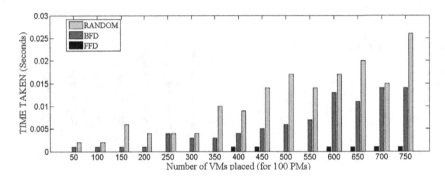

Figure 9. Time taken vs VMs placed (150 PMs)

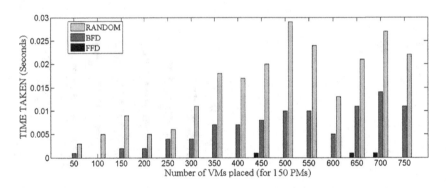

Figure 10. Time taken vs VMs placed (200 PMs)

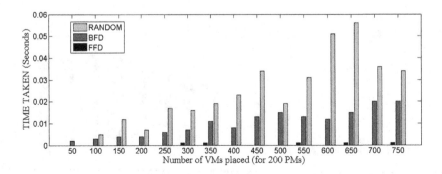

Consequently in modified BFD, smaller bins are utilized first, so even though modified BFD uses larger number of bins, the bins used are smaller in size and it was found that the utilization or the packing efficiency in the modified BFD is generally higher than that of modified FFD.

Conclusion

From the observations in the previous section it is concluded that the BFD algorithm for VM placement provides better results than the FFD algorithm. Therefore, it would be more feasible to use the BFD algorithm for placing the VMs, in the authors' consolidation scheme.

DYNAMIC VM CONSOLIDATION

Introduction

After initial placement of the VMs, dynamic consolidation is required. The demands of the VMs constantly change over time. It is thus imperative that the underlying resources be provisioned from time to time to serve the VMs adequately while conserving energy and keeping the level of SLA violations down.

The problem of Dynamic VM consolidation can be broken down into 5 parts:

1. **Initial VM Placement:** Initially, the VMs need to be placed on the hosts.
2. **Detecting Overloaded Hosts:** The overload detection algorithm checks all hosts for overload. If any of the host is overloaded, the VMs need to be migrated away from the hosts.
3. **Detecting Underloaded Hosts:** The underload detection algorithm checks all hosts for underload so that the hosts can be switched to a power conserving state by migrating all the VMs away to other hosts.
4. **Selecting the VMs for Migration from the Hosts:** The VM selection algorithm returns the combined migration map for the overloaded and underloaded hosts, which indicates where to place the VMs chosen for migration.
5. **VM Placement:** Finally, the VM placement is done according to the migration map.

Problem Statement

The problem of dynamic VM consolidation has been presented as minimization problem, to minimize the total cost incurred due to SLA violations and power consumption of data centers. The problem in this work assumes that the centralized cloud is hosted on a data center that has a large number of heterogeneous servers. Each of the servers may be assigned to carry out different or similar functions. A cloud computing infrastructure can be modelled with PM as a set of physical servers or machines $PM_1, PM_2, \ldots, PM_n$. The resources of cloud infrastructure can be used by the virtualization technology, which allows one to create several virtual machines $VM_1, VM_2, \ldots, VM_m$ on a physical machine and therefore, reduces the amount of hardware in use and improves the resource utilization. So with the help of virtual machines, cloud resources are utilized.

The problem addressed in this work is to minimize the total energy consumption of data centers as well as to minimize the amount of SLA violations. The metric that has been used to measure it is Energy and SLA violation (ESV) metric, which is to be minimized.

The Power Consumption and Performance Metrics

Fan et al. (2007) and Kusic et al. (2009) have shown that the power consumed by the nodes can be estimated by taking into consideration the CPU utilization alone. So to reduce the energy consumption the CPU utilization in the data centers needs to be improved. For calculating the power consumption, the following model is generally assumed:

$$P\left(u\right) = k * P_{full} + \left(1 - k\right) * P_{full} * u \tag{7}$$

Here, u is the CPU utilization, P_{full} is the power consumption of the node when it is fully utilized which signifies the maximum power consumed and k denotes the fraction of the power that the idle server consumes. According to Beloglazov et al. (2010), value of k generally is around the range 0.7, so the value of k is chosen as 0.7.

The modified Power consumption model then becomes:

$$P\left(u\right) = P_{full} * \left(0.7 + 0.3 * u\right) \tag{8}$$

The Energy consumed by all the hosts for computation (18) is given by:

$$E_{comp} = \sum_{i=1}^{N} \int P\left(u_i\left(t\right)\right) dt \tag{9}$$

The computation cost depends on the energy consumed by all the servers. Apart from the computation cost, they also considered costs related to Virtual Machine migration and the switching costs.

The energy consumed for migration (18) is given by:

$$E_{migr} = 4 * \sum_{j=1}^{MV} P_m * \frac{C_j}{BW_j} \tag{10}$$

MV denotes the number of migrated Virtual Machines. P_m denotes a unit power consumption for migrating a Virtual Machine (P_m is a constant according to Baliga et al. (2011)). C_j denotes the memory size of migrated VM j and BW_j denotes the Bandwidth available for migrating the VM j.

The switching cost is incurred when a server is switched on from sleep state and is given by Addis et al. (2010) and Kusic et al. (2009):

$$E_{switch} = \sum_{i=1}^{K} \frac{P_{si} * T_{si}}{2} \tag{11}$$

Here, K denotes the number of servers that are rebooted. P_{si} denotes the difference in power consumed by the server i when in sleep mode and in active mode. T_{si} denotes the time taken by the server i to turn on and start functioning, from sleep mode. So the total energy consumed is given by:

$$E_{total} = E_{comp} + E_{migr} + E_{switch} \tag{12}$$

Beloglazov and Buyya (2012), in their work, point out that large amount of memory being used by the physical hosts these days, have begun to dominate the power consumption by the hosts and that it is also very difficult to develop an accurate power consumption model for multi-core CPU architectures. So, instead of formulating a complex analytical model for power consumption, they have used real data provided by the *SPECpower* benchmark and the authors adopt the same. The data-set defines the power consumed by each host at various workloads based on collected data and uses these values to calculate the energy consumed by the hosts. The power consumption by the hosts at different load levels is benchmarked as follows:

Table 1 represents the power consumed by the servers at different load levels, measured in Watts. From the table, it can be observed that the load level and the power consumed follow a linear relationship.

Calculating the Cost of Virtual Machine Migrations

Live VM migration is required to migrate the VMs from the overloaded and underloaded hosts with only a small downtime. However, VM migration when carried out while the applications are running leads to performance degradation to a considerable extent. According to Voorsluys et al. (2009), the performance degradation experienced by the applications is directly related to the number of memory pages it updates while executing. But it was also found out in these studies that the performance degradation including the downtime in the case of web applications can be estimated to be nearly 10% of the CPU utilization. Thus the performance degradation experienced by a VM_j is modelled by Beloglazov et al. (2010) as:

$$U_{dj} = 0.1 * \int_{t_0}^{t_0 + T_{mj}} u_j(t) dt \tag{13}$$

Table 1. Server power consumption at different load levels

Server	0%	10%	20%	30%	40%	50%	60%	70%	80%	90%	100%
HP ProLiant G4	86	89.4	92.6	96	99.5	102	106	108	112	114	117
HP ProLiant G5	93.7	97	101	105	110	106	121	125	129	133	135

$$T_{mj} = \frac{M_j}{B_j} \tag{14}$$

where, U_{dj} denotes the degradation in performance experienced by the j_{th} VM, t_0 is the time of start of the migration of j_{th} VM and $t_0 + T_{mj}$ is the ending time of the migration of j_{th} VM. $U_j(t)$ denotes the CPU utilization of the j_{th} VM, M_j denotes the memory used by the j_{th} VM, and B_j denotes the network bandwidth available to the j_{th} VM.

Modeling the SLA Violations and Performance Metrics

An SLA violation will occur when less CPU capacity is being provided than what is demanded. The total SLA violation is defined as the ratio of the sum of unallocated MIPS to the sum of the requested MIPS. Hence, the overall SLA violation is given by:

$$\frac{\sum_{i=1}^{m} RequestedMIPS(i) - AllocatedMIPS(i)}{\sum_{i=1}^{m} AllocatedMIPS(i)} \tag{15}$$

where, $RequestedMIPS(i)$ denotes the MIPS requested by the i_{th} VM for running the application, and $AllocatedMIPS(i)$ denotes the actual MIPS that were allotted to the i_{th} VM. The SLA is assumed to be violated when for a particular VM, the Requested MIPS is less than the actual allocated MIPS.

According to Beloglazov and Buyya (2012) and Huang et al. (2014), two kinds of SLA violation metrics are used to estimate the level of SLA violations.

The first one (16) is the SLA violations due to over-loaded hosts and will be denoted as *SLATAH*. It denotes the ratio of total time spent experiencing SLA violations to the total active time of hosts.

$$SLATAH = \frac{\frac{1}{N} \sum_{i=1}^{N} T_{si}}{\sum_{i=1}^{N} T_{ai}} \tag{16}$$

T_{si} denotes the time for which Host i has experienced SLA violations, T_{ai} denotes the total active time of Host i, N denotes the number of hosts.

The second SLA violation metric quantifies the performance degradation of the Virtual Machines due to migration. Voorsluys et al. (2009) have considered this since SLA violations are also caused by VM migrations. This is denoted as:

$$PDM = \frac{1}{M} \sum_{j=1}^{M} \frac{C_{dj}}{C_{rj}} \tag{17}$$

C_{dj} is an estimate of the performance degradation caused due to migration of VM_j, C_{rj} denotes the total CPU MIPS requested by VM_j. The value of C_{dj} is taken as the 10% of the CPU MIPS during migrations of VM_j.

The following metric denotes the total SLA violations taking into account both the above types of SLA violations, since both *SLATAH* and *PDM* with equal importance denote the SLA violation level of the cloud:

$$SLAV = SLATAH * PDM \tag{18}$$

The metric combining both Energy consumption and SLA violations is given by Beloglazov and Buyya (2012) as:

$$ESV = E_{total} * SLAV \tag{19}$$

Dynamic VM Placement Optimization

Huang et al. (2014) have divided the overall process of VM consolidation into following five steps:

Initial Placement of the Virtual Machines

Initially the VMs are placed on the Physical Machines, based on the resources they demand. But their demands may change while running, so they are consolidated dynamically using the following steps.

Detecting Overloaded Hosts

This phase of the VM consolidation process is used to reduce the load on the overloaded hosts. The traditional approach is the *STA* (Static Threshold Algorithm). The *STA* defines an upper threshold for the hosts beforehand and the provisioning schemes have to keep the total utilization of the CPU under the threshold limit. If the threshold limit is exceeded, some VMs have to be migrated from the host to reduce the load on the CPU so that a SLA violation can be prevented. But, since STA defines static threshold limits, they are not suitable for dynamically changing workloads and conditions, so Overload detection schemes which can handle the dynamically changing environments are needed. Beloglazov and Buyya (2012) in their study proved that local regression method, which was proposed by Cleveland (1979) achieves most suitable results with dynamic, variable workload. It was shown by Beloglazov et al. that local regression can obtain the best results when compared to other popular methods of detection like, Median Absolute Detection, and Interquartile range. Beloglazov et. al in their work have shown that *LrMMT 1.2* is the best detection algorithm for detecting overloaded hosts.

To migrate the VMs from the physical machines, an upper threshold needs to set, such that when the CPU utilization of the particular host reaches above this value, the VMs are migrated iteratively from the host, until the host is no longer overloaded. But in an environment where the workload is dynamic and is changing by the minute, we need a more accurate estimate of the threshold value and it cannot be fixed to a particular value.

The authors have proposed a new algorithm *MEANMAD MMM 2.5* by improving upon the existing algorithm proposed by Beloglazov et al. *MEANMAD MMM* uses *MEANMAD*(Mean of absolute deviation from median) for dynamically varying the upper threshold limit for overload detection based on a statistical analysis of the historical data of CPU utilization by application workloads on the hosts. The *MEANMAD MMM* is used to estimate the threshold value by measuring the deviation of previous values of the CPU utilization of the host. If the deviation of these values is large enough, it is more likely that the CPU utilization will reach 100% and the CPU will get overloaded. So, for a larger deviation, they need to lower the upper threshold and migrate the VMs from the host.

MEANMAD is defined as:

$$MEANMAD = mean\left(\left|CPUutilization_i - median\left(CPUutilization[]\right)\right|\right) \tag{20}$$

where, *CPUutilization[]* denotes the list of all CPU utilizations, $CPUutilization_i$ denotes the CPU utilization value of the i_{th} element in the list and the upper threshold is given by:

$$T_u = 1 - s * MEANMAD \tag{21}$$

where, *s* is a safety parameter and we can define it as per our requirement. If we want to focus more on the energy conservation, then *s* can be assigned a larger value so that migrations are more and energy consumed is also less. By varying *s* suitably, they found that for the workload of the nature used, 2.1 comes out to be a good value and is effective in reducing the overall energy and SLA violation metric to a great extent.

MEANMAD is a measure of statistical dispersion, but it is not a robust statistic unlike the MAD used by Beloglazov and Buyya (2012). The main idea behind the MEANMAD is not to entirely discard the outlier data, as the outliers do also play an important role in deciding the overload threshold as even a few instances of high CPU utilization could cause the CPU to be overloaded and cause SLA violations. This is why their algorithm succeeds in reducing the SLA violations to a great extent and even the combined metric of Energy and SLA violations is reduced greatly.

Detecting Underloaded Hosts

We have already seen that idle hosts may consume up-to 70% of the peak energy consumption. It will therefore be feasible to migrate all the Virtual Machines from an underloaded host and switch it off or put it in a power saving state. The procedure to be followed for handling under-loaded hosts is:

1. First, the host with least utilization is considered for migrating all VMs from it.
2. The selected VMs are migrated to other servers while not over-loading them.
3. This process is then repeated for all under-loaded hosts.

Selecting the VMs for Migration from the Hosts

After the list of overloaded and underloaded hosts is determined, the next logical step is to determine which Virtual Machines to migrate from these hosts. Various schemes exist, including the Minimum Migration Time (MMT) policy by Beloglazov and Buyya (2012) which migrates a VM that needs the minimum time to migrate compared to the other VMs in the same host. The algorithm runs iteratively to migrate the VMs one by one until the host is no longer overloaded. Zhang et al. (2014) proposed the MNM policy which selects the minimum number of the VMs to migrate from a host so that the CPU utilization falls below the specified upper threshold.

The authors have proposed a new VM selection scheme "Migrate Maximum MIPS (MMM)". The overload detection scheme has already decided that a host is overloaded and then some VMs need to be chosen to migrate from the host so that the host may no longer be overloaded. According to this scheme, for choosing which VMs to migrate they take the CPU power (MIPS) of each VM the host is using, into consideration. Among all the VMs running in the host, they choose that VM for migration which is consuming the maximum MIPS. After the first VM is chosen for migration, the host is again checked for overload, if it is still overloaded the selection scheme is applied again and this process is carried out iteratively until the host in consideration is no longer overloaded.

The idea behind choosing MIPS for selecting the VMs is that it is desired to migrate those VMs first which consume the maximum amount of the host's CPU power. When VMs consuming larger CPU power are migrated first, chances are the number of VM migrations will go down and ultimately lead to a reduction in the consumption of energy, which is the case as demonstrated in the experiments.

Optimal VM Placement

The VM placement problem is an NP hard one. However, various heuristics have been developed to approach closer to the optimal solution. Algorithms used for the placement of the Virtual Machines can be broadly categorized as using the:

1. Power Based Approach
2. Application QoS based approach.

The first approach tries the placement in such a way so as to utilize servers to their maximum efficiency by server consolidation and hence minimize energy consumption. While the second approach aims at enhancing the Quality of Service (QoS) as defined in the Service Level Agreements (SLA) by maximizing the resources given to the applications. This work tries to take both the approaches into account and to arrive at a trade-off between the two which will be most beneficial to the Cloud service providers.

The Virtual Machine placement problem is modelled as a bin packing problem. The bin packing problem is NP-Hard, so no polynomial time algorithm exists to solve this problem. So various heuristics have been used in placement models which give good results in a short period of time. The most popular algorithm used for this purpose is the constraint based Best Fit Decreasing modified suitably to take the energy model into consideration. Best Fit decreasing is the most suitable choice in scenarios where the workload is dynamically changing. Though it may not always give optimal results, but it makes up for it in speed of achieving the placements. While these may not give optimal solutions, they perform the placements in quicker time, which is an acceptable trade-off in cloud computing environment, where time is of utmost importance. One such algorithm is the LIP (Least Increase Power) algorithm which was named so by Huang et al. (2014). This algorithm first sorts the selected Virtual Machines in the decreasing order of CPU utilization and then for each VM, it allocates it to that particular host which will lead to the least increased power in the host. Huang et al. also proposed LIP with host sort which sorts the hosts in descending order of current CPU utilization. They also proposed an algorithm of allocating VM in that host which would lead to the highest utilization in the host. This was predicted using local regression techniques. Zhang et al. (2014) have used an improved version of the Best-Fit decreasing algorithm which is power aware (PBFDH). The authors use the Power aware version of the Best Fit decreasing algorithm as proposed by Beloglazov et al. (2012), which is what is implemented in the CloudSim 3.0.3 toolkit which is used to conduct their experiments.

Performance Evaluation

CloudSim toolkit 3.0.3 has been used to simulate the existing and proposed algorithms. The cloud consists of a data center consisting of 800 heterogeneous physical nodes. Of these, half are HP ProLiant ML110 G4 servers, having 1860 MIPS capacity on each core and other half are HP ProLiant ML110 G5 servers, having 2660 MIPS capacity on each core. Each server has a network bandwidth capacity of 1 GBPS. Both type of hosts have 4GB of RAM.

The types of VMs used are

1.   2500 MIPS, 0.85 GB(RAM),
2.   2000 MIPS, 3.75 GB,
3.   1000 MIPS, 1.7 GB,
4.   500 MIPS, 613 MB.

The objective is to minimize both energy and SLA violation costs, so the metrics: Energy and SLAV both have to be taken into account. Thus, the metric *ESV = Energy * SLAV* is used to compare the consolidation schemes which gives equal weight-age to both energy and the level of SLA violations.

The following plots show the comparison between *LrMMT 1.2*, the best VM consolidation scheme used by Beloglazov and Buyya (2012) and proposed scheme of authors: *MEANMAD MMM 2.5*. The algorithm is run for 10 sets of data as provided in the CloudSim toolkit, which denotes the CPU utilization values from PlanetLab collected on the 10 different dates. The data is provided as part of the CoMon project, according to Park et al. (2006).

Figure 12 shows the number of VM migrations, which are a bit less in comparison to *LrMMT 1.2*. From Figure 11, it can be observed that their proposed scheme consumes lesser energy while consolidating the VMs, and from Figure 13, Figure 14 and Figure 15 it is observed that the level of SLA violations is much less in their scheme than in *LrMMT 1.2*. But the objective is to minimize both Energy and cost incurred due to SLA violations. So the most important metric is the ESV metric (Figure 16), which clearly shows that their proposed scheme gives much better results for minimizing both Energy and SLA violations.

Table 2 shows the percentage improvement in the ESV metric in each of the cases obtained in their scheme, over *LrMMT 1.2*:

Figure 11. Comparison based on Energy consumed

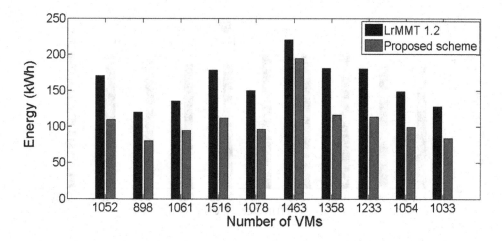

Figure 12. Comparison based on number of migrations

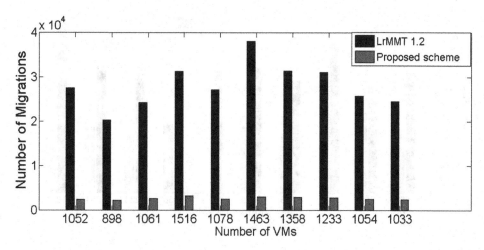

Figure 13. Comparison based on PDM metric

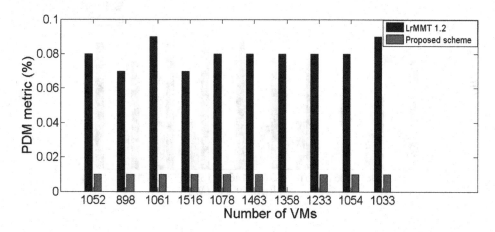

Figure 14. Comparison based on SLATAH metric

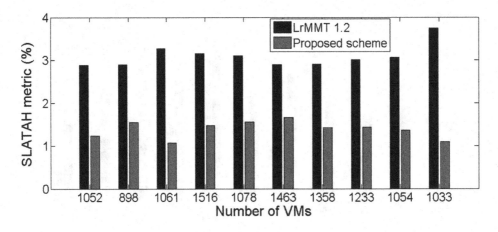

Figure 15. Comparison based on SLAV metric

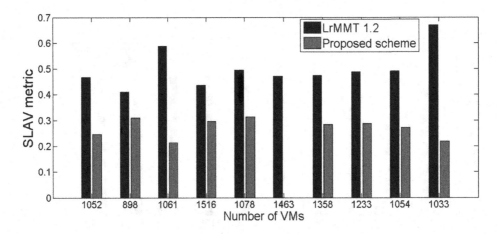

Figure 16. Comparison based on ESV metric

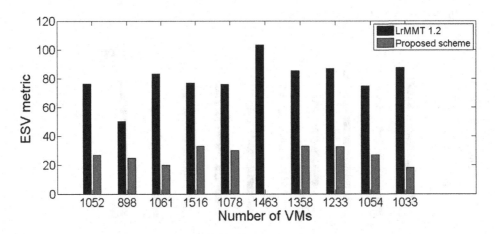

Table 2. Percentage improvement in ESV metric over LrMMT 1.2

Number of VMs	1052	898	1061	1516	1078	1463	1358	1233	1054	1033
% improvement in ESV metric	63.48	49.06	74.06	53.63	58.16	NA	61.06	61.32	61.37	77.37

Conclusion

1. Performance evaluation has indicated that the authors' proposed consolidation scheme, MEANMAD MMM 2.5 has improved upon the results obtained by Beloglazov et al. in their paper, in terms of reducing both energy and the level of SLA violations as a whole. These will in-turn lead to a better ROI for the cloud service users.
2. As per Beloglazov and Buyya (2012) the local regression based overload detection schemes significantly outperform the adaptive threshold based schemes. But the results obtained in authors' work indicate otherwise. The adaptive threshold based consolidation schemes outperform the local regression based consolidation schemes when an appropriate measure of statistical dispersion is used.

CONCLUSION AND FUTURE WORK

In this work, the problem of an effective Virtual Machine consolidation scheme to reduce energy consumption is undertaken. Reducing Energy consumption is one of the most serious concerns for the cloud service providers. Even in idle mode the data center is able to consume about 70% of the peak energy. Effective VM consolidation scheme can help the cloud data centers save more energy and hence reduce their costs of operation and increase the ROI. The authors have proposed a new algorithm for overload detection: the *MEANMAD 2.5* and combined with the minimum migration time policy of selecting the VMs for migration, they get the method *MEANMAD MMM 2.5,* which has improved upon the results obtained by Beloglazov et al. in their paper, in terms of reducing both energy and the level of SLA violations as a whole leading to a better ROI for the cloud service users. Also, as per Beloglazov et al. (2012) the local regression based overload detection schemes significantly outperform the adaptive threshold based schemes. But the results obtained from adaptive threshold based consolidation schemes outperform the local regression based consolidation schemes when an appropriate measure of statistical dispersion is used.

The future direction of this work includes modifying other phases of the VM provisioning scheme which can reduce energy consumption and SLA violations even further than what is already achieved.

REFERENCES

Addis, B., Ardagna, D., Panicucci, B., & Zhang, L. (2010). Autonomic management of cloud service centers with availability guarantees. *IEEE 3rd International Conference on Cloud Computing* (CLOUD). doi:10.1109/CLOUD.2010.19

Anily, S., Bramel, J., & Simchi-Levi, D. (1994). Worst-case analysis of heuristics for the bin packing problem with general cost structures. *Operations Research*, *42*(2), 287–298. doi:10.1287/opre.42.2.287

Baliga, J., Ayre, R. W., Hinton, K., & Tucker, R. (2011). Green cloud computing: Balancing energy in processing, storage, and transport. *Proceedings of the IEEE*, *99*(1), 149–167. doi:10.1109/JPROC.2010.2060451

Belady, C.L. (2007). In the data center, power and cooling costs more than the it equipment it supports. *Electronics Cooling*, *13*(1), 24.

Beloglazov, A., Abawajy, J., & Buyya, R. (2012). Energy-aware resource allocation heuristics for efficient management of data centers for cloud computing. *Future Generation Computer Systems*, *28*(5), 755–768. doi:10.1016/j.future.2011.04.017

Beloglazov, A., & Buyya, R. (2010). Adaptive threshold-based approach for energy-efficient consolidation of virtual machines in cloud data centers.*Proceedings of the 8th International Workshop on Middleware for Grids, Clouds and e-Science*. doi:10.1145/1890799.1890803

Beloglazov, A., & Buyya, R. (2012). Optimal online deterministic algorithms and adaptive heuristics for energy and performance efficient dynamic consolidation of virtual machines in cloud data centers. *Concurrency and Computation*, *24*(13), 1397–1420. doi:10.1002/cpe.1867

Berkey, J. O., & Wang, P. Y. (1994). A systolic-based parallel bin packing algorithm. *IEEE Transactions on Parallel and Distributed Systems*, *5*(7), 769–772. doi:10.1109/71.296322

Bobroff, N., Kochut, A., & Beaty, K. (2007). Dynamic placement of virtual machines for managing SLA violations.*10th IFIP/IEEE International Symposium on Integrated Network Management, IM'07*. doi:10.1109/INM.2007.374776

Buyya, R., Yeo, C. S., Venugopal, S., Broberg, J., & Brandic, I. (2009). Cloud computing and emerging IT platforms: Vision, hype, and reality for delivering computing as the 5th utility. *Future Generation Computer Systems*, *25*(6), 599–616. doi:10.1016/j.future.2008.12.001

Calheiros, R. N., Ranjan, R., Beloglazov, A., De Rose, C. A., & Buyya, R. (2011). Cloudsim: A toolkit for modelling and simulation of cloud computing environments and evaluation of resource provisioning algorithms. *Software, Practice & Experience*, *41*(1), 23–50. doi:10.1002/spe.995

Cleveland, W. S. (1979). Robust locally weighted regression and smoothing scatterplots. *Journal of the American Statistical Association*, *74*(368), 829–836. doi:10.1080/01621459.1979.10481038

Coffman, E. G. Jr, Garey, M. R., & Johnson, D. S. (1996). *Approximation algorithms for bin packing: a survey. Approximation algorithms for NP-hard problems*. PWS Publishing Co.

Fan, X., Weber, W. D., & Barroso, L. A. (2007). Power provisioning for a warehouse-sized computer. *ACM SIGARCH Computer Architecture News*, *35*(2), 13–23. doi:10.1145/1273440.1250665

Fleszar, K., & Hindi, K. S. (2002). New heuristics for one-dimensional bin-packing. *Computers & Operations Research*, *29*(7), 821–839. doi:10.1016/S0305-0548(00)00082-4

Gupta, M., & Singh, S. (2003). Greening of the internet.*Proceedings of the 2003 conference on Applications, technologies, architectures, and protocols for computer communications*. ACM.

Hanne, F. Z. (2011). Green-it: Why developing countries should care? *International Journal of Computer Science Issues*, *8*(4).

Huang, J., Wu, and K., Moh, M. (2014). Dynamic virtual machine migration algorithms using enhanced energy consumption model for green cloud data centers. *IEEE International Conference on High Performance Computing & Simulation* (HPCS). doi:10.1109/HPCSim.2014.6903785

Huang, Q., Gao, F., Wang, R., & Qi, Z. (2011). Power consumption of virtual machine live migration in clouds.*IEEE Third International Conference on Communications and Mobile Computing (CMC)*. doi:10.1109/CMC.2011.62

Hwang, K., Dongarra, J., & Fox, G. C. (2013). *Distributed and cloud computing: from parallel processing to the internet of things*. Morgan Kaufmann.

Jung, G., Joshi, K. R., Hiltunen, M. A., Schlichting, R. D., & Pu, C. (2008). Generating adaptation policies for multi-tier applications in consolidated server environments.*IEEE International Conference on Autonomic Computing (ICAC)*. doi:10.1109/ICAC.2008.21

Jung, G., Joshi, K. R., Hiltunen, M. A., Schlichting, R. D., & Pu, C. (2009). A cost-sensitive adaptation engine for server consolidation of multitier applications.*Proceedings of the 10th ACM/IFIP/USENIX International Conference on Middleware*. Springer. doi:10.1007/978-3-642-10445-9_9

Kumar, S., Talwar, V., Kumar, V., Ranganathan, P., & Schwan, K. (2009). vManage: loosely coupled platform and virtualization management in data centers.*Proceedings of the 6th international conference on Autonomic computing*. ACM. doi:10.1145/1555228.1555262

Kusic, D., Kephart, J. O., Hanson, J. E., Kandasamy, N., & Jiang, G. (2009). Power and performance management of virtualized computing environments via lookahead control. *Cluster Computing*, *12*(1), 1–15. doi:10.1007/s10586-008-0070-y

Mell, P., & Grance, T. (2011). *The NIST definition of cloud computing*. NIST.

Nathuji, R., & Schwan, K. (2007). Virtualpower: Coordinated power management in virtualized enterprise systems. *Operating Systems Review*, *41*(6), 265–278. doi:10.1145/1323293.1294287

Park, K., & Pai, V. S. (2006). Comon: A mostly-scalable monitoring system for planetlab. *Operating Systems Review*, *40*(1), 65–74. doi:10.1145/1113361.1113374

Sahoo, J., Mohapatra, S., & Lath, R. (2010). Virtualization: A survey on concepts, taxonomy and associated security issues.*IEEE Second International Conference on Computer and Network Technology (ICCNT)*. doi:10.1109/ICCNT.2010.49

Scholl, A., Klein, R., & J¨urgens, C. (1997). Bison: A fast hybrid procedure for exactly solving the one-dimensional bin packing problem. *Computers & Operations Research*, *24*(7), 627–645. doi:10.1016/S0305-0548(96)00082-2

Srikantaiah, S., Kansal, A., & Zhao, F. (2008). Energy aware consolidation for cloud computing.*Proceedings of the 2008 conference on Power aware computing and systems.*

Verma, A., Ahuja, P., & Neogi, A. (2008). pMapper: power and migration cost aware application placement in virtualized systems. *Proceedings of the ACM/IFIP/USENIX 9th International Middleware Conference.* Springer-Verlag.

Voorsluys, W., Broberg, J., Venugopal, S., & Buyya, R. (2009). *Cost of virtual machine live migration in clouds: A performance evaluation. Cloud Computing.* Heidelberg, Germany: Springer.

Yang, J., & Leung, J. Y. T. (2003). The ordered open-end bin-packing problem. *Operations Research, 51*(5), 759–770. doi:10.1287/opre.51.5.759.16753

Zhang, X., Yue, Q., & He, Z. (2014). Dynamic energy-efficient virtual machine placement optimization for virtualized clouds. *Proceedings of the 2013 International Conference on Electrical and Information Technologies for Rail Transportation* (EITRT2013). Heidelberg, Germany: Springer. doi:10.1007/978-3-642-53751-6_47

Chapter 10
Network Virtualization:
Network Resource Management in Cloud

Kshira Sagar Sahoo
National Institute of Technology Rourkela, India

Ratnakar Dash
National Institute of Technology Rourkela, India

Bibhudatta Sahoo
National Institute of Technology Rourkela, India

Mayank Tiwary
C. V. Raman College of Engineering, India

Sampa Sahoo
National Institute of Technology Rourkela, India

ABSTRACT

Cloud computing is a novel paradigm which relies on the vision of resource sharing over the Internet. The concept of resource virtualization, i.e. hiding the detail specification of the resources from the end users is the key idea of cloud computing. But the tenants have limited visibility over the network resources. The Network-as-a-Service (NaaS) framework integrates the cloud computing services with direct tenant access to the network infrastructure. The Network virtualization (NV) is such a platform that acts as a mediation layer to provide NaaS to tenants. NV supports the coexistence of multiple virtual networks, which is the collection of virtual nodes and virtual links on the same underlying physical infrastructure. Prior to set up a virtual network in an NV Environment, resource discovery and resource allocation are the primary job. In this chapter, we have discussed on basic NV architecture, surveyed the previous work on the resource allocation along with ongoing research projects on network virtualization.

INTRODUCTION

The term virtualization means it is the creation of a virtual version of the actual one, such as an operating system, a server, a storage device or network resources. Anyone who uses computers, video games, cell phones, PDAs, or the Internet, it means virtualization is being used.

Virtualization is an old but very popular technique for resource sharing like CPU, memory, storage and almost all other system resources. Fundamentally, virtualization is an abstract concept that hides

DOI: 10.4018/978-1-5225-1721-4.ch010

hardware details. It refers to the technologies designed to provide a layer of abstraction between computer hardware systems and the software running on them. By providing a logical view of computing resources, rather than a physical view, virtualization technology provides numerous benefits to the industries and end users. The most common thing in the various virtualization method has generally divided a single piece of hardware into two or more segments. Each segment operates as its own independent environment.

Recently, virtualization has moved its trend from server virtualization to network virtualization. Server virtualization is a decade ago popularized technology. Server virtualization also termed as host or computer virtualization. It is a masking method of server resources, including the identity of physical server being used, processors, and operating system for the server uses. The server administrator uses an application which divides one physical server into multiple isolated virtual environment. These virtual environments sometimes known as a guest, instance or emulation. This server virtualization is a key enabler of cloud computing. It has been more popularize due to numerous benefit of it, among them sustainability of computing resources, on-demand provisioning, flexible management, reliability management etc.

The most common usage of this technology is in Web servers. Using virtual Web servers is a popular way to provide low-cost Web hosting services. Instead of demanding a separate computer for each Web server, dozens of virtual servers can co-reside on the same computer. Network Interfaces are virtualized in server virtualization, but ignores any kind of virtualization of the network devices, such as switches and routers.

The network virtualization decouples the network infrastructure from its provided services and it allows many isolated virtual networks to share the same physical network infrastructure. Similar to VMs in server virtualization, the virtual networks can be deployed on demand and resource are dynamically allocated which maximizes the reusability. Each virtual network gets the functionalities ranging from simple connectivity to performance guarantee and new protocol provisioning.

In this article we are emphasizing on the architecture, design goal, resource allocation in network virtualization and current research projects on network virtualization.

CONCEPT BEHIND VIRTUALIZATION AND ITS BENEFITS

The concept of virtualization has been used since the sixties when the time sharing concept was introduced. Later, M44/44X Project had started from the IBM Watson Research Centre. Testing of timesharing was the main subject of this research. Then after the virtual machine monitor (VMM) came, which had the ability to create multiple virtual machines (VM). A VM is a self-contained operating environment that performs as if it is a distinct computer. It is also termed as a "guest" that created and run within another computing environment referred as a "host". At a particular time multiple VMs can run within a single host. Each instance of VMM have capable of running its own operating system. After four decades, industries are generalizing the fundamental technologies of virtualization where they are managing the resources in a more efficient way and provide services to the customers.

The virtualization mechanism provides a number of benefits to the service providers and everyday users. Some important benefits are described below.

Flexibility

Virtualization brings more flexibility to the IT industry. The administrator can expand, shrink or transfer the data without hardware any dedicated hardware. Data in no longer confined to the physical hard drives, so industries having more flexibility to change and grow their data size. Using this, data can smoothly transfer without affecting other data.

Reduce Cost

Now a days organizations are typically used virtualized environment in their data centers, which drastically reduces the infrastructure cost. Instead of buying new hardware devices, older devices can run new applications with the help of virtualized servers. Virtualization offers significant cost benefits due to the shared and scalability of computing resources. Large task can be executed with a pool of computing VM resources and unutilized VMs can be powered off remotely from a centralized location which reduces utility cost.

Less Complexity

Virtualization helps you reduce the number of servers you need to manage every day, but also helps you simplify management of your remaining servers. By centralizing services, you can more easily maintain operational insight into the condition of your servers, and ensure optimal server utilization by balancing workloads to achieve the greatest possible efficiency.

Reliability

Ensuring to the user's requirement by the technology is the primary goal. At some point of time the system may fail due to link failure, data centre crash or disaster happens. Many techniques are there to provide a robust and reliable system to the users. But virtualization provides an additional layer which ensures the enhanced reliability of the system. In such above situation the critical system can be replicated or migrate to other locations at any time thus eliminate the failure situation.

Security

Virtualization limits the communication between processes running on different virtual machines, hence isolating processes from each other. For example, the effect of malware can be limited, without affecting the hardware or other applications running outside the specific virtual environment.

Research on Operating System

Virtualization allows for the development and debugging of a new instance of an OS on the same hardware. This allows for new research ideas to be implemented and tested.

Software Testing and Debugging

Virtualization offers a stable and convenient way to create a reproducible environment for software testing. This provides an easy way to test and debug new software before and during deployment into production environments.

Optimization of Hardware Utilization

Virtualizing hardware equipment makes it possible to accommodate multiple processor environments, hence it is possible to aggregate multiple servers on the same machine, up to capacity, and reduce the hardware number and costs.

Job Migration

While one task is being executed that can be moved transparently from one hardware system to another in case of emergency. Migration of job can be used for efficient load balancing in a virtualized environment. Energy saving accomplished by moving jobs from a lightly loaded machine and then powering down the hardware. In the fault tolerant model, machine virtualization enables the transparent migration of running processes to a different machine.

Virtual Storage

Due to the virtual storage technique, the actual storage becomes independent of the services, and the management functionality becomes easier. Addressing of individual storage devices, e.g. hard-drives, it becomes transparent to the service, administrator, as well as to the user.

Easy Step to Deploy of Bundle Applications

Placement of applications is not so easy, as they require specific versions of operating system libraries and may not coexist on the same machine. Virtual machines can alleviate this problem by introducing a separate virtual machine for the incompatible applications. The ISO images containing the correct OS version and hence the necessary applications can easily be placed in one virtual machine, without changing the current configuration of the machine.

NETWORK VIRTUALIZATION IN BRIEF

As discussed in the introduction section, virtualization technologies have recently shifted from server virtualization to network virtualization. Though it is not strictly a new concept, but when it has realized that network virtualization can deliver a new platform upon which new network architecture can fabricate and experimented, from that onwards it has brought a new dimension of research. Besides, network virtualization has been appearing as the basis of a new global Internet architecture, which overcoming the present Internet "ossification" problem and motivating the development and deployment of new network technologies and advanced applications. In addition, it is expected to facilitate a new way of doing business by letting the dealing of network resources among multiple providers and customers (Villela, Campbell, & Vicente, 2001). Before going to discuss a deep detail about it, let us discuss one example, which will illustrate the network virtualization.

Among many, the telephone network is a good example of a virtual network. We can use cell phones to talk to a traditional land-based telephone, we call and talk to someone reside elsewhere in the world, and we connect our computer into a phone line for dialup connection to the Internet. The same network can be used for carrying voice, video, and data, including faxes over different carriers like wireless, fibre optic cabling.

A virtual storage network similar to a telephone network supports many different interfaces. For instance fibre channel, Ethernet, InfiniBand, SATA, SAS, and others, as well as multiple storage networking protocols including SCSI, FCP, FCIP, iFCP, TCP/IP and others. A virtual storage network can access via block, file (NAS), and object-based to meet the different needs of applications and adapt to support different technology resources (virtual bridged local area networks, 2006).

In a close analogy to the virtual machine, a virtualized network is a software container that presents logical network components—logical switches, routers, firewalls, load balancers, VPNs and more—to connect workloads. These virtualized networks are created and managed programmatically by the underlying physical network serving as a simple packet-forwarding backplane.

BASIC STRUCTURE OF NETWORK VIRTUALIZATION

In virtualization technologies a VMM or a hypervisor manages the physical resources, and maintaining isolation among VMs (Mudigonda, Yalagandula, Mogul, Stiekes & Pouffary, 2011). The assumption of general architecture for network virtualization (Khan, Zugenmaier, Jurca & Kellerer, 2012) is presented in Figure 1.

Figure 1. Comparison of Server virtualization and network virtualization

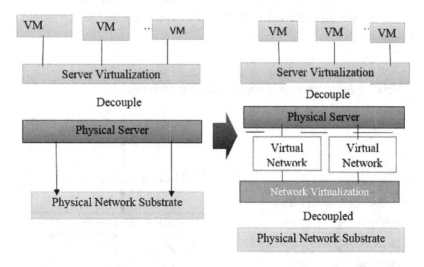

As stated above the network virtualization handles multiple virtual networks on the physical network infrastructure. This paradigm decouples the network infrastructure from the services it being served. Then, just like VM in server virtualization, the VM can be allocated dynamically to the physical network.

The business model in network virtualization is depicted in Figure 2. A two-layer virtualization model is depicted on the left side, where infrastructure providers (InPs) are responsible for dispensing physical resources, to service providers (SPs). Thus, VN working on top of the physical substrates (Niebert, et al., 2008). The network resources include CPU, memory, bandwidth which is likely to share among SPs.

This practice permits InPs to deal with their physical substrate independently while SPs focus on upgrading end to end service provisioning (Martin, Völker, & Zitterbart 2011). In (Schaffrath, et al., 2009) authors introduced a four-layer network virtualization business model, which is shown in right side of Figure 2. This four-layer business model states that, the actual virtualization process is carried out among In Ps, virtual network provider (VNP), a virtual network operator (VNO), and Service Provider (SP). In this model, SPs focus on providing services to users by asking resources from VNP, VNP is accountable for creating virtual networks based on requests received from SPs, whereas VNO is accountable for handling the establishment of virtual networks. VNP and VNO are eliminating the burden of creating and managing tasks from SPs, enabling these to focus only on providing services.

NETWORK VIRTUALIZATION ENVIRONMENT

In the previous section we have already discussed the overall model of the network virtualization. Dissimilar to the current all-IP Internet, a virtualized systems administration environment is a gathering of various heterogeneous system architectures from distinctive SPs (Service Provider). Each SP rents assets from one or more infrastructure Provider (InP) to make Virtual Network (VN), and deploys customized protocols and services.

Basic Model

The main distinction between the participants in the network virtualization model and the traditional model is the presence of two different roles, InPs and SPs, as opposed to the single role of the ISPs (Chowdhury & Boutaba, 2010).

Figure 2. Two business model in network virtualization environment

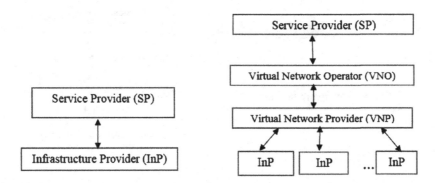

Figure 3. Network virtualization environment

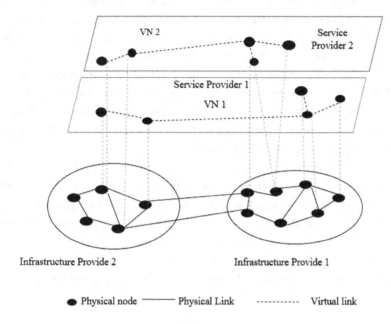

- **InP:** (Infrastructure Provider) InPs really deal with the underlying physical resources. They offer their assets through programmable interfaces to diverse SPs. InPs separate themselves through the nature of assets they give, the flexibility they delegate to their clients, and the devices they give to endeavour that opportunity.
- **SP:** SPs lease resources from numerous InPs to create and deploy VNs by programming allocated network resources to offer end-to-end services to the users. One SP can also provide network services to other SPs. In another sense, it can also create child VNs by partitioning its resources and act as a virtual InP by leasing those small networks to other SPs (Figure 3).
- **End User:** End users in the network virtualization model are similar to those of the existing Internet. An end user can connect to multiple VNs from different SPs for different services.

Design Goals

The design goals for successfully understanding network virtualization have been addressed by different researchers:

- **Flexibility:** Network virtualization technique must provide independence in every aspect of networking. Each SP should be free to implement arbitrary network topology, routing and forwarding functionalities, and customized control protocols independent of the underlying physical network.
- **Manageability:** By separating SPs from InPs, network virtualization creates accountability at every layer. It modularizes network management tasks which eases network administrator's responsibility. It must provide complete end-to-end control of the VNs to the SPs, so that it can avoid the requirement of administrative boundaries seen in the existing Internet.

- **Scalability:** Coexistence of multiple networks is one of the essential principles of network virtualization. It is important to have scalability for the existence of multiple virtual network in NVE.
- **Isolation:** To improve fault tolerance, security, and privacy Network virtualization must provide isolation among coexisting VNs. Network protocols are prone to misconfigurations and implementation faults. Misconfiguration in one VN must not affect to other coexisting VN.
- **Programmability:** Programmability of the network element is another essential design aspect. This feature can implement customized applications and deploy varied services.
  It enabling a secure programming paradigm with a considerable level of flexibility for SPs without much compromise from infrastructure providers.
- **Heterogeneity:** Service Provider need to provide the resources to the VNs without any technology specific requirement. Heterogeneous protocols implemented by different SPs and heterogeneous devices used by end users must be supported by the underlying infrastructures.
- **Legacy Support:** Theoretically legacy support (backward compatibility) in network virtualization can easily integrate by considering the existing Internet as another VN in its collection of networks. But finding the efficient way is a big challenge.
- **Nesting:** Nesting is one of the major design goals of network virtualization, which ensures the child derived from a parent VN.

Historical Perspective

In the past, the concept of multiple coexisting logical networks has appeared in the literatures numerous times. This section presents a survey on important network virtualization technologies that are already popularized. NV is often associated with virtual private network, virtual local area network, Software Defined Network and a number of different technologies.

In (Wang, Iyer, Dutta, Rouskas, & Baldine, 2013), the authors summarize basic network virtualization concepts and discussed selected virtualization testbeds developed by different research communities. This article (Chowdhury & Boutaba, A survey of network virtualization, 2010), is an extension of (virtual bridged local area networks, 2006) by presenting additional commercial technologies and formulating its own unified definition for network virtualization.

Figure 4. A classification of various Network virtualization technologies

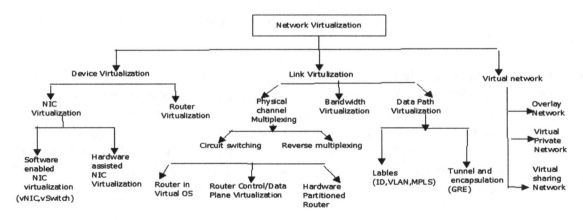

Figure 4 represents a reconstruction of that classification. In this section we will discuss virtualization technologies related to network devices, links, and virtual networks.

Device Virtualization

We shall start our discussion on network virtualization primary on Network Interface Card (NIC) and router like fundamental network devices.

NIC Virtualization

NIC virtualization may be software or hardware aided virtualization. We have already come across VMware, Citrix System, and Oracle like hypervisor. The main task of such platform is Operating System(OS) virtualization, along with sharing of actual NIC among different instances of OS. VNIC is a software emulator that helps to realize such virtualization. Having dedicated IP and MAC addresses this emulator can be connected to a physical NIC by a VNet driver of VMware that is loaded in the host OS. The below Figure 5 illustrates the general architecture of NIC virtualization. A VNIC that is connected to a virtual network does not require an Ethernet interface on the host. A VNIC client contains virtual machine and implicitly VNIC implemented via a piece of code in VMM.

Unlike a physical switch, a vSwitch may not perform all functions, but it can perform certain operations like traffic switching, multiplexing, bridge VNIC with physical NIC. NIC virtualization provides a package of virtual servers, virtual NICs, virtual switches and links, which is often called as "Network-in-a-box".

Figure 5. Basic network virtualization

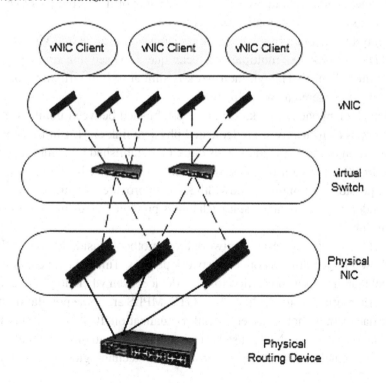

Peripheral component interconnect express (PCIe) is a bidirectional serial bus that provides lower latency and higher data transfer than parallel buses such as PCI. PCIe was developed for high speed interconnects such as Gigabit Ethernet, InfiniBand etc. The VM-centric servers facing a lot of I/O bottleneck, since one PCIe channel is available in a regular NIC. Single root I/O virtualization (SR-IOV) is a hardware improvement that could produce multiple instances of PCI functions by its Virtual Functions (VFs). Instead of connecting vNIC clients to a vSwitch, every VM could be directly mapped to a VF for direct access of NIC resource, which normally provides better throughput, and lower CPU utilization (Chowdhury & Boutaba, 2010).

Router Virtualization

In a typical router, both hardware and software are tightly coupled. CISCO, IOS, VxWorks, and Linux are the router based OS, they have designed in such a way that, hardware can be utilized efficiently. Various efforts have been applied on separation of router software from the hardware. A VM is an application environment or we can simply call an OS that is installed in a host machine that imitates as a dedicated hardware. The end user would get the same experience on a VM as they would have a dedicated hardware. Router in the virtual OS like VMware or Xen called virtual router. These routers share the CPU, memory, Network Infrastructure Card (NIC), hard drive, such hardware resources. We had discussed "Network-in-a-box" in the earlier section. Virtual routers are VNIC client in a virtualization environment. These Vrouters enhance the idea of "Network-in-a-box".

Link Virtualization

Link virtualization creates multiple separate virtual links over a shared physical link. In today's Internet era variety of link virtualization techniques are available. Some of the techniques like ATM, Ethernet, 802.1q, MPLS, etc. follows the link virtualization principle.

Multiplexing of physical medium in the network transmission is alike link virtualization. It may be wired or wireless; TDM, CDMA like multiplexing techniques are used in a single physical medium to multiple different distinct channel. Though their work is similar to link virtualization generally multiplexing technique is not considered as virtualization.

In a circuit switched telephone network, a route is established between points over the network in such a way that it appears as if there were a dedicated physical link exist. But this connection session set up only for the duration of the connection. This circuit is established by combing a number of channels along with the links of the path between source and destination. In the reverse concept optical technology makes it possible to combine bandwidth so as to provide flexible services. These services are independent of underlying physical capacity. Channels produced by using this above technique are referred to as virtual link.

Tunnelling protocols encapsulate various network layer protocols inside various P2P link over an IP network. Tunnels allow a logical link to connect network devices. Tunnels create an illusion that protocols in the device feel that there is a connection to other device, even when no physical connection exist among devices. Generic routing protocols like PSec, GTS, MPLS are some popular tunnelling protocol. Virtualization of the data path is another aspect of link virtualization. It allows to manipulate the data on the data path rather than the channel. Nodes use various technologies to direct the data along the virtual link named as label and tunnelling. Various link virtualization technologies are listed in the Table 2.

Virtual Networks

A virtual network is a type of computer network that consists of virtual network links in a limited extend. Till now, we have come across two types of virtual networks: link and device virtualization. In the next session we will review virtual networks that are the subject of academic research.

- **Overlay Networks** : An overlay network is a virtual network that built upon the physical topology of another network. Tunneling and encapsulation technologies are used to achieve this virtual link in the application layer. The main advantage of overlay network is free from geographical restriction along with adapting to change and easily deployable in any environment (Galán-Jiménez & Gazo-Cervero, 2011).

For instance, consider Figure 6. In the Figure 6, three physical substrates with physical links are available. Let's say a new network service has to implement between node A and C. Only A and C node has to modify to realize this service through tunnelling technique through A-a-b-C. Node C need not to be modified, it continues to forward the data between A and C but not aware of the new service. The Table 1 shows the available physical link and a link overlay upon it.

Figure 6. Instance of Overlay network

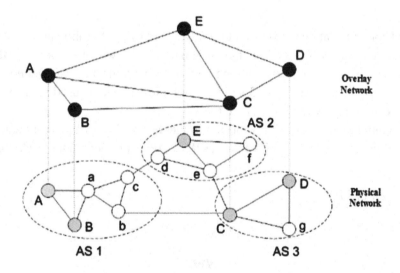

Table 1. Link overlay for various path

Underlying Physical Path	Link Overlay
A-B	A-B
A-C	A-a-b-C
A-E	A-a-c-d-E
B-C	B-a-b-C
D-E	D-C-e-E
C-E	C-e-E

Table 2. Examples of link virtualization technologies

Link virtualization Technologies	Examples
Bandwidth Virtualization	Reverse multiplexing, PSTN circuit
Data Path Virtualization	VLAN, GRE tunnels, MPLS
Physical Channel Multiplexing	FDM, TDM

Many overlay networks have been constructed on the existing network by adding new features to it. Such overlay network includes a digital subscriber line or cable network overlaid upon older public switch telephone network or cable TV. In the similar fashion MBone and 6Bone create multicast and IPv6 capabilities in the Internet (Rockell & Fink, 2000). Many overlay network has been designed in the recent years. Basically, they are addressing performance and availability, supporting multicasting, improve QoS, provides security. Sometimes it has also used as a test bed to design new architecture. Overlay technology is the key technology behind VPN, VLAN, active and programming network.

VLAN

VLANs are adaptable as far as system organization, network administration, and reconfiguration. It is a set of hosts having a common interest that are logically carried together under a single broadcast domain irrespective of their physical availability. As VLAN is a logical association between hosts, so management of the network is less complex than physical LAN.

In VLAN all the frames contain an identifier (VLANID) in the header of the MAC. VLAN enabled switches contain both VLANID and MACID for transmission of a frame. Many VLANs on multiple switches can be linked together, which allows information from multiple VLANs to be carried over a single link between switches.

VPN

VPN is a dedicated communication network that is constructed by using public network such as Internet to connect to a private network like a company's internal network which is shown in the Figure 7. In other words, VPN is the logical connection among host. VPN contains the customer edge (CE) devices. Among many technology layers 2 and layer 3 VPN technologies are widely used in the networking stack. In many cases VPN service provider taking care the VPN.

In the implementation point view VPN working in the various layer of network stack (Wang, Iyer, Dutta, Rouskas, & Baldine, 2013). Layer 3 VPN uses IP or MPLS protocol in the backbone for transmis-

Figure 7. Logical view of VPN

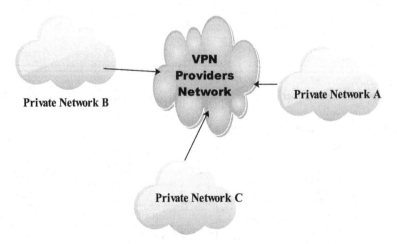

sion of frames. Layer 2 VPN runs in the top of different protocols. It provides an end to end data link between distributed sites by using ATM/ frame relay techniques.

L2 and L3 VPN uses packet switching technique, whereas L1 extends this concept to circuit switching principle. Multiservice architecture is supported by L1VPN, which allows each service to have independent address space, independent resource view and policies. VPWS and VPLS are two variants of L1VPN (Takeda, 2007). VPWS services are point to point, whereas VPLS can be pointed to multi-point.

Active and Programmable Networks

It may not be considered as an example of network virtualization, but most of the projects in this area use the concept of co-existing networks on a same network substrate by using network programming. To allow multiple external parties to run probably conflicting codes on the same physical network elements, active and programmable networks offers an isolated environment to avoid code conflicts. Two research communities named as telecommunications community and the other for the IP network community have defined the implementation concept of programmable networking (Campbell, et al., 1999).

Two approaches may realize the concept of active and programmable networks one is open signalling approach and another is active networks approach.

Active networks approach (Tennenhouse, Smith, Sincoskie, Wetherall, & Minden, 1997) enhanced the flexibility through complex programming model on network elements such as routers and switches to perform custom operation based on contents of the packets, and also allow them to modify packets.

RESEARCH CHALLENGES IN NETWORK VIRTUALIZATION

The research direction of NV, mostly focusing on some of the old problems, which creates other research challenges like programing capability, security, instantiation to the NVE etc. Here we have discussed few research challenges on NVE.

Resource Allocation

In the resource allocation mechanism, virtual network embedding in an NVE is a very challenging issue. In the previous section we had stated that the VN embedding is NP-hard problem. Inter-domain embedding is an unexplored domain in Network Virtualization, where VN request needs to segregate among various InPs and each fragmented embedding must be coordinated to each other using inter InP policy.

Resource Discoveries

The resource discovery process performed before the resource allocation in NV. In a communication system admission control is an important validation process. Before the communication establish, it checks the status of the current resource availability, if it lacks the required resources communication stopped. Most of the solution to this part are static in nature, but require dynamic resizing.

Virtual Node and Link

In VN, the devices or link is the main resources to be virtualized. Many commercial router vendors have started implementing virtual router mechanism in their devices. Virtual router migration is an effective technique to handle node failure and improve the manageability (Wang, Keller, Biskeborn, van der Merwe, & Rexford, 2008).

But, while migrating a virtual router several constraints like link capacity, platform compatibility issues are the main hindrance. Similar to the virtual node, the overhead to the virtual link should be minimized. These are the main research issues related to the virtual node and link.

Scheduling of Resources

To provide the required services to the service provider, InPs create a dedicated network to each SP. To perform this, InP must employ an efficient scheduling algorithm to all network elements such as physical link, node etc. which is another key research area.

Mobility Management

In a wireless environment, movement of end users from one place to another causes the migration of virtual router from one device to another creates a big challenge. Getting the actual location of any resource at a particular time and routing packets to that location is another research area.

Security and Privacy

Security and privacy are being always a big concern for any network system. Attacks like Denial of Services (DOS) to the physical network in NVE, affects all the VN present in the network. To overcome the above problem, CABO provides a flexible solution. A detailed survey on various possible security threats and solutions to the known attacks are explained in (Milanova, Fahmy, Musser, & Yener, 2006.).

Green Cloud Computing

A fascinating truth is that energy utilization in Data Centre Network (DCN) is required to keep the server running, but much more energy is required to keep the server cool. Energy consumption in a DCN can be reduced by switching off some network devices, but this method creates again some additional problem. One research area is more prevalent regarding energy consumption is that dynamic relocation of active resources. Dynamic relocation of resources can minimize the energy consumption, for example VM migration. VM migration can drastically reduce the energy consumption by demanding the resources at fossil fuel based energy site, but transfer and execute the VM at renewable energy site. Hence, research on renewable energy in DCN is explained in (Mandal, Habib, Mukherjee & Tornatore, 2013).

Interfacing

Every Infrastructure Provide (InP) must provide some standard interface, so that Service Providers (SPs) can communicate with them in an efficient manner.

Network Virtualization Economics

In NV the bandwidth is an essential commodity where SPs are the buyers and InPs are the sellers and brokers who act as mediators between the buyers and sellers. End users participate as buyers of services from different SPs. Efficient traditional concepts like centralized and decentralized marketplaces could be used in network virtualization environments for achieving better economy.

RESOURCE DISCOVERY AND ALLOCATION IN NETWORK VIRTUALIZATION

In network virtualization environment the VNs (Virtual Networks) are the combination of virtual node and virtual links. Also the number of VNs shares their resources offered by underlying network. Among many challenging issues, efficient resource allocation is one of them, because the efficient allocation mechanism reduces congestion, enhance QoS in the physical substrate. The objective here is to select and assign the underlying nodes having sufficient CPU, bandwidth and other hardware capabilities to VNs such that it minimizes the total resources of physical network. The mapping of VNs onto the substrate network is commonly known as resource allocation can be static or dynamic in nature.

In static allocation resources are known before and cannot change during lifetime of a VN. But to enhance the network performance, dynamic resource allocations have a key role. Due to unpredictable traffic pattern allotted resources to VNs may also vary, it needs to be readjusted which can be possible in dynamic allocation. In this section we concisely describe the resource discovery and resource allocation in virtual networks through a system-theoretical model.

Resource Discovery

The resource discovery process starts before the resource allocation in network virtualization. This resource discovery phase come into the picture when VNPs are trying to discover the resources in the underlying physical substrate. Resource discovery is an important process typically when multiple InPs are providing infrastructures. By mutual communication with the InP and VNP this can be achieved.

When a VNP got the VN requests from the customers, it selects an InP on which it built a VNs.

In 4WARD model, a framework has involved in resource discovery which comprises: InP, VNP, and VN user (Houidi, Louati, Zeghlache, & Baucke, 2009). The main objective is to choose an appropriate InP from a number of possibilities. This framework has two main sections: resource description and resource clustering. The basic component of resource description which is a part of resource discovery could be a network element, which can be a link, an interface or a node. Again, each element can have functional and non-functional attributes. Various QoS parameters, performance parameters, cost/price are under non-functional attributes, whereas the execution environment, virtualization software, operating system etc. is the functional attributes.

According to the customers' resource requirement the VNP searches the standard repository where available resources are stored. If the resource requirement are satisfying, the appropriate InP will be selected otherwise the user's request will be rejected. The resource discovery process helps to VNP to select the best InP for a customer's VN request. It basically considers the functional attributes of a physical substrate that are announced by the InPs.

Resource Allocation in Network Virtualization

Resource allocation is also known as VN mapping; is a process which performed by Infrastructure Providers (InP) upon getting requests from the users to construct a Virtual Network (VN) through VNP. The instantiation of a VN starts after carrying out the virtualization of physical resources. This virtual network resources must be provisioned and discovered before the resource allocation phase.

In simple term, a VM topology consists of virtual nodes and virtual links without considering CPU capacity, storage capacity and location of the virtual node. The requested VN are serviced and managed by a management plane. In the following we are presenting a mathematical model described in (Belbekkouche, Hasan, Karmouch, et al 2012).

Mathematical Formulation

The resource allocator assigns the resources to VN from the physical network can be thought of as a queuing system in which VN request is served, in a FCFS (First Come First Serve) manner or any other mechanism which is shown in the Figure 8.

Let the physical topology of an underlying substrate network be represented by a graph $G_s = \{V_s, E_s\}$; where V_s is the set of physical nodes and E_s is the set of physical links. Again the VN will be considered as another graph $G_v = \{V_v, E_v\}$; where V_v is the set of virtual nodes and E_v is the set of virtual links. There are some constraintassociated with each virtual node ($n_i^v \in V_v$) such as location ($loc(n_i^v)$) and the required CPU capacity ($CPU(n_i^v)$) must be characterized into a single physical node ($n_k^v \in V_s$) along th all the constraints. Similar to the virtual node, in each virtual link ($l_k^v \in E_v$) is having certain constraints. They required bandwidth and propagation delay i.e. $B\binom{v}{k}$ and $D(l_k^v)$ respectively over a physical path (P_j^s) . (P_j^s). is the set of continuous physical links i.e. l_r^s.

Figure 8. Conceptual model for resource allocation in VN
Source: Haider, Potter, & Nakao, 2009

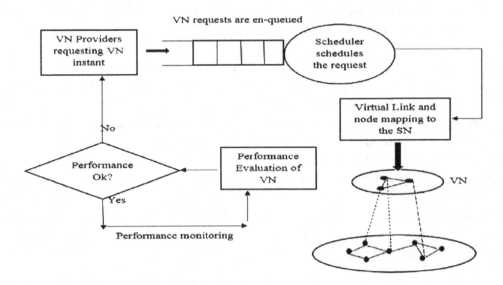

It must satisfy the following inequalities $B(P_j^s) = \min B\left(l_r^s\right)$.

Resource Allocation Approaches in Virtual Network

Resource allocations to VNs can be static or dynamic allocation. In static allocation the resource assignment is fixed during the life span of a VN, whereas in dynamic approach, on the basis of the present demand, resources are being allocated during the life span of the VNs. Dynamic allocation of VN is more challenging and careful scheduling is required. In communication system admission control is a validation process that monitors whether the current available resources are sufficient for the connection in the network (Haider, Potter, & Nakao, 2009). During allocation, admission control mechanisms are provided by the VN providers to handle the unpredictable request generate by VNs.

Static Mechanism

Since resources are predefined in static resource allocation, it creates a major problem due to stricter requirement of minimizing node and link load. To avoid this problem many heuristic techniques are adopted. Selecting a cluster having lightly loaded links assign to the VN carried out in the assignment phase. This is the basic static mechanism.

Many authors claimed that basic method is very cost effective and having large search space. By restricting the VN topologies to back bone star topologies the search space can be reduced, and the problem can be addressed. In (Botero & Hesselbach, 2009) authors describe resource at a node is the product of CPU capacity and link bandwidth. In order to assign and improve the efficiency of link mapping k-shortest path algorithm and path spitting has been proposed.

Dynamic Mechanism

Static allocation mechanism suffers from underutilization of underlying resources, lower performance and QoS. So, it is important to have an adaptive mechanism to reassign the resources to various VN. Some authors worked on reconfiguration of the resources to the assigned VN by pointing out the heavily loaded link and node in the physical network, and then the reconfiguring occurs of the VNs. DaVinci is a new framework which has periodically reassign bandwidth among multiple VMs by sharing underlying virtual resources.

Resource Allocation Categories in Network Virtualization

Authors in (Belbekkouche, Hasan, Karmouch, & others, 2012) describe resource allocation in network virtualization can be categorized into 4 types. The allocation might be centralized, distributed, reconfiguration and survivability.

In centralized resource allocation method, a single entity is responsible for receiving VN request and perform the task present in the InP. Among the main disadvantages of this approach are the communication overhead between the central entity and other nodes in the physical network during the update information of available resource on the network and scalability cannot be well addressed for large scale network. If the central entity fails, the whole system might not work.

Where as in distributed method, the allocation process is distributed among all physical nodes in the InP. Physical nodes take part in the process and use local knowledge and cooperation protocols to accomplish the process.

In reconfiguration approach the resource allocation is readjusted, because the initial resource allocation to VNs, might not optimal which may affect the performance of the overall system. Virtual node and link migration like techniques are used in this approach, which may not be acceptable in real-time application because of its longer service time.

Physical links and nodes in the network virtualized environment are vulnerable to failure. In survivability mode, additional resources are allocated to the critical services hosted by the VNs during the failure period.

Below tables summarize the resource allocation techniques used in various approaches. It is clear that most of the authors have used heuristic techniques in their work. In the early work, the virtual network topology is used as the only requirement, but in later research bandwidth, CPU, location of the node is being considered as the equal importance.

Table 3. Centralized resource allocation techniques used in network virtualization

Sl. No	Techniques used	Requirement for virtualization
1. (Zhu & Ammar, 2006)	Heuristic	Topology
2 (Chowdhury & Boutaba, 2009)	Heuristic	Topology, CPU, bandwidth, location of the node
3 (Lu & Turner, 2006)	Heuristic	Topology, traffic, location of the node
4. (Botero & Hesselbach, 2009)	Heuristic	Topology
5. (Szeto, Iraqi, & Boutaba, 2003)	Maximum concurrent flow	Bandwidth
6. (Razzaq & Rathore, 2010)	Heuristic	Topology, node and link capacity

Table 4. Distributed resource allocation techniques used in network virtualization

Sl No.	Techniques used	Requirement for virtualization
1. (N. Chowdhury)	Heuristic	Physical network resources
2. (Amarasinghe, 2012)	Policy based	Topology, node location
3. (Wang, Wang, & Yuan, 2009)	Game Theory	Bandwidth

Table 5. Reconfiguration and survivability techniques used in network virtualization

Sl No.	Techniques used	Requirements for virtualization
1. (Marquezan, et al., 2009)	Heuristic	Storage capacity
2. (He, et al., 2008)	Congestion control	Bandwidth
3. (Yeow, Westphal, & Kozat, 2011)	Heuristic	Bandwidth

RUNNING PROJECTS ON RESOURCE MANAGEMENT OF NETWORK VIRTUALIZATION

The network Virtualization idea arose when a large scale test bed was required for the development and testing of next generation network research. In this section we shall discuss on some running project working on network virtualization in the industry and academia also. Research communities are mostly working on overlay network, VPN and programmable network, etc. Many organizations are working on Network virtualization over the year. Due to the lack of a proper taxonomy, different research group having their own set of jargon for the project. But a set of characteristics is regulating all the prototypes used in network virtualization.

Projects like CABO, NauVeau etc. projects are focusing on virtualizing the available network resources, like link virtualization, node virtualization, etc. Some of the network virtualization protocols are determined by the technology they are using. Like X-Bone is a wired based virtual architecture, Tempet is targeting for ATM network, etc. Many research group characterizing their protocols in a layered manner. Efforts have been given on virtualizing different layer of the network stack. One of the examples of physical layer network virtualization protocol is UCLP, whereas PlanetLab is an application layer protocol. Certain projects have emphasized on architectural aspects of network virtualization. Like VNRMS focusing on network management, similarly Genesis emphasizes on spawning network.

In the next section it has discussed some running projects on network virtualization in this section.

X-Bone

The X - Bone system is a dynamically deployed and managing an Internet overlay network that has proposed to increase resource sharing and reduce configuration effort, it supports automatic configuration (Touch, Wang, & Eggert, 2003). This was the first proposed overlay network built by the IP network, having enhanced security features. Other features like isolation and resource allocation among multiple overlay network are included in X-Bone. Then the concept further enhanced with other technology, called Virtual Internet (VI) (Sundararaj & Dinda, 2004). VN is an IP system made out of tunnelling among an arrangement of virtual switches and hosts. All internet component like host, routers, and link can be virtualized by a VI.

Multihoming refers to a computing node or device connected to more than one computer network. All components participating in the VI must support multihoming. For example, it can be used to increase the reliability of an Internet Protocol network, such as a user served by more than one ISP. In recent times, P2P-XBone, has developed which is a peer-to-peer based synthesis of X-Bone, supports creation and release of dynamic IP tunnels, and customized routing table configuration.

The overall architecture of X-Bone consists of overlay manager, multicast control protocol and resource daemon. The task of different components of X-Bone as follows: configuration of an overlay, controlled by the overlay manger, which is managed by the overlay manager. Overlay manager is usually running at user side. It is controlled by user interface or API. Resource daemon monitors the resources and runs at each resource. It provides security, access control to the resources. Discovering available resources for the communication is the task of multicast control protocol.

VNET

It is used by means of virtual LAN and uses layer 2 tunnelling protocol (L2TP). Each hosted VM runs VNET process, use tunnelling tunneling techniques for communication. The recipient is also another VM, and can be contacted through VNET directly. For an external host, an operation carried out by VNET proxy node. The overlay system supports both TCP and UDP to routing the overlay. Without participation of any OS, one VM can migrate from one machine to another.

VIOLIN

Virtual Internetworking on Overlay Infrastructure (VIOLIN) is an application level network architecture. Various isolated virtual network created upon the overlay infrastructure, by VIOLIN software. It was implemented on PlanetLab, in the early stage. Entities like virtual end host, routers and switches of VIOLIN implemented and managed by software and hosted by physical overlay. One of the main features of VIOLIN is, it has own address space. As per demand entities of VIOLIN can be created, deleted and migrated dynamically. Other value added network services can be used and deployed in VIOLIN, may not supported in legacy network. Without any modification in legacy application can run in VIOLIN. It creates testbed for experiment related to networking.

VIOLIN architecture can be divided into 3 levels. The lower level is the physical IP network, middle level plane is an overlay infrastructure like PlanetLab and on the top VIOLIN environment created on the overlay infrastructure. As VIOLIN is not dependent on PlanetLab, Emulab like tested can easily embed into it.

VNRMS

Resource management is the main goal of Virtual Network Resources Management System (VNRMS). Network resources can be easily customizable using VNRMS. It provides a programmable environment where multiple virtual network can be created from a single physical network. Virtual Network Resources (VNR) of VNRMS framework can be similar to PNR of physical network. VNR is a logical subnet of PNR. Abstract views of resources that are allocated to a particular VN provided by MIBlets. The management information base (MIB) of the PNR is logically partitioned of multiple disjoint MIBs, known as MIBlets. It hides the details of network resources.

NetScript

It is a middleware which facilitates programming of intermediate nodes. Routing, packet analyzer and signalling functions are the main focus of this language. These programs are acting like mobile agent; programs are dispatched dynamically to the remote system and execute under the control of local or remote system. It is used for composing, providing and managing the network abstraction (Da Silva, Florissi, & Yemini, 1998).

GENESIS

It is a variant of open programmable networks. The main advantages of Genesis are it allows multiple heterogeneous child virtual networks to operate on top of subsets of their parent's resources, and provides isolation among them (Kounavis, et al., 2001). It automates the different stages of a life cycle process starting from creation to the designing of networks.

FEDERICA

FEDERICA (Szegedi, Figuerola, Campanella, Maglaris, & Cervelló-Pastor, 2009) addresses data plane, control plane, and management plane challenges in the virtualization capable network infrastructure. Its goal is to provide transparent infrastructure, which will support isolated coexisting slices along with complete user control to the lowermost possible layer. Interconnection among multiple slices can be provisioned and connect to external networks and services to create large groups. A dedicated proxy keeps user slices from unauthorized accesses.

PlanetLab

PlanetLab (Brett, et al., 2004) is a research testbed, jointly devPrincetonthe year 2002 by Princenton University, UC Berkeley, and The University of Wasington. It is composed of PlanetNodes distributed throughout the universe. PlanetNodes are the dedicated servers running PlanetOS, a customized Linux OS. PlanetLab does not have dedicated links, so communication between PlanetNodes is possible through the Internet.

There are four design principles of PlanetLab. Among them the first one is sliceability. It ensures that each application acquires and runs in a slice of the overlay. The decentralized control structure, enable the nodes to act according to local policies. An important principle is subservices that run on their own slices, instead of a centralized one. Lastly, overlay support an existing and widely adopted programming interface, to promote actual long term service development instead of just being a temporary testbed.

GENI

The Global Environment for Network Innovations (GENI) is one of the largest and a complex virtualization enabled test-bed. Its main goal is to build an open, large scale experimental facility for evaluating new network architecture on the existing Internet. GENI provides an opportunity to create a customized virtual network to do experiments on the Internet to the researchers. GENI has been paving the ways to researchers to explore the challenges in the network virtualization area in many ways. GENI is a collection of research projects which are coming under four control frameworks: PlanetLab, ProtoGENI (a descendent of Emulab), ORCA (open resource control architecture) and ORBIT (Ott, Seskar, Siraccusa, & Singh, 2005). GENI provides the programmability ability to the researchers to change the behaviour of computing, storage, and routing etc. in the virtualization model. In GENI, end users who do not directly interact with an experimental team, may communicate with the experimental GENI slice. It provides such a physical connectivity mechanism to a large community, so that they can easily join more than one experimental services.

CABO

Presently, ISPs handle the network infrastructure and provide network service to end users. Adopting a new technology not only requires changes in hardware, but also to host software, but for this it is essential that ISPs should jointly agree to any architectural change. CABO (Wang, Keller, Biskeborn, van der Merwe, & Rexford, 2008) end this impasse by promoting separation between the infrastructure providers and service providers. Automatic migration of virtual routers from one physical node to another is supported by it.

4WARD

Due to the lack of adequate facilities to design and test new network protocols, network research had forced to stop. 4WARD overcome this problem by a set of radical architectural approach. It is a combination of multiple network working on a single platform. It is a part of European Union (EU) 7th framework program. It can run on both wired and wireless architectures, having heterogeneous network. On demand instantiation and interoperation among heterogeneous virtual network is supported by this project.

4WARD business model introduces three roles: infrastructure providers, virtual network providers (VNP), virtual network operators (VNO). Infrastructure provider manages the underlying network resources, VNP creates virtual networks; and VNO helps to connect customers to the services provided within dissimilar virtual networks. However, the promising factor of 4WARD is to bring network virtualization to the end users.

CONCLUSION

Network virtualization stands at a unique point in the virtualization design space. It can efficiently utilize the physical resources by allowing multiple virtual resources to coexist in a physical resource. These physical resources can be networked components, such as routers, switches, hosts, virtual machines, etc. Hence, this virtualization technique can reduce the total cost by sharing network resources.

In this paper, we have conducted a review of network virtualization efforts by various industry and academic research groups. We also discussed a set of research issues and challenges that will arise in network virtualization and later focused on resource discovery and allocation issues. In future work, our research directions will be investigated on its support of reliable cloud computing networks.

REFERENCES

Amarasinghe, H. (2012). *Utilization of Dynamic Attributes in Resource Discovery for Network Virtualization* (Ph.D. dissertation). University of Ottawa.

Belbekkouche, A., Hasan, M., Karmouch, A., & others. (2012). Resource discovery and allocation in network virtualization. *IEEE Communications Surveys & Tutorials, 14*(4), 1114-1128.

Botero, J. F., & Hesselbach, X. (2009). The bottlenecked virtual network problem in bandwidth allocation for network virtualization. *Communications, 2009. LATINCOM'09. IEEE Latin-American Conference on*, (pp. 1-5). doi:10.1109/LATINCOM.2009.5305042

Brett, P., Bowman, M., Sedayao, J., Adams, R., Knauerhase, R. C., & Klingaman, A. (2004). Securing the PlanetLab Distributed Testbed: How to Manage Security in an Environment with No Firewalls, with All Users Having Root, and No Direct Physical Control of Any System. *LISA*, *4*, 195–202.

Campbell, A. T., De Meer, H. G., Kounavis, M. E., Miki, K., Vicente, J. B., & Villela, D. (1999). A survey of programmable networks. *Computer Communication Review*, *29*(2), 7–23. doi:10.1145/505733.505735

Chowdhury, N. F. S. (n.d.). Polyvine: Policy-based virtual network embedding across multiple domains. *Proc. ACM*.

Chowdhury, N., & Boutaba, R. (2009). Network virtualization: State of the art and research challenges. *Communications Magazine, IEEE*, *47*(7), 20–26. doi:10.1109/MCOM.2009.5183468

Chowdhury, N. M., & Boutaba, R. (2010). A survey of network virtualization. *Computer Networks*, *54*(5), 862–876. doi:10.1016/j.comnet.2009.10.017

Da Silva, S., Florissi, D., & Yemini, Y. (1998). *NetScript: A language-based approach to active networks. Tech. Rep.* New York: Computer Science Dept., Columbia Univ.

Galan-Jimenez, J., & Gazo-Cervero, A. (2011). Overview and challenges of overlay networks: A survey. *Int J Comput Sci Eng Surv, 2*, 19-37.

Haider, A., Potter, R., & Nakao, A. (2009). Challenges in resource allocation in network virtualization. *20th ITC Specialist Seminar, 18*, 20.

He, J., Zhang-Shen, R., Li, Y., Lee, C.-Y., Rexford, J., & Chiang, M. (2008). Davinci: Dynamically adaptive virtual networks for a customized internet.*Proceedings of the 2008 ACM CONEXT Conference*, (p. 15). doi:10.1145/1544012.1544027

Houidi, I., Louati, W., Zeghlache, D., & Baucke, S. (2009). Virtual resource description and clustering for virtual network discovery.*Proceedings of ICC*. doi:10.1109/ICCW.2009.5207979

Khan, A., Zugenmaier, A., Jurca, D., & Kellerer, W. (2012). Network virtualization: A hypervisor for the Internet? *Communications Magazine, IEEE*, *50*(1), 136–143. doi:10.1109/MCOM.2012.6122544

Kounavis, M. E., Campbell, A. T., Chou, S., Modoux, F., Vicente, J., & Zhuang, H. (2001). The genesis kernel: A programming system for spawning network architectures. Selected Areas in Communications. *IEEE Journal on*, *19*(3), 511–526.

Lu, J., & Turner, J. (2006). *Efficient mapping of virtual networks onto a shared substrate*. Academic Press.

Marquezan, C. C., Nobre, J. C., Granville, L. Z., Nunzi, G., Dudkowski, D., & Brunner, M. (2009). Distributed reallocation scheme for virtual network resources. *Communications, 2009. ICC'09. IEEE International Conference on*, (pp. 1-5). doi:10.1109/ICC.2009.5198934

Martin, D., Völker, L., & Zitterbart, M. (2011). A flexible framework for Future Internet design, assessment, and operation. *Computer Networks*, *55*(4), 910–918. doi:10.1016/j.comnet.2010.12.015

Mudigonda, J., Yalagandula, P., Mogul, J., Stiekes, B., & Pouffary, Y. (2011). NetLord: A scalable multi-tenant network architecture for virtualized datacenters. *Computer Communication Review*, *41*, 62–73.

Niebert, N., El Khayat, I., Baucke, S., Keller, R., Rembarz, R., & Sachs, J. (2008). Network virtualization: A viable path towards the future internet. *Wireless Personal Communications*, *45*(4), 511–520. doi:10.1007/s11277-008-9481-6

Ott, M., Seskar, I., Siraccusa, R., & Singh, M. (2005). ORBIT testbed software architecture: supporting experiments as a service. null, (pp. 136-145).

Razzaq, A., & Rathore, M. S. (2010). An approach towards resource efficient virtual network embedding. *Evolving Internet (INTERNET), 2010 Second International Conference on*, (pp. 68-73). doi:10.1109/INTERNET.2010.21

Rockell, R., & Fink, R. (2000). *6Bone Backbone Routing Guidelines*. Tech. rep., RFC 2772, February.

Schaffrath, G., Werle, C., Papadimitriou, P., Feldmann, A., Bless, R., & Greenhalgh, A. et al. (2009). Network virtualization architecture: proposal and initial prototype. *Proceedings of the 1st ACM workshop on Virtualized infrastructure systems and architectures*, (pp. 63-72). doi:10.1145/1592648.1592659

Sundararaj, A. I., & Dinda, P. A. (2004). Towards Virtual Networks for Virtual Machine Grid Computing. Virtual machine research and technology symposium, (pp. 177-190).

Szegedi, P., Figuerola, S., Campanella, M., Maglaris, V., & Cervello-Pastor, C. (2009). With evolution for revolution: managing FEDERICA for future internet research. *IEEE Communications Magazine*, *47*(7), 34-39.

Szeto, W., Iraqi, Y., & Boutaba, R. (2003). A multi-commodity flow based approach to virtual network resource allocation. *Global Telecommunications Conference, 2003. GLOBECOM'03*. IEEE. doi:10.1109/GLOCOM.2003.1258787

Takeda, T. (2007). *Framework and requirements for layer 1 virtual private networks*. Academic Press.

Tennenhouse, D. L., Smith, J. M., Sincoskie, W. D., Wetherall, D. J., & Minden, G. J. (1997). A survey of active network research. *Communications Magazine, IEEE*, *35*(1), 80–86. doi:10.1109/35.568214

Touch, J., Wang, Y., & Eggert, L. (2003). *A Virtual Internet Architecture*. ISI Technical Report ISI-TR-570. Workshop on Future Directions in Network Architecture (FDNA).

Villela, D., Campbell, A. T., & Vicente, J. (2001). Virtuosity: Programmable resource management for spawning networks. *Computer Networks*, *36*(1), 49–73. doi:10.1016/S1389-1286(01)00150-5

Wang, A., Iyer, M., Dutta, R., Rouskas, G. N., & Baldine, I. (2013). Network virtualization: Technologies, perspectives, and frontiers. Lightwave Technology. *Journalism*, *31*(4), 523–537.

Wang, C., Wang, C., & Yuan, Y. (2009). Game based dynamical bandwidth allocation model for virtual networks. *Information Science and Engineering (ICISE), 2009 1st International Conference on*, (pp. 1745-1747). doi:10.1109/ICISE.2009.616

Wang, Y., Keller, E., Biskeborn, B., van der Merwe, J., & Rexford, J. (2008). Virtual routers on the move: Live router migration as a network-management primitive. *Computer Communication Review*, *38*(4), 231–242. doi:10.1145/1402946.1402985

Yeow, W.-L., Westphal, C., & Kozat, U. C. (2011). Designing and embedding reliable virtual infrastructures. *Computer Communication Review*, *41*(2), 57–64. doi:10.1145/1971162.1971173

Zhu, Y., & Ammar, M. H. (2006). Algorithms for Assigning Substrate Network Resources to Virtual Network Components. *INFOCOM*, *1200*, 1–12.

KEY TERMS AND DEFINATIONS

Network Substrate: It is required an efficient mapping technique to map the VN onto the underlying physical network. This physical network, usually consists of physical nodes and physical links which is also known as network substrate.

NVE: NV is the coexistence of multiple virtual networks and each VN is the collection of virtual node and virtual link decoupled and independly run on the top of the physical network. In a typical NVE, multiple service providers (SP) provide VN to the end users.

Resource Allocation: Resource allocation is an integral part of any computing system. The resource allocation mechanism is used in virtual machine placement in data centers, network virtualization, multipath network routing, etc. Since it is NP-hard problem many suitable solutions have been devised for the resource allocation problem.

Resource Discovery: The process starts before the resource allocation in network virtualization. This resource discovery phase come into the picture when VNPs are trying to discover the resources in the underlying physical substrate.

vSwitch: Virtual switch is also known as vSwitch is a software emulator, used to connect virtual machines to communicate with each other and working on layer -2 of the virtual network. It performs functions like traffic switching, multiplexing and bridge, vNIC with physical NIC etc.

Chapter 11
Software as a Service, Semantic Web, and Big Data:
Theories and Applications

Kijpokin Kasemsap
Suan Sunandha Rajabhat University, Thailand

ABSTRACT

This chapter explains the overview of software as a service (SaaS); SaaS and application service provision (ASP); the security concern of SaaS; the perspectives on SaaS adoption; the challenges of SaaS in the digital age; the overview of the Semantic Web; the current trends in the Semantic Web services; the overview of Big Data; the concept of Big Data analytics; and the prospects of Big Data in the digital age. SaaS offers a wide range of business applications through the cloud computing service providers toward enhancing organizational performance. The Semantic Web extends beyond the capabilities of the current Web 2.0, thus enabling more effective collaborations and smarter decision making in modern operations. Big Data from the cloud computing platforms provides the significant advantage, if the essential data sources are hosted by the same SaaS and enhanced by the Semantic Web technologies.

INTRODUCTION

Software as a service (SaaS) represents a radical shift in how software is created, delivered, and purchased (Savelyev, 2014). SaaS refers to an on-demand software delivery service model (Marston, Li, Bandyopadhyay, Zhang & Ghalsasi, 2011), which is part of the cloud computing phenomenon. Cloud computing is the specialized pattern of grid and utility computing, and that takes grid computing style when the dynamic connection service and the virtual resources service are available through the Internet (Jasim, Abbas, El-Horbaty & Salem, 2016). With the rapid development in the availability of computer services and the widespread application of the Internet technology, SaaS has become an important approach for new product development within various information technology (IT), the Internet, and software companies (Du, Lu, Wu, Li, & Li, 2013). The distributed SaaS environments significantly sup-

DOI: 10.4018/978-1-5225-1721-4.ch011

port the provision of scalable and virtualized resources as a service over the Internet (Aisopos, Tserpes & Varvarigou, 2013).

The Semantic Web (also known as Web 3.0) is an extension of the current Web 2.0 in which information has a well-defined meaning (Çelik & Elçi, 2013). Khan et al. (2013) indicated that the Semantic Web technologies (e.g., the Semantic Web services) can effectively cater the requirements for achieving interoperability. The main goal of the Semantic Web is to enrich Web 2.0 with semantics and make Web 2.0 be understood by computers, in order to communicate between people and computers (Zhongzhi, Mingkai, Yuncheng & Haijun, 2005). The Semantic Web can be considered as an example of a semantic network (Guns, 2013). The Semantic Web consists of the distributed environment of shared and interoperable ontologies, which have emerged as the common formalisms for knowledge representation (Wei, Guosun & Lulai, 2006).

Big Data is a collection of enormous data that it becomes difficult to process using current database management tools or traditional data processing applications (Xu, Zhao, Chiang, Huang, & Huang, 2015). Regarding Big Data applications, the increases in the volume of data, the velocity with which they are generated and captured, and the variety of formats in which they are delivered all must be taken into account (Kimble & Milolidakis, 2015). Big Data computing demands a huge storage and computing for data processing that can be delivered from on-premise or cloud computing infrastructures (Kune, Konugurthi, Agarwal, Chillarige & Buyya, 2016). Hashem et al. (2015) stated that Big Data utilizes the distributed storage technology based on cloud computing rather than the local storage attached to a computer or electronic device.

In modern operations, the deployment, the integration, and the operation of a Big Data infrastructure are complex and require human resources and special skills. More and more organizations are no longer interested in keeping complex infrastructures in their own data center. Loading large data sets is often a challenge. Another shift of this Big Data processing is the move toward cloud computing (Vaidya, 2016). Big Data from cloud computing-related SaaS and the Semantic Web can be an attractive alternative, relieving the organizations from pre-investments and all operational tasks. The efforts regarding installation, configuration, and maintenance of the systems are completely omitted. Capacity planning is no longer necessary regarding SaaS and the Semantic Web.

Major Internet services (e.g., the Semantic Web) are required to execute the tremendous amount of data at real time (Yıldırım & Watson, 2016). Big Data storage and processing are essential for cloud computing services (Pokorny & Stantic, 2016). The required capacities can be flexibly adjusted to the changing demands, in particular during peak loads in modern operations. Big Data services from SaaS and the Semantic Web provide the great potential for cost reduction toward obtaining various Big Data benefits. Big Data from the cloud computing platforms provides the significant advantage, if the essential data sources are hosted by the same SaaS and enhanced by the Semantic Web technologies.

This chapter aims to bridge the gap in the literature on the thorough literature consolidation of SaaS, the Semantic Web, and Big Data. The extensive literature of SaaS, the Semantic Web, and Big Data provides a contribution to practitioners and researchers by describing the current issues and trends with SaaS, the Semantic Web, and Big Data in order to maximize the technological impact of SaaS, the Semantic Web, and Big Data in modern operations.

Background

The Internet bandwidth and the requirement of businesses for effectiveness with business partners enhance organizations to adopt the IT infrastructures toward promoting organizational performance in modern business (Dubey & Wagle, 2014). There is a growing application of modern platform services, such as cloud computing, infrastructure-as-a-service (Iaas), and platform-as-a-service (Paas), representing a large pool of usable resources, such as hardware and software, that are easily accessible through the Internet (Cusumano, 2010). Cloud computing includes network access to storage, processing power, development platforms, and software (Kasemsap, 2015a). Cloud computing changes the form and function of IT infrastructures in global supply chain (Kasemsap, 2015b).

Enterprise resource planning (ERP) systems are offered on the cloud computing under the SaaS model (Seethamraju, 2015). In SaaS-based electronic procurement (e-procurement) and ERP business model of software provisioning, the consumer does not manage the underlying cloud infrastructure including network, servers, operating systems, storage, or even individual application capabilities, with the possible exception of limited user-specific application configuration settings. ERP is a software-driven business management system that integrates all perspectives of business, including planning, manufacturing, sales, and marketing (Kasemsap, 2015c).

The Web operating system is an operating system that users can access from any hardware at any location. Use of Semantic technology in Web operating systems is an emerging field that improves the management and discovery of resources and services (Javanmardi, Shojafar, Shariatmadari, Abawajy & Singhal, 2014). In the Semantic Web vision of the World Wide Web, content will not only be accessible to humans, but also will be available in machine interpretable form as ontological knowledge bases (Rettinger, Rettinger, Tresp, d'Amato & Fanizzi, 2012). The rapid development of the Internet has led to the diverse applications of accessing various Web 2.0 resources (Kao & Hsu, 2007).

The development of IT has enabled an exponential growth on the data that is produced, processed, stored, shared, analyzed, and visualized (López, del Río, Benítez & Herrera, 2015). Big Data has instigated many areas of investigation, such as computer sciences and statistics (Xu, Cai & Liang, 2015). Big Data encompasses data and information that exceed human comprehension, that exist at a volume unmanageable by standard computer systems, and that arrive at a velocity not under the control of the investigator toward having a level of imprecision not found in traditional inquiry (Brennan & Bakken, 2015). Big Data applications demand and consequently lead to the developments of diverse large-scale data management systems in different organizations, ranging from traditional database vendors to new emerging Internet-based enterprises (Wu, Yuan, & You, 2015).

ASPECTS OF SOFTWARE AS A SERVICE, SEMANTIC WEB, AND BIG DATA

This section describes the overview of SaaS; SaaS and ASP; the security concern of SaaS; the perspectives on SaaS adoption; the challenges of SaaS in the digital age; the overview of the Semantic Web; the current trends in the Semantic Web services; the overview of Big Data; the concept of Big Data analytics; and the prospects of Big Data in the digital age.

Overview of Software as a Service

Software as a service (SaaS) can be defined as applications and computer-based services delivered and managed from a remote center to multiple customers through the Internet or a virtual private network (Lee, Park, & Lim, 2013). SaaS is a software delivery paradigm where the software is hosted off-premises, developed by service providers and delivered through the Internet and the payment mode follows a subscription model (Espadas, Concha & Molina, 2008). Saas shares common themes with on-demand service (Jeong & Stylianou, 2010). Because SaaS is delivered to users over networks, many issues arise concerning service quality that impact customer acceptance of SaaS (Wu, 2011).

SaaS has the potential to provide a stable, reliable, and flexible experience, with access to software regardless of time and location (Goncalves & Ballon, 2011). There are three basic characteristics common to most SaaS applications: under the typical SaaS business model, providers charge a subscription fee for each application which users pay in relation to the level of service they access (Ma & Seidmann, 2008); the software and data are centrally hosted by the service provider utilizing a single-instance, multi-tenant architecture (Susarla, Barua & Whinston, 2010); and SaaS relies predominantly on the World Wide Web and is accessed by customers over the Internet. SaaS has not only its business models, but also its unique development processes and computing infrastructure (Tsai, Bai, & Huang, 2014).

SaaS takes advantage of the thin client technology and provisions SaaS based upon the Internet and semantic technologies, where all the software and the data reside on the server and the client side needs an interface application like the browser, as against the packaged software provisioning model where the software is sold as a product (Mital, Pani & Ramesh, 2014). The most important benefits for independent software vendors include potential economies of scale in both production and distribution costs, more predictable revenues, the development of software with lighter operating systems and hardware requirements, and shorter sales cycles (Goncalves & Ballon, 2011).

SaaS offers major business and IT benefits that organizations are looking to take advantage of (Tang & Liu, 2015). SaaS vendors increasingly offer Web-based services at a subscription fee (Daas, Hurkmans, Overbeek & Bouwman, 2013). Regarding SaaS applications, users use software through the Internet and only pay for what they use, so they do not have to worry about the complicated management of software and hardware (Han, Chung, & Kim, 2015). SaaS is dependent on network integrity for service delivery (Goode, Lin, Tsai, & Jiang, 2015). Much attention has been focused upon trying to objectively measure e-service quality in system and software performance (Benlian, Koufaris & Hess, 2011).

Saas provider acts as a mediator, mediating services between independent software vendors (Lee et al., 2013). SaaS providers aim at minimizing their operational cost by efficiently using resources from IaaS providers, and improving customer satisfaction level by satisfying service level agreement (SLA), which is used to guarantee the quality of service (QoS) requirements of accepted users (Wu, Garg & Buyya, 2012). QoS discovery determines the feasibility of services composition directly (Xuemei, Lizhen, Yisheng & Yongli, 2006).

Software as a Service and Application Service Provision

Saas is the important type of application service provision (ASP) (Lee et al., 2013). IT providers have viewed SaaS as an excellent approach to addressing the shortcomings of previous on-demand software solutions, such as ASP (Benlian & Hess, 2011). On-demand software delivery service models have been developed since the late 1990s and have come in many forms and varieties, including ASP and business service provision (Benlian & Hess, 2011). These types of demand-driven application services provide users and firms with the Internet-based access to resources, expertise, and an integrated portfolio of complex applications spanning firms' complete virtual value chain (Valente & Mitra, 2007).

As the ASP market worsens, it is essential to improve ASP planning and management, as it is harder for many ASP providers to survive (Currie, 2003). For ASP services to be successful, system and service qualities must be well prepared (Kim & Kim, 2008). In small and medium-sized enterprises (SMEs), both ASP service and information quality are the significant factors in enhancing user satisfaction, trust, and the intention to use (Lee, Kim, & Kim, 2007). ASPs are recognized to have the achieved considerable success with big businesses, but their success has been less notable with SME markets (Altaf & Schuff, 2010). Lack of ASP customization options and concerns about financial stability, service reliability, and functional capability flexibility are the major problems for SMEs (Lee et al., 2013).

Security Concern of Software as a Service

A key business problem hence lies in the fact that poor security of the SaaS service undermines the client's trust and satisfaction with that service (Goode et al., 2015). Security is important to SaaS customers (Mouratidis, Islam, Kalloniatis & Gritzalis, 2013). Wu (2011) found no relationship between security and behavioral intention to use SaaS services. Heart (2010) surveyed 143 SaaS clients, and found no significant relationship between the perceived risk of data insecurity and intention to adopt SaaS services. Du et al. (2013) surveyed 1399 SaaS end-customers and found no significant relationship between security perceptions and intention to adopt SaaS. The ability to actively control for security threats is an important factor in a firm's decision to entrust their IT services to SaaS firms (Lee & Kim, 2007). From the client's perspective, security relates to their own operations depending on the threats they experience (Mouratidis et al., 2013).

Perspectives on Software-as-a-Service Adoption

Perceived service quality has a positive influence, and management attitude toward ownership and control has a negative influence on SaaS adoption for both types of operations (Cho & Chan, 2015). The role of perceived risk in IT adoption processes in general and in IT outsourcing decisions in particular is widely supported in various application contexts (Benlian & Hess, 2011). For example, perceived risk has been shown to affect users' intention to adopt the Internet-based applications and services (e.g., bill payment services) at the individual consumer level (Kim, Ferrin, & Rao, 2008). At the organizational level, perceived risk has been found to negatively affect IT managers' intention to increase the level of business process outsourcing (Gewald & Dibbern, 2009). Chwelos et al. (2001) found that the perceived benefits of electronic data interchange (EDI) have a significant influence on IT managers' EDI adoption intentions.

Challenges of Software as a Service in the Digital Age

SaaS becomes an important foundation of the Internet of Services (Benlian, Hess & Buxmann, 2009). SaaS, which offers the possibility to cover both core and non-core business operations of a company, has profoundly transformed traditional outsourcing approaches (Cho & Chan, 2015). Software vendors increasingly aim to apply the SaaS delivery model instead of the traditional on-premise model (Walraven, Truyen & Joosen, 2014).

Software packages evaluation and selection is one of the most important activities encountered by SaaS users in the high performance networked computing environment, especially for SMEs (Ergu & Peng, 2014). SaaS multi-tenancy in cloud-based applications helps service providers to save cost, improve resource utilization, and reduce service customization and maintenance time (Almorsy, Grundy, & Ibrahim, 2014). SaaS has significant effects on enterprise costs and return on investment (ROI) in IT and information systems (Rodrigues, Ruivo & Oliveira, 2014).

SaaS provides access to applications to end users over the Internet without the investment in infrastructure and software (Wu et al., 2012). SaaS providers aim at minimizing the payment of using virtual machines from cloud providers, and want to maximize the profit earned through serving the SaaS users' requests (Li & Li, 2012). SaaS providers derive their profits from the margin between the operational cost of infrastructure and the revenue generated from customers (Li & Li, 2013). By varying size of SaaS products, SaaS providers can improve their market position and profits by successfully acting in the tension area of customer acquisition, pricing, and costs (Katzmarzik, 2011).

Overview of the Semantic Web

The Semantic Web targets the sharing of structured information and formal knowledge pursuing objectives of achieving collective intelligence on the Web 2.0 (Janik, Scherp & Staab, 2011). Web 2.0 allows groups of people to work on a document or spreadsheet simultaneously, while in the background a computer keeps track of who made what changes where and when. Semantic Web technology utilizes ontologies to describe a domain. Ontologies explicitly define the concepts, relationships among the concepts, and the relevant terminology in a domain of interest (Gruber, 1993). Ontologies can be imported and used for knowledge representation. This gives computer applications awareness of the organizations of the data distributed over the Internet (Niknam & Karshenas, 2015).

The Semantic Web technique can help users solve the disadvantages of keyword-based Web service matching (Zou, Xiang, Gan & Chen, 2011). d'Amato et al. (2012) indicated that the Semantic Web search is currently one of the hottest research topics in both Web search and the Semantic Web. In the Semantic Web, vocabularies are shared among knowledge workers to describe linked data for scientific, industrial, and daily life usage (Zhang, Cheng, Ge & Qu, 2009). Security is one of the key challenges for the development of distributed collaborative manufacturing systems regarding the Semantic Web applications (Yang, Chen, Zhang, & Zhang, 2011).

Technological ideas and tools developed for the Semantic Web can be integrated with engineering tools and software (McCorkle & Bryden, 2007). The Semantic Web enables creating data models, drawing the meaningful conclusions from encoded knowledge, and sharing information on the Web and between computer applications (Hitzler, Krotzsch & Rudolph, 2011). With the enormous amount of information presented on the Web, the retrieval of relevant information has become a serious problem and is the topic of research for last few years (Chahal, Singh & Kumar, 2014).

Current Trends in the Semantic Web Services

The Semantic Web services technology is developed to overcome the shortcomings of traditional standards, such as Web services description language (WSDL) and universal description, discovery, and integration (UDDI), and enable maximal automation in all aspects of Web services (Si, Chen, Deng, & Yu, 2013). SaaS based on the Semantic Web technologies has two parts: service orchestration and semantic base (Mital et al., 2014). SaaS based e-procurement and ERP publish the descriptions of service interfaces on the Web 2.0 using WSDL. These descriptions include information about how to invoke the services using hypertext transfer protocol (HTTP), simple object access protocol, and other protocols.

The Semantic Web vision allows people to share the ontology (i.e., a set of conceptual terms labeled by uniform resource locator (URL). The Semantic Web services aim at the automated discovery, selection, and orchestration of Web services on the basis of machine-interpretable semantic descriptions (Dietze, Gugliotta, Domingue, Yu & Mrissa, 2010). The benefits of flexibility, integration and functionality are only achievable because of the Semantic Web capabilities of SaaS-based solution (Mital et al., 2014).

The purpose of the Semantic Web services discovery is to utilize semantic knowledge to find the effective services that can be composed to form an admissible answer to a query (Benbernou & Hacid, 2005). The Semantic Web service matchmaking, as one of the most challenging problems in the Semantic Web services, aims to filter and rank a set of services with respect to a service query by using a certain matching strategy (Wei, Wang, & Wang, 2012). Bell et al. (2007) stated that the Web service-based development represents an emerging approach for the development of distributed information systems. Web services technology is critical for the success of business integration and other application fields, such as bioinformatics (Wang, Zhang & Sunderraman, 2006).

The Semantic Web services are a set of related functionality that can be programmatically accessed through the Web (Medjahed & Bouguettaya, 2005). Verma et al. (2005) stated that the Semantic Web services are the new paradigm for distributed computing. The Semantic Web services have been regarded as software building blocks that can be assembled to construct the distributed business applications of the next generation and assist enterprises to promote operational efficiency and organizational flexibility (Li, Huang, Yen, & Sun, 2011). Semantic Web services effectively support interactions between machines over the Internet (Saboohi & Kareem, 2013).

Semantic Web services possess the potential to help unify the computing resources and knowledge scattered on the Internet into a large platform for collaborative design (Liu, Gao, Shen, Hao, & Yan, 2009). The Semantic Web services ascribe meanings to the published service descriptions so that software systems can automatically interpret and invoke them (Huhns, 2002). The Semantic Web service-based model configures, executes, and disengages one or more services to meet a specific set of requirements instantly and automatically (Turner, Budgen & Brereton, 2003).

Overview of Big Data

Big Data is defined as the quantity of data that exceeds the processing capabilities of a given system (Minelli, Chambers, & Dhiraj, 2013), in terms of time and memory consumption. Big Data is attracting much attention in a wide variety of areas (e.g., industry, medicine, and financial businesses) because they have progressively acquired a lot of raw data (Triguero, Peralta, Bacardit, García & Herrera, 2015). However, the analysis and knowledge extraction process from Big Data become very difficult tasks for most of the classical and advanced data mining and machine learning tools (Woniak, Graña & Corchado, 2014).

The advent of Big Data delivers a cost-effective prospect for the improved decision making in critical development areas, such as health care, economic productivity, and security (Hilbert, 2016). Fundamentals of good modeling and statistical thinking are crucial for the success of Big Data projects (Hoerl, Snee & de Veaux, 2014). The collection and aggregation of massive datasets and the development of analytical tools by which to study these data is part of cutting-edge efforts across scientific disciplines, with social, behavioral, and economic sciences leading the way in many of these efforts (White & Breckenridge, 2014).

Many organizations have always collected lots of data but most of it was discarded (Parham, Mooney, & Cairney, 2015). Big Data includes the growing amount of less-structured data from ERP systems, social media, customer relationship management (CRM) programs, and other sources (Fanning & Grant, 2013). The emergence of social media (e.g., Facebook, Twitter, and blog) has a strong and positive influence on the development of modern communication and business growth (Kasemsap, 2014). The use of social media improves effective communication, increases thought leadership, enhances sales, and provides better customer service (Kasemsap, 2016a). CRM becomes one of the most important competitive business strategies in the digital age, thus involving organizational capability of managing business interactions with customers in an effective manner (Kasemsap, 2015d).

Many modern businesses have embraced Big Data with enthusiasm (Walker & Fung, 2013). There are four main areas where Big Data has potential for promoting positive social change (i.e., advocacy; analysis and prediction; facilitating information exchange; and promoting accountability and transparency) (Taylor, Cowls, Schroeder, & Meyer, 2014). The processing and analysis of Big Data now play a central role in decision making, forecasting, business analysis, product development, customer experience, and loyalty (Casado & Younas, 2014).

Due to massive technological advances, Big Data is broadly applied to include social and commercial environments (Kwon, Lee, & Shin, 2014). Andrejevic (2013) emphasized socio-cultural efforts to understand the social world through Big Data applications. The subject of Big Data has been a major item on the national agenda and is considered as a significant part of technological infrastructure (Esposti, 2013). Although Big Data technology has the potential to provide powerful competitive advantages, many companies are struggling to establish effective privacy in connection with Big Data initiatives (Shin & Choi, 2015).

Concept of Big Data Analytics

Big Data analytics aims to generate new insights that can meaningfully and, often in real time, complement traditional statistics, surveys, and archival data sources that remain largely static (Xiang, Schwartz, Gerdes & Uysal, 2015). Big Data analytics can be used to understand customers, competitors, market characteristics, products, business environment, impact of technologies, and strategic stakeholders, such as alliance and suppliers (Xiang et al., 2015). Many examples and cases have been cited to illustrate the applications of Big Data analytics in order to solve business problems (Mayer-Schönberger & Cukier, 2013).

The emergence of Big Data offers not only a potential advantage for social scientific inquiry, but also raises distinct epistemological issues for this new area of research (Cowls & Schroeder, 2015). Although Big Data analytics does not preclude hypothesis testing, it is often applied to explore novel patterns or predict future trends from the data. While Big Data analytics is widely accepted as a new approach to knowledge creation, there has been recently voice of concerns about the potential pitfall of spurious correlations and calls for theory-based approaches to Big Data analytics (Boyd & Crawford, 2012).

Prospects of Big Data in the Digital Age

The Big Data era has arisen, driven by the increasing availability of data from multiple sources, such as social media, online transactions, network sensors, and mobile devices (Fernández, Gómez, Lecumberry, Pardo & Ramírez, 2015). Big Data is used to refer to the challenges and advantages derived from collecting and processing vast amounts of data (Marx, 2013). Big Data is the emerging trend in IT areas (Fanning & Drogt, 2014) and encompasses large volume of complex structured, semi-structured, and unstructured data, which is beyond the processing capabilities of conventional databases (Casado & Younas, 2014).

Triguero et al. (2015) stated that in the era of Big Data, analyzing and extracting knowledge from large-scale data sets is a very interesting task. The ability to analyze large data sets is a central factor for competitiveness that is underpinning the new trends of productivity, growth, and innovation (Kitchin, 2014). The advancements in data storage and mining technologies allow for the preservation of increasing amounts of data described by a change in the nature of data held by modern organizations (Cumbley & Church, 2013). Big Data applications are characterized by a non-negligible number of complex parallel transactions on a huge amount of data that continuously varies, generally increasing over time (Castiglione, Gribaudo, Iacono & Palmieri, 2015). Financial managers who can derive actionable information from Big Data are able to achieve more corporate growth by making better decisions (Fanning & Grant, 2013).

Big Data is an emerging paradigm applied to data sets whose size is beyond the ability of commonly used software tools to capture, manage, and process the data within a tolerable elapsed time (Wigan & Clarke, 2013). Big Data is the foundation on which policy making is based (McNeely & Hahm, 2014). Big Data has to be of high value (Xu, Liu, Mei, Hu & Chen, 2015). Various technologies are recognized to support the management of Big Data, such as massively parallel processing databases (Yuan et al., 2013), cloud computing platforms, and MapReduce (Zhang, Yang, Liu, & Chen, 2013). MapReduce is a paradigm of parallel programming (Dean & Ghemawat, 2010), designed to generate large data sets. MapReduce is a good example of Big Data processing in a cloud computing environment and allows for the processing of large amounts of datasets stored in parallel in the cluster (Dean & Ghemawat, 2008).

Hashem et al. (2015) indicated that addressing Big Data is a challenging and time-demanding task that requires a large computational infrastructure to ensure successful data processing and analysis. Dealing with Big Data with uncertainty distribution is one of the most important issues of Big Data research (He, Wang, Zhuang, Shang, & Shi, 2015). Big Data techniques are considered as the powerful tool to exploit the potential of the Internet of Things (IoT) and the smart cities (Jara, Genoud, & Bocchi, 2015). The IoT deployments typically generate large amounts of data that require computing as well as storage (Alohali, 2016). There is a great deal of enthusiasm about the prospects for Big Data held in health care systems around the world (Keen, Calinescu, Paige & Rooksby, 2013). New sources of data in the Big Data domain provide an opportunity to deliver a more effective statistical service (Tam & Clarke, 2015).

Guo et al. (2015) indicated that data variety is viewed as one of the most critical features for the Big Data-related multimedia. Multimedia has become a form of Big Data which gives the users valuable information, such as event occurrence, networks computing, purchase recommendation, and workflow control (Wang, Jiang, Wu & Xiong, 2014). The unlimited potential of a data-driven economy is widely recognized, and there is the increasing enthusiasm for the notion of Big Data (Shin & Choi, 2015). Advancements in Big Data analysis offer the cost-effective opportunities for the improvements in the critical decision-making development areas, such as health care, employment, economic productivity, security, and resource management (Tinati, Halford, Carr & Pope, 2014).

FUTURE RESEARCH DIRECTIONS

The classification of the extensive literature in the domains of SaaS, the Semantic Web, and Big Data will provide the potential opportunities for future research. Data mining is the computational procedure of pioneering schemes in the large data sets regarding methods at the integration of artificial intelligence, machine learning, statistics, and database systems (Kasemsap, 2015e). Business analytics can be used to validate the causal relationships within traditional input, process, output, and outcome categories (Kasemsap, 2015f). Business intelligence involves creating any type of data visualization that provides insight into a business for the purpose of making a decision or taking an action (Kasemsap, 2016b). Business process modeling is the documentation of a business system using a combination of text and graphical notation (Kasemsap, 2016c). The relationships among SaaS, the Semantic Web, Big Data, data mining, business analytics, business intelligence, and business process modeling in modern operations would seem to be viable for future research efforts.

CONCLUSION

This chapter emphasized the overview of SaaS; SaaS and ASP; the security concern of SaaS; the perspectives on SaaS adoption; the challenges of SaaS in the digital age; the overview of the Semantic Web; the current trends in the Semantic Web services; the overview of Big Data; the concept of Big Data analytics; and the prospects of Big Data in the digital age. SaaS, the best-known branch of cloud computing, is a delivery model in which applications are hosted and managed in a service provider's datacenter, paid for on a subscription basis and accessed through a browser over an Internet connection. SaaS significantly provides more power and control to the corporate buyer than traditional software license models.

SaaS applications are sold on a subscription basis for a monthly recurring fee. With SaaS, corporate buyers only pay for the active users of the system. SaaS applications typically have limited customization of features and the user interface. As a result, there are no delays resulting from the need for internal IT organizations to perform the development, enhancement, and deployment of SaaS applications. SaaS vendors typically deliver two to four major upgrades per year and several minor updates that the user gets automatically. Users of SaaS-based applications can always be certain that they are using the latest version of the software provided by the cloud computing vendor.

The Semantic Web is an aggregation of intelligent websites and data stores accessible by an array of semantic technologies, conceptual frameworks, and well-recognized contracts of interaction to allow machines to do more of the work to respond to service requests, providing better information relevance and performing intelligent reasoning. The emergence of the Semantic Web is a natural progression in accredited information theories, borrowing concepts from the knowledge representation and knowledge management worlds as well as from revised thinking within the World Wide Web community.

Big Data represents an important trend in technology that leads the way to a new aspect in understanding the modern business world and making business decisions. Big Data can enhance the significant value by making information transparent and usable at much higher frequency in modern operations. As modern organizations create and store more transactional data in digital form, they can collect more accurate and detailed performance information on everything. The utilization of Big Data becomes an essential basis of competition and growth in the digital age. When the adoption of Big Data is properly aligned to the business, existing governance structures can be easily adjusted to address security, assurance, and general approach to embracing new technologies.

The applications of SaaS, the Semantic Web, and Big Data are critical for modern organizations that seek to serve suppliers and customers, increase business performance, strengthen competitiveness, and achieve continuous success in modern operations. Therefore, it is necessary for modern organizations to apply their SaaS, the Semantic Web, and Big Data toward satisfying the requirements of suppliers and customers. Applying SaaS, the Semantic Web, and Big Data has the potential to enhance organizational performance and reach strategic goals in modern operations.

REFERENCES

Aisopos, F., Tserpes, K., & Varvarigou, T. (2013). Resource management in software as a service using the knapsack problem model. *International Journal of Production Economics*, *141*(2), 465–477. doi:10.1016/j.ijpe.2011.12.011

Almorsy, M., Grundy, J., & Ibrahim, A. S. (2014). Adaptable, model-driven security engineering for SaaS cloud-based applications. *Automated Software Engineering*, *21*(2), 187–224. doi:10.1007/s10515-013-0133-z

Alohali, B. (2016). Security in Cloud of Things (CoT). In Z. Ma (Ed.), *Managing Big Data in cloud computing Environments* (pp. 46–70). Hershey, PA: IGI Global. doi:10.4018/978-1-4666-9834-5.ch003

Altaf, F., & Schuff, D. (2010). Taking a flexible approach to ASPs. *Communications of the ACM*, *53*(2), 139–143. doi:10.1145/1646353.1646389

Andrejevic, M. (2013). *Infoglut: How too much information is changing the way we think and know?* New York, NY: Routledge.

Bell, D., de Cesare, S., Iacovelli, N., Lycett, M., & Merico, A. (2007). A framework for deriving Semantic Web services. *Information Systems Frontiers*, *9*(1), 69–84. doi:10.1007/s10796-006-9018-z

Benbernou, S., & Hacid, M. S. (2005). Resolution and constraint propagation for Semantic Web services discovery. *Distributed and Parallel Databases*, *18*(1), 65–81. doi:10.1007/s10619-005-1074-8

Benlian, A., & Hess, T. (2011). Opportunities and risks of software-as-a-service: Findings from a survey of IT executives. *Decision Support Systems*, *52*(1), 232–246. doi:10.1016/j.dss.2011.07.007

Benlian, A., Hess, T., & Buxmann, P. (2009). Drivers of SaaS-adoption: An empirical study of different application types. *Business & Information Systems Engineering*, *1*(5), 357–369. doi:10.1007/s12599-009-0068-x

Benlian, A., Koufaris, M., & Hess, T. (2011). Service quality in software-as-a-service: Developing the SaaS-QUAL measure and examining its role in usage continuance. *Journal of Management Information Systems*, *28*(3), 85–126. doi:10.2753/MIS0742-1222280303

Boyd, D., & Crawford, K. (2012). Critical questions for Big Data: Provocations for a cultural, technological, and scholarly phenomenon. *Information, Communication and Society*, *15*(5), 662–679. doi:10.1080/1369118X.2012.678878

Brennan, P. F., & Bakken, S. (2015). Nursing needs Big Data and Big Data needs nursing. *Journal of Nursing Scholarship*, *47*(5), 477–484. doi:10.1111/jnu.12159

Casado, R., & Younas, M. (2014). Emerging trends and technologies in Big Data processing. *Concurrency and Computation*, *27*(8), 2078–2091. doi:10.1002/cpe.3398

Castiglione, A., Gribaudo, M., Iacono, M., & Palmieri, F. (2015). Modeling performances of concurrent Big Data applications. *Software: Practice & Experience*, *45*(8), 1127–1144. doi:10.1002/spe.2269

Çelik, D., & Elçi, A. (2013). A broker-based semantic agent for discovering Semantic Web services through process similarity matching and equivalence considering quality of service. *Science China: Information Sciences*, *56*(1), 1–24. doi:10.1007/s11432-012-4697-1

Chahal, P., Singh, M., & Kumar, S. (2014). An efficient web page ranking for Semantic Web. *Journal of The Institution of Engineers (India): Series B*, *95*(1), 15–21. doi:10.1007/s40031-014-0070-7

Cho, V., & Chan, A. (2015). An integrative framework of comparing SaaS adoption for core and non-core business operations: An empirical study on Hong Kong industries. *Information Systems Frontiers*, *17*(3), 629–644. doi:10.1007/s10796-013-9450-9

Chwelos, P., Benbasat, I., & Dexter, A. S. (2001). Research report: Empirical test of an EDI adoption model. *Information Systems Research*, *12*(3), 304–321. doi:10.1287/isre.12.3.304.9708

Cowls, J., & Schroeder, R. (2015). Causation, correlation, and Big Data in social science research. *Policy & Internet*, *7*(4), 447–472. doi:10.1002/poi3.100

Cumbley, R., & Church, P. (2013). Is "Big Data" creepy? *Computer Law & Security Report*, *29*(5), 601–609. doi:10.1016/j.clsr.2013.07.007

Currie, W. L. (2003). A knowledge-base risk assessment framework for evaluating Web-based application outsourcing projects. *International Journal of Project Management*, *21*(3), 207–217. doi:10.1016/S0263-7863(02)00095-9

Cusumano, M. (2010). Technology strategy and management: Cloud computing and SaaS as new computing platforms. *Communications of the ACM*, *53*(4), 27–29. doi:10.1145/1721654.1721667

d'Amato, C., Fanizzi, N., Fazzinga, B., Gottlob, G., & Lukasiewicz, T. (2012). Ontology-based semantic search on the Web and its combination with the power of inductive reasoning. *Annals of Mathematics and Artificial Intelligence*, *65*(2), 83–121. doi:10.1007/s10472-012-9309-7

Daas, D., Hurkmans, T., Overbeek, S., & Bouwman, H. (2013). Developing a decision support system for business model design. *Electronic Markets*, *23*(3), 251–265. doi:10.1007/s12525-012-0115-1

Dean, J., & Ghemawat, S. (2008). MapReduce: Simplified data processing on large clusters. *Communications of the ACM*, *51*(1), 107–113. doi:10.1145/1327452.1327492

Dean, J., & Ghemawat, S. (2010). MapReduce: A flexible data processing tool. *Communications of the ACM*, *53*(1), 72–77. doi:10.1145/1629175.1629198

Dietze, S., Gugliotta, A., Domingue, J., Yu, H. Q., & Mrissa, M. (2010). An automated approach to Semantic Web services mediation. *Service Oriented Computing and Applications*, *4*(4), 261–275. doi:10.1007/s11761-010-0070-7

Du, J., Lu, J., Wu, D., Li, H., & Li, J. (2013). User acceptance of software as a service: Evidence from customers of China's leading e-commerce company, Alibaba. *Journal of Systems and Software*, *86*(8), 2034–2044. doi:10.1016/j.jss.2013.03.012

Dubey, A., & Wagle, D. (2007). Delivering software as a service. *The McKinsey Quarterly*, *6*, 1–12.

Ergu, D., & Peng, Y. (2014). A framework for SaaS software packages evaluation and selection with virtual team and BOCR of analytic network process. *The Journal of Supercomputing*, *67*(1), 219–238. doi:10.1007/s11227-013-0995-7

Espadas, J., Concha, D., & Molina, A. (2008). *Application development over software-as-a-service platforms*. Paper presented at the 3rd International Conference on Software Engineering Advances (ICSEA 2008), Sliema, Malta. doi:10.1109/ICSEA.2008.48

Esposti, S. (2013). *Big Data or dataveillance? The rise of the scientific enterprise*. Paper presented at the 38th Annual Meeting of the Society for Social Studies of Science (4S 2013), San Diego, CA.

Fanning, K., & Drogt, E. (2014). Big Data: New opportunities for M&A. *Journal of Corporate Accounting & Finance*, *25*(2), 27–34. doi:10.1002/jcaf.21919

Fanning, K., & Grant, R. (2013). Big Data: Implications for financial managers. *Journal of Corporate Accounting & Finance*, *24*(5), 23–30. doi:10.1002/jcaf.21872

Fernández, A., Gómez, A., Lecumberry, F., Pardo, A., & Ramírez, I. (2015). Pattern recognition in Latin America in the "Big Data" era. *Pattern Recognition*, *48*(4), 1185–1196. doi:10.1016/j.patcog.2014.04.012

Goncalves, V., & Ballon, P. (2011). Adding value to the network: Mobile operators' experiments with software-as-a-service and platform-as-a-service models. *Telematics and Informatics*, *28*(1), 12–21. doi:10.1016/j.tele.2010.05.005

Goode, S., Lin, C., Tsai, J. C., & Jiang, J. J. (2015). Rethinking the role of security in client satisfaction with software-as-a-service (SaaS) providers. *Decision Support Systems*, *70*, 73–85. doi:10.1016/j.dss.2014.12.005

Gruber, T. R. (1993). A translation approach to portable ontology specifications. *Knowledge Acquisition*, *5*(2), 199–220. doi:10.1006/knac.1993.1008

Guns, R. (2013). Tracing the origins of the Semantic Web. *Journal of the American Society for Information Science and Technology*, *64*(10), 2173–2181. doi:10.1002/asi.22907

Guo, K., Pan, W., Lu, M., Zhou, X., & Ma, J. (2015). An effective and economical architecture for semantic-based heterogeneous multimedia Big Data retrieval. *Journal of Systems and Software*, *102*, 207–216. doi:10.1016/j.jss.2014.09.016

Han, J. S., Chung, K. Y., & Kim, G. J. (2015). Policy on literature content based on software as service. *Multimedia Tools and Applications*, *74*(20), 9087–9096. doi:10.1007/s11042-013-1664-9

Hashem, I. A. T., Yaqoob, I., Anuar, N. B., Mokhtar, S., Gani, A., & Khan, S. U. (2015). The rise of "Big Data" on cloud computing: Review and open research issues. *Information Systems*, *47*, 98–115. doi:10.1016/j.is.2014.07.006

He, Q., Wang, H., Zhuang, F., Shang, T., & Shi, Z. (2015). Parallel sampling from Big Data with uncertainty distribution. *Fuzzy Sets and Systems*, *258*, 117–133. doi:10.1016/j.fss.2014.01.016

Heart, T. (2010). Who is out there?: Exploring the effects of trust and perceived risk on SaaS adoption intentions. *ACM SIGMIS Database*, *41*(3), 49–68. doi:10.1145/1851175.1851179

Hilbert, M. (2016). Big Data for development: A review of promises and challenges. *Development Policy Review*, *34*(1), 135–174. doi:10.1111/dpr.12142

Hitzler, P., Krotzsch, M., & Rudolph, S. (2011). *Foundations of Semantic Web technologies*. Boca Raton, FL: Chapman & Hall/CRC.

Hoerl, R. W., Snee, R. D., & de Veaux, R. D. (2014). Applying statistical thinking to "Big Data" problems. *Wiley Interdisciplinary Reviews: Computational Statistics*, *6*(4), 222–232. doi:10.1002/wics.1306

Huhns, M. N. (2002). Agents as Web services. *IEEE Internet Computing*, *6*(4), 93–95. doi:10.1109/MIC.2002.1020332

Janik, M., Scherp, A., & Staab, S. (2011). The Semantic Web: Collective intelligence on the Web. *Informatik Spektrum*, *345*(5), 469–483. doi:10.1007/s00287-011-0535-x

Jara, A. J., Genoud, D., & Bocchi, Y. (2015). Big Data for smart cities with KNIME a real experience in the SmartSantander testbed. *Software: Practice & Experience*, *45*(8), 1145–1160. doi:10.1002/spe.2274

Jasim, O. K., Abbas, S., El-Horbaty, E. M., & Salem, A. M. (2016). CCCE: Cryptographic cloud computing environment based on quantum computations. In Z. Ma (Ed.), *Managing Big Data in cloud computing environments* (pp. 71–99). Hershey, PA: IGI Global. doi:10.4018/978-1-4666-9834-5.ch004

Javanmardi, S., Shojafar, M., Shariatmadari, S., Abawajy, J. H., & Singhal, M. (2014). PGSW-OS: A novel approach for resource management in a Semantic Web operating system based on a P2P grid architecture. *The Journal of Supercomputing*, *69*(2), 955–975. doi:10.1007/s11227-014-1221-y

Jeong, B. K., & Stylianou, A. C. (2010). Market reaction to application service provider (ASP) adoption: An empirical investigation. *Information & Management*, *47*(3), 176–187. doi:10.1016/j.im.2010.01.007

Kao, S. J., & Hsu, I. C. (2007). Semantic Web approach to smart link generation for Web navigations. *Software: Practice & Experience*, *37*(8), 857–879. doi:10.1002/spe.789

Kasemsap, K. (2014). The role of social media in the knowledge-based organizations. In I. Lee (Ed.), *Integrating social media into business practice, applications, management, and models* (pp. 254–275). Hershey, PA: IGI Global. doi:10.4018/978-1-4666-6182-0.ch013

Kasemsap, K. (2015a). The role of cloud computing adoption in global business. In V. Chang, R. Walters, & G. Wills (Eds.), *Delivery and adoption of cloud computing services in contemporary organizations* (pp. 26–55). Hershey, PA: IGI Global. doi:10.4018/978-1-4666-8210-8.ch002

Kasemsap, K. (2015b). The role of cloud computing in global supply chain. In N. Rao (Ed.), *Enterprise management strategies in the era of cloud computing* (pp. 192–219). Hershey, PA: IGI Global. doi:10.4018/978-1-4666-8339-6.ch009

Kasemsap, K. (2015c). Implementing enterprise resource planning. In M. Khosrow-Pour (Ed.), *Encyclopedia of information science and technology* (3rd ed., pp. 798–807). Hershey, PA: IGI Global. doi:10.4018/978-1-4666-5888-2.ch076

Kasemsap, K. (2015d). The role of customer relationship management in the global business environments. In T. Tsiakis (Ed.), *Trends and innovations in marketing information systems* (pp. 130–156). Hershey, PA: IGI Global. doi:10.4018/978-1-4666-8459-1.ch007

Kasemsap, K. (2015e). The role of data mining for business intelligence in knowledge management. In A. Azevedo & M. Santos (Eds.), *Integration of data mining in business intelligence systems* (pp. 12–33). Hershey, PA: IGI Global. doi:10.4018/978-1-4666-6477-7.ch002

Kasemsap, K. (2015f). The role of business analytics in performance management. In M. Tavana & K. Puranam (Eds.), *Handbook of research on organizational transformations through big data analytics* (pp. 126–145). Hershey, PA: IGI Global. doi:10.4018/978-1-4666-7272-7.ch010

Kasemsap, K. (2016a). Utilizing social media in modern business. In I. Lee (Ed.), *Encyclopedia of e-commerce development, implementation, and management* (pp. 2171–2182). Hershey, PA: IGI Global. doi:10.4018/978-1-4666-9787-4.ch156

Kasemsap, K. (2016b). The fundamentals of business intelligence. *International Journal of Organizational and Collective Intelligence, 6*(2), 12–25. doi:10.4018/IJOCI.2016040102

Kasemsap, K. (2016c). The roles of business process modeling and business process reengineering in e-government. In J. Martins & A. Molnar (Eds.), *Handbook of research on innovations in information retrieval, analysis, and management* (pp. 401–430). Hershey, PA: IGI Global. doi:10.4018/978-1-4666-8833-9.ch015

Katzmarzik, A. (2011). Product differentiation for software-as-a-service providers. *Business & Information Systems Engineering, 3*(1), 19–31. doi:10.1007/s12599-010-0142-4

Keen, J., Calinescu, R., Paige, R., & Rooksby, J. (2013). Big Data + politics = open data: The case of health care data in England. *Policy & Internet, 5*(2), 228–243. doi:10.1002/1944-2866.POI330

Khan, W. A., Hussain, M., Latif, K., Afzal, M., Ahmad, F., & Lee, S. (2013). Process interoperability in healthcare systems with dynamic Semantic Web services. *Computing, 95*(9), 837–862. doi:10.1007/s00607-012-0239-3

Kim, D. J., Ferrin, D. L., & Rao, H. R. (2008). A trust-based consumer decision-making model in electronic commerce: The role of trust, perceived risk, and their antecedents. *Decision Support Systems, 44*(2), 544–564. doi:10.1016/j.dss.2007.07.001

Kim, G., & Kim, E. (2008). An exploratory study of factors influencing ASP (application service provider) success. *Journal of Computer Information Systems, 48*(3), 118–124.

Kimble, C., & Milolidakis, G. (2015). Big Data and business intelligence: Debunking the myths. *Global Business and Organizational Excellence*, *35*(1), 23–34. doi:10.1002/joe.21642

Kitchin, R. (2014). *The data revolution: Big Data, open data, data infrastructures and their consequences*. London, UK: Sage Publications. doi:10.4135/9781473909472

Kune, R., Konugurthi, P. K., Agarwal, A., Chillarige, R. R., & Buyya, R. (2016). The anatomy of Big Data computing. *Software: Practice & Experience*, *46*(1), 79–105. doi:10.1002/spe.2374

Kwon, O., Lee, N., & Shin, B. (2014). Data quality management, data usage experience and acquisition intention of Big Data analytics. *International Journal of Information Management*, *34*(3), 387–394. doi:10.1016/j.ijinfomgt.2014.02.002

Lee, H., Kim, J., & Kim, J. (2007). Determinants of success for application service provider: An empirical test in small businesses. *International Journal of Human-Computer Studies*, *65*(9), 796–815. doi:10.1016/j.ijhcs.2007.04.004

Lee, S., Park, S. B., & Lim, G. G. (2013). Using balanced scorecards for the evaluation of "software-as-a-service". *Information & Management*, *50*(7), 553–561. doi:10.1016/j.im.2013.07.006

Li, C., & Li, L. (2012). Optimal resource provisioning for cloud computing environment. *The Journal of Supercomputing*, *62*(2), 989–1022. doi:10.1007/s11227-012-0775-9

Li, C., & Li, L. (2013). Efficient resource allocation for optimizing objectives of cloud users, IaaS provider and SaaS provider in cloud environment. *The Journal of Supercomputing*, *65*(2), 866–885. doi:10.1007/s11227-013-0869-z

Li, S. H., Huang, S. M., Yen, D. C., & Sun, J. C. (2011). Semantic-based transaction model for Web service. *Information Systems Frontiers*, *15*(2), 249–268. doi:10.1007/s10796-013-9409-x

Liu, M., Gao, Q., Shen, W., Hao, Q., & Yan, J. (2009). A semantic-augmented multi-level matching model of Web services. *Service Oriented Computing and Applications*, *3*(3), 205–215. doi:10.1007/s11761-009-0045-8

López, V., del Río, S., Benítez, J. M., & Herrera, F. (2015). Cost-sensitive linguistic fuzzy rule based classification systems under the MapReduce framework for imbalanced Big Data. *Fuzzy Sets and Systems*, *258*, 5–38. doi:10.1016/j.fss.2014.01.015

Ma, D., & Seidmann, A. (2008). The pricing strategy analysis for the "software-as-a- service" business model. In J. Altmann, D. Neumann, & T. Fahringer (Eds.), *Grid economics and business models* (pp. 103–112). Berlin, Germany: Springer–Verlag. doi:10.1007/978-3-540-85485-2_8

Marston, S., Li, Z., Bandyopadhyay, S., Zhang, J., & Ghalsasi, A. (2011). Cloud computing: The business perspective. *Decision Support Systems*, *51*(1), 176–189. doi:10.1016/j.dss.2010.12.006

Marx, V. (2013). The big challenges of Big Data. *Nature*, *498*(7453), 255–260. doi:10.1038/498255a

Mayer-Schönberger, V., & Cukier, K. (2013). *Big Data: A revolution that will transform: How we live, work, and think*. New York, NY: Houghton Mifflin Harcourt.

McCorkle, D. S., & Bryden, K. M. (2007). Using the Semantic Web technologies in virtual engineering tools to create extensible interfaces. *Virtual Reality (Waltham Cross)*, *11*(4), 253–260. doi:10.1007/s10055-007-0077-3

McNeely, C. L., & Hahm, J. O. (2014). The Big (Data) bang: Policy, prospects, and challenges. *Review of Policy Research*, *31*(4), 304–310. doi:10.1111/ropr.12082

Medjahed, B., & Bouguettaya, A. (2005). A dynamic foundational architecture for Semantic Web services. *Distributed and Parallel Databases*, *17*(2), 179–206. doi:10.1007/s10619-004-0190-1

Minelli, M., Chambers, M., & Dhiraj, A. (2013). *Big Data, big analytics: Emerging business intelligence and analytic trends for today's businesses*. Hoboken, NJ: John Wiley & Sons. doi:10.1002/9781118562260

Mital, M., Pani, A., & Ramesh, R. (2014). Determinants of choice of Semantic Web based software as a service: An integrative framework in the context of e-procurement and ERP. *Computers in Industry*, *65*(5), 821–827. doi:10.1016/j.compind.2014.03.002

Mouratidis, H., Islam, S., Kalloniatis, C., & Gritzalis, S. (2013). A framework to support selection of cloud providers based on security and privacy requirements. *Journal of Systems and Software*, *86*(9), 2276–2293. doi:10.1016/j.jss.2013.03.011

Niknam, M., & Karshenas, S. (2015). Integrating distributed sources of information for construction cost estimating using Semantic Web and Semantic Web service technologies. *Automation in Construction*, *57*, 222–238. doi:10.1016/j.autcon.2015.04.003

Parham, A. G., Mooney, J. L., & Cairney, T. D. (2015). When BYOD meets Big Data. *Journal of Corporate Accounting & Finance*, *26*(5), 21–27. doi:10.1002/jcaf.22059

Pokorny, J., & Stantic, B. (2016). Challenges and opportunities in Big Data processing. In Z. Ma (Ed.), *Managing Big Data in cloud computing environments* (pp. 1–24). Hershey, PA: IGI Global. doi:10.4018/978-1-4666-9834-5.ch001

Rettinger, A., Rettinger, U., Tresp, V., d'Amato, C., & Fanizzi, N. (2012). Mining the Semantic Web. *Data Mining and Knowledge Discovery*, *24*(3), 613–662. doi:10.1007/s10618-012-0253-2

Rodrigues, J., Ruivo, P., & Oliveira, T. (2014). Software as a service value and firm performance: A literature review synthesis in small and medium enterprises. *Procedia Technology*, *16*, 206–211. doi:10.1016/j.protcy.2014.10.085

Saboohi, H., & Kareem, S. A. (2013). An automatic subdigraph renovation plan for failure recovery of composite Semantic Web services. *Frontiers of Computer Science*, *7*(6), 894–913. doi:10.1007/s11704-013-2248-6

Savelyev, A. (2014). Software-as-a-service – Legal nature: Shifting the existing paradigm of copyright law. *Computer Law & Security Report*, *30*(5), 560–568. doi:10.1016/j.clsr.2014.05.011

Seethamraju, R. (2015). Adoption of software as a service (SaaS) enterprise resource planning (ERP) systems in small and medium sized enterprises (SMEs). *Information Systems Frontiers*, *17*(3), 475–492. doi:10.1007/s10796-014-9506-5

Shin, D. H., & Choi, M. J. (2015). Ecological views of Big Data: Perspectives and issues. *Telematics and Informatics*, *32*(2), 311–320. doi:10.1016/j.tele.2014.09.006

Si, H., Chen, Z., Deng, Y., & Yu, L. (2013). Semantic Web services publication and OCT-based discovery in structured P2P network. *Service Oriented Computing and Applications*, *7*(3), 169–180. doi:10.1007/s11761-011-0097-4

Susarla, A., Barua, A., & Whinston, A. B. (2010). Multitask agency, modular architecture, and task disaggregation in SaaS. *Journal of Management Information Systems*, *26*(4), 87–118. doi:10.2753/MIS0742-1222260404

Tam, S. M., & Clarke, F. (2015). Big Data, official statistics and some initiatives by the Australian Bureau of Statistics. *International Statistical Review*, *83*(3), 436–448. doi:10.1111/insr.12105

Tang, C., & Liu, J. (2015). Selecting a trusted cloud service provider for your SaaS program. *Computers & Security*, *50*, 60–73. doi:10.1016/j.cose.2015.02.001

Taylor, L., Cowls, J., Schroeder, R., & Meyer, E. T. (2014). Big Data and positive change in the developing world. *Policy & Internet*, *6*(4), 418–444. doi:10.1002/1944-2866.POI378

Tinati, R., Halford, S., Carr, L., & Pope, C. (2014). Big Data: Methodological challenges and approaches for sociological analysis. *Sociology*, *48*(4), 663–681. doi:10.1177/0038038513511561

Triguero, I., Peralta, D., Bacardit, J., García, S., & Herrera, F. (2015). MRPR: A MapReduce solution for prototype reduction in Big Data classification. *Neurocomputing*, *150*, 331–345. doi:10.1016/j.neucom.2014.04.078

Tsai, W. T., Bai, X. Y., & Huang, Y. (2014). Software-as-a-service (SaaS): Perspectives and challenges. *Science China: Information Sciences*, *57*(5), 1–15. doi:10.1007/s11432-013-5050-z

Turner, M., Budgen, D., & Brereton, P. (2003). Turning software into a service. *IEEE Computer*, *36*(10), 38–44. doi:10.1109/MC.2003.1236470

Vaidya, M. (2016). Handling critical issues of Big Data on cloud. In Z. Ma (Ed.), *Managing Big Data in cloud computing environments* (pp. 100–131). Hershey, PA: IGI Global. doi:10.4018/978-1-4666-9834-5.ch005

Valente, P., & Mitra, G. (2007). The evolution of Web-based optimisation: From ASP to e-services. *Decision Support Systems*, *43*(4), 1096–1116. doi:10.1016/j.dss.2005.07.003

Verma, K., Sivashanmugam, K., Sheth, A., Patil, A., Oundhakar, S., & Miller, J. (2005). METEOR-S WSDI: A scalable P2P infrastructure of registries for semantic publication and discovery of Web services. *Information Technology & Management*, *6*(1), 17–39. doi:10.1007/s10799-004-7773-4

Walker, D., & Fung, K. (2013). Big Data and big business: Should statisticians join in? *Significance*, *10*(4), 20–25. doi:10.1111/j.1740-9713.2013.00679.x

Walraven, S., Truyen, E., & Joosen, W. (2014). Comparing PaaS offerings in light of SaaS development. *Computing*, *96*(8), 669–724. doi:10.1007/s00607-013-0346-9

Wang, G., Jiang, W., Wu, J., & Xiong, Z. (2014). Fine-grained feature-based social influence evaluation in online social networks. *IEEE Transactions on Parallel and Distributed Systems*, *25*(9), 2286–2296. doi:10.1109/TPDS.2013.135

Wang, H., Zhang, Y. Q., & Sunderraman, R. (2006). Extensible soft Semantic Web services agent. *Soft Computing*, *10*(11), 1021–1029. doi:10.1007/s00500-005-0029-3

Wei, D., Wang, T., & Wang, J. (2012). A logistic regression model for Semantic Web service matchmaking. *Science China: Information Sciences*, *55*(7), 1715–1720. doi:10.1007/s11432-012-4591-x

Wei, W., Guosun, Z., & Lulai, Y. (2006). Semtrust: A semantic reputation system in P2P-based Semantic Web. *Wuhan University Journal of Natural Sciences*, *11*(5), 1137–1140. doi:10.1007/BF02829224

White, P., & Breckenridge, R. S. (2014). Trade-offs, limitations, and promises of Big Data in social science research. *Review of Policy Research*, *31*(4), 331–338. doi:10.1111/ropr.12078

Wigan, M., & Clarke, R. (2013). Big Data's big unintended consequences. *Computer*, *46*(6), 46–53. doi:10.1109/MC.2013.195

Woniak, M., Graña, M., & Corchado, E. (2014). A survey of multiple classifier systems as hybrid systems. *Information Fusion*, *16*, 3–17. doi:10.1016/j.inffus.2013.04.006

Wu, L., Garg, S. K., & Buyya, R. (2012). SLA-based admission control for a software-as-a-service provider in cloud computing environments. *Journal of Computer and System Sciences*, *78*(5), 1280–1299. doi:10.1016/j.jcss.2011.12.014

Wu, L., Yuan, L., & You, J. (2015). Survey of large-scale data management systems for Big Data applications. *Journal of Computer Science and Technology*, *30*(1), 163–183. doi:10.1007/s11390-015-1511-8

Wu, W. W. (2011). Developing an explorative model for SaaS adoption. *Expert Systems with Applications*, *38*(12), 15057–15064. doi:10.1016/j.eswa.2011.05.039

Xiang, Z., Schwartz, Z., Gerdes, J. H. Jr, & Uysal, M. (2015). What can Big Data and text analytics tell us about hotel guest experience and satisfaction? *International Journal of Hospitality Management*, *44*, 120–130. doi:10.1016/j.ijhm.2014.10.013

Xu, M., Cai, H., & Liang, S. (2015). Big Data and industrial ecology. *Journal of Industrial Ecology*, *19*(2), 205–210. doi:10.1111/jiec.12241

Xu, W. J., Zhao, C. D., Chiang, H. P., Huang, L., & Huang, Y. M. (2015). The RR-PEVQ algorithm research based on active area detection for Big Data applications. *Multimedia Tools and Applications*, *74*(10), 3507–3520. doi:10.1007/s11042-014-1903-8

Xu, Z., Liu, Y., Mei, L., Hu, C., & Chen, L. (2015). Semantic based representing and organizing surveillance Big Data using video structural description technology. *Journal of Systems and Software*, *102*, 217–225. doi:10.1016/j.jss.2014.07.024

Xuemei, Y., Lizhen, X., Yisheng, D., & Yongli, W. (2006). Web service description and discovery based on semantic model. *Wuhan University Journal of Natural Sciences*, *11*(5), 1306–1310. doi:10.1007/BF02829257

Yang, X., Chen, Y., Zhang, W., & Zhang, S. (2011). Exploring injection prevention technologies for security-aware distributed collaborative manufacturing on the Semantic Web. *International Journal of Advanced Manufacturing Technology*, *54*(9), 1167–1177. doi:10.1007/s00170-010-2983-x

Yıldırım, A. A., & Watson, D. (2016). A cloud-aware distributed object storage system to retrieve large data via HTML5-enabled Web browsers. In Z. Ma (Ed.), *Managing Big Data in cloud computing environments* (pp. 25–45). Hershey, PA: IGI Global. doi:10.4018/978-1-4666-9834-5.ch002

Yuan, D., Yang, Y., Liu, X., Li, W., Cui, L., Xu, M., & Chen, J. (2013). A highly practical approach towards achieving minimum datasets storage cost in the cloud. *IEEE Transactions on Parallel and Distributed Systems*, *24*(6), 1234–1244. doi:10.1109/TPDS.2013.20

Zhang, X., Cheng, G., Ge, W. Y., & Qu, Y. Z. (2009). Summarizing vocabularies in the global Semantic Web. *Journal of Computer Science and Technology*, *24*(1), 165–174. doi:10.1007/s11390-009-9212-9

Zhang, X., Yang, T., Liu, C., & Chen, J. (2013). A scalable two-phase top-down specialization approach for data anonymization using MapReduce on cloud. *IEEE Transactions on Parallel and Distributed Systems*, *25*(2), 363–373. doi:10.1109/TPDS.2013.48

Zhongzhi, S., Mingkai, D., Yuncheng, J., & Haijun, Z. (2005). A logical foundation for the Semantic Web. *Science in China Series F: Information Sciences*, *48*(2), 161–178. doi:10.1360/03yf0506

Zou, G., Xiang, Y., Gan, Y., & Chen, Y. (2011). A novel approach to annotating Web service based on interface concept mapping and semantic expansion. *Soft Computing*, *15*(5), 929–938. doi:10.1007/s00500-010-0548-4

ADDITIONAL READING

Chawla, N. V., & Davis, D. C. (2013). Bringing Big Data to personalized healthcare: A patient-centered framework. *Journal of General Internal Medicine*, *28*(3), 660–665. doi:10.1007/s11606-013-2455-8

Cheng, Y., Chen, Y., Wei, R., & Luo, H. (2015). Development of a construction quality supervision collaboration system based on a SaaS private cloud. *Journal of Intelligent & Robotic Systems*, *79*(3), 613–627. doi:10.1007/s10846-014-0108-8

Chou, S. W., & Chiang, C. H. (2013). Understanding the formation of software-as-a-service (SaaS) satisfaction from the perspective of service quality. *Decision Support Systems*, *56*, 148–155. doi:10.1016/j.dss.2013.05.013

Choudhary, P. K., Mital, M., Sharma, R., & Pani, A. K. (2015). Cloud computing and IT infrastructure outsourcing: A comparative study. *International Journal of Organizational and Collective Intelligence*, *5*(4), 20–34. doi:10.4018/IJOCI.2015100103

Coronado, M., Iglesias, C. A., & Serrano, E. (2015). Modelling rules for automating the Evented WEb by semantic technologies. *Expert Systems with Applications*, *42*(21), 7979–7990. doi:10.1016/j.eswa.2015.06.031

Daniel, B. (2015). Big Data and analytics in higher education: Opportunities and challenges. *British Journal of Educational Technology*, *46*(5), 904–920. doi:10.1111/bjet.12230

Espadas, J., & Monila, A. (2011). A tenant-based resource allocation model for scaling software-as-a-service applications over cloud computing infrastructures. *Future Generation Computer Systems*, *29*(1), 273–286. doi:10.1016/j.future.2011.10.013

Fan, H., Hussain, F. K., Younas, M., & Hussain, O. K. (2015). An integrated personalization framework for SaaS-based cloud services. *Future Generation Computer Systems*, *53*, 157–173. doi:10.1016/j.future.2015.05.011

Fortino, G., Parisi, D., Pirrone, V., & Di Fatta, G. (2014). BodyCloud: A SaaS approach for community body sensor networks. *Future Generation Computer Systems*, *35*, 62–79. doi:10.1016/j.future.2013.12.015

Fuller, M. (2015). Big Data: New science, new challenges, new dialogical opportunities. *Zygon*, *50*(3), 569–582. doi:10.1111/zygo.12187

Gandomi, A., & Haider, M. (2015). Beyond the hype: Big Data concepts, methods, and analytics. *International Journal of Information Management*, *35*(2), 137–144. doi:10.1016/j.ijinfomgt.2014.10.007

Gutierrez-Milla, A., Borges, F., Suppi, R., & Luque, E. (2015). Crowd evacuations SaaS: An ABM approach. *Procedia Computer Science*, *51*, 473–482. doi:10.1016/j.procs.2015.05.271

Huang, K. C., & Shen, B. J. (2015). Service deployment strategies for efficient execution of composite SaaS applications on cloud platform. *Journal of Systems and Software*, *107*, 127–141. doi:10.1016/j.jss.2015.05.050

Kim, W., Lee, J. H., Hong, C., Han, C., Lee, H., & Jang, B. (2012). An innovative method for data and software integration in SaaS. *Computers & Mathematics with Applications (Oxford, England)*, *64*(5), 1252–1258. doi:10.1016/j.camwa.2012.03.069

Koumenides, C. L., & Shadbolt, N. R. (2014). Ranking methods for entity-oriented Semantic Web search. *Journal of the Association for Information Science and Technology*, *65*(6), 1091–1106. doi:10.1002/asi.23018

Lee, S. G., Chae, S. H., & Cho, K. M. (2013). Drivers and inhibitors of SaaS adoption in Korea. *International Journal of Information Management*, *33*(3), 429–440. doi:10.1016/j.ijinfomgt.2013.01.006

Lin, Y. D., Thai, M. T., Wang, C. C., & Lai, Y. C. (2015). Two-tier project and job scheduling for SaaS cloud service providers. *Journal of Network and Computer Applications*, *52*, 26–36. doi:10.1016/j.jnca.2015.02.008

Paydar, S., & Kahani, M. (2015). A Semantic Web enabled approach to reuse functional requirements models in Web engineering. *Automated Software Engineering*, *22*(2), 241–288. doi:10.1007/s10515-014-0144-4

Rahmani, A., Amine, A., & Hamou, R. M. (2015). De-identification of health data in Big Data using a novel bio-inspired apoptosis algorithm. *International Journal of Organizational and Collective Intelligence*, *5*(3), 1–15. doi:10.4018/IJOCI.2015070101

Rohitratana, J., & Altmann, J. (2012). Impact of pricing schemes on a market for software-as-a-service and perpetual software. *Future Generation Computer Systems*, *28*(8), 1328–1339. doi:10.1016/j.future.2012.03.019

Rosaci, D. (2015). Finding semantic associations in hierarchically structured groups of Web data. *Formal Aspects of Computing*, *27*(5), 867–884. doi:10.1007/s00165-015-0337-z

Song, J., Guo, C., Wang, Z., Zhang, Y., Yu, G., & Pierson, J. M. (2015). HaoLap: A Hadoop based OLAP system for Big Data. *Journal of Systems and Software*, *102*, 167–181. doi:10.1016/j.jss.2014.09.024

Svajlenko, J., Keivanloo, I., & Roy, C. K. (2015). Big Data clone detection using classical detectors: An exploratory study. *Journal of Software: Evolution and Process*, *27*(6), 430–464. doi:10.1002/smr.1662

Wu, W. W., Lan, L. W., & Lee, Y. T. (2011). Exploring decisive factors affecting an organization's SaaS adoption: A case study. *International Journal of Information Management*, *31*(6), 556–563. doi:10.1016/j.ijinfomgt.2011.02.007

Xu, B., Luo, S., Yan, Y., & Sun, K. (2012). Towards efficiency of QoS-driven Semantic Web service composition for large-scale service-oriented systems. *Service Oriented Computing and Applications*, *6*(1), 1–13. doi:10.1007/s11761-011-0085-8

Yang, Z., Sun, J., Zhang, Y., & Wang, Y. (2015). Understanding SaaS adoption from the perspective of organizational users: A tripod readiness model. *Computers in Human Behavior*, *45*, 254–264. doi:10.1016/j.chb.2014.12.022

Yao, Y. (2015). Cloud computing: A practical overview between year 2009 and year 2015. *International Journal of Organizational and Collective Intelligence*, *5*(3), 32–43. doi:10.4018/ijoci.2015070103

KEY TERMS AND DEFINITIONS

Analytics: The field of data analysis that involves studying the historical data to explore the potential trends, to analyze the effects of certain decisions, and to evaluate the performance of the given tool.

Big Data: The large sets of data that are produced by people using the Internet, and that can only be stored, understood, and used with the assistance of special tools and methods.

Cloud Computing: The process where a task is solved by using a wide variety of technologies, including computers, networks, servers, and the Internet.

Enterprise Resource Planning: The computerized management system that connects the multiple business operations.

Information Technology: The set of tools, processes, and associated equipment employed to collect, manage, and present the information.

Internet: The method of connecting a computer to other computers through the dedicated routers and servers.

Semantic Web: The extension of the World Wide Web that catalogs information on a web page and reprocesses it so that other machines including computers can understand the information.

Software as a Service: A software distribution model in which applications are hosted by the service providers and are made available to customers over the Internet.

Chapter 12
Software Development Methodology for Cloud Computing and Its Impact

Chhabi Rani Panigrahi
C. V. Raman College of Engineering, India

Rajib Mall
Indian Institute of Technology Kharagpur, India

Bibudhendu Pati
C. V. Raman College of Engineering, India

ABSTRACT

This chapter emphasizes mainly on the software development methodology basically agile methods of software development in cloud computing platforms and its impact on software development processes. This chapter also covers the benefits of agile development methodology in cloud computing platform. Along with this all traditional software development phases are analyzed to discuss the differences between the traditional software development processes and software development in cloud computing environment. This chapter also includes a brief description of programming models such as MapReduce, BSPCloud, and Dryad etc. available in the literature to handle big data in SaaS cloud. Finally, we highlight the challenges and future scope of software development process in cloud computing environment.

INTRODUCTION

Software development process models are continuously evolving. They are affected by the type of the developed products, the nature of the project, and several other environmental factors. It is known that a particular software process development model cannot work well for all types of projects. The different constraints such as time, budget, and resources play also a significant role in deciding the best way to proceed in developing particular software. In this chapter, the main focus is given on how software projects can be developed in cloud computing platform and the impacts of cloud computing on software development.

DOI: 10.4018/978-1-5225-1721-4.ch012

In terms of software product models, the widely known object oriented model is currently competed by possible alternatives. For cloud computing, service oriented model and service oriented architecture (SOA) seems as a possible successor of the object oriented paradigm. In SOA, design abstractions are built around the concept of services. Systems are decomposed based on the number and type of services they are offered to clients or users. Services are expected to be designed, implemented and deployed in very agile manners that can allow different types of users to call and use such services with the least amount of possible efforts. Some of the popular object orientated (OO) concepts such as abstraction and encapsulation can still be used and applied to good SOA design and such concepts are seen now as good software design principles rather than OO design principles. In abstraction, it is always important to decompose the system to the right level and number of services in the right granularity. Each service should have the right and relevant attributes, methods, associations, etc. that can help minimize its coupling with other services. Similarly, to apply encapsulation, services should be offered in ways that can relief the clients or users from any type of commitment or dependency in the implementation details of the service. This makes it easy to change the implementation details of such services with the least possible impact on clients. On the service side itself, encapsulation plays also an important role in separating the service representation or interface from its detail implementation. This can make it easy to update and change such service without impacting its interface or service clients. In SOA, focus is on Web services rather than Web applications. SOA helps in isolating service provider from user and provides generic services that are not intended for specific users and that are themselves unaware of the nature of use in the client side.

The rest of the chapter is organized as follows. First, the traditional software development process is revisited. Next, the cloud computing platform along with the benefits of software development with cloud platform is identified. Then the software process model for cloud platform is discussed. Subsequently, impacts of cloud computing platform on software development processes are identified and then different programming models for cloud computing platform are presented. Finally, future scope and challenges of software development with cloud platform are highlighted.

BACKGROUND

In this section, traditional method of software development is summarized. Subsequently, the cloud computing platform has been described and the benefits of software development on cloud computing platform are also highlighted.

Traditional Software Development Life Cycle

Software Development Life Cycle (SDLC) is a process followed in software industry to produce high quality software (Roger et al., 2014). The SDLC is aimed at meeting customer expectations, complete the project within times and cost budgets. Traditional software development requires different hardware technologies and the development process involves different stakeholders. The quality and success of a software project depends on various factors such as time, budget, efficiency, maintainability, dependability, and usability of the product (Farooq & Quadri, 2012). Since 1968, software engineering evolves as a systematic, disciplined, and quantifiable engineering approach to develop software which makes the software development easy and manageable (Mall, 2014).

Traditional SDLCs follow a framework of activities such as identifying requirements, planning, design, coding, testing, deployment, and maintenance. Requirements gathering is one of the important activity among them as the error in requirement identification will propagate to all subsequent activities during software development. There are many traditional SDLC models used to develop software and the most popular traditional SDLC models that are followed in industry include *Waterfall Model*, *Iterative Waterfall Model*, *Spiral Model*, *V-Model*, and *Evolutionary Model*. Again the type of process model used to develop a particular system depends on several factors such as type of project, size of the project, time requirement to deliver the software, and budget etc.

Success of a software product is more difficult as compared to the products from other engineering domains such as electronics, mechanical, and civil engineering etc. This may be due to the fact that software is intangible during its development period. For this, different SDLC framework activities such as project planning and control, risk management, quality assurance, configuration management etc. are carried out by software project managers to monitor the progress of the project. Even after considering all measures, many software projects failed and it was found that 50% of the software projects failed due to factors such as slippage of schedule and budget, inflexibility in software maintenance, unfriendly interface, and changes made in the software. This was mainly due to lack of communication and co-ordination among different stakeholders involved in the software project.

Now-a-days, one of the major problems in any software project is the frequent change in customer's requirements. The changes in requirements lead to increase the complexity of the project as well as results in budget and schedule slippage. But, when the changes are incorporated at a later phase of SDLC model, the cost of the projects increase exponentially. Figure 1 shows the cost of change at a later phase in the development life cycle. Hence, it is important for any software project that the early phases in SDLC such as requirements gathering, planning, and design phase must be performed involving all stakeholders of the project from very beginning. For this, during mid-1990 a couple of agile process models such as Extreme Programming (XP), Crystal, Scrum etc. have been developed. These models were developed to handle the projects which involve continuous changes in requirements during development. The agile process model is described in more details in subsequent section.

Figure 1. Cost of change in different phases of SDLC

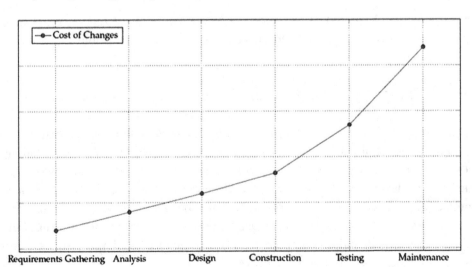

Cloud Computing Platform

Cloud computing is an evolving area of research now-a-days and is emerged not just as a piece of technology but as an easier means for development of software product. The idea behind cloud computing is that computing environments as well as resources can be used in an optimal manner. With this new emerging technology, several changes are expected to happen in the Information Technology (IT) fields as well as systems that adopt this technology. Day by day, industries are adopting cloud computing platform and according to Gartner research, "worldwide cloud services revenue is on pace to surpass $56.3 billion in 2009, 21.3% increase from 2008 revenue of $46.4 billion. The market is expected to reach $150.1 billion in 2013" (Gartner. (n.d.)).

Cloud Computing Service Models

The cloud computing service models are basically categorized into three types: *Infrastructure as a Service (IaaS), Platform as a Service (PaaS),* and *Software as a Service (SaaS)* (Dillon et al., 2010). SaaS among them has got great recognition in the software industry and it influence how software is developed and delivered. It is also considered as the representative of the next generation software development process. It provides multi-tenant and on-demand access to software and applications. SaaS refers to all kinds of applications and services that are created by vendors in the cloud systems. It provides service to the customers on the basis of Service Level Agreement (SLA) with cloud providers and functions as a Web-based service. The cloud users can access the SaaS services using various devices and for that they need not have to install the applications in their devices (Dillon et al., 2010; Bibi et al., 2010). To access the services provided by SaaS, the users have to subscribe to these services and then can execute them as on-demand, scalable, and pay-per-use charges (Bibi et al., 2010; Laplante et al., 2008). In SaaS, the vendors who host services in the cloud platform known as service providers are the owners of these services.

PaaS model provides different platforms for software development which are hosted in the cloud and are accessed via any network (Bibi et al., 2010). This model provides on-demand elastic and scalable run-time environment for the users. The service provider is responsible for providing scalability and to manage fault tolerance. One of the major differences between SaaS and PaaS is that services provided by the cloud are hosted by SaaS and are complete and un-modifiable whereas, PaaS offers both complete and in-progress applications that can be used to develop new software (Dillon et al., 2010). The third category of cloud service model that is IaaS provides physical computing resources such as storage, processing capabilities, and networks (Dillon et al., 2010) etc. The vendors or the cloud providers use virtualization technique to provide the shared computing resources to many customers. Based on resource demand of the customers, the resources can be either scaled-up or scaled-down in IaaS model. IaaS is similar to PaaS and SaaS for cloud users. PaaS provides means to build new software than can be considered as SaaS and IaaS provide means to end user to access to these new SaaS services (Bibi et al., 2010).

Cloud Computing Deployment Models

The four deployment models proposed to deploy and access cloud platform include: *private, public, community,* and *hybrid* clouds (Mell & Grance, 2011). Among them, public cloud is the most popular one in which the necessary infrastructure required for any user is established by a third-party service

Figure 2. Cloud deployment models
Source: Cloud or Not: 4 Cloud Deployment Models. (n.d.)

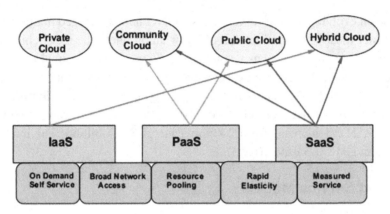

provider and can be accessed on a subscription basis. Figure 1 shows the cloud deployment models along with the three cloud service models defined for cloud computing. The three cloud service models: IaaS, PaaS, and SaaS were developed based on five essential features such as *on-demand self service*, *resource pooling*, *rapid elasticity, broad network access*, and *measured service* of cloud computing and is shown in Figure 1. The different service models of cloud platform can be used either individually or can be combined with other service models to form different deployment models such as *private*, *public*, *community*, or *hybrid cloud*.

- **Private Cloud** : Private clouds are also called as enterprise clouds. The cloud infrastructure in this type of deployment model is created solely for a single organization. The ownership, operation, and management of the cloud are the responsibility of that organization (Mell & Grance, 2011). The private cloud aims at providing a flexible and private infrastructure to users within their administrative domains (Sotomayor, 2009). Sometimes the terms Virtual Private Cloud (VPC) and private cloud are used interchangeably. But, these two terms are not exactly same. A VPC is a kind of private cloud and uses a third party cloud provider's infrastructure while a private cloud uses internal infrastructure. This type of clouds is more secured as compared to other cloud deployment models.

- **Public Cloud** : This is intended for the public use of cloud resources and is operated by commercial vendors or service providers. It provides a remote interface for creating as well as managing cloud instances which is publicly accessible (Sotomayor, 2009). This is a type of service model for provisioning storage as well as computational services to the general public. This model uses *pay-per-use* pricing model to access computational and storage resources from cloud. The public cloud software, infrastructure, and other back-end architecture in a multi-tenant environment are managed by the service providers and the customers are free from the responsibility of managing the cloud resources. The customers can access freely the services available in the cloud, but they may suffer from small resources due to their openness. For example, when a person creates a Gmail account he or she can store up to 15 GB of data only.

- **Community Cloud:** The community cloud is meant for providing services to a limited number of organizations. The organizations that use community cloud are governed, managed, and secured commonly by either all the participating organizations or by a service provider. This type of cloud is meant for those organizations who work on joint projects, and applications having common requirements such as similar usage, security, and policy compliance (Mell & Grance, 2011) for building, executing, and managing such projects etc. The community cloud is a hybrid form of private clouds which is meant for specific targeted groups and the aim of these groups is to achieve their business objectives. The participating organizations in this type of cloud take the advantages such as *multi-tenancy* and *pay-per-use* billing from public cloud but with increasing level of security, privacy, and policy compliance.

- **Hybrid Cloud** : This type of cloud combines infrastructures from two or more above-mentioned deployment models. When private cloud resources are unable to meet users' QoS requirements, hybrid cloud is used to meet the organization's needs. It is considered as a separate cloud in which different clouds are connected via interfaces which helps in sharing data, applications as well as computational resources among different clouds (Mell & Grance, 2011; Sotomayor, 2009).

Benefits of Software Development on Cloud Computing Platform

In this section, the benefits associated with software development on cloud computing platform are identified and are listed as follows:

- Cloud computing provides highly customizable environment.
- Provides flexibility to its users to have access to their resources at any time through a standard internet connection.
- There is no requirement of specific hardware or software to use cloud services and hence it reduces the computer cost.
- Provides unlimited storage capacity that is offers virtually limitless storage
- Supports mobility that means a user can have the ability to access data and applications at anytime and anywhere.
- Provides increased data reliability.
- Provides easier group collaboration.
- It can be easily combined with other enterprise solutions.
- Results in quicker deployment of software with less probability of failures.
- It helps in utilization of internal resources in an optimal way.
- Provides scalability that means users can have access to any amount and any type of resources as and when required.
- The *pay-per-use* pricing model of cloud allows an organization to only pay for the used resources and there is no infra-structure maintenance or up-gradation costs. So, it involves low infrastructure cost.

MAIN FOCUS OF THE CHAPTER

Software Process Model for Cloud Platform

In this section, first the agile process model for traditional software development is presented. Then the agile development with cloud computing is presented. Subsequently, the benefits of agile method of software development in cloud computing platform are highlighted. Finally, the impacts of cloud platform on software development are presented.

Agile Process Model

During mid-1990s, agile development methodology was developed to incorporate frequent changes in requirements during SDLC. Agile process model emphasizes on shorter development cycles and faster customer feedback. The developers do not have to estimate the time required for the next version to be delivered in advance. The agile methods are considered as *lightweight software development* methods which have evolved as a criticism against traditional process models for software development called *heavyweight methods*. The heavy weight methods are *regulated, regimented,* and *micromanaged* and provide very little flexibility and visibility to the users. On the other hand, agile methods support *adaptive planning, evolutionary development*, early delivery, and encourage *flexible response to change* (Agile Alliance, 2013).

Agile software development has common features based on the 12 basic principles of the Agile software development manifesto (Agile Manifesto. (n.d.)) that is published by 17 software developers at Utah in February 2001. The most popular agile methods are Extreme Programming (XP), Agile Modeling, Agile Unified Process (AUP), Crystal methodologies family, Dynamic Systems Development Methods (DSDM), Essential Unified Process (EssUP),, Feature-Driven Development (FDD), Lean Software development, Open Unified Process (OpenUP), Kanban Development, Scrum, Adaptive Software Development etc. and among them some of which were existed in practice before the publication of Agile manifesto (Agile Manifesto. (n.d.)).

The agile models have originated from the existing conventional process models for software development such as Prototyping, Iterative, Incremental, Evolutionary, and RAD. Among the various agile models, DSDM, Scrum, and XP are the most popular methods and are generally followed in software industry. Most of the agile methods promote features such as *teamwork, collaboration,* and *process adaptability* throughout the development life cycle of the project (Agile Alliance, 2013). The software development process is generally controlled by adopting a *time-boxed* iterative approach. In agile methods, tasks are divided into small *increments* which involve minimal planning. Each iteration involves a short time frame called a *time box* and a *time box* typically exists for a period of one to four weeks. During each iteration, a *cross functional team* works. At the end of each iteration, a working product is developed and is demonstrated to the stakeholders. This allows the projects to adapt to changes rapidly and reduces the overall risk of the project.

The customer satisfaction is one of the important considerations in agile methods. So, the agile methods are considered as communication intensive. Agile software development works better when the software development team contains motivated, talented, self-organized, and experienced software developer. Unlike the conventional heavy weight methods that emphasize on formal documentation, agile methods prefer to use *face-to-face communication* among the members in a team. In agile methods, teams mostly work in a single office to improve communication among them. To promote communication and collaboration, the typical team size is kept as 5 to 9 people. Each agile team has one customer representative who is selected by the stakeholders of the software project. His role is to answer requirements and development related questions on behalf of the customer during the planning and execution of the iterations. The development team keeps a progress review meeting with the stakeholders and the customer representative at the end of each iteration to prioritize the requirements for the next iteration. The objective is to ensure that the project outcome is aligned with the needs of the customer and the goals of the company, while optimizing the *return on investment*. Agile development has been widely used for certain types of projects such as projects having less complexity, experienced developers, often change in requirements, less number of developers, and flexibility to respond to changes.

AGILE DEVELOPMENT WITH CLOUD COMPUTING

Cloud computing provides benefits such as collecting immediate feedback, providing valuable functionality to the customers quickly, and able to make rapid changes based on the customers' feedback etc. for agile development. In 2010, CapGemini conducted a survey in association with HP in order to analyze the industry trends regarding adoption of agile methods with cloud computing (Lean Agile Methodologies Accentuate Benefits of Cloud Computing (n. d.).). Their survey included around 30,000 cloud experts, engineers, IT managers, and quality assurance managers who were working in leading companies across Asia, Europe, and North America (Lean Agile Methodologies Accentuate Benefits of Cloud Computing (n. d.)). Their survey report also indicated that about 60% of the organizations that participated in the survey were expected to adopt lean agile methods for their forthcoming cloud projects.

Agile development methodologies and cloud computing are complement to each other in the sense that cloud computing provides services that meet user requirements vary fast by delivering services according to their need. But, agile development methodologies need user collaboration in requirements identification. The aim of agile methods is to break down the requirements of a project into small and manageable pieces which guarantees to meet user feedback. Each small piece can be planned, developed, and tested individually to achieve high quality of the product. However, lean agile methods emphasize on developing a collaborative relationship between software developers and end users (Amber, 2002; Lean Agile Methodologies). End users involvement throughout the development process is one of the important features of agile methods and feedbacks from end users are accepted during all phases of development.

Agile development methodology provides a lot of functionality to the customers such as collecting quick feedback, making instant changes based on the collected feedback, faster cycles for development etc. But, it is lack of a key component that is a development platform which is required in agile development to provide faster development cycles. In traditional software development environment, a new software distribution requires patches, reinstallation, as well as support from the development team. Therefore, traditional software development involves months or even years to provide a new distribution of software. Again, incorporating the user feedback into next release version involves huge amount of time. In this scenario, cloud computing plays a vital role and makes a notable difference between traditional and cloud computing software development environment. Cloud computing helps in eliminating the unwieldy distribution requirements of software unlike conventional software development environment. In cloud computing platform, new distributions of software are installed on hosted servers and can be available

Figure 3. Agile development process at salesforce.com
Source: The Landmark, White Paper (n.d.)

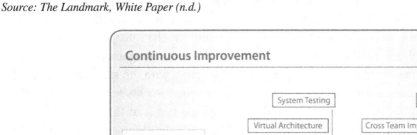

to users. Hence, it is possible in cloud environment that the application or service that is run today was modified just the night before or even an hour ago.

One of the best examples that motivated people to adopt agile development with cloud computing is the experience of R & T team at salesforce.com. In late 2006, the R&D team at salesforce.com shifted to agile development (The Landmark, White Paper (n.d.)). The R&D team at salesforce.com said that cloud computing is the ideal environment for agile development (The Landmark, White Paper (n.d.)). The agile development process at salesforce.com is shown in Figure 3. According to the view given by the R & D team, just after two weeks of training, the development staffs which consist of 30 teams were able to adopt agile methodology at salesforce.com. The R&D team at salesforce.com also shared its experience with its customers about agile development on the Force.com platform and it was found that many had reported similar successes (The Landmark, White Paper (n.d.)). Figure 4 shows the transformation results of pre and post agile development methodology at salesforce.com. From Figure 4, it is clear that the days between major releases decreases largely after adoption of cloud computing platform with agile development at salesforce.com.

Guha, R. proposed an extended version of XP model for software development in cloud computing platform and named it as *Extreme Cloud Programming* (Guha, R., 2009). The *Extreme Cloud Programming* model is shown in Figure 5. In this model, all phases of a SDLC model need communication between the cloud providers and the software engineers unlike the XP model. The author in (Guha, R., 2009) distinguished the role of software developer and cloud service provider during different phases of SDLC for the proposed model. Guha, R. reported that resource accounting activity need to be done during requirement gathering phase of SDLC by the cloud service provider. The other activities of the project such as defining software architecture, mapping of software architecture to hardware architecture, user interface design, cost and schedule estimation of the project etc. should also be carried out in

Figure 4. Pre and post agile development at salesforce.com
Source: The Landmark, White Paper (n.d.)

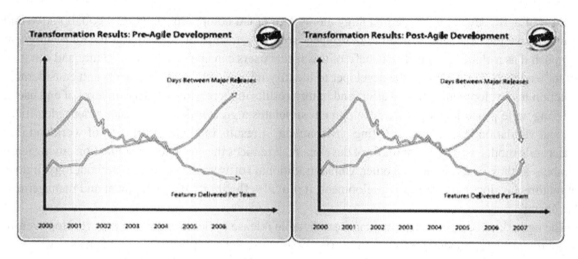

collaboration with cloud service providers. During the construction phase of software development, if web services are integrated with the development then error should be corrected by the developers along with the cloud service providers as web services involve many enterprises. The customers should do the maintenance contract for a project with the cloud provider according to the SLA signed by the customers.

The author's experimental results indicate that *Extreme Cloud Programming* model increases the interaction between software engineers and cloud provider. The improved communication in this model is an inherent benefit and helps in resolving the issues associated with the software development process on cloud computing platform.

Figure 5. Extreme cloud programming model
Source: Guha, R., 2009

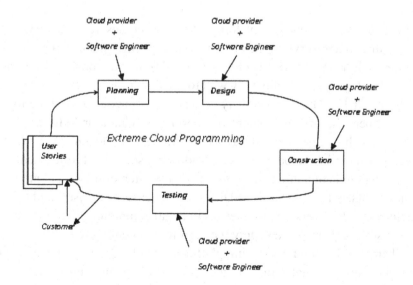

Benefits of Agile Development with Cloud Computing

The use of agile development methodology along with cloud computing supports a collaborative and an interactive environment. When the developers resolve a feature of software, at the same moment they push it as a cloud service. The benefit of this is that users can analyze the new feature and can give instant feedback. Thus, it helps the developer to identify misunderstood requirements and considerable reduction in development time and effort and in turn results in increasing satisfaction level of end users.

Using agile process in software development simulates a greater degree of requirement identification and validation in a cloud computing environment. It results in higher utilization of workload that means agile model uses a fixed number of developers. It reduces the cost of communication among team members as they sit closer to each other. Unlike traditional software development methodology, it does not require any documents during development. It provides flexibility if development and management plan change.

The agile development results in a more predictable release cycle through *time-boxing*. However, in conventional SDLC models, software industries have to predict what functionality of the software can be delivered after 6 months or 1 year. It may happen that they may not keep their promises they make with the customer because of large unknown cycles in the development process.

The transparency is made possible in agile methods by using certain tools and techniques such as continuous integration, automation of unit testing, daily meetings, and information *radiators* etc. This helps in building trust with the customers. This practice of agile method in cloud platform contrasts with the traditional method of software development where the problems are hidden from the customers.

Agile development in cloud computing platform help in recapturing the spirit of creativity and excitement of tem members as it decentralizes the process by impelling decision-making and other responsibilities of the project to the development teams. Continuous improvement characteristics of agile development provides better experience to all team members of the project starting from developers, quality assurance engineers to documentation writers.

IMPACT OF CLOUD COMPUTING PLATFORM ON SOFTWARE DEVELOPMENT

In cloud computing platform, software development now becomes very challenging. Software development involves distributed services, heterogeneous platforms, and enterprises are now globally dispersed. Therefore, Global Software Development (GSD) now is considered as the most popular model for software development that suits very well to medium or large size organizations (Chauhan, M. A. & Babar, M. A., 2012). GSD's popularity among IT businesses is growing rapidly because of potential economical benefits as development outsourcing to China or India might make software development process much cheaper and faster (Hashmi, S., (2011); Mockus, A. & Herbsleb, J., 2001).

Software development process models exist for traditional software development are not adequate to develop software in cloud computing environment unless interaction with cloud service providers is included. Requirements gathering phase of SDLC includes customers, users and software engineers. Now, it has to include the cloud service providers as in cloud computing environment, it is the responsibility of the cloud service provider to supply the required computing resources to the customers as well as maintain them too. In cloud computing platform, the cloud service providers only know the size, details of architectures, virtualization strategy used, and resource utilization percentage of the cloud resources. So, the planning and design phases of SDLC also have to include the cloud service providers as mediator along with the software engineers. Again, only the cloud service providers can decide the size of the development team for a particular project, reusability of components, cost and schedule estimation, risk and configuration management etc. Because of the components reuse during software development in cloud platform, the size of the newly developed software in terms of Kilo-Lines Of Code (KLOC) or number of Function Points (FP) will be reduced but complexity of the project will increase to many folds due to lack of implementation details documents of the software to be developed and also their integration requirements.

In cloud computing platform, the coding and testing phase of SDLC can be carried out independently and this adds huge benefit to the project as everybody will have easy access to the software. This reduces the cost as well as time required during testing and validation phase. For this, developers need to use the open-source software and the web services that are freely available in the cloud. Software developers need to have more expertise in developing software from off-the-shelf components rather than writing it from scratch. Refactoring of existing application is one of the best methods for effective utilization of cloud resources. Maintenance phase of SDLC in cloud platform should include the cloud service providers. Now, due to involvement of the cloud service providers in all phases of SDLC, the customers need to sign a contract with them so that the *"Software Engineering code of ethics"* will not be violated by the cloud service providers. So, one can conclude that there is a complete shift of responsibility in all phases of SDLC from software developers to cloud service providers in cloud computing platform. Cloud service providers insist that software should be developed in modular fashion as to maintain load balancing in cloud, the tasks need to be migrated from one server to another (Singh, A., 2008).

In addition to above discussed considerations, protection and security of the data is one of the important issues that need to be considered while developing software in cloud platform. Also there may be occasional demand of higher usage of computing resources by certain applications that may prevent the benefits of *pay-by-use* model of cloud computing. This is because multiple applications may need higher resource usage all at the same time. Especially in SaaS model, the customers may have occasional high resource requirements which cannot be predicted in advance. Cloud service providers use virtualization technique to provide resources in an efficient way to many customers on demand. For higher resource utilization in cloud, the cloud service providers need to do migration of applications from one server to another or from one storage to another. As the customers in cloud want resources with high availability and reliability for their applications, so there may be a conflict of interest among the customers. To avoid this conflict, cloud service providers need to define QoS provisions for higher priority tenants in SLA.

The level of interaction between software engineers and cloud providers depends on type of cloud deployment models used by them. In private cloud, the customer has more control over the cloud resources as compared to public and other types of clouds. In order to assure the availability and reliability of the high priority applications, customers should prefer to use private cloud rather than other types of clouds. The private cloud provides the benefits like less interaction with cloud service provider, self-managed, increased security, high availability and reliability of data. These features of private cloud results in reducing the complexity of software development but the infrastructure costs increase hugely and are shown as in Figure 6. The public cloud provides cheaper computing which is more significant than the private cloud which involves less complexity of software development and hence the public cloud becomes more useful and attractive.

Figure 6. Economics vs. software complexity on different types of cloud
Source: Guha, R., 2009

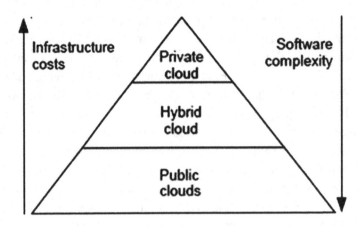

PROGRAMMING MODELS IN CLOUD

In this section, some of the cloud computing programming models such as MapReduce, BSPCloud, All-pairs, SAGA, Dryad, and Transformer proposed in the literature for cloud platforms along with their advantages and disadvantages are presented. Finally, the current issues and future trends have also been discussed. Nowadays, in many applications the amount of data has been increased from tera byte to petabyte level, and even higher. Massive data is generated from various fields such as social media, medical, agriculture etc. However, the cost of computer hardware is declined day by day. Cloud computing takes the advantage of this (Foster, I. et al., 2008) as it promises to support on-demand and flexible IT services, which go beyond conventional programming models. To handle such big data, different programming models in cloud platform such as Map Reduce, BSP, and SAGA etc. have been developed. But, the choice of the programming model depends on the choice of the problem and the QoS expected from the cloud. Due to the development of SaaS model, software is now rented and not purchased. Softwares for consumers are hosted on the cloud and are maintained by different cloud service providers. For example, Social Network Service (SNS) usage has become more widely used and such trend results in increase in the size of data that need to be processed by enterprises. This necessitates the consideration of data in the prospective of big data. According to Cisco, *"Cloud applications will account for 90% of total mobile data traffic by 2018, compared to 82% by the end of 2013. Mobile cloud traffic is expected to grow twelve fold from 2013 to 2018, attaining a compound annual growth rate of 64%"* (Cisco (n.d.), 2014). To handle such big data, different programming models for cloud computing platform have been developed. A cloud computing programming model helps users to use cloud computing resources without concern about the implementation details.

Advantages of cloud computing programming models include:

- Allows parallel processing
- Provides fault tolerant functionality
- Supports heterogeneity.
- Takes care of load balancing.

MapReduce

This programming model is one of the most widely accepeted programming models in cloud computing platform. It was introduced by Google. It is used to process massive data. It is basically built on two operations that are *map* and *reduce* (Patel, A. B. et al., 2012; Dean, J. & Ghemawat, S., 2004; Dean, J. & Ghemawat, S. 2008) and is shown in Figure 8. Map-reduce work basically on two stages. The role of map-reduce technique is to schedule the task among various nodes. The map function is used for processing the input file and generates small chunks of data. The master and slave nodes are used for processing the inputs. The master nodes divide the input stream into smaller sub-modules and then again divided by the slave nodes. After computation, the slave nodes send the final results to the master node. Reduce function collects the results from various sub-modules and produces the final output by combining the different results.

The computation of tasks using MapReduce is shown in Figure 7. The task is executed in four phases: *Map, Sort, Merge,* and *Reduce.* In MapReduce model, a user defined Map function is used that takes a key-value pair as input and results in a collection of key-value pairs as output. The Sort and Merge phases group the data to produce an array where, each element is a group of values for each key. The Reduce phase takes the output of Sort and Merge phase. The various hash functions are used in map and reduce functions and are user defined and varies with the application of the model.

The main shortcoming of this approach is that certain applications are hardly expressed by MapReduce. It is difficult to maintain and reuse code in MapReduce. This model is time consuming and more prone to errors. The basic requirements in MapReduce are communication, coordination, and synchronization between the nodes.

BSPCloud

Initially, Block Synchronous Parallel (BSP) model was developed to bridge parallel computation software and architecture. This programming model was developed by Valiant, L.G. (Valiant, L. G., 1990). The advantages of BSP Model include:

Figure 7. Computation of MapReduce

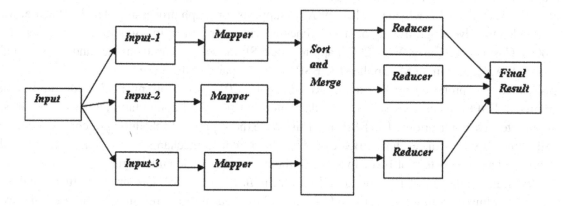

Figure 8. BSPCloud programming model architecture
Source: Xiaodong, L., 2013

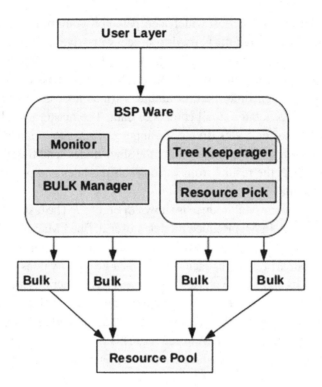

- Performance of the model can be predicted.
- There is no possibility of deadlock during message passing.
- Easy to write program in BSP model.

Due to the advantages of BSP model as mentioned above, some improved models based on BSP were developed in different programming environments. Williams *et al.* (Williams et al., 2000) proposed a Heterogeneous Bulk Synchronous Parallel (HBSP) model which can be used to write program for heterogeneous environment. Google's Pregel is a distributed programming model based on BSP model (Malewicz, A. et al., 2010) which is able to provide supports for graph processing. The BSP model was also extended to solve programming on heterogeneous grid environment in (Bonorden, 2007; Righir et al., 2009). Costa et al. (Costa, V.G., 2005) applied the BSP model on search engines and Hassan et al. (Hassan, M. A. H. & Bamha M.) applied the BSP model on parallel database.

BSPCloud was proposed by Xiaodong (Xiaodong, L., 2013) by adopting BSP model into cloud environment. BSPCloud can be used both for data intensive as well as computation intensive and input or output intensive applications. The BSPCloud also have the support of scheduling of computing tasks as well as the allocation of resources. BSPCloud uses hierarchical mechanism for communication with other nodes. The architecture of BSPCloud programming model is shown in Figure 8.

The central component of BSPCloud architecture is *BSPWare*. BSPWare provides functionalities such as scheduling of computing tasks and efficient allocation of cloud resources. The users interact with BSPWare through user layer. The BSPWare consists of mainly 4 components as shown in Figure

8. *Monitor* helps in monitoring all resources in the cloud. *TreeKeeper* component is used to construct as well as maintain the tree of resources. *ResourcePick* component is responsible for choosing the required resources from virtual resource tree and can perform computation. *BulkManager* acts as a controller of the application and splits an application program into many bulks and these bulks can run in parallel using resources from resource pool and is also responsible for fault tolerant.

But, Google's MapReduce programming model (Dean, J. & Ghemawat, S. (2008)) hides the details of parallelization, fault tolerance, and load balance. In MapReduce, users specify the computation only in terms of map and reduce function, and then the runtime system automatically parallelizes the computation across large-scale clusters of machines.

All-Pairs

All-pairs problem is defined as: when all elements of a set X are compared with all elements of another set Y via a function F, which results in a matrix M, such that $M[i, j] = F(X[i], Y[j])$ (Moretti, C. et al., 2008). All-pairs programming model is used to solve problems with all-pairs in various domains such as data mining, biometrics, etc. (Moretti, C. et al., 2008).

Dryad

Dryad is a parallel computing platform released by Microsoft for computation of coarse-grained data (Isard, M. et al., 2007). A job in Dryad is a Directed Acyclic Graph (DAG) where, a vertex represents a program and an edge is used to represent data channels. The vertices provided by the application developer are simple and are written as sequential programs. The data channel abstraction has several implementations that use shared memory, TCP pipes etc. Dryad automatically maps the DAG to physical resources. Vertices in a DAG are executed in parallel. Dryad is more flexible as compared to MapReduce. It allows multiple inputs and multiple outputs and the programming is easier. But, it is not a suitable model for iterative and nested program.

SAGA

MapReduce was emerged as a popular programming model for data-intensive applications. But, most of the implementations of MapReduce are meant for a specific infrastructure. To overcome the disadvantages of MapReduce programming model, another parallel programming model named as SAGA was developed. SAGA provides a high level Application Programming interface (API) known as SAGA API. This API can be used to create distributed applications and is infrastructure independent. SAGA provides support to implement different programming models such as MapReduce and All-pairs. It also focuses on the issues associated with interoperability on grid and cloud infrastructures (Miceli, Chris et al., 2009).

The architecture of SAGA is shown as in Figure 9. The main components of SAGA include *SAGA engine, Programmer's interface*, and *Functional adapters*. SAGA API is written using C++ and this has support for other programming languages such as Python, C, and JAVA (Chris, M. et al., 2009). SAGA has a unique feature that is creation of the required adapter that distinguishes SAGA from other programming models. The different adapters provide different functionalities. This feature of SAGA allows extending applications to different systems without much overhead. SAGA en-

Figure 9. SAGA architecture

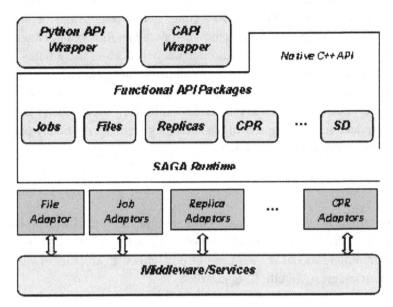

gine supports run-time decision making that helps in loading relevant adaptors at run-time as shown in Figure 9. SAGA also provides various functionalities such as job submission across distributed platforms check point recovery and service discovery.

The SAGA API supports implementation of MapReduce and All-Pairs programming models (Chris, M. et al., 2009). SAGA MapReduce does not have support for multi threading. But, creating adapters in SAGA involves less overhead and makes it easy to deploy SAGA implementation on different clouds. The implementation of All-Pairs model using SAGA is described in (Chris, M. et al., 2009). The major disadvantage of this model includes the complexity of the implementation for each new system added to SAGA.

Transformer

Several programming models such as MapReduce, Dryad, SAGA etc. exist for cloud platforms. But, all suffer from certain disadvantages. For example, the programmers have to master about the details of the whole APIs present for a particular model in order to use that model. Among these models, most are designed for specific programming abstractions such as C++ and JAVA and are developed for a particular kind of problems. These programming models do not have support for a universal distributed software framework to process massive datasets. To overcome these problems, a new framework called *Transformer* was developed by Wang, P. et al. (2010). The three popular parallel programming models such as Map-Reduce, Dryad, and All-Pairs programming models can be implemented using *Transformer* and is not problem specific (Wang, P. et al., 2010).

Transformer model is based on two primitive operations: *send* and *receive*. The architecture of the Transformer programming model is shown in Figure 10. From Figure 10, it is clear that the architecture of *Transformer* is basically consists of two layers: *Common Runtime* and *Model Specific System*. Runtime system deals with tasks such as flow of data between machines and execution of tasks on different

Figure 10. Architecture of transformer programming model
Source: Wang, P. et al., 2009

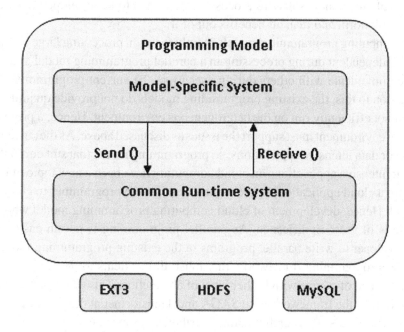

machines using *send ()* and *receive ()* functions. Model-specific system layer handles tasks such as data partitioning, mapping, and data dependencies etc.

Transformer is designed based on master-slave architecture. Run time system layer of *Transformer* has components such as manager, supervisor, worker, file, and message sender or receiver and Model specific system layer includes only one component named as *controller*. Every node in Transformer consists of two communication components: *sender* and *receiver*. The master node issues commands for execution of task on the slave nodes. Then after execution of the task, the status of execution is returned to master node by the slave node. Failure of task in *Transformer* is detected by the run-time system layer and fault-recovery is performed by the controller.

Transformer uses *Actor Model* design pattern and is coded in Python. Massage passing mechanism in *Transformer* is used to provide communication among nodes rather than using semaphores and conditions as used in multi-threading approach. It uses asynchronous message passing mechanism and the messages need to be serialized before sending. For a detailed analysis of all the three models mentioned above, interested reader can refer to (Wang, P. et al., 2009).

FUTURE SCOPE AND CHALLENGES

Cloud computing is the result of advancement in different technologies which ranges from increased processing, storage, provisioning of computational resources on demand, ubiquitous high-bandwidth network access, and increased security of Internet. However, agile development methodologies for software development effectively utilize the opportunity provided by cloud computing. It helps in releasing software iteratively and getting rapid and continuous user feedback. Therefore, combining agile development processes with cloud computing will bring the best of both worlds. Cloud computing being a popular computing platform, new software process models need to be developed that can mitigate the challenges of cloud platform and reap all benefits out of it.

Current cloud computing programming models mainly focus on processing large volume of data. The blocks of data are independent during processing in a parallel programming model and when one block of data needs to communicate with others during execution, the current programming models are not applicable. In addition to this, the existing programming models do not provide quantitative estimate of algorithms and cannot efficiently run on the heterogeneous environment. Hence, a programming model for cloud computing environment must support the issues as discussed above. As the current programming models work well for data intensive applications, so programming model that suit computation intensive and input or output intensive applications on cloud computing have been a new topic of research. Again, when programming a cloud application, it's very important for the programmer to choose a simple and realistic cost model. Hence, development of cloud computing programming model whose performance can be predictable is of great significance. As parallel programming is not an easy task, it becomes difficult for the developer to write parallel programs in the existing programming models. So, there is the need of parallel programming frameworks that must allow clients to develop robust and scalable programming models and of course with higher label of abstraction. This can be achieved by using only the set of APIs as used by the frameworks like SAGA and Transformer at the cost of performance rather than going through the details of the architecture, distributed hardware etc.

With the development of cloud computing and network techniques, more and more companies start to offer their testing systems based on the cloud. However, there are still some challenges which hinder the utilization of cloud testing that include testing security, environment construction, integration and interoperability, and scalability.

CONCLUSION

Software development in the cloud environment can be more efficient and more cost-effective than traditional software development. However, the cloud approach may neither automatically suitable nor profitable for all kinds of software. Business and IT managers need to take into consideration many technical aspects before migrating to cloud development. It can be argued that cloud approach is profitable to organizations who start to build new web-based services and who do not have redundant server capacity. Also services that may encounter sudden or occasional increase in demand can take benefits from the scalability of cloud systems.

On the other hand, public cloud systems do not necessarily suit systems that require extreme availability, need real-time computational capabilities or handle sensitive information. Also if an organization already has large data centers with ample processing power, the need for public cloud is limited. But, even within these situations cloud computing can sometimes be useful. Organizations can create their own private clouds to create similar scalable systems as public clouds. Also, they can utilize some services from the public clouds to improve their own systems and create some form of a hybrid cloud that best suits to their needs.

REFERENCES

Agile Manifesto. (n. d.). Retrieved from http://agilemanifesto.org/principles.html

Alliance, A. (2013). *What is Agile Software Development?*. Retrieved April, 4, 2015, from https://www.agilealliance.org/

Amber, S. (2002). *When and when aren't you Agile Modeling?* Retrieved Sept, 22, 2004, from http://www.agilemodeling.com/essays/whenAreYouAgileModeling.html

Bibi, S., Katsaros, D., & Bozanis, P. (2010). Application Development: Fly to the clouds or stay in-house?. In *Proceedings of 19th IEEE International Workshops on Enabling Technologies: Infrastructures for Collaborative Enterprises, ser. WETICE '10*. IEEE Computer Society. doi:10.1109/WETICE.2010.16

Bonorden, O. (2007). Load balancing in the bulk-synchronous-parallel setting using process migrations. In *Proceedings of IEEE International Parallel and Distributed Processing Symposium (IEEE Cat No07TH8938)*. doi:10.1109/IPDPS.2007.370330

Chang, V., Mills, H., & Newhouse, S. (2007). *From Open Source to long-term sustainability: Review of Business Models and Case studies*. Nottingham, UK: UK e-Science All Hands Meeting.

Chris, M. (2009). Programming Abstractions for data Intensive Computing on Clouds and Grids. In *Proceeding of 9th IEEE/ACM International Symposium on Cluster Computing and the Grid*.

Cisco. (n.d.). *Cisco Visual Networking Index: Global Mobile Data Traffic Forecast Update (2014), 2013–2018*. Retrieved from http://www.forbes.com/sites/louiscolumbus/2014/03/14/roundup-of-cloud-computingforecasts-and-market-estimates-2014/

Cloud or Not 4 Cloud Deployment Models. (n.d.). Retrieved from http://blog.thehigheredcio.com/2011/02/22/cloud-deployment-models/

Costa, V. G., Prinrista, A., & Marin, M. (2005). *A parallel search engine with BSP*. IEEE.

Dean, J., & Ghemawat, S. (2004). MapReduce: Simplified data processing on large clusters. In Proceedings of USENIXSymposium on Operating Systems Design and Implementation.

Dean, J., & Ghemawat, S. (2008). Mapreduce: Simplified data processing on large clusters. *Communications of the ACM, 51*(1), 107–113. doi:10.1145/1327452.1327492

Dillon, T., Wu, C., & Chang, E. (2010). Cloud Computing: Issues and challenges. In *Proceedings of 24th IEEE International Conference on Advanced Information Networking and Applications (AINA 2010)*. doi:10.1109/AINA.2010.187

Farooq, S. U., & Quadri, S. M. K. (2012). Quality Practices in Open Source Software Development Affecting Quality Dimensions. *Trends in Information Management, 7*(2), 116–134.

Foster, I., Yong, Z., Raicu, I., & Lu, S. (2008). Cloud computing and grid computing 360-degree compared. *2008 Grid Computing Environments Workshop*. doi:10.1109/GCE.2008.4738445

Gartner. (n.d.). Retrieved from http://www.gartner.com/it/page.jsp?id=920712

Guha, R. (2009). Towards the Intelligent Web Systems. In *Proceedings of IEEE CS, First International Conference on Computational Intelligence, Communication Systems, and Network.*

Hadoop. (n.d.). Retrieved from http://hadoop.apache.org/

Hassan, M. A. H., & Bamha, M. (2008). *Parallel processing of group-by join queries on shared nothing machines. Springer-Verlag* .

Isard, M., Budiu, M., Yuan, Y., Birrell, A., & Fetterly, D. (2007). Dryad: Distributed data-parallel programs from sequential building blocks. *Operating Systems Review, 41*(3), 59–72. doi:10.1145/1272998.1273005

Laplante, P., Zhang, J., & Voas, J. (2008). What's in a name? Distinguishing between SaaS and SOA. *IT Professional, 10*(3), 46–50. doi:10.1109/MITP.2008.60

Lean Agile Methodologies Accentuate Benefits of Cloud Computing. (n.d.). Retrieved fromwww.thetechnologygurus.com/.../LACC_white_paper_ed_v5.320180428

Malewicz, A., Gregorz, H., Matthew, J. C., Bik Aart, H., Llan, L., Naty, & Grzegorz, C. (2010). Pregel: A system for large-scale graph processing. In *Proc. of the International Conference on Management of Data.* doi:10.1145/1807167.1807184

Mall, R. (2014). *Fundamentals of Software Engineering* (4th ed.). Prentice Hall.

Mell, P. & Grance, T. (2011). *The NIST definition of cloud computing* (draft). U.S. National Institute of Standards and Technology special publication, 800.

Miceli, C. (2009). Programming Abstractions for Data Intensive Computing on Clouds and Grids. *9th IEEE/ACM International Symposium on Cluster Computing and the Grid.* doi:10.1109/CCGRID.2009.87

Moretti, C., Bulosan, J., Thain, D., & Flynn, P. J. (2008). All-pairs: an abstraction for data-intensive cloud computing. In *Proc. of the 2008 IEEE International Parallel & Distributed Processing Symposium.* doi:10.1109/IPDPS.2008.4536311

Patel, A. B., Birla, M., & Nair, U. (2012). *Addressing Big Data Problem Using Hadoop and Map Reduce.* doi:10.1109/NUICONE.2012.6493198

Righir, D., Pilla, L., & Carissimi, A. (2009). *MigBSP: A Novel Migration Model for Bulk-Synchronous Parallel Processes Rescheduling.* New York: IEEE.

Roger, S. P., & Bruce, R. M. (2014). *Software Engineering a Practitioner's Approach* (8th ed.). Tata: McGraw Hill.

Singh, A., Korupolu, M., & Mahapatra, D. (2008). Server-Storage Virtualization: Integration and Load Balancing in Data centers. IEEE/ACM Supercomputing (SC).

Sotomayor, B., Montero, R. S., Llorente, I., & Foster, I. (2009). Virtual infrastructure management in private and hybrid clouds. *IEEE Internet Computing, 13*(5), 14–22. doi:10.1109/MIC.2009.119

The Landmark. (n.d.). *Agile Development Meets Cloud Computing for Extraordinary Results at Salesforce.com.* Retrieved from http://www.developerforce.com/media/ForcedotcomBookLibrary/WP_Agile_112608.pdf

Valiant, L. G. (1990). A bridging model for parallel computation. *Communications of the ACM, 33*(8), 103-11.

Wang, P., Meng, D., Han, J., Zhan, J., Tu, B., Shi, X., & Wan, L. (2010). Transformer: A New Paradigm for Building Data Parallel Programming Models. *IEEE Micro, 30*(4), 55–64. doi:10.1109/MM.2010.75

Williams, T. L., & Parsons, R. J. (2000). *The Heterogeneous Bulk Synchronous Parallel model. In ROLIM J. Parallel and Distributed Processing, Proceedings*. Berlin: Springer-Verlag Berlin.

Compilation of References

AAIRM. (2002). *A risk management standard.* London UK: The Institute of Risk Management, the National Forum for Risk Management in the Public Sector and the Association of Insurance and Risk Managers.

Abatan, P. (2011). *What could Happen if you don't Employ Enterprise Rights Management.* Retrieved July 01, 2014, from www.enterprisedrm.info/

Abram, T. (2009). The hidden values of it risk management. *Information Systems Audit and Control Association Journal, 2009*(2), 40-45.

Ackermann, T. (2012). *IT Security Risk Management: Perceived IT Security Risks in the Context of Cloud Computing.* Berlin, Germany: Springer-Gabler.

Addis, B., Ardagna, D., Panicucci, B., & Zhang, L. (2010). Autonomic management of cloud service centers with availability guarantees. *IEEE 3rd International Conference on Cloud Computing* (CLOUD). doi:10.1109/CLOUD.2010.19

Agile Manifesto. (n. d.). Retrieved from http://agilemanifesto.org/principles.html

Ahmed, S., & Abdullah, A. (2011). E-Healthcare and Data Management Services in a Cloud. *8th International Conference on High-capacity Optical Networks and Emerging Technologies.* Retrieved on June 10, http://ieeexplore.ieee.org/xpl/articleDetails.jsp?arnumber=6149827&newsearch=true&queryText=E-Healthcare%20and%20Data%20Management%20Services%20in%20a%20Cloud

Ai, L., Tang, M., & Fidge, C. J. (2010). *QoS-oriented resource allocation and scheduling of multiple composite web services in a hybrid cloud using a random-key genetic algorithm.* Academic Press.

Aiber, S., Gilat, D., Landau, A., Razinkov, N., Sela, A., & Wasserkrug, S. (2004). Autonomic self-optimization according to business objectives. In *Proceedings of International Conference on Autonomic Computing* (ICAC'04).

Aib, I., Salle, M., Bartolini, C., & Boulmakoul, A. (2005). A business driven management framework for utility computing environments. In *Proceedings of the Ninth IFIP/IEEE International Symposium on Integrated Network Management (IM'05).* IEEE.

Ai, L., Tang, M., & Fidge, C. (2011). *Resource allocation and scheduling of multiple composite web services in cloud computing using cooperative coevolution genetic algorithm.* Neural Information Processing. doi:10.1007/978-3-642-24958-7_30

Aisopos, F., Tserpes, K., & Varvarigou, T. (2013). Resource management in software as a service using the knapsack problem model. *International Journal of Production Economics, 141*(2), 465–477. doi:10.1016/j.ijpe.2011.12.011

Alahmadi, A., Alnowiser, A., Zhu, M. M., Che, D., & Ghodous, P. (2014). Enhanced first-fit decreasing algorithm for energy-aware job scheduling in cloud. *Computational Science and Computational Intelligence (CSCI), 2014 International Conference on.*

Alliance, A. (2013). *What is Agile Software Development?*. Retrieved April, 4, 2015, from https://www.agilealliance.org/

Almorsy, M., Grundy, J., & Ibrahim, A. S. (2014). Adaptable, model-driven security engineering for SaaS cloud-based applications. *Automated Software Engineering, 21*(2), 187–224. doi:10.1007/s10515-013-0133-z

Alnowiser, A., Aldhahri, E., Alahmadi, A., & Zhu, M. M. (2014). Enhanced weighted round robin (ewrr) with dvfs technology in cloud energy-aware. *Computational Science and Computational Intelligence (CSCI), 2014 International Conference on.*

Alnuem, M., Alrumaih, H., & Al-Alshaikh, H. (2015). *Enterprise risk management from boardroom to shop floor.* Paper presented in The Sixth International Conference on Cloud Computing, GRIDs, and Virtualization, Nice, France.

Alohali, B. (2016). Security in Cloud of Things (CoT). In Z. Ma (Ed.), *Managing Big Data in cloud computing Environments* (pp. 46–70). Hershey, PA: IGI Global. doi:10.4018/978-1-4666-9834-5.ch003

Alsolami, F. (2013). N-Cloud: Improving performance and security in cloud storage. *2013 IEEE 14th International Conference on High Performance Switching and Routing.* doi:10.1109/HPSR.2013.6602319

Altaf, F., & Schuff, D. (2010). Taking a flexible approach to ASPs. *Communications of the ACM, 53*(2), 139–143. doi:10.1145/1646353.1646389

Amarasinghe, H. (2012). *Utilization of Dynamic Attributes in Resource Discovery for Network Virtualization* (Ph.D. dissertation). University of Ottawa.

Amazon EC2. (n.d.). Retrieved from http://aws.amazon.com/ec2/instance-types

Amber, S. (2002). *When and when aren't you Agile Modeling?* Retrieved Sept, 22, 2004, from http://www.agilemodeling.com/essays/whenAreYouAgileModeling.html

Amundson, I., & Koutsoukos, X. D. (2009). A Survey on Localization for Mobile Wireless Sensor Networks. Mobile entity localization and tracking in GPS-less environments. *Lecture Notes in Computer Science, 5801,* 235-254. Retrieved on June 8, http://link.springer.com/chapter/10.1007%2F978-3-642-04385-7_16

Andrejevic, M. (2013). *Infoglut: How too much information is changing the way we think and know?* New York, NY: Routledge.

Anily, S., Bramel, J., & Simchi-Levi, D. (1994). Worst-case analysis of heuristics for the bin packing problem with general cost structures. *Operations Research, 42*(2), 287–298. doi:10.1287/opre.42.2.287

Anisseh, M., & Yussuf, R. b. (2011). A Fuzzy Group Decision Making Model for Multiple Criteria based on Borda Count. *International Journal of the Physical Sciences, 6*(3), 425–433.

Ararez, L., Chaouchi, H., & Gurkas, Z. (2011). Performance Evaluation and Experiments for Host Identity Protocol. *International Journal of Computer Science, 8*(2), 74-83. Retrieved on June 8, http://ijcsi.org/papers/IJCSI-8-2-74-83.pdf

Ardagna, D., Panicucci, B., & Passacantando, M. (2013). Generalized nash equilibria for the service provisioning problem in cloud systems. IEEE Transactions on Services Computing, 6(4), 429–442.

Ardagna, D., Panicucci, B., & Passacantando, M. (2011). A game theoretic formulation of the service provisioning problem in cloud systems. In *Proceedings of the 20th ACM international conference on world wide web*. doi:10.1145/1963405.1963433

Ardagna, D., Trubian, M., & Zhang, L. (2004). SLA based profit optimization in multi-tier web application systems. In *Int'l Conference On Service Oriented Computing*.

Armbrust, M. (2009). *Above the clouds: A berkeley view of cloud computing*. EECS Department, University of California, Berkeley, Tech. Rep. UCB/EECS-2009-28.

Assuncao, M. D., Calheiros, R. N., Bianchi, S., Netto, M. A., & Buyya, R. (2015). Big Data computing and clouds: Trends and future directions. *Journal of Parallel and Distributed Computing*, *79*, 3–15. doi:10.1016/j.jpdc.2014.08.003

Assun, M., Costanzo, A., & Buyya, R. (2009). Evaluating the Cost-benefit of Using Cloud Computing to Extend the Capacity of Clusters. In *Proceedings of the 18th ACM International Symposium on High Performance Distributed Computing (HPDC 2008)*.

Aven, T. (2008). *Risk analysis: Assessing uncertainties beyond expected values and probabilities*. West Sussex, UK: John Wiely and Sons, Ltd. doi:10.1002/9780470694435

AXELOS. (2011). *ITIL® glossary and abbreviations*. Retrieved April 07, 2016 from https://www.exin.com/assets/exin/frameworks/108/glossaries/english_glossary_v1.0_201404.pdf

Ayyub, B. M. (2001). *Elicitation of Expert Opinions for Uncertainty & Risks*. CRC Press LLC. doi:10.1201/9781420040906

Ayyub, B., & Lai, K.-L. (1992). Structural Reliability Assessement with Ambiguity & Vagueme=ness in Failure. *Naval Engineers Journal*, *104*(3), 21–35. doi:10.1111/j.1559-3584.1992.tb02221.x

Ayzenberg, Y., & Picard, R. W. (2014). FEEL: A System for Frequent Event and Electrodermal Activity Labeling. *IEEE Journal of Biomedical And Health Informatics*, *18*(1), 266-277. Retrieved on June 1, http://ieeexplore.ieee.org/xpl/articleDetails.jsp?arnumber=6579690&newsearch=true&queryText=FEEL:%20A%20System%20for%20Frequent%20Event%20and%20Electrodermal%20Activity%20Labeling

Bai, X. (2010). Affordance of Ubiquitous Learning through Cloud Computing. *Fifth International Conference on Frontier of Computer Science and Technology*. Retrieved on June 8, http://ieeexplore.ieee.org/xpl/articleDetails.jsp?arnumber=5575671&newsearch=true&queryText=Affordance%20of%20Ubiquitous%20Learning%20through%20Cloud%20Computing

Baliga, J., Ayre, R. W., Hinton, K., & Tucker, R. (2011). Green cloud computing: Balancing energy in processing, storage, and transport. *Proceedings of the IEEE*, *99*(1), 149–167. doi:10.1109/JPROC.2010.2060451

Banerjee, D., Biswas, S., Daigle, C., & Siegford, J. M. (2012). Remote activity classification of hens using wireless body mounted sensors. *The 9th International Conference on Wearable and Implantable Body Sensor Networks*. Retrieved on June 6, http://ieeexplore.ieee.org/xpl/articleDetails.jsp?arnumber=6200546&newsearch=true&queryText=Remote%20activity%20classification%20of%20hens%20using%20wireless%20body%20mounted%20sensors

Baya, V., Mathaisel, B., & Parker, B. (2010). The cloud you don't know: An engine for new business growth. PWC Journal of Technology Forecast, 1(4), 4-16.

Beg, I., & Ashraf, S. (2009). Similarity Measures of Fuzzy Sets. *Applications & Computational Mathematics*, *8*(2), 192–202.

Belady, C.L. (2007). In the data center, power and cooling costs more than the it equipment it supports. *Electronics Cooling, 13*(1), 24.

Belbekkouche, A., Hasan, M., Karmouch, A., & others. (2012). Resource discovery and allocation in network virtualization. *IEEE Communications Surveys & Tutorials, 14*(4), 1114-1128.

Bell, D., de Cesare, S., Iacovelli, N., Lycett, M., & Merico, A. (2007). A framework for deriving Semantic Web services. *Information Systems Frontiers, 9*(1), 69–84. doi:10.1007/s10796-006-9018-z

Beloglazov, A., Buyya, R., Lee, Y. C., Zomaya, A., & others. (2011). A taxonomy and survey of energy-efficient data centers and cloud computing systems. *Advances in Computers, 82*(2), 47-111.

Beloglazov, A., Abawajy, J., & Buyya, R. (2012). Energy-aware resource allocation heuristics for efficient management of data centers for cloud computing. *Future Generation Computer Systems, 28*(5), 755–768. doi:10.1016/j.future.2011.04.017

Beloglazov, A., & Buyya, R. (2010). Adaptive threshold-based approach for energy-efficient consolidation of virtual machines in cloud data centers. *Proceedings of the 8th International Workshop on Middleware for Grids, Clouds and e-Science.* doi:10.1145/1890799.1890803

Beloglazov, A., & Buyya, R. (2012). Optimal online deterministic algorithms and adaptive heuristics for energy and performance efficient dynamic consolidation of virtual machines in cloud data centers. *Concurrency and Computation, 24*(13), 1397–1420. doi:10.1002/cpe.1867

Benbernou, S., & Hacid, M. S. (2005). Resolution and constraint propagation for Semantic Web services discovery. *Distributed and Parallel Databases, 18*(1), 65–81. doi:10.1007/s10619-005-1074-8

Benlian, A., & Hess, T. (2011). Opportunities and risks of software-as-a-service: Findings from a survey of IT executives. *Decision Support Systems, 52*(1), 232–246. doi:10.1016/j.dss.2011.07.007

Benlian, A., Hess, T., & Buxmann, P. (2009). Drivers of SaaS-adoption: An empirical study of different application types. *Business & Information Systems Engineering, 1*(5), 357–369. doi:10.1007/s12599-009-0068-x

Benlian, A., Koufaris, M., & Hess, T. (2011). Service quality in software-as-a-service: Developing the SaaS-QUAL measure and examining its role in usage continuance. *Journal of Management Information Systems, 28*(3), 85–126. doi:10.2753/MIS0742-1222280303

Berkey, J. O., & Wang, P. Y. (1994). A systolic-based parallel bin packing algorithm. *IEEE Transactions on Parallel and Distributed Systems, 5*(7), 769–772. doi:10.1109/71.296322

Berners-Lee, T., Hendler, J., & Lassila, O. (2001). The Semantic Web. *Scientific American Magazine.*

Bibi, S., Katsaros, D., & Bozanis, P. (2010). Application Development: Fly to the clouds or stay in-house?. In *Proceedings of 19th IEEE International Workshops on Enabling Technologies: Infrastructures for Collaborative Enterprises, ser. WETICE '10.* IEEE Computer Society. doi:10.1109/WETICE.2010.16

Birman, K., Chockler, G., & van Renesse, R. (2009). *Toward a cloud computing research agenda.* SIGACT News.

Bisong, A., & Rahman, S. (2011). An overview of the Security concerns in Enterprise Cloud Computing. *International Journal of Network Security & Its Applications, 3*(1), 30–45. doi:10.5121/ijnsa.2011.3103

Bobroff, N., Kochut, A., & Beaty, K. (2007). Dynamic placement of virtual machines for managing sla violations. In *10th IFIP/IEEE International Symposium on Integrated Network Management, IM'07.* doi:10.1109/INM.2007.374776

Bonorden, O. (2007). Load balancing in the bulk-synchronous-parallel setting using process migrations. In *Proceedings of IEEE International Parallel and Distributed Processing Symposium (IEEE Cat No07TH8938).* doi:10.1109/IPDPS.2007.370330

Botero, J. F., & Hesselbach, X. (2009). The bottlenecked virtual network problem in bandwidth allocation for network virtualization. *Communications, 2009. LATINCOM'09. IEEE Latin-American Conference on*, (pp. 1-5). doi:10.1109/LATINCOM.2009.5305042

Boyd, D., & Crawford, K. (2012). Critical questions for Big Data: Provocations for a cultural, technological, and scholarly phenomenon. *Information, Communication and Society, 15*(5), 662–679. doi:10.1080/1369118X.2012.678878

Brennan, P. F., & Bakken, S. (2015). Nursing needs Big Data and Big Data needs nursing. *Journal of Nursing Scholarship, 47*(5), 477–484. doi:10.1111/jnu.12159

Brett, P., Bowman, M., Sedayao, J., Adams, R., Knauerhase, R. C., & Klingaman, A. (2004). Securing the PlanetLab Distributed Testbed: How to Manage Security in an Environment with No Firewalls, with All Users Having Root, and No Direct Physical Control of Any System. *LISA, 4*, 195–202.

Broder, J. (2006). *Risk analysis and the security survey*. Burlington, MA: Butterworth-Heinemann Elsevier.

Brotby, W. (2006). *Information security governance: Guidance for boards of directors and executive management*. Rolling Meadows, IL: IT Governance Institute.

Brown, W. A., Moore, G., & Tegan, W. (2006). *SOA governance—IBM's approach*. Somers, NY: IBM Corporation.

Burge, J., Ranganathan, P., & Wiener, J. (2007). Cost-aware scheduling for heterogeneous enterprise machines (CASH'EM). In *Cluster Computing, 2007 IEEE International Conference on*.

Burrell, J., Brooke, T., & Beckwith, R. (2004). Vineyard Computing: Sensor Networks in Agricultural Production. *Pervasive Computing, 3*(1), 38-45. Retrieved on June 9, http://ieeexplore.ieee.org/xpl/articleDetails.jsp?arnumber=1269130&newsearch=true&queryText=Vineyard%20Computing:%20Sensor%20Networks%20in%20Agricultural%20Production

Buyya, R., Pandey, S., & Vecchiola, C. (2013). *Market-Oriented Cloud Computing and the Cloudbus Toolkit*. The University of Melbourne. doi:10.1002/9781118640708.ch14

Buyya, R., Yeo, C. S., Venugopal, S., Broberg, J., & Brandic, I. (2009). Cloud computing and emerging IT platforms: Vision, hype, and reality for delivering computing as the 5th utility. *Future Generation Computer Systems, 25*(6), 599–616. doi:10.1016/j.future.2008.12.001

Calheiros, R., Ranjan, R., Beloglazov, A., De Rose, C. A. F., & Buyya, R. (2011). CloudSim: A Toolkit for Modeling and Simulation of Cloud Computing Environments and Evaluation of Resource Provisioning Algorithms. *Software: Practice and Experience, 41*(1), 23-50.

Calheiros, R. N., Ranjan, R., Beloglazov, A., De Rose, C. A., & Buyya, R. (2011). Cloudsim: A toolkit for modelling and simulation of cloud computing environments and evaluation of resource provisioning algorithms. *Software, Practice & Experience, 41*(1), 23–50. doi:10.1002/spe.995

Campbell, A. T., De Meer, H. G., Kounavis, M. E., Miki, K., Vicente, J. B., & Villela, D. (1999). A survey of programmable networks. *Computer Communication Review, 29*(2), 7–23. doi:10.1145/505733.505735

Casado, R., & Younas, M. (2014). Emerging trends and technologies in Big Data processing. *Concurrency and Computation, 27*(8), 2078–2091. doi:10.1002/cpe.3398

Castane, G. G., Nunez, A., & Carretero, J. (2012). iCanCloud: A Brief Architecture Overview. *Parallel and Distributed Processing with Applications (ISPA), 2012 IEEE 10th International Symposium on*. doi:10.1109/ISPA.2012.131

Castiglione, A., Gribaudo, M., Iacono, M., & Palmieri, F. (2015). Modeling performances of concurrent Big Data applications. *Software: Practice & Experience, 45*(8), 1127–1144. doi:10.1002/spe.2269

Çelik, D., & Elçi, A. (2013). A broker-based semantic agent for discovering Semantic Web services through process similarity matching and equivalence considering quality of service. *Science China: Information Sciences, 56*(1), 1–24. doi:10.1007/s11432-012-4697-1

Chahal, P., Singh, M., & Kumar, S. (2014). An efficient web page ranking for Semantic Web. *Journal of The Institution of Engineers (India): Series B, 95*(1), 15–21. doi:10.1007/s40031-014-0070-7

Chandramouli, R., & Mell, P. (2010). State of Security readiness. *Crossroads, 16*(3), 23–25. doi:10.1145/1734160.1734168

Chang, V., Mills, H., & Newhouse, S. (2007). *From Open Source to long-term sustainability: Review of Business Models and Case studies*. Nottingham, UK: UK e-Science All Hands Meeting.

Chen, K. R., Lin, Y. L., & Huang, M. S. (2011). A Mobile Biomedical Device by Novel Antenna Technology for Cloud Computing Resource toward Pervasive Healthcare. *11th IEEE International Conference on Bioinformatics and Bioengineering*. Retrieved on June 9, http://ieeexplore.ieee.org/xpl/articleDetails.jsp?arnumber=6089820&newsearch=true&queryText=A%20Mobile%20Biomedical%20Device%20by%20Novel%20Antenna%20Technology%20for%20Cloud%20Computing%20Resource%20toward%20Pervasive%20Healthcare

Chen, W.-N., Zhang, J., & Yu, Y. (2007). Workflow scheduling in grids: an ant colony optimization approach. *Evolutionary Computation, 2007. CEC 2007. IEEE Congress on*, (pp. 3308-3315).

Chen, Y., Shen, W., Huo, H., & Xu, Y. (2010). A Smart Gateway for Health Care System Using Wireless Sensor Network. *Fourth International Conference on Sensor Technologies and Applications 2010*. Retrieved on June 5, http://ieeexplore.ieee.org/xpl/articleDetails.jsp?arnumber=5558128&queryText=A%20Smart%20Gateway%20for%20Health%20Care%20System%20Using%20Wireless%20Sensor%20Network&newsearch=true

Chen, Y.-L., Yang, Y.-C., & Lee, W.-T. (2014). The study of using game theory for live migration prediction over cloud computing. Springer Intelligent Data analysis and its Applications, 2, 417–425. doi:10.1007/978-3-319-07773-4_41

Chen, Q., Guo, M., Deng, Q., Zheng, L., Guo, S., & Shen, Y. (2013). HAT: History-based auto-tuning MapReduce in heterogeneous environments. *The Journal of Supercomputing, 64*(3), 1038–1054. doi:10.1007/s11227-011-0682-5

Chen, Y., & Sion, R. (2011). To cloud or not to cloud? Musings on costs and viability. In *Proc. of Symp. on Cloud Computing, SOCC '11*. doi:10.1145/2038916.2038945

Cho, V., & Chan, A. (2015). An integrative framework of comparing SaaS adoption for core and non-core business operations: An empirical study on Hong Kong industries. *Information Systems Frontiers, 17*(3), 629–644. doi:10.1007/s10796-013-9450-9

Chowdhury, N. M., & Boutaba, R. (2010). A survey of network virtualization. *Computer Networks, 54*(5), 862–876. doi:10.1016/j.comnet.2009.10.017

Chowdhury, N., & Boutaba, R. (2009). Network virtualization: State of the art and research challenges. *Communications Magazine, IEEE, 47*(7), 20–26. doi:10.1109/MCOM.2009.5183468

Chowdhury, N. F. S. (n.d.). Polyvine: Policy-based virtual network embedding across multiple domains. *Proc. ACM*.

Chris, M. (2009). Programming Abstractions for data Intensive Computing on Clouds and Grids. In *Proceeding of 9th IEEE/ACM International Symposium on Cluster Computing and the Grid*.

Chun, B. N., & Culler, D. E. (2002). User-centric performance analysis of market-based cluster batch schedulers. In *Proceedings of the 2nd IEEE/ACM International Symposium on Cluster Computing and the Grid (CCGRID)*. doi:10.1109/CCGRID.2002.1017109

Chwelos, P., Benbasat, I., & Dexter, A. S. (2001). Research report: Empirical test of an EDI adoption model. *Information Systems Research*, *12*(3), 304–321. doi:10.1287/isre.12.3.304.9708

Cisco. (n.d.). *Cisco Visual Networking Index: Global Mobile Data Traffic Forecast Update (2014), 2013– 2018*. Retrieved from http://www.forbes.com/sites/louiscolumbus/2014/03/14/roundup-of-cloud-computingforecasts-and-market-estimates-2014/

Cleveland, W. S. (1979). Robust locally weighted regression and smoothing scatterplots. *Journal of the American Statistical Association*, *74*(368), 829–836. doi:10.1080/01621459.1979.10481038

Cloud Computing. (n.d.). In *Wikipedia*. Retrieved on June 5, 2016 https://en.wikipedia.org/wiki/Cloud_computing

Cloud or Not 4 Cloud Deployment Models. (n.d.). Retrieved from http://blog.thehigheredcio.com/2011/02/22/cloud-deployment-models/

Cloud Security Alliance. (2012). *Security guidance for critical areas of Mobile Computing*. Available: https://downloads.cloudsecurityalliance.org/initiatives/mobile/Mobile_Guidance_v1.pdf

Coffman, E. G. Jr, Garey, M. R., & Johnson, D. S. (1996). *Approximation algorithms for bin packing: a survey. Approximation algorithms for NP-hard problems*. PWS Publishing Co.

Coleman, K., Norris, J., Candea, G., & Fox, A. (2004). Oncall: defeating spikes with a free-market application cluster. In *Proceedings of the 1st International Conference on Autonomic Computing*.

Conejero, J., Rana, O., Burnap, P., Morgan, J., Caminero, B., & Carrion, C. (2016). Analyzing hadoop power consumption and impact on application qos. *Future Generation Computer Systems*, *55*, 213–223. doi:10.1016/j.future.2015.03.009

Conti, M., Giordano, S., May, M., & Passarella, A. (2010). From Opportunistic Networks to Opportunistic Computing. *IEEE Communications Magazine*, *48*(9), 126-139. Retrieved on June 3, http://ieeexplore.ieee.org/xpl/articleDetails.jsp?arnumber=5560597&newsearch=true&queryText=From%20Opportunistic%20Networks%20to%20Opportunistic%20Computing

Cook, D. J., & Das, S. K. (2012). Pervasive Computing at Scale: Transforming the State of the Art. *Journal Pervasive and Mobile Computing*, *8*(1), 22-35. Retrieved on June 1, http://www.sciencedirect.com/science/article/pii/S1574119211001416

COSO. (2012). Enterprise Risk Management for Cloud Computing. Durham, NC: The Committee of Sponsoring Organizations of the Treadway Commission (COSO).

Costa, V. G., Prinrista, A., & Marin, M. (2005). *A parallel search engine with BSP*. IEEE.

Cowls, J., & Schroeder, R. (2015). Causation, correlation, and Big Data in social science research. *Policy & Internet*, *7*(4), 447–472. doi:10.1002/poi3.100

CSA (The Cloud Security Alliance). (2011). *Security guidance for critical areas of focus in cloud computing v3.0*. Retrieved September 09, 2015, from https://downloads.cloudsecurityalliance.org/initiatives/guidance/csaguide.v3.0.pdf

CSA. (2010). *Top Threats to Cloud Computing V1.0*. CSA.

CSA. (2011). *Security Guidance for Critical Areas of Focus in Cloud Computing V3.0*. CSA.

Cumbley, R., & Church, P. (2013). Is "Big Data" creepy? *Computer Law & Security Report, 29*(5), 601–609. doi:10.1016/j. clsr.2013.07.007

Currie, W. L. (2003). A knowledge-base risk assessment framework for evaluating Web-based application outsourcing projects. *International Journal of Project Management, 21*(3), 207–217. doi:10.1016/S0263-7863(02)00095-9

Cusumano, M. (2010). Technology strategy and management: Cloud computing and SaaS as new computing platforms. *Communications of the ACM, 53*(4), 27–29. doi:10.1145/1721654.1721667

d'Amato, C., Fanizzi, N., Fazzinga, B., Gottlob, G., & Lukasiewicz, T. (2012). Ontology-based semantic search on the Web and its combination with the power of inductive reasoning. *Annals of Mathematics and Artificial Intelligence, 65*(2), 83–121. doi:10.1007/s10472-012-9309-7

Da Silva, S., Florissi, D., & Yemini, Y. (1998). *NetScript: A language-based approach to active networks. Tech. Rep.* New York: Computer Science Dept., Columbia Univ.

Daas, D., Hurkmans, T., Overbeek, S., & Bouwman, H. (2013). Developing a decision support system for business model design. *Electronic Markets, 23*(3), 251–265. doi:10.1007/s12525-012-0115-1

Dabbagh, M., Hamdaoui, B., Guizani, M., & Rayes, A. (2015). Toward energy-efficient cloud computing: Prediction, consolidation, and overcommitment. *IEEE Network, 29*(2), 56–61. doi:10.1109/MNET.2015.7064904

Daneshyar, S., & Razmjoo, M. (2012). Large-scale data processing using Mapreduce in cloud computing Environment. *International Journal on Web Service Computing, 3*(4), 1–13. doi:10.5121/ijwsc.2012.3401

DARPA. (2016). *The DARPA agent mark-up language.* Retrieved from http://www.daml.org/

Dash, D., Kantere, V., & Ailamaki, A. (2009). An Economic Model for Self-Tuned Cloud Caching. In *Proc of the 25th IEEE International Conference on Data Engineering.* doi:10.1109/ICDE.2009.143

Datatorrent. (n.d.). Retrieved from https://www.datatorrent.com/product/architecture/

Davis, C., Schiller, M., & Wheeler, K. (2006). *IT auditing: Using controls to protect information assets.* Emeryville, CA: McGraw-Hill Osborne Media.

Dawoud, W., Takouna, I., & Meinel, C. (2010). Infrastructure as a service security: Challenges and solutions. In *The 7th International Conference on Informatics and Systems* (INFOS). Potsdam, Germany: IEEE Computer Society.

De Haes, S., & Grembergen, W. (2009). *Enterprise governance of information technology: Achieving strategic alignment and value.* New York: Springer. doi:10.1007/978-0-387-84882-2

Dean, J., & Ghemawat, S. (2004). MapReduce: Simplified data processing on large clusters. In Proceedings of USE-NIXSymposium on Operating Systems Design and Implementation.

Dean, J., & Ghemawat, S. (2008). MapReduce: Simplified data processing on large clusters. *Communications of the ACM, 51*(1), 107–113. doi:10.1145/1327452.1327492

Dean, J., & Ghemawat, S. (2010). MapReduce: A flexible data processing tool. *Communications of the ACM, 53*(1), 72–77. doi:10.1145/1629175.1629198

Delavar, A. G., & Aryan, Y. (2011). *A Synthetic Heuristic Algorithm for Independent Task Scheduling in Cloud System.* IJCSI.

Deng, Y., Kang, B. Y., Zhang, Y. J., Deng, X. Y., & Zhang, H. X. (2011). *A Modified Similarity Measure of Generalized Fuzzy Numbers. In Chinese Control & Decision Conference* (pp. 2173–2175). CCDC.

Dept. of Homeland Security. (2006). *Security Guidelines for the Petroleum Industry.* American Petroleum Institute (API) Publications.

Dhillon, J. S., Purini, S., & Kashyap, S. (2013). Virtual machine coscheduling: A game theoretic approach. In *2013 IEEE/ACM 6th International Conference on Utility and Cloud Computing (UCC)*, (pp. 227–234).

Dhillon, G., & Torkzadeh, G. (2006). Value-focused Assessment of Information System Security in Organizations. *Information Systems Journal, 16*(3), 293–314. doi:10.1111/j.1365-2575.2006.00219.x

Dietze, S., Gugliotta, A., Domingue, J., Yu, H. Q., & Mrissa, M. (2010). An automated approach to Semantic Web services mediation. *Service Oriented Computing and Applications, 4*(4), 261–275. doi:10.1007/s11761-010-0070-7

Dillon, T., Wu, C., & Chang, E. (2010). Cloud Computing: Issues and challenges. In *Proceedings of 24th IEEE International Conference on Advanced Information Networking and Applications (AINA 2010).* doi:10.1109/AINA.2010.187

Dowsley, R., Muller-Quade, J., & Nascimento, A. C. A. (2009). *A cca2 secure public key encryption scheme based on the mceliece assumptions in the standard model.* In CT-RSA. doi:10.1007/978-3-642-00862-7_16

Dubey, A., & Wagle, D. (2007). Delivering software as a service. *The McKinsey Quarterly, 6*, 1–12.

Du, J., Lu, J., Wu, D., Li, H., & Li, J. (2013). User acceptance of software as a service: Evidence from customers of China's leading e-commerce company, Alibaba. *Journal of Systems and Software, 86*(8), 2034–2044. doi:10.1016/j.jss.2013.03.012

Dutta, A., Peng, G. C., & Choudhary, A. (2013). Risks in enterprise cloud computing: The perspective of IT experts. *Journal of Computer Information Systems, 53*(4), 39–48. doi:10.1080/08874417.2013.11645649

Egami, K., Matsumoto, S., & Nakamura, M. (2011). Ubiquitous Cloud: Managing Service Resources for Adaptive Ubiquitous Computing. *IEEE International Conference on Pervasive Computing and Communications Workshops.* Retrieved on June 10, http://ieeexplore.ieee.org/xpl/login.jsp?tp=&arnumber=5766853&url=http%3A%2F%2Fieeexplore.ieee.org%2Fxpls%2Fabs_all.jsp%3Farnumber%3D5766853

Ergu, D., & Peng, Y. (2014). A framework for SaaS software packages evaluation and selection with virtual team and BOCR of analytic network process. *The Journal of Supercomputing, 67*(1), 219–238. doi:10.1007/s11227-013-0995-7

Escobedo, L., Tentori, M., Quintana, E., Favela, F., & Garcia-Rosas, D. (2014). Using Augmented Reality to Help Children withAutism Stay Focused. *IEEE Pervasive Computing / IEEE Computer Society [and] IEEE Communications Society, 13*(1), 38–46. doi:10.1109/MPRV.2014.19

Espadas, J., Concha, D., & Molina, A. (2008). *Application development over software-as- a-service platforms.* Paper presented at the 3rd International Conference on Software Engineering Advances (ICSEA 2008), Sliema, Malta. doi:10.1109/ICSEA.2008.48

Esposti, S. (2013). *Big Data or dataveillance? The rise of the scientific enterprise.* Paper presented at the 38th Annual Meeting of the Society for Social Studies of Science (4S 2013), San Diego, CA.

Fanning, K., & Drogt, E. (2014). Big Data: New opportunities for M&A. *Journal of Corporate Accounting & Finance, 25*(2), 27–34. doi:10.1002/jcaf.21919

Fanning, K., & Grant, R. (2013). Big Data: Implications for financial managers. *Journal of Corporate Accounting & Finance, 24*(5), 23–30. doi:10.1002/jcaf.21872

Fan, X., Weber, W. D., & Barroso, L. A. (2007). Power provisioning for a warehouse-sized computer. *ACM SIGARCH Computer Architecture News, 35*(2), 13–23. doi:10.1145/1273440.1250665

Farooq, S. U., & Quadri, S. M. K. (2012). Quality Practices in Open Source Software Development Affecting Quality Dimensions. *Trends in Information Management, 7*(2), 116–134.

Feller, E., Ramakrishnan, L., & Morin, C. (2015). Performance and energy efficiency of big data applications in cloud environments: A hadoop case study. *Journal of Parallel and Distributed Computing, 79*, 80–89. doi:10.1016/j.jpdc.2015.01.001

Fernandez, E. B., Yoshioka, N., & Washizaki, H. (2009). Modeling Misuse Patterns. In *Proceedings of the 4th Int. Workshop on Dependability Aspects of Data Warehousing and Mining Applications (DAWAM 2009), in conjunction with the 4th Int.Conf. on Availability, Reliability, and Security (ARES 2009)*. Fukuoka, Japan: IEEE Computer Society. doi:10.1109/ARES.2009.139

Fernandez, A., del Rio, S., Lopez, V., Bawakid, A., del Jesus, M. J., Benitez, J. M., & Herrera, F. (2014). Big Data with Cloud Computing: An insight on the computing environment, MapReduce, and programming frameworks. *Wiley Interdisciplinary Reviews: Data Mining and Knowledge Discovery, 4*(5), 380–409.

Fernández, A., Gómez, A., Lecumberry, F., Pardo, A., & Ramírez, I. (2015). Pattern recognition in Latin America in the "Big Data" era. *Pattern Recognition, 48*(4), 1185–1196. doi:10.1016/j.patcog.2014.04.012

Ferrari, L., Berlingerio, M., Calabrese, F., & Curtis-Davidson, B. (2013). Measuring Public-Transport Accessibility Using Pervasive Mobility Data. *IEEE Pervasive Computing, 12*(1), 26-33. Retrieved on June 1, http://ieeexplore.ieee.org/xpl/login.jsp?tp=&arnumber=6353419&url=http%3A%2F%2Fieeexplore.ieee.org%2Fiel5%2F7756%2F5210084%2F06353419.pdf%3Farnumber%3D6353419

Filippi, P. D. (2013). Ubiquitous Computing in the Cloud: User Empowerment vs. User Obsequity. In *User Behavior in Ubiquitous Online Environments*. IGI Global. Retrieved on June 1, https://halshs.archives-ouvertes.fr/hal-00855712/document

Fisch, E., & White, G. (2000). *Secure Computer & Networks: Analysis, Design & Implementation*. Boca Raton, FL: CRC Press.

Fleszar, K., & Hindi, K. S. (2002). New heuristics for one-dimensional bin-packing. *Computers & Operations Research, 29*(7), 821–839. doi:10.1016/S0305-0548(00)00082-4

Foster, I., Yong, Z., Raicu, I., & Lu, S. (2008). Cloud computing and grid computing 360-degree compared. *2008 Grid Computing Environments Workshop*. doi:10.1109/GCE.2008.4738445

Galan-Jimenez, J., & Gazo-Cervero, A. (2011). Overview and challenges of overlay networks: A survey. *Int J Comput Sci Eng Surv, 2*, 19-37.

Garfinkel, T., & Rosenblum, M. (2005). When virtual is harder than real: Security challenges in virtual machine based computing environments. In *Proceedings of the 10th conference on Hot Topics in Operating Systems*. USENIX Association.

Gartner. (n.d.). Retrieved from http://www.gartner.com/it/page.jsp?id=920712

Ge, Y., & Wei, G. (2010). GA-based task scheduler for the cloud computing systems. *Web Information Systems and Mining (WISM), 2010 International Conference on.*

Ghazizadeh, A. (2012). Cloud Computing Benefits And Architecture In E-Learning. *Seventh IEEE International Conference on Wireless, Mobile and Ubiquitous Technology in Education*. Retrieved on June 8, http://ieeexplore.ieee.org/xpl/articleDetails.jsp?arnumber=6185026&newsearch=true&queryText=Cloud%20Computing%20Benefits%20And%20Architecture%20In%20E-Learning

Gheorghe, G., Neuhaus, S., & Crispo, B. (2010). ESB: An Enterprise Service Bus for Access and Usage Control Policy Enforcement. In *Proc. Annual IFIP WG 11.11 International Conference on Trust Management*.

Giacobbe, M., Celesti, A., Fazio, M., Villari, M., & Puliafito, A. (2015). A Sustainable Energy-Aware Resource Management Strategy for IoT Cloud Federation. *IEEE International Symposium on Systems Engineering* (ISSE). Retrieved on June 8, http://ieeexplore.ieee.org/xpl/articleDetails.jsp?arnumber=7302751&newsearch=true&queryText=A%20Sustainable%20EnergyAware%20Resource%20Management%20Strategy%20for%20IoT%20Cloud%20Federation

Goncalves, V., & Ballon, P. (2011). Adding value to the network: Mobile operators' experiments with software-as-a-service and platform-as-a-service models. *Telematics and Informatics*, *28*(1), 12–21. doi:10.1016/j.tele.2010.05.005

Goode, S., Lin, C., Tsai, J. C., & Jiang, J. J. (2015). Rethinking the role of security in client satisfaction with software-as-a-service (SaaS) providers. *Decision Support Systems*, *70*, 73–85. doi:10.1016/j.dss.2014.12.005

Gorai, M., & Agarwal, K. (2012). A Survey on Pervasive Computing. *International Journal of Scientific & Engineering Research*, *3*(6), 1-7. Retrieved on June 2, http://www.ijser.org/researchpaper%5CA-Survey-on-Pervasive-Computing.pdf

Goranson, H. (1999). *The agile virtual enterprise: Cases, metrics, tools*. New York: Quorum Books.

Grobauer, B., Walloschek, T., & Stocker, E. (2011, March/April). Understanding Cloud Computing Vulnerabilities. *IEEE Security and Privacy*, *9*(2), 50–57. doi:10.1109/MSP.2010.115

Gruber, T. R. (1993). A translation approach to portable ontology specifications. *Knowledge Acquisition*, *5*(2), 199–220. doi:10.1006/knac.1993.1008

Gu, H., Diao, Y., Liu, W., & Zhang, X. (2011). The Design of Smart Home Platform Based on Cloud Computing. *International Conference on Electronic & Mechanical Engineering and Information Technology*. Retrieved on June 8, http://ieeexplore.ieee.org/xpl/articleDetails.jsp?arnumber=6023915&newsearch=true&queryText=The%20Design%20of%20Smart%20Home%20Platform%20Based%20on%20Cloud%20Computing

Guha, R. (2009). Towards the Intelligent Web Systems. In *Proceedings of IEEE CS, First International Conference on Computational Intelligence, Communication Systems, and Network*.

Gu, J., Hu, J., Zhao, T., & Sun, G. (2012). A new resource scheduling strategy based on genetic algorithm in cloud computing environment. *Journal of Computers*, *7*(1), 42–52. doi:10.4304/jcp.7.1.42-52

Gunasekera, K., Hunter, J., Canto, M., & Weeks, S. (2015). *Accelerating Satellite Image Processing through Cloud Computing*. Academic Press.

Guns, R. (2013). Tracing the origins of the Semantic Web. *Journal of the American Society for Information Science and Technology*, *64*(10), 2173–2181. doi:10.1002/asi.22907

Guo, K., Pan, W., Lu, M., Zhou, X., & Ma, J. (2015). An effective and economical architecture for semantic-based heterogeneous multimedia Big Data retrieval. *Journal of Systems and Software*, *102*, 207–216. doi:10.1016/j.jss.2014.09.016

Guo-ning, G., Ting-lei, H., & Shuai, G. (2010). Genetic simulated annealing algorithm for task scheduling based on cloud computing environment. *2010 International Conference on Intelligent Computing and Integrated Systems*.

Guo, Z., & Fox, G. (2012). Improving mapreduce performance in heterogeneous network environments and resource utilization.*Proceedings of the 12th IEEE/ACM International Symposium on Cluster, Cloud and Grid Computing (Ccgrid 2012).* doi:10.1109/CCGrid.2012.12

Gupta, M., & Singh, S. (2003). Greening of the internet.*Proceedings of the 2003 conference on Applications, technologies, architectures, and protocols for computer communications.* ACM.

Hadoop. (n.d.). Retrieved from http://hadoop.apache.org/

Haider, A., Potter, R., & Nakao, A. (2009). Challenges in resource allocation in network virtualization. *20th ITC Specialist Seminar, 18,* 20.

Hameed, A., Khoshkbarforoushha, A., Ranjan, R., Jayaraman, P. P., Kolodziej, J., & Balaji, P. (2014). A survey and taxonomy on energy efficient resource allocation techniques for cloud computing systems. *Computing,* 1–24.

Han, J. S., Chung, K. Y., & Kim, G. J. (2015). Policy on literature content based on software as service. *Multimedia Tools and Applications, 74*(20), 9087–9096. doi:10.1007/s11042-013-1664-9

Hanne, F. Z. (2011). Green-it: Why developing countries should care? *International Journal of Computer Science Issues, 8*(4).

Hardy, G. (2006). New roles for board members on IT. *Governance Journal, 13*(151), 11–14.

Harnik, D., Pinkas, B., & Shulman-Peleg, A. (2010). Side channels in Cloud services: Deduplication in Cloud Storage. *IEEE Security and Privacy, 8*(6), 40–47. doi:10.1109/MSP.2010.187

Hashem, I. A. T., Yaqoob, I., Anuar, N. B., Mokhtar, S., Gani, A., & Khan, S. U. (2015). The rise of "Big Data" on cloud computing: Review and open research issues. *Information Systems, 47,* 98–115. doi:10.1016/j.is.2014.07.006

Hashizume, K., Yoshioka, N., & Fernandez, E. B. (2013). Three misuse patterns for Cloud Computing. In D. G. Rosado, D. Mellado, E. Fernandez-Medina, & M. Piattini (Eds.), *Security engineering for Cloud Computing: approaches and Tools* (pp. 36–53). IGI Global. doi:10.4018/978-1-4666-2125-1.ch003

Hassan, M. A. H., & Bamha, M. (2008). *Parallel processing of group-by join queries on shared nothing machines. Springer-Verlag* .

Hassan, M. M., Song, B., & Huh, E.-N. (2011). Game-based distributed resource allocation in horizontal dynamic cloud federation platform. In *Algorithms and Architectures for Parallel Processing* (pp. 194–205). Springer. doi:10.1007/978-3-642-24650-0_17

HBR (Harvard Business Review). (2011). *Harvard Business Review on Aligning Technology with Strategy.* Boston: Harvard Business School Publishing.

Heart, T. (2010). Who is out there?: Exploring the effects of trust and perceived risk on SaaS adoption intentions. *ACM SIGMIS Database, 41*(3), 49–68. doi:10.1145/1851175.1851179

Hefner, K. (2012). *Search cloud storage, community cloud.* Retrieved from http://searchcloudstorage.techtarget.com/definition/community-cloud

He, J., Zhang-Shen, R., Li, Y., Lee, C.-Y., Rexford, J., & Chiang, M. (2008). Davinci: Dynamically adaptive virtual networks for a customized internet.*Proceedings of the 2008 ACM CONEXT Conference,* (p. 15). doi:10.1145/1544012.1544027

He, Q., Wang, H., Zhuang, F., Shang, T., & Shi, Z. (2015). Parallel sampling from Big Data with uncertainty distribution. *Fuzzy Sets and Systems, 258*, 117–133. doi:10.1016/j.fss.2014.01.016

Hermann, D. S. (2003). *A Practical Guide to Security Engineering & Information Assurance*. Auerbach Publications, CRC Press.

Hermenier, F., Lorca, X., Menaud, J.-M., Muller, G., & Lawall, J. (2009). Entropy: a consolidation manager for clusters. In *Proceedings of the 2009 ACM SIGPLAN/SIGOPS international conference on Virtual execution environments*. doi:10.1145/1508293.1508300

Hilbert, M. (2016). Big Data for development: A review of promises and challenges. *Development Policy Review, 34*(1), 135–174. doi:10.1111/dpr.12142

Hillson, D. (2008). Why risk includes opportunity. *The Risk Register Journal of PMI's Risk Management Special Interest Group, 10*(4), 1–3.

Hitzler, P., Krotzsch, M., & Rudolph, S. (2011). *Foundations of Semantic Web technologies*. Boca Raton, FL: Chapman & Hall/CRC.

Hoerl, R. W., Snee, R. D., & de Veaux, R. D. (2014). Applying statistical thinking to "Big Data" problems. *Wiley Interdisciplinary Reviews: Computational Statistics, 6*(4), 222–232. doi:10.1002/wics.1306

Hoseiny Farahabady, M., Dehghani Samani, H. R., Leslie, L., Lee, Y. C., & Zomaya, A. (2013). Handling Uncertainty: Pareto-Efficient BoT Scheduling on Hybrid Clouds. *Parallel Processing (ICPP), 2013 42nd International Conference on*.

Hotz, H., (2006). *A short introduction to game theory*. Academic Press.

Houidi, I., Louati, W., Zeghlache, D., & Baucke, S. (2009). Virtual resource description and clustering for virtual network discovery.*Proceedings of ICC*. doi:10.1109/ICCW.2009.5207979

Hsu, C.-H., Slagter, K. D., Chen, S.-C., & Chung, Y.-C. (2014). Optimizing energy consumption with task consolidation in clouds. *Information Sciences, 258*, 452–462. doi:10.1016/j.ins.2012.10.041

Hsu, C.-H., Slagter, K. D., & Chung, Y.-C. (2015). Locality and loading aware virtual machine mapping techniques for optimizing communications in MapReduce applications. *Future Generation Computer Systems, 53*, 43–54. doi:10.1016/j.future.2015.04.006

Hsu, H.-M., & Chen, C.-T. (1996). Aggregation of Fuzzy Opinions Under Group Decision Making. *Fuzzy Sets and Systems, 79*(3), 279–285. doi:10.1016/0165-0114(95)00185-9

Hu, L., Jin, H., Liao, X., Xiong, X., & Liu, H. (2008). Magnet: A novel scheduling policy for power reduction in cluster with virtual machines. *Cluster Computing, 2008 IEEE International Conference on*, (pp. 13-22).

Huang, J., Wu, and K., Moh, M. (2014). Dynamic virtual machine migration algorithms using enhanced energy consumption model for green cloud data centers. *IEEE International Conference on High Performance Computing & Simulation (HPCS)*. doi:10.1109/HPCSim.2014.6903785

Huang, Q., Gao, F., Wang, R., & Qi, Z. (2011). Power consumption of virtual machine live migration in clouds.*IEEE Third International Conference on Communications and Mobile Computing (CMC)*. doi:10.1109/CMC.2011.62

Huhns, M. N. (2002). Agents as Web services. *IEEE Internet Computing, 6*(4), 93–95. doi:10.1109/MIC.2002.1020332

Hwang, K., Dongarra, J., & Fox, G. C. (2013). *Distributed and cloud computing: from parallel processing to the internet of things*. Morgan Kaufmann.

Hyser, C., Mckee, B., Gardner, R., and Watson, B. J., (2008). *Autonomic virtual machine placement in the data center.* Academic Press.

Ibrahim, S., Jin, H., Lu, L., Wu, S., He, B., & Qi, L. (2010). Leen: Locality/fairness-aware key partitioning for mapreduce in the cloud. *Second IEEE International Conference on Cloud Computing Technology and Science (CloudCom).*

Isard, M., Budiu, M., Yuan, Y., Birrell, A., & Fetterly, D. (2007). Dryad: Distributed data-parallel programs from sequential building blocks. *Operating Systems Review, 41*(3), 59–72. doi:10.1145/1272998.1273005

ISO. (2005). *27001: Information Security Management – Specification with Guidance for Use.* London: ISO.

ISO-International Organization for Standardization. (2009). *ISO GUIDE 73:2009.* Geneva, Switzerland: International Organization for Standardization.

ITU-T. (2005). *International Telecommunications Union (ITU) - Telecoms Standards Recommendation X.805.* Geneva: ITU.

ITU-T. (2006). Security in Telecommunications and Information Technology: An Overview of Issues and the Deployment of Existing ITU-T Recommendations for Secure Telecommunications. Geneva: International Telecommunications Union (ITU).

ITU-T. (2007). Cyber-security Guide for Developing Countries. Geneva: International Telecommunications Union (ITU).

Jackson, M. O., (2011). *A brief introduction to the basics of game theory.* Academic Press.

Jaeger, T., & Schiffman, J. (2010). Outlook: Cloudy with a chance of Security challenges and improvements. *IEEE Security and Privacy, 8*(1), 77–80. doi:10.1109/MSP.2010.45

Janik, M., Scherp, A., & Staab, S. (2011). The Semantic Web: Collective intelligence on the Web. *Informatik Spektrum, 345*(5), 469–483. doi:10.1007/s00287-011-0535-x

Jara, A. J., Genoud, D., & Bocchi, Y. (2015). Big Data for smart cities with KNIME a real experience in the Smart-Santander testbed. *Software: Practice & Experience, 45*(8), 1145–1160. doi:10.1002/spe.2274

Jasim, O. K., Abbas, S., El-Horbaty, E. M., & Salem, A. M. (2016). CCCE: Cryptographic cloud computing environment based on quantum computations. In Z. Ma (Ed.), *Managing Big Data in cloud computing environments* (pp. 71–99). Hershey, PA: IGI Global. doi:10.4018/978-1-4666-9834-5.ch004

Jasti, A., Shah, P., Nagaraj, R., & Pendse, R. (2010). Security in multi-tenancy cloud. In *IEEE International Carnahan Conference on Security Technology (ICCST).* IEEE Computer Society.

Javanmardi, S., Shojafar, M., Shariatmadari, S., Abawajy, J. H., & Singhal, M. (2014). PGSW-OS: A novel approach for resource management in a Semantic Web operating system based on a P2P grid architecture. *The Journal of Supercomputing, 69*(2), 955–975. doi:10.1007/s11227-014-1221-y

Jeong, B. K., & Stylianou, A. C. (2010). Market reaction to application service provider (ASP) adoption: An empirical investigation. *Information & Management, 47*(3), 176–187. doi:10.1016/j.im.2010.01.007

Jin, J., Luo, J., Song, A., Dong, F., & Xiong, R. (2011). BAR: an efficient data locality driven task scheduling algorithm for cloud computing. *Proceedings of the 11th IEEE/ACM International Symposium on Cluster, Cloud and Grid Computing.* doi:10.1109/CCGrid.2011.55

JISC Legal Information. (2014). *User Guide: Cloud Computing Contracts, SLAs and Terms & Conditions of Use.* Retrieved February 5, 2016, from http://www.webarchive.org.uk/wayback/archive/20150703224546/http://www.jisclegal.ac.uk/ManageContent/ViewDetail/ID/2141/User-Guide-Cloud-Computing-Contracts-SLAs-and-Terms-Conditions-of-Use-31082011.aspx

Jones, M. T. (2010). *Anatomy of an open source cloud.* Retrieved from http://www.ibm.com/developerworks/opensource/library/oscloud-anatomy

Joseph, C. T., Chandrasekaran, K., & Cyriac, R. (2015). A novel family genetic approach for virtual machine allocation. *Procedia Computer Science, 46,* 558–565. doi:10.1016/j.procs.2015.02.090

Ju, J., Wang, Y., Fu, J., Wu, J., & Lin, Z. (2010). Research on Key Technology in SaaS. In *International Conference on Intelligent Computing and Cognitive Informatics (ICICCI).* Hangzhou, China: IEEE Computer Society.

Jung, G., Joshi, K. R., Hiltunen, M. A., Schlichting, R. D., & Pu, C. (2008). Generating adaptation policies for multi-tier applications in consolidated server environments.*IEEE International Conference on Autonomic Computing (ICAC).* doi:10.1109/ICAC.2008.21

Jung, G., Joshi, K. R., Hiltunen, M. A., Schlichting, R. D., & Pu, C. (2009). A cost-sensitive adaptation engine for server consolidation of multitier applications.*Proceedings of the 10th ACM/IFIP/USENIX International Conference on Middleware.* Springer. doi:10.1007/978-3-642-10445-9_9

Kalra, M., & Singh, S. (2015). A review of metaheuristic scheduling techniques in cloud computing. *Egyptian Informatics Journal, 16*(3), 275–295. doi:10.1016/j.eij.2015.07.001

Kamburugamuve, S., Christiansen, L., & Fox, G. (2015). A framework for real time processing of sensor data in the cloud. *Journal of Sensors, 2015,* 1–11. doi:10.1155/2015/468047

Kamei, K., Nishio, S., Hagita, N., & Sato, M. (2012). Cloud networked robotics. *IEEE Network Magazine, 26*(3), 28–34. Retrieved on June 8, http://ieeexplore.ieee.org/xpl/articleDetails.jsp?arnumber=6201213&newsearch=true&queryText=Cloud%20networked%20robotics

Kant, A., Sharma, A., Agarwal, S., & Chandra, S. (2010). An ACO approach to job scheduling in grid environment. In Swarm, Evolutionary, and Memetic Computing (pp. 286-295). Springer. doi:10.1007/978-3-642-17563-3_35

Kao, S. J., & Hsu, I. C. (2007). Semantic Web approach to smart link generation for Web navigations. *Software: Practice & Experience, 37*(8), 857–879. doi:10.1002/spe.789

Kao, Y.-C., & Chen, Y.-S. (2016). Data-locality-aware mapreduce real-time scheduling framework. *Journal of Systems and Software, 112,* 65–77. doi:10.1016/j.jss.2015.11.001

Kaplan, R., & Mikes, A. (2012). Managing Risks: A new framework. *Harvard Business Review, 90*(6), 48–63.

Karve, A., Kimbrel, T., Pacifici, G., Spreitzer, M., Steinder, M., Sviridenko, M., & Tantawi, A. (2006). Dynamic Placement for Clustered Web Applications. In *15th International Conference on World Wide Web.* ACM. doi:10.1145/1135777.1135865

Kasemsap, K. (2014). The role of social media in the knowledge-based organizations. In I. Lee (Ed.), *Integrating social media into business practice, applications, management, and models* (pp. 254–275). Hershey, PA: IGI Global. doi:10.4018/978-1-4666-6182-0.ch013

Kasemsap, K. (2015a). The role of cloud computing adoption in global business. In V. Chang, R. Walters, & G. Wills (Eds.), *Delivery and adoption of cloud computing services in contemporary organizations* (pp. 26–55). Hershey, PA: IGI Global. doi:10.4018/978-1-4666-8210-8.ch002

Kasemsap, K. (2015b). The role of cloud computing in global supply chain. In N. Rao (Ed.), *Enterprise management strategies in the era of cloud computing* (pp. 192–219). Hershey, PA: IGI Global. doi:10.4018/978-1-4666-8339-6.ch009

Kasemsap, K. (2015c). Implementing enterprise resource planning. In M. Khosrow-Pour (Ed.), *Encyclopedia of information science and technology* (3rd ed., pp. 798–807). Hershey, PA: IGI Global. doi:10.4018/978-1-4666-5888-2.ch076

Kasemsap, K. (2015d). The role of customer relationship management in the global business environments. In T. Tsiakis (Ed.), *Trends and innovations in marketing information systems* (pp. 130–156). Hershey, PA: IGI Global. doi:10.4018/978-1-4666-8459-1.ch007

Kasemsap, K. (2015e). The role of data mining for business intelligence in knowledge management. In A. Azevedo & M. Santos (Eds.), *Integration of data mining in business intelligence systems* (pp. 12–33). Hershey, PA: IGI Global. doi:10.4018/978-1-4666-6477-7.ch002

Kasemsap, K. (2015f). The role of business analytics in performance management. In M. Tavana & K. Puranam (Eds.), *Handbook of research on organizational transformations through big data analytics* (pp. 126–145). Hershey, PA: IGI Global. doi:10.4018/978-1-4666-7272-7.ch010

Kasemsap, K. (2016a). Utilizing social media in modern business. In I. Lee (Ed.), *Encyclopedia of e-commerce development, implementation, and management* (pp. 2171–2182). Hershey, PA: IGI Global. doi:10.4018/978-1-4666-9787-4.ch156

Kasemsap, K. (2016b). The fundamentals of business intelligence. *International Journal of Organizational and Collective Intelligence, 6*(2), 12–25. doi:10.4018/IJOCI.2016040102

Kasemsap, K. (2016c). The roles of business process modeling and business process reengineering in e-government. In J. Martins & A. Molnar (Eds.), *Handbook of research on innovations in information retrieval, analysis, and management* (pp. 401–430). Hershey, PA: IGI Global. doi:10.4018/978-1-4666-8833-9.ch015

Kashihara, S., Tsukamoto, K., & Oie, Y. (2007). Service-Oriented Mobility Management Architecture For Seamless Handover in Ubiquitous Networks. *IEEE Wireless Communications, 14*(2), 28 - 34. Retrieved on June 8, http://ieeexplore.ieee.org/xpl/articleDetails.jsp?arnumber=4198163&newsearch=true&queryText=Service-Oriented%20Mobility%20Management%20Architecture%20For%20Seamless%20Handover%20in%20Ubiquitous%20Networks

Katsaros, G., Subirats, J., Fitó, J. O., Guitart, J., Gilet, P., & Espling, D. (2013). A service framework for energy-aware monitoring and VM management in Clouds. *Future Generation Computer Systems, 29*(8), 2077–2091. doi:10.1016/j.future.2012.12.006

Katsikas, S. K. (2009). Risk Management. In J. R. Vacca (Ed.), Computer & Information Security Handbook (pp. 605-625). Morgan-Kaufmann, Inc.

Katzmarzik, A. (2011). Product differentiation for software-as-a-service providers. *Business & Information Systems Engineering, 3*(1), 19–31. doi:10.1007/s12599-010-0142-4

Kaur, K., Chhabra, A., & Singh, G. (2010). Heuristics based genetic algorithm for scheduling static tasks in homogeneous parallel system. *International Journal of Computer Science and Security, 4*(2), 183.

Keene, C. (2009). *The Keene View on Cloud Computing.* Available: http://www.keeneview.com/2009/03/what-is-platform-as-service-paas.html

Keen, J., Calinescu, R., Paige, R., & Rooksby, J. (2013). Big Data + politics = open data: The case of health care data in England. *Policy & Internet, 5*(2), 228–243. doi:10.1002/1944-2866.POI330

Kenndy, J., & Eberhart, R. (1995). Particle swarm optimization. *Proceedings of IEEE International Conference on Neural Networks.* doi:10.1109/ICNN.1995.488968

Kessaci, Y., Melab, N., & Talbi, E.-G. (2011). A pareto-based GA for scheduling HPC applications on distributed cloud infrastructures. *High Performance Computing and Simulation (HPCS), 2011 International Conference on,* (pp. 456-462).

Khajemohammadi, H., Fanian, A., & Gulliver, T. A. (2014). Efficient Workflow Scheduling for Grid Computing Using a Levelled Multi-objective Genetic Algorithm. *Journal of Grid Computing, 12*(4), 637–663. doi:10.1007/s10723-014-9306-7

Khalifa, A., & Eltoweissy, M. (2012). A Global Resource Positioning System for Ubiquitous Clouds. *International Conference on Innovations in Information Technology* (IIT). Retrieved on June 2, http://ieeexplore.ieee.org/xpl/articleDetails. jsp?arnumber=6207720&queryText=A%20Global%20Resource%20Positioning%20System%20for%20Ubiquitous%20 Clouds&newsearch=true

Khan, A., Zugenmaier, A., Jurca, D., & Kellerer, W. (2012). Network virtualization: A hypervisor for the Internet? *Communications Magazine, IEEE, 50*(1), 136–143. doi:10.1109/MCOM.2012.6122544

Khan, W. A., Hussain, M., Latif, K., Afzal, M., Ahmad, F., & Lee, S. (2013). Process interoperability in healthcare systems with dynamic Semantic Web services. *Computing, 95*(9), 837–862. doi:10.1007/s00607-012-0239-3

Khattak, A. M., Pervez, Z., Ho, K. K., Lee, S., & Young-Koo Lee, Y. K. (2010). Intelligent Manipulation of Human Activities using Cloud Computing for u-Life Care. *10th IEEE/IPSJ Annual International Symposium on Applications and the Internet.* Retrieved on June 10, http://ieeexplore.ieee.org/xpl/articleDetails.jsp?arnumber=5598159&newsearch =true&queryText=Intelligent%20Manipulation%20of%20Human%20Activities%20using%20Cloud%20Computing%20 for%20u-Life%20Care

Khodadadi, F., Calheiros, R. N., & Buyya, R. (2015). A data-centric framework for development and deployment of Internet of Things applications in clouds. *Tenth IEEE International Conference on, Intelligent Sensors, Sensor Networks and Information Processing (ISSNIP).* doi:10.1109/ISSNIP.2015.7106952

Kim, H. K., Kim, J. K., & Ryu, Y. U. (2009). Personalized Recommendation over a Customer Network for Ubiquitous Shopping. *IEEE Transactions on Services Computing, 2*(2), 140-151. Retrieved on June 8, http://ieeexplore.ieee.org/xpl/ articleDetails.jsp?arnumber=4815203&newsearch=true&queryText=Personalized%20Recommendation%20over%20 a%20Customer%20Network%20for%20Ubiquitous%20Shopping

Kimble, C., & Milolidakis, G. (2015). Big Data and business intelligence: Debunking the myths. *Global Business and Organizational Excellence, 35*(1), 23–34. doi:10.1002/joe.21642

Kim, D. J., Ferrin, D. L., & Rao, H. R. (2008). A trust-based consumer decision-making model in electronic commerce: The role of trust, perceived risk, and their antecedents. *Decision Support Systems, 44*(2), 544–564. doi:10.1016/j. dss.2007.07.001

Kim, G., & Kim, E. (2008). An exploratory study of factors influencing ASP (application service provider) success. *Journal of Computer Information Systems, 48*(3), 118–124.

Kirci, P., Chaouchi, H., & Laouiti, A. (2014). Cluster-Based Protocol Structures in WSNs. *21st International Conference on Systems, Signals and Image Processing* (IWSSIP 2014). Retrieved on June1, http://ieeexplore.ieee.org/xpl/articleDetails.jsp?arnumber=6837661&newsearch=true&queryText=Cluster-Based%20Protocol%20Structures%20in%20WSNs

Kirci, P., Chaouchi, H., & Laouiti, A. (2014). Wireless Sensor Networks and Efficient Localisation. *2014 International Conference on Future Internet of Things and Cloud.* Retrieved on June 4, http://ieeexplore.ieee.org/xpl/articleDetails.jsp?ar number=6984181&newsearch=true&queryText=Wireless%20Sensor%20Networks%20and%20Efficient%20Localisation

Kirci, P., Kurt, G., & Omercikoglu, M. A. Y. (2014). Remote Monitoring of Heart Pulses with Smart Phone. *CIE44&IMSS14 Proceedings.* Retrieved on June 5, https://www.researchgate.net/publication/289263211_Remote_monitoring_of_heart_ pulses_with_smart_phone

Kitchin, R. (2014). *The data revolution: Big Data, open data, data infrastructures and their consequences.* London, UK: Sage Publications. doi:10.4135/9781473909472

Kliem, K., Koner, M., Weißenborn, S., & Byfield, M. (2015). The Device Driver Engine - Cloud enabled Ubiquitous Device Integration. *IEEE Tenth International Conference on Intelligent Sensors, Sensor Networks and Information Processing* (ISSNIP). Retrieved on June 8, http://ieeexplore.ieee.org/xpl/login.jsp?tp=&arnumber=7106921&url=http%3A%2F%2Fieeexplore.ieee.org%2Fxpls%2Fabs_all.jsp%3Farnumber%3D7106921

Kong, Z., Xu, C.-Z., & Guo, M. (2011). Mechanism design for stochastic virtual resource allocation in non-cooperative cloud systems. In *2011 IEEE International Conference on Cloud Computing (CLOUD).* doi:10.1109/CLOUD.2011.82

Ko, R., & Lee, S. S. (2013). Cloud Computing Vulnerability Incidents: A Statistical Overview. *IEEE Spectrum, 49*(12).

Kortchinsky, K. (2009). *CloudBurst: A VMware Guest to Host Escape Story.* Las Vegas, NV: Immunity, Inc.

Koufi, V., Malamateniou, F., & Vassilacopoulos, G. (2010). Ubiquitous Access to Cloud Emergency Medical Services. *Proceedings of the 10th IEEE International Conference on Information Technology and Applications in Biomedicine.* Retrieved on June 10, http://ieeexplore.ieee.org/xpl/articleDetails.jsp?arnumber=5687702&newsearch=true&queryText=Ubiquitous%20Access%20to%20Cloud%20Emergency%20Medical%20Services

Kounavis, M. E., Campbell, A. T., Chou, S., Modoux, F., Vicente, J., & Zhuang, H. (2001). The genesis kernel: A programming system for spawning network architectures. Selected Areas in Communications. *IEEE Journal on, 19*(3), 511–526.

Kousalya, K., & Balasubramanie, P. (2009). To Improve Ant Algorithm's Grid Scheduling Using Local Search. *International Journal of Intelligent Information Technology Application, 2*(2).

KPMG. (2010). *From hype to future: KPMG's 2010 Cloud computing survey.* Available: http://www.techrepublic.com/whitepapers/from-hype-to-futurekpmgs-2010-cloud-computing survey/2384291

Kramer, F. (2012). *Musings on the Cloud - A Customer Oriented Comcept Formation to Cloud computing with respect to SME.* EMCIS2012 European Mediterranean & Middle Eastern Conference on Information Systems, Munich, Germany.

Kulkarni, R. V., Förster, A., & Venayagamoorthy, G. K. (2011). Computational Intelligence in Wireless Sensor Networks: A Survey. *IEEE Communications Surveys & Tutorials, 13*(1), 68 - 96. Retrieved on June1, http://ieeexplore.ieee.org/xpl/articleDetails.jsp?arnumber=5473889&newsearch=true&queryText=Computational%20Intelligence%20in%20Wireless%20Sensor%20Networks:%20A%20Survey

Kumar, D., & Sahoo, B. (2014). *Energy efficient heuristic resource allocation for cloud computing.* Academic Press.

Kumar, S., Talwar, V., Kumar, V., Ranganathan, P., & Schwan, K. (2009). vManage: loosely coupled platform and virtualization management in data centers.*Proceedings of the 6th international conference on Autonomic computing.* ACM. doi:10.1145/1555228.1555262

Kune, R., Konugurthi, P. K., Agarwal, A., Chillarige, R. R., & Buyya, R. (2016). The anatomy of Big Data computing. *Software: Practice & Experience, 46*(1), 79–105. doi:10.1002/spe.2374

Kunzler, R., Muller-Quade, J., & Raub, D. (2009). *Secure computability of functions in the IT setting with dishonest majority and applications to long-term security.* In TCC. doi:10.1007/978-3-642-00457-5_15

Kusic, D., Kephart, J. O., Hanson, J. E., Kandasamy, N., & Jiang, G. (2009). Power and performance management of virtualized computing environments via lookahead control. *Cluster Computing, 12*(1), 1–15. doi:10.1007/s10586-008-0070-y

Kwong, K. H., Sasloglou, K., Goh, H. G., Wu, T. T., Stephen, B., Gilroy, M., . . . Andonovic, I. (2009). Adaptation of wireless sensor network for farming industries. *Sixth International Conference on Networked Sensing Systems* (INSS). Retrieved on June 3, http://ieeexplore.ieee.org/xpl/login.jsp?tp=&arnumber=5409951&url=http%3A%2F%2Fieeexplo re.ieee.org%2Fxpls%2Fabs_all.jsp%3Farnumber%3D5409951

Kwon, O., Lee, N., & Shin, B. (2014). Data quality management, data usage experience and acquisition intention of Big Data analytics. *International Journal of Information Management, 34*(3), 387–394. doi:10.1016/j.ijinfomgt.2014.02.002

Lai, C.-F., Chang, J.-H., Hu, C.-C., Huang, Y.-M., & Chao, H.-C. (2011). CPRS: A cloud-based program recommendation system for digital TV platforms. *Future Generation Computer Systems, 27*(6), 823–835. doi:10.1016/j.future.2010.10.002

Lai, K.-L. (1992). *Generalized Uncertainty in Structural Reliability Assessment.* College Park, MD: University of Maryland.

Laplante, P., Zhang, J., & Voas, J. (2008). What's in a name? Distinguishing between SaaS and SOA. *IT Professional, 10*(3), 46–50. doi:10.1109/MITP.2008.60

Lauro, R. D., Lucarelli, F., & Montella, R. (2012). SIaaS - Sensing Instrument as a Service Using cloud computing to turn physical instrument into ubiquitous service. *10th IEEE International Symposium on Parallel and Distributed Processing with Applications.* Retrieved on June 8, http://ieeexplore.ieee.org/xpl/articleDetails.jsp?arnumber=6280396 &newsearch=true&queryText=SIaaS%20-%20Sensing%20Instrument%20as%20a%20Service%20Using%20cloud%20 computing%20to%20turn%20physical%20instrument%20into%20ubiquitous%20service

Lean Agile Methodologies Accentuate Benefits of Cloud Computing. (n.d.). Retrieved from www.thetechnologygurus. com/.../LACC_white_paper_ed_v5.320180428

Lee, C., Suzuki, J., Vasilakos, A., Yamamoto, Y., & Oba, K. (2010). An evolutionary game theoretic approach to adaptive and stable application deployment in clouds. In *Proceedings of the 2nd workshop on Bio-inspired algorithms for distributed systems.* doi:10.1145/1809018.1809025

Lee, H., Kim, J., & Kim, J. (2007). Determinants of success for application service provider: An empirical test in small businesses. *International Journal of Human-Computer Studies, 65*(9), 796–815. doi:10.1016/j.ijhcs.2007.04.004

Lee, S., Park, S. B., & Lim, G. G. (2013). Using balanced scorecards for the evaluation of "software-as-a-service". *Information & Management, 50*(7), 553–561. doi:10.1016/j.im.2013.07.006

Lee, Y. C., & Zomaya, A. Y. (2012). Energy efficient utilization of resources in cloud computing systems. *The Journal of Supercomputing, 60*(2), 268–280. doi:10.1007/s11227-010-0421-3

Li, J., & Chinneck, J. (2009). Performance Model Driven QoS Guarantees and Optimization in Cloud. *Software Engineering Challenges of Cloud Computing.* doi:10.1109/CLOUD.2009.5071528

Li, J., Lu, Q., Zhu, L., Bass, L., Xu, X., Sakr, S., . . . Liu, A. (2013). Improving Availability of Cloud-Based Applications through Deployment Choices. *IEEE 6th International Conference on Cloud Computing.*

Liang, X., Zhang, K., Shen, X., & Lin, X. (2014). Security And Privacy in Mobile Social Networks: Challenges And Solutions. *IEEE Wireless Communications, 12*(1), 33–41. doi:10.1109/MWC.2014.6757895

Liao, X., Jin, H., & Liu, H. (2012). Towards a green cluster through dynamic remapping of virtual machines. *Future Generation Computer Systems, 28*(2), 469–477. doi:10.1016/j.future.2011.04.013

Li, C., & Li, L. (2012). Optimal resource provisioning for cloud computing environment. *The Journal of Supercomputing, 62*(2), 989–1022. doi:10.1007/s11227-012-0775-9

Li, C., & Li, L. (2013). Efficient resource allocation for optimizing objectives of cloud users, IaaS provider and SaaS provider in cloud environment. *The Journal of Supercomputing, 65*(2), 866–885. doi:10.1007/s11227-013-0869-z

Li, K., Xu, G., Zhao, G., Dong, Y., & Wang, D. (2011). Cloud task scheduling based on load balancing ant colony optimization.*Chinagrid Conference (ChinaGrid), 2011 Sixth Annual,* (pp. 3-9). doi:10.1109/ChinaGrid.2011.17

Linkedin-samza. (n.d.). Retrieved from http://www.infoq.com/articles/linkedin-samza

Lin, Y.-K., & Chong, C. S. (2015). Fast GA-based project scheduling for computing resources allocation in a cloud manufacturing system. *Journal of Intelligent Manufacturing,* 1–13.

Li, S. H., Huang, S. M., Yen, D. C., & Sun, J. C. (2011). Semantic-based transaction model for Web service. *Information Systems Frontiers, 15*(2), 249–268. doi:10.1007/s10796-013-9409-x

Litoiu, M., Woodside, M., Wong, J., Ng, J., & Iszlai, G. (2010). A business driven cloud optimization architecture. *Proceedings of 2010 ACM SAC.*

Litoiu, M., Ng, J., & Iszlai, G. (2010). A Business Driven Cloud Optimization Arcitecture. In *Proceedings of 2010* (pp. 380–385). ACM SAC.

Liu, B., Chen, Y., Blasch, E., Pham, K., Shen, D., & Chen, G. (2014). A holistic cloud-enabled robotics system for real-time video tracking application. In Future Information Technology. doi:10.1007/978-3-642-40861-8_64

Liu, H., Xu, D., & Miao, H. (2011). Ant colony optimization based service flow scheduling with various QoS requirements in cloud computing. *Software and Network Engineering (SSNE), 2011 First ACIS International Symposium on,* (pp. 53-58).

Liu, Y., Wu, M., & Hou, H. (2012). The Design and Implement of Mobile Heath Management Software Base on the Android Platform. *International Symposium on Information Science and Engineering 2012.* Retrieved on June 6, http://ieeexplore.ieee.org/xpl/articleDetails.jsp?arnumber=6495353&newsearch=true&queryText=The%20Design%20and%20Implement%20of%20Mobile%20Heath%20Management%20Software%20Base%20on%20the%20Android%20Platform

Liu, H., Abraham, A., & Hassanien, A. E. (2010). Scheduling jobs on computational grids using a fuzzy particle swarm optimization algorithm. *Future Generation Computer Systems, 26*(8), 1336–1343. doi:10.1016/j.future.2009.05.022

Liu, M., Gao, Q., Shen, W., Hao, Q., & Yan, J. (2009). A semantic-augmented multi-level matching model of Web services. *Service Oriented Computing and Applications, 3*(3), 205–215. doi:10.1007/s11761-009-0045-8

Londono, J., Bestavros, A., & Teng, S. H. (2009). *Collocation games and their application to distributed resource management. Tech. Rep.* Boston University Computer Science Department.

López, V., del Río, S., Benítez, J. M., & Herrera, F. (2015). Cost-sensitive linguistic fuzzy rule based classification systems under the MapReduce framework for imbalanced Big Data. *Fuzzy Sets and Systems, 258,* 5–38. doi:10.1016/j.fss.2014.01.015

Lord CrusAd3r. (n.d.). *Problems Faced by Cloud Computing.* Retrieved from dl.packetstormsecurity.net/.../Problems-FacedbyCloudComputing.pdf

Lu, J., & Turner, J. (2006). *Efficient mapping of virtual networks onto a shared substrate.* Academic Press.

Luiz, F. B. (2011). HCOC: A Cost Optimization Algorithm for Workflow Scheduling in Hybrid Clouds. *Journal of Internet Services and Applications, 2*(3).

Luo, L., Wu, W., Di, D., Zhang, F., Yan, Y., & Mao, Y. (2012). A resource scheduling algorithm of cloud computing based on energy efficient optimization methods.*Green Computing Conference (IGCC), 2012 International*, (pp. 1-6).

Luo, L., Wu, W., Tsai, W., Di, D., & Zhang, F. (2013). Simulation of power consumption of cloud data centers. *Simulation Modelling Practice and Theory, 39*, 152–171. doi:10.1016/j.simpat.2013.08.004

Lu, Z., Wen, X., & Sun, Y. (2012). A game theory based resource sharing scheme in cloud computing environment. In *2012 IEEE World Congress on Information and Communication Technologies (WICT)*. doi:10.1109/WICT.2012.6409239

Ma, M., Yang, Y., & Zhao, M. (2013). Tour Planning for Mobile Data-Gathering Mechanisms in Wireless Sensor Networks. *IEEE Transactions on Vehicular Technology, 62*(4), 1472 - 1483. Retrieved on June 2, http://ieeexplore.ieee.org/xpl/articleDetails.jsp?arnumber=6359890&queryText=Tour%20Planning%20for%20Mobile%20DataGathering%20Mechanisms%20in%20Wireless%20Sensor%20Networks&newsearch=true

Ma, D., & Seidmann, A. (2008). The pricing strategy analysis for the "software-as-a- service" business model. In J. Altmann, D. Neumann, & T. Fahringer (Eds.), *Grid economics and business models* (pp. 103–112). Berlin, Germany: Springer–Verlag. doi:10.1007/978-3-540-85485-2_8

Malewicz, A., Gregorz, H., Matthew, J. C., Bik Aart, H., Llan, L., Naty, & Grzegorz, C. (2010). Pregel: A system for large-scale graph processing. In *Proc. of the International Conference on Management of Data*. doi:10.1145/1807167.1807184

Mall, R. (2014). *Fundamentals of Software Engineering* (4th ed.). Prentice Hall.

Mao, Z., Yang, J., Shang, Y., Liu, C., & Chen, J. (2013). A game theory of cloud service deployment. In *2013 IEEE Ninth World Congress on Services*. doi:10.1109/SERVICES.2013.35

MapReduce. (n.d.). Retrieved from https://www.quora.com/How-does-Facebook-Twitter-and-Google-use-Map-Reduce-paradigm

Marinescu, D. (2014). *Cloud Computing: Cloud Vulnerabilities*. Retrieved July 6, 2014, from TechNet Magazine: www.technet.microsoft.com/en-us/magazine/dn271884.aspx

Marinescu, D. C. (2012). Cloud Computing and Computer Clouds Department of Electrical Engineering & Computer Science. Orlando, FL: University of Central Florida. Retrieved from https://www.cs.ucf.edu/~dcm/Teaching/CDA5532-CloudComputing/LectureNotes.pdf

Marks, N. (2015). *The myth of IT risk*. Retrieved September 09, 2015, from https://normanmarks.wordpress.com/2015/08/28/the-myth-of-it-risk/

Marquezan, C. C., Nobre, J. C., Granville, L. Z., Nunzi, G., Dudkowski, D., & Brunner, M. (2009). Distributed real-location scheme for virtual network resources. *Communications, 2009. ICC'09. IEEE International Conference on*, (pp. 1-5). doi:10.1109/ICC.2009.5198934

Marrocco, G. (2010). Pervasive Electromagnetics: Sensing Paradigms By Passive Rfid Technology. *IEEE Wireless Communications, 17*(6), 10-17. Retrieved on June 6, http://ieeexplore.ieee.org/xpl/articleDetails.jsp?arnumber=5675773&newsearch=true&queryText=Pervas%C4%B1ve%20Electromagnetics:%20Sensing%20Paradigms%20By%20Passive%20Rf%C4%B1d%20Technology

Marshall, P., Keahey, K., & Freeman, T. (2010). Elastic Site Using Clouds to Elastically Extend Site Resources. In *Proceedings of the 10th IEEE/ACM International Symposium on Cluster, Cloud and Grid Computing (CCGrid 2010)*. doi:10.1109/CCGRID.2010.80

Marston, S., Li, Z., Bandyopadhyay, S., Zhang, J., & Ghalsasi, A. (2011). Cloud Computing: The Business Perspective. *Decision Support Systems, 51*(1), 176–189. doi:10.1016/j.dss.2010.12.006

Martin, D., Völker, L., & Zitterbart, M. (2011). A flexible framework for Future Internet design, assessment, and operation. *Computer Networks, 55*(4), 910–918. doi:10.1016/j.comnet.2010.12.015

Maruthanayagam, D., & Umarani, R. (2010). Enhanced ant colony algorithm for grid scheduling. *International Journal of Computer Technology and Applications, 1*(1), 43–53.

Marx, V. (2013). The big challenges of Big Data. *Nature, 498*(7453), 255–260. doi:10.1038/498255a

Mastorakis, G., Mavromoustakis, C., & Pallis, E. (2015). *Resource Management of Mobile Cloud Computing Networks and Environments.* Hershey, PA: IGI Global. doi:10.4018/978-1-4666-8225-2

Mayer-Schönberger, V., & Cukier, K. (2013). *Big Data: A revolution that will transform: How we live, work, and think.* New York, NY: Houghton Mifflin Harcourt.

McCorkle, D. S., & Bryden, K. M. (2007). Using the Semantic Web technologies in virtual engineering tools to create extensible interfaces. *Virtual Reality (Waltham Cross), 11*(4), 253–260. doi:10.1007/s10055-007-0077-3

McEachem, C. (2001). Technology Risks: Don't Panic - Financial Services Firms Seem to Have Cyber-Risk Under Control. *Wall Street Technology, 38.*

McKinsey & Co. (2012). *Perspectives of Digital Business.* McKinsey Center for Business Technology.

McNeely, C. L., & Hahm, J. O. (2014). The Big (Data) bang: Policy, prospects, and challenges. *Review of Policy Research, 31*(4), 304–310. doi:10.1111/ropr.12082

Medjahed, B., & Bouguettaya, A. (2005). A dynamic foundational architecture for Semantic Web services. *Distributed and Parallel Databases, 17*(2), 179–206. doi:10.1007/s10619-004-0190-1

Mell, P. & Grance, T. (2011). *The NIST definition of cloud computing* (draft). U.S. National Institute of Standards and Technology special publication, 800.

Mell, P., & Grace, T. (2011). The NIST Definition of Cloud Computing. NIST Special Publication, 800-145. Gaithersburg, MD: National Institute of Standards and Technology (NIST).

Mell, P., & Grance, T. (2009). *A NIST definition of cloud computing.* National Institute of Standards and Technology. NIST SP 800–145. Retrieved from: http://www.nist.gov/itl/cloud/upload/cloud-def-v15.pdf

Mell, P., & Grance, T. (2011). *The NIST definition of cloud computing.* Academic Press.

Mell, P., & Grance, T. (2011). *The NIST Definition of Cloud Computing.* National Institute of Standards and Technology (NIST). Retrieved June 2014, from www.csrc.nist.gov/publications/nistpubs/800-145/SP800-145.pdf

Mell, P., & Grance, T. (2011). *The NIST definition of cloud computing.* NIST.

Menken, I., & Blokdijk, G. (2008). *Virtualization: The complete cornerstone guide to virtualization best practices.* Brisbane, Australia: Emereo Pty Ltd.

Metheny, M. (2013). *Federal Cloud Computing: The Definitive Guide for Cloud Service Providers.* Waltham, MA: Elsevier.

Miceli, C. (2009). Programming Abstractions for Data Intensive Computing on Clouds and Grids. *9th IEEE/ACM International Symposium on Cluster Computing and the Grid.* doi:10.1109/CCGRID.2009.87

Microsoft. (2005). *Security Guide for Small Businesses.* Microsoft Corporation. Retrieved from www.asbdc-us.org

Milchtaich, I. (1996). Congestion games with player-specific payoff functions. *Games and Economic Behavior, 13*(1), 111–124. doi:10.1006/game.1996.0027

Minas, L., & Ellison, B. (2009). Energy Efficiency for Inf ormation Technology: How to Reduce Power Consumption in Servers and Data Centres (Computer System Design). Energy Efficiency for Information Technology: How to Reduce Power Consumption in Servers and Data Centres (Computer System Design). Intel Press.

Minelli, M., Chambers, M., & Dhiraj, A. (2013). *Big Data, big analytics: Emerging business intelligence and analytic trends for today's businesses.* Hoboken, NJ: John Wiley & Sons. doi:10.1002/9781118562260

Mishra, S. K., Deswal, R., Sahoo, S., & Sahoo, B. (2015). *Improving Energy Consumption in Cloud.* Academic Press.

Mital, M., Pani, A., & Ramesh, R. (2014). Determinants of choice of Semantic Web based software as a service: An integrative framework in the context of e-procurement and ERP. *Computers in Industry, 65*(5), 821–827. doi:10.1016/j.compind.2014.03.002

Mkoba, E. S., & Saif, M. A. (2014). A survey on energy efficient with task consolidation in the virtualized cloud computing environment. *International Journal of Research in Engineering and Technology, 3.*

Mocanu, E. M., Florea, M., & Andreica, M. I. (2012). Cloud computing task scheduling based on genetic algorithms. *Systems Conference (SysCon), 2012 IEEE International,* (pp. 1-6).

Moise, D., & Carpen-Amarie, A. (2012). *Mapreduce applications in the cloud: A cost evaluation of computation and storage.* Springer.

Mora Mora, H., Gil, D., Colom Lopez, J. F., & Signes Pont, M. T. (2015). *Flexible Framework for Real-Time Embedded Systems Based on Mobile Cloud Computing Paradigm.* Mobile Information Systems.

Moretti, C., Bulosan, J., Thain, D., & Flynn, P. J. (2008). All-pairs: an abstraction for data-intensive cloud computing. In *Proc. of the 2008 IEEE International Parallel & Distributed Processing Symposium.* doi:10.1109/IPDPS.2008.4536311

Mouratidis, H., Islam, S., Kalloniatis, C., & Gritzalis, S. (2013). A framework to support selection of cloud providers based on security and privacy requirements. *Journal of Systems and Software, 86*(9), 2276–2293. doi:10.1016/j.jss.2013.03.011

Mudigonda, J., Yalagandula, P., Mogul, J., Stiekes, B., & Pouffary, Y. (2011). NetLord: A scalable multi-tenant network architecture for virtualized datacenters. *Computer Communication Review, 41*, 62–73.

Murad, S. E. (2013). Using Semantic Services in Service-Oriented Information Systems. *IEEE Potentials Magazine., 32*(1), 36–46. doi:10.1109/MPOT.2012.2187806

Must Have Metrics for Your SaaS Business. (2012). Retrieved from https://blog.kissmetrics.com/5-metrics-for-saas

Nathuji, R., & Schwan, K. (2007). Virtualpower: Coordinated power management in virtualized enterprise systems. *Operating Systems Review, 41*(6), 265–278. doi:10.1145/1323293.1294287

Ngai, E., & Wat, F. (2005). Fuzzy Decision Support System for Risk Analysis in e-Commerce Development. *Decision Support Systems, 40*(2), 235–255. doi:10.1016/j.dss.2003.12.002

Niebert, N., El Khayat, I., Baucke, S., Keller, R., Rembarz, R., & Sachs, J. (2008). Network virtualization: A viable path towards the future internet. *Wireless Personal Communications, 45*(4), 511–520. doi:10.1007/s11277-008-9481-6

Niknam, M., & Karshenas, S. (2015). Integrating distributed sources of information for construction cost estimating using Semantic Web and Semantic Web service technologies. *Automation in Construction, 57*, 222–238. doi:10.1016/j.autcon.2015.04.003

NIST (National Institute of Standards and Technology). (2015). *Cloud computing service metrics description.* Retrieved September 09, 2015, from http://www.nist.gov/itl/cloud/upload/RATAX-CloudServiceMetricsDescription-DRAFT-20141111.pdf

NIST. (2008). *Taxonomies of Security Metrics. National Institute of Standards & Technology (NIST). doi:Elizabeth Chew.* Marianne Swanson, Kevin Stine, Nadya Bartol, Anthony Brown & Will Robinson.

Niyato, D., Zhu, K., & Wang, P. (2011). Cooperative virtual machine management for multi-organization cloud computing environment. In *Proceedings of the 5th International ICST Conference on Performance Evaluation Methodologies and Tools, ICST (Institute for Computer Sciences, Social-Informatics and Telecommunications Engineering).*

Obaidat, M. S., Denko, M., & Woungang, I. (2011). *Pervasive Computing and Networking.* John Wiley & Sons. Retrieved on June 8, http://eu.wiley.com/WileyCDA/WileyTitle/productCd-0470747722.html

Okada, H., Itoh, T., Suzuki, K., Tatsuya, T., & Tsukamoto, K. (2010). Simulation study on the wireless sensor-based monitoring system for rapid identification of avian influenza outbreaks at chicken farms. *IEEE Sensors Conference.* Retrieved on June 4, http://ieeexplore.ieee.org/xpl/articleDetails.jsp?arnumber=5690089&newsearch=true&queryText=Simulation%20study%20on%20the%20wireless%20sensorbased%20monitoring%20system%20for%20rapid%20identification%20of%20avian%20influenza%20outbreaks%20at%20chicken%20farms

Olson, D. & Peters, S. (2011). Managing Software Intellectual Assets in Cloud Computing, Part 1. *Journal of Licensing Executives Society International, H*(3), 160-165.

Oltsik, J. (2010). *What's Needed for Cloud Computing? - Focus on Networking and WAN Optimization. Enterprise Security Group.* ESG.

Opelt, A., Gloger, B., Pfarl, W., & Mittermayr, R. (2013). *Agile Contracts: Creating and Managing Successful Projects with Scrum.* Hoboken, NJ: John Wiley & Sons. doi:10.1002/9781118640067

Oracle. (n.d.). *Oracle VM Server for SPARC 3.1 Security Guide.* Retrieved from Oracle Technology Network: www.docs.oracle.com/cd/E38405_01/

Oriol, F., & Guitart, J. (2011). Initial Thoughts on Business-driven IT Management Challenges in cloud Computing Providers. *6th IFIP/IEEE International Workshop on Business Driven IT Management.*

OSGi Alliance. (2015). *OSGi Core Release Specification 5.0.* Retrieved on June 8, http://www.osgi.org/

Osterwalder, A. (2004). *The Business Model Ontology - A Proposition In A Design Science Approach* (Doctoral thesis). University of Lausanne.

Ott, M., Seskar, I., Siraccusa, R., & Singh, M. (2005). ORBIT testbed software architecture: supporting experiments as a service. null, (pp. 136-145).

Owens, K. (n.d.). *Securing virtual compute infrastructure in the Cloud.* SAVVIS. Available: http://www.savvis.com/en-us/info_center/documents/hoswhitepaper securingvirutalcomputeinfrastructureinthecloud.pdf

Ozier, W. (2002). Risk Assessment. In *Information Security Management Handbook.* CRC Press.

Palanisamy, B., Singh, A., & Liu, L. (2015). Cost-effective resource provisioning for mapreduce in a cloud. *IEEE Transactions on Parallel and Distributed Systems*, *26*(5), 1265–1279. doi:10.1109/TPDS.2014.2320498

Pande, D., & Jog, V. (2014). Study of Security Problem in Cloud. *International Journal of Engineering Trends & Technology*, 34-36.

Pappis, C., & Karacapilidis, N. (1993). A Comparative Assessment of Measures of Similarity of Fuzzy Values. *Fuzzy Sets and Systems*, *56*(2), 171–174. doi:10.1016/0165-0114(93)90141-4

Parham, A. G., Mooney, J. L., & Cairney, T. D. (2015). When BYOD meets Big Data. *Journal of Corporate Accounting & Finance*, *26*(5), 21–27. doi:10.1002/jcaf.22059

Park, K., & Pai, V. S. (2006). Comon: A mostly-scalable monitoring system for planetlab. *Operating Systems Review*, *40*(1), 65–74. doi:10.1145/1113361.1113374

Patel, A. B., Birla, M., & Nair, U. (2012). *Addressing Big Data Problem Using Hadoop and Map Reduce*. doi:10.1109/NUICONE.2012.6493198

Pedrycz, W., & Gomide, F. (2007). *Fuzzy Systems Engineering: Towards Human Centric Computng*. John Wiley & Sons. doi:10.1002/9780470168967

Phan, L. T., Zhang, Z., Zheng, Q., Loo, B. T., & Lee, I. (2011). An empirical analysis of scheduling techniques for real-time cloud-based data processing. *IEEE International Conference on, Service-Oriented Computing and Applications (SOCA)*. doi:10.1109/SOCA.2011.6166240

Piccoli, G. (2013). *Information Systems for Managers: Text & Cases* (2nd ed.). John Wiley & Sons, Inc.

Pingale, S.H., & Mogal, V. (2015). New Approach to Schedule Bag of Tasks (BoTs) with Increase in Parallel Process. *International Journal of Innovative Research in Computer and Communication Engineering*, *3*(7).

Pokorny, J., & Stantic, B. (2016). Challenges and opportunities in Big Data processing. In Z. Ma (Ed.), *Managing Big Data in cloud computing environments* (pp. 1–24). Hershey, PA: IGI Global. doi:10.4018/978-1-4666-9834-5.ch001

Pooranian, Z., Shojafar, M., Abawajy, J. H., & Abraham, A. (2015). An efficient meta-heuristic algorithm for grid computing. *Journal of Combinatorial Optimization*, *30*(3), 413–434. doi:10.1007/s10878-013-9644-6

Popovic, K., & Hocenski, Z. (2010). Cloud Computing Security issues and challenges. In *Proceedings of the 33rd International convention MIPRO*. IEEE Computer Society.

Porter, M. E. (1980). *Competitive Strategy: Techniques for Analyzing Industries & Competitors*. New York: Free Press.

Pretschner, A., Hilty, M., Schutz, F., Schaefer, C., & Walter, T. (2008). Usage control enforcement: Present and future. In *Security & Privacy* (pp. 44–53). IEEE.

Puthal, D., Sahoo, B., Mishra, S., & Swain, S. (2015). Cloud computing features, issues, and challenges: a big picture. *Computational Intelligence and Networks (CINE), 2015 International Conference on*, (pp. 116-123).

Puthal, D., Sahoo, B., Mishra, S., & Swain, S. (2015). Cloud computing features, issues, and challenges: a big picture. *International Conference on, Computational Intelligence and Networks (CINE)*. doi:10.1109/CINE.2015.31

QoS. (n.d.). Retrieved from http://www.nptel.ac.in/courses/106105086/pdf/module6.pdf

Raghavan, S., Marimuthu, C., Sarwesh, P., & Chandrasekaran, K. (2015). Bat algorithm for scheduling workflow applications in cloud. *Electronic Design, Computer Networks \& Automated Verification (EDCAV), 2015 International Conference on*, (pp. 139-144).

Rahman, M., Li, X., & Palit, H. (2011). Hybrid heuristic for scheduling data analytics workflow applications in hybrid cloud environment. *Parallel and Distributed Processing Workshops and Phd Forum (IPDPSW), 2011 IEEE International Symposium on,* (pp. 966-974).

Ramezani, F., Lu, J., & Hussain, F. K. (2014). Task-based system load balancing in cloud computing using particle swarm optimization. *International Journal of Parallel Programming, 42*(5), 739–754. doi:10.1007/s10766-013-0275-4

Ranjith, P., Chandran, P., & Kaleeswaran, S. (2012). On covert channels between virtual machines. *Journal in Computer Virology Springer, 8*(3), 85–97. doi:10.1007/s11416-012-0168-x

Rao, K. V., & Ali, M. A. (2015). *Survey on Big Data and applications of real time Big Data analytics.* Academic Press.

Rao, L., Liu, X., Xie, L., & Liu, W. (2010). Minimizing electricity cost: Optimization of distributed internet data centers in a multi-electricity-market environment. *Proceedings of the IEEE,* 1–9.

Raychoudhury, V., Cao, J., Kumar, M., & Zhang, D. (2013). Middleware for pervasive computing: A survey. *Pervasive and Mobile Computing, 9*(2), 177-200. Retrieved on May 27, http://www.sciencedirect.com/science/article/pii/S1574119212001113

Razzaq, A., & Rathore, M. S. (2010). An approach towards resource efficient virtual network embedding. *Evolving Internet (INTERNET), 2010 Second International Conference on,* (pp. 68-73). doi:10.1109/INTERNET.2010.21

Rettinger, A., Rettinger, U., Tresp, V., d'Amato, C., & Fanizzi, N. (2012). Mining the Semantic Web. *Data Mining and Knowledge Discovery, 24*(3), 613–662. doi:10.1007/s10618-012-0253-2

Reuben, J. S. (2007). *A survey on virtual machine Security.* Seminar on Network Security. Retrieved from http://www.tml.tkk.fi/Publications/C/25/papers/Reuben_final.pdf.

Righir, D., Pilla, L., & Carissimi, A. (2009). *MigBSP: A Novel Migration Model for Bulk-Synchronous Parallel Processes Rescheduling.* New York: IEEE.

Ristenpart, T., Tromer, E., Shacham, H., & Savage, S. (2009). Hey, you, get off of my cloud: exploring information leakage in third-party compute clouds. In *Proceedings of the 16th ACM conference on Computer and communications security.* ACM. doi:10.1145/1653662.1653687

Rockell, R., & Fink, R. (2000). *6Bone Backbone Routing Guidelines.* Tech. rep., RFC 2772, February.

Rodrigues, J., Ruivo, P., & Oliveira, T. (2014). Software as a service value and firm performance: A literature review synthesis in small and medium enterprises. *Procedia Technology, 16,* 206–211. doi:10.1016/j.protcy.2014.10.085

Roger, S. P., & Bruce, R. M. (2014). *Software Engineering a Practitioner's Approach* (8th ed.). Tata: McGraw Hill.

Roxin, A., Gaber, J., Wack, M. & Nait-Sidi-Moh, (2007). A Survey of Wireless Geolocation Techniques. *IEEE Globecom Workshops 2007.* Retrieved on June 9, http://ieeexplore.ieee.org/xpl/articleDetails.jsp?arnumber=4437809&newsearch=true&queryText=A%20Survey%20of%20Wireless%20Geolocation%20Techniques

Roy, A., & Dutta, D. (2013). Dynamic Load Balancing: Improve Efficiency in Cloud Computing. *International Journal of Emerging Research in Management &Technology, 2*(4).

Saboohi, H., & Kareem, S. A. (2013). An automatic subdigraph renovation plan for failure recovery of composite Semantic Web services. *Frontiers of Computer Science, 7*(6), 894–913. doi:10.1007/s11704-013-2248-6

Sadasivam, S. G., & Selvaraj, D. (2010). A novel parallel hybrid PSO-GA using MapReduce to schedule jobs in Hadoop data grids. *Nature and Biologically Inspired Computing (NaBIC), 2010 Second World Congress on,* (pp. 377-382).

Sahandi, R., Alkhalil, A., & Opara-Martins, J. (2013). Cloud Computing from SMEs Perspectives: A Survey-based Investigation. *Journal of Information Technology Management, 24*(1), 1–12.

Sahoo, A. K., Sahoo, K. S., & Tiwary, M. (2014). Signature based malware detection for unstructured data in Hadoop. *International Conference on, Advances in Electronics, Computers and Communications (ICAECC).* doi:10.1109/ICAECC.2014.7002394

Sahoo, S., Nawaz, S., Mishra, S. K., & Sahoo, B. (2015). *Execution of real time task on cloud environment.* Academic Press.

Sahoo, J., Mohapatra, S., & Lath, R. (2010). Virtualization: A survey on concepts, taxonomy and associated security issues. *IEEE Second International Conference on Computer and Network Technology (ICCNT).* doi:10.1109/ICCNT.2010.49

Salem, M., Adinoyi, A., Yanikomeroglu, H., & Falconer, D. (2010). Opportunities and Challenges in OFDMA-Based Cellular Relay Networks: A Radio Resource Management Perspective. *IEEE Transactions on Vehicular Technology, 59*(5), 2496 – 2510. Retrieved on June 3, http://ieeexplore.ieee.org/search/searchresult.jsp?newsearch=true&queryText=Opportunities%20and%20Challenges%20in%20OFDMABased%20Cellular%20Relay%20Networks:A%20Radio%20Resource%20Management%20Perspective

Samza. (n.d.). Retrieved from http://thenewstack.io/apache-samza-linkedins-framework-for-stream-processing

Sanaei, Z., Abolfazli, S., Khodadadi, T., & Xia, F. (2014). Hybrid Pervasive Mobile Cloud Computing: Toward Enhancing Invisibility. *Information, 16*(11), 8145-8181. Retrieved on June 10, https://umexpert.um.edu.my/file/publication/00001293_110375.pdf

Sani, A., Rajab, M., Foster, R., & Hao, Y. (2010). Antennas and Propagation of Implanted RFIDs for Pervasive Healthcare Applications. *Proceedings of the IEEE, 98*(9), 1648-1655. Retrieved on June 6, http://ieeexplore.ieee.org/xpl/articleDetails.jsp?arnumber=5523906&newsearch=true&queryText=Antennas%20and%20Propagation%20of%20Implanted%20RFIDs%20for%20Pervasive%20Healthcare%20Applications

Sauv'e, J., Marques, F., Moura, A., Sampaio, M., Jornada, J., & Radziuk, E. (2005). SLA Design from a Business Perspective. In *Proceedings of the 16th IFIP/IEEE International Workshop on Distributed Systems: Operations and Management* (DSOM'05). Citeseer.

Savelyev, A. (2014). Software-as-a-service – Legal nature: Shifting the existing paradigm of copyright law. *Computer Law & Security Report, 30*(5), 560–568. doi:10.1016/j.clsr.2014.05.011

Sawant, S. (2011). *A genetic algorithm scheduling approach for virtual machine resources in a cloud computing environment.* Academic Press.

Schaer, J., & Eshelman, L. (1993). Real-Coded Genetic Algorithms and Interval Schemata.Foundations of Genetic Algorithms-2-, D. Morgan-Kaufmann.

Schaffrath, G., Werle, C., Papadimitriou, P., Feldmann, A., Bless, R., & Greenhalgh, A. et al. (2009). Network virtualization architecture: proposal and initial prototype.*Proceedings of the 1st ACM workshop on Virtualized infrastructure systems and architectures*, (pp. 63-72). doi:10.1145/1592648.1592659

Schlarman, S. (2009). IT risk exploration: The IT risk management taxonomy and evolution. *Information Systems Audit and Control Association Journal, 2009*(3), 27-30.

Scholl, A., Klein, R., & J¨urgens, C. (1997). Bison: A fast hybrid procedure for exactly solving the one-dimensional bin packing problem. *Computers & Operations Research, 24*(7), 627–645. doi:10.1016/S0305-0548(96)00082-2

Schoofs, A., Daymand, C., Sugar, R., Mueller, U., Lachenman, A., Kamran, S. M., . . . Schuster, M. (2009). IP-based testbed for herd monitoring. *International Conference on Information Processing in Sensor Networks, 2009* (IPSN 2009). Retrieved on June 4, http://ieeexplore.ieee.org/xpl/articleDetails.jsp?arnumber=5211913&newsearch=true&queryText =IP-based%20testbed%20for%20herd%20monitoring

Schubert, L., & Jeffrey, K. (2012). *Advances in clouds, research in future cloud computing*. European Union. Retrieved on June 10, http://cordis.europa.eu/fp7/ict/ssai/docs/future-cc-2may-finalreport-experts.pdf

Security Guidance for Critical Areas of Focus in Cloud Computing V2 . 1. (2009). Cloud Security Alliance. Retrieved on June 1, https://cloudsecurityalliance.org/csaguide.pdf

Seethamraju, R. (2015). Adoption of software as a service (SaaS) enterprise resource planning (ERP) systems in small and medium sized enterprises (SMEs). *Information Systems Frontiers, 17*(3), 475–492. doi:10.1007/s10796-014-9506-5

Segal, S. (2011). *Corporate Value of Enterprise Risk Management: The Next Step in Business Management*. Hoboken, NJ: John Wiley & Sons.

Shamsi, J., Khojaye, M. A., & Qasmi, M. A. (2013). Data-intensive cloud computing: Requirements, expectations, challenges, and solutions. *Journal of Grid Computing, 11*(2), 281–310. doi:10.1007/s10723-013-9255-6

Shaurette, K. M. (2002). The Building Blocks of Information Security. In Information Security Management Handbook. Academic Press.

Shawish, A., & Salama, M. (2014). Cloud Computing: Paradigms and Technologies. In F. Xhafa & N. Bessis (Eds.), *Inter-cooperative Collective Intelligence: Techniques and Applications* (pp. 39–67). Berlin, Germany: Springer-Verlag. doi:10.1007/978-3-642-35016-0_2

Shelly, G. B., & Vermaat, M. E. (2011). *Discovering Computers: Living in a Digital World*. Course Technology, Cengage Learning.

Shetch, A., & Ranabahu, A. (2010, August). Semantic Modeling for Cloud Computing. *IEEE Internet Computing*.

Shin, D. H., & Choi, M. J. (2015). Ecological views of Big Data: Perspectives and issues. *Telematics and Informatics, 32*(2), 311–320. doi:10.1016/j.tele.2014.09.006

Shinder, D. (2013). *Selecting a Cloud Provider*. Retrieved September 09, 2015, from http://www.cloudcomputingadmin. com/articles-tutorials/architecture-design/selecting-cloud-provider-part1.html

Shojafar, M., Javanmardi, S., Abolfazli, S., & Cordeschi, N. (2015). FUGE: A joint meta-heuristic approach to cloud job scheduling algorithm using fuzzy theory and a genetic method. *Cluster Computing, 18*(2), 829–844. doi:10.1007/ s10586-014-0420-x

Si, H., Chen, Z., Deng, Y., & Yu, L. (2013). Semantic Web services publication and OCT-based discovery in structured P2P network. *Service Oriented Computing and Applications, 7*(3), 169–180. doi:10.1007/s11761-011-0097-4

Singh, A., Korupolu, M., & Mahapatra, D. (2008). Server-Storage Virtualization: Integration and Load Balancing in Data centers. IEEE/ACM Supercomputing (SC).

Singh, P., Pandey, B. K., Mandoria, H. L., & Srivastava, R. (2013). Review of Energy Aware policies for Cloud Computing Environment. *i-Manager's Journal of Information Technology, 3*(1), 14.

Singh, S. (2013). *Data Security Issues and Strategy on Cloud Computing. Moradabad: International Journal of Science, Engineering and Technology Research*.

Siva, M., & Poobalan, A. (2012). Semantic Web Standard in Cloud Computing. *International Journal of Soft Computing and Engineering, 1.*

Smallwood, R. F. (2012). *Safeguarding Critical e-Documents: Implementing a Program for Securing Confidential Information Assets.* John Wiley & Sons, Inc. doi:10.1002/9781119204909

Smyth, P. (2009). *Cloud Computing A Strategy Guide for Board Level Executives.* Kynetix Technology Group.

Somani, U., Lakhani, K., & Mundra, M. (2010). Implementing digital signature with RSA encryption algorithm to enhance the data Security of Cloud in Cloud Computing. In *1st International conference on parallel distributed and grid Computing* (PDGC). IEEE Computer Society. doi:10.1109/PDGC.2010.5679895

Sood, A., & Enbody, R. (2013). Targeted Cyber-attacks: A Superset of Advanced Persistent Threats. *IEEE Security and Privacy, 11*(1).

Sotomayor, B., Montero, R. S., Llorente, I., & Foster, I. (2009). Virtual infrastructure management in private and hybrid clouds. *IEEE Internet Computing, 13*(5), 14–22. doi:10.1109/MIC.2009.119

Spark. (n.d.). Retrieved from http://www.infoq.com/articles/apache-spark-introduction

Srikantaiah, S., Kansal, A., & Zhao, F. (2008). Energy aware consolidation for cloud computing.*Proceedings of the 2008 conference on Power aware computing and systems.*

Stantchev, V., & Stantcheva, L. (2013). Applying IT-Governance Frameworks for SOA and Cloud Governance. In M. D. Lytras, D. Ruan, R. D. Tennyson, P. Ordonez De Pablos, F. J. García Peñalvo, & L. Rusu (Eds.), *Information Systems, E-learning, and Knowledge Management Research* (pp. 398–407). Berlin, Germany: Springer-Verlag. doi:10.1007/978-3-642-35879-1_48

Steiner, T. (2012). *An Introduction to Securing a Cloud Environment.* SANS Institute.

Storm. (n.d.). Retrieved from http://www.infoq.com/news/2011/09/twitter-storm-real-time-hadoop

Summingbird. (n.d.). Retrieved from http://www.infoq.com/news/2014/01/twitter-summingbird

Sun, D., Chang, G., Wang, C., Xiong, Y., & Wang, X. (2010). Efficient nash equilibrium based cloud resource allocation by using a continuous double auction. In *2010 International Conference on Computer Design and Applications (ICCDA).*

Sundararaj, A. I., & Dinda, P. A. (2004). Towards Virtual Networks for Virtual Machine Grid Computing.Virtual machine research and technology symposium, (pp. 177-190).

Sun, M., Zhuang, H., Li, C., Lu, K., & Zhou, X. (2016). Scheduling algorithm based on prefetching in MapReduce clusters. *Applied Soft Computing, 38,* 1109–1118. doi:10.1016/j.asoc.2015.04.039

Sun, W., Zhang, D., Zhang, N., Zhang, Q., & Qiu, T. (2014). Group participation game strategy for resource allocation in cloud computing. In *Network and Parallel Computing* (pp. 294–305). Springer. doi:10.1007/978-3-662-44917-2_25

Susarla, A., Barua, A., & Whinston, A. B. (2010). Multitask agency, modular architecture, and task disaggregation in SaaS. *Journal of Management Information Systems, 26*(4), 87–118. doi:10.2753/MIS0742-1222260404

Szegedi, P., Figuerola, S., Campanella, M., Maglaris, V., & Cervello-Pastor, C. (2009). With evolution for revolution: managing FEDERICA for future internet research. *IEEE Communications Magazine, 47*(7), 34-39.

Szeto, W., Iraqi, Y., & Boutaba, R. (2003). A multi-commodity flow based approach to virtual network resource allocation. *Global Telecommunications Conference, 2003. GLOBECOM'03.* IEEE. doi:10.1109/GLOCOM.2003.1258787

Takeda, T. (2007). *Framework and requirements for layer 1 virtual private networks.* Academic Press.

Tam, S. M., & Clarke, F. (2015). Big Data, official statistics and some initiatives by the Australian Bureau of Statistics. *International Statistical Review, 83*(3), 436–448. doi:10.1111/insr.12105

Tang, C., & Liu, J. (2015). Selecting a trusted cloud service provider for your SaaS program. *Computers & Security, 50,* 60–73. doi:10.1016/j.cose.2015.02.001

Tang, Q., Gupta, S. K., & Varsamopoulos, G. (2008). Energy-efficient thermal-aware task scheduling for homogeneous high-performance computing data centers: A cyber-physical approach. *Parallel and Distributed Systems. IEEE Transactions on, 19*(11), 1458–1472.

Tawfeek, M. A., El-Sisi, A., Keshk, A. E., & Torkey, F. A. (2013). Cloud task scheduling based on ant colony optimization. *Computer Engineering & Systems (ICCES), 2013 8th International Conference on,* (pp. 64-69).

Taylor, L., Cowls, J., Schroeder, R., & Meyer, E. T. (2014). Big Data and positive change in the developing world. *Policy & Internet, 6*(4), 418–444. doi:10.1002/1944-2866.POI378

Teng, F., & Magoules, F. (2010). A new game theoretical resource allocation algorithm for cloud computing. In *Advances in Grid and Pervasive Computing* (pp. 321–330). Springer. doi:10.1007/978-3-642-13067-0_35

Teng, F., Magoules, F., Yu, L., & Li, T. (2014). A novel real-time scheduling algorithm and performance analysis of a MapReduce-based cloud. *The Journal of Supercomputing, 69*(2), 739–765. doi:10.1007/s11227-014-1115-z

Tennenhouse, D. L., Smith, J. M., Sincoskie, W. D., Wetherall, D. J., & Minden, G. J. (1997). A survey of active network research. *Communications Magazine, IEEE, 35*(1), 80–86. doi:10.1109/35.568214

Tenorth, M., Kamei, K., Satake, S., Miyashita, T., & Hagita, N. (2013). Building Knowledge-enabled Cloud Robotics Applications using the Ubiquitous Network Robot Platform. *IEEE/RSJ International Conference on Intelligent Robots and Systems* (IROS). Retrieved on June 8, http://ieeexplore.ieee.org/xpl/articleDetails.jsp?arnumber=6697184&newsearch=true&queryText=Building%20Knowledgeenabled%20Cloud%20Robotics%20Applications%20using%20the%20Ubiquitous%20Network%20Robot%20Platform

The Landmark. (n.d.). *Agile Development Meets Cloud Computing for Extraordinary Results at Salesforce.com.* Retrieved from http://www.developerforce.com/media/ForcedotcomBookLibrary/WP_Agile_112608.pdf

Tinati, R., Halford, S., Carr, L., & Pope, C. (2014). Big Data: Methodological challenges and approaches for sociological analysis. *Sociology, 48*(4), 663–681. doi:10.1177/0038038513511561

Tiwari, N., Sarkar, S., Bellur, U., & Indrawan, M. (2015). Classification framework of MapReduce scheduling algorithms. *ACM Computing Surveys, 47*(3), 49. doi:10.1145/2693315

Torres, J., Nogueira, M., & Pujolle, G. (2013). A Survey on Identity Management for the Future Network. *IEEE Communications Surveys & Tutorials, 15*(2), 787-802. Retrieved on June 7, http://ieeexplore.ieee.org/xpl/articleDetails.jsp?arnumber=6275425&queryText=A%20Survey%20on%20Identity%20Management%20for%20the%20Future%20Network&newsearch=true

Touch, J., Wang, Y., & Eggert, L. (2003). *A Virtual Internet Architecture.* ISI Technical Report ISI-TR-570. Workshop on Future Directions in Network Architecture (FDNA).

Townsend, M. (2009). Managing a security program in a cloud computing environment. In *Information Security Curriculum Development Conference* (pp. 128–133). ACM. doi:10.1145/1940976.1941001

Triguero, I., Peralta, D., Bacardit, J., García, S., & Herrera, F. (2015). MRPR: A MapReduce solution for prototype reduction in Big Data classification. *Neurocomputing*, *150*, 331–345. doi:10.1016/j.neucom.2014.04.078

Tsai, C.-W., & Rodrigues, J. J. (2014). Metaheuristic scheduling for cloud: A survey. *Systems Journal, IEEE*, *8*(1), 279–291. doi:10.1109/JSYST.2013.2256731

Tsai, W. T., Bai, X. Y., & Huang, Y. (2014). Software-as-a-service (SaaS): Perspectives and challenges. *Science China: Information Sciences*, *57*(5), 1–15. doi:10.1007/s11432-013-5050-z

Tsakalozos, K., Kllapi, H., Sitaridi, E., Roussopoulos, M., Paparas, D., & Delis, A. (2011). *ICDE '11 Proceedings of the 2011 IEEE 27th International Conference on Data Engineering*.

Turban, E., Leidner, D., McLean, E., & Wetherbe, J. (2008). *Information technology for management: Transforming organizations in the digital economy*. John Wiley and Sons Inc.

Turner, M., Budgen, D., & Brereton, P. (2003). Turning software into a service. *IEEE Computer*, *36*(10), 38–44. doi:10.1109/MC.2003.1236470

Turocy, T. L., & Von Stengel, B. (2001). *Game theory: Draft prepared for the encyclopedia of information systems*. Tech. Rep. CDAM Research Report LSE-CDAM-2001-09.

Tziritas, N., Khan, S. U., Xu, C.-Z., Loukopoulos, T., & Lalis, S. (2013). On minimizing the resource consumption of cloud applications using process migrations. *Journal of Parallel and Distributed Computing*, *73*(12), 1690–1704. doi:10.1016/j.jpdc.2013.07.020

Unruh, D., & Muller-Quade, J. (2010). Universally composable incoercibility. In IACR Cryptology. doi:10.1007/978-3-642-14623-7_22

US Gov't. (2009, May). *The White House*. Retrieved July 01, 2014, from The Comprehensive National Cybersecurity Initiative: www.whitehouse.gov/issues/foreign-policy/cybersecurity/national-initiative

Vaidya, M. (2016). Handling critical issues of Big Data on cloud. In Z. Ma (Ed.), *Managing Big Data in cloud computing environments* (pp. 100–131). Hershey, PA: IGI Global. doi:10.4018/978-1-4666-9834-5.ch005

Valente, P., & Mitra, G. (2007). The evolution of Web-based optimisation: From ASP to e-services. *Decision Support Systems*, *43*(4), 1096–1116. doi:10.1016/j.dss.2005.07.003

Valentini, G. L., Khan, S. U., & Bouvry, P. (2013). Energy-efficient resource utilization in cloud computing. In Large Scale Network-centric Computing Systems. John Wiley & Sons.

Valiant, L. G. (1990). A bridging model for parallel computation. *Communications of the ACM*, *33*(8), 103-11.

Van den Bossche, R., Vanmechelen, K., & Broeckhove, J. (2010). Cost-Optimal Scheduling in Hybrid IaaS Clouds for Deadline Constrained Workloads. In *3rd International Conference on Cloud Computing*, (pp. 228–235). doi:10.1109/CLOUD.2010.58

Vaquero, L. R.-M., & Moran, D. (2011, January). Locking the Sky: A Survey on IaaS Cloud Security. *Computing*, *91*(1), 93–118. doi:10.1007/s00607-010-0140-x

Venkatesha, S., Sadhu, S., & Kintali, S. (2009). *Survey of virtual machine migration techniques*. Technical report, Dept. of Computer Science, University of California, Santa Barbara. Retrieved from http://www.academia.edu/760613/Survey_of_Virtual_Machine_Migration_Techniques

Verma, A., Ahuja, P., & Neogi, A. (2008). pMapper: power and migration cost aware application placement in virtualized systems. *Proceedings of the ACM/IFIP/USENIX 9th International Middleware Conference.* Springer-Verlag.

Verma, K., Sivashanmugam, K., Sheth, A., Patil, A., Oundhakar, S., & Miller, J. (2005). METEOR-S WSDI: A scalable P2P infrastructure of registries for semantic publication and discovery of Web services. *Information Technology & Management, 6*(1), 17–39. doi:10.1007/s10799-004-7773-4

Viat-Blanc, P., Goglin, B., Guillier, R., & Soudan, S. (2011). *Computing Networks from cluster to cloud computing.* Wiley. Retrieved on June 10, http://eu.wiley.com/WileyCDA/WileyTitle/productCd-1848212860.html#

Vice, P. (2015). *Should IT Risks Be Part of Corporate Governance?* Retrieved September 09, 2015, from http://insurance-canada.ca/blog/2015/08/30/should-it-risks-be-part-of-corporate-governance/

Vice, P. (2015). *Taking risk management from the silo across the enterprise.* Retrieved September 9, 2015, from http://www.aciworldwide.com/-/media/files/collateral/aci_taking_risk_mgmt_from_silo_across_enterprise_tl_us_0211_4572.pdf

Vidalis, S., & Jones, A. (2005). Analyzing Threat Agents & Their Attributes. Pontypridd, UK: School of Computing, University of Glamorgan.

Villela, D., Campbell, A. T., & Vicente, J. (2001). Virtuosity: Programmable resource management for spawning networks. *Computer Networks, 36*(1), 49–73. doi:10.1016/S1389-1286(01)00150-5

Vogl, S. (n.d.). Secure Hypervisor. *Technische Universitat Muncheon.*

Voorsluys, W., Garg, S. K., & Buyya, R. (2011). Provisioning Spot Market Cloud Resources to Create Cost-effective Virtual Clusters. In *Proceedings of the 11th IEEE International Conference on Algorithms and Architectures for Parallel Processing* (ICA3PP-11). Springer.

Voorsluys, W., Broberg, J., Venugopal, S., & Buyya, R. (2009). *Cost of virtual machine live migration in clouds: A performance evaluation. Cloud Computing.* Heidelberg, Germany: Springer.

Wahner, K. (2014). *Real-Time Stream Processing as Game Changer in a Big Data World with Hadoop and Data Warehouse.* InfoQ.

Walker, J. (2009). Internet Security. In J. R. Vacca (Ed.), Computer & Information Security Handbook (pp. 93-117). Morgan-Kaufmann, Inc. doi:10.1016/B978-0-12-374354-1.00007-8

Walker, D., & Fung, K. (2013). Big Data and big business: Should statisticians join in? *Significance, 10*(4), 20–25. doi:10.1111/j.1740-9713.2013.00679.x

Walraven, S., Truyen, E., & Joosen, W. (2014). Comparing PaaS offerings in light of SaaS development. *Computing, 96*(8), 669–724. doi:10.1007/s00607-013-0346-9

Wang, C., Wang, C., & Yuan, Y. (2009). Game based dynamical bandwidth allocation model for virtual networks. *Information Science and Engineering (ICISE), 2009 1st International Conference on,* (pp. 1745-1747). doi:10.1109/ICISE.2009.616

Wang, T., Liu, Z., Chen, Y., Xu, Y., & Dai, X. (2014). Load balancing task scheduling based on genetic algorithm in cloud computing. *Dependable, Autonomic and Secure Computing (DASC), 2014 IEEE 12th International Conference on,* (pp. 146-152).

Wang, A., Iyer, M., Dutta, R., Rouskas, G. N., & Baldine, I. (2013). Network virtualization: Technologies, perspectives, and frontiers. Lightwave Technology. *Journalism, 31*(4), 523–537.

Wang, C., Wang, Q., Ren, K., & Lou, W. (2009). Ensuring data Storage Security in Cloud Computing. In *The 17th International workshop on quality of service*. IEEE Computer Society. doi:10.1109/IWQoS.2009.5201385

Wang, G., Jiang, W., Wu, J., & Xiong, Z. (2014). Fine-grained feature-based social influence evaluation in online social networks. *IEEE Transactions on Parallel and Distributed Systems, 25*(9), 2286–2296. doi:10.1109/TPDS.2013.135

Wang, H., Zhang, Y. Q., & Sunderraman, R. (2006). Extensible soft Semantic Web services agent. *Soft Computing, 10*(11), 1021–1029. doi:10.1007/s00500-005-0029-3

Wang, P., Meng, D., Han, J., Zhan, J., Tu, B., Shi, X., & Wan, L. (2010). Transformer: A New Paradigm for Building Data Parallel Programming Models. *IEEE Micro, 30*(4), 55–64. doi:10.1109/MM.2010.75

Wang, X., Wang, Y., & Cui, Y. (2016). An energy-aware bi-level optimization model for multi-job scheduling problems under cloud computing. *Soft Computing, 20*(1), 303–317. doi:10.1007/s00500-014-1506-3

Wang, X., Wang, Y., & Zhu, H. (2012). Energy-efficient task scheduling model based on MapReduce for cloud computing using genetic algorithm. *Journal of Computers, 7*(12), 2962–2970. doi:10.4304/jcp.7.12.2962-2970

Wang, Y., Keller, E., Biskeborn, B., van der Merwe, J., & Rexford, J. (2008). Virtual routers on the move: Live router migration as a network-management primitive. *Computer Communication Review, 38*(4), 231–242. doi:10.1145/1402946.1402985

Wang, Z., & Jiang, X. (2010). HyperSafe: a lightweight approach to provide lifetime hypervisor control-flow integrity. In *Proceedings of the IEEE symposium on Security and privacy*. IEEE Computer Society. doi:10.1109/SP.2010.30

Wang, Z., Shuang, K., Yang, L., & Yang, F. (2012). Energy-aware and revenue-enhancing Combinatorial Scheduling in Virtualized of Cloud Datacenter. *Journal of Cases on Information Technology, 7*(1), 62–70.

Wark, T., Corke, P., Sikka, P., Klingbeil, L., Guo, Y., & Crossman, C. … Bishop-Hurley, G. (2007). Transforming Agriculture through Pervasive Wireless Sensor Networks. *IEEE Pervasive Computing, 6*(2), 50-57. Retrieved on June 9, http://ieeexplore.ieee.org/xpl/articleDetails.jsp?arnumber=4160605&newsearch=true&queryText=Transforming%20Agriculture%20through%20Pervasive%20Wireless%20Sensor%20Networks

Warrier, S., & Shandrashekhar, P. (2006). A Comparison Study of Information Security Risk Management Frameworks in. Paper presented in the Asia Pacific Risk and Insurance Conference, Tokyo, Japan.

Wei, D., Wang, T., & Wang, J. (2012). A logistic regression model for Semantic Web service matchmaking. *Science China: Information Sciences, 55*(7), 1715–1720. doi:10.1007/s11432-012-4591-x

Wei, G., Vasilakos, A. V., Zheng, Y., & Xiong, N. (2010). A game-theoretic method of fair resource allocation for cloud computing services. *The Journal of Supercomputing, 54*(2), 252–269. doi:10.1007/s11227-009-0318-1

Weiser, M. (1991). The Computer for the 21st Century. *Scientific Am., 265*(3), 66-75. Retrieved on May 17, https://www.ics.uci.edu/~corps/phaseii/Weiser-Computer21stCentury-SciAm.pdf

Wei, W., Guosun, Z., & Lulai, Y. (2006). Semtrust: A semantic reputation system in P2P-based Semantic Web. *Wuhan University Journal of Natural Sciences, 11*(5), 1137–1140. doi:10.1007/BF02829224

White, P., & Breckenridge, R. S. (2014). Trade-offs, limitations, and promises of Big Data in social science research. *Review of Policy Research, 31*(4), 331–338. doi:10.1111/ropr.12078

Whitman, M. E., & Mattord, H. (2005). Principles of Information Security (2nd ed.). Thomson Course Technology.

Wigan, M., & Clarke, R. (2013). Big Data's big unintended consequences. *Computer, 46*(6), 46–53. doi:10.1109/MC.2013.195

Williams, T. L., & Parsons, R. J. (2000). *The Heterogeneous Bulk Synchronous Parallel model. In ROLIM J. Parallel and Distributed Processing, Proceedings*. Berlin: Springer-Verlag Berlin.

Winkler, V. (2011). *Securing the Cloud: Cloud computer Security techniques and tactics*. Waltham, MA: Elsevier Inc.

Woniak, M., Graña, M., & Corchado, E. (2014). A survey of multiple classifier systems as hybrid systems. *Information Fusion, 16*, 3–17. doi:10.1016/j.inffus.2013.04.006

Wood, T., Shenoy, P. J., Venkataramani, A., & Yousif, M. S. (2007). *Black-box and gray-box strategies for virtual machine migration* (Vol. 7, pp. 17–17). NSDI.

Wu, H., Ding, Y., Winer, C., & Yao, L. (2010). Network Security for virtual machine in Cloud Computing. In *5th International conference on computer sciences and convergence information technology* (ICCIT). IEEE Computer Society.

Wu, L., Garg, S. K., & Buyya, R. (2012). SLA-based admission control for a software-as-a-service provider in cloud computing environments. *Journal of Computer and System Sciences, 78*(5), 1280–1299. doi:10.1016/j.jcss.2011.12.014

Wu, L., Yuan, L., & You, J. (2015). Survey of large-scale data management systems for Big Data applications. *Journal of Computer Science and Technology, 30*(1), 163–183. doi:10.1007/s11390-015-1511-8

Wu, W. W. (2011). Developing an explorative model for SaaS adoption. *Expert Systems with Applications, 38*(12), 15057–15064. doi:10.1016/j.eswa.2011.05.039

Xhafa, F., & Kolodziej, J. (2010). Game-theoretic, market and meta-heuristics approaches for modelling scheduling and resource allocation in grid systems. In *2010 IEEE International Conference on P2P, Parallel, Grid, Cloud and Internet Computing (3PGCIC)*. doi:10.1109/3PGCIC.2010.39

Xiang, Z., Schwartz, Z., Gerdes, J. H. Jr, & Uysal, M. (2015). What can Big Data and text analytics tell us about hotel guest experience and satisfaction? *International Journal of Hospitality Management, 44*, 120–130. doi:10.1016/j.ijhm.2014.10.013

Xiaopeng, G., Sumei, W., & Xianqin, C. (2010). VNSS: a Network Security sandbox for virtual Computing environment. In *IEEE youth conference on information Computing and telecommunications (YC-ICT)* (pp. 395–398). Washington, DC: IEEE Computer Society. doi:10.1109/YCICT.2010.5713128

Xu, K., Zhang, X., Song, M., & Song, J. (2009). Mobile Mashup: Architecture, Challenges and Suggestions. In *International Conference on Management and Service Science*. IEEE Computer Society.

Xu, X., He, G., Zhang, S., Chen, Y., & Xu, S. (2013). On Functionality Separation for Green Mobile Networks: Concept Study over LTE. *IEEE Communications Magazine, 51*(5), 82-90. Retrieved on June 4, http://ieeexplore.ieee.org/xpl/articleDetails.jsp?arnumber=6515050&newsearch=true&queryText=On%20Functionality%20Separation%20for%20Green%20Mobile%20Networks:%20Concept%20Study%20over%20LTE

Xu, Z. (2005). An Approach Based on Similarity Measure to Multiple Attribute Decision Making with Trapezoid Fuzzy Linguistic Variables. In J. C. Siekmann (Ed.), Fuzzy Systems & Knowledge Discovery (LNAI), (Vol. 3613, pp. 110-117). Springer. doi:10.1007/11539506_13

Xuemei, Y., Lizhen, X., Yisheng, D., & Yongli, W. (2006). Web service description and discovery based on semantic model. *Wuhan University Journal of Natural Sciences, 11*(5), 1306–1310. doi:10.1007/BF02829257

Xu, J., & Fortes, J. A. (2010). Multi-objective virtual machine placement in virtualized data center environments. In *2010 IEEE/ACM Int'l Conference on Green Computing and Communications (GreenCom) & Int'l Conference on Cyber, Physical and Social Computing (CPSCom)*. doi:10.1109/GreenCom-CPSCom.2010.137

Xu, M., Cai, H., & Liang, S. (2015). Big Data and industrial ecology. *Journal of Industrial Ecology*, *19*(2), 205–210. doi:10.1111/jiec.12241

Xu, W. J., Zhao, C. D., Chiang, H. P., Huang, L., & Huang, Y. M. (2015). The RR-PEVQ algorithm research based on active area detection for Big Data applications. *Multimedia Tools and Applications*, *74*(10), 3507–3520. doi:10.1007/s11042-014-1903-8

Xu, Z., Liu, Y., Mei, L., Hu, C., & Chen, L. (2015). Semantic based representing and organizing surveillance Big Data using video structural description technology. *Journal of Systems and Software*, *102*, 217–225. doi:10.1016/j.jss.2014.07.024

Yang, X.-S. (2010). A new metaheuristic bat-inspired algorithm. In Nature inspired cooperative strategies for optimization (NICSO 2010) (pp. 65-74). Springer. doi:10.1007/978-3-642-12538-6_6

Yang, X.-S., & Press, L. (2010). Nature-Inspired Metaheuristic Algorithms (2nd ed.). Academic Press.

Yang, J., & Leung, J. Y. T. (2003). The ordered open-end bin-packing problem. *Operations Research*, *51*(5), 759–770. doi:10.1287/opre.51.5.759.16753

Yang, S.-J., & Chen, Y.-R. (2015). Design adaptive task allocation scheduler to improve MapReduce performance in heterogeneous clouds. *Journal of Network and Computer Applications*, *57*, 61–70. doi:10.1016/j.jnca.2015.07.012

Yang, X., Chen, Y., Zhang, W., & Zhang, S. (2011). Exploring injection prevention technologies for security-aware distributed collaborative manufacturing on the Semantic Web. *International Journal of Advanced Manufacturing Technology*, *54*(9), 1167–1177. doi:10.1007/s00170-010-2983-x

Yeboah-Boateng, E. O. (2013c, December). Of Social Engineers and Corporate Espionage Agents: How Prepared Are SMEs in Developing Economies? *Journal of Electronics and Communication Engineering Research*, 14-22.

Yeboah-Boateng, E. O., & Essandoh, K. A. (2013, November). Cloud Computing: The Level of Awareness amongst Small and Meduim Enterprises (SMEs) in Developing Economies. *Journal of Emerging Trends in Computing & Information Sciences*, 832-839.

Yeboah-Boateng, E. O. (2013a). *Cyber-Security Challenges with SMEs in Developing Economies: Issues of Confidentiality, Integrity & Availablity (CIA)*. Aalborg University.

Yeboah-Boateng, E. O. (2013b, February). Fuzzy Similarity Measures Approach in Benchmarking Taxonomies of Threats against SMEs in Developing Economies. *Canadian Journal on Computing in Mathematics, Natural Sciences. Engineering in Medicine*, 34–44.

Ye, N. (2008). *Secure Computer & Network Systems: Modeling, Analysis & Design*. John Wiley & Sons. doi:10.1002/9780470023273

Yeow, W.-L., Westphal, C., & Kozat, U. C. (2011). Designing and embedding reliable virtual infrastructures. *Computer Communication Review*, *41*(2), 57–64. doi:10.1145/1971162.1971173

Yıldırım, A. A., & Watson, D. (2016). A cloud-aware distributed object storage system to retrieve large data via HTML5-enabled Web browsers. In Z. Ma (Ed.), *Managing Big Data in cloud computing environments* (pp. 25–45). Hershey, PA: IGI Global. doi:10.4018/978-1-4666-9834-5.ch002

Yu, G. J., & Wang, S. C. (2007). A Hierarchical MDS-based Localization Algorithm for Wireless Sensor Networks. *16th IST Mobile and Wireless Communications Summit*. Retrieved on June 1,http://ieeexplore.ieee.org/xpl/articleDetails.jsp?arnumber=4299079&queryText=A%20Hierarchical%20MDSbased%20Localization%20Algorithm%20for%20Wireless%20%20%20Sensor%20Networks&newsearch=true

Yu, J., Buyya, R., & Tham, C. (2005). Cost-based Scheduling of Scientific Workflow Applications on Utility Grids. In *Proceedings of the 1st International Conference on e-Science and Grid Computing* (e-Science 2005).

Yuan, D., Yang, Y., Liu, X., Li, W., Cui, L., Xu, M., & Chen, J. (2013). A highly practical approach towards achieving minimum datasets storage cost in the cloud. *IEEE Transactions on Parallel and Distributed Systems, 24*(6), 1234–1244. doi:10.1109/TPDS.2013.20

Yu, J., & Buyya, R. (2006). A Budget Constrained Scheduling of Workflow Applications on Utility Grids using Genetic Algorithms. In *Workshop on Workflows in Support of Large-Scale Science (WORKS)*. doi:10.1109/WORKS.2006.5282330

Yu, J., & Buyya, R. (2006). Scheduling scientific workflow applications with deadline and budget constraints using genetic algorithms. *Science Progress, 14*(3-4), 217–230.

Zadeh, L. (1978). Fuzzy Sets as a Basis for a Theory of Possibility. *Fuzzy Sets and Systems, 1*(1), 3–28. doi:10.1016/0165-0114(78)90029-5

Zafar, F., & Omer, A. (2013). *Social, Dynamic and Custom-Based Clouds: Architecture, Services and Frameworks*. Springer London.

Zaharakis, I. D., & Komninos, A. (2012). Ubiquitous Computing – a Multidisciplinary Endeavour. *IEEE Latin America Transactions, 10*(3), 1850 – 1852. Retrieved on May 27, http://ieeexplore.ieee.org/xpls/abs_all.jsp?arnumber=6222593&tag=1

Zhang, J., Wang, W., Zhao, Y., & Cattani, C. (2012). Multiobjective quantum evolutionary algorithm for the vehicle routing problem with customer satisfaction. Mathematical Problems in Engineering.

Zhang, S., Zhang, S., Chen, X., & Huo, X. (2010). Cloud Computing Research and Development Trend. In *Second International Conference on Future Networks* (ICFN'10). IEEE Computer Society. doi:10.1109/ICFN.2010.58

Zhang, W., Duan, P., Li, Z., Lu, Q., Gong, W., & Yang, S. (2015). A Deep Awareness Framework for Pervasive Video Cloud. *IEEE Access, 3*, 2227 - 2237. Retrieved on June 2, http://ieeexplore.ieee.org/xpl/articleDetails.jsp?arnumber=7315021&newsearch=true&queryText=Zhang,%20W.,%20Duan,%20P.,%20Li,%20Z.,%20Lu,%20Q.,%20Gong,%20W.%20AND.%20Yang,%20S.%20A%20

Zhang, X., Yue, Q., & He, Z. (2014). Dynamic energy-efficient virtual machine placement optimization for virtualized clouds. *Proceedings of the 2013 International Conference on Electrical and Information Technologies for Rail Transportation* (EITRT2013). Heidelberg, Germany: Springer. doi:10.1007/978-3-642-53751-6_47

Zhang, F., Cao, J., Khan, S. U., Li, K., & Hwang, K. (2015). A task-level adaptive MapReduce framework for real-time streaming data in healthcare applications. *Future Generation Computer Systems, 43*, 149–160. doi:10.1016/j.future.2014.06.009

Zhang, L. M., Li, K., Lo, D. C.-T., & Zhang, Y. (2013). Energy-efficient task scheduling algorithms on heterogeneous computers with continuous and discrete speeds. *Sustainable Computing: Informatics and Systems, 3*(2), 109–118.

Zhang, X., Cheng, G., Ge, W. Y., & Qu, Y. Z. (2009). Summarizing vocabularies in the global Semantic Web. *Journal of Computer Science and Technology, 24*(1), 165–174. doi:10.1007/s11390-009-9212-9

Zhang, X., Yang, T., Liu, C., & Chen, J. (2013). A scalable two-phase top-down specialization approach for data anonymization using MapReduce on cloud. *IEEE Transactions on Parallel and Distributed Systems, 25*(2), 363–373. doi:10.1109/TPDS.2013.48

Zhao, G., Liu, J., Tang, Y., Sun, W., Zhang, F., Ye, X., & Tang, N. (2009). Cloud Computing: A Statistics Aspect of Users. In *First International Conference on Cloud Computing (CloudCom)*. Springer Berlin. doi:10.1007/978-3-642-10665-1_32

Zhao, J., Tao, J., & Streit, A. (2016). Enabling collaborative MapReduce on the Cloud with a single-sign-on mechanism. *Computing*, *98*(1-2), 55–72. doi:10.1007/s00607-014-0390-0

Zheng, Z., Wang, R., Zhong, H., & Zhang, X. (2011). An approach for cloud resource scheduling based on Parallel Genetic Algorithm. *Computer Research and Development (ICCRD), 2011 3rd International Conference on*.

Zheng, Z., Wang, P., Liu, J., & Sun, S. (2015). Real-time big data processing framework: Challenges and solutions. *Applied Mathematics & Information Sciences*, *9*(6), 3169.

Zhongzhi, S., Mingkai, D., Yuncheng, J., & Haijun, Z. (2005). A logical foundation for the Semantic Web. *Science in China Series F: Information Sciences*, *48*(2), 161–178. doi:10.1360/03yf0506

Zhou, Y., Xie, J., Li, L., & Ma, M. (2014). Cloud model bat algorithm. *The Scientific World Journal*. PMID:24967425

Zhu, J. (2010). Cloud Computing Technologies and Applications. In B. F. Escalante (Ed.), Handbook of Cloud Computing (pp. 21-45). Springer Science & Business Media. doi:10.1007/978-1-4419-6524-0_2

Zhu, K., Song, H., Liu, L., Gao, J., & Cheng, G. (2011). Hybrid genetic algorithm for cloud computing applications. *Services Computing Conference (APSCC), 2011 IEEE Asia-Pacific*, (pp. 182-187). doi:10.1109/APSCC.2011.66

Zhu, Y., & Ammar, M. H. (2006). Algorithms for Assigning Substrate Network Resources to Virtual Network Components. *INFOCOM*, *1200*, 1–12.

Zomaya, A. Y. (2011), Maximizing Profit and Pricing in Cloud Environments. *12th International Conference on Web Information System Engineering (WISE 2011)*.

Zou, G., Xiang, Y., Gan, Y., & Chen, Y. (2011). A novel approach to annotating Web service based on interface concept mapping and semantic expansion. *Soft Computing*, *15*(5), 929–938. doi:10.1007/s00500-010-0548-4

Zuo, X., Zhang, G., & Tan, W. (2014). Self-adaptive learning PSO-based deadline constrained task scheduling for hybrid IaaS cloud. *Automation Science and Engineering. IEEE Transactions on*, *11*(2), 564–573.

About the Contributors

Ashok Kumar Turuk is working as an associate professor in Department of Computer Science and Engineering at National Institute of Technology, Rourkela, India. He obtained his Ph.D. degree in Computer Science and Engineering from Indian Institute of Technology, Kharagpur, India and his M.Tech. and B.Tech. from National Institute of Technology, Rourklea, India. He has more than 18 years of teaching experience in undergraduate and graduate levels in the field of Computer Science and Engineering. His current research area includes Optical Networking, Cloud Computing, and Wireless Sensor Network. He has handled several technical projects.

Bibhudatta Sahoo obtained his M. Tech. and Ph.D. degree in Computer Science & Engineering from NIT, Rourkela. He has 24years of Teaching Experience in undergraduate and graduate level in the field of computer Science & Engineering. He is presently Assistant Professor in the Department of Computer Science & Engineering, NIT Rourkela, INDIA. His technical interests include Data Structures & Algorithm Design, Parallel & Distributed Systems, Networks, Computational Machines, Algorithms for VLSI Design, Performance evaluation methods and modeling techniques Distributed computing system, Networking algorithms, and Web engineering. He is a member of IEEE & ACM.

Sourav Kanti Addya is pursuing Ph.D. in Department of computer science Engg at National Institute of Technology, Rourkela, India. His area of research is cloud computing. He obtained his M. Tech and B. Tech in computer science & Engg form NIT Rourkela, India and West Bengal University of Technology, India respectively. His technical interests include Algorithm Design, Computer Networks, Optimization techniques, Information security and Web Technologies.

* * *

Ratnakar Dash received his PhD degree from National Institute of Technology, Rourkela, India, in 2013. He is presently working as assistant professor in the Department of Computer Science and Engineering at National Institute of Technology, Rourkela, India. His area of interests include signal processing, image processing, Machine learning, intrusion detection system. He has published more than 10 papers in journals of international repute.

Subrat Kumar Dhal obtained Bachelor of Technology degree in Computer Science and Engineering with first class from National Institute of Technology, Rourkela. His interests are Parallel and Distributed Systems and High Performance Computing.

Salah Dowaji is an Associate Professor at Information Technology Engineering Faculty. Dean of faculty since 2013. Teaching Compiler Design, Parallel Programming and Software Engineering courses to 4th year engineering students. National Expert in CMMI-DEV. Researcher in many fields: Cloud Computing, Parallel Processing, IoT and Wireless Sensor Networks.

Sanjay Kumar Jena received his M.Tech in computer science and engineering from the Indian Institute of Technology Kharagpur and Ph.D. from the Indian Institute of Technology Bombay in 1982 and 1990, Respectively. He is a fulltime professor in the Department of Computer Science and Engineering, National Institute of Technology Rourkela. He is a senior member of IEEE and ACM and a life member of IE(I), ISTE and CSI. His research interests include data engineering, information security, parallel computing and privacy preserving techniques.

Kijpokin Kasemsap received his BEng degree in Mechanical Engineering from King Mongkut's University of Technology, Thonburi, his MBA degree from Ramkhamhaeng University, and his DBA degree in Human Resource Management from Suan Sunandha Rajabhat University. He is a Special Lecturer in the Faculty of Management Sciences, Suan Sunandha Rajabhat University, based in Bangkok, Thailand. He is a Member of the International Association of Engineers (IAENG), the International Association of Engineers and Scientists (IAEST), the International Economics Development and Research Center (IEDRC), the International Association of Computer Science and Information Technology (IACSIT), the International Foundation for Research and Development (IFRD), and the International Innovative Scientific and Research Organization (IISRO). He also serves on the International Advisory Committee (IAC) for International Association of Academicians and Researchers (INAAR). He has had numerous original research articles in top international journals, conference proceedings, and books on the topics of business management, human resource management, and knowledge management, published internationally.

Pınar Kırcı received the BSc degree in mathematics and computer from the Beykent University, Istanbul, Turkey, in 2002 and the MSc degree in computer engineering and the Ph.D. degree in computer engineering from the Istanbul University, Istanbul, Turkey, in 2005 and 2011, respectively.

Rajib Mall is currently Professor & Head in the Department of Computer Science & Engineering, Indian Institute of Technology (IIT), Kharagpur, India. He is a Senior Member in IEEE. He has published over 150 refereed research papers and has authored several books. His current research interests include analysis and testing of object-oriented programs.

Sambit Kumar Mishra is a Ph.D. scholar in Computer Science and Engineering at National Institute of Technology, Rourkela, India. He received his M.Tech. degree in Computer Science from Utkal University, Bhubaneswar, India in 2014 and M.Sc. degree in Computer Science from Utkal University, Bhubaneswar, India in 2011. His research interests include Cloud computing, Distributed computing, Wireless sensor network.

Salah Eddin Murad received his MSc in Software Engineering and Information Systems from Damascus University in 2012. He is certified trainer and holds many certificates in project and risk management including PMP, PMI-RMP, IPMA. He occupied various positions including Head of PMO, Head of System Development Department, Trainer\Consultant, and Engineering Instructor. Currently, he is a PhD candidate in Software Engineering and Information Systems. His research interests include Cloud Computing, Software Engineering, Project and Risk Management, Agile Management, Business Driven IT Management, SOA, Semantic Web, System Integration and Software Architecture, BI and Big Data.

Chhabi Panigrahi is currently working as an Associate Professor at C. V. Raman College of Engineering, Bhubaneswar in the department of Computer Science and Engineering. She received her Ph.D. degree in Computer Science and Engineering from IIT Kharagpur, India. Her research interests include Cloud Computing, Big data, and Testing Object-Oriented Programs. She has nearly 15 years of experience in teaching and research. She is the author of several scholarly research papers.

Bibudhndu Pati is currently working as an Associate Professor and Head in the Department of Computer Science and Engineering at C.V. Raman College of Engineering, Bhubaneswar. He received his PhD from IIT Kharagur, India. His current research interests include Big Data, Internet of things, Cloud Computing, and Wireless Sensor Networks. He has over 17 years of teaching, research, and industry experience.

Arnab Kumar Paul is a PhD student in the Department of Computer Science at Virginia Tech, USA.

Kshira Sagar Sahoo is a Ph.D. scholar in Computer Science and Engineering at National Institute of Technology, Rourkela, India.He received his M.Tech degree in Information and Communication Technology from IIT, Kharagpur, India in 2014. His research interests include Software Defined Network, network virtualization, Big Data Analytics. He is a member of IEEE computer society.

Sampa Sahoo is pursuing a Ph.D. in Departmnet of Computer Science & Engg at National Institute of Technology, Rourkela, India. Her area of research is Cloud Computing, Parallel and Distributed Computing System. She obtained her M.Tech. and B.Tech. in Computer Science & Engg. from Berhampur University, India and Biju Patnaik University of Technology (BPUT), India respectively. She has 7 years of teaching experience.

Mohammad Shalan is a Professional Engineer, with international working experience since 1995 in telecommunications, cloud computing, SMAC contracting, enterprise architecture, project management, risk analysis, audit and governance. He graduated with a Master degree in Telecommunication Engineering, 2005 and a B.Sc. in Electrical Engineering in 1995 from the University of Jordan. He is an author of several articles and published chapters in edited books. He is a holder of several active memberships in many professional organizations with unique certifications including: Project Management Professional, PMP® and Risk Management Professional, PMI-RMP® from Project Management Institute (PMI) Certified in the Governance of Enterprise Information Technology, CGEIT®, Certified Information System Auditor, CISA® and Certified in Risk and Information Systems Control, CRISC® from Information Systems Audit and Control Association (ISACA) Certification in Risk Management Assurance, CRMA® from The Institute of Internal Auditors (The IIA), Information Technology Infrastructure Library, ITIL foundations certification, with high level experience, Jordan Engineers Association (JEA) and the Institute of Electrical and Electronic Engineers (IEEE).

Sai Sruti is pursuing her B.Tech in Computer Science & Engineering at IGIT Sarang, India.

Mayank Tiwary is currently a B.Tech student in the Department of Information Technology at C.V. Raman College of Engineering, Bhubaneswar, India. He is currently working in the field of Cyber Foraging, Mobile Cloud Computing and Software Defined Networks. He is a student member of IEEE and CSI.

Harshit Verma received the B.Tech degree in Computer Science and Engineering from the National Institute of Technology, Rourkela in 2015. His Research interests include Cloud Computing, Virtualization, Energy Efficiency, Algorithms. Since then he has been with SAP Labs India, where he is currently a Software Engineer.

Ezer Osei Yeboah-Boateng has a Ph.D. in Cyber-Security from the center for Communications, Media & Information technologies (CMI), Aalborg University in Copenhagen, Denmark. Ezer holds an M.S. degree in Telecommunications (Magna cum Laude), with concentrations in Wireless Network Security and digital signal processing (DSP) with Biometric based Interactive Voice Response (IVR) systems, from the Stratford University, Virginia, USA, and a B.Sc. (Honors) in Electrical & Electronic Engineering from the University of Science & Technology (U.S.T.) in Kumasi, Ghana. He is currently a Senior Lecturer and acting Dean at the Faculty of Informatics, GTUC.

Index

A

ACO 168, 172, 179-180, 183
Agile Development 286, 292-296, 303
Analytics 199, 205, 264, 266, 271, 273, 285
and BFD 220
Appropriating 115, 135
ARPANET 31
Availability 19, 22-23, 37, 39, 66, 71, 76, 87, 106-107,
    110, 113-114, 116-117, 125, 127-129, 137, 139,
    148, 168, 191-193, 196, 200, 208, 250-251, 264,
    272, 297, 304

B

Bandwidth 16, 31, 39, 93, 109, 111, 121, 173, 179-180,
    189-190, 192-194, 201, 205, 216-218, 226, 228,
    232, 244, 248, 253-256, 266
BAT 168, 172, 182-183
Benchmarking 116, 135
Best Fit Algorithm 157-158, 160, 163
Big Data 22, 192-193, 199, 201-202, 205, 264-266,
    270-274, 285-286, 298
Business Driven IT Management 38, 60

C

Carrier 31
challenges 36, 38-39, 62, 68, 72-73, 79, 81, 89, 95,
    101, 106-107, 109, 112, 118, 126, 129, 135-136,
    147, 192-193, 204-205, 251, 259-260, 264, 266,
    268-269, 272-273, 286-287, 303-304
Client Enterprise (CE) 87-88
Cloud Computing (CC) 1, 17-23, 33-40, 47, 50, 60-62,
    67, 81, 89-92, 98, 101, 105-107, 109-115, 118,
    121-122, 125-126, 128, 130, 136-139, 142-143,
    145, 148-149, 167-171, 173-174, 179, 189-193,
    201-202, 204-205, 210-212, 217, 225, 231,
    239-240, 252, 260, 264-266, 272-273, 285-287,
    289-299, 303-304

Cloud Distribution 31
Cloud Service Footprint (CSF) 61-64, 66, 71, 81, 87
Cloud Service Provider (CSP) 87
cloud services 19, 31-32, 36, 41, 63, 101, 109, 112-114,
    116, 121-122, 128-129, 148, 169, 191, 217, 289
CloudSim 40, 50-51, 179-181, 210, 215, 232
Computer 2, 8, 11, 15, 17, 20-21, 31-32, 37, 73, 91,
    110, 145, 172, 188-189, 209, 218, 240, 243, 249,
    257, 264-266, 269, 285, 298
Concerns 61, 63, 65, 78-79, 101, 105-109, 111-114,
    117-118, 122, 125-130, 135, 235, 268, 271
Consolidation Scheme 210, 214-215, 225, 232, 235
Cooperative Game Theory 145, 147, 153-156, 165, 167
Customer satisfaction 33, 38, 40, 42-44, 47, 53-54,
    56, 60, 267, 292
Cyber-Security 105-109, 111, 113-114, 117-118, 122,
    125-126, 128-129, 135

D

Data Centers 112, 136, 139-140, 145, 167, 172-174,
    193, 202, 210-215, 217, 225-226, 235, 241, 263,
    304
Data Locality 193, 196-197, 200-202, 205, 208
Database 5, 34, 37, 70, 75, 265-266, 273, 300
Distributed computing 1-2, 5, 21, 31, 106, 112, 168, 270
Distributed System 21, 31
Dynamic Resource Discovery 60

E

Enterprise Resource Planning 266, 285

F

FFD 218-221, 224-225

G

GA 168, 172, 177-179, 183

Game Theory 144-145, 147-149, 153-157, 165, 167
General Packet Radio Service (GPRS) 31
Global System for Mobile Communications (GSM) 31-32
Governance 38, 61-62, 64, 66, 68-70, 73, 81-82, 87, 120, 273
Grid Computing 17, 32, 105-106, 110, 212, 264

H

Hadoop 193-194, 196-204, 208-209
Hadoop Distributed File System 193, 208
HDFS 193, 196, 198-199, 202, 208-209
healthcare system 10
Host 45, 47, 74, 90, 93-94, 101, 149, 171-174, 188-189, 191, 194, 203-204, 210, 213-214, 216-217, 227-232, 240, 247-248, 250, 257-258, 260, 289

I

Information Technology 47, 88, 101, 264, 285, 289
Infrastructure 2-3, 6, 15, 17-19, 21-23, 33-35, 38-39, 41, 47-49, 66, 68, 72-73, 77, 79, 89, 93, 106, 109, 111-112, 130, 137, 148, 169, 171, 173-174, 191-194, 196, 201, 203, 205, 211-213, 215, 220, 225, 239-241, 244, 248, 252, 254, 258-260, 265-267, 269, 271-272, 289, 297, 301
Infrastructure Provider 39, 49, 244, 260
Internet 1, 3-4, 6, 11-15, 17, 19, 21-22, 34, 60-61, 90, 96, 106, 110-113, 125, 168, 173-174, 190, 192, 205, 211, 216, 239, 242-244, 248, 250, 257, 259, 264-270, 272-273, 285, 303
issues 6, 15-16, 33, 36-37, 47, 61, 65, 89-92, 94-96, 98, 101, 105-108, 112, 116, 127-128, 130, 135, 168, 174, 181, 183-184, 193-194, 198, 202, 205, 252-253, 260, 265, 267, 271-272, 295, 297-298, 301, 303-304

K

Knowledge 20-21, 71, 79, 112, 114, 117, 124-125, 127, 181, 184, 218, 256, 265-266, 269-273

L

link virtualization 248, 257

M

Mainframe Computer 32
MapReduce 190, 192-205, 209, 272, 286, 298-299, 301-302

Maturity 62, 64, 66, 69-70, 81-82
Middle Circle Contractor (MCC) 87
Mobile Endpoints-Fixed Endpoints 32
mobility 2, 4-6, 9, 14, 16, 19, 72-73, 96, 252

N

Nash Equilibrium 144-149, 157, 159-160, 165
Network Substrate 251, 263
Non-Cooperative Game Theory 145, 148, 157, 167
NP-Complete 148, 173-174, 210
NVE 251-252, 263

P

Peer-to-Peer 32, 257
pervasive computing 1-2, 9, 13-14, 21, 23
Physical Machine 140, 156-157, 159, 167, 169, 191, 203, 212, 217, 219, 224-225
programmability 259
Programming Models 286-287, 298-299, 301-302, 304
PSO 168, 172, 176, 181-183

Q

QoS 15, 37, 39, 112, 137-139, 147, 149, 153, 172-173, 180-181, 191-192, 195, 208, 217, 231, 250, 253, 255, 267, 297-298
Quality of Services 208

R

Resource Allocation 37, 39, 139, 147-149, 171, 173, 179-180, 194, 203, 211-212, 216, 239-240, 251, 253-257, 263
Resource Discovery 23, 60, 239, 251, 253, 260, 263
Resource Management 60, 112, 138, 148, 171, 197, 199, 213, 217, 239, 257-258, 272
Response Time 33, 36-40, 42, 49, 54, 140, 184, 197, 200-201, 203, 209
Risk 7, 13-14, 61-67, 69, 81-82, 87, 89, 107, 114, 116-120, 122, 130, 268, 288, 292, 297
Risk Management 62-63, 66-67, 87, 288
Risk Management (RM) 62, 66

S

Scalability 18, 66, 81, 106, 109, 137, 169, 191, 193, 197, 201-202, 205, 209, 241, 255, 289, 304
SDLC 287-288, 292, 294, 296-297

Security 2, 4, 7, 14, 16, 18-21, 23, 36, 64, 73-75, 77, 89-96, 98, 101, 105-107, 109, 111-113, 115-116, 118-119, 121-122, 125-130, 135, 169, 190-191, 199, 204-205, 241, 250-252, 257, 264, 266, 268-270, 272-273, 297, 303-304

Semantic Web 39-40, 47, 56, 60, 264-266, 269-270, 273-274, 285

sensors 2, 4-11, 13, 18-19, 21, 192, 272

Service 2, 4, 12-14, 16-22, 31-42, 45, 47, 49-50, 56, 61-67, 69-82, 87, 89-93, 98-99, 105-106, 108-113, 125, 127-129, 135-139, 145, 148-149, 153, 169-173, 181, 189, 191-192, 195, 199, 202-203, 208-213, 216-217, 231, 235, 240, 242, 244, 249-252, 256, 259-260, 263-266, 268-273, 285, 287, 289-290, 294-298, 302

Service Deployment 32, 64, 148

Service Level Agreement (SLA) 36, 75, 138, 153, 169, 189, 191, 209-210, 213, 267, 289

Service Momentum 70-71, 87

Service Provider 36, 39, 42, 45, 69-70, 87, 89, 110-111, 139, 145, 169, 171, 181, 191, 209-210, 244, 250, 252, 267, 273, 287, 289, 294, 296-297

Service-oriented Architecture (SOA) 32

smart spaces 2

Software 2, 4, 17, 32, 34-35, 39, 63, 76-77, 90, 93-96, 101, 106, 116, 130, 171, 189, 191, 197, 204, 240, 242-243, 246-248, 253, 258, 260, 263-264, 266-270, 272-273, 285-289, 291-299, 302-304

Software as a Service 34-35, 93, 264, 266-268, 285, 289

Strategy 21, 33, 37, 39, 56, 62, 65-70, 73, 77, 80, 87, 96, 106, 108-109, 121, 128-130, 135, 145-146, 156-157, 159, 181, 216, 218, 270, 296

T

Take-Down Policy 79, 87

Task 12, 20-21, 38-39, 47, 61, 87, 114, 139, 168, 171-183, 189-190, 192, 194-198, 201-205, 209, 215, 241-242, 247, 255, 257, 272, 285, 299, 303-304

Task Allocation 171, 201, 203, 215

Task Consolidation Problem 168, 172-175, 178, 180-182, 189

Technology 3-8, 11, 13-14, 17, 20-21, 36, 47, 60-66, 68-69, 72-73, 81-82, 87-88, 90-91, 101, 105-106, 108, 110, 127, 135, 169, 171-172, 174, 192, 209, 211, 216, 225, 240-241, 243, 248, 250, 257, 260, 264-267, 269-271, 273, 285, 289

Technology Organization (TO) 62, 65, 81, 88

U

ubiquitous system 1, 12, 16, 18

V

Value metrics measurement 39

Value-Added 106, 115, 118, 121, 127, 135

Value-Based Metric 60

Vendor 49, 64, 90, 101, 113, 273

Virtual Machine (VM) 47, 93, 112, 136-137, 139-143, 145, 147, 151, 155, 157, 165, 167, 169, 173, 180, 189, 191, 194, 201-202, 209-210, 212-213, 215, 217, 226-227, 231, 235, 240, 242-243, 247, 263

Virtual Machine Monitor (VMM) 137, 140, 189, 212, 240

Virtual Machine Placement 136-137, 139-143, 145, 147, 155, 157, 165, 167, 217, 231, 263

Virtual networks 100, 239-240, 244, 247, 249, 253, 259-260, 263

Virtual Resource 60, 301

Virtualization 17, 20, 35, 90-91, 93, 98, 101, 105-106, 109-110, 112, 127, 130, 137, 140, 167, 169, 171-172, 174, 189-191, 209, 211-212, 216, 225, 239-249, 251, 253-255, 257, 259-260, 263, 289, 296-297

vSwitch 247-248, 263

W

Web 2.0 20, 264-266, 269-270

Wireless networks 4, 6, 8, 15-16

Y

Yet Another Resource Negotiator 209

Become an IRMA Member

Members of the **Information Resources Management Association (IRMA)** understand the importance of community within their field of study. The Information Resources Management Association is an ideal venue through which professionals, students, and academicians can convene and share the latest industry innovations and scholarly research that is changing the field of information science and technology. Become a member today and enjoy the benefits of membership as well as the opportunity to collaborate and network with fellow experts in the field.

IRMA Membership Benefits:

- **One FREE Journal Subscription**

- **30% Off Additional Journal Subscriptions**

- **20% Off Book Purchases**

- Updates on the latest events and research on Information Resources Management through the IRMA-L listserv.

- Updates on new open access and downloadable content added to Research IRM.

- A copy of the Information Technology Management Newsletter twice a year.

- A certificate of membership.

IRMA Membership $195

Scan code to visit irma-international.org and begin by selecting your free journal subscription.

Membership is good for one full year.

Printed in the United States
By Bookmasters